THE ROAD GANG

Copyright © 2025 by Keith Mexsom

First Published March 2025

ISBN: 978-0-6485129-6-7

Cover Design: Graham Kennedy
Index: Daphne Lawless

Acknowledgements

First and foremost, my thanks to The Bruce Jesson Foundation which, way back in 2008, thought my ambition to write of the commercial influences on Auckland transport planning worthy of the Bruce Jesson Critical Writing Award for that year.

That initial research resulted in the publication of *Waka Paddle to Gas Pedal — The First Century of Auckland Transport*, followed by *Gas Pedal to Back-Pedal — The Second Century of Auckland Transport* and this final volume, *The Road Gang*.

Ultimately, both this volume and its predecessors are anthologies; collections of the observations of many learned researchers, journalists, witnesses, and commentators, many obtained from Papers Past and elsewhere — the voices of both past and presently-living individuals who have either influenced or recorded the events that constitute New Zealand's transport history. It is they who deserve the greatest credit for having provided the essence upon which these stories is based.

Dedication
In Memory Of my dear brother, David, and my fishing buddy, Roger.
Both gone too soon.

ABOUT THE AUTHOR

Keith Mexsom has been writing fiction and non-fiction for more than 40 years. During that time, he has acquired a good deal of magazine and newspaper experience in both New Zealand and Australia as a publisher, editor, sub-editor, journalist, magazine feature writer, and copywriter — working in both a team environment and as a freelancer. He now lives in New South Wales after having lived in Auckland for many years.

Previously-published books include **Waka Paddle to Gas Pedal** and **Gas Pedal to Back-Pedal** — as featured at: https://keithmexsom.pubsitepro.com.

CONTENTS

Introduction
Chapter One:	The Transport Curtain Rises	1
Chapter Two:	Enter the Machines	10
Chapter Three:	Enter the Road Gang	39
Chapter Four:	First Vehicle Assemblers	45
Chapter Five:	The Component Industry	88
Chapter Six:	The Assemblers Disassembled	139
Chapter Seven:	Vehicle Importers and Dealers	179
Chapter Eight:	Oil Exploration	201
Chapter Nine:	The Petrol & Oil Suppliers	256
Chapter Ten:	Roads…Roads…Roads…	292
Chapter Eleven:	Consequences	367
Afterword		381
References		382
Index		461

Introduction

Unlike my previous volumes, *Waka Paddle to Gas Pedal* and *Gas Pedal to Back-Pedal*, this third volume of transport history necessarily encompasses the history of the whole of New Zealand and not just the city of Auckland.

This third volume does not pretend to include a <u>complete</u> list of individuals and entities that have comprised New Zealand's Road Gang over the years. It is simply a selection of the more prominent and interesting of the many, who, from the late 1890s, sought to make a (mostly legitimate) living from New Zealand's motor vehicle and road transport industry.

As with most occupations, the prime motivation of Road Gang members was simply to profit from their activities in order to feed their families and satisfy personal and professional ambition. At the same time, their endeavours met the needs of a motoring public conditioned by market forces and transport necessity to acquire their goods and services.

Here are some of their stories...

Chapter One

The Transport Curtain Rises

The Bad Years

As described by William Sutch in his book, Poverty and Progress in New Zealand, the commercial reality that existed in New Zealand between 1865 and about 1900 was uncertain, to say the least, for many of its citizens:

"Between 1870 and 1890 the foundations of the country's economy were laid, but in 1870 it was not clear that the country had any future other than that of an exporter of wool from large land-holdings. These were mainly in the South Island, which at that time had two-thirds of the population and four-fifths of the 10 million sheep in New Zealand. The gold rushes were over, and gold production was beginning to decline. After 1865 the prices of the main exports, wool and wheat, had continued to fall abroad; those with sheep-runs experienced a heavy fall in income, and those without (four out of five in the census of 1871 were not farmers) suffered the threat of poverty and prolonged unemployment. Towards the end of the depressed late 'sixties thousands of former immigrants had left New Zealand…

"The long depression which began in 1865 and ended in 1895 was interrupted for a period of four or five years in the 'seventies by an increase in economic activity caused by investment spending by the government and lending by the banks and loan companies.

"Julius Vogel, the New Zealand Treasurer in 1870, planned to end the isolation of the New Zealand settlements by linking them by road and rail and also by unifying the railway gauges, of which there were three. The various provinces had gone ahead separately with their less than 50 miles of railways, were heavily in debt, and found it difficult to borrow more in London; also no province would build for the country as a whole and the areas where there were no immediate profits to be made were neglected." [1]

Political Ends Gained

In her book, *By Design: A brief history of the Public Works Department, Ministry of Works 1870-1970*, Rosslyn J Noonan described the state of the country's railway network as a result of parochial and entrepreneurial influences during the 1870s and later:

"According to the (Public Works) department's critics, inefficient and confused administration was the reason for the working railways' failure to pay the interest on the loans raised for their construction. As well as providing an insufficient return on the money invested in them, the railways were also offering allegedly inadequate services…

"In the [eighteen] seventies public works in an area assured prosperity through employment opportunities, rising land values, and increased settlement. Public pressure for works, particularly railway lines, was widespread…

"As the depression became apparent the position of the Public Works Department became increasingly insecure. There were several reasons for this. The proclaimed potential of Vogel's public works proposals had fostered utopian-type aspirations. When these were not fulfilled Vogel's scheme and everything associated with it came under the most critical scrutiny…

"Well into the eighties the myth of overseas borrowing and extensive public works as a panacea for all ills was firmly believed by many New Zealanders…

"In 1880 it was still believed by many that the railways alone could solve the country's problems: the 1880 Public Works report was ever optimistic: 'We need not despair…of ultimately attaining a good result. We have covered the country with these stimulating and civilising agencies [railways]: in their neighbourhood settlement will extend, population and industries will increase…'" [2]

Local Selfishness

Unfortunately, the construction of these *stimulating and civilising agencies* in the form of haphazard railway lines, many to nowhere, rarely resulted in the local progress envisaged. Instead of railways to riches, many of the lines proved to be ephemeral fancies of parochial, private and political interests, as described by Rosslyn J Noonan:

"Of course politicians pressured for railway lines not only for private ends but also for political ones - and parochial interests served usually meant political ends gained. The Minister of Public Works, James MacAndrew, was described as 'the very impersonation of local selfishness'.

"In the 1878 public works proposals, his province of Otago was allocated eight branch lines, including 160 miles of the Otago Central railway. This despite the unfavourable report on the latter line…The Otago Central and the Midland line were classic examples…Three unfavourable reports were compiled by department staff on the latter line. But it went ahead because of the private interests of some politicians including Vogel and Stout. [Robert Stout, MP Dunedin East] [3]

"Historian K Sinclair has pointed out that by twentieth century standards there were quite unacceptably close links between business and politics. [4]

"These links should not be judged by twentieth century standards. The politicians of the 1870s and 1880s were predominantly laissez faire liberals who believed 'that to seek private advantage was to serve social well-being'.

"W H Oliver in the *Story of NZ* [5] acknowledges that 'Vogel used the state to facilitate the quest for personal riches' but adds that according to his political philosophy, 'to make money was a social virtue'." [6]

Land Speculation

From the first Pakeha settlement to the present day, there has been no easier way to make money in New Zealand than by on-selling real estate.

However, as the Daily Southern Cross pointed out in its editorial of 1 September 1871, reporting on the turning of the first sod for the Kaipara Railway, the *social virtue* of land speculation had its limits:

"The ruinous spirit of land speculation which is so characteristically condemned by Dieffenbach's 'Travels in New Zealand' which he observed springing up from the very time that Auckland was selected by Captain Hobson for the site of the capital of the colony, were very observable in 1864.

"We could name many instances where people purchased allotments and blocks of land on or near the supposed line of the Auckland and Drury Railway, after it was spoken about and before anything definitely was done, a few months afterwards demanding the most exorbitant price for the same land when wanted by the Railway Commissioners. That was the 'public spirit' and that was the conduct which prevented the Auckland and Drury Railway from ever becoming an accomplished fact.

"Had the Assembly passed a short Act enabling the Provincial Government or the Railway Commissioners to take the land they required at a reasonable price, the position of Auckland would have been different to-day; for, by unscrupulous greed, the goose was killed which would have laid the golden eggs in the future…" [7]

System of Log Rolling

By the late 1870s, the cronyism, the perceived waste of public money, and the poor economic performance of the rail network became so concerning that an inquiry, by way of a Royal Commission, was decided upon.

In an editorial published on 23 December 1879, the West Coast Times repeated the concerns previously reported by the Lyttelton Times:

"The Lyttelton Times, in a recent article, pointed out the reckless manner in which the Public Works Policy is administered. Neither the Ministry nor anyone else seems to know or care whether money is thrown away or not. Mr Oliver [Richard Oliver – Minister of Public Works] confessed that Ministers had no time to devote to a close inquiry into the manner in which the ever recurring loans are spent…

"Hence the proposal for a Royal Commission to examine into the prospects of the railways under construction is proposed. It is indeed high time that the system adopted by successive Ministries, since the Vogel scheme of public works was first introduced, should be altered. The Lyttelton Times truly observes that some of the railways of New Zealand represent the result of a gigantic system of log rolling.

"One member voted for a railway to another member's paddock, because he of the paddock had agreed to the construction of a railway which would make his stable site valuable. Another insisted on a railway because his constituents wanted it, and Governments pressed forward railways because votes were given accordingly…

"The Royal Commission, if it does its work properly, will discover that many districts have been scandalously neglected, that people who have for years contributed largely to the revenue, have received no adequate return, and that certain parts of the Colony have been left in comparative isolation, while railway communication far in excess of what was wanted has been given in other quarters." [8]

Report of the Railway Commission

Indeed, that is just what the Railway Commissioners found in their report to Parliament on 26 July 1880:

"7. In some—indeed, in many—instances the opinions and recommendations which we shall submit to your Excellency in this report are at variance with the tenor of the evidence taken in the districts interested in proposals for the construction of railways.

"It is perhaps scarcely necessary to point out that settlers in all parts of the colony take an especial and not unnatural pride in their own particular district and in the progress it has made, and that they are prone to attach a greater value to its existing resources, and to take a more sanguine view of its future, than can be acquiesced in by a dispassionate and unprejudiced observer.

"8. At the outset of our investigation we were met by the fact that the already constructed railways of New Zealand do not, as a whole, yield a return sufficient to pay one-half of the interest upon their cost; and we felt it to be necessary, before we could take upon ourselves the responsibility of recommending the extension of existing or the construction of new lines, that we should endeavour to learn the causes to which this unsatisfactory state of things is attributable, and the extent, if any, to which those causes may be removed or their operation modified.

"9. One leading cause is sufficiently apparent, and can only be remedied by time and the gradual progress of settlement which the resources of the colony will undoubtedly secure—we refer to the making of railways in some parts of the colony far in advance of existing settlement, and consequently of an amount of traffic adequate to their support." [9]

Road Construction

As settlements grew, the arbitrary provision of railway access had soon to be augmented by improved roads — in those early days, dray roads for carts and bridle roads for horse riders.

During the year to October 1895, some 677 miles of road were constructed nationwide, of which 368 miles were for wheel-traffic and 309 miles for horse riders.

The total length of the country's roads was then said to be some 1827 miles of which 502 miles had been constructed in the Auckland provincial district.

However, ever the poorer cousin to rail services, settlers were still waiting for road access to their properties months after settling them — as pointed out by the Minister for Public Works, the Hon. R J Seddon, in his 21 October 1895 Statement to Parliament:

"…one of the greatest drawbacks to settlement arises from the fact that it is almost ruinous to the poorer class of settlers for them to be in occupation of their holdings for months prior to the construction of roads giving access thereto.

"In other words, the lands should be roaded first, or, wherever practicable, the roading and clearing should proceed simultaneously." [10]

The increasing predominance of roads over rail as the main means of access to settlements at the start of the twentieth century was highlighted by the Hon. William Fraser, Minister of Works, in his Statement to Parliament on 18 October 1912:

"In my opinion, to give the settlers of the Dominion access to their holdings by means of roads should be the first consideration in any scheme of public works. I have no desire to minimize the value of railways to the Dominion, but these are of secondary importance if the settlers cannot reach them.

"Now, road-making in New Zealand is difficult and expensive, owing to the configuration of the country and to the absence in many localities of suitable metal. Hence considerable sums have to be provided each year for this class of work." [11]

Road Expenditure

The Public Account Statement for the Financial Year 1911-1912 recorded a total spend on Auckland District roads (including the Coromandel, Waikato, and Franklin Districts) of £39,646, including £335 contributed by local bodies. [12]

By 1928, that expenditure on Auckland District roads had increased to £316,787 — an increase that obviously reflected not only the construction of more roads but also the evolving of road surface construction from *suitable metal* to the concrete and tarmac needed for the conveyance of motor vehicle traffic. [13]

Motorways

A shortage of men and material during the Second World War resulted in a slowdown of all infrastructure building. However, by the late 1940s, road construction had fully resumed and even included the formation of motorways as State Highways — as described by the Minister of Works, Hon. Robert Semple, in his 1948 Ministry of Works Statement to Parliament:

"Further legislation passed during the year in the form of the Public Works Amendment Act, 1947, made provision for the declaration of motor-ways, and these limited access highways, some of which are already under construction, will be of great benefit to the community and one of the most important milestones in the development of the road transport of the Dominion. They will provide safe and more economic transport, and will in this way pay for themselves in a few years after being brought into use.

"With a view to assisting some local authorities and in order to help round off the State highways system, the Main Highways Board, with my approval, classified 1,330 miles of main highways as State highways as from 1st April, 1948. As a result of this further length of State highways the whole of the cost of construction and maintenance, in accordance with the standard prescribed by the Board, will from the date of classification be the sole responsibility of the State." [14]

By 1950, road and motorway construction costs nationwide had increased dramatically with the Ministry of Works expenditure recorded for the 1949-1950 financial year as Roads: £464,649 and Highways: £2,342,139. [15]

Roads Supplant Rail

The Public Works Amendment Act 1947 amended the Public Works Act 1928, Sections 216 and 217 of which pertained to the acquirement of land for the construction of railways. Section 4 (2) of the 1947 amendment prepared for the now more predominant, new construction of motorways:

"Where under the powers conferred upon him by this Act the Governor-General desires to construct a motor-way he may issue a Proclamation defining the middle-line of the motor-way or any part thereof, and in every such case the provisions of sections two hundred and sixteen and two hundred and seventeen of the principal Act shall, as far as they are applicable and with the necessary modifications, apply in respect of the construction of the motor-way in like manner as if a railway were to be constructed." [16]

Land Speculation (Again)

Just as there had been prior to the construction of the Drury Railway in the late nineteenth century, there was no shortage of land speculators eager to profit from the Government's plans to expand the nation's road network — as described by Finlay J MacDonald in his 2014 essay, *Primate City*:

"A plan to develop Auckland along transport corridors, with rail loops and bus routes linking the spokes, was ditched. Rail fell out of favour. Motorways and the private car were promoted as the way of the future. Land speculation, held in check by wartime price controls, gathered pace as developers snapped up cheap rural acreages that could be sold for handsome profits once the motorways arrived.

"Those motorways were funded from road and petrol taxes, creating a self-sustaining cycle of road-based development — in effect, a public subsidy for private gain." [17]

The First Highway Lobby

As previously observed, the construction of New Zealand's railway network was greatly influenced by political and parochial bias and mostly paid for by the taxpayer. In America, at the turn of the twentieth century, the reverse occurred when the shareholders of privately-owned railways paid to construct their own right-of-ways and rolling stock. The railways thrived as they opened America to the hordes of immigrants seeking their fortunes and a new life.

However, as in New Zealand, the railways of America were inevitably replaced by the motor vehicle and its need for more and better roads — as described in January 1922 by 'Demon' of the Otago Witness:

"With such excellent roads as America is getting the use of the motor truck is extending, and whole fleets can be seen hauling merchandise from town to town. It had been found that fewer handlings and rapid dispatch are points which weigh in favour of the motor as against the railway in what is known as 'short haul traffic'. On long-distance traffic the railway is still unassailable, but the motor has a distinct niche in the matter of transport, and where you have good roads the motor comes into its own." [18]

David Young of the Chicago Tribune wrote in 1995:

"So it is with the epic struggle between railroads and highways in the 20th century. On one side, railroads were the monopolistic playthings of the robber barons, who got exactly what they deserved when government regulation nearly strangled them. They were replaced in the pantheon of perfidy by an insidious cabal called the highway lobby, which conspired to enrich itself at taxpayer expense…

"By 1880 cyclists had formed the League of American Wheelmen and were campaigning for better roads so they could pedal across the countryside. This was the beginning of the highway lobby. Over the years it was joined by farmers who wanted to be able to move their grain to the nearest railroad, the early motorists and their clubs, the Post Office Department, which had been required by Congress to provide rural mail delivery, vehicle manufacturers, truckers, bus companies, highway builders, the states, purveyors of cement and shippers tired of poor service from the monopolistic railroads. Even the railroads campaigned for better roads until they figured out they were slitting their own throats...

"Railroad enthusiasts...tend to ignore the advances in technology that resulted in more efficient transportation than the railroads were able to provide. Just as railroads were technologically superior to the primitive roads and sluggish canals of the 19th century, motor vehicles and airplanes proved technologically superior to trains in many, but not all, markets in the 20th century." [19]

Getting There

David Young's comments were part of a review of Stephen B Goddard's 1994 book, *Getting There: The Epic Struggle between Road and Rail in the American Century*. In his book, Stephen Goddard explained the evolving of America's road lobby from the *League of American Wheelmen* to the *Road Gang* of later years:

"By 1910, nearly a half-million motor vehicles were on American roads, 187,000 of them produced in that year alone...In 1900, automobiling was a sport; by 1910, it had become a business...

"To counter the perceived drift toward White House control, the highway coalition went underground in 1942 to seek common ground. Meeting for lunch each Thursday behind closed doors in Washington, 240 oil, rubber, and auto bigwigs, top highway bureaucrats, trade association executives, and public relations specialists debated how to maintain hegemony in the highway field. No press releases issued from this secret society, referred to by Washington insiders as simply the 'Road Gang'.

"General Motors' President William Durant recalled years later the beginnings of the American highway lobby: 'The whole network taken for granted in later generations was woven in these years – the highways, the fuel and service stations, the mechanisms of registration, insurance and policing – all simply enlarged upon and refined in the following half-century.'

"To the industrialists, who were now selling glass, rubber, steel, concrete and their end products in numbers beyond their wildest dreams, whatever needed to be done to sustain the boom and to build pressure for good roads simply had to be accomplished...

"Whole new industries now joined the highwaymen to protect their hard-won gains by bankrolling the campaigns of highway-friendly congressmen. The American Automobile Association, the Auto Manufacturers Association, the American Petroleum Institute, and the American Road Builders Association (ARBA) were old hands at the game. But the interstate highways' pervasiveness would bring new beneficiaries into the fold: hotel and motel operators, housing and restaurant developers, real estate agencies, and Wall Street bankers — literally anyone who contributed to or benefited from superhighways...

"The highwaymen had learned that the hot buttons that would sell the public on their program: 'talk of privacy, of private property, of individualism.' But little effort was made in the increasingly pluralistic American society to seek umbrella values and from that, to chart a course of action. And so each interest looked to its own particular needs apart from the whole, just as each transport mode had been doing for generations. Independent individuals all, following the American way." [20]

Rail or Road?

The concept of *independent individuals following the American way* was nothing new to the same type of industrialists, importers, retailers, and financiers who, by the 1920s, made up New Zealand's own 'Road Gang'. As described in previous volumes, Aucklanders, in particular, have relied upon the reluctance of successive governments to interfere in their commercial enterprises since the day the city was founded. This laissez-faire environment soon engendered a distinct class of individuals who became known as Auckland's *limited circle* — gentlemen of fortune who used their commercial resources to shape the city's early growth regardless of government aspirations.

During the 1930s, many of those government aspirations included social reform and public works, mostly financed internally. However, this government policy often conflicted with the more ambitious intentions of the limited circle who sought to finance many of their entrepreneurial projects by means of overseas borrowing — particularly from Britain.

As described by William Sutch in his book, *the quest for security in New Zealand 1840 to 1966*:

"The pressure groups in the community limiting the actions of the government were still farmers, importers, merchants, and those concerned with the lending of money." [21]

Access to the City

Whereas New Zealand's first roads were essential to service the rural community, the flood of motor vehicles and the growth of cities meant that good urban roads also became an increasingly important need for the country. Just like the laying of railway tracks before them, new roads for the motor car were lobbied for by those with speculative and political ambition.

Such lobbying was evident during a meeting held to discuss road access into Wellington — as reported by the Evening Post on 28 April 1919: (The 'George' Magnus referred to is thought to be Godfrey William Magnus. He is described in a later chapter as one of New Zealand's first motor vehicle dealers, with the founding of Magnus Motors Limited of Wellington in 1907, and as a partner of Magnus Sanderson, cycle company.)

"At the monthly meeting of the Wellington Automobile Club, Mr. George Magnus attended by invitation with a view to putting before the meeting his ideas with regard to the new road to Paekakariki, via Plimmerton, Pukerua, and the sea coast.

"Mr Magnus stated that the proposed new road had been surveyed and no serious engineering difficulties presented themselves. The suggested road would be a saving of four or five miles in distance and not less than 570 ft of elevation by not going over the Paekakariki Hill. The new scheme affected all motorists, and he thought that now was the time and opportunity to stress the necessity of it to Cabinet." [22]

National Monument

Just in case such a road was not seen to be essential in itself, its construction as a national monument was proposed in the hope it might generate more interest:

"Mr Magnus stated that Mr W H Field MP was in sympathy with the proposition, and it had been suggested that the new road should be a national monument in memory of the New Zealand boys who had fallen in the war. Mr Magnus also suggested that at different parts of the road tablets should be erected naming the different battles that the New Zealanders engaged in. He had secured the sympathy of at least two members of the Cabinet who had promised support if the scheme matured." [23]

The Shape of Things to Come

While these pressure groups sought to flood the country with motor vehicles, the Ministry of Work's 1946 ten-year plan, *The Shape of Things to Come*, planned for a suburban railway network serving Auckland and its region. This government-sponsored project was to include an underground railway from the Beach Road station to join the Western Line at Kingsland, (the route proposed as early as 1914 as the Auckland-Morningside Deviation) and the electrification and duplication of existing suburban lines. [24]

There was also the commissioned report of Halcrow Thomas (March 1950) which recommended greater use of suburban rail as a public transport service for the greater Auckland region. [25]

Subsequent studies by De Leuw Cather, the first of which was reported in July 1965, also recommended suburban rail and buses as a necessary alternative to private road transport. Such plans were a distinct threat to the supremacy of motor vehicles and to those who sought to profit from them. [26]

But, the motor lobby for the Road Gang need not have worried. Their wants would prevail, and lead to:

"…a political/philosophical change to a less planned approach to city building and national development…This approach was very much driven by vested interests and by land speculation and resulted in sprawling subdivisions characteristic of modern Auckland." [27]

Indeed, it was not until 2016 before another real threat to the road transport members of the Road Gang was posed — by a study which recommended the expansion of Auckland's rail-freight network with the intention of replacing much of the freight carried along South Auckland roads. The expansion was also needed to facilitate the more efficient running of the City's passenger services in anticipation of the start of the City Rail Link.

Wiri to Westfield

KiwiRail Holdings Limited was formed in 2008 as a state-owned enterprise responsible for rail and inter-island ferry operations in New Zealand. The country's rail network thus became subject to Government financial and political control.

In December 2016, KiwiRail, the New Zealand Transport Agency, and Auckland Transport, in association with one of the world's leading engineering and professional service firms, WSP/Parsons Brinckerhoff, presented a business case to the Government for the improvement of freight movements in South Auckland.

Entitled 'Wiri to Westfield (W2W) — The Case for Investment' the business case presented ten options by which greater freight-carrying efficiency could be achieved along the Wiri to Westfield section of the North Island Main Trunk railway — described as:

"…a key link in the national and regional rail network. It carries a mix of suburban passenger services, inter-regional freight trains and freight shuttles between Ports of Auckland and Wiri. It is a major conduit for the movement of goods across New Zealand and a key public transport artery connecting South Auckland with the CBD and the wider region.

"The current twin track configuration has reached the maximum operational capacity. At the same time, the parallel State Highway network operates over-capacity during extended periods of the day. Consequently the transport system in South Auckland is under significant pressure and suffers from poor levels of resilience…"

"The investigation undertaken by the project partners concluded that completing the 3rd Main Line for the W2W section of the [line] would best meet the investment objectives for the project and to address the agreed problems affecting the network.

"This option is economically inefficient, as the forecast benefits significantly exceed the expected costs…Completing the 3rd Main Line significantly reduces the W2W constraint by separating passenger and freight services on this critical section of the national rail network…

"Completing the W2W Third Main will immediately deliver the following outcomes:
- 3 minute travel time saving for five million rail passenger journeys per annum
- At least 400 fewer heavy vehicles on the State Highway network each week with associated decongestion and road safety benefits

"The 3rd Main Line between Wiri and Westfield is compatible with any future requirement for more capacity and operational flexibility on the critical portion of the Auckland rail network spanning the Port of Auckland through to Westfield/Southdown and further south to Wiri and ultimately to Pukekohe.

"This would likely involve the construction of a 4th Main Line, possibly in combination with, or as a substitute for, other improvements at Westfield Junction which is another significant constraint in the Auckland rail network.

"The preferred timing for implementation of the 4th Main (or other intervention) was not the subject of this business case and continues to be assessed by Auckland Transport and KiwiRail as part of the Auckland Rail Development Program (ARDP) work." [28]

The Uncomfortable Truth

Following its completion in June 2016, KiwiRail refused to release the full business case — only a heavily-redacted version. After a good deal of public pressure, the unredacted study was finally released in July 2017 and, as described by Ben Ross in his article, 'Finally revealed: report shows rail destroys roading for Auckland freight', published by the Spinoff on 27 July 2017:

"…its contents are a shocking indictment of government policy…The business case for greater freight efficiency in South Auckland has finally been released, and it turns out that a new 'Third Main' rail line is the best of 10 options. Guess what's worst? Putting greater reliance on road freight. So why…does the government still insist on favouring trucks instead of funding the rail option?

"Why was the business case [initially] redacted?

"The answer is surely politics. It seems to come down to an attempt to protect the position taken by the government.

"The redacted material wasn't commercially sensitive and nor would its publication have harmed the free and frank debate between officials and the minister. Instead, it contains a clear-cut case to build the Third and Fourth Mains as quickly as possible, and definitely before the CRL opens (2023 on current estimates). The redacted MCA [Multi Criteria Analysis] also completely demolishes the roads-first argument,

"Why does the government persist with the option of more roads for more road freight?

"This question has been asked repeatedly by all the media organisations and many analysts following the issue, including politicians at central and local level representing nearly all non-government parties…they *all* recommend that the extra rail line or lines be built as quickly as possible.

"The government's continued support of the road freight industry in preference to expanding the role of rail, in the face of the data in this report, makes a complete mockery of its claim to prudent economic management. It makes, instead, a pretty good case for incompetence, or cronyism, or both." [29]

Unsurprisingly, the government referred to was a Road Gang favourite — the Fifth National-Party Government which governed New Zealand from 19 November 2008 to 26 October 2017.

Chapter Two

Enter the Machines

The First Horseless Carriages

Many of the most successful of man's inventions have proved to be so because they fulfilled a need at the time and added to the fortunes of humanity long after their introduction and refinement. Such was the case during the nineteenth century when the first prototypes of horseless carriages were put together. There was then an overriding need to improve on the staying power of the horse and rid the streets of its smelly by-product.

However, the potential of an innovative idea is sometimes suppressed by competing interests and it is only after a change of circumstances that a discarded concept may be rejuvenated at a much later date.

Such was the case with the horseless carriage during its progression through various stages of power generation — from the very first, wind-powered land vehicles of China (sailing chariots) to those of the steam, internal combustion, and electrical drive systems developed in Europe during the eighteenth and nineteenth centuries.

"One of the first men to suggest using steam to propel a vehicle was Sir Isaac Newton, the English scientist. His vehicle, built about 1680, consisted of a spherical steam boiler with a jet pointed to the rear. The reaction of the steam on the air was supposed to move the vehicle…

General Motors Canada provides an historical overview of the development of the horseless carriage at its website, a part of which includes:

"It was…in the 18th century that various inventors began experimenting with piston and cylinder engines powered by steam or the explosion of gunpowder. In 1769, Captain Nicolas Cugnot of France built and ran an artillery tractor which was powered by a steam engine. His efforts were far from a complete success, but the vehicle did travel about 4 ½ kilometers per hour between stops to build up steam.

"In 1801, Richard Trevithick of England built and ran a steam-powered carriage. In the 1820s and '30s many Englishmen constructed, and commercially operated, steam vehicles, which carried passengers and cargo. However, their efforts were severely hampered by conservative countrymen who restricted them from using the public roads. They were forced to turn their attention to operating trains or carriages on private rails; thus giving birth to railroads.

"In 1860, a French engineer named Etienne Lenoir invented an internal combustion engine that used illuminating gas for fuel and an electric spark for ignition. It was used to drive machinery and became the first commercial gas engine. In 1866, Otto and Langen of Germany improved upon the gas engine by developing the four-stroke cycle which is still used today.

"In 1885, [Gottlieb] Daimler, another German, used the Otto cycle in a gas vapour engine which he manufactured in quantity. The following year he applied his petrol engine to a motor car. Daimler's engine was used in France by Emile Levassor who designed a vehicle which set the basic mechanical pattern for modern automobiles." [1]

Across the Channel, in Britain, the future of the petrol-powered automobile was assured — as reported by the Otago Witness on 12 July 1900:

"It is admitted that the great motor trial run of 1000 miles just completed in England has fully served the purpose for which it was instituted. The course was from London, west to Bristol, north to Edinburgh, via Birmingham and Lancaster, thence south to London, through Newcastle, and Leicester.

"Included also in the itinerary were two or three divergences, consisting of side runs to certain hills, upon which were tested the climbing capabilities of the various motors. It must be understood that this run was not a time trial, but simply a test in which the fittest survived.

"One of the trade papers states that in the first place it served the indubitably valuable purpose of showing motor engineers wherein the motor as at present constructed fails; and, equally important, how far their efforts may be said to be crowned with success.

"All things considered, it is not unreasonable to look for a certain influx of valuable improvements, some affecting the actual design of the cars, others in matters of detail, but all introduced with good cause, and tending to release the motor car from the stigma of being still in the experimental stage.

"This trial has been the first real attempt to educate a rather incredulous public up to the proper understanding of the value of these vehicles.

"At the finish of the trip some 50 of the motors were exhibited at the Crystal Palace, and appeared in all stages of dirt, mud, and dust. It was evident that some of the cars had had a very rough time, judging by the cut tyres, twisted frames, and damaged steering gear." [2]

The First Electric Vehicles

Sometime between 1832 and 1839, Robert Anderson of Scotland built a motorized carriage powered by galvanic cell batteries but the batteries were not rechargeable so had to be replaced after a short distance.

"Another Scot, Robert Davidson of Aberdeen, built a prototype electric locomotive in 1837. A bigger, better version, demonstrated in 1841, could go 1.5 miles at 4 mph towing six tons. Then it needed new batteries. This impressive performance so alarmed railway workers (who saw it as a threat to their jobs tending steam engines) that they destroyed Davidson's devil machine, which he'd named Galvani.

"Batteries that could be recharged came along in 1859, making the electric-car idea more viable.

"Around 1884, inventor Thomas Parker helped deploy electric-powered trams and built prototype electric cars in England. By 1890, a Scotland-born chemist living in Des Moines, Iowa, William Morrison, applied for a patent on the electric carriage he'd built perhaps as early as 1887. It appeared in a city parade in 1888, according to the Des Moines Register. With front-wheel drive, 4 horsepower, and a reported top speed of 20 mph, it had 24 battery cells that needed recharging every 50 miles…" [3]

The first electric tram replaced the horse-drawn version in Auckland in November 1902. Those early trams could be described as the hybrid of their day as the electricity needed to power the tramway was supplied by the city's steam power stations. By 1904, the city was described by New Zealand's Registrar General as one of the most progressive in the colonies by virtue of its electric tramway system. [4]

As described by Allan Dick in his book to mark the centenary of the Motor Trade Association of New Zealand, published in 2017:

"As the 19th century was coming to a close and the world was gearing up for a future without horses, the electric car was a major contender. Putting aside steam cars, the two main contenders to rule the beckoning future of the motor vehicle were the simple and straight-forward electric cars and the complex, unreliable machines powered by internal combustion engines (ICE), fuelled by a liquid that was highly explosive, gasoline.

"If you look back to the year 1898, you would have to say that of the two propulsion systems, electricity was the winner. The cars were simpler, quieter, they had no smell, they were reliable — and they were fast.

"The first World Land Speed Record was established on 18 December 1898, by Comte Gaston de Chasseloup-Laubat at 39.24 mph. He was driving a Jeantaud electric car powered by a single electric motor generating 36 bhp…

"But for almost all of last [20th] century, the electric car was consigned to being a mere curiosity, hampered by the need for bulky batteries that only provided sufficient storage capacity for a short distance…there was minimal advancement in battery technology and we are left asking, if the motor industry had collectively decided in 1898 to go electric rather than ICE [internal combustion engine], where would the motor vehicle be today?" [5]

No Competition

"History doesn't [specifically] record how it was that the oil barons won the battle to provide the fuel (and thus decide the technology) for the motor vehicle for the next 110-plus years…" [6] But their plentiful supply of oil during the early twentieth century enabled petroleum-powered vehicles to be operated far more cheaply than their electric competition. More and better roads were being built to accommodate the needs of an increasing number of motorists but the length of many roads proved to be a mile too far for the battery capacity of even the most modern of electric vehicles then operating.

Meanwhile, improvements continued to be made to the internal combustion-powered vehicles. The muffler, invented in 1897, significantly reduced engine noise, and the invention of the electric starter by Charles Kettering in 1912 eliminated the need for energy-sapping, hand cranking to start the engine. The latter invention encouraged more of the fairer sex to learn to drive.

Such improvements progressively added to the popularity of the internal combustion engine-driven vehicles supplied to the eager buyer by Henry Ford and others who saw the prices of their products reduced significantly by their mass-production methods. [7]

By 1912, an electric car sold for almost double that of a gasoline-powered car and, although battery power would progress to power low-mileage vehicles such as milk floats and forklifts, the electric motor vehicle as a mass conveyance was soon overtaken by the internal combustion engine eagerly promoted by the Road Gang's manufacturers, dealers, and oil producers. It would be more than a century before the fortunes of modern electric vehicles improved — after a greater sense of preservation of the human species prevailed — triggered by changing climatic conditions that provoked the need for a less carbon-consuming and polluting mode of transportation.

W A Ryan and Company

One of the first importations into New Zealand of a very early model, internal combustion engine arrived, in fact, as a power source for a launch — then known as a 'vapour' or 'oil' engine — as reported by The New Zealand Herald on 9 November 1894:

"By the Monowai, yesterday afternoon from San Francisco, arrived a novel vessel to these colonies in the shape of a launch 22½ feet long, fitted with a four-horse power vapour engine (marine type). There are several thousands of these engines now in use in the United States, and it is claimed that they can be run far more cheaply than by steam power.

"No engineer is required, neither fire heat, boiler pumps, or other appliances, that are of necessity used with steam engines…After getting on board, all that is necessary is to oil the engine, give the flywheel a few revolutions, and the boat is under headway, and after starting requires next to no attention. There is no smoke, ashes, or dirt, everything is perfectly clean about this motor…

"Boats similar to the one just arrived may be obtained through the owners, Messrs. W A Ryan and Co., of this city, who are also agents for the manufacturers, or the engines can be supplied separately from one up to twenty horse power.

"Although this 'specimen' is in the shape of a boat engine, motors on the same principle are largely used for electric lighting, pumping, running printing presses, factories, elevators, turning and woodworking machinery, street cars, shearing machines, cream separators, in fact for anything where a cheap and handy motor is required, and can be driven with ordinary gas, gasoline, or naphtha." [8]

At the time W A Ryan and Co of Quay Street, Auckland were the Australasian agents for the engine which was quickly utilised as an alternative to steam power in early 1895:

"Mr C E Button…has erected a building as a creamery, with a 4 horse-power gasoline engine, manufactured by the Union Gas Engine Company of San Francisco and imported by W A Ryan and Co., of this city. The engine was started by the engineer and in full operation in 10 seconds, and by the press representative in 15 seconds.

"The motive power of the engine is gasoline, and it will run with ordinary gas. The oil [gasoline] is supplied at 1s 9d per gallon, and it takes a gallon per horse-power, working for eight working hours. It flows into a little chamber called the 'vaporiser' where it mixes with air, and is thence drawn into the cylinder, at a certain point of which it is exploded by a spark from the electric battery.

"The engine is at present used for chaff-cutting…in Hobson Street…" [9]

By April 1903, W A Ryan and Co was advertising itself as "General Engineers — Sole agents for New Zealand for the Oldsmobile trading from Railway Wharf, Quay Street, Auckland" [10]

With John Mowbray as Chairman of Directors, W A Ryan and Co opened a branch at Christchurch in August 1905 [11] and in September 1905, the company was offering "…a good stock of second-hand Motor-cars." [12]

During a Labour Day parade of trades and industries held at Auckland in October 1905, the Auckland Star described the presentation of W A Ryan and Co:

"An instructive exhibit was the motor waggon of Messrs W A Ryan and Co. Its great power was shown by the ease with which it moved along under its towering load of six tons of sacked wheat. Another display by the Ryan Company was much more aesthetic, but represented equally the usefulness of motor-power. It was a motor-car smothered in a wealth of beautiful arum lilies, driven by a chauffeur in white, several charming girls in white being the passengers." [13]

In August 1906, the company informed that it had not abandoned steam power altogether:

"Appointed sole New Zealand agents for all goods manufactured by John L Thorneycroft and Co. Limited, London — including "Marine Oil and Steam Motors, Steam Lorries, Commercial Vehicle Motors, and Direct Coupled Oil Electric Light Sets — Thorneycroft Steam Motor Waggons 4-ton £915 5-ton £985…" [14]

However, the bubble was soon to burst, as reported by the Christchurch Press on 9 April 1910:

"Samuel Vaile and Sons, auctioneers of Auckland announce in our advertising columns that they are offering for sale by auction on the 19th prox. a valuable brick property on Quay street in that city for W. A. Ryan and Co., Ltd. (in liquidation)." [15]

New Zealand's First Motor Cars

The first recorded importation of the motor car to New Zealand is said to have been "…two knocked-down Benz cars which had arrived in Wellington aboard the steamer Rotomahana…" and received by businessman and Member of Parliament, William McLean, in 1898. "He gave them the pet names 'Lightning' and 'Petrolette' which indicated how they would be viewed — as novelties both intriguing and a nuisance. The horseless carriage had arrived." [16]

However, under the legislation that then existed, neither William McLean nor anyone else could legally drive such contraptions on Wellington streets. Not for long though. He soon arranged for the introduction of appropriate legislation to Parliament.

When first introduced to Parliament, it was stated that the "McLean Light Locomotive Bill…was not intended to confer any special privilege on the promoter (McLean), who only wished to be placed in a position to use the cars which he had imported." [17]

Accordingly, what would become the McLean Motor-car Act of 1898 also enabled "…other Persons to obtain Permits and Licenses for a like Purpose, and also to authorise the Storage of Inflammable Substances used in driving such Motor-cars." [18]

The provision of the Act allowing others to be licensed to operate motor cars came after some criticism of the original Bill — as reported by The New Zealand Times on 16 July 1898:

"Whatever credit may be due to the gentlemen who have first brought motor cars on to the streets of Wellington, there is no reason why Parliament should pass a measure conferring on them or anyone else a monopoly of the rights of running such vehicles here or anywhere else in the colony. We are informed that monopoly is not to be asked for; that the proposal made to Parliament will merely be for the granting of a right not necessarily exclusive. That, it appears to us, is the only form in which the Legislature should grant the concession to run motor cars." [19]

The New Zealand Times editorial also foretold of the motor vehicle becoming a necessity — a future development not all that obvious in 1898:

"For, as is indicated by the petition of local motor-constructing tradesmen to the City Council on Thursday night, there are likely to be several interests at stake in this connection. It may be said with as much certainty as is possible in these fast-moving, inventive days, that the motor car has 'come to stay'. It is a new thing now, but will presently come into general use. Parliament should therefore be very chary of doing anything which may confer monopoly in a means of transit which promises to become a general necessity." [20]

One of the first petrol-driven motor cars to be successfully driven any distance in the South Island was reported by the Nelson Evening Mail on 12 July 1900. This was no Benz or Star imported from overseas but of local construction — perhaps one of the first to be assembled in New Zealand:

"The Oamaru Mail states that Mr. F. R. Denniston, mechanical engineer, of Christchurch, arrived in Oamaru recently on a motor car which he has constructed from his own model. It is driven by a gasoline engine, and Mr. Denniston proved the practical nature of its construction by riding down from Christchurch upon it. The car, which is admittedly only roughly built, can attain a speed of 15 or 16 miles an hour under favourable circumstances." [21]

Auckland's First Motor Cars

What is thought to have been Auckland's first motor car, the Star, was made by the Star Engineering Company of Wolverhampton, England and delivered to its sole Auckland agent, Skeates and Bockaert, in 1899. The Star "…featured a 3.5-horsepower engine, had one cylinder and was belt-driven." [22]

An interview of Arthur Marychurch, said to have been the importer of the Star was published by the Manawatu Standard on 13 January 1936:

"The car…was brought to Auckland by the steamer, Whakatane, arriving in Auckland in September 1899. It was run in Auckland until December of that year, and was then taken to Christchurch by steamer.

"'I paid £168 for the car new at the works, and was given the agency,' said Mr Marychurch in an interview in Auckland. On my arrival back, I gave the agency to Messrs Skeates and Bockaert, and they paid the freight and duty, amounting to £90. That is how Skeates and Bockaert came to handle the car…The car was sold to Messrs Wardell Bros. of Christchurch, for £130.'

"'The Star was capable of 20 miles an hour on high gear and eight miles an hour on low. Built early in 1899, it was powered by a single-cylinder motor of 4 9-16 in. bore and stroke, with an open-fronted crankshaft with two driving pulleys for two speeds on the crankshaft. There was one fixed and two loose pulleys on the intermediate shaft, from which there was chain drive to the rear wheels. The car was equipped with wire wheels with pneumatic tyres, the front ones being smaller in diameter than the rear ones.'" [23]

The Motoring Lobby

Subsequent arrivals of motor cars to Auckland were described by Dr F J Rayner, the founder and first president of the Auckland Automobile Association:

"Motoring in Auckland first began in 1902 when the firm of Ryan and Co. indented four Oldsmobile cars. These were sold to Dr Rayner, Dr Owen, Mr Spinks, and Dr Lowe. About the same time Mr Geo. Henning imported a steam-car for himself, and shortly afterward a shipment of Darracq cars arrived, indented by Messrs Skeates and Bockaert.

"Mr Smith, of Smith and Caughey, and Mr Leyland, of Leyland O'Brien were two early owners of these cars. About the only other car on the market at this time was the single-cylinder Cadillac, for which Messrs Dexter and Crozier were agents.

"These few motorists got together and formed a club, known as the Auckland Automobile Association, which used to meet in a rented room in 52 Queen Street. This club was formed to organise outings and trips, and to safeguard the interests of motorists by promotion of traffic by-laws, and the examination of prospective motor drivers. In those days there were no City Council by-laws or even tests for drivers' certificates, so the club early formulated an examination on both the theory and practice of motoring." [24]

A study entitled 'The Motoring Lobby in New Zealand, 1898-1930', undertaken by historians Austin Gee and Alexander Trapeznik examined the activities of some automobile organisations "…in the context of wider pressure group activity…" The study was published in the Journal of New Zealand Studies (Victoria University, Wellington) in 2018 — excerpts from which include:

"Though New Zealand's first motor car was imported only in 1898, and there were no local manufacturers, within a quarter of a century the country had one of the highest levels of car ownership worldwide. In 1907 it was estimated there were about 3,000 private cars in the country, or one for every 316 people. In the second decade of the century car ownership grew markedly as a result of the availability of cheaper and more practical vehicles, not least the Ford Model T, and the development of a second-hand market for cars.

"Accurate figures are first available for 1925, by which time there were 71,403 cars, or one for every 19 people; a decade later, despite the effects of the Depression, the ratio had reached one in 12…

Regional motor clubs were formed throughout New Zealand from 1903 onwards. By 1915 there were 11 of them, and by 1928, 15. They varied widely in size, from the large Auckland and Canterbury associations to the smaller Nelson and Wairarapa clubs. Some of them briefly sought to exclude members of the motor trade, but in general they sought to attract as wide a membership as possible…

"From the incomplete figures available, it seems that motoring organisations rarely represented more than a quarter of all motorists. Early local authority vehicle registration records survive only patchily, but of the 175 owners of cars registered in Dunedin in 1911, only 35 — a fifth — had joined the Otago Motor Association by the following year.

"Matters seem not to have improved substantially by 1927, when the Southland Motor Association estimated that its membership constituted only about a quarter of all car owners in its province. By the end of 1934, the Otago club's membership had reached 2,651, representing about 22 percent of the approximately 12,000 cars registered in the province. The organisations were naturally open to accusations they did not represent the views of motorists in general…

"Though they had a clear political agenda and several of them adopted the name 'automobile association', the New Zealand motor clubs were not campaigning organisations on the model of the Automobile Association (AA) in Britain. This had been formed in 1905 to take direct action against police speed traps and other forms of what it saw as official harassment of motorists…

"On one occasion in 1925, a committee member of the Otago Motor Club stood in the middle of the road to warn fellow motorists of a nearby police speed trap. He was reported by a fellow club member and charged with obstructing the police. The magistrate rejected his defence that he merely sought to prevent the commission of an offence, lamented that the motor club had sanctioned his behaviour, and fined him £10…

"Motor clubs sought to protect their members' interests through lobbying, self-regulation and self-policing, but some saw their main purpose as social…

"Motor clubs had an obvious interest in the state of public roads and bridges, and so were in regular contact with urban and rural councils. They sought to avoid the implication of special pleading by arguing that remedying dangerous grades and bends, or cutting back overhanging vegetation, would benefit 'all kinds of traffic', not just motor cars…

"An early attempt was made to form a 'good roads' association in Christchurch in 1905, and one formed in Auckland by members of the regional automobile association in 1918 was more successful and long-lived. It had national influence and cooperated closely with motor clubs to pressure local and national government…

When clubs wished to influence local government decisions, whether on road building or traffic regulations, they often sent delegations to the city or county councils. The delegation that approached the Dunedin City Council in 1915, asking for 'more equitable treatment between motors and other vehicles', was typical…

"Before the First World War, motorists were inclined to imply that resistance to their demands was based on ignorance of the benefits of motoring. Hostility to motor vehicles would fade, they believed, once those in influential positions acquired cars of their own. For instance, motorists campaigning in 1915 to have a rural road widened and fenced met strong resistance from local farmers. This was before motor vehicles became important for rural transport, and the ratepayers could see only disadvantages in the increased costs and wear caused by 'pleasure' motoring. The car owners concluded that 'it seemed that the only way to get the road opened would be to wait till the [farmers] had cars of their own and then they would change their minds…'

"The routine consultation of motoring organisations on proposed legislation was well established by 1924, when the centralised registration of motor vehicles was introduced. The Motor Vehicles Bill was 'the outcome of a series of conferences' with motor associations and local bodies, and the Minister of Public Works declared it 'the nearest we can get to giving something to fit in with the expression given at that time of the various interests'…

"When the early motoring lobby is examined in detail, it is clear that it comprised a series of shifting alliances between public bodies and private interest groups…The initiative for action on matters affecting motorists could come from either local government or the motor clubs, either individually or coordinated by the motor unions.

"They applied pressure to the national government by such means as writing letters, sending telegrams, commissioning specialist reports and sending delegations to ministers in person…Motorists' demands were much less likely to succeed at the national level if government revenue was at stake…" [25]

Imports Galore
"…by the end of the decade [1910] more and more [New Zealand] people were shelling out hard-earned cash to join the horseless carriage brigade. In 1903 the value of car imports was £16,598. By 1910 it was more than a quarter of a million pounds. The era of mass ownership seemed about to begin." [26]

"Figures from ACC [Auckland City Council] records show 64 motorcars were registered in 1910 and 1,224 in 1913…" [27]

Freight Without The Horse
While the first imports of the horseless carriage catered for the about-town transport of doctors and the bon-vivants, it was the cost-saving factor of motorised vehicle transport of goods and material, compared to that of horse-drawn vehicles, that made all the difference — as reported by the Nelson Evening Mail on 3 February 1921:

"Better Roads for Less Money — Severe Test By Waimea County

"…a demonstration was given yesterday, before the chairman, Mr Best, and members and Engineer, Mr Menzies, of the Waimea County Council, of the merits of the Thornycroft Dump Truck for carting and spreading road metal.

"The test was carried out under the supervision of Mr W Vaughan, of the South Island Motors Ltd., Christchurch, who control the agency for this make of vehicle for the South Island in the interests of Messrs A. Hatrick and Co., Ltd., Wellington, who are distributors for Australia and New Zealand.

"The test selected for this demonstration by the Waimea County Council was to transport metal from the bins at Appleby bridge over the Moutere Hills, and spread at a point some distance beyond Muntz's store, a total distance of 10½ miles.

"During a period of eight hours' running time, four loads of metal consisting each of three full yards per trip, were loaded, transported, and spread. It is estimated that two horses and a dray could cart only a yard and a quarter of metal per day over this route. Thus the Thornycroft motor in actual test, outstripped the horses and dray, by 12 yards to a yard and a quarter.

"The Chairman and members of the Council present expressed themselves as agreeably surprised with the capabilities of this modern method of transport, no doubt being left in their minds that such methods were not only desirable but essential…" [28]

Competing with Rail

While the greater efficiency and economic value of transporting goods by motor transport was good news for the average consumer, such was not the case for the competition — the railways — as reported by the Evening Star in December 1921:

"In some parts of New Zealand the railways are meeting with strong opposition from motor lorries. This is particularly the case on the west coast of the North Island, and the attention of the Acting Minister of Railways was called to the matter by Mr E. Newman today.

"He said that benzine is being carried into the Manawatu district from Wellington by lorry at 2s a case, whereas the rail charge is 3s 8d. Wool was being taken to Wellington from the Manawatu by motor at the same rates as the railway, with the additional advantage that there is no cartage to the store.

"A quotation had been made to carry butter to Wellington at railway rates by motor, while passenger traffic from Marton Junction to Wanganui by motor car was rapidly growing. The result of present conditions was that the bulk of the traffic was being diverted from the rail to the road.

"The Hon. D. H. Guthrie replied that the position was under consideration. He knew there was strong competition by motor lorries, where wool could be taken to port and benzine brought in return, benzine being one of the highest freight commodities carried on the railway…

"He realised that in the South Island motors were competing with the railways. The department had the matter under consideration, with a view to keeping up the revenue and not allowing undue competition." [29]

The First Vehicle & Parts Dealers

Despite the country's roads being more suited to horse-drawn carriages than mechanised traffic, and some initial concern that the motor vehicle might be just a short-lived wonder, many coach builders and business entrepreneurs set out to capitalise on the novelty while it lasted.

While the New Zealand marketplace for motor vehicles and ancillaries would eventually be dominated by a comparatively few entities and their principals, during the very early years of the twentieth century, a great number of small manufacturers, importers, and dealers emerged from the clip-clop of hooves and the ding-ding of bicycle bells to meet the challenges and opportunities presented by the motor car.

Competitive Advertising

The competition generated by the first motor mechanics, motor body fabricators, importers, and retailers of ancillary products soon required city billboards and newspaper classifieds to be emblazoned with the great number of constantly-improved models on offer to entice the prospective buyer. Although the advertising medium would change over time, the precedent for inciting and maintaining motor car mania was set in place for many decades.

The Warranty

A particular selling point promoted by motor vehicle dealers was the warranty — a guarantee that the buyer was not being sold a lemon.

"The concept of an auto warranty originated from Ford Motor Company's Buggies in 1908, which provided customers a guarantee for repairs for up to nine months after purchase." [30]

As early as 1924, vehicle dealers such as The Dominion Motors were providing car warranties as an incentive to sell used vehicles with low mileage. [31]

In April 1972, Ford reduced its new car and light commercial vehicles warranty from 12 months or 12,000 miles to six months or 6000 miles. Heavy vehicle warranties were also reduced to six months or 12,000 miles:

"The company's president (Mr R B Fawcett) told The Press yesterday that the cuts had been made possible by improvements in engineering and quality control at local assembly plants. Asked if one would not expect this to be a reason for maintaining or extending warranty periods rather than reducing them, Mr Fawcett said this would be a logical thought for someone not directly involved in the motor industry.

"'The motoring public would not be at any disadvantage,' he said.

"'The company's experience had shown that engineering and quality advances meant most defects were minor, and appeared during the first six months or 6000 miles. Reducing the period would mean the same service to the public, but a halving of the administration needed to maintain a 12-months record for the 20,000-plus Ford vehicles sold in 12 months. The man in the street is going to get exactly the same kind of deal.

"'Competitors might possibly suggest to buyers they would be better with a longer warranty, but while warranty periods might be a motivating factor in the choice of a new car, confidence in the product was more important…Warranty periods had changed over the years,' he said, 'and overseas the trend was now away from some of the very long periods of past years to shorter terms.'" [32]

Early Newspaper Advertisements

A selection of advertisements for motor vehicles for sale and wanted, published between 1911 and 1920, by The New Zealand Herald and Auckland Star, included:

Pullen, Armitage & Company

"Carriage and Car Body Builders, corner of Albert and Federal Streets — For Sale. Cheap — Hansom Cabs, two four-wheel Dogcarts, four Spring Carts…" [33]

"Just Arrived. A new shipment of the famous North British Motor Car Tyres and Tubes. Prices on application." [34]

"Motor Car Salesman. Written applications will be received up to October 6, 1917, from men qualified to Sell Studebaker Cars, 'North British Baud' and 'Clincher Cross' Tyres. Send previous records and testimonials to Stanley G Chambers, Managing Director…" [35]

"The Auckland Home of Republic Trucks…we stock a complete line of Republic Parts, we employ specially trained mechanics and transportation engineers and we are always ready to serve Republic owners in an efficient manner." [36]

Cousins And Atkin — "Coachbuilders, Beach Road — Are Builders of Business and Pleasure Vehicles, also Motor Bodies…" [37]

Harrison and Gash, Carriage and Motor Works, Newmarket — "Ford Motor Car for Sale, with up-to-date local body…" [38]

C Jephson, Wairiki Road, Mt Eden — "Car, Cadillac, for Sale; equal to new; suitable for taxi or motor service work…"

Haydock and Spragg Central Garage — Wakefield Street — "Daimler 15-20 h.p. £250; 8 h.p. Auto-Carrier £90…"

G A Haydon, Engineer, 50 Hobson Street — "Ford Cars — Several 5-seater Cars in good order. Also 2 and 5-seater Cars wanted to Purchase…"

Walker and Co Limited, The Ferry Garage, Quay Street — "An Up-To-The-Minute Car. The Maxwell '25'. A Beautiful 5-Seater with streamline body, electric lighting, and self-starter, and the latest equipment. Built for hard wear and economical running. A smart, sterling and durable car at a low price…No Better Proposition Offering…"

P Faithfull and Co, 39-41 Wakefield Street — "Chalmers 30 h.p. 5-seater £180 Daimler S K 15 h.p. 5-seater £230 Hupmobile 2-seater £125 Overland 1914 Model 5-seater £280 S.C.A.T. Chassis for Delivery Van £180 And several other Cars…" [39]

Russell and Co Garage, Little Queen Street — "Car, 5-seater B.S.A English in first-class condition…"

Hoiland and Gillett Ltd, Customs Street West — "Hallford Motor Lorry 2-1/2 ton; 2 bodies and complete; in perfect order…" [40]

Laird Bros, Corner Customs and Hobson Streets — "Metz Motor Cars. Mr Motorist. If you want a car having a first-class appearance, thoroughly reliable, obtainable at a fair Price, and as simple as a bicycle, buy a Metz. After 3-1/2 years' daily use in and about Auckland the Metz Cars have proved beyond argument that the Friction-driven Car, either as a business or pleasure proposition, stands alone. The pleasure or profit of motoring depends on the running cost, and anyone can afford to run a Metz Car…Five-seater 25 h.p. 4-cylinder, electric light and starter, speedometer, and full equipment £250, subject to increase. Two-seater £180, no electric equipment."

S E Moe and Co. Motor Garage, Great South Road, Papatoetoe — "Motor and Cycle Importers, Engineers, Etc…" [41]

John W Andrew, Eden Terrace — "Motors For Sale. Be Up-To-Date And Motorise Your Delivery, Get A Chase Truck — The Best Money Can Buy. I have Two 1-Ton Chassis arriving at an early date…" [42]

"— has Second hand Ford Cars, Trucks, and Delivery Vans for sale. Price on application…" [43]

Skeates And White, Motor Garage, Customs Street — "Motor Car For Sale £295 A Beautiful Five-Seater Arrol Johnston Car. British Built in absolutely perfect condition…" [44]

Blomeley and Sons, Motor Builders, Eden Terrace — "Oldsmobile 30 h.p. 5-seater, first-class chassis for Sale: suitable for delivery work, cheap…" [45]

Dexter and Crozier Ltd, Albert Street — "The Burford Motor Lorry. Two Ton Chassis. The Highest Grade Truck Manufactured. Those interested invited to inspect. Trials by Appointment…" [46]

Miller's Motor Garage, Khyber Pass — "Miller's Special Motor Bargains — 3-seater Sunbeam, 1912 model, good running order £275; 3-seater Kissel 40 horse electric light and starter, equal to new, stream line body £275; Turee 5-seater B.S.A. good running order £250…Several 2-seater English and American Cars, low price…" [47]

The Canadian Motor Co of New Zealand Limited, Little Queen Street — "We, the leading dealers in Ford Cars, have the right to sell in the City of Auckland and in the territory extending from Waiwera to Cambridge and thence to Rotorua. Send to us for your Ford Touring, Runabout, or Commercial Car, and we will give you immediate delivery. A E Roxburg, Manager." [48]

The Queen Street Garage, Just above Town Hall — "New Cars Are Practically Unobtainable. See this Bargain List: Ford 2-seater £140; Ford 5-seater £160; Cadillac 5-seater £260; Chevrolet 5-seater £260; Studebaker 7-seater £325; Ford Bus £225; A.C. 3-seater £270; We specialise in car repairs…" [49]

Empire Motor Garage, 181-183 Karangahape Road — "Fords(3), 2 and 5-Seaters in Perfect Running Order, £140 to £160. Briscoe 3-Seater, electric lighting, starter, etc. £180 R.C.H. 2-Seater, £120 any trial. Princess 2-Seater, electric lighting, starter, etc. £150. We specialise in Ford Repairs. Only Genuine Ford Parts Used…" [50]

The Campbell Motor Co., 13 Customs Street East — "Dodge Bros Cars To Arrive. Book for October Shipment. See the latest Creation in Motor Cars. The 6 cyl Columbia Sports Model. Nothing to equal it has ever been seen in NZ for design and finish. Price £600…Trucks…for immediate delivery. No waiting…" [51]

[Campbell Motors was started by George Campbell and Les 'Snowy' Bedford "…selling Firestone tyres, used cars and four-gallon tins of petrol, then Dodge cars, in 1919 for Northern Automobiles, who had previously had that franchise for Auckland." [52]

As detailed later, Campbell Motors Limited was incorporated in 1926, and acquired by Wright Stephenson & Co Limited in 1969. Throughout the company's long existence, its many subsidiaries included Campbell Motor Imports, Campbells Wholesale, Campbell Tube Products, Campbell Industries, Olympus Motors Limited, and Motorlife Sales Co Limited.] [53]

Schofield and Denton, Newmarket — "A Bargain. English Car, five-seater, tip-top condition; great hill climber; light benzine consumption. £275 Cash. Also Cadillac Car, 1915 model; condition as new. Snip for Cash…" [54]

"Motor Cars For Sale — 5-Seater Krit Car in good order £140 for quick sale. 1914 Cadillac Car electric light, self-starter; only done 9000 miles, perfect order £440. English 5-seater car, light, good hill climber, tyres 30 by 3-1/2, splendid order, bargain £250. B.S.A. Car 5-seater, electric light, self-starter, as new £465. Also would Exchange an unencumbered Section for a Car Value £155…" [55]

"Smith Form A Trucks. Let us convert your Ford Car and improve your haulage facilities. We have a limited number of these Attachments in stock…" [56]

Private Sales

Many of the advertised motor vehicles were offered by private owners…some with an apparently very patriotic reason for an urgent sale…

"2-seater 15.9 h.p. Arrol-Johnston Car for Sale, good as new: owner leaving for front immediately — Phone 179…" [57]

"For Immediate Sale — Nearly new 2-1/2 ton Hallford Motor Lorry 23 h.p. Very strong machine. Two 14-passenger 23 h.p. Motor Buses, good order…Owners off to war…R H Wood and Co. Exchange Lane, 93 Fort Street…" [58]

Two-Car Family

It wasn't long before the concept of a two-car family was eagerly promoted by some dealers:

"Spragg's Garage, Lorne Street — Scripps Booth Motor-Cars, the Smartest and Most Attractive Two-Seaters in Auckland, Light Weight And Will Do 80 Miles To Gallon Of Benzine. If you possess a big, heavy car and want an economical runabout of stylish appearance, or if you want an ideal lady's car, you'll never regret investing in a Scripps Booth…" [59]

The Motor Trade Association

The Motor Trade Association (MTA) was founded at Feilding in 1917 as the Motor Garage Proprietors' Association of New Zealand. "By 1918 a national council had been formed and could report a membership of 173. In 1919 the name of the organisation became The Motor Garage Proprietors and Cycle Traders Association of New Zealand. In 1921 the name became the more embracing one of The New Zealand Motor Trade Association, which remained until 1933, when it was amended to the New Zealand Garage Proprietors' Association. The association, together with the New Zealand Petrol Resellers' Association which was formed in

1934, combined to form the New Zealand Retail Motor Trade Association in 1940. The name was amended to the Motor Trade Association (Incorporated) in 1974." [60]

As Allan Dick pointed out in his centenary history of the Motor Trade Association, published in 2017:

"Many workshops and garages had originally been blacksmiths, used to shoeing horses and repairing buggies and farm implements, and that was really all that many were interested in. But after the MTA was founded (and became a national organisation) its Wellington head office spent the next decade imploring all members to become all-things to the motorist and to not just sell them the car if they were a dealer, or repair the car if they were a garage, but to sell them tyres, petrol, oil — everything else that their car needed…" [61]

As well as the dealers previously listed, there were many entrepreneurs ready, willing, and able to heed the advice of the MTA and 'become all-things to the motorist':

Leonard F Wallis

L F Wallis and Company Limited was registered as a private company at Wellington on 17 December 1914 with a capital of £10,000 divided into 10,000 shares of £1 each. Subscribers at the time included L (Leonard) F Wallis 3334 shares, G (George) A Wallis 3333 shares, and E J Stephens 3333 shares.

The objects of the company were stated as: "To acquire as a going concern the business heretofore carried on by L F Wallis under the style of 'L S Wallis and Co.' as wholesale and retail merchants and importers, manufacturers and traders of and in motor vehicles, etc." [62]

One of the first motoring accessories provided by L F Wallis and Co included a puncture seal device described by The New Zealand Herald in August 1913:

"Ever since the invention of motor-cars tyres have been a trouble and a vexation to the motorist. Detachable wheels were introduced to overcome puncture delays, but punctures themselves seemed beyond the inventive mind of man. The slightest perforation of the inner tube meant instant stoppage of the car, and the occupants, if the speed was fast, were pitched headlong on to the ground, with risk to life and limb.

"The inner tubes no doubt will still remain open to puncture, but a new invention called puncture seal will, if used, prevent you knowing it. The wheels will remain inflated if this solution has been first injected to the inner tube through the valve, and you will reach your destination without knowledge of a puncture.

"The method of overcoming the effects of puncture is to inject this non-inflammable patented substance, which resembles an ordinary rubber solution of a thick consistency. As the wheels revolve it moistens and adheres to the inside of the tube. It adds no perceptible weight, and does not displace the air.

"The tube may be pumped to 80lb or 90lb pressure, and the moment a puncture occurs the air pressure forces this new substance into the wound, and automatically heals it up. Not enough air is lost to blow out a match. Nails up to 3in in length may be driven into the tube and withdrawn, but the inflation does not suffer, and not an ounce of air pressure is lost." [63]

A demonstration of the effectiveness of the product by Leonard Wallis was reported in September 1914:

"It is not often that we see a motorist deliberately hammering nails into the tyres of his car, yet this is what a Tribune reporter witnessed at Napier last night, and to his astonishment no air came out of the tubes nor did the tyres appear to be affected in the least by having holes bored in them.

"The motorist, Mr L F Wallis, who at first appeared to be playing the fool with his tyres, was a representative of Puncture Seal Limited, and he was demonstrating the absolute immunity from punctures which follows their treatment by Puncture Seal.

"The reporter who investigated last night's experiments satisfied himself that Puncture Seal did all that is claimed for it, and possesses nothing but advantages. Puncture Seal Limited, are now erecting a plant at Messrs Davis and Boyd's garage, Hastings, and will be prepared to execute orders in a day or two." [64]

A further advancement for the motorist in the early years was the inclusion of a Stepney Spare Wheel…invented by Thomas Morris Davies of Llanelli, South Wales in 1904.

"At that time, early motor cars were made without spare wheels, so a puncture was an event dreaded by all drivers. Mr Davies' brilliant idea was to make a spokeless wheel rim fitted with an inflated tyre…In 1922 the company became Stepney Tyres Limited…" [65]

By July 1915, L F Wallis & Co had become the sole agent in New Zealand for the Stepney:

"The demonstrations given at the South Taranaki Winter Show by Mr L F Wallis, agent for the Stepney tyres and puncture proof tubes, have aroused much interest, as is proved by the fact that already no fewer than thirty-three local motorists have booked orders. This invention has efficiently withstood severe tests, and in practical use has proved satisfactory to owners of cars.

"The Stepney was introduced into New Zealand only twelve months ago. The earliest users are satisfied with the reliability, of the patent, and declare that nails, which immediately puncture an ordinary tube, enter their Stepneys without any effect. When the nails are extracted there is no reduction of the air pressure in the tube. The sole agency is held by Messrs L. F. Wallis and Co. Ltd. of Wellington." [66]

By 1915, L F Wallis and Co had become the New Zealand agents for the Maxwell motor car… [67]

However, the company's attempt to sell Chevrolet motor-cars on behalf of Dominion Motor Vehicles Limited was not so successful and led to court proceedings that dragged on for many months:

"Mr Skerrett, in opening the case for the plaintiffs [L F Wallis and Co Ltd], submitted that by an agreement dated October 7 last year the plaintiffs were appointed solo agents and granted the sole right of selling Chevrolet motor-cars for that part of the South Island north of a line drawn from Hurunui to Ross.

"The agreement was signed by C B Norwood, managing director of the defendant company [Dominion Motor Vehicles Ltd] and the selling basis was fixed at 20 per cent…Acting on this agreement, the plaintiffs went to the expense of introducing the cars in the territory mentioned.

"They also paid £25 as a deposit upon a demonstration car, but neither such car nor such deposit had been yet delivered or returned. Indeed, the defendants violated their agreement, and caused plaintiffs loss, although the plaintiffs were ready and willing to proceed, and had proceeded to carry out their part of the agreement.

"Under this part of the agreement plaintiffs claim they lost the sale of at least sixty cars bearing a profit of £60 each had the defendants fulfilled their part of the agreement entered into. A second cause of action was for the refund of the deposit of £25. A third cause of action was the non-delivery of cars for sale within the City of Wellington, which right, by a letter dated August 25, 1915, was conferred to plaintiffs by defendants and confirmed by them by agreement six weeks later.

"An order and deposit for a car was accepted by the defendants in confirmation of this arrangement, but neither of the cars had been delivered. By defendant's action plaintiffs considered they lost the profit on at least 20 cars…In pursuance of the contract the plaintiffs ordered thirty cars, but they were not delivered…" [68]

"His Honour the Chief Justice was engaged, yesterday in the further hearing of the case in which L. F. Wallis and Co. Ltd claimed £9875 from the Dominion Motor Vehicles Ltd for alleged breach of agreement. The hearing was adjourned to admit of the evidence of Cyril W Bradford being taken. Mr Bradford is the factory representative of the Chevrolet Motor Company of New York, and his evidence will be taken on commission on a date to be fixed after his arrival in New Zealand." [69]

"The Chief Justice heard further evidence in a protracted case on Saturday. This is a claim for £9875 by L F Wallis and Co. Ltd. against the Dominion Motor Vehicles Ltd for alleged breach of contract. When the dispute was before the court in July last evidence was heard concerning an agency for a particular model of the Chevrolet car. The case was adjourned." [70]

While the court proceedings continued, the principals of L F Wallis & Company took the opportunity to pursue other motor industry interests and resolved to wind up the company on 24 August 1916 after having disposed of its principal assets to a new company, Combined Buyers Limited. [71]

Combined Buyers

"Combined Buyers Limited of 58 Taranaki Street, Wellington was registered in August 1916 with a capital of £100,000 — 10,000 shares of £10 each. The subscribers were then recorded as G (George) A Wallis, E J Stevens, Ella Barry, F E Petherick, L (Leonard) F Wallis, M King, and O Beere.

The objects of the new company were stated as: "To acquire as a going concern the business heretofore carried on by L F Wallis & Co Ltd at Wellington and to carry on the business of merchants and importers of motors and motor vehicles, etc." [72]

By November 1916, Combined Buyers Limited was advertising itself as a wholesale motor warehouse…[73] and had purchased a "Three-storied building at corner of Dixon and Quinn Streets [Wellington]…for £5350…" [74]

However, not everyone was impressed with the incorporation of what was described as "a one-sided semi-co-operative idea" by NZ Truth commentator, Cambist, in July 1917:

"Ten Shares to Control a £100,000 Company And Carry a Third of the Profits Without any Liability. There are many dodges for getting into business, especially when the supply of cash is scarce. 'Cambist' is constrained to open this article with the foregoing remark, for the prospectus of the Combined Buyers Limited has just come to hand..." [75]

Later that year, in December 1917, Cambist commented on the first Annual Report and Balance Sheet published by Combined Buyers, voicing his concerns as to the legitimacy of the business:

"Without the fullest particulars as to the landed cost of these goods, and the full amount of the trading turnover, no one can guess how the customers fare in their dealings. That partly goes to prove that the oft reiterated demand for details made by Cambist has a great deal to commend itself to the thoughtful members of all joint stock trading, and other concerns that hold out special inducements for patronage.

"Have the founders' shares enjoyed a 'cut' out of this year's profits? and will any more premiums be demanded on the future emissions of the company? are two points that Cambist would like to raise…" [76]

Nevertheless, despite the criticism and the trading difficulties experienced during the war years, the economic outlook for the company was encouraging — as evidenced by the Shareholders' report published by The Dominion in March 1918:

"Supplies from overseas were arriving freely and manufacturers generally were showing an anxiety for trade. Cabled advice just to hand stated that a large parcel of orders for accessories had already been shipped, and although trading was still mainly confined to tyres, the time was rapidly approaching when we could be stocking all the necessities of the trade…the following motion was carried unanimously:- That the capital of the company be increased to the amount of £250,000 by the creation of additional capital of the amount of £150,000, divided into 15,000 shares of £10 each…" [77]

Later that year, at the Annual Meeting of the company, that optimism was maintained:

"At the Annual Meeting of Combined Buyers Limited held at Wellington on 29 November 1918, the Chairman of Directors, W S Bennett, advised of a net profit for the year of £524 11s 6d.

"…notwithstanding the strenuous times, the abnormal trade conditions of the past year, and the insistent opposition of the trade, the turnover had shown considerable expansion over that of the previous year. They had been able to maintain more than a sufficiency of stocks of tyres and tubes and had also secured large supplies of accessories thus enlarging the company's usefulness to shareholders at rates considerably below the ordinary prices levied by others.

"The company had accepted the Dominion agency for the 'Paige' car, built by the Paige Detroit Motor Car Company, and by repute quite equal to the 'Buick', and it was anticipated that these cars would be available to shareholders at a very reasonable rate compared with present ruling prices…Supplies of lubricating oil have been arranged for, and the first two shipments are now on the water.

"At September 30 [1918], 2498 shareholders were allied to the company…Running costs of cars and other motor vehicles would be appreciably reduced by members placing the whole of their orders for tyres, tubes and accessories with the company…" [78]

One of the many accessories promoted by Combined Buyers Limited included what must have been the forerunner of the windscreen wiper, marketed as "The Outlook Cleaner". This single-bladed device was affixed to the vehicle windscreen and hand-operated by the driver —

"Why run into danger when you can drive in any storm with clear vision and comfort. Operated without leaving your seat. — An Insurance for 10 shillings Post Free…From Combined Buyers Limited, Motor Merchants, 91-93 Dixon Street, Wellington." [79]

By December 1919, vehicles offered for sale by Combined Buyers Limited included:

"Motor Trucks! 1½ to 2 and 2 to 2½-ton 'Wichita' Trucks complete with Acetylene Lamps, Driver's Seat, and full equipment. Price: 1½ to 2-ton, £705; 2 to 2½ ton £805, at Wellington. Combined Buyers Limited, 91-97 Dixon Street, Wellington." [80]

By 1925, Leonard Wallis had expanded his interests to Australia "…where he founded the Combined Buyers Ltd of Australia, which has shown profit during the last couple of years…

"…Mr L. F. Wallis had been so successful in importing motor spirit for his Australian shareholders at very favourable prices, that the directors of the New Zealand company, with the single exception of Mr. Robieson, invited him to spend eight months here to organise the importation and distribution of motor spirit for the New Zealand…" [81]

However, as the previous publicity implied, not all within the company were in favour of expanding their operations to include motor spirit — as reported by The New Zealand Herald:

"The chairman referred to a circular issued by a South Island shareholder, Mr Wallis, and said that statements in the circular imputed that Mr. Bennett's connection with his own firm as well as with Combined Buyers was a hindrance to the sale of motor spirit by Combined Buyers. Mr. Bennett declared that the statements in the circular were not true, and that his firm had never been agents for certain oil companies.

"Mr L F Wallis said that just after the armistice he had suggested that the company should import benzine. He had found Mr Bennett unfavourable and taxed him with being in a position which would not let him support the idea, as his firm was interested in the sale of benzine and Combined Buyers would appear as a competitor." [82]

Perhaps as a result of internal strife, the later trading results for Combined Buyers showed a distinct downturn, as reported in December 1928:

"The directors of the Motor Company of Combined Buyers Limited, Wellington, report in their profit and loss account a net loss of £23,621 for the year. A proposal will be made at an extraordinary general meeting to wind up the company." [83]

Indeed, the shareholders of Combined Buyers Limited subsequently voted for voluntary liquidation of the company and liquidators were appointed on 18 January 1929. [84]

As before, Leonard F Wallis had other motor industry interests with which to busy himself, including:

National Service Stations (1)

The importation of motor spirit and oils continued under another Leonard Wallis company, National Service Stations Limited, which found itself subject to an application to restrict its trading activities in October 1928:

"A new phase of the recent price war in the sale of petrol is indicated by an application lodged in the Supreme Court at Christchurch by the Vacuum Oil Company (Pty) Ltd which seeks an injunction restraining National Service Stations Ltd from allegedly selling as Canterbury Automobile Association petrol spirit which is stated to be a mixture of Plume and another kind of petrol. The Vacuum Oil Company alleges that any such action by National Service Stations Ltd which acts as selling agent for Canterbury Automobile Association petrol, is calculated to be prejudicial to the operation of the company, in that the addition of its motor spirit would lead the public to believe that C.A.A. spirit was possessed of qualities higher than was considered to be actually the case." [85]

However, the application was unsuccessful — as reported by the Ashburton Guardian on 23 October 1928:

"Mr Justice Adams this morning heard a case in which the Vacuum Oil Company Proprietary Ltd of Wellington, sought an injunction against National Service Stations Ltd of Christchurch with the object of preventing them mixing Plume motor spirit with a mixture sold as Canterbury Automobile Association spirit. Plaintiffs alleged that defendants mixed petrol and as a result the mixture came to he regarded as superior to Plume. The Judge held that plaintiff had not established the right to an injunction and dismissed the case with costs." [86]

The Christchurch Press subsequently explained the circumstances of the matter:

"Mr A T Donnelly, who appeared for the Vacuum Oil Company, said that the writ of injunction arose out of the method employed by defendants in their petrol filling station business. They had pumps for well-known brands of spirit and also for C.A.A. spirit which was sold to Automobile Association members at the cut price of 1s 10d.

"The station proprietors decided, or were compelled, to mix some of the plaintiff's brand of petrol, Plume spirit, with the anonymous C.A.A. spirit. The question was whether they were justified in doing this under the agreement entered into with the proprietors of Plume…

"For the defence, Mr Gresson said the station did not want to terminate the agreement. The kerbside pump, under the agreement was expressly used by the station to sell the company's petrol. The only thing done was to take some of the spirit, mix it with other spirit and sell the mixture, but not through the company's pump. The plaintiffs' case must fail because the law never allowed, except by express agreement, a fetter to be placed on the sale of goods after once sold. The mixture was in no way inferior to Plume spirit and was sold at the same price. Indeed it was the sale of C.A.A. spirit at 1s 10d which made the oil companies reduce their prices from 2s 1d to this figure." [87]

National Service Stations Limited owned Sydenham Service Station in 1927 and Cashel Street Service Station in March 1929…leasing them to private individuals…[88] By February 1941, the company also leased the establishment known as the Petrol Supplies Service Station situated at Lower Taranaki Street, Wellington. [89]

In September 1938, the Dominion Battery Company Limited of Lower Hutt was registered with a capital of £1000. The subscribers were then E N Cunningham 500 shares and National Service Stations Limited 500 shares. Objects were stated as: "Battery manufacturers, importers, petrol and service station proprietors and incidental." [90]

National Service Stations (2)

A second Wallis-related company by the name of National Service Stations Limited was registered on 15 March 1942. As of 3 May 2023, the company remains a registered entity with John Gregory Wallis as a Director and Shareholder along with an Anthony Bruce Wallis.

The Anglo Petroleum Oil Company

"The Anglo Petroleum Oil Company Limited of Wellington, as importers and vendors of lubricating oils, greases and machinery oils of all kinds, etc. was incorporated in October 1932 with a capital of £2000 in £1 shares. Subscribers were L F Wallis, 1999 shares and K A Wallis, 1 share." [91]

A licence to act as a wholesaler at Wellington, was granted to the company on 26 April 1933 [92] and cancelled as of 10 May 1937. [93]

Most of the products distributed in New Zealand by the Anglo Petroleum Oil Company were, as the name suggests, of British origin — as reported by the Wairarapa Daily Times in October 932:

"The Masterton branch of the Anglo Petroleum Oil Company, for which Mr S M Baird is the Wairarapa representative, is making a most comprehensive display of motor oils covering a wide range. Anglo super motor oils are 100 per cent refined in England by Glico Petroleum Ltd., London, from the crude product of the Anglo-Persian wells, controlled by the British Government..." [94]

(Glico — also known as G. L. I. Co, the Gas Lighting Improvement Co, was established in Britain in 1888 before a change of name to Glico Petroleum Company in 1924, producing Glico Motor Spirit and similar products.) [95] Registered on 26 April 1948, the Anglo Petroleum Oil Company Limited had a name change to Flex Grip Rubber Industries Limited. [96]

Victory Rubber Industries

In July 1942, F A Warner and L F Wallis of Lower Hutt filed applications for letters patent: the formation of treads on vehicle wheels or tyres — as reported by their agents, Messrs. Baldwin Son and Carey, Patent Attorneys... [97]

Victory Rubber Industries Limited was registered on 4 May 1943 [98] as a private company at Wellington with a capital of £2500. "Objects: Vulcanising, retreading, and repairs of motor and other tyres." [99]

(The same company is now registered as Wallis Gas Limited and, before that, Victory Developments Limited, with the current Director named as John Gregory Wallis. The current Shareholders are Atta Service Station Limited and Diana Wallis.) [100]

New Zealand Flex Grip

By July 1948, another Leonard Wallis company, New Zealand Flex Grip Limited, had managed to obtain the exclusive right to retread all Government motor vehicles with the Government having provided most the company's capital — as reported by the Christchurch Press and the Ashburton Guardian:

"Notice of his intention to ask the Minister in charge of State Advances (Mr W Nash) to give reasons for the investment by the State Advances Corporation of £6000 in a £7000 company registered under the name of New Zealand Flex Grip Ltd to exploit certain patents dealing with retreads, was given by Mr C M Bowden (Opposition, Karori) in the House of Representatives to-day..." [101]

"The reason for the State Advances Corporation's investment of £6000 in New Zealand Flex Grip Ltd (capital £7000) was explained by the Minister of Finance (the Rt. Hon. W Nash) in the House of Representatives yesterday. He said the company was formed solely to retread and recap tyres for Government vehicles under a patented process. A licence to use the process for this purpose had been given the company by the holder of the patent. By becoming a shareholder in the company, the Government not only shared in the profits from retreading its own tyres, but ensured that its vehicles were efficiently serviced in this respect." [102]

However, others engaged in the retreading industry, of which there were many to meet the obvious demand, took exception to what they viewed as favouritism by the Government:

"A return by the Government to the hitherto established method of calling for tenders for the retreading or recapping of Government tyres was sought in a petition presented to the House of Representatives yesterday by Mr J T Watts (Oppos., St. Albans), on behalf of Hawke's Bay Tyre Rebuilders Limited and 13 others, all members of the New Zealand Tyre Retreaders' Association.

"The petitioners asked that the work be not confined to the company known as New Zealand Flex Grip Limited. As an alternative to the calling of tenders, petitioners wanted the work of retreading Government tyres to be distributed fairly among retreaders throughout New Zealand without the calling of tenders on the basis of the current price list less 20 per cent.

"Arrangements had been made by the Government with certain companies to retread Government tyres with 'flex grip' treads or conventional treads, said the petitioner. They claimed that the operations of New Zealand Flex Grip Limited had created what was in effect largely a Government monopoly in the work of retreading Government tyres, and that such action was calculated to do harm and damage to the petitioners and members of the association." [103]

The following is a transcript of part of the debate entitled "Retreading of Government Tires" that ensued in the House of Representatives on 13 October 1949. The debate explains the controversy stirred by the Government's investment in Leonard Wallis' private company and the retreading monopoly it had created:

"Mr Petrie (Otahuhu) — Sir, I am directed by the Industries and Commerce Committee to present the report of the Committee on the petition of Hawkes Bay Tyre Re-Builders, Limited, and thirteen others, being members of the New Zealand Tyre Retreaders' Association (Incorporated), praying that the retreading or recapping of Government tires shall not be confined solely to the Flex Grip Company, and that the method of calling for tenders for the work be reintroduced; or, alternatively, that the work be fairly distributed among retreaders throughout New Zealand…

"Mr. Bowden (Karori) — Sir, the prayer of this petition is that the retreading or recapping of Government tires shall not be confined to the Flex Grip Company, but that the Government revert to the hitherto established method of calling for tenders for this work or, alternatively, that the work of retreading Government tires be fairly distributed among retreaders throughout New Zealand without calling for tenders, on the basis of the current list price less 20 per cent…

"This petition was presented last year; in fact, an earlier question was asked about the investment by the Government of £6,000 out of a total capital of £7,000 in a company formed for this purpose. It appears that the Government has put practically up the whole of the capital of this company to exploit certain patents dealing with the retreading of motor tires.

"As to whether or not those patents are valuable I leave the House to judge when I recite certain facts. One is that this proposal was put to the Inventions Board during the war, but was turned down at not being a worth-while process.

"The work that was formally done by recognized retreaders throughout New Zealand, of whom there are sixty-three, was the recapping and retreading of tires by what is known as the conventional method. The system adopted by this company was in operation for only six weeks when it was found necessary to depart substantially from the process which it first adopted. Earlier, when the work was done by the conventional retreaders, it was done at prices negotiated between the Government and the retreaders on the basis of prices authorised by the Price Tribunal, the Government getting certain discounts, again as a matter of arrangement…

"There was a considerable amount of work done in respect of retreading, so much so that, as I have said, there were about 63 retreaders throughout New Zealand, some of them with a substantial investment in plant and machinery. During the war, one large company was given a special licence to import 30,000 dollars' worth of retreading machinery; that company, in common with others, is now being bypassed by this new Government organisation.

"It appears, therefore, that the Government put up £6,000 against £1,000 on the part of the proprietor, who has a licence of the patent, to develop a process which at that time was not proved, and which, after a few weeks' operation, was found not to be a success and had to be adapted. In fairness, I must say the adaptation appears to have given more satisfactory results and the original scheme.

"The extraordinary thing is that this company into which the Government has put the £6,000 does not own the patents. The letters patent are in the hands of one of the directors of the company who, however, transferred it to another company of which he is also a director; and the company that is financed by the Government actually has only got a letter by way of licence and apparently the terms are not definite…

"In this company to which the original licence was assigned the director of the company that the Government has financed holds the great majority of the shares, in fact, at the time of registration he held £2,000 out of £2,500 worth of capital. He is also the landlord of one of the premises hired by the company since to carry on business operations.

"The process originally was not successful. There have been substantial departures since, and now they seem to be getting better results. None the less, several agents dropping the process in many instances and are proceeding to cap tires by the conventional process. The position obtains that those companies that have been appointed agents for this process have a great advantage in that they have Government work directed to them. One estimate is that the Government work is worth £100,000 a year. That gives them a substantial benefit at the cost of the others.

"An extraordinary point emerges. There is evidence that the cost of the new process is no cheaper — in fact, it is costing the Government more, because there are only two of those agents in the whole of the South Island. It will be seen that the cost of freights, sending the tires for recapping and returning them, is an additional item of cost. There is delay. This work is undertaken by the agents without tenders being called for, and it seems to be definitely unfair to the others.

"It seems an extraordinary investment by the Government that it should put up £6,000 out of a capital of £7,000 to try an unproved process, with no advantage to the Government, with interference with established businesses some of which have idle plants now and have had to dispense with staff as a result of the loss of Government work.

"The monopoly established by this company, owned, controlled and directed…though the Government has two directors out of four. The control is not in the hands of the Government, however, because the decision is in the hands of certain of the other directors…

"In fairness to all the retreaders throughout New Zealand who ask that they be given an opportunity to obtain a share of the Government's business, my suggestion is that the Government should consider its interests and take steps to call the members of the New Zealand Tyre Retreaders' Association into consultation to see whether some scheme cannot be adopted under which the retreaders could be given a share of Government business.

"Mr Mathison (Avon) — …I do not agree…that the Government should have nothing to do with a company of this kind — on the contrary I think the Government has shown wisdom in investing money in this company which has a process for retreading tires which is equal if not superior to the conventional methods of retreading. In spite of the arguments advanced by the petitioners and the honourable member for Karori to the contrary, the evidence adduced by the petitioners, as I shall demonstrate in a moment or two, was quite misleading…

"First of all it is well known that certain vested interests purchase inventions from time to time not for the purpose of utilizing them in interest of their own business, but for the purpose of suppressing them to enable them to keep up their own profits.

"It would be interesting to ascertain the real basis for the hostility generated for a long time past against this company. For instance we have the affirmation of Mr T M Smallwood, chairman of directors of New Zealand Flex Grip Limited, under date 9th August to this effect:

"'The New Zealand Tyre Retreaders' Association has been consistently hostile to the New Zealand Flex Grip Limited ever since its incorporation as a company. The Association has intimated to its members, in effect, that if any work is done for New Zealand Flex Grip Limited, the membership of such company in the New Zealand Tyre Retreaders' Association would be terminated…'

"(Mr Mathison) I know that to a certain extent a monopoly has been created, and there is a very good reason for the creation of that monopoly. There is an atmosphere of hostility against the Flex Grip Company, but I am sure that can be resolved provided the New Zealand Tyre Retreaders' Association is prepared to work as the agents of the Flex Grip Company are working today. The New Zealand Tyre Retreaders' Association has no objection to a monopoly provided it has the monopoly. Its principal objection is that it is outside the monopoly.

"On the figures, Flex Grip is slightly more costly than the conventional retread, but the evidence showed that it has a longer life than the conventional retread.

"Mr. Rae (Parnell) — I was impressed by the statement that there are now only seven of these Flex Grip retreading depots in New Zealand, two in the South Island and five in the North Island, and it does not need much imagination to realize that the transport of tires to and from repairing depots must incur heavy increased costs…I agree with the honourable member for Karori when he states that the Government should give more than consideration to this case, and that it should go into the whole matter thoroughly instead of leaving the monopoly with New Zealand Flex Grip Limited. There are sixty-three companies in New Zealand, and they should have a fair share of this important work which they can do just as cheaply and as efficiently as this privileged company…

"Mr Watts (St. Albans) …I am not satisfied and with the position disclosed to us; nor am I satisfied that the whole story behind this transaction came out in evidence. I agree there is a lot more to be found out about it, if we were able to do so.

"The story involved in this petition is an example of Government interference, and of its entry into private business. Briefly, a man named Wallis, well known in business circles in Wellington, invented what he thought was a new process for recapping or retreading tires. He placed it before the Inventions Board during the war, but the Board turned it down. Evidence was given before the Patents Commission, and there were some doubts expressed as to whether this was an invention at all, or whether there was anything original about it.

"Nevertheless, the Commissioner of Patents finally registered the invention. This gentleman somehow or other managed to persuade the Minister of Finance, and I think, the Minister of Works to invest £6,000 in a company with a capital of £7,000 — £6,000 from the Government and £1,000 from Wallis or his associates. The company was formed to retread Government tires by this process…

"In addition, the Government, through the State Advances Corporation, has advanced a further £1,000 by way of debenture. So, out of the total capital of £8,000 which has been put into this company, £7,000 has been supplied by the Government.

"When the Government put that money into that company, Mr Wallis told us the experiments were not complete, and the process was not a proven success. He had to change the method of retreading a few weeks after the company was formed, and it started retreading Government tires. The Minister of Finance put all that money into a process which had not been proved a success, and which…had to be changed at a later date…

"There was no valid reason for the Government creating a monopoly for this man. The petitioners ask for a fair share of Government work. They wish to do it by their own process, but, if the Government does not desire the conventional process to be used, they are prepared to use the Flex Grip process in order to get their share of the Government work, although they know that that is not the best process or the process that gives the best results…

"The Right Hon. Mr Nash [Minister of Finance] — The suggestion has been made that this process is of no value but in answer to that I would quote the following letter from the managing director of Motorways Limited which is one of the largest concerns of its kind in the South Island:

"'In support of the Government's interest in the above company, we have to advise that Mr L F Wallis, Managing Director of New Zealand Flex Grip Ltd, has been with us for the last two days assisting us with the production of Flex Grip Retreading.

"'Its patent process undoubtedly has many advantages over ordinary retreading, as it enables us to apply a much heavier, permanent, non-skid tread than can be provided with ordinary camelback.

"'From the writer's examination of Flex Grip bus tires which have run over 40,000 miles, we are completely satisfied that this process is revolutionary and in addition to the increased road safety factor to which Flex Grip insures, there will be a national saving of thousands of pounds annually, owing to the decreased accident rate and increased safety mileage per tire which is now made possible by the use of Flex Grip.'" [104]

The name of New Zealand Flex Grip Limited was changed to Tyreways (N.Z.) Limited, registered on 24 June 1952 [105] and again to Motorways (Wellington) Limited registered on 16 September 1954. [106]

An associated company, Flex Grip Rubber Industries Limited, also had a name change to FlexGrip Treads Limited registered on 22 November 1951 [107] and again to Tyreways (1955) Limited registered on 18 October 1955. [108]

Presumably in order to facilitate a change of proprietorship, Tyreways (1955) Limited (1953/150) was placed in voluntary liquidation on 13 July 1960 [109] and eventually struck off on 10 February 1964. [110]

Louis Emil Laugesen

In November 1896, Louis Emil Laugesen & Son were advertising for "…two or three good Sawmill Hands" to work at their small sawmilling business at Kaikoura. [111]

Midland Motorways Services

By December 1915, L E Laugesen & Co was promoting itself as the proprietor of the Kaikoura Express Motor Service, a daily service between Kaikoura and Parnassus (between Kaikoura and Christchurch). [112]

That bus service had expanded by November 1926 when Louis Laugesen was granted a licence by the Christchurch City Council to run a feeder service from Cathedral Square to Darfield as a supplement to the City's trams. [113] However, this contract was taken over by the Tramways Board from 1 November 1930. [114]

Nevertheless, the company continued to expand its rural bus services — as illustrated by a Christchurch Press article reporting on a Government announcement in February 1933 that an additional tax on petrol of 3d a gallon was to be introduced. A number of firms using petrol-driven vehicles in their business protested, including Louis Laugesen's son, Louis Keith Laugesen, then the manager of Midland Motorways:

"Every penny added to the price of petrol costs us a pound a week, said Mr Laugesen…Midland Motorways, Mr Laugesen told a reporter, uses just under 15,000 gallons of petrol a year, and during the year 1931-32 paid nearly £500 in petrol tax and more than £750 in taxation on petrol, tyres and licenses.

"The average taxation worked out at 1.21d a mile for the total mileage of the five buses used by the company and the additional petrol tax would bring this figure up to 1.3d or 1.4d a mile.

"Transport companies of this kind are in a difficult position, because, according to Mr Laugesen, they can hardly pass on any increase in costs. The farmers will simply stop travelling if we increase our rates…" [115]

Midland Motorways Services registered as a limited liability company on 3 May 1935 with a Capital of £2000. Subscribers: Louis Emil Laugesen 1000 shares and Louis Keith Laugesen 1000 shares. "Objects: Omnibus service car and cartage proprietors and incidental." [116]

The company then traded from 250 Durham Street, Christchurch [117] but, in October of that year, announced its intention to build a bus terminal station at a recently-purchased property at 29 Lichfield Street. The proposed bus station was then described as "…the first of its kind in New Zealand." [118]

The new bus station was open for business by late February 1936:

"When the firm of Midland Motorways Services Ltd moves into its new bus station at 29 Lichfield street next Wednesday, the city will have not only an up-to-date transport service depot, but a handsome addition to its architecture.

"Built at a cost of £6000, the station will house the Midland Motorways fleet, will contain an up-to-date workshop, and will provide a parking area for private cars on Friday and Saturday evenings in the centre of the city. Midland Motorways have found it necessary to build this large new station because of the great increase in their business. With nine buses, the depot in Durham street has become much too small, but the spaciousness of the new building will overcome many difficulties which the firm has had to contend with in the last year or so…In one Corner, there will be a tyre and battery service store run by Midland Motorways…" [119]

The Midland Motorways fleet continued to expand — as reported by the Christchurch Press in June 1938:

"Delivery was taken yesterday by Midland Motorways Services of its fifteenth passenger bus. The new vehicle has a completely locally-built body on a Bedford bus chassis, altered to the requirements of the firm. It seats 31 passengers, and is attractively finished in green leather, with sponge rubber seats and backs…" [120]

The company's continued coach building business was described by a Christchurch Press article published in 1976:

"Soon after the war ended, Midland began building bus bodies. This has developed into a highly specialised body-building department. Both the company's coachworks and panelworks have seen centralised on a two-acre central city site…Next year [1977], the coachworks will build 20 more new buses.

"Early bodies were constructed of Southland beech and aluminium sheathing. Now, a new luxury tour coach, which costs $60,000, is all aluminium." [121]

In the meantime, the fortunes of Midland Motorways Services Limited continued to prosper with an increase in capital of £80,000 to £100,000 in 1948. [122] At about the same time, the company converted from a private to a public company. [123]

Described as "…one of the pioneers of the motor transport industry in Canterbury", the Christchurch Press of 26 May 1955 reported that, at the age of 85, Louis Emil Laugesen had retired from the directorate of Midland Motorways Services. [124] Louis Emil Laugesen died on 31 May 1966. He was 95. [125]

Having already incorporated Tasman Rental Cars (Christchurch) Limited as a subsidiary, Midland Motorways Services purchased all the shares in Tasman Rental Cars (Wellington) Limited and Tasman Rental Cars (Hutt) Limited in October 1967. [126]

Expansion continued in February 1969:

"Midland Motorways Services Ltd the Christchurch coach operator, has extended its coach interests to the North Island with the purchase of all the shareholding in Edward Motors Ltd and associated companies in Auckland…

"Edwards Motors operates regular timetable services to Matamata, Tauranga and Mount Maunganui, and newspaper, mail contracts and passenger services from Auckland to Rotorua, Taupo, Napier and Hastings.

"The purchase involves 22 coaches, a number of rental cars in Auckland and Matamata, terminal buildings in Auckland and Matamata, and property in Morrinsville and Mount Maunganui. New Zealand Scenic Tours Ltd an associated company which conducts sightseeing tours in Auckland city and which operates from a sales office in Lower Queen Street, is also included in the purchase…

"The parent company has a number of tour and charter services in the South Island, and operates a nightly coach each way between Christchurch and Dunedin." [127]

On 11 December 1969, the name of the company was changed from Midland Motorways Services Limited (C1935/25) to Midland Coachlines Limited [128] and by September 1976, the company was described by the Christchurch Press as "...one of New Zealand's largest commercial bus and tour operators...[from] only small beginnings when the company was founded...in 1929." [129]

On the occasion of the retirement of Louis Keith Laugesen in 1976, the company's beginnings and history were recalled by Ken Coates in an article published by the Christchurch Press on 9 December 1976, part of which includes:

"Today tourism is a big business for the company which handles about 50,000 tourists, mostly Australians, a year. This excludes group charters. Pioneer Midland Ltd is an associate company which has links with Ansett-Pioneer in Australia. Midland has 100 buses — 60 based in Christchurch and 40 in Auckland...In almost 50 years, the company has grown from a small family business to a public company of 1200 shareholders and a paid-up capital of more than $2M. Assets are worth nearly $8½M and revenue last year was almost $7M...

"Keith Laugesen is retiring as managing director but is not withdrawing from the business he has built over the years. He will remain as chairman of the board..." [121]

In October 1985, the Christchurch Press published a brief history of various companies that by then were no longer members of the stock exchange, including:

"Midland Motorways Services Ltd which ran bus services throughout Canterbury in 1980 bought a 20 per cent stake in Bunting and Company from H W Smith Ltd. Mr C. T. Giltrap, an Auckland motor magnate, bought 51 per cent of Midland. A half-share in Midland's Hertz rental-car franchise in New Zealand, Tasman Rental Cars, was then sold to Marac Holdings Ltd.

"In June 1981, Midland bought the tours, transport, and marketing arms of Trans Tours Ltd, an Auckland-based subsidiary of UEB Ltd. Midland was then taken over by Ceramco, Ltd. Its bus activities were sold eventually to H and H Travel Lines, Ltd of Invercargill. Its service to outlying towns and settlements was largely taken over by the Christchurch Transport Board." [130] Louis Keith Laugesen died in February 1986 at the age of 80. [131]

Motorways Limited

Following the death of Louis Emil Laugesen in June 1966, the Christchurch Press, with reference to the founding of Midland Motorways Services, described him as "...a pioneer in the road passenger transport industry in the South Island...The Press obituary also referred to his establishment of Motorways Limited, garage proprietors and tyre retreaders:

"In 1929, Mr Laugesen, with his two younger sons, founded the firm of Motorways Limited which has service stations at Hornby, Sockburn, and Channeys. A few years later the firm established a tyre retreading factory at Hornby. This factory was later moved to Sockburn where it is now the headquarters of the Dominion's largest tyre retreading company, having factories in all the main centres." [125]

Indeed, Motorways' first line of business was the selling of petrol from its stations, as advertised in September 1932:

"Cheaper Petrol. Special to Tractor Owners. 40-Gallon Drums filled at 1/8 per gallon. At Motorways Limited, Hornby. [132]

At a time of intense competition among petrol brands, independence became a selling point of difference — as advertised in November 1932:

"Motorways Limited, Hornby are in no way connected with an Association for the fixation of prices. Purchasers of One Quart of Oil are able to obtain Petrol at cost. Open Day and Night. L Laugesen and Son, Proprietors." [133]

During the years 1933 and 1934, Motorways expanded its selling of petrol and other garage services from one to three stations, as shown by its advertising at that time:

"Petrol Always Cheaper at Motorways Limited. 2 Service Stations. Main South Road, Hornby. Bring your Drums and fill up at 1/9 per gallon. L Laugesen and Son, Proprietors." [134]

"Plume and Voco obtainable at our stations at 1/6 per gallon with quart of oil. Motorways Limited. Hornby and Sockburn." [135]

"Motorists. Chaneys Corner Service Station now owned by Motorways Limited. Prices right. Two Attendants and No Waiting. Motorways Ltd. Louis E Laugesen, Secretary." [136]

By March 1935, the importance of being seen to be an independent retailer remained:

"It having been reported to us that certain persons in Christchurch are spreading reports to the effect that our business is being financed by the major Oil Companies, we take this opportunity of giving such reports an emphatic denial. Legal action will be taken against anyone repeating these false statements after this date. Motorways Limited, Louis E. Laugesen, Managing Director. Hornby, Sockburn, Chaney's Corner." [137]

Tyre Retreading

As well as the selling of motor spirit and oil, Motorways Limited recognised an opportunity in the retreading of tyres — a service desperately needed by the fleet of buses run by its sister company, Midland Motorways Services. The company's retreading service was announced on 13 May 1937:

"Car Owners! Truck Owners!! Bus Owners!!! Your Tyre Costs Are Too High. To lead in any field of endeavour one must keep abreast of the times. No better example of leadership can be quoted than Motorways installation of One Piece Circular Moulds For Retreading Tyres. This is the first plant of its kind in New Zealand with the complete range of moulds for the Retreading of Car, Truck and Bus Tyres.

"Motorways plan to cut your Tyre costs in half — Midland are doing it on their Buses — we can do it for you. Full particulars and prices on application. A Motorways Guarantee behind every job turned out. Motorways Limited, Chaney's Corner, Sockburn, and Bus Station: 31 Lichfield Street." [138]

In October 1949, the company advertised good stocks of both new and second-hand tyres for sale:

"Sound Second-Hand Tyres…Holding Good Stocks of New Tyres. Call and See Our Tyre Men? Motorways Limited, Sockburn and Chaneys" [139]

By 1950, the retreading business had expanded — as reported by the Christchurch Press on 30 March of that year:

"The biggest tyre retreading mould in the southern hemisphere, and one which will save New Zealand hundreds of thousands of dollars, is now in operation in a factory operated by Motorways Limited at Sockburn.

"The mould, which weighs three tons and a half, was made by two engineering firms in Christchurch, and it is designed to retread tyres used by the Public Works Department's 12-yard and 15-yard carry-alls and similar privately-owned equipment.

"The Public Works Department planned as long ago as 1933 to get equipment for retreading the tyres on its earth-moving equipment, as they had to be replaced from the United States at considerable expense. When the department decided to buy the equipment there was an urgent need to save dollars, and the plan would have been abandoned, but Motorways Limited undertook to provide a mould made entirely in New Zealand. The tyres retreaded will carry a new tyre guarantee.

"The mould and other equipment necessary for the work were installed at a cost of about £6000. The firm has signed a contract with the Government to undertake the retreading of tyres for all its earth-moving vehicles. There are about 200 of them in operation at present. The mould will also be able to handle other large tyres used by contractors.

"A senior member of the firm said yesterday that there were only about a dozen similar moulds in existence anywhere in the world, and none of them was bigger than the Sockburn one.

A ceremony will be held at the factory this afternoon to mark the production of the first tyres." [140]

By January 1961 the tyre business of Motorways continued to operate from its Lichfield Street premises providing tyre servicing as well as undersealing and stem cleaning services to the motorist. [141] However, the business was now known as Tyreways (1960) Limited after a name change on 7 October 1960. [142]

Urban Sprawl

As described by Mark Webster in *Assembly — A History of New Zealand Car Production 1921-1998*:

"By 1921, the automobile was changing the shape of New Zealand cities: 'People are now able to buy cheaper sections in less crowded localities and live healthier lives because of cheap and swift means of transportation' (New Zealand Motor Life, November 20, 1921). The seeds of urban sprawl were being sown…This seems ironic now, but public opinion was swinging solidly in behind motor transport as clean and environmentally-friendly after years of concerns nationally about the disgraceful mess horses made in our towns and cities." [143]

A Slow Transition

Nevertheless, the transition from horse-drawn vehicles to those driven by the petrol engine was not a rapid one, as the exhibitors at various shows around the country demonstrated, still with a foot in both camps — as reported by the Waikato Times on 20 November 1925:

"As the years go by the various exhibits at the Waikato A. and P. Show come and go, but the record from an exhibitor's point of view must surely be held by the Arthur Atkin Vehicle Co., which has this year completed its 34th exhibition.

"For years past the winners in the show-ring have driven to victory in one of the firm's vehicles, and this year the Atkin Sulkies were again prominent in the Grand Parade. At the stand a nicely arranged assortment of smart gigs and sulkies, splendidly appointed, well sprung and upholstered, attracted much attention. Waggons and carts for farm purposes are also shown and to the discriminating buyer the quality of workmanship and materials used must make an instant appeal.

"Other activities of the firm include motor coach work, springs, painting and upholstering. Now that the summer season is with us no doubt motor-car owners will take advantage of the excellent service offered by the Arthur Atkin Vehicle Factory. Only the best of enamels are used for motor painting, whilst upholstery and hood work receive the same careful attention, and the quality of materials used is of the best that can be procured. To those requiring further particulars regarding prices, etc., a hearty invitation is extended by the manager (Mr Chas Speight) to visit the works, which are situated at the corner of Grey and Bridge Streets, Hamilton East." [144]

Record Imports

While vehicles of the horse-drawn kind were still being made and purchased in 1925, storm clouds of motor exhaust and noise were flooding across the wharves of New Zealand — as reported by the Evening Post on 3 April 1926:

"Imports of motor vehicles into New Zealand last year constituted a record. The total number, excluding motor-cycles, was 22,321 for 1925, as against 18,629 in 1924. According to country of origin, 15.33 per cent, of the total came from Britain, 44 per cent, from Canada, 38.33 per cent, from the United States, and 21.5 per cent, from Europe.

"The percentage of British cars has risen from 6½ per cent in 1924 to 15.33 per cent last year. The numbers in 1925 were 2882 against 1015 in 1924…

"In regard to commercial vehicles the proportions from the various countries are: Britain 15 per cent; Canada 47 per cent; U.S.A. 37 per cent; and Continental 1 per cent.

"On a financial reckoning Britain makes a better showing, taking 24½ per cent of the business, as against Canada's 35 per cent, and U.S.A.'s 38 per cent…

"In regard to motor-cycles, Britain holds now an easy lead, with 3211 machines, against America's 1621. The total number of motor-cycles imported in 1925 was 4836, as against 2296 in 1924…

"The value of tires imported last year was £1,148,075.

"The total value of cars, trucks, tires, and spares imported last year was £4,966,129, made up as follows:— Cars, £2,435,303; trucks, £485,870; tires, £1,803,959; and spares, £240,997. The figures are taken from the excellent compilation by 'The Radiator'." [145]

More Cars Than Quality Roads?

As the importation of complete motor vehicles, parts for assembly, and the buying and selling of vehicles, became an increasingly profitable commercial activity, meeting the insatiable demand, Auckland city roads, already choked with horse-drawn traffic, trams, pedestrians, and cyclists, soon struggled to accommodate them. Even with the construction of more roads and the eventual demise of horse-drawn traffic and the trams, road congestion would continue well into the next century.

The question of enough quality road space to accommodate all these vehicles rolling off the assembly lines was, of course, of considerable importance to the vehicle manufacturers — as reported by the Waikato Times on 24 December 1927:

"'Everybody tells me you are turning the corner; there seems to be a happy feeling all through New Zealand that the worst is over. You have a wonderful country, and I think there are good times ahead for all.'

"With these words Mr A. S. Murray, vice-president of General Motors, Export Company, New York, who is in Wellington, summed up his observations during a tour he has just made of the North Island and a part of the South Island.

"'Since my arrival in the Dominion a fortnight ago I have been over many of your roads, which I consider are in surprisingly good condition,' he told a Dominion representative.

"Discussing the motor industry, Mr Murray said that by entering a little more deeply into the commerce of the countries in which his firm operated they hoped to dispel the idea that they were a foreign enterprise.

"'Our policy…is to purchase more and more in those countries. That, of course, is a little difficult in New Zealand, because it is not a large manufacturing country…From my own observation, I believe New Zealand is rapidly approaching the saturation point, and that it will soon become a stabilised market for replacement; the population cannot absorb many more motor cars. The next development…will be toward an improvement in the existing cars rather than in the production of new models; I don't think we can look in the immediate future for any new product. Our volume of trade in America, where there is one car to every five people, is not increasing very rapidly. The market there is just about stabilised. The changes are taking place among the manufacturers rather than in the trade itself.'" [146]

Planned Obsolescence

While the vice-president of General Motors may well have thought that New Zealand was not then ready to assemble newer models of his company's vehicles, the concept of regular replacement of the old with the new had been expressed about two years earlier by the head of General Motors, Alfred P Sloan Jnr. — as recounted by Graham Hawkes in his book, *On the Road — The Car In New Zealand*:

"To enemies of the consumer society Sloan is an arch villain because it was he who introduced the idea of the annual model change and planned obsolescence. He advocated that 'the change in the new model should be so novel and attractive as to create demand for the new value and, so to speak, create a certain amount of dissatisfaction with past models as compared with the new one.' Car buyers recognised the ploy but came to love it anyway." [147]

"Does the car industry manipulate public opinion and decide in advance what cars people will buy two or three years hence? The industry says it can only sell cars the public is willing to buy. But in the 1950s the formidable power of the Madison Avenue advertising agencies was turned loose on the motoring public of America. Appealing to people's aspirations to status and power, the wordsmiths and illustration artists created an aura of motorised romance, almost fantasy, that has never been repeated since." [148]

Man Arrests His Friend

Fervently promoted by means of press advertisements, billboards, the cinema and, eventually, television, that same *aura of motorised romance* seemingly targeted prospective New Zealand motorists since long before the 1950s — with ads often disguised as news — as published by the Christchurch Press on 3 June 1921:

"Mild excitement was caused in Cathedral square yesterday morning by the actions of two men. They were engaged in animated conversation when suddenly one was observed to seize the other by the coat collar and propel him with great force across the Square.

"Followed by an ever-increasing crowd they turned into Worcester street West, and continued past the Scott Monument and over the bridge, halting just outside David Crozier, Ltd.

"Here it became evident what the trouble was. It appears that the 'victim' and his aggressor are both very close friends and the 'victim' was about to buy a motor-car. The 'aggressor', being a recognised authority on car values, was very keen that his friend should invest in a Briscoe Sedan, and to make sure that he investigated its merits had run him along to David Crozier's in the manner shown.

"The sequel was made known last evening when he confirmed his friend's judgement by becoming the proud owner of a Briscoe Sedan. It is no uncommon thing for Briscoe Sedan owners to be so enthusiastic in their praise of this beautiful light car. David Crozier Ltd will be pleased to demonstrate." [149]

The Vanguard of New Prosperity

Despite their 'tackiness', such advertisements produced results — particularly after the Second World War as statistics for vehicle registrations show:

"…new car registrations rose sharply from 3500 in 1933 to 16,000 in 1935, 23,000 in 1936 and 30,000 in 1937." [150]

"In 1938 [there were] 207,242 cars on the road in NZ with one of every two cars less than 6 years old. By 1948, [there were] 228,044 cars on the road [and] only one in six was less than 6 years old.

"By late 1940s, one car to every six New Zealanders (1:6) compared to U.S. 1:4, Canada 1:8, Australia 1:9, England 1:18, South Africa 1:24. It was estimated that one in 12 New Zealanders was directly supported by earnings of the motor industry." [151]

As outlined later, "Canada and the US were the major sources until the 1930s. British cars then dominated until the 1960s. With imports from Commonwealth countries receiving preferential treatment, Australia emerged as another important source…" [152]

"During the 1952 calendar year, sales in New Zealand of passenger cars and commercial vehicles manufactured in the United Kingdom reached the highest figure ever recorded said Mr A W Hamilton Brown, New Zealand representative of the Society of Motor Manufacturers and Traders…

"Mr Brown said that during the year the total number of cars sold was 32,298, and 11,351 commercial vehicles were sold. Ninety per cent of the cars and 95 per cent of the trucks had been exported from the United Kingdom.

"The best year for all car sales until 1952 was 1937, when sales totalled 29,994. The previous highest total of commercial vehicles sold was 10,687, registered in 1951…In 1951, 25,826 cars were sold.

"These vehicle shipments from the United Kingdom represented in 1951 an amount of £11,300,000 to Britain…

"'The motor-vehicle share of total New Zealand imports in 1952 was estimated at 9.8 per cent, compared with an average of 10.1 per cent for the years from 1936 to 1938, and an average of 5.4 per cent for the years from 1946 to 1951,' he said." [153]

As observed by Graham Hawkes in 'On The Road — The Car in New Zealand':

"The car, then, was perceived as being the vanguard of the new prosperity, the measure of our civilisation…During the 1950s the car plants of Wellington's Hutt Valley were in full swing, bolting together a large array of cars that today could never be profitably attempted. But for the time, it was evidence of some kind of industrial miracle. The media of the time seemed hell-bent on establishing the car industry as a mighty monolith that would put a car in every garage and a smile on everyone's face…Of course, the reality was that New Zealand was supporting only a car assembly operation, and its size and efficiency could have been strongly debated…" [154]

Nevertheless, by the 1960s, "Local car production increased, as did imports, resulting in greater numbers of cars available and a broader range of vehicles to choose from…Whereas in 1960 & 1961 new registrations totalled 33,000 and 38,000, by 1963 they had reached 58,000 and the years 1964 and 1965 saw 65,000 and 67,000 new car registrations." [155]

"…by the mid-sixties sustained prosperity meant that many households could afford a second car…our sprawling suburbs made it a necessity…Retailing was changing, shifting from the traditional corner store that had served only a small community. The supermarket had arrived. In 1958 Foodtown had opened its first premises in Otara…with a carpark of 150 spaces. Newer suburbs were being served by giant shopping centres or malls, a complex of specialist shops with the essential supermarket at its core. The country's first, Lynnmall, opened in 1963…Suddenly 'mum' needed a shopping basket on wheels and the birth of the two-car family spawned an explosion in used car dealerships." [156]

Depreciable Consumer Durable

Despite various import restrictions, new vehicle industry volumes peaked in 1973, and again in 1984, at around 125,000 new vehicles. In 1992 just 66,500 new vehicles were sold. 2005, with just over 100,000 new vehicle sales, was the highest for 20 years…" [157]

However, contrary to normal supply and demand principles that usually ensure lower prices in a saturated market, "Inflation, devaluation, increasing sales tax, the desire for car companies to protect their profits, inefficiencies within the assembly industry, penalties on imported cars — all these forced [new car] prices higher and higher…for what New Zealanders considered an essential item of transport…" [158]

Consequently, by the late 1980s, used vehicles had become an increasingly more affordable alternative for the average motorist:

"Over the 1980s and 1990s government protection of the NZ auto-assembly industry was reduced and restrictions on importing used cars were eased resulting in a flood of used Japanese cars entering the market." [159]

"The change from cars being seen as an investment to a depreciable consumer durable, was brought about by the advent of imported used vehicles from Japan, completely changing the shape of the industry with used import sales being up to double the level of new registrations for over a decade…" [160]

The Japanese Flood

The importation of used vehicles from Japan certainly upset the traditional market that had evolved over many decades. According to a Christian Science Monitor report of 30 June 1992:

"Over the past two years, New Zealand has imported 141,694 Japanese used cars; the remaining 123,482 cars sold have either been imported new or assembled locally. Used cars are selling faster because they are cheaper…"

"They've made quite a significant change' reports George Fairbairn, secretary general of the New Zealand Automobile Association. They've made such a change that the New Zealand automobile assemblers lobbied for a tariff, which the government installed last year.

"But the $1200 (New Zealand…) duty has not stopped the docks from filling up with used cars…

"The importers of new Japanese cars are also unhappy and sometimes refuse to supply parts to repair the used cars. 'They don't feel the cars give the right image since they were not intended for the New Zealand market,' explains Mr Fairbairn…" [161]

In February 2024, New Zealand Autocar Magazine, quoting Customs data, reported that New Zealand imported "…approximately 115,753 used cars with 113,462 coming from Japan…mainly because we are one of the few right-hand drive countries that will happily accept them." [162]

Chapter Three

Enter the Road Gang

William Stanley (Stan) Goosman
"During the depression of the 1920s William Stanley (Stan) Goosman took up cream cartage to supplement his earnings. His horse and wagon business grew into a large cartage concern which he gradually set aside as he became involved in politics…" [1]

By 1925, William Goosman had entered the motor age as a carting contractor, operating three motor lorries from Waitoa in the Matamata-Piako district of the Waikato carrying out large contracts for local authorities. [2]

He was also working as a roading contractor by 1931 and had expanded his road haulage business with the purchase of another local concern. At about the same time, William Goosman incorporated W S Goosman and Company Limited, of which he was a Director and Shareholder until the company was voluntarily wound up in April 1954. [3]

The extent of his company's business can be gauged by a July 1937 New Zealand Gazette entry that records the company's leasing of a quarry in the Gisborne District, presumably to supply his road construction business. [4]

Given his commercial history, William Goosman obviously had a more than passing interest in transport matters during his time as a Member of Parliament from 1938 to the time of his retirement in 1963. In the First National Government, from 1949 to 1954, he served as the Minister of Transport, Minister of Works, Minister of Railways, and Minister of Marine. Between 1960 and 1963, William Goosman held the Minister of Works and Minister of Electricity portfolios in the Second National Government. [5]

Decision Time
A 1950 Transport Department Annual report stated:

"The number of motor vehicles licensed in New Zealand at 31st March 1950 (413,363) showed an increase of 26,408, or 6.39 per cent over the figure for the previous year and is the highest level yet reached. [6]

According to Graham Hawkes, in his book, On the Road — The Car In New Zealand:

"In Auckland in 1950, there were an estimated 50,000 motor vehicles and two-thirds of these were private cars — an average of one car to every two houses…An Automobile Association bulletin editorial of the time…saying the numbers driving cars in Auckland between 7 a.m. and 8 a.m. averaged 69,000 — nearly equalling the number travelling on buses, trains and ferries, and more than half the total number of people using trams…" [7]

The need for more road space to accommodate so many vehicles became so dire in Auckland and other New Zealand cities that urgent decisions had to be made. There was also a pressing need to upgrade and better maintain existing roads to cope with the heavier types of vehicles…the trolleybuses, omnibuses, and trucks.

Roading Investigation Committee
In order to establish what roads had to be built and upgraded nationally to deal with the motor vehicle phenomenon, and at what cost, William Goosman, as Minister of Works, appointed a Roading Investigation Committee in March 1952.

The six Committee members appointed included representatives from the Ministry of Works, the New Zealand Counties Association, the Municipal Association of New Zealand, the Treasury, and the Transport Department. In lieu of direct representation, interested organisations such as the North and South Island Motor Unions and the Industrial Transport

Association of New Zealand, were allowed to have representatives present as observers during the hearing of evidence.

However, due to the Minister's stated need for a quick report, the Committee's hearings were confined to Wellington during its investigation. As a result, a good deal of the evidence heard was restricted to hearsay delivered by witnesses from around the rest of the country.

Indeed, when the Roading Investigation Committee delivered its 170-page report on 7 February 1953, it contained an almost apologetic admission that their investigation was incomplete because of the Committee's inability "…to travel outside Wellington both to meet interested parties and to inspect actual roading conditions in the different districts of New Zealand." [8]

National Roads Fund

Unsurprisingly, the Roading Investigation Committee report managed to conclude "…user payments must be increased substantially if the financial requirements of our roading system are to be adequately met…" To that end, the report recommended the pooling of all motor taxation and national roading revenues in a proposed National Roads Fund.

The Committee also proposed that a National Roads Board should administer the Fund which would comprise revenue obtained from petrol and mileage tax, tyre tax, heavy traffic fees, registration and licence fees, and an annual contribution from central government. [9]

Part of the Roading Investigation Committee Report emphasised "…the importance of an adequate roading system to the whole economic and social life of New Zealand. Road transport…plays such a vital part in the general economic activity of the community, and private motoring is such a strongly established feature of modern life, that the provision of good roads is of first-rank importance to every citizen." [10]

But despite that *first-rank importance*, there remained not only the question of cost to provide *good roads* but of how that cost would be shared between the individual road user and the general taxpayer represented by central government. There was also the perennially parochial fear of local governments losing control of their historical responsibility for the construction and maintenance of its local roads.

The latter concern was expressed by Roading Investigation Committee member, J L Burnett:

"This, I consider, would lead to bureaucratic control, which would sound the death-knell of our democratic local government system…" [11]

Undeterred by such conflicting interests and divergent viewpoints, the management and funding of roading was facilitated by legislation with the passage of the National Roads Act 1953 which established the National Roads Board and National Roads Fund. [12]

Urban Choices

Once the question of who would pay for the country's roads was settled, the planners and engineers could get on with the job of deciding where and when they would be constructed. Easily enough in the rural areas. However, in the cities, there were the usual conflicting interests to be reconciled, particularly in Auckland where the choice was simple — prioritise the construction of roads, particularly motorways, to accommodate the increasing use of motor vehicles by its citizens or, in accordance with the findings of the many expensive and exhaustive studies undertaken over many decades, provide Auckland commuters with a cheap and efficient, public transport service so good that they would be only too glad to leave their cars at home.

As with most decisions to be made by governments and public bodies in a democracy, particularly those involving comparatively large public expenditure, yet another inquiry was called for to decide the matter.

But not any inquiry. From a political point of view, the choice in favour of road-based transport and not rail had already been decided as the right option, both economically and in terms of future needs.

Auckland was already committed to the construction of a long-awaited, harbour bridge and approach roads following the signing of a contract on 29 October 1954. What became known as the 'austerity' bridge was to accommodate only four road lanes with no provision for public transport or pedestrian traffic.

While this omission was to be regretted for decades later, a road-only, main arterial route across the harbour fitted very well with the National Government's preference for roads as determined by the findings of Minister Goosman's Roading Investigation Committee.

However, a general election loomed in late 1954 so the commissioning of an inquiry beforehand avoided the issue becoming an election topic for Sidney Holland's National Party which had previously provided limited support for suburban rail for Auckland.

Any potential volatility of the matter was further diluted by its portrayal as a 'technical matter' — not one to be decided by politicians or the general public, but by qualified engineers and planners.

Accordingly, following a proposal by the Hon. W. S. Goosman, Minister of Works, "…that Auckland consider the advisability of giving preference to a system of express motorways into and through the city area, instead of the underground rail project, to which the government was committed," that Mr A. J. Dickson, the Auckland City Council Engineer, suggested that an overall Master Transportation Plan be prepared, with a view to ascertaining which proposal — express motorways or underground railway — should be given priority." [13]

In keeping with the apparent need for a 'technical approach', the Auckland City Council's Technical Advisory Committee was supplemented by local body engineers and planners charged with undertaking:

"…a complete survey of all the Metropolitan Area's transport and traffic problems and prepare a detailed report and a master transportation plan for the area." [14]

The Master Transportation Plan

The resulting Master Transportation Plan for Metropolitan Auckland was produced in July 1955, decided upon by four committees (executive, general information, traffic, and transport). Each committee comprised at least six members with overall supervision by Arthur Dickson. At the time of the study, almost all members were Registered Municipal Engineers, Associate Members of the Institution of Civil Engineers or members of what was then the New Zealand Institution of Engineers. There was only one representative from the Railways Department. [15]

Technical Advisory Committee
Members of the Technical Advisory Committee inquiry team included:
Arthur James Dickson OBE, BE, MICE, FRSA, MNZIE, MRSanI, JP (Chairman)
    — Auckland City Engineer from 1944 to 1969
Neville Longbourne Vickerman MICE MNZIE — Chief Engineer, Auckland Harbour Board from 1947 to 1956 and on the advisory panel to the Auckland Harbour Bridge Authority from 1951 to 1960 and 1968 to 1969. He started with the Harbour Board in 1910 and became an assistant engineer in 1925.
Cecil Bland MIAE — Auckland City Engineer, Auckland City Traffic Superintendent from June 1935. He was described as an expert motor mechanic by his employer in 1917 and in December 1945 he visited England and the USA to investigate the latest traffic control methods.
William L Bell MICE MNZIE — District Commissioner of Works, Auckland from 1948 to March 1960.
O G Thornton — District Engineer, Ministry of Works, Auckland from 1943.
Professor Cyril Roy Knight (1909-1989) MA, B Arch (Liverpool) Dean of the Faculty of Architecture, Auckland University College and member of the City Council town planning
    committee
Cyril W Firth MSc, AMICE, MNZIE (1903-2003) — Auckland City Waterworks Engineer

Wilfred E Begbie MIHE (England) — Resident Engineer, Mt Albert Borough
Charles Ernest Henry Putt MTPI — Auckland City Town Planning Officer, Engineering Department from 1928.
T S Roe MSI (NZ) — Chief Surveyor, Lands and Survey Department
A Greville Walker AMICE, MNZIE — Ellerslie & Otahuhu Boroughs Engineer
H H Thompson AMNZIE — Borough Engineer, Mt Roskill from 1950 (formerly in charge of all highways from Auckland to Wellsford, including the construction of the new Riverhead road around the head of the Waitemata Harbour, and the new deviation and bridge at Silverdale).
Ralph P Worley MSc, AMICE, MNZIE, AMIE (Aust), MRSanI, MSI (NZ) — Birkenhead, Northcote & Manurewa Boroughs Engineer (Worley, Downey, Muir & Partners)
J Hall — New Lynn, Glen Eden & Henderson Boroughs Engineer
William G Macky BSc, AMICE, AMNZIE — Manukau County Council Engineer
Charles Hewson McCormick — Borough Engineer, Mt Eden
C R Gribble FRANZ, FCIS — General Manager, Auckland Transport Board
C E H Putt MTPI — Auckland City
A T Griffiths Registered Municipal Engineer — Devonport & Takapuna Boroughs
L B Boyce — Auckland City Council Traffic Engineer
E G McLeod AMICE AMNZIE — Auckland District Railways Engineer
William Ivan Gardiner Registered Municipal Engineer — Onehunga Borough
Charles C Collom BSc (Engineering London), MICE, MIMunE, MNZIE — Chief Engineer, Auckland Metropolitan Drainage Board
L E A Turrell — Assistant District Traffic Manager, NZ Railways
M Moir — Assistant Manager, Auckland Transport Board
Frederick William Osborn Jones BE, MTPI, AMICE, AMI Structural Engineering — Auckland Regional Planning Officer from 1946 then Director of Planning for the Auckland Regional Planning Authority until retirement in 1970s. (With Arthur Dickson, Jones undertook the initial planning of the motorway network when the Auckland Harbour Bridge was planned.)

Local Body Representatives Not On the Various Committees:
J E Fitzgerald — Mount Wellington
H A Truman — One Tree Hill
P E Fraser — Papatoetoe [16]

Superior Knowledge

As there was only <u>one</u> representative from the Railways Department, it is little wonder that the findings of the Committee unanimously favoured express motorways and not suburban rail as the future of Auckland's transport systems.

By entrusting the investigation to the engineers, politicians had also relinquished the ultimate decision-making process to what Stephen B Goddard described as the "Engineers' Superiority Complex —Engineers, by believing in their own intellectual and moral superiority over policy makers (an attitude thoroughly in the mainstream of Progressivism) did not endear themselves to legislators. As one engineer described his role: 'It is not sufficient for an engineer, or any other educated man, to know. He must act. A part of the engineer's duty is to help in molding public opinion by educating and guiding the public in those matters in which engineers by virtue of their training and occupation have superior knowledge.'" [17]

The Road Gang Wins

The education and guidance of the Auckland public was achieved by means of the subsequent publication of the Master Transportation Plan as a glossy misrepresentation of many facts to suit the cause, supported by a good deal of political and civic hype. After that, there was no going back for Auckland — there was to be no real competition from rail or any other transport service for many decades.

With the full approval of the engineers who would design and build the needed roads, motorways, and bridges, the Road Gang had free rein to fill them with as many vehicles as it could while the farmers and speculators could sell rural land for satellite settlements served by petrol stations far from the reach of straight-line rail corridors. The bottom feeders could also profit — anyone who contributed to or benefited from superhighways and roads — hotel and motel operators, housing and restaurant developers, real estate agencies and, of course, the bankers.

Defaults…

The win for Auckland's Road Gang had been achieved partly by default…

During the 1950s, few of the numerous mayors, councillors and officials elected to Auckland's multiple local bodies possessed a collective vision as to what Auckland could achieve by way of a diverse, future-proof transport system. If any had promoted such a vision on behalf of their electors, parish-pump parochialism prevented any collective agreement of the type reached by the Technical Advisory Committee in favour of the Road Gang.

Auckland's citizens were thus deprived of any objective reasoning. Instead, they were led down the roads favoured by a biased, ad hoc body. Auckland's factionalism also provided central government with good reason to withhold funding from the City for any projects of which it disapproved, including the various transport systems opposed for many decades.

And Deceits…

The win for Auckland's Road Gang had been achieved partly by deceit…

There were a number of misrepresentations included by the Technical Advisory Committee in its final version of the Master Transportation Plan. One of the most glaringly obvious but most believed of those misrepresentations was the Committee's finding that Auckland did not have the density of population to support a suburban railway service.

The Plan's Auckland density measurement of only four persons per acre was later shown to be an intended underestimation using a grossly overestimated urbanised area. According to a study of the Master Transportation Plan undertaken by the late Paul Mees, an Australian academic specialising in urban planning and public transport, the true density figure that should have been used by the Technical Advisory Committee was fifteen residents per acre. [18]

As outlined by Peter Nunns in a November 2014 'Greater Auckland' post, 'Was Auckland's motorway network built on strategic misrepresentations?', the Technical Advisory Committee found "…it was necessary to lie with statistics…" at a time when "…58% of motorised trips in Auckland were taken by public transport (and only 42% by car) and that the average Aucklander took 290 PT trips per year…" [19]

The Plan's argument that the country could only afford one transport system for Auckland and that road construction was the cheapest option would eventually be found to be another deception.

As Peter Nunns pointed out: "While both rail investment and road investment carried a substantial price-tag, the decision to choose roads was made on the basis of the fact that they wouldn't be *that much* more expensive than rail." [20]

The Transportation Plan estimated the cost of the proposed railway development scheme, which included the Morningside Deviation and electrification of the line from Papakura to Henderson, at £11,710,000 and the Road Development Scheme of Urban Motorways at just £12,000,000. [21]

Even allowing for a few years of inflation and a slight variation in proposals, the Committee's railway cost estimate inexplicably exceeded that provided by the two Halcrow Thomas studies reported in March 1950 and April 1954. The first Halcrow Thomas estimate of £5,456,500 for construction of the Morningside Deviation and electrification of the line and their second estimate of £4,450,000 for a modified version of suburban line improvements were far less than the Technical Advisory Committee, of mostly road engineers, came up with. [22]

Nevertheless, the Committee was smug enough to advise:

"It is evident from the survey that if the £11,000,000 required for construction of the Morningside Deviation Scheme were to be made available by the Government for expenditure on the road system, it would achieve very much greater results." [23]

Obviously, looking back from a twenty-first century perspective, those *very much greater results* took far longer to achieve and the cost far exceeded that suggested by the Technical Advisory Committee. However, in the meantime, as described by Peter Nunns:

"I imagine at the time, the people in charge thought it was necessary to twist the truth so people would willingly give up the great public transport system they were using. There was a lot of passionate protest in NZ about getting rid of the trams…I imagine they thought they were doing Aucklanders a favour by delivering to them the amazing future we would all have once everyone was driving their car on these wide open and free flowing motorways. Which was probably true for a few months." [24]

In his book, *the quest for security in New Zealand 1840 to 1966*, William Sutch also commented on what he described as *the discrimination in favour of motor roads*:

"The discrimination in favour of motor roads, though it can partly be explained in terms of cement, motorcar, and oil companies, construction firms, equipment suppliers, local authorities, and engineers is, at bottom, the choice that the politician thinks the voter would prefer." [25]

Voter Preference

Of course, what *the voter would prefer* was unduly influenced to a great extent by the supposed experts of a stacked Technical Advisory Committee who misrepresented the case for an efficient and affordable transport system with glossy photos of sunny highways free-flowing through Los Angeles, and statistical distortions contained in their Master Transportation Plan for Metropolitan Auckland.

At the same time, the 1950s voter, the average citizen, the consumer, was bombarded by advertising:

"Appealing to people's aspirations to status and power…" the car industry "…created an aura of motorised romance, almost fantasy…" [26]

As long as influential persons and industry favoured the construction of roads and not the development of public transport, the Road Gang had no competition. And the voter, the average citizen, the consumer, with his and her cars garaged at their new home, only a few kilometres from the new shopping centre and its huge car park, and within an easy drive of their place of work, seemed relatively happy — to begin with.

Chapter Four

First Vehicle Assemblers

The Cart Before The Horse

A previous chapter referred to the transition from horse-drawn carriage building to that of motor vehicle assembly at the beginning of the twentieth century. That transition to modern-day transport was not necessarily a smooth one — as described by Mr A G Howland, said to be the oldest coachbuilder of Christchurch, when he commented on a September 1901 Arbitration Court minimum pay award affecting coachbuilding employees:

"Now I understand, the Union intends interfering further with what the labourers shall or shall not do, and by limiting the work to be done by them will still further hamper the trade. All this together with the competition we have to contend in the shape of bicycles, motor-cars, cheap imported machine-made work from America, second-hand carriages sent out from England, tramcars which serve the suburbs, and railway conveniences which allow the people to travel a great deal without horse vehicles, is becoming too much. I think you will agree with me, after what I have told you, that it is indeed a difficult matter for the coachbuilders to carry on business at all successfully.

"The conditions of trade have altered so much of late years that employers had to work right on each day like their men even before the award, and now the Union wants to do everything in the way of managing our business for us — except make them pay their way…" [1]

By 1909, a Department of Labour report included the building of 'motor bodies':

"Coachbuilding: This trade, which embraces the building of coaches, carriages, wagons, and motor bodies, has had a very successful year, and all tradesmen engaged in the different branches of the trade have made full time." [2]

But, by 1912, the building of coaches, carriages, and wagons was in steep decline, gradually replaced by the fabrication of motor car bodies which faced stiff competition from overseas — as reported by the Evening Star:

"A deputation of four journeymen coachbuilders waited on the Hon. G. Laurenson [Minister of Customs] at Christchurch yesterday to discuss the condition of the coachbuilding industry. The deputation stated that the coachbuilding trade had drifted down, and was in danger that in a few years it would be extinct. Its place would be taken by the motorbuilding trade. The wages paid in this trade were not responsible for the decline. Journeymen only got 1s 3d, compared with 1s 4½d in the cabinetmaking trade.

"In 1910 only 6 per cent of motor car bodies were made in New Zealand. One of the biggest establishments had closed down and the journeymen drifted away to Australia or elsewhere. It appeared as though the shops would have to cease building and become mere repairing shops.

"Motor car bodies were even coming in in sections. They had only to be put together before being sent out. The deputation submitted the following rough tariff:—(1) That all chassis with bodies attached be taxed 25 per cent on the total value including chassis; (2) that all chassis without bodies be admitted free, as at present; (3) that all motor bodies without chassis be taxed at the following rates: Single-seaters £25, double-seaters and taxis £35 ; (4) that a tax of 30 per cent, be placed on all material pertaining to motor bodies otherwise than in the raw.

"It was contended that frequently the invoice price was faked, and that the body usually cost more than was shown. The last proposal was devised to prevent foreign makers sending parts into New Zealand, where they could be 'slapped up' by anyone. The Minister, in reply, said he hoped to be able to do something to assist the industry, either by increasing the duty on the bodies or by putting a duty on motor cars. He believed the industry could be established in this country." [3]

The First Motor Vehicle Assemblers

As outlined in the previous chapter, when introduced to Parliament in 1898, the 'McLean Light Locomotive Bill' was intended to allow businessman and Member of Parliament, William McLean, to operate his recently-imported motor vehicles on the streets of Wellington. However, an increasing number of those contemplating the growth of a motor industry were wary of any legislation that conferred a monopoly on any one person or section of that industry.

To those of an entrepreneurial outlook, it was blatantly obvious, and more than amply justified by future events, that there would eventually be a lot more vehicle operators to be licensed — not just in Wellington, but throughout the country.

But it wasn't just the importers and drivers to be legislated for. Little known at the time were the New Zealand engineers constructing their own versions of petrol-driven motor cars — as revealed by a report published by the Evening Post on 15 July 1898:

"Ten local tradesmen interested in Mr W McLean's Light Locomotives Bill, petitioned the City Council last night against the Bill being allowed to pass on the ground that it proposes to grant a practical monopoly. They claim to be specially interested in the subject inasmuch as they have already been to considerable expense, and are daily incurring further expense, in the manufacture of motors.

"The work already gives employment to many hands, and will probably continue to do so. They further state that the motors which they are manufacturing are of more recent design than those imported by Mr. McLean, and that it will be advantageous to the public if they and others are given equal rights to run motors and motor-cars with him.

"The various local bodies in the colony should be given the right of issuing licenses to all manufacturers of motors and motor-cars, and the petitioners ask the Council to endeavour to secure an amendment of the existing law in this direction. The Council took no action, it being understood that the Mayor would do what he considered necessary when the Bill was before the Local Bills Committee of the House." [4]

The 'tradesmen's' objections were supported by a Letter to the Editor published the next day by the Evening Post:

"Sir —In your article in last night's Post re motor cars and the private Bill that has been proposed in the interest of Mr. McLean and his business associates you wisely say it would be objectionable to give Mr. McLean a monopoly until someone else comes along with motor cars.

"I beg to state for your information that there are at present two engineering firms in Wellington now engaged in making motors for public conveyances in New Zealand. They employ many men; the motors will soon be running; they are of the latest design for street traffic.

"Now, sir, is it right in the face of the many monopolies we have to bear of this kind to grant any one man or company this privilege for the whole colony? I say it is detrimental to this city and the colony.

"Where does the enterprise come in, when we have two firms spending four times the money in wages and material than the two motors cost Mr. McLean to import? No Act should be passed to confer the right to any one company. Any person should be permitted to run motors when certified to by someone competent, appointed by the City Council. Hoping some of our wise legislators will stop the present monopolies, I am, &, Enterprise. Wellington…" [5]

By the time the McLean Motor-car Act of 1898 became law, the legislators had 'wisely' refrained from granting any monopolies. For the time being at least, the legislation left the Wellington 'tradesmen' and others free to construct motor vehicles 'of the latest design for street traffic'.

Some of the first and more prominent of these entities to emerge as motor vehicle assemblers in New Zealand included:

F R Denniston

As mentioned in the previous chapter, one of the first to construct a gasoline-powered motor car from his own design in New Zealand was the Christchurch mechanical engineer, F R Denniston, who drove his creation from Christchurch to Oamaru in July 1900.

Described by the Nelson Evening Mail at the time as "only roughly built", [6] Mr Denniston's car was nevertheless the forerunner of the tens of thousands to be assembled in New Zealand over many decades.

But F R Denniston was more than just a manufacturer and assembler of motor vehicles — he was very much an inventor as well — as evidenced by the patents he applied for in 1906 and 1913:

"F. R. Denniston, Oamaru, an improved variable speed gear for motor vehicles…" [7]

"F. R. Denniston, Oamaru, Spare wheel attachment…" [8]

By May 1910, F R Denniston was also a South Island agent for the Ford Motor Company. [9]

No doubt having found it easier to represent the American import than to build his own, Mr Denniston represented Ford at the A & P Association annual exhibition held at Waimate in November 2014 — as reported by the Timaru Herald:

"F R Denniston — The popular and cheap Fords were exhibited by Mr Denniston of the Ford Garage. The many features and the suitability of the Fords for all practical purposes, as well as its low price, have made it a big favourite, and it was largely inspected yesterday." [10]

On 12 September 1924, F R Denniston teamed up with A. E. Shipley of Christchurch to register Denniston and Shipley Limited with a capital of £2500. Objects: "To acquire and take over as a going concern the business of motor car dealers, manufacturers, importers and sellers of motor cars and accessories lately carried on at Timaru by F. R. Denniston." [11]

However, by September 1926, the business of Denniston and Shipley Limited as motor car dealers, manufacturers and importers had been taken over by Timaru businessmen, T. L. Johnston and W. L. Johnston who had formed a new company with a capital of £2000. [12]

In the race to meet consumer demand and the pursuit of profit, such takeovers were common in the motoring world of New Zealand during the first three decades of the twentieth century.

And, continuing the trend set by Henry Ford in America, it was inevitable that the concept of mass production would eventually replace the vast number of small, New Zealand entities providing custom body-building and the garage-assembly of motor vehicles

Progress and the need for competitive pricing called for greater local production efficiency that only larger companies with a guaranteed supply of vehicle parts from overseas could provide.

W G Vining Limited

An immigrant from London to Nelson in 1892, William Graeme Vining was another example of a bicycle dealer who eventually moved with the times into motor vehicle dealing and assembly. [13]

His origins were summed up in a Nelson Evening Mail advertisement published 24 March 1900:

"Vining's Cycle Depot. W G VINING begs to inform Cyclists and the Public generally that he is carrying on his Cycle Business at the old address, but under his own name and personal supervision.

"Having secured the services of a Skilled Mechanic, he is prepared to undertake all kinds of Cycle Repairs at moderate charges and Promptly.

"Prior to re-building, the whole stock of Bicycles will be offered at greatly reduced prices. Up-to date Machines (both new and second-hand), can be obtained at a low cost previously unheard of in Nelson. Inspection invited before purchasing elsewhere. W G Vining Cycle Depot, Trafalgar-street, Nelson." [14]

By June 1907, the transition was complete with W G Vining having been appointed "Sole accredited Agent for Nelson and District" for the Cadillac — as advertised in the Nelson Evening Mail:

"To Intending Motor Car Buyers. The famous Cadillac will meet with your requirements. Delivery in 10 days. There is no car at any price that is less expensive to maintain than a Cadillac. There is no car at any price that will travel any road that cannot be travelled by a Cadillac. There is no car at any price that will climb any hill that cannot be climbed by a Cadillac. There is no car as good as a Cadillac at the price of a Cadillac. Do not be persuaded to purchase an underpowered car (either English or Foreign) which depends upon getting along by having a number of gears which are difficult to manipulate, noisy, and bad to drive on country roads as it will not track in cart ruts. The Cadillac is bristling with good points..." [15]

By March 1913, with the motor trade obviously booming, W G Vining had disposed of his cycle business to another in the bicycle trade. [16]

"While Dominion Motors of Wellington was the distributor for Hudson and Essex motor vehicles for North Island, from 1912, distributorship for the South Island went to W.G. Vining Limited...

"Vining had built a 31,500 square feet (2,926.5 square meters) garage in 1908 which was the largest garage in New Zealand at the time. A car assembly plant was established at the premises and shortly thereafter Vinings obtained additional licenses to import and assemble Cadillac, Maxwell, Haynes, and Ford vehicles from the United States; Bean cars from the United Kingdom; and Darracq and Unic vehicles from France.

"The plant later assembled Chevrolet and Rover vehicles until they established their own New Zealand assembly operations. The business ceased when it was sold on 30 September 1927 upon W.G. Vining's retirement." [17]

Vining's son, Phillip Vining, and an associate, Chas B Scott, formed a new business, P Vining & Scott and they continued the Hudson and Essex franchise from new premises at Nelson. [18]

Cooper and Pryce

Cooper and Pryce was founded in 1908 by Arthur Sidney Cooper (died April 1945) [19] and William Pryce at 120 Victoria Street, Christchurch, premises from which they traded for 55 years until death and retirement resulted in the closure of the business in June 1963.

About 1903, Welshman William Pryce met Arthur Cooper in Christchurch when they both worked for Boon and Company, building bodies for that city's first electric trams. After setting up in business together, "...Cooper and Pryce received their first batch of motor-vehicles, for which various types of bodies were required. These were twin-cylinder Renaults.

"With the growing use of motor-vehicles, the business of the firm increased...[building] just about everything from fire engines to hearses...the firm would get an order for three or four hundred bodies at a time, and they were produced on assembly-line methods; but provision had to be made for the occasional customer who wanted something a little different." [20]

In May 1914, the Christchurch Press reported that Cooper and Pryce had made the body for one of the city's first meat vans to replace the "Ordinary horse lorries, covered with cloths, the whole arrangement not being in keeping with modern requirements in regard to the sanitary handling of meat...between the abattoirs and the shop..." [21]

The commercial activities of Cooper and Pryce were further described during a Christchurch Sun report of the Canterbury A and P Association's Annual Show at Addington during November 1915:

"Messrs Cooper and Pryce, motor car body-builders, make a remarkable demonstration of what can be produced by local industry. As one admires the handsome body of a motor car it seldom enters the head that it is possible to produce the same article in New Zealand.

"The firm of Cooper and Pryce commenced as upholsterers in carriage and coach-work, but for the last six years their inventive genius has been centred on mastering the work of building and fitting motor car bodies. How well they have succeeded is proved by a glance round the exhibits and photographs in the stall on the grounds. There are prominently displayed several varieties of hides used in the manufacture of seats, while motor car bodies are shown from the bare steel frame to the graceful finished car. The proprietors are justly proud of their latest triumph, the building of a splendid body for one of Adams, Ltd.'s six-cylinder Studebaker cars. The renovating of old cars is a specialty of this firm…" [22]

After retiring the previous July, William Pryce died on 30 October 1963. [23]

J Bett and Bayly Limited

The transition from horse-drawn vehicles to those of the petrol-driven variety remained a gradual transformation well into the second decade of the twentieth century, as illustrated by newspaper reports of a Manawatu Dairy Show held in June 1912:

"[John Bett and William Mason Bayly trading as J Bett and Bayly Limited]…carry on a very extensive carriage-building and motor-car agency in Palmerston North, and are, as is their usual custom, making a display of vehicles at the Show, and visitors are specially invited to inspect this fine exhibition of motor cars, carriages, and other vehicles…

"Among the vehicles exhibited are some beautiful gigs of modern design, finished in perfect style and undoubtedly more than equal to the imported article both in finish, style, and workmanship.

"Messrs Bett and Bayly's exhibit is a source of great attraction and to country visitors is of special interest. Side by side can be seen the daintiest little pony carts and the strongest and most useful farm cart, while the motor cars — the more modern means of locomotion — are also exhibited in great variety." [24]

"Among the outside exhibitions the marquee of J Bett and Bayly, Ltd., is a leading feature. The old established firm has joined forces with Mr William Mason Bayly. The new company is now J Bett and Bayly, Ltd., whose carriage building and motor car business [at Palmerston North] now run hand in hand.

"There are here dog-carts, gigs and carriages side by side with the latest types of motor — Wolseley, Metallurgique, Daimler, F.N. motor cars for which Mr Bayly secured the agency. These are three of the newest models manufactured by the Wolseley Tool and Motor Car Company, a branch of the famous firm of Vickers, Ltd., at Birmingham…

"Two of the Wolseley cars are 16-20 h.p., fitted with the latest bodies, hoods, screens, head lights, and wire wheels. One has a full Lucas electric lighting set, including dynamo head lights…

"This company is making a speciality of motor coach work and has all the most up-to-date machinery for making and repairing motor bodies, hoods and screens." [25]

By May 1915, J Bett and Bayly had moved into what the Manawatu Times described as an "extensive factory" in King Street, Palmerston North where the paper's reporter was able to inspect "…the latest model Buick cars. [26]

A few months later, the same newspaper reported that while a rapid expansion of the motor business necessitated the building of premises more suited to that activity, the company's traditional carriage-building continued apace:

"There is not another firm in New Zealand that carries on motor and carriage building on such a large scale as Messrs Bett and Bayly. In the motor division of their extensive factory there is not a single part that cannot be supplied or repaired, hence the rapid growth and ever increasing demand for new space.

"At the present time the firm are erecting in Rangitikei Street handsome new brick buildings for their motor business which will do duty as a workshop, garage, offices and showroom. The new buildings are two storey, being 200 by 52 feet.

"At the rear of the premises there will be a large power house where a suction gas plant will supply the power for the machinery and lighting installation. The firm have now under order a large amount of new machinery, and when this is installed they will have one of the most up-to-date plants in Australasia.

"The repairs to motor cars are now carried on in King Street but when the new premises are ready by October or November next the machinery will be transferred to Rangitikei Street.

"The very best mechanics are employed in the motor works, and at the time of the visit, they were working at top pressure with repairs and the fitting up of new cars. The firm hold the agency for Sunbeam, F.N., Buick, A.Cc., Wolseley, and Colcott light cars…

"In the carriage factory were a large number of cars undergoing various stages of repairs. Some were turned out finished, while others were having new bodies fitted. The firm build a large number of bodies for cars, the owners preferring to have them built locally, as they know that the quality of the workmanship will be all that could be desired, and in addition they are able to get any particular design they order.

"In the factory can also be seen a large number of gigs, drays, etc., any design being built to order. The carriage building works were established in 1885 and have extended in conformity with the times. Even with the advent of motors it is surprising the number of orders that pour into the factory…it was wonderful where they all go to, but many find their way into the back country…" [27]

The new motor car premises were in full production by September 1916:

"J. Bett and Bayly Ltd., Palmerston North agents for Buick cars, advise the arrival of another shipment of these popular American cars which have become universal favourites in the district. Buick cars are renowned for their quality, and have never been the cheapest car in its class.

"The Buick 'Six', with its wonderful valve-in-head motor, can justly be said to fulfil this aspiration. The firm are now showing a fine 3-seater car on which is fitted a body built in the firm's own workshop. This car is a wonderful work, and has been greatly admired by all who have seen it.

"Bett and Bayly Ltd. claim to have the largest and most up-to-date motor garage in the Dominion and invite inspection of their fine new premises. They employ a very large staff of very expert workmen who undertake all classes of motor car building and repair work.

"This is a branch of the trade that the firm specialise in and they guarantee to give satisfaction. Full stocks of motor spirits, benzine, tyres and accessories are stocked and a night porter is kept on the premises." [28]

[As an aside, it is noticeable that J. Bett and Bayly Limited retained its legacy business of horse-drawn carriage manufacturing well into the twentieth century while the company successfully invested in the horseless carriages of the future. However, as well as diversifying its carriage-building business to include that of motor cars, the company also operated as funeral directors — thus initially capitalising on both the cause and effect of both industries. Given the carnage caused by the increasing numbers of vehicles to later choke the nation's roads, one could speculate that by selling its undertaking business in April 1918 the company lost a very profitable complement to the motor car business.]

Nevertheless, health and old age were soon to influence the fortunes of Messrs. J. Bett and Bayly. William Mason Bayly retired from the firm due to ill health in May 1918 and moved to the Bay of Islands. [29]

In December 1923, John Bett announced that the firm was to "…relinquish the coach-building branch of the business and henceforth devote their sole time and attention to the motor trade and repair work associated therewith.

"The firm's premises are being remodelled and reconstructed to facilitate the new conditions, and motorists will please note that the firm's operations have been transferred to Cuba Street, where the entrance to the offices, Buick showrooms, and workshops are now situated.

"The firm wish to specially thank their many, clients for past favours, and desire it to be known far and wide that the 'Buick' Service Station and Agency will continue to be conducted on up-to-date lines under Mr. J. Bett's personal supervision, as heretofore.

"In connection with the above it is interesting to note that the coachbuilding branch of the firm's trade, which has just been relinquished, was established by the late Mr. Felix Stratford in 1882, and was taken over by Mr. J. Bett, who was an employee of Mr. Stratford, in 1885…" [30]

"This was the first, coachbuilding business to commence operations in Palmerston North. In those days motor cars were unknown and Rangitikei Street was a grass road and the horse coaches used to pull up on the grass patch in front of our premises. Time brought many changes, however…" [31]

"Everyone recognises, as Messrs. Bett and Bayly do, that the days of coaches and carts are fast passing away, hence the firm's determination to concentrate all their efforts on the new order of things." [32]

J Bett and Bayly Limited was placed in voluntary liquidation on 28 January 1924 [33] and John Bett retired. He died in 1929. [34]

Nevertheless, the legacy of the J Bett and Bayly business continued with its 'chief man', W Richardson, who advertised in the Evening Post of 15 June 1927:

"Motor Hood and Screen Maker, Cuba street, Palmerston North. Good workmanship, prompt service, and moderate charges is Mr. Richardson's motto. In order to facilitate the prompt dispatch of work a fine roomy brick workshop has been added to the premises. Patrons leaving their cars in Mr. Richardson's care for repair need have no fear of fire as the new works are entirely constructed in brick with concrete floors.

"Mr. Richardson was Messrs. Bett and Bayly's chief man when that firm were in business. It will be remembered that they had departments for every phase of the motor trade, and Mr. Richardson now carries on business on the same lines. His plant is a first-class one and his extensive connection is a result of his reliability and good workmanship. He can fit your car to perfection at a very moderate cost…" [35]

Stevens and Sons

The original proprietor of Stevens and Sons was William John Stevens, born about 1845, who first partnered with John Reed Glanville as coachbuilders at Christchurch. However, that partnership was dissolved on 25 January 1877 [36] and William Stevens later partnered with Joseph Kitson Boon to form Boon and Stevens, a partnership that lasted for some nineteen years. [37]

In April 1894, Boon and Stevens, described as coach and tramcar builders, applied for a patent for "…an improved tramcar lifeguard." [38]

By October 1898, William Stevens was operating as a coachbuilder on his own account; as Stevens and Sons, "Builders of Carriages, Gigs, Cabs, Dog Carts, Buggies, etc." [39]

At the Christchurch Metropolitan Agricultural Show of November 1898, Stevens and Sons exhibited nine examples of its coaches. However, it appears from press reports of the time that the New Zealand Motor Car Company's exhibit of the 'Petrolette' motor car "…was constantly surrounded by an interested crowd." [40]

Not surprisingly, then, by 1912, Stevens and Sons had progressed to constructing the body work of the horseless carriage — as reported by the Christchurch Press:

"On the finish and painting of the locally-made bodies Messrs Stevens and Sons must be congratulated. This firm were entrusted with building the body-work for the Navy League art union car, which is fitted on a 12-16 Wolseley chassis. This is a very fine specimen of the carriage-builder's art.

"Messrs Stevens and Sons have laid themselves out to provide for the motorist in body fittings of every description. The address of the firm is 22 Lower High street, Christchurch…where they are at present erecting new buildings to cater for the motoring public." [41]

In November 1919, William Stevens retired, passing the business to his sons, E W Stevens, S H Stevens, A J Stevens, and Herbert C F Stevens, who established the limited liability company of Stevens and Sons Limited. [42] Nevertheless, the building of motor car bodies continued — as reported by the Wanganui Chronicle in July 1920:

"Another model which prominently arrests the eye is a 4-cylinder Hupmobile with a colonial body. The chassis for these cars are imported, and the bodies built by Stevens and Sons, Ltd., of Christchurch. The builders have done their work splendidly, the lines, finish, and upholstering being superior to those of most imported cars.

"These cars are fitted with the Stewart extra air device, which gives greater mileage on benzine consumption, a valuable factor with benzine at the present high cost. These cars are beautifully sprung, and are fitted with every facility for storing luggage conveniently, a little rack even being supplied for the driver's pipe." [43]

While Stevens and Sons had much earlier built tramcar bodies, by 1936, its expertise had grown to include the motor passenger bus:

"An interesting vehicle which might have been noticed in the city one day recently was a new motor-bus built by Stevens and Sons, Ltd., on a Morris chassis, to the order of Porter's Carrying and Passenger Service, Ashburton. [44]

Of course, the advent of the war and its effects on supply, affected all motor vehicle assembly production, particularly the relatively smaller businesses such as Stevens and Sons — as reported by the Gisborne Herald in July 1940:

"Because no import licenses for motor vehicles are available for the fourth period, a number of men in a motor assembly plant in Christchurch will be out of work after this month. This was revealed by Mr. H. C. F. Stevens, managing director of the motor car assembly and body-building works of Stevens and Sons, Limited. A year ago a total of 171 men were employed, but after July 17 the total will be 11.

"On Friday the last chassis was received in the assembly works, which operates on the chain system. Already the last body has passed through the paint shop, and the work for the men engaged in this stage has ended. As the remaining cars in the works pass along the assembly line the jobs of more and more men will have ended until on July 17 the last car passes out of the shop. Then the plant will have to close down.

"During the peak period in the last four years 116 men have been employed in the assembly at the works, and this number already has been reduced to 45, and after July 17 there will not be any work for these men.

"Mr. Stevens stated that the stopping of the work of assembling cars was a direct result of the import restrictions and petrol restrictions. 'At the peak we were turning out nine units a day, and employing 88 men on the body assembly, and 28 on the chassis assembly, giving a total of 116 employees engaged on car assembly,' stated Mr. Stevens." [45]

By this time, Stevens and Sons had been working closely with South Island Motors Limited, perfecting their body-building expertise in conjunction with the latter's motor vehicle assembly. [46]

Seabrook, Fowlds & Company

Seabrook, Fowlds & Co, formed by John Seabrook, William Fowlds, and Philip Seabrook, "…started life [in 1919] with a Vauxhall agency and as a Leyland truck agent for the Auckland region, with a sub-agency for Citroens…" [47]

According to an Auckland Star promotional article published 14 December 1922:

"Few people in and about this city and district are unacquainted with the name [Seabrook, Fowlds & Co.] and the fact that it is linked with the sale and distribution of the finest motor vehicles on the market. This is not surprising with an appreciation that the partners are vigorous young men with a fine experience in motor spheres here and abroad. They are the type whom discriminating overseas manufacturers and sale representatives seek to entrust with high-class productions…But the progress of Messrs. Seabrook, Fowlds & Co. could not be adequately chronicled without reference to its intimate connection with commercial transport in the distribution of Leyland motor vehicles, made by the most formidable and comprehensive organisation in Great Britain…" [48]

By December 1935, Seabrook, Fowlds was importing Austins in semi-knocked-down (SKD) form and assembling them at a small factory on St George's Bay Road, Parnell. [49]

The 1936 easing of Customs tariffs for CKD imports encouraged Seabrook, Fowlds to expand its Austin assembly business as reported by the Auckland Star on 1 July 1936:

"The firm of Seabrook, Fowlds, Ltd., has decided to build an assembly factory at Manukau Road, near the junction with the Great South Road, in order to comply with the Customs regulations governing the importation of motor vehicles. A staff of skilled labour will be engaged for assembling, trimming, painting and upholstering work.

"Tenders have been called for, the building, which will cover a large portion of the section, which extends 300 feet to Williamson Street. The plans are for a single-storey structure of two brick walls and two iron walls, and the plant will be of the most modern kind.

"In the paint shop an air-conditioning plant will be installed to absorb paint vapour, and a new system to check exhaust fumes will be used.

"Mr. J. Seabrook said that the work to be carried out would typify the progress of the motor industry, and that of the British car, particularly in the Auckland Province, also the effect of the new Customs regulations in creating local employment. [50]

The Seabrook, Fowlds Newmarket factory was running at full capacity by November 1937 when an Auckland Star report compared the new assembly line as a "Modern Magic Carpet" and then proceeded to document the progress of an Austin car from the unpacking of its parts to its final road test.

The report commented that the output of Austin cars averages 20 a week and concluded:

"There are 54 on the office and works staff of this efficient and up-to-date factory…" [51]

Philip Seabrook (1901-1972), who featured as number six on The Rich List for January 1936, was described, at the time, as "…a distinguished motor racer and part-owner of Auckland car dealership Seabrook Fowlds (later part of the New Zealand Motor Corporation), which held the valuable Austin franchise." [52]

In 1965, Seabrook Fowlds expanded its body-building activities with the purchase of Hawke Bros. Limited, a motor body builder of Takanini, and its associate company, Bus Sales Limited. [53]

A Christchurch Press article of 2 July 1966 reported that, despite government restrictions on the importation of new cars, "The consolidated net profit of Seabrook Fowlds Ltd…rose £7258, or 6.9 per cent, to £113,201 in the year to March 31…A greatly increased volume in used car trading had been undertaken to meet the reduction in new cars…" [54]

As described later, Seabrook Fowlds and four other prominent motor vehicle importers and dealers became part of the New Zealand Motor Corporation Limited in 1970. [55]

South Island Motors

South Island Motors Limited was registered as a company at 147 Armagh Street, Christchurch on 3 November 1920 with a Capital of £30,000 in £1 shares. Initial shareholders included: William W Vaughan 22,500 shares and A Hatrick & Co. Limited 7,500 shares. Objects: Importers and sellers of motor-cars, trucks, aeroplanes. [56]

In February 1921, South Island Motors was described as the firm "…who control the agency for [the Thornycroft Dump Truck] for the South Island in the interests of Messrs A Hatrick & Co., Ltd., Wellington who are the distributors for Australia and New Zealand." [57]

At the same time, South Island Motors was advertising itself at the distributors for the American Overland Four car, then said to be the most economical for petrol consumption. [58]

By March 1923, the company was also offering the 'Great Performance' and 'Sleeve-Valve Engine Supremacy' of the Willys-Knight cars, another Overland model produced by the Ohio firm between 1914 and 1933. [59]

As of 20 December 1924, V J McKibbin was the manager of South Island Motors [60] and managing director by September 1932. [61]

South Island Motors Limited was licensed as a manufacturing retailer in July 1935 [62] following a report that the firm "…in conjunction with Stevens and Sons, Limited, motor-body builders, are experimenting with a new scheme of motor assembly which promises to prove successful and which is giving employment directly to 30 men and increased business to several industries. Their present workshops are capable of producing 80 cars a month, and there is some chance of the scheme being extended to different makes of cars and of its establishment on a permanent basis." [63]

"…the McKibbin and Newburgh families…retained their interest in the business until 1969, when the company merged with David Crozier Motors." [64]

South Island Motors was voluntarily wound up on 20 September 1982. [65]

Amuri Motors

"Formed in 1910 by Duncan Rutherford after acquiring the business of the motor company of J S Hawkes Limited and erecting a garage at Gloucester Street…Christchurch. The name Amuri Motors was adopted in 1920…A workshop and assembly shop were constructed…and the firm was agents for Dodge cars and products of the North East Electric Company, and Sunbeam cars.

"The agency for Standard vehicles was gained in 1931. The company is the oldest overseas distributor of the Standard Motor Company. The company is still [in 1965] a direct importer of Studebaker cars, and the Standard Triumph range has become a mainstay of the firm.

"The company covers the whole of Canterbury, Nelson, Marlborough, Westland, the Wellington province and the Hawke's Bay province. The head office is in Christchurch, and there is a branch office in Wellington. The Wellington branch handles the distribution in the North Island, and the Christchurch office deals with South Island distribution." [66]

Descendants of Duncan Rutherford retained an interest in Amuri Motors together with Christchurch barrister, Garth Hamilton Gould, and his brother, George Arthur Churchill Gould. Amuri Motors was later to become Amuri Corporation Limited and then South Eastern Utilities Limited, a subsidiary of Pyne Gould Corporation. [67]

In 1966, "Amuri began its successful association with Mazda…and began importing and distributing Mazda vehicles nationally through its subsidiary company, Champion Motors Ltd. Six years later, in 1975, Mazda Motors of NZ Ltd was formed to import Mazda vehicles in volume, with Amuri Motors a substantial shareholder in this company through Champion Motors Ltd." [68]

Champion Motors

"Champion Motors Limited was incorporated on 19 December 1955 with a Capital of £500. Initial Shareholders included Christchurch: Amuri Motors Limited, Dunedin: Cossens and Black Limited, Invercargill: P. H. Vickery Limited, New Plymouth: Newton King Limited, Auckland: Northern Automobiles Limited (100 shares each). Objects: agents and dealers in motor-vehicles, etc." [69]

By 1983, "Amuri Motors had shareholders' funds of $9.2 million including paid capital of $1.2 million…"[70]

The firm's business success continued through to 1985 — as reported by the Christchurch Press:

"Amuri Motors' shift to new premises represents only one part of a $5 million expansion programme by the Amuri Group of Companies…Other developments by the Amuri group involves adding parts and service facilities to the existing showroom and used car departments of Moorhouse Mazda.

"This will convert the Moorhouse Mazda dealership to a full dealership. The expansion of Moorhouse Mazda and the relocation of Amuri Motors complement the expansion plans of Mazda Motors N.Z. Ltd.

"Mazda's current $22 million investment in assembly facilities and major, improvement of plant and equipment is structured to cope with increased demand for Mazda vehicles.

"Through a subsidiary company, Champion Motors Ltd, (which began its association with Mazda in 1966), the Amuri Group is one of only four shareholders in Mazda Motors.

"The company's acquisition of the Volvo franchise means Amuri Motors now markets two of the most highly respected brand names in the world — Mazda of Japan and Volvo of Europe." [71]

The name of Amuri Motors Limited was changed to Amuri Corporation Limited on 15 August 1986. [72]

In October 1989, it was announced: "Amuri Motors, Ltd, a wholly owned subsidiary of the Christchurch-based listed investment and property company, Amuri Corporation, will become a General Motors car and light commercial franchise holder for Wellington from December 4.

"During the last 80 years Amuri Motors has held franchises for many marques, and more recently those for Mazda, Volvo and BMW.

"Amuri Motors will acquire General Motors franchise-related assets of Wrightcars Wellington branch, subject to Commerce Commission approval. These assets include new vehicle stock, parts and accessories, and special tools and equipment. Most of the General Motors trained staff are being re-employed by Amuri Motors.

"General Motors and Mazda products are to be located in separate facilities on Amuri's Kent Terrace site. The entire dealership is being completely renovated to incorporate the additional requirements, and a multi-level car park building will be constructed at the rear of the site for customer parking and vehicle storage...

"The general manager of Amuri Corporation's motor division, Mr Charles Deans, said that the acquisition of the General Motors franchise would give Amuri the ability to retail high volumes of vehicles through the expanded Wellington branch." [73]

The name of Amuri Corporation Limited was changed to South Eastern Utilities Limited (a Pyne Gould Corporation subsidiary) on 12 July 1996.

The Colonial Motor Company

The Colonial Motor Company "…originated from William Black's coach-building factory which started operations in 1859 at 89 Courtenay Place, Wellington.

"In 1881 it was taken over by Rouse & Hurrell, who expanded the business with new three storied premises calling it *Rouse & Hurrell's Empire Steam and Carriage Works*. This partnership was formed into a limited liability company in 1902…The Ford Motor Car Agency was taken up in 1908 and in August 1911 a new name *The Colonial Motor Company Limited* was registered.

"On Ford Canada's recommendation a dominant shareholding and control was acquired by Mr Charles Corden Larmour and the sale of this majority holding and control to Mr Hope Gibbons and his family interests was concluded in April 1918 after negotiations in 1916. At that time there were 17 Authorised Ford Dealers in New Zealand of which 10 were in the South Island."

"In 1919 The Colonial Motor Company restructured with a new memorandum and articles but the 1911 name was retained.

"The nine storied building at 89 Courtenay Place, designed by architect J M Dawson to Ford plans, opened as the tallest Wellington construction in 1922. It was the first motor vehicle assembly plant in New Zealand — vehicles starting in boxes at the top and driving out completed at the bottom. The Company later built assembly plants at Fox Street, Parnell, Auckland and Sophia Street, Timaru. This was the age of the Model T with Ford market share reaching a peak of 27% in 1926." [74]

"By 1922 Model T Fords were big business…Car components shipped from the Ford factory in Canada were assembled with locally-manufactured fittings." [75]

As Standard Motor Bodies Limited, the Colonial Motor Company also "…built various truck bodies to order on Model T chassis." [76]

"In 1936, the Ford Motor Company of New Zealand Limited established [its own] assembly plant at Seaview, Lower Hutt, and took over the distribution of Ford products in New Zealand. The Colonial Motor Company then concentrated on the retail side of the business, operating the retail garages it then owned." [77]

The Colonial Motor Company continues to trade as a new and used, motor vehicle dealer [2023] with some twenty dealerships at major centres throughout the country. Descendants of Hope Gibbons, including Graeme Durrad Gibbons, Stuart Barnes Gibbons, James Picot Gibbons, Alexander Peter Gibbons, and other family members, remain in control of the company and/or its various dealerships as directors and/or shareholders.

The January 1936 edition of The Rich List recorded the Gibbons family (car dealing) as the fifth wealthiest individuals/families in New Zealand at that time. By 1987, the family had slipped to tenth position (car and truck dealing) with an estimated wealth of $50 million. [78]

General Motors New Zealand

A New Zealand assembler of American vehicles was incorporated as General Motors New Zealand Limited in January 1926. The company soon established an early assembly plant at Petone where, "On 31 August 1926 the first car, a four-cylinder Chevrolet sedan, rolled off the production line… Just before Christmas the first Pontiac was produced, soon followed by the first Buick.

In March 1927 the 1000th vehicle — a Chevrolet — was produced at Petone, a mere eight months after the plant began operation. In 1928 General Motors began assembling Oldsmobile sedans, and by 1929 total production had reached 12,000 cars and trucks, with staff numbers at the plant having increased from 250 to 500." [79]

Keen to promote its place as a pioneer in New Zealand motor car manufacture and to emphasise its employment of local labour and purchase of locally-made parts, General Motors invited the press to its Petone factory in November 1929 for a bit of a chin-wag with the company's managing director, W. M'Hardy Forman .

During the diatribe, Mr M'Hardy Forman advised that during the New Zealand production of motor cars, General Motors used "…a considerable percentage of New Zealand materials in the construction of our cars and trucks. Dominion-grown wool is fast being absorbed in the manufacture of New Zealand-made upholstery, and eventually approximately 33,000 yards will be used annually. In body building for commercial vehicles we are using miro, a native wood, at the rate of 150,000 super feet annually, and 120,000 feet of English glass will be replaced by the New Zealand article as soon as a suitable product is offered.

"For some time we have been consuming New Zealand-made varnishes, glues, enamels, and numerous small parts, but other articles that should be manufactured are carpets (we use 6000 yards), top material (13,000 yards), padding (28,000 lb). We might mention, too, that much is being done by way of encouraging the colour printing trade, as all General Motors advertising literature is produced entirely on New Zealand presses…

"We do not need to look very far to recognise the benefits that the motor car has brought. It is no mere coincidence that national standards of living are higher in almost direct proportion to the extent that the motor car is used in our country. New Zealanders may be well proud of the fact that their country is the third most highly motorised in the world.

"It is the ideal of General Motors (New Zealand) Ltd to add to the material benefits derived by the use of motor cars, the economic benefits that result from building these motor cars locally, and in contributing directly to the wealth of the country, in providing lucrative employment to hundreds of New Zealanders, in wonderfully organised sales help to its retail distributors, and in the employment of industrial methods that enable vast economies to be passed on to car buyers — in these ways, then is not General Motors helping New Zealand grow?" [80]

By 1936 more than 37,000 vehicles had been assembled at the General Motors Petone plant which eventually closed in 1984 — as reported by the Christchurch Press in August that year:

"Vehicle production has ended at New Zealand's oldest motor-assembly plant. General Motors' Petone plant was the first big one to build cars in New Zealand, beginning in August 1926, with a four-cylinder Chevrolet sedan. Assembly of Bedford trucks began in 1931.

"During the war the plant produced Bren gun carriers. It resumed car production in 1947 and produced its 100,000th vehicle, a Vauxhall series E, in 1952.

"Holdens were first produced at Petone in 1957. With the opening of GM's Trentham plant in 1967, the Petone works concentrated on refrigerator production and the assembly of commercial vehicles and components. It began assembling Bedford CF vans in 1977, and 9072 were built by the time the final unit came off the assembly line last week.

"Axle tubes continue to be assembled at Petone, but only until the end of this month when the plant will close. When GM announced last year that the plant would close, 277 people were employed there…" [81]

Australia produced the first Holden in 1948 and within a couple of years had manufactured some 20,000 vehicles. A number of different models were available to New Zealand motorists from about the mid-1950s. From July 1994 General Motors New Zealand Limited became Holden New Zealand Limited before reverting to its original name in September 2020. [82]

New Zealand Motor Bodies

On 15 June 1925, Wellington's Dominion newspaper reported the recent formation of the Wellington Motor Bus Company, in time for the arrival of three new motor buses from Auckland and the near-completion of two more buses built upon Republic chassis by the Wellington firm of Munt, Cottrell, & Co. [83]

Munt, Cottrell, & Co., general carriers, Customs, and forwarding agents of Wellington since at least 1903, had expanded into the motor body building industry by April 1922. By the end of May 1926, Munt, Cottrell had merged its motor body building business with another, C L Neilsen & Co. of Dannevirke, to form Munt, Cottrell, Neilsen & Co. Limited. The new company consolidated its motor body building business at a new factory at Jackson Street, Petone. [84]

By 1937, the company was trading at Petone as New Zealand Motor Bodies Limited "…building metal frame bus and coach bodies and other commercial superstructures, hoists and other truck equipment." [85]

In October 1946, New Zealand Motor Bodies purchased the motor-body building business of Stevens & Sons Limited which had operated from Ferry Road, Christchurch for many years. Following the purchase, New Zealand Motor Bodies continued to operate its 'Standard Steel Frame Omnibus Body Assembly Works' from its Tuam Street, Christchurch factory. [86]

By October 1948, New Zealand Motor Bodies had also established a new factory at Auckland from where it produced what the Te Awamutu Courier described as the "Most Modern Passenger Vehicle in Waikato…The bus, which is called the 'Te Awamutu Flyer', is a Canadian Ford Mercury bus chassis. The body was the first all steel body to be manufactured by New Zealand Motor Bodies Ltd. in their new factory in Auckland. It seats 33 passengers and the seats are 'Dunlopillo' cushions with brown leather trimmings." [87]

When the Wanganui City Council started to develop its public transport system in 1949, its Transport Committee chose New Zealand Motor Bodies to build part of its proposed fleet, comprising "…the latest model Ford V 8 forward control bus chassis incorporating many new features not previously marketed in New Zealand. These chassis will be fitted with the New Zealand Motor Bodies, Ltd., Wellington, all-steel safety 31-passenger bodies." [88]

New Zealand Motor Bodies continued to profitably assemble cars and manufacture omnibus, trolley-bus, and coach bodies at its Christchurch, Petone, and Auckland plants as illustrated by a few of its annual reports through to 1970:

"A rise of £11,100 to £28,686 in profit is shown in the accounts of New Zealand Motor Bodies Ltd Petone for the year ended March 31 [1951]…Net income from sales, after deducting cost of material and manufacturing wages was £35,007 higher than last year at £128,505…The directors state that production was a record and 133 omnibus, trolley-bus, and coach bodies were built during the year compared with 90 in the previous year…" [89]

"Net profit of New Zealand Motor Bodies Ltd. For the year to March 31, 1960 rose sharply to £30,832 against £19,191 the previous year." [90]

"Net profit of New Zealand Motor Bodies, Ltd., Petone increased by £7339 or 20.6 per cent, to £43,016 after record output in the year ended March 31 [1963]…The three factories worked at full capacity during the year, the chairman (Mr G D. Stewart) says in the annual report. A total of 150 bus bodies was built compared with 104 in 1962." [91]

"Current orders for bus bodies and the recent improvement in the assembly division are sufficient reasons to expect the coming year to be a favourable one for New Zealand Motor Bodies, Ltd., in spite of the credit and other restrictions, says' the chairman (Mr G. D. Stewart) in his annual report. Net profit rose by £1404, or 3.4 per cent, to £42,468 in the year to March 31[1967]…" [92]

"Net profit of New Zealand Motor Bodies, Ltd, Petone, was $51,104 for the year to March 31 [1970], compared with $79,254 for the I previous year…The board decided it was essential to secure sufficient orders to keep the three factories running and to maintain the skilled staff as an effective organisation pending a return to improved trading conditions.

"Sales of bus bodies were reduced from 149 in the previous year to 120 by the reluctance of passenger service operators to place orders until the findings of the transport commission were known but volume in the car assembly and commercial body building departments increased.

"The directors say the company is now well placed to handle expected increased demands. Orders have increased in recent months. 'The expected demand from the market gives us confidence to budget for increased and improved results,' they say." [93]

However, by 1973, management problems at its Auckland plant were said to have caused a considerable reversal of fortunes for New Zealand Motor Bodies:

"New Zealand Motor Bodies, Ltd, the Petone-based motor-body builder, with factories also in Christchurch and Auckland, has again incurred problems with the Auckland branch and has advised shareholders that the profit for the year is 'disappointing'.

"The directors, in a report to shareholders, said that although on March 21 [1974] they had advised shareholders that the profit position was expected to improve, as it did in Petone and Christchurch, the Auckland branch operated at a loss…

"In March 1973, the company reported that while earnings had been maintained in the bus building activities, management problems had arisen in the subsidiary assembly company which had had a considerable effect on production and operated at a loss.

"The chairman of the company (Mr G. D. Stewart) in the annual report, described) the result for the year as 'most unsatisfactory' and put the failure of past management at the Auckland branch as one of the main reasons for it.

"Monthly figures had led the directors to expect a profit, but stock shortages incurred through plant damage, revealed by stocktaking, proved the operating results had been overstated…" [94]

"New Zealand Motor Bodies, Ltd, has reported an audited net loss for the year to June 30 [1974] of $195,408 after checking the books of the Auckland plant.

"The problems in the Auckland plant have taken considerable longer to resolve than anticipated, but substantial progress has been achieved.

"The Petone and Christchurch branches have continued to operate profitably in spite of shortages of labour and materials, the report says...The motor division had to contend with substantial increases in sales tax on new motor vehicles, the tightening of hire purchase regulations, and increasing fuel prices, all of which have had some effect on sales..." [95]

Nevertheless, the promising and profitable future represented by New Zealand Motor Bodies attracted serious interest from other industry players in 1975 — as reported by the Christchurch Press:

"N.Z. Motor Bodies, Ltd has become the subject of a battle for control by the distributors of rival brands of Japanese motor vehicles. Nissan Motor Distributors N.Z., Ltd the franchise holder for Datsun...The Nissan bid comes two days before Motor Bodies shareholders were to be asked to approve a deal which would give Moller Holdings, Ltd, New Zealand Honda franchise holder, an interest in the company...

"N.Z. Forest Products Ltd has a 32 per cent interest in Nissan Motor Distributors. The attraction of N.Z. Motor Bodies for both Moller and Nissan is its assembly plant at Auckland." [96]

An agreement between New Zealand Motor Bodies and Moller Holdings Limited to proceed with a scheme of association was reached in May 1975 — as reported by the Christchurch Press:

"'The proposals agreed to by the Motor Bodies and Moller boards were in the nature of a partnership between two companies,' [chairman of Motor Bodies] Mr Stewart said. Motor Bodies was the largest manufacturing company in the transport industry in New Zealand, and Moller was one of the leading car franchise and distribution companies. Their activities were complementary in the transport field, and would lead to further development, he said.

"Motor Bodies would continue to control the bus manufacturing plants, the vehicle assembly plant, and contracts for building vehicles, and assembling cars. It would gain an assured supply of vehicles for assembly, rather than being dependent on franchise holders not financially interested in the company.

"Moller would retain its car franchises, marine motors, and the spare parts business associated, with the franchises, and retail outlets. Moller would obtain priority rights to assembly in the Motor Bodies assembly plant at Auckland.

"Recent moves by the Government, in favour of the importation of completely knocked-down cars, made the division attractive to franchise holders." [97]

New Zealand Motor Bodies' association with Moller Holdings and some Government encouragement for local industry in turn encouraged the company to expand its operations — as reported by the Christchurch Press in October 1975:

"An assurance from the Government that full encouragement will be given to the New Zealand bus-building industry has prompted New Zealand Motor Bodies, Ltd, to take an option on an area of land at Palmerston North, the chairman (Mr G. D. Stewart) says in his annual report.

"This is after talks with the Government on the proposal that New Zealand industry could supply the needs of bus operators, which would overcome the necessity to provide overseas funds for imports.

"Local industry could make bus bodies comparable with the highest overseas standards, and it had achieved 90 per cent local content, significantly greater than other automotive production in New Zealand, Mr Stewart says." [98]

Indeed, the new Motor Bodies' factory at Palmerston North was opened on 3 July 1977. [99]

As a result, the company's car and light commercial vehicle assembly plant at Mount Wellington, Auckland was shut down in 1978 but reactivated and expanded in late 1979 to cater for the needs of Mazda Motors of New Zealand Limited. [100]

After several mergers, New Zealand Motor Bodies Limited changed its name to Coachwork International Limited on 20 September 1984. [101]

"By 1987, it [Coachwork International Limited] had an 80% share of the New Zealand coach body market…The company ceased trading in 1993." [102]

The Dominion Motors

Dominion Motor Vehicles Limited, founded in Wellington in 1912 by (Sir) Charles Norwood (1871-1966), began with wholesale distribution of imported vehicles and would eventually become the sole assemblers of Morris vehicles in New Zealand, operating from the same Courtenay Place site for some eight decades. [103]

"In 1919 Dominion Motors amalgamated with a Christchurch business, J A Redpath's Universal Motor Co., and opened new retail departments in Christchurch as well as in Wellington. Distributorships included Oldsmobile, Crossley, Chevrolet, Stutz, Rolls-Royce, Hudson and Essex, and Vauxhall.

"For the first nine months of 1927 Essex would become the third most popular car brand in New Zealand, behind Chevrolet in second place, and Ford in first place.

"Auckland operations were run from premises at Albert Street…where there was one of a number of small workshops run in the main centres by Dominion Motors that finished assembly of partly knocked down cars. In 1928 the…Albert Street 'assembly line' took one hour to assemble each new car." [104]

"Just before Christmas 1930, at a dinner held at Wellington, the secretary and director of British Morris Motors (1926) Limited, S G K Smallbone, announced the appointment of Dominion Motors to control the distribution of Morris cars and commercial vehicles in New Zealand.

According to a report of the event, the Otago Daily Times described The Dominion Motors Limited (chairman of directors, Mr C. J. B. Norwood) as then a company with:

"…a head office, 10 branches, and 80 points of distribution, was in the front rank of motor interests in the Dominion. Its capital, direction, and staff, numbering over 300, are supplied entirely by New Zealanders. The company has grown from a very modest concern in 1911 to one of very big dimensions, with an annual turnover in normal times in excess of £1,000,000." [105]

[It is of interest to note here that, in anticipation of the influx of used Japanese cars imported several decades later, an Auckland motor dealer by the name of Charles Eustace Gray imported second-hand Morris cars from England and sold them in New Zealand. His company, Morris Motors Limited, was successfully sued by Morris Motors (1926) Limited in May 1929 for piracy — appropriating the name and reputation of the British company.] [106]

"In 1938, [Dominion Motors] built in Mortimer Pass Newmarket a real assembly plant on 1½ acres of bare land…The building was completed at the end of February 1939 when it was expected the necessary plant would be installed by the middle of the year. The new plant would turn out 10 vehicles a day at the Mortimer Pass frontage. War was declared on 3 September 1939 but the plant was opened and began production. By the start of the 1950s it employed more than 600 people. A new extra plant was built in Panmure in 1953. Opened in 1954, it continued to grow until 1961 and built Morris Minor commercial models until 1975." [107]

[By 1960] "In New Zealand nearly 70,000 units (Morris Minor 1000) were sold, initially imported fully built up but later assembled by Dominion Motors at its plant in Newmarket, Auckland." [108]

The Rover Company of New Zealand

The Rover Company of New Zealand Limited was the first English company to establish an overseas chassis assembly and body building plant in any part of the Empire when its new factory at Petone was officially opened by New Zealand's Prime Minister, George Forbes, on 17 February 1932.

During the ceremony, great emphasis was placed on the use of locally-sourced raw materials with the only imported material in the bodywork expected to be the leather and the steel panels

Mention was also made of the value of the mutual trade that existed between New Zealand and the Mother Country, pointing out that England was practically New Zealand's only market and how right and proper it was to reciprocate by providing a market for English cars. [109]

"However, the depressed financial conditions didn't help sales and already by December 1932 the company was unable to buy the cars from its English parent — Rover UK was struggling under huge losses of £96,000, of which the money spent on the NZ plant formed a significant proportion…In September 1932, the Rover Company of New Zealand changed its name to the British Sales Company Ltd, but the company went into voluntary liquidation in February 1933." [110]

As reported by the Christchurch Press on 10 January 1933:

"The Rover Company's accounts for the year to July 31 last, show a trading loss of £95,983, and this is increased to £225,413, after allowing for depreciation, loss on investments, etc. To this figure is added a further sum of £112,507 as a reserve for loss on property and plant, and after deducting the balance brought forward of £58,895 there will be a debit of £279,024 to be carried forward." [111]

By August 1933, the Rover factory at Petone, opened with such fanfare just eighteen months previously, was offered for sale or lease. [112] The premises were eventually occupied by the makers of petrol cans, J Gadsden and Co Limited.

South Road Services

South Road Services Limited was registered as a private company on 15 November 1933 with a Capital of £2,000. The company's shareholders included William R. O'Fee and F. M. O'Fee, both of Dunedin; J. M. Doggart of Balclutha; and J. Galbraith of Tahakopa. Objects; To construct, equip, maintain, repair, and work omnibuses, buses, taxi motor cars, trucks, lorries, drays, aeroplanes, or other vehicles, and general incidental." [113]

The bus services operated by South Road Services were taken over by the Government in September 1936 [114] to be operated by the Railways Department. [115]

Todd Corporation

The Todd conglomerate's beginnings in the motor industry began with what is said to have been the first importation by Charles Todd (junior) of a De Dion Bouton motor car into Otago and the acquisition of a Ford dealership at Dunedin with his brother, James Todd, in 1908. [116]

What is today known as The Todd Corporation Limited began with the company's incorporation as Todd. Brothers Limited in June 1919, and the Todd Motor Company in 1923 under Desmond Todd.

The Todd Motor Company started with the Otago dealership for Ford but that was relinquished with the acquirement of the franchise for the importation of the US Gray car in 1923. Gray went out of business in 1926 but, by then, the Todd company had founded a strong dealer network up and down the country. [117]

The Todd Motor Company moved its headquarters to Wellington in 1924. By then, the company had acquired the rights to distribute General Motors vehicles in the Wellington region and became the sole distributor for Chrysler in 1925. [118]

In 1928, the business became the New Zealand franchisee of the British automobile manufacturer, the Rootes Group, and opened an Auckland dealership selling Hillman, Humber, and Commer models.

In 1934, what had become Todd Motor Industries Limited, led by Andrew Todd, opened an automotive assembly plant at Petone to assemble and sell vehicles from imported Chrysler (USA) and Rootes (United Kingdom) parts. [119]

"The first motorcars from the Todd line were Plymouths in 1935 (from US Chrysler Corporation) at the rate of seven per day. In April, Rootes Hillman and Humber cars from England followed." [120]

Todd Motor Industries was one of the leading manufacturers in the country when the business acquired the Mitsubishi franchise in 1970 and expanded to the Todd Park motor vehicle assembly plant at Porirua in 1975.

As reported by the New Zealand Motor Vehicle Dealers Institute, from August 1979, Todd Motors held the number two market share position in the New Zealand automobile industry behind Ford…"boosted no doubt by excellent sales of the Mitsubishi Mirage…" [121]

Indeed, Todd Motors continued to assemble a wide range of cars and light and heavy commercial vehicles and maintained its market share for much of the 1980s.

However, the Todd Corporation sold its motor vehicle businesses to Mitsubishi in 1987 and thereafter   concentrated on the family's other interests of oil and gas exploration and production, electricity generation and retailing, property development, minerals, healthcare, and technology. [122]

As described later, those additional business interests included the importing and retailing of Europa oil with terminal services at four major ports and a chain of petrol stations across New Zealand. [123]

Those descendants of the original Charles Todd (senior), his sons Charles and James, then Desmond and Andrew, now include David Malfroy Todd, Michael John Todd, Jennifer Ann Todd, and Katrina Margot Todd as those now most active in the family business.

Motor Assemblies (South Island)

In June 1935, P H Vickery, Amuri Motors Limited, Boon and Co., and Cossens and Black Limited, all of the South Island, established Motor Assemblies (South Island) Limited to assemble Dodge cars and trucks at Christchurch. This followed an amendment to Customs duties that favoured cars shipped in a knocked-down (CKD) for assembly in New Zealand. [124]

As well as the sale of completely built vehicles imported from Britain and America, in 1935 the comparatively smaller retailers saw the chance to profit further from the assembly of those vehicles in New Zealand following the Government's encouragement:

"Four firms are concerned in the organisation to control an assembly factory for cars imported in the knocked-down condition, known in the trade as c.k.d., which is to be established in Christchurch. Orders have been placed for material, and operations will begin as soon as the plant arrives.

"The four firms are Amuri Motors, Ltd., Christchurch, Boon and Co., Christchurch, P. H. Vickery, Ltd., Invercargill, and Cossens and Black, Ltd., Dunedin.

"The premises used by Boon and Co. for the making and assembly of tramcars will be the site of the new factory. Under a recent amendment to Customs duties, cars shipped in a knocked-down condition are specially favoured. It was the intention of the Legislature when making the change in the tariff that the development of motor assembly business should be encouraged in order to provide employment. The Christchurch factory will be the first of its kind to be established in the city." [125]

A Christchurch Press promotion of November 1935 described the establishment of Motor Assemblies (South Island) Limited at Tuam Street, Christchurch as:

"A New Christchurch Industry — An Important Business — Work For Unemployed Men…Metals, materials, fittings — to take a pile of them 'in the rough' and mould them by a process of intricacy and art into a beautifully finished article. That is the romantic business for which Motor Assemblies (South Island) Ltd. was recently established in Christchurch. From this factory, one new DODGE car is being turned out every day ready for its work upon the roads. That in itself is an impressive indication of the industrial importance of this new business…" [126]

In 1939, the Motor Assemblies factory was also assembling Studebaker cars from ckd packs imported from America. While "…imports of American cars were severely curtailed during the war…In 1946, some hundreds of post-war Studebaker models were assembled for the distributors holding the franchise [Amuri Motors Limited] who were also the owners of the assembly company at that time." [127]

However, a report published by the Christchurch Press on 2 March 1955, described Motor Assemblies Limited as the only motor assembly works in the South Island…"where all the c.k.d. imports of one English firm's cars are assembled…it employs 218 men and 13 women…and its production in 1953-54 was about 2000 cars…" [128]

The English firm referred to was Standard-Triumph whose ckd vehicles had since replaced those of the American models because of the much lower, preferential tariffs that then applied to British imports.

In May 1957, Motor Assemblies was planning to build a second motor assembly plant at Hornby, Christchurch occupying some 200,000 square feet and costing about £750,000. Negotiations were then continuing in England with the parent firm of Standard Motor Company of New Zealand which was backing the plant. [129]

As described by the Christchurch Press, the proposed factory was to be "…the most modern assembly plant in the country, there would be a mixed-model production schedule and that the present staff of more than 200 would be almost doubled." [130]

However, by the end of the year, the Government had announced a 25 per cent reduction in imports of knocked-down cars. Consequently, when asked in January 1958 about the proposed expansion to Hornby, the general manager of Motor Assemblies, Mr A R Cutler, replied:

"The situation looks grim and it appears that we may have to call a halt to any expansion and improvement of plant after such a drastic cut." [131]

The British vehicle manufacturer, Standard-Triumph, had acquired a financial interest in Motor Assemblies by 1960 and both entities were taken over by the British Leyland Group in 1961.

In March 1962, press reports indicated that negotiations between Standard-Triumph New Zealand and the Government had started for the purchase of partly-completed buildings intended for a cotton mill at Nelson.

Commenting on speculation that if the negotiations were successful, Motor Assemblies would be expected to transfer its Christchurch assembly plant to Nelson, the general manager, Mr A R Cutler, replied: "It should be remembered that we have completed plans for a new assembly project at Hornby, and this has only been held up over the last three or four years by the uneven level of import licences for knocked-down cars…In the event of the Nelson project proving a more central and therefore economic proposition it could only be expected that the directors would take advantage of it." [132]

In the meantime, by early 1964, Motor Assemblies continued to produce Standard-Triumph vehicles at its two Christchurch assembly plants despite the Government's import licensing restrictions and what were described as unreliable allocations:

"In a circular to all employees, dated March 5 [1964] Mr Cutler stated that because of circumstances beyond the control of the company, production had to be cut back sooner and in a greater degree than was ever anticipated.

"…factors involved were the lack of information about motor vehicle import licences for the period July 1964 to June 1965; the allocation to Standard-Triumph (NZ)Limited of a disappointingly small proportion of licences from the £2.5 million additional funds made available by the Government last year…

"The company was at a loss to understand why although production was increased by some 64 per cent for the six months to December 1963, compared with the preceding six months, Standard-Triumph (NZ) Ltd was allocated what appeared to be a ridiculously small amount of licences.

"Even if a protest is successful the additional licence gained is not likely to be very great for it is believed that cars imported and built between June and December 1963, exceeded in licence value by some millions of pounds the extra £2.5 million the Government had allotted for this period, Mr Cutler stated in the circular.

"Within a short time the company would be reduced to a production rate of approximately five Triumph Heralds and three Triumph 2000 saloons at the Tuam street plant. At the Ensors road plant the situation would improve a little as the production of the Standard 15cwt van and similar units was stepped up to two or more a day, said Mr Cutler." [133]

While Motor Assemblies complained of not receiving its rightful share of the Government's £2.5 million bonus allocation, its Hutt Valley competitors professed no such grievance and reported that their firms had been able to keep production near last year's [1963] record level as a result of the share of the allocation they received.

"Spokesmen for these firms — Todd Motor Industries Ltd., Ford Motors Ltd., and General Motors Ltd. said…The shares were determined by sales performance of each assembly firm in the second half of last year. Motor Assemblies was a relatively small concern and probably had not increased its production sufficiently to gain any sizeable portion of the bonus allocation…" [134]

A relatively small concern or not, Motor Assemblies was about to get closer to the competition, according to a Christchurch Press article in July 1964 that reported:

"The Government and Standard-Triumph (NZ) Ltd are expected to announce this week that agreement has been reached for the company to buy the Nelson cotton mill building…It is expected that with an extension of work to Nelson up to 300 employees may be engaged there…It is believed that as an encouragement to the car firm, special contracts with concession rates have been arranged with the Railways Department and the Nelson Harbour Board for the moving of parts and built-up cars." [135]

While the move to Nelson may well have pleased the British owners of Motor Assemblies, not all New Zealanders approved of the arrangement — as outlined by a Christchurch Press editorial published 20 July 1964:

"The sale [for £75,000] of the uncompleted building and 27 acres of land at the Nelson cotton mill site for a motor-car assembly works will enable the Government to close its cotton mill account…

"The Government has offered Standard-Triumph many inducements to move to Nelson. Those of a 'once-and-for-all' nature include import licences for plant and for assembled vehicles during the move, and State Advances Corporation assistance with employees' housing.

"These are all of value to Standard-Triumph which appears to have driven a hard bargain with the Government; but their real cost to the community is slight. Of more significance are the permanent subsidies the firm will receive.

"The Railways Department will allow the firm a special discount for distributing vehicles from Nelson to the rest of the South Island and to the southern half of the North Island; and presumably the firm will also get the benefit of the notional railway between Nelson and Picton.

"The firm will also be subsidised by the Nelson Harbour Board's ratepayers or by other users of the port; but this is of little concern outside Nelson.

"The grants, subsidies and other inducements offered to Standard-Triumph to move to Nelson rather than stay in Christchurch or move to Auckland or Whangarei are substantial; but they have purchased a desirable diversion of industry, population, and employment opportunities from a major centre to a minor one.

"Taxpayers are entitled to know, however, how much it is costing them to re-site this plant in Nelson; and they have been given no details of the subsidies and grants involved…There is a further cost to the community in this deal though it would presumably be incurred whether the enlarged assembly plant was sited at Nelson or anywhere else: the increased cost of protecting an uneconomic industry.

"That the industry is uneconomic is no fault of individual firms, but an inevitable result of protection by import licence – the policy followed by successive governments since World War II.

"It has resulted in the establishment of 17 assembly works which shared in 1963 (a year of record imports) 62,000 vehicles for assembly…With the help of a tariff (but not import control) one motor works might be able to compete with imports; but not 17.

"The chances of a rational reorganisation of the industry are even more remote now that the Government has agreed to subsidise the operations of one producer in this highly-protected industry." [136]

In anticipation of the start of production at Nelson in October 1965, the assembly of cars and light commercial vehicles by Motor Assemblies ceased at Ensors Road, Christchurch on 24 August of that year. The Tuam Street plant remained operational but run by the parent company, Leyland, which continued to assemble special purpose heavy vehicles there and at Auckland. [137]

"Twenty-five [Motor Assemblies] staff transferred from Christchurch, and a further 75 [Nelson] locals were employed over the next few months. In October [1965] the first Nelson vehicle was produced. The model mix was Triumph Heralds and 2000s, and Leyland light commercials…" [138]

By 1970, the Nelson assembly plant was not short of work — as reported by the Christchurch Press in September of that year:

"New Zealand-assembled Rover cars are to be exported to Australia in a $2.5 million agreement negotiated under the New Zealand-Australia Free Trade Agreement. They will be the first New Zealand-assembled cars to be sold in Australia…

"During the first year, a total of 800 built-up Rover 2000s and Rover 3500s with an f.o.b. value of more than $2.5 million will be exported from New Zealand. The cars will supply most of Australia's requirements for these two models now met by the importing of built-up models from Britain.

"The agreement was announced today by the deputy chairman and managing director of the British Leyland Corporation of New Zealand Ltd (Mr A R Cutler). Mr Cutler said that the export order would mean expanding the labour force at the Nelson plant by about 60 men; the factory itself would not need extending. It was hoped to ship the cars direct from Nelson." [139]

"The Nelson plant was successively owned by Standard Triumph NZ, British Leyland Corporation of New Zealand, New Zealand Motor Corporation (NZMC) and finally Honda New Zealand." [140]

The Austin of England Agency

The Austin Motor Company was founded by Englishman, Herbert Austin, who started production of the first models at Longbridge, Birmingham in 1906.

"Although the first recorded [New Zealand] sale of an Austin car by David Crozier, Ltd, was in 1919, one of the first Austins was bought by a New Zealander, Mr G. [George] H. Scott, in 1909. This was a 15 horsepower model, and was one of the first two cars to be exported by the Austin Motor Company, the other being an Austin 18/24 which went to South Africa.

"Mr Scott was the man responsible for introducing the make to New Zealand and he used his first car as a demonstrator and began with it an association with Austin that continued until his retirement 32 years later." [141]

"George H Scott became the Austin of England company agent in Wellington in 1909 so effectively that, within four years, Austin was the top-selling British make." [142]

"In 1913, only three years after the landing of the first Austin, the number of Austins shipped to New Zealand exceeded the total number of all other British cars exported to New Zealand.

"Mr Scott ultimately appointed seven distributors for New Zealand, each controlling a province. The first two to be appointed were David Crozier, Ltd, in Christchurch, and P. H.

Vickery, Ltd, in Invercargill. In the early years the cars were imported either 'fully built up or as complete chassis, the bodies being built in New Zealand. In Christchurch, Cooper and Pryce, a well-known coach-building firm, was responsible for building many bodies for cars imported by David Crozier, Ltd." [143]

In 1919, George Scott became New Zealand's official Austin factory representative and established the Austin Distributors Federation comprising the original distributors appointed by him to assemble and sell their own Austins.

"The notorious 'slump' involved the motor industry in New Zealand in serious problems between 1930 and 1933 and import restrictions reduced sales of all makes of cars for the years 1931 to 1934 to almost one half of the figures for the previous four years. In 1935 a change of Government brought more problems. Very soon after taking office the Labour Government enacted regulations which required that motor vehicles be imported in completely-knocked-down condition.

"This suddenly created a major problem for Austin distributors and also the New Zealand importers of motor vehicles none of whom, with the exception of Ford and General Motors, had assembly plants here.

"In one respect at least the distributors were prepared for the change-over which was to introduce large-scale car assembly to New Zealand. During 1933 and 1934 Mr Scott negotiated and succeeded in obtaining the consent of the Customs Department and the Austin Motor Company to a plan regarding imports which enabled the seven Austin distributors to establish and function as a federation. This step formed the nucleus for wider and more important developments later as a federation." [144]

Austin Motor Industries

On 23 May 1939, P H Vickery, Boon and Co., J Black, and David Crozier Limited incorporated Austin Motor Industries Limited, to assemble Austin models at their Motor Assemblies' Christchurch premises. [145]

In anticipation of the new venture, the Christchurch Press of 14 March 1939 commented:

"When a new motor-car assembly factory in Christchurch is in full operation, 125 men will be employed. The factory will cover one acre and a half of a six acres and a quarter block adjacent to the Christchurch-Lyttelton railway line.

"The factory, which is expected to be in production in four months, will be built by a privately-owned company, comprising David Crozier, Ltd., Messrs D. Clive Crozier (Christchurch), P. H. Vickery (Invercargill), and John Black (Dunedin), and the Boon Investment Company. The share capital is £10,000.

"All Austin cars for the South Island will be assembled at the works, the plans for which have been prepared. Modern in its lay-out, the factory will be single storeyed and finished with stucco. In the crane bay, car cases will be stacked four high. Other departments are for painting, trimming, and assembly, while space for 60 cars ready for the road is provided in the plans.

"The factory will be located in a new 'heavy industries' locality approved by the town planning committee of the City Council, whose final approval of the building plans has yet to be obtained. A section of the land is being reserved for the future erection of workers' dwellings and for a site for another factory. A siding from the railway will run into the crane bay, while access to a paved road will be given by a new road to be constructed by the company alongside the railway.

"The nucleus of the staff is already obtainable in Christchurch, because David Crozier, Ltd., have been operating two small assembly plants for some years, and employment will be given to a number of new employees. The latest in changing, dining, and recreation rooms has been planned for the staff at the factory, which will be capable of expansion at a minimum of expense. Overtures were made that the factory should be built at Wellington. The claims of Christchurch as the site were too strong, however." [146]

Associated Motor Industries

"In 1938, the Austin Distributors Federation created Associated Motor Industries (AMI) as its assembly division and incorporated the entity as a company after the war in 1945.

Associated Motor Industries Limited was incorporated on 2 August 1945 [147] with a capital of £20,000 in shares of £1 each. The original shareholders were Magnus Motors Limited, Wellington (5600 shares); Austin Motors (Otago) Limited, Dunedin (1200 shares); David Crozier Limited, Christchurch (2800 shares); P H Vickery Limited, Invercargill (1200 shares); Farmers' Co-op Organisation Society, Hawera (1600 shares); Aorangi Limited, Napier (1200 shares); and Seabrook, Fowlds Limited, Auckland (6400 shares).

"Object: Manufacturers, dealers, repairers, etc., of motor-cars, motor vehicles, aeroplanes, and incidental." [148]

"In 1946, Associated Motor Industries purchased three large disused military stores on leased NZ Railway land in Petone…In August 1946, still using SKD [semi-knocked-down] kits the first post-war, locally-assembled Austin rolled off the line at Petone. The model mix was mainly Austin 8s and 10s and locally manufactured trim items accounted for about 5 percent of car content…Between 1948 and 1954 8000 Austins were assembled…

"The Petone plant was extended in 1953 as well as increased production space the opportunity was taken to bring the entire Austin Distributors Federation under the same roof for the first time. The additions were officially opened…on 17 November 1955." [149]

In 1969, economies of scale to suit the commercial environment of the time called for a merger of New Zealand's assemblers of British cars — as reported by the Christchurch Press:

"The five companies which control the assembly and distribution of Austin and Morris vehicles in New Zealand have agreed in principle to merge. They include two listed companies— Seabrook Fowlds (N.Z.), Ltd, Auckland, and Magnus Motors, Ltd, Wellington.

"The others are Dominion Motors, Ltd, which is a public company whose shares are not listed, David Crozier, Ltd, Christchurch and Dunedin, and P. H. Vickery, Ltd, Invercargill.

"Dominion Motors assembles and distributes Morris vehicles. It has an assembly plant in Auckland.
The other four own the Petone assembly plant for Austin vehicles and form the Austin Distributors' Federation (N.Z.), Ltd

"It is understood that the Leyland franchises such as Jaguar, Rover and Triumph, are not involved in the merger. Any rearrangement of these would be a matter for Leyland and fall outside the scope of the Austin and Morris companies, which are all New Zealand owned." [150]

As detailed later, the merger did progress to become part of the New Zealand Motor Corporation Limited.

First Austin Assemblers and Distributors

Those first Austin assemblers and distributors included:

David Crozier Limited

"Dexter and Crozier had originally been established in 1896 in Auckland by Rueben Dexter and David Crozier at premises on Victoria Street East. At first the company was a cycle importer and manufacturer specialising in Ramblers Cycles which were brought into NZ from the USA.

"By the later 1890s, largely as a result of the foresight of David Crozier, the company had pioneered the importing of motorcycles beginning with a 'Thomas Autoley' in 1899, and an 'Indian' in 1901.

"In 1903 David Crozier saw the future potential of the motor car and travelled to the United States to investigate first-hand the motor industry there. As a result of that visit he was successful in gaining the agency for Cadillac in New Zealand.

"These early Cadillac cars were single cylinder machines, chain driven, with just two seats. Within two years Dexter and Crozier were able to advertise that there were more Cadillacs in New Zealand than any other make of car…

"In 1908 Dexter and Crozier opened a branch [at Manchester Street], Christchurch and David Crozier moved down from Auckland to manage the office…

"…in 1912, a new brick and stucco building of more than 1000m² was opened [at 57-59 Worcester Street West]…it included a showroom garage, and work and assembly shops. These new premises of Dexter and Crozier known as 'The Motor House' were considered to be the most exclusive and up-to-date of their type in New Zealand at that time.

"…in March 1912 Dexter and Crozier imported 30 new Cadillacs. These were self-starting with electric rather than kerosene or carbide lamps. Between 1912 and 1918 other models were added to their showroom floor including; Oakland Paige, Detroit D & C, Briscoe, Saxon, Maudin, Bean, Beloise and Thornycroft.

"In 1915 the company imported the first V type 8 cylinder vehicles…Most of these vehicles were from the United States but in 1918 this was to change when the company went British and gained an agency for Austin cars, thereby terminating a 14 year exclusive association with Cadillac.

"The early Austin cars were imported from the Longbridge works in England and were either fully assembled or just a chassis, the bodies being made in Christchurch by the coach builders Cooper and Pryce…

"In 1919 David Crozier and Rueben Dexter dissolved their partnership. Dexter continued to run the Auckland branch as Dexter Limited. On 20 November 1919 [151] a new company was registered for the Worcester Street address as David Crozier Limited. The two principal shareholders were David Crozier and Andrew Hughes, who was in charge of the workshop and car assembly." [152]

The Worcester Street premises of David Crozier Limited were described by the Christchurch Sun on 8 November 1920:

"The modern garage of David Crozier Ltd. covers a floor space of 13,500 square feet…the growth of business has been phenomenal. Splendidly ventilated and well-lighted by day and night, the garage is up-to-date in every respect, and must rank as one of the best in New Zealand…David Crozier holds one of the finest supplies of spares and accessories in the Dominion; for instance, the motorist can obtain spares from the time of the 1903 10 h.p. Cadillac. Austin Bean, Cadillac, and Briscoe cars appear in the firm's stand at the [1920 Motor] Exhibition." [153]

By November 1937, the growing business of Davis Crozier Limited required some expansion of its Worcester street premises — as reported by the Christchurch Press:

"The opening last evening by the Mayor of Christchurch (Mr J W Beanland) of the new garage premises of David Crozier Ltd., in Worcester street, makes available to the motoring public a notable addition to the service facilities of the city. The new building will almost double the floor space of the firm, which is one of the oldest in the motor trade in New Zealand. The garage, though not among the largest in the country, is now one of the most modern and most completely equipped…

"The recent extension of the premises, which now gives a total floor space of 25,000 square feet, has been made necessary by the growing clientele of the firm. Altogether 44 hands are now employed." [154]

The business continued to prosper:

"By September 1969…a new 1600m² showroom was opened…By 1970 they also held the dealership for the Massey Ferguson tractor…

"The late 1960s saw some more changes which started in December 1968 when the company merged with South Island Motors and then with Austin Motors, Otago. In 1970, after 51 years,

David Crozier Limited was absorbed into the national New Zealand Motor Corporation which in turn was also consumed in a 1980s take-over…" [155]

P H Vickery Limited

English immigrant, Percy Harry Vickery (1873-1965) was another who progressed from repairing, assembling, and importing bicycles to that of motor vehicles and accessories in the early 1900s. He is said to have been "…one of the first to import petrol (in tins and cases) and tyres to keep the cars on the road." [156]

"He began distributing Michelin tyres throughout Southland and eventually secured a direct franchise to sell Dodge cars and trucks. His close association with Lord Austin in England allowed him to also arrange the distribution of the Austin motor vehicle." [157]

In July 1906, tenders were invited "…for the erection of a three-storey building in Tay street [Invercargill] for Mr P H Vickery, who intends to open an extensive motor and cycle warehouse." [158]

P H Vickery secured the agency for Southland of the B.S.A. motorcycle in July 1911 [159] and for the Humber motorcycle later that year. [160] The latter machine, often referred to as a 'motor bicycle', was propelled by either a 3½ or 2-horse-power motor. [161]

At the December 1911 Annual Show of the Southland Metropolitan A & P Association, P H Vickery not only displayed the B.S.A and Humber motorcycles but also the American 30 h.p. E.M.F. and the 20 h.p. Flanders motor cars. At that time, the business was also reported "…to control the agency and sale of Renault cars and Commercial vehicles, for Southland." [162]

At the 1916 A & P 'Jubilee Show', it was reported: "P H Vickery…has an extensive exhibit of Motor Cars and Motor Tyres. Motor enthusiasts will be interested in the latest production of Dodge Bros. Cars. They are shown in the Touring five-seater, also the Roadster single-seater." [163]

In July 1919, P H Vickery became P H Vickery Limited when Percy's brother, T W Vickery joined the firm as a director and manager. [164]

In 1923, the Austin Motor Company of England offered its overseas agents a cut-price deal by which it would supply chassis and cars at the same prices as those charged to its home market providing:

"(1) The Agent bear his share of the burden by working on a close margin and (2) A fixed firm price ex coast town to be settled, approved by us, and not altered without our consent in writing.

"The prices fixed for New Zealand are less than English prices, plus the Customs duty into New Zealand. These Cars are creating quite a sensation in the North. There are fourteen models ranging from £510 for the 12-h.p. to £1035 for the Mayfair Limousine.

The first shipment of the Austin 12-h.p. cars has arrived at Bluff, ex s.s. Trocarrel, so that those who are looking for a beautiful piece of British workmanship can inspect same in the Showroom of P H Vickery Ltd." [165]

By May 1931, P H Vickery continued to prosper selling Austin and Dodge motor vehicles, and a little subtle advertising disguised as a general interest piece didn't go amiss:

"The owner of a 44 h.p. car bought in 1904 one of the first motor cars sold in Southland by P. H. Vickery has decided for sentimental reasons to bury it." [166]

Boon and Company

"… Joseph Kitson Boon, one of the early coachbuilders of Christchurch and founder of Boon and Company…" died May 1935 at the age of 91. His career started with the local blacksmith at the age of ten.

Joseph Boon entered into a partnership with Mr [William John] Stevens forming the firm Boon and Stevens for 19 years before partnership was dissolved and he formed Boon and Company with his two sons. Boon and Company designed and built the 'Brougham Hansom' cab which was the most popular means of conveyance until the advent of the motor car. [167]

First Vehicle Assemblers **69**

The advent of the motor car started early for Boon and Co — with an exhibit at the 1902 Christchurch Metropolitan Show:

"Evidence of the advent of the motor-car as a popular method of locomotion in our streets and roads was given by some exhibits, which, however, were not nearly so numerous as might have been expected, and by no means represented the extent of the position the new industry has already attained.

"First to claim attention was a very fine motor-car shown in the tent of Messrs Boon and Co., carriage builders, by Messrs Oates, Lowry and Co. It is a large and luxuriously equipped vehicle, made to seat from four to five persons, weighs 14cwt, and is fitted with a 10 h.p. motor.

"The motive power is the explosion caused by the mixture of air and petrol flashed by electricity. Messrs Oates and Lowry have manufactured the car, with the exception of the body and wheels, which have been constructed by Messrs Boon and Co. The automobile is a distinct credit to the two firms mentioned. In the same tent is shown a Zealandia motor-bicycle fitted with a Thomas (American motor)." [168]

However, the construction of larger bodies was retained by the company with the winning of the Christchurch Tramway Board's 1904 tender for the construction of five car bodies for the City's new electric trams at £365 per car. [169]

Boon and Co went on to build "…practically all the tram cars for service in Christchurch, Napier, Gisborne, and Wanganui." [170]

In the meantime, Boon and Co was not only praised for the quality of its car, bus, and tram bodies but also for its manufacture of car windscreens, hoods, and other fittings. [171]

Following his retirement about 1918, Joseph Kitson was succeeded by his son, W J Boon, as Managing Director, and by his grandson, A A Boon, who was the manager of the firm in 1930. [172]

By 1930, Boon and Co had progressed from the construction of body work for trams to that of the first trolley-bus bodies for the Christchurch City Council at a cost of £719 each. [173]

Cossens and Black

In 1873, Thomas Cossens and Alexander John Black set themselves up in Dunedin as engineers and ironfounders. [174]

In its early days, trading as Britannia Iron Works, Cossens and Black advertised "…every description of Agricultural Implements for Sale…" [175] The partnership was also engaged in the ironwork construction of a number of rock-crushing and brick-making machines, as well as some of Otago's infrastructure — as reported by the Otago Daily Times in October 1879:

"The ironwork required for the construction of the suspension bridge which is to cross the Manuherikia River near Ophir (or Black's) township, in the Vincent County, has just been finished by the firm of Messrs Cossens and Black, of Dunedin. Altogether the ironwork weighs 25 tons. The span between the two piers of the bridge, when erected, will be 207 feet. [176]

In 1882, in what would be the start of the firm's vehicle assembly work, Cossens and Black were awarded the contract for the construction of 50-person cars for Dunedin's Mornington Cable Tramway. [177]

Thomas Cossens died at the very young age of 47 in March 1891 but Cossens and Black continued to trade with trustees representing the Cossens and Black families. Alexander Black continued as the head of the business. [178]

The business was incorporated as a limited liability company on 18 March 1899. [179]

By the turn of the century, Cossens and Black Limited was manufacturing gold dredges and had exported hydraulic mining plants to Australia and Russia. [180]

In October 1916, Cossens and Black were appointed sole agents for the Dodge Bros. Roadster Car. [181] By the time of the Otago Metropolitan Show of November 1917, a newspaper report described Cossens and Black as "well-known motor engineers, importers, and dealers in [motor vehicle] supplies." [181]

Those supplies included "…a good array of the new non-shod French Michelin tyres." [182]

Cossens and Black Limited announced in April 1919 that it had been appointed sole Otago agents for Sterling Motor Trucks. [183]

By February 1921, what was described as "…the most comprehensive exhibit of motor cars ever seen in Dunedin is being made at present by Messrs Cossens and Black (Ltd.) in their spacious garage and showrooms…" was reported by the Otago Daily Times. New and used models for sale included the American Dodge and Moon, the British Sunbeam, and the Guy truck. [184]

In December 1924, Leyland Motors announced that it was "…now supplying the New Zealand market with special overseas types [of motor vehicles] which are of unusual strength in every part. The local [Otago] agents are Cossens and Black." [185]

Alexander Black died 21 November 1926 at the age of 79. [186]

The Later Motor Vehicle Assemblers
The Ford Motor Company of New Zealand

The Ford Motor Company of New Zealand Limited was registered as a private company on 9 January 1936 with a registered office at the Hope Gibbons Building, 7-13 Dixon street, Wellington. The company started with Capital of £400,000 divided into 400,000 shares of £1 each. Original shareholders included the Ford Motor Company of Canada Limited with 399,996 shares; and W R Campbell, G H Jackson, T B Cavaghan, and G G Gibbes Watson, all of Wellington, with 1 share each.

The objects of the new company were stated to be: "Manufacturers, assemblers, importers, exporters, and shippers of and agents and merchants for and wholesale and retail dealers in traction engines, road and other rollers, motor wagons, motor lorries, motor cars, and incidental." [187]

In order to produce Ford vehicles at a more competitive cost than those previously imported and assembled by the Colonial Motor Company, Ford intended to build its own New Zealand factory, as reported by the Evening Post on 25 February 1936:

"Some details of the new Ford factory which is now in course of construction on an estate of over 13 acres at Sea View Road, Lower Hutt, at an estimated cost for land, plant, and equipment of £160,000, were given by Mr. G. H. Jackson, managing director of Ford Motor Company of New Zealand Limited…" [188]

"By establishing its own assembly works in New Zealand, Ford would be able to benefit from more favourable import tariffs that gave British cars a decided price advantage. The British Preferential Tariff that then applied to most goods imported from Britain was all about butter and wool and New Zealand's need to export as much of it to Britain as it could, whether the British needed it or not. The British Preferential Tariff was no more than a goodwill gesture to the Mother Country.

"While Canada was very much a country of the Commonwealth, the trading relationship between it and New Zealand did not offer the quite same benefits. In fact, there was a distinct imbalance of trade between the two countries in favour of Canada — particularly during the five years to 1936.

"In the year 1931 the exports from New Zealand were £222,942 (sterling) and the imports into New Zealand £1,224,569; 1932: £208,315 and £1,007,096; 1933: £433,861 and £1,012,213; 1934: £554.931 and £1,677,704; 1935: £522,441 and £1,960,493." [189]

As a result, although the New Zealand Trade Agreement with Canada, ratified in April 1932, provided for tariff rates that "…shall in no case be higher than the rates chargeable on similar goods under the British Preferential Tariff of New Zealand" certain additional duties were payable on some goods.

For instance, Article VI of the 1932 Trade Agreement provided for motor vehicles and parts for motor vehicles 'having bodies suited or designed for carrying passengers' were subject to an additional 'body duty' charge of some 11¼ per cent. [190]

When it was agreed in 1932, the New Zealand Trade Agreement with Canada was to last for only one year but was extended several times before a final expiry date of 31 July 1936.

In the meantime, the New Zealand Government sought to amend and clarify the tariffs and customs duties charged on imports received from every country by means of the Customs Acts Amendment Act, 1934, passed in October of that year.

With regard to the importation of unassembled parts of motor vehicles, the Customs Acts Amendment Act provided for a British Preferential Tariff of 10 per cent and a General Tariff of 55 per cent up to and including 31 December 1934 and for a British Preferential Tariff of 5 per cent and a General Tariff of 50 per cent on and after 1 January 1935. [191]

Section 16 (1) of the Act stated: "The Minister shall from time to time, by notice in the *Gazette* determine the goods which may be entered under Tariff item 389 *(a)* as motor-vehicles unassembled or completely knocked down, and may in like manner determine the conditions under which such goods shall be imported into and used in New Zealand and the purposes for which those goods shall be so used." [192]

Such a Gazette notice advised of an Order In Council of 18 November 1935 modifying certain provisions of the trade agreement to include reduced tariffs for unassembled or completely knocked down (c.k.d.) motor vehicles from 1 May 1936.

The new tariff schedule of 10 to 12½ per cent of the value of the finished article confirmed the British Preferential Tariff as applying to the importation of unassembled parts of motor vehicles. [193]

When asked to comment on the development, the president of the Ford Motor Company of Canada, Wallace B. Campbell, replied that the New Zealand plant would be ready to operate from 1 July 1936.

"We are enthusiastic about the agreement…The revision of the treaty will help us maintain business in New Zealand which we were in danger of losing to England and the United States. We also hope to increase our market for cars in New Zealand…" [194]

Ford's new assembly plant at Seaview, Lower Hutt was officially opened by the Minister of Transport, Robert Semple, on 7 April 1937. By then, the plant employed some 650 New Zealanders with one complete unit turned out every 15 minutes. [195]

During the opening ceremony, the Minister provided his audience with a number of facts describing the growth of the vehicle industry:

"The number of cars in New Zealand in 1914 was 20,000, in 1925 123,000, in 1930 195,000, in 1935 214,000 and at the end of last year [1936] 241,915. "As far as we have been able to ascertain 118 additional cars are going on the road every day in New Zealand.

"The cost of vehicles Imported into the Dominion in 1936 was £3,550,000; the annual cost of the operation of all vehicles was over £30,000,000. The number of persons engaged in the motor industry was estimated at 50,000, with a wages bill of at least £10,000,000 a year. Users of motor-vehicles paid in direct taxation over £6,000,000 a year.

"The motor industry, said Mr Semple, had not only revolutionised the transport system, but it had also revolutionised methods of road construction. In 1925 New Zealand had 700 miles of paved roads and in 1935 3000 miles. In 1925 there were 28,000 miles of metalled roads, and in 1935 37,000. New Zealand was now the second most highly-motorised country in the world, being second only to the United States of America." [196]

In its first year of operation, Ford's Seaview plant "…produced 8691 passenger and commercial vehicles and 115 tractors…" [197]

In 1964, Ford purchased land at Wiri, Manukau City, and opened a National Parts Depot there in 1965. This was followed by the establishment of a transmission and chassis manufacturing facility in 1972 and the completion of its assembly plant and production of Falcons at Wiri the following year.

In 1981, an alloy wheel plant was opened at Wiri and, by 1987, most operations had been moved from the Seaview plant at Lower Hutt to Wiri. The Seaview plant was closed in 1988 after 52 years. [198]

Mazda Motors of New Zealand

Mazda was founded as the Toyo Cork Kogyo Company at Horoshima, Japan in 1920 and one of its first manufactured products was a 250cc two-stroke engine later used to drive a prototype motorcycle. By 1931, the company had progressed to a three-wheel truck with a load capacity of 200 kg — the 'Mazda-go'. The prototype of a small passenger car was produced in 1940 and, by 1950, the company was manufacturing small four-wheeled trucks with a load capacity of one ton.

By the early 1960s, early-model passenger cars, vans, and pickups were supplementing the trucks produced and, in 1965, the company's first bus was introduced. [199]

When the dedicated roll-on vehicle transporter, Jinyo Maru, berthed at Lyttelton in early January 1972:

"…186 Mazda pick-up trucks consigned to Champion Motors Limited of Christchurch…" were discharged.

"The Jinyo Maru has already discharged 210 mixed vehicles from Hiroshima at Melbourne and, after she has discharged her trucks at Lyttelton, she will discharge 206 mixed vehicles at Wellington and another 182 at Auckland. The Jinyo Maru is reported to be able to discharge 100 vehicles an hour under normal work." [200]

Mazda Motors of New Zealand Limited was established in February 1972 [201] in conjunction with its Japanese parent, Motor Holdings Limited of Otahuhu, Champion Motors Limited of Christchurch (a subsidiary of Amuri Motors), and William Scollay and Company Limited of Wellington were also minority shareholders.

The company formation was in anticipation of the establishment of a Mazda vehicle assembly plant in New Zealand, approval for which was granted in April 1972 — as reported by the Christchurch Press:

"New Zealand Government approval for the Mazda assembly programme has now been granted, according to the announcement today. But the joint venture agreement signed by all parties is still subject to Japanese Government approval because of the planned equity investment by the Japanese interest in the new company.

"Initially, assembly of Mazdas at the Motor Holdings Otahuhu plant will be of the rotary-engined Capella coupe and sedan, the conventionally-engined Capella coupe and sedan, and the 81600 pick-up.

"The new company, Mazda Motors of New Zealand, will act as importer and wholesale distributors of the new vehicles and the parts for them and the retail sales will be handled through the existing Champion Motors and Motor Holdings dealership chains." [202]

By mid-1974, Mazda Motors of New Zealand was quite optimistic about its ability to sell vehicles in New Zealand:

"The company says it is increasing Mazda production from 10 to 20 vehicles a day by the end of this month, and is encouraged by Mazda sales in Australia, where the marque recently took 10 per cent of new registrations for the first time." [203]

However, the Motor Holdings assembly plant at Otahuhu was feeling the strain by August 1979 — as reported by the Christchurch Press:

"In the assembly of motor vehicles, the company [Motor Holdings] was faced with long lead-times to achieve assembly rates and the provision of necessary componentry from local manufacturers.

"It was in these areas the company had found the greatest difficulties for its Subaru franchise, and also for the assembly of the Mazda range — the 28 per cent owned associate company,

Mazda Motors of N.Z., Ltd. However, the assembly plant at Otahuhu was continuing to operate to limit, Mr Robinson [Chairman of Motor Holdings Limited] said." [204]

As a result, Mazda needed some additional assembly room and acquired it in early 1980:

"Mazda Motors of New Zealand Ltd has bought the Mount Wellington plant of New Zealand Motor Bodies, Ltd, for an undisclosed sum and expects to begin production there in June. A Mazda spokesman said yesterday it was intended to continue producing Mazda vehicles at the Otahuhu plant of Motor Holdings, Ltd.

"The decision to buy the Motor Bodies plant had been made because Mazda was having difficulty in assembling enough vehicles at Otahuhu to meet demand.

"The Mount Wellington plant [at Sylvia Park] had been built originally [by New Zealand Motor Bodies] for the assembly of cars. In recent years it had been producing buses. Staff becoming redundant would be offered employment by Mazda, which expected to need a workforce of about 175 at Mount Wellington by the end of the year." [205]

As reported by the Christchurch Press in October 1984, Mazda was soon to be independently operating both the Mount Wellington and Otahuhu assembly plants:

"Motor Holdings, Ltd, and Mazda Motors (NZ), Ltd, have announced restructuring plans which will see Motor Holdings increase its shareholding in Mazda while Mazda will buy Motor Holdings' Otahuhu assembly plant." [206]

But by November 1985: "Motor Holdings, Ltd, has negotiated the sale of its 44 per cent interest in Mazda Motors (NZ), Ltd, to Mazda Corporation and Sumitomo Corporation of Japan." [207]

Further restructuring of the motor assembly industry continued when Mazda Motors and the Ford Motor Company announced a joint plan "…to reduce their vehicle assembly lines to Ford's Manukau City plant and Mazda's Sylvia Park Plant.

"The two companies have had reciprocal assembly contracts for commercial vehicles for the last five years, and the new arrangement will boost their investments in assembly plant by $20 million, the companies said. The investment represented an increase to Ford New Zealand's previously announced $45 million expansion and modernisation programme at Manukau City and Mazda New Zealand's recently completed $15 million modernisation at Sylvia Park.

"The added investment would permit the gradual phasedown of Mazda's Otahuhu plant by early 1988, the companies said. The Otahuhu plant has been assembling vehicles for almost 40 years. It employs 256 people, but would require substantial investment to remain competitive in the future." [208]

The Ford Motor Company & Mazda Motors

Ford acquired a 7 per cent financial stake in the Mazda Motor Company in 1979. During the 1980s, Ford gained another 20 per cent financial interest and a controlling interest of 33.4 per cent in May 1996, partly as a result of losses related to the 1997 Asian financial crisis. [209]

"The partnership resulted in various joint projects with Mazda including large and small efforts in all areas of the automotive landscape — most notably in the realm of pick-up trucks (such as the Mazda B-Series, which spawned a Ford Courier variant in North America in 1972) and smaller cars." [210]

Ford relinquished all its shareholdings in Mazda in 2015 giving Mazda full ownership of the company. [211]

Vehicle Assemblers New Zealand

The pooling of vehicle assembly resources by Ford and Mazda continued in New Zealand from late 1986 — as reported by the Christchurch Press:

"All cars common to Ford New Zealand, Ltd, and Mazda Motors of New Zealand, Ltd, will be assembled by Ford in its Manukau City plant in future. Likewise, all the light commercial vehicles common to both companies will be assembled by Mazda Motors at its Sylvia Park plant.

That, in essence, is the plan to improve the motor vehicle assembly operation that was announced in a joint statement by both companies towards the end of September…" [212]

To facilitate the partnership, the two companies established Vehicle Assemblers New Zealand Limited (VANZ). The company was registered from 23 December 1986 to 24 February 2001 with the Ford Motor Company of New Zealand Limited and Mazda Motors of New Zealand Limited as shareholders in the ratio of 74 per cent to 26 per cent, respectively. [213]

"New Zealand's largest motor assembly company…Vehicle Assemblers New Zealand, Ltd, own two, large assembly plants both in Auckland at Manukau City and Sylvia Park, and will employ about 1220 people when both plants are fully operational.

"It will have a paid-up share capital of $59 million…headed by Mr Peter Shaw, currently Ford New Zealand's assembly operations manager, and vice-president will be Mr James Morikawa, Mazda New Zealand's managing director.

"The two assembly plants are being extensively modernised. Advances, which place emphasis on an improved working environment, include an automatic final paint process and an advanced overhead conveyor system for moving vehicles through the assembly process. Distribution and marketing of Ford and Mazda in New Zealand will remain independent." [214]

"However, free-market reforms in New Zealand in the late 1980s saw the lowering of import tariffs and a flood of used imports from Japan. Many of these were mechanically identical Mazda Capellas (as the 626 was known in Japan), as well as Ford Telstars and Mondeos. In addition, Australian-built Fords like the Falcon, and its GM rival, the Holden Commodore, could now be imported New Zealand duty-free. With the demise of local car assembly looking inevitable, VANZ announced it would cease operations in 1997. The alloy wheel plant was sold in 2001." [215]

Motor Holdings Group

Joseph Noel Turner founded Car Auctions Limited with his father and brother in 1936 and acquired the car importer Jowett and Bradford (Jowett Motors) in 1937. By 1953 the Turner family had moved to the assembly and distribution of Volkswagen vehicles, trading as V. W. Motors (New Zealand) Limited from 1955.

As well as the Turner family, both Christopher Albert Spencer and Michael Peter Spencer held large shareholdings (via Caspex Corporation Limited) and Peter Albert Spencer and John Berridge Spencer (via Catonia Corporation Limited) in the Motor Holdings Group at various times.

From 1958 to 1988, the Motor Holdings Group operated from its large assembly and distribution plant at [Fort Richard Road] Otahuhu [216] and during that time, some 127,000 vehicles were built there.

Volkswagen production began strongly, completing 2066 in the first year of operation and the 10,000th Beetle rolled out of the Otahuhu plant in 1962. [217]

The Trekka — Due to New Zealand's restrictive import licensing regime of the 1960s, Motor Holdings decided to produce a light utility vehicle — the Trekka — "…New Zealand's first significant foray into car design and manufacture, with around 2,500 built between 1966 and 1973. The vehicles were powered by Skoda engines from Czechoslovakia, while the bodies were manufactured in New Zealand. They were not a major success…" [218]

The first assembled Trekkas were exported from New Zealand to Fiji and other Pacific Island nations from 1968 and one hundred packs of unassembled vehicles were exported to Indonesia in March 1971. [219]

In 1966, Motor Holdings acquired Butcher and Company (NZ) Limited and its franchise to import and distribute Simca motor vehicles. [220]

The right to import front-wheel-drive Subarus was also acquired by Motor Holdings in 1971. [221]

Noel Turner began to acquire other franchises and assemble on behalf of other smaller makes. Peugeot 403 and 404 sedans for Campbell Motors, Fiat 500s after Noel Turner acquired the Italian franchise, Ramblers, Studebakers, and the first Japanese Datsuns…French Simcas, Skodas from then communist Czechoslovakia…later Datsun 1200s and even Vauxhall Vivas were built there…

Motor Holdings Limited had a shareholding in Mazda Motors of New Zealand Limited when the latter company was established in February 1972. Motor Holdings assembled Mazdas at its Otahuhu plant and renewed the contract in May 1981:

"Motor Holdings Limited has announced that a new contract for the assembly of Mazda vehicles has been signed with Mazda Motors of New Zealand, Limited. Under the new contract the Motor Holdings subsidiary company, Motor Industries (International), Limited, will assemble at least 24 Mazda units a day including the very successful new 323 series, and the revised 626 saloon.

"It is also announced that Ford Courier trucks will be assembled on a limited contract arrangement in the Otahuhu plant. This volume now completely utilises the Otahuhu plant capacity and follows on the company's announcement that the No 2 plant at Waitara is now at full capacity to meet rising Subaru demand." [222]

However, such were the vagaries of the New Zealand vehicle assembly industry that, by August 1982, Motor Industries were laying off some 65 workers following "…a request from Mazda to reduce assembly volumes." [223]

Of course, after Mazda had recently purchased the former Motor Bodies assembly plant at Mount Wellington, it had become somewhat independent of the Motor Industries facility.

In 1986, Motor Holdings "…produced its 30,000th Volkswagen in Otahuhu. This also represented the final assembly of Volkswagens in New Zealand." [224]

"Motor Holdings sold the Otahuhu plant to Mazda in the 1980s, and it was closed not long after it built its last vehicle, a Mazda utility in 1987." [225]

Wilton Motor Body Company

In 1945, Wilton Motor Bodies Limited, then of 1 Wilton Street, Grey Lynn, Auckland, advertised its services in the Auckland Star — "About Trucks, Vans, Cars, Caravans — For all classes [of] Coachbuilding and Repair Work…" [226]

Wilton Motor Bodies, headed by J J C [Joe] Gardner and J L Griffiths was licensed as a 'Manufacturing Retailer' under the Sales Tax Act on 1 March 1947 [227] and the company was chosen by the Wanganui City Council's Transport Committee to design and build the bodies of its proposed bus fleet — as reported by the Wanganui Chronicle on 11 November 1949:

"The Wanganui Civic Transport Committee held its final meeting this week, when the new company which will take over Wanganui's public passenger transport system, Greyhound Buses, Ltd., went to allotment.

"It was unanimously felt that the very best should be purchased for the new transport system and that a mixed fleet of heavy and light vehicles would suit best, the heavy vehicles to do the hard running and the light vehicles to do the easier portions of the work.

"'Every available bus chassis was considered from every point and hours of consideration have been given to each type,' Mr Seivewright [of the Wanganui Civic Transport Committee] added. 'It was finally decided unanimously by the directorate to purchase a mixed fleet of Daimler heavy-duty omnibus chassis, fitted with 37-passenger bodies designed and built by Wilton Motor Bodies, Ltd. Auckland…" [228]

In September 1950, The Wilton Motor Body Co. Limited advertised its presence at 49 Tutanekai Street, Grey Lynn, Auckland and its services as: "Builders of Quality Buses, Luxury Coaches, Station Wagons, Tankers and all Commercial Vehicle Bodies." [229]

New Zealand Gazette entries record that in May 1954, "The Wilton Motor Body Company Ltd…applied for a licence to resell motor spirit from one pump to be installed on garage premises at 16-24 Westmoreland Street, Auckland"; [230] that the company was granted a Wholesalers' Licence Under the Sales Tax Act 1932-33 on 1 February 1955; [231] and was approved as a 'Vendor of Motor Vehicles for Purposes of New Registration' as of 20 February 1957. [232]

Indeed, the Wilton Motor Body Company occupied the Westmoreland Street premises from about 1954, extending the ground floor in 1956, and adding mezzanine floors in 1958. [233]

An advertisement in the March 1957 edition of Beaded Wheels, a publication of the Vintage Car Club of New Zealand, listed the services provided by the Wilton Motor Body Company as: Upholstery, Panel Beating, Body Building, Welding, and Motor Repair. The advertisement also promoted Proofkote applications provided by our subsidiary, R Goldingham & Co. Limited. [234]

"Nissan Motor Distributors NZ Ltd was formed over the shell of the Wilton Motor Body Company Limited in late 1965: H E Melhop Ltd had acquired the companies that held the Nissan Datsun license from Joe Gardner; J Gardner Motors, Newmarket, though, retailed them..." [235]

Wilton Motor Body Company Limited was de-registered from the Companies Office register on 13 June 1975. [236]

The New Zealand Motor Corporation

The New Zealand Motor Corporation Limited was incorporated on 7 November 1956 and traded as such until the name of the company was changed to EMCO Group Limited, a subsidiary of Steel & Tube Holdings Limited, on 2 April 1982. [237]

"On its formation, NZMC had over 3000 staff, 40 retail branches, a bus and coachwork factory, a commercial, industrial and earthmoving equipment arm, and four car assembly plants, namely, Dominion Motors, at Newmarket, Auckland; Dominion Motors Commercials, at Panmure, Auckland; AMI, at Petone; and Standard Triumph/ Leyland Commercial, at Nelson.

"Land Rover assembly was carried out under contract by New Zealand Motor Bodies in Sylvia Park, Auckland, while some local pressing of Land Rover panels was carried out in New Zealand Motor Bodies Petone plant." [238]

In April 1970, the New Zealand Motor Corporation acquired a number of motor vehicle dealers in a merger reported by the Christchurch Press on 27 June 1970:

"The New Zealand Motor Corporation resulted from the merger of five motor companies, The Dominion Motors Ltd, Magnus Motors Ltd, Seabrook Fowlds Ltd, David Crozier Ltd, and P H Vickery Ltd. It is now one of the 12 largest companies listed on the New Zealand Stock Exchange.

"The company has about 100 dealers and 100 service centres, and its staff totals about 3000. Its dealers market Austin, Morris, Wolseley and MG cars and commercial vehicles, and Pontiac, Bentley and Rolls-Royce cars, as well as tractors and earth-moving equipment." [239]

At the time of the merger, the Corporation's chairman and managing director, Walter Norwood, commented: "Integration will ensure that a large segment of the New Zealand motor industry will be consolidated under New Zealand ownership and control...It is felt that as a consequence of these moves, the integration and rationalisation of New Zealand's motor vehicle assembly and distribution industry will have taken a big step forward and that the benefits to the national economy and motor vehicle owners will be far-reaching..." [240]

Further consolidation of the motor industry in New Zealand was proposed in December 1971 when British Leyland invited the New Zealand Motor Corporation to acquire all its trading interests in New Zealand. As reported by the Christchurch Press on 6 May 1972:

"The New Zealand Motor Corporation Ltd has taken over the assets and liabilities of the British Leyland Motor Corporation in New Zealand for cash payment of $15m and an issue of two million N.Z.M.C. shares. This will increase the issued capital of N.Z.M.C. from $13m to $15m, of which British Leyland will hold 13.3 per cent...

"The chairman of the N.Z.M.C. (Sir Walter Norwood) said that the agreement marked the completion of negotiations which grew out of the original discussions between the N.Z.M.C. and British Leyland on the possibility of setting up a joint assembly plant…To some extent a merger of this nature was inevitable…if the old situation had been allowed to continue it would have meant that British Leyland and N.Z.M.C. would have been increasingly in competition with each other and this in turn would have meant a perpetuation of duplicated assembly operations, spare parts stocks, servicing facilities and so on." [241]

As a result of the merger:

"The new corporation will control four assembly plants, all of them with surplus production capacity.

"The plants are: Newmarket, producing Morris and Austin 1100 and 1300 cars, and preparing for assembly of the Morris Marina early next year.

"Panmure, producing Austin-Morris Commercial;

"Petone, producing Austin Maxi and Austin-Morris Mini, Tasman and Kimberley cars;

"Nelson, producing Triumph, Rover, Jaguar and Daimler cars. (The New Zealand assets of British Leyland of course included the Nelson plant of Motor Assemblies, Limited which then became a subsidiary of the New Zealand Motor Corporation.) [242]

"The N.Z.M.C. cars involved in the merger are: Austin, Morris, M.G.-Wolseley, Pontiac, Rolls-Royce, and Bentley. The New Zealand-assembled British Leyland cars involved are Triumph, Rover, Jaguar, Daimler, and Landrover. Besides Austin and Morris Commercial trucks, the new corporation will take over Leyland franchises for Leyland, Albion, Scamell and A.E.C. vehicles.

"The odd-man-out is the Landrover, the assembly of which is under contract to New Zealand Motor Bodies, Ltd, in Auckland, until 1974." [243]

As reported by the Christchurch Press, the New Zealand Motor Corporation was selling the most motor vehicles by mid-1975:

"The latest registration figures for the first five months of 1975 show that N.Z.M.C. has a commanding lead…N.Z.M.C. has 22.2 per cent of the market, with Ford second on 19.2 per cent; Todds with 16.6 per cent is third, while General Motors are fourth with 15.3 per cent. The three Japanese models—Datsun, Toyota and Mazda — have market shares ranging between 6.0 per cent and 7.8 per cent each." [244]

"However by December 1975, Japanese vehicles accounted for 27 percent of all New Zealand car sales. UK-sourced cars had 51 percent, Australia 16 percent and others the remaining 6 percent. So it was not surprising that the New Zealand Motor Corporation realised they needed a Japanese car. They chose Honda, despite the franchise being already held by The Moller Group, who had sold over 3000. The Honda franchise was to be additional to that for the BL marques. The first Honda Civic rolled off the Petone lines in February [1976]…

"The first NZMC factory to close was the former Dominion Motors Morris plant in Mortimer Pass, Newmarket; it closed in 1978 and production was transferred to Panmure…The second plant to close was Petone, in May 1983…An entry in Petone, a History, gives production figures from 1946 to August 1977 as 135,399 vehicles…The Panmure plant was closed in 1987…

"Honda New Zealand was formed in August 1988 with a paid-up capital of NZ$36 million. The new company purchased all Honda-related assets from The Steel and Tube Group (the owners of NZMC Limited), including the former Standard Triumph/Rover/Jaguar assembly plant in Nelson. This plant was closed 1996…" [245]

The British Origins of The New Zealand Motor Corporation
The British Leyland Motor Corporation of New Zealand

The Leyland Motor Corporation "…started out in 1896 as the Lancashire Steam Motor Company…" [246]

By November 1919, the British Leyland Motor Corporation of New Zealand, trading as Leyland Motors, had established a branch at Wellington from which it co-ordinated the importation and sale of its motor lorries through various New Zealand dealers such as Seabrook, Fowlds & Co.

Following on from their successful performance during the First World War, British Leyland trucks continued to be popular as utility and transport vehicles with New Zealand farmers and businesses.

By way of an advertisement published by The New Zealand Herald on 28 November 1919, Leyland Motors proclaimed itself as:

"…the first and only builders of Motor Lorries to establish a Branch — NOT and Agency — in New Zealand. Such a departure is an indication of the progressive spirit of modern British Commerce. Thus Leyland's own comprehensive Service will be here on the spot at the immediate call of the Leyland-owner." [247]

By August 1921, the 'Leyland owner' was said to include the NZ Post and Telegraph Department, with seventeen Leylands recently purchased, and the Wellington City Council which had purchased two Leyland Tip-Wagons. [248]

By 1968, British Leyland was producing buses, trucks, tractors, and Rover cars…selling to some 140 countries…providing one of Britain's most glittering export stories…

In January of that year, British Leyland merged with British Motor Holdings, the makers of the Mini and Jaguar cars, in what was then described as the "…biggest industrial merger in Britain…to form Britain's largest vehicle builder and its biggest single exporter."

The combined company became known as the British Leyland Motor Corporation with sales of £800m and some 200,000 employees. [249]

In New Zealand, the merger resulted in a change of name from The Leyland Motor Corporation of New Zealand Limited to British Leyland Motor Corporation of New Zealand Limited on 3 March 1969 [250] and the centralisation of activities incorporating the Leyland Motor Corporation, Rover New Zealand Limited, and Aveling-Barford (NZ) Limited.

"The company then had six divisions: heavy vehicles, cars and light commercial vehicles, construction equipment, assembly division, spare parts division, and the administration and finance division." [251]

Triumph Motor Company

The Triumph Motor Company originated in London in 1885 when a Nuremburg native by the name of Siegfried Bettmann set up a company, S Bettmann & Co Import Export Agency, to import bicycles.

The company was renamed New Triumph Co Limited in 1886 and then the Triumph Cycle Co Limited in 1897 after the company began manufacturing its own bicycles and, eventually, motorcycles.

The first Triumph motorcycle was produced in 1902 and small-scale car making was soon to follow with the Triumph Motor Company established in 1930.

However, the bicycle and motorcycle businesses were sold in the late 1930s and the Triumph Motor Company was placed into receivership in 1939 and subsequently acquired by the Standard Motor Company Limited in 1944. [252]

The Standard Motor Company

The Standard Motor Company Limited was founded in Coventry, England in 1903 by Reginald Maudslay. The company constructed its first car-making workshops there at the outbreak of the First World War in 1914. [253]

In July 1931, the company appointed H H Robinson (a former South Island Manager for the automobile and motor accessories importer, Combined Buyers Limited) to develop the company's interests and establish a headquarters at Wellington. [254]

A news release published by the Christchurch Press at the time stated:

"Standard Cars. Big Range of 1932 Models — According to Mr H. H. Robinson, who is the representative of the manufacturers a range of 1932 models of Standard (English) motor-cars is shortly to be landed in the Dominion in time, it is hoped, for the Olympia Motor Exhibition to be held in Christchurch next month, or soon afterwards.

"The range will be a wide one and will be found very suitable for local conditions. Distributors are being appointed throughout the Dominion and special attention is to be paid to the question of servicing, the intention being to establish a big station in Wellington, where large quantities of spare parts will be stocked under the supervision of an expert, so that they may be obtained from any part of the Dominion at short notice." [255]

One of the first in New Zealand to be appointed as a 'Direct Factory Distributor' of Standard Cars was Amuri Motors Limited of Durham Street, Christchurch (Managing Director, L Treleaven), appointed in November 1931. The distributor chosen for the Auckland province was Northern Automobiles Limited of Albert Street, Auckland (and later of Hamilton & Tokoroa — Managing Director, T A Low & Director, J Epps), appointed July 1932. [256]

Subsequent distributors of Standard Motor Company vehicles and parts included:
Newton King Limited, New Plymouth (H Ashton, Director)
T R Taylor Limited, Dunedin and Invercargill (Managing Director, T R Taylor)
E Reynolds & Co Limited, Wellington (Managing Director, H L Rogers)
Reynolds & Co Limited, Wellington (Director, F Sinclair)
C C Wakefield & Co Limited, Wellington (New Zealand Manager, Walter Ingle)
Magnus Motors Limited, Wellington (Managing Director, Godfrey Magnus)
Carlton-Carruthers Limited, Wellington (Managing Director, Sinclair Carruthers)
Kensley & Co Pty Limited, Wellington (H H McLean) [257]

Standard Motor Company (New Zealand)

By August 1953, the British Standard Motor Company was trading as a New Zealand-registered, limited liability company, The Standard Motor Company (New Zealand) Limited, with Athol William Hamilton Brown of Wellington as Managing Director. [258] (After Athol William Hamilton Brown died in a drowning accident in May 1959, he was succeeded as managing director by K R Hougham in March 1960.) [259]

In January 1954, The Standard Motor Company (New Zealand) Limited, was granted a wholesale licence, to sell motor vehicles on its own account at Wellington. [260]

Following the takeover of the Triumph Motor Company by the Standard Motor Company in 1944, the combined companies became known as Standard-Triumph International. Standard's presence in New Zealand became the Standard Motor Co. (New Zealand) Limited with its head office in Auckland, and then Standard-Triumph (New Zealand) Limited on 27 November 1959. [261]

As both The Standard Motor Co. (New Zealand) Limited and Standard-Triumph, the company advertised in October 1957 that its "…nationwide network of distributors and dealers, service facilities, and full stocks of genuine 'Stanpart' spares…" were available "…at some 67 points between North Cape and the Bluff." [262]

Standard-Triumph (New Zealand)

A wholesale Licence was granted to Standard-Triumph (New Zealand) Limited at Christchurch on 1 September 1959 [263] after the company had acquired a financial interest in the Motor Assemblies Christchurch plant which went on to assemble Standard and Triumph vehicles. [264]

Standard-Triumph was also granted a wholesale Licence at Wellington on 1 October 1959. [265]

The British Standard-Triumph Motor Company became a subsidiary of British Leyland after a successful £20m bid in April 1961. [266] The Standard name was dropped in favour of just Triumph in 1963.

The Japanese Influence

After the Second World War, vehicle manufacturers in Japan worked under severe restrictions but, by the 1960s, the industry was booming. In 1967, car output reached 750,000 and the manufacturers expected to produce 1,350,000 cars in 1968. By then, all the big names in the Japanese industry were represented in New Zealand and in Australia where the Japanese car makers were claiming 13 per cent of the market. [267]

In February 1967, the Christchurch Press reported:

"Assembly in Christchurch of the Toyota Corona car is another step in what might become a major thrust by the Japanese car industry if sufficient import licences were granted.

"Although Japanese car sales in New Zealand are still modest—about 1000 a year—the industry now claims to be the world's third largest producer of motor-vehicles after the United States and Germany.

"During 1966, Japanese factories overtook the British vehicle industry after increasing production by nearly 22 per cent over the 1965 output. Mergers and business alliances in 1966 were partly responsible for the big increase in production.

"Nissan, makers of the Datsun car—already being assembled in Auckland at the rate of about 300 units a year — merged with the Prince company last August. Steel Bros., Ltd., at Addington who are now beginning to assemble Toyota cars, have been assembling Prince cars for the New Zealand market.

"Toyota, one of Japan's two largest car companies, concluded a business co-operation agreement with the Hino firm last October. Hino's Contessa 1300 car has been assembled by the Campbell Motors, Ltd., plant at Thames since last July.

"In December, Isuzu and Fuji Heavy Industries signed a similar co-operation agreement. An Auckland company has the New Zealand franchise to distribute Fuji's Subaru cars. A New Plymouth firm, H. H. Moller, Ltd., has obtained a licence to import the Isuzu Bellet, also to be assembled at Thames..." [268]

Steel Bros (NZ)

"Steel Bros (NZ) Limited began as a coach-building business in 1878 in premises on Lincoln Road [Christchurch]. The founding brothers, Joseph and David Steel, emigrated to New Zealand in 1860 from the Bendigo goldfields with their widowed mother, four brothers, and three sisters.

"They built farm carts, spring drays, gigs of many styles, including the celebrated Seddon pattern gig, designed for the Prime Minister, Richard John Seddon, waggonettes, buggies, and station waggons.

"They entered the age of the motor-vehicle slowly. World War II directed the company [then known as Steel Bros. (Addington) Limited] into converting trucks into army vehicles, making dummy aeroplanes and 80ft barges and repairing war vehicles.

"Post-war production spread into van and coach bodies, ambulances, decks, tippers, and a general run of commercial vehicles...From 1960 to 1970 it diversified its engineering, producing all types of transport trailers, notably the Hiab crane, truck-mounted or stationary, enabling an entire goods-handling operation be carried out single-handed.

"The first motor-body assembly work began in 1939. By 1952, International Harvester cabs and Austin and Morris commercial chassis and cabs were being produced. By 1954, there were 100 people on the staff and the Lincoln Road premises were enlarged to 40,000 sq. ft." [269]

In 1964, Steel Bros. (Addington) Limited was assembling Japanese "...Prince, International, Nissan, and Mazda vehicles. Production was at the rate of three vehicles per day..." [270]

By January 1965, Steel Bros was advertising for mechanics and assembly line workers to start at its new second factory at Buchanans Road, Hornby. [271]

"In 1967, Steel Bros assembled the first Toyota Corona in New Zealand on behalf of Consolidated Motor Industries Limited which then had the New Zealand Toyota franchise. [272]

The Hornby factory was extended and opened by the Minister of Customs (Mr Adams-Schneider) on 31 October 1970. At the time of the opening, Steel Bros Chairman, Sir Clifford Plimmer, advised that although the capacity of the new plant was 23 units per day, the lack of completely-knocked-down licences meant that the plant was running at only 16 units per day and this unused capacity was causing some concern. [273]

Steel Bros & Consolidated Motor Distributors

The company name, Steel Bros. (Addington) Limited, was changed to Steel Bros. NZ Limited on 14 October 1970 [274] and the company joined Consolidated Motor Distributors Limited in a joint shareholding to form Steel's Motor Assemblies Limited.

Steel's Motor Assemblies Limited opened a new factory at Traffers Road, Christchurch in 1974 at which were assembled various models of Toyotas, Datsuns, and Mazdas.

"When Steel Bros decided to withdraw from the contract [in 1977] and consolidate its engineering operation, production was running at 30 units a day." [275]

The decision resulted in the buyout by Consolidated Motor Distributors of Steel's Motor Assemblies' share of the company in February 1977. [276]

As well as Christchurch, Steel Bros. NZ Limited "…then had offices and workshops at Auckland and Wellington and service agencies in 15 centres…" [277]

In the early 1970s, Steel Bros had acquired the rights to assemble the English Lotus cars.

"The company also had the rights to use the Lotus name and became the only Lotus manufacturer based outside the UK…In Christchurch production of the cars began in a sub-factory in Buchanans Road…The first cars were finished in December 1973…Locally produced content of the car was 75% which made the government quite happy…In 1975 production was transferred to the main Steel Bros site at Treffers Road. It is believed that 98 cars were built at the Steel Bros plant before supply of the engines dried up [about March 1979]. All were fully assembled and ready to drive. Of these 8 were sold in Australia…" [278]

The decision to concentrate more on the needs of heavy road transport was brought about by a change in regulation that would lead to more trucks using the country's roads:

"In 1983 the New Zealand railways system was deregulated and road transport operators were relieved of the restrictions under which they had been forced to operate. Steelbro (as the company was now known) began to wind down its vehicle assembly and motor body building business and concentrate more on the production of trailers." [279]

Nissan New Zealand

Nissan built its first Dat Car (Datsun) for the Japanese market in 1914 [280] and following its merger with Prince Motors in August 1966, the Nissan Motor Company became the largest producer and exporter of motor vehicles in Japan. [281]

Nissan opened a New Zealand headquarters in 1963 and became Nissan Motor Distributors (New Zealand) Limited in March 1966. The name of the company was subsequently changed to Nissan Datsun Holdings Limited from December 1975 and again to the present name of Nissan New Zealand Limited in April 1999. [282]

"The first Japanese cars constructed in New Zealand were Nissans, then known as Datsuns. Datsun Bluebird P312s were built at the Motor Holdings plant in Mount Wellington from March 1963. [283]

"NZ Forest Products bought a substantial shareholding in the [Nissan] company…Forest Products then bought all their vehicles from Nissan — they had a big requirement for utes, trucks, and all their company cars became Nissans too. So Forest Products were a source of finance and a market." [284]

"Until it built its own permanent plant in Wiri, south Auckland, in the late 1970s, Nissans were assembled all over New Zealand by NZ Motor Bodies in Mount Wellington (early Bluebirds) Campbell Industries in Thames (1200 and 1600, 120Y, 180B), Motor Holdings, Waitara (1200 wagon, 120Y wagon), Todd Motors, Porirua (180B) a Nissan-owned 'temporary' plant in Mt Roskill, Auckland (1200, 120Y) and commercial vehicle plants in Glen Innes and Mangere. [285]

Plans to replace the Nissan plant at Glen Innes were under-way by late 1973 — as reported by the Christchurch Press.

"A new 65,000 sq ft assembly plant—formerly a printing house building—is being set up at Mount Roskill by Nissan Motor Distributors N.Z., Ltd. The plant will be four times the size of the firm's present facilities at Glen Innes, and will assemble Datsun 1200 cars, commercial vehicles, and four-wheel-drive utilities. The company says it plans production of 5000 vehicles a year." [286]

Indeed, "The Nissan Motor Distributors assembly plant in Stoddard Road, Mt Roskill, was opened on 25 March 1974. It will assemble sedans, utilities and heavy trucks for Nissan Datsun." [287]

A second Nissan Datsun Holdings assembly plant was opened at Wiri by Prime Minister Muldoon on 22 October 1977 [288] and this was followed by the addition of a parts centre in October 1979 — as reported by the Christchurch Press:

"Early last month the Nissan Datsun national parts centre near Auckland was opened. The centre has a warehouse for 41,000 line items with a computer-controlled stock system. Parts are held for every Datsun sold in New Zealand since 1962; 20 different body shapes and 12 different engines. The Nissan Datsun Group invited public inspection recently and on view was a $6 million investment in the future of motoring in New Zealand.

"On the 21.5 ha site, the group's facilities for assembly, vehicle distribution, and parts supply, make up a complex which is the nucleus of Nissan Datsun's service in New Zealand. In 1965, Datsun had placed a modest 300 vehicles on the roads of New Zealand. By the start of the 1980s, the needs of nearly 60,000 vehicles with the Datsun and Nissan marques will be serviced from the parts centre. Orders at the rate of 200 a day can be processed, priority being given to vehicles off the road. Datsun dealers hold stocks of fast-moving items and replenish their shelves from the centre…60 Datsun dealers throughout New Zealand…

"Working at capacity, the staff of 400 assemble 30 passenger vehicles a day at Wiri. A second commercial vehicle assembly plant works nearby at Otahuhu.

"The new vehicle distribution centre is sited at the rear of the complex and was first established at Wiri in 1974. Dealers receive vehicles by transporter or drive-away system. South Island orders are shipped weekly." [289]

<u>Campbell Motors</u>

Campbell Motors traded from Auckland's Customs Street East as early as December 1920. Indeed, the business was advertising a 7-passenger Cadillac for sale at £450 [290] and a 5-passenger Dodge for £425 in October 1921. [291]

A subsequent advertisement published by the Auckland Star in July 1922 commented:

"Campbell Motors specialise in Dodge car repairs and reconditioned Dodge cars. This is the only firm in New Zealand who make that claim. They have sold hundreds of Dodges, and their premises in Customs Street East are looked on as the 'home of the Dodge car owners and buyers in Auckland'. Another branch of their business is exchange. They are always ready to make a reasonable exchange…" [292]

Campbell Motors was also the Auckland agent for the ill-fated Durant motor car, assembled at New York until 1932 [293] — advertised as "The wonder car for colonial use…Real leather upholstery. Light on benzine. A cheap car to run." [294]

For the New Zealand market, the Durant Company renamed one of its models the 'Rugby'. The first shipment of 50 was said to have been sold by Campbell Motors within 30 days. [295]

By February 1926, the business was advertising itself as New Campbell Motors Limited of Anzac Avenue, Auckland with new showrooms opening "…in the heart of Queen Street". [296]

Campbell Motors was registered as Campbell Motors Limited on 12 July 1926, [297] with a capital of £30,000 divided into £1 shares. The initial shareholders were William Norton, Victor Cecil Bedford, Henry Laidlaw Turnbull, Leslie Frederick Bedford, and Josiah Daniel Webster each allocated 6000 shares. [298]

In December 1926, Campbell Motors announced that it had taken over the Lambton Garage, 15 Thorndon Quay…"…the new home of Rugby, Flint and Singer Cars." [299]

A month later, in January 1927, Campbell Motors announced that it had opened an "Up-to-date Garage in Cuba Street, Palmerston North" and that the firm was agents for Rugby, Flint, Locomobile and Singer Cars." [300] Another dealership was opened at New Plymouth with the registration of Campbell Motors (New Plymouth) Limited in September 1927 with a capital of £3000. The business traded as Campbell and Telfar, motor proprietors. [301]

By early 1933, Campbell Motors had established a number of new and used car dealerships around the North Island, including at J Wyllie's Garage, Whangarei, from which they were selling a "…phenomenally large number of cars…at keen Auckland prices…and such attractive terms as to enable almost anyone to have a good sound car, or to change their older machine for a better and more recent model, with better riding and lower running costs." [302]

In August 1938, Campbell Motors "…opened a depot for the sale of fine used cars at N Jonassen's Garage, Pollen Street, [Thames]." It was to be the start of what would later become the company's expanded business of parts manufacture, car assembly, and distributorship at Thames. [303]

A subsidiary of Campbell Motors Limited, Campbell Tube Products, began the manufacture of vehicle parts, such as exhaust pipes and mufflers, at Thames in 1939. In 1963, Campbell Motors bought land from the Thames local council on which the company built a car assembly plant.

"The assembly business was named Campbell Motor Industries, beginning with assembly of the Peugeot 404. The first 404 left the factory on 3 September 1964.

"Earlier in the year Campbell Motors acquired the rights to assemble American Motors Rambler which had previously been assembled by VW Motors in Otahuhu, Auckland.

"The first Rambler to be assembled by Campbell Motors Industries in Thames came off the assembly line also in September 1964.

"A total of 590 Rebel sedans were built by CMI and an additional 177 wagons and hardtops were fully imported. For 1970 only, CMI brought in a small number of fully assembled, right-hand-drive 1970 AMC Ambassador sedans.

"From 1966 CMI acquired the rights to assemble Hino Contessas and Isuzu Belletts. Renaults were added in 1967. New Zealand's first Toyota Corollas were assembled by CMI in April 1968 as a joint venture with Consolidated Motor Industries, followed by Datsun in 1970." [304]

However, by 1975 Challenge Corporation had become the major shareholder of the Campbell Motors Group — as anticipated by the Christchurch Press:

"Challenge Corporation. Ltd. appears to have won control of a unique and extremely valuable motor vehicle importing, assembling and retailing group.

"In the last few weeks, Challenge has acquired at least 37 per cent of the shareholding of Campbell Motors, Ltd, Auckland. Reliable sources say it has also been successful in acquiring another 49 per cent of the company, giving it almost full control. If this is so, Challenge would now control:

"Campbell Motors, retailer of Toyota, Renault, Peugeot, Daihatsu, and American Motors vehicles in Auckland, Takapuna, Whangarei, and Thames.

"Campbell Industries, which assembles Toyota. Renault and Peugeot vehicles at Thames.

"Campbell Tube Products, manufacturer of motor vehicle mufflers, exhaust systems, and roof racks, and other companies involved in motor vehicle importing and distributing…

"Consolidated Motor Distributors, holder of the Toyota franchise in New Zealand and itself associated with a Christchurch car assembly plant, Steel's Motor Assemblies.

"Challenge is involved in motor vehicles throughout its subsidiary, Wrightcars Ltd, which runs a chain of 32 motor dealerships throughout New Zealand, selling mainly Toyotas.

"Wrightcars was also a third equal shareholder in Consolidated Motor with Campbell, and C.P.D. [Cable Price Downer] Ltd." [305]

Cable Price Downer & Challenge Corporation

Cable Price Downer Limited was originally incorporated as William Cable and Company Limited in 1911. The company was known as William Cable Holdings Limited from December 1951 to August 1962 when the company's name was again changed — to Cable Price Downer Limited. [306]

Challenge Corporation Limited was originally incorporated as Wright Stephenson & Co Limited in 1906. The company was known as NMA Wright Stephenson Holdings Limited from March 1972 to October 1973 when the company's name was again changed — to Challenge Corporation Limited. [307]

As William Cable Holdings Limited, Cable Price Downer acquired F Butler Limited of Hamilton in 1952. At that time, the activities of F Butler (incorporated in June 1946) [308] were described as "…distributors of engineering and equipment lines. Butlers operate a heavy transporter service throughout the North Island, and they service farm and construction equipment." [309]

In November 1965, the name of F Butler Limited was changed to Consolidated Motor Industries Limited, [310] formed as a joint partnership between Cable Price Downer and Challenge Corporation (then Wright Stephenson & Co), with the franchise to assemble and distribute Toyota vehicles in New Zealand — as advertised in the Christchurch Press in February 1966:

"A new Company Consolidated Motor Industries Limited in which Cable Price Downer Limited and Wright Stephenson and Company Limited are the major Share Holders, has been formed to operate the Toyota Motor Franchise in New Zealand, and they require a General Manager." [311]

It was soon announced that the Toyota Corona would be the first to be assembled by the joint venture:

"A popular Japanese car, the Toyota Corona, will be assembled in quantity at the Addington works of Steel Brothers, motor body builders. The first will be completed in December.

"A new company, Consolidated Motor Industries, Ltd., in which Cable-Price-Downer, Ltd., has a 50 per cent interest, has been formed and plans to assemble a range of vehicles produced by the giant Toyota Company.

"Plans are being made to increase the percentage of local components to go into the Toyota cars assembled in Christchurch. Cable-Price officials say the proportion of local components, which is already well above the minimum approved by the Department of Industries and Commerce will be increased.

"The Cable-Price corporation will be responsible for the distribution of Toyota cars throughout New Zealand. About 300 a year will be assembled." [312]

Assembly of the first Toyota Corona at the Steel Brothers Addington plant was completed on 2 February 1967. The event was attended by the Minister of Finance, Mr Lake, who commented:

"'New Zealand was unable to raise the overseas funds the motor industry would like to see. More Coronas than would become available would be wanted but he hoped this shortage would be only temporary.'

The chairman of Consolidated Motor Industries, J H Ingram, replied:

"'New Zealand's current overseas exchange position, coupled with our import licensing policy, restricts, for the time being, our initial annual output to 300 units and inhibits our rate of growth and penetration of the New Zealand market.'" [313]

Consolidated Motor Industries Limited became Consolidated Motor Distributors Limited from November 1970 [314] and Cable Price Downer and Challenge Corporation subsequently held 80 per cent of the equity capital of the company in equal shares. Toyota of Japan held 20 per cent of the capital in the form of specified preference shares. With the growth of the franchise, Consolidated Motor Distributors had expanded and owned Steels Motor Assemblies at Christchurch and Campbell Industries at Thames. [315]

Toyota New Zealand

"All aspects of the Japanese Toyota Motor Corporation's vehicle manufacture, distribution, parts and service within New Zealand were consolidated in May 1979. This consolidation resulted in the incorporation of Consolidated Motor Distributors Limited, Campbell Industries Limited, and the Toyota parts distribution centre at Palmerston North as Toyota New Zealand Limited.

"The respective assembly plants of Steel's Motor Assemblies Limited at Christchurch and Campbell Industries Limited at Thames were also included as Toyota New Zealand entities." [316]

European Motor Distributors

European Motor Distributors Limited was incorporated by car dealer, Colin John Giltrap, on 17 August 1977 [317] following his acquisition of the Volkswagen franchise relinquished by the Motor Holdings Group.

"Giltraps already handle vehicles from Audi, a Volkswagen subsidiary, and a new building under construction at Mount Wellington will handle the importing and distribution of all VW, Audi and Porsche lines to the national dealer chain.

"The new company also plans to assemble VWs at the South Pacific Vehicle Assemblers' plant in Wanganui, where the Suzuki range is assembled…" [318]

South Pacific Vehicle Assemblers

South Pacific Vehicle Assemblers Limited, incorporated on 14 May 1976, [319] was owned by the Coleman Group, George Palmer and Sons of Hamilton [George Palmer Motors Limited], and Colin Giltrap [320]

"Percy Coleman, [founder of the Coleman Group] was a nationally known motorcyclist in the 1920s and 1930s…His sons Rod and Bob…jointly ran the firm's assembly and distribution interests at Wanganui.

"The Colemans began importing Suzuki motorcycles in 1959…With the easing of import restrictions in 1972, the Colemans' imports reached 30,000 units a year. In 1973, planning began for the setting up of an assembly plant for Suzuki four-wheel vehicles.

In February 1984, "The Coleman family's three-generation love of motor-cycling paid off with a multi-million-dollar sale of their business interests to…Suzuki…" [321]

Suzuki New Zealand

Suzuki New Zealand Limited was incorporated on 1 December 1983 [322] to take over the South Pacific Suzuki Vehicle Assemblers and South Pacific Suzuki Distributors previously run by the Coleman Group.

"The firm will import and distribute Suzuki motorcycles, outboard motors and generators, and will assemble Suzuki four-wheel drive vehicles and mini cars…the emphasis in New Zealand operations would be on vehicles for use in agriculture such as farm bikes." [323]

However, the competitive and regulatory nature of the New Zealand marketplace did not accommodate the Suzuki brand for long — as reported by the Christchurch Press on 30 November 1988:

"Suzuki New Zealand Ltd has announced it will mothball its Wanganui vehicle assembly plant from December 31 — with the loss of 16 jobs. Suzuki's managing director in Wanganui, Mr Kaz Adachi, said a depressed market and the company's battle to compete against other brands had brought about the shut-down of the assembly line.

"'We were down to four vehicles a day and that was simply not sufficient to maintain efficiency there,' Mr Adachi said. Suzuki had been bringing its models into New Zealand as C.K.D. units, which meant they were assembled at the Wanganui plant for distribution. But Mr Adachi said C.K.D. production meant Suzuki had to have a bigger lead time, getting the parts into New Zealand months ahead of its competitors, who were bringing [in] completed models. He said he had to make it clear that it was not the company's intention to sell the assembly plant." [324]

Peter Greenslade in his 'Behind The Wheel' column, published by the Christchurch Press on 9 December 1988, described what he thought was the reason for the demise of Suzuki's local assembly line:

"Suzuki started out by producing pint-sized cars which, since the British Leyland Mini disappeared from dealers' showrooms, have not proved popular in New Zealand. Admittedly, the Suzuki has grown into the 1324 cu cm Swift, the four-wheel-drive Samurai and, more recently, the 1500 cu cm Vitara, but the old three cylinder Alto image is apparently still strong and overshadows the larger vehicles.

"Maybe it's because of that image that Suzuki New Zealand is at least temporarily abandoning local assembly, although it is more likely that, like the Daihatsu, being handled by the Turners and Growers Group and now imported completely built up from Japan, Suzuki has come to realise that New Zealand's Motor Industry Plan has won yet another battle in the continuing war. It seems that you've just got to be big to succeed." [325]

Chapter Five

The Component Industry

As described by Eric Pawson in his 'Cars and the motor industry' history published by the Encyclopedia of New Zealand:

"The motor assembly industry relied on a wide range of local component manufacturers and suppliers. These had developed since the 1930s, when industry was encouraged with tariff protection, and later with local content requirements for cars imported unassembled.

"Component manufacturers included Exide batteries, Dulux paints, Tubular Steel exhaust systems, and makers of bumpers, upholstery, rubber components and tyres. In the 1990s such companies were also affected by the reduction in tariffs on imported vehicles.

"Jobs were lost in South Auckland and Masterton when automotive-wiring manufacturers closed in the late 1990s. Pilkington Automotive in Hutt Valley had supplied glass to all New Zealand car assemblers. Despite moving into export markets, it closed in 2003. Radiola Corporation lost its car radio business, because imported cars arrived with radios.

"Companies that had been geared towards export were less affected. One was Southward Engineering, which made exhaust systems for Australia. Another was Firestone, which built a plant in Christchurch after the Second World War. In the early 2000s it still manufactured tyres for the domestic market, and for export to Australia and the Pacific. [1]

According to the New Zealand Official Year Book of 1920, the imported value of automobiles, motor-cars, motor cycles, and materials for them totalled £2,244,741 during the 1919 financial year. [2]

During the 1957 financial year, motor vehicle parts were accounted for separately with the value of imports of that class for that year amounting to £2,591,000. [3]

At about the time that the last motor vehicle assembly plant closed, the New Zealand Official Year Book of 1999 reported:

"There are around 40 manufacturers of automotive components whose production is around $400 million per year, with exports totalling around $180 million. Exports include tyres, alloy wheels, wiring harnesses, springs and windscreens. The automotive component sector employs around 4,000 people." [4]

Automotive Component Manufacturers

As related by Mark Webster in his book, 'Assembly — A History of New Zealand Car Production 1921-1998':

"Local assembly wasn't cheap. New Zealand-manufactured components for locally assembled cars cost at least a third more than the cost of their Japanese-manufactured equivalents, even with freight factored in, according to The New Zealand Motor Car Industry After the Plan by Dan Witt, page 85."

"Lots of companies took huge hits as models came to the end of New Zealand assembly. There were colossal closures or cutbacks throughout the ancillary industries…Like the car dynasties, local supply dynasties had been created…There were [makers of] fabric and trim, fastener and sealant supplies, battery makers, tyre makers…the quality of product from these manufacturers was up there with anything produced anywhere in the world…" [5]

A few of those component manufacturers included:

Glass Makers
Pilkington Brothers

Pilkington Brothers was founded by the brothers, William and Richard, who started making glass at St Helens in England in 1826. [6]

"Early [New Zealand] settlers brought window glass with them from Europe, protected from the rigours of sea transport by straw and crates. In April 1840, the *New Zealand Gazette* advertised the sale of 'window glass'. It had arrived on the New Zealand Company's ship *Glenbervie*, which docked safely in Wellington on 2 October 1839 after a 5-month journey from London. Included in her cargo were 78 boxes of glass and 24 pairs of windows. Until the late 1950s, New Zealand's growing glass market was serviced entirely by imports." [7]

It was not until 1949 that a glass factory to be built in New Zealand was first proposed — as reported by the Bay of Plenty Times in May of that year:

"One of the world's greatest glassmaking concerns, the 125-year-old firm of Pilkington Brothers Ltd of England, is to establish a factory in Randwick Road, Lower Hutt. Approval in principle for the erection of the factory has been obtained from the Government. This plant will not actually be for glass manufacture, but will process glass into safety glass for the motor assembly plants of New Zealand…There is only one plant actually manufacturing glass in New Zealand. That is at Penrose, making bottles only." [8]

Pilkington Brothers (New Zealand) Limited was incorporated on 16 September 1949 [9] and the Lower Hutt plant was opened in 1953 to service the local vehicle assembly industry. [10]

McKendrick Glass Manufacturing Company

The McKendrick Glass Manufacturing Company Limited was established by McKendrick Brothers Limited on 25 May 1960 with an initial capital of £150,000 and the intention of constructing a sheet-window glass factory at Whangarei. [11]

The company built a major plant around a glass tank feeding two Fourcault machines, and started trials on 11 July 1962. [12]

By September 1962, with the optimism reminiscent of that used by New Zealand's first oil explorers, intended more to reassure his company's shareholders, managing director, G A R McKendrick:

"…said the company had made amazing progress in production. 'We claim that the 20 tons a day we are producing is better than that achieved by many of the top factories in the world in the same period…I see potentially great development in our supplying special automobile glass for export.'" [13]

However, despite some financial assistance from the Government attempting to save a wholly-owned New Zealand entity, by January 1963, McKendrick Glass Company Limited was in receivership with the receiver advertising for any interested parties to buy the glassworks as a going concern. [14]

Following the company's collapse, the Christchurch Press commented:

"The proposed sale of the Whangarei glassworks will end one of New Zealand's most unfortunate industrial ventures in recent years. Responsibility for the present owners' difficulties, however, can scarcely be laid upon the National Party Government, which erred on the side of generosity in upholding its predecessor's promise of a protected market, and subsequently in guaranteeing an £80,000 bank overdraft.

"The Government's wisdom in declining the McKendrick Glass Manufacturing Company's representations for further financial aid is today more than ever apparent. Nevertheless, it is a matter for regret that although raw materials for glassmaking are available within New Zealand, the company has encountered such formidable problems in manufacturing, at competitive prices, acceptable substitutes for imports." [15]

In May 1963, it was announced that Pilkington and the Australian glassmaker, Australian Consolidated Industries, had purchased the assets of the McKendrick Glass Company for £380,000 cash. [16]

Trading as New Zealand Window Glass Limited, commercial production began in April 1964.

"Some 30,000 tonnes of glass were produced each year, ranging in thicknesses from 2 to 6 mm…By 1988, the plant employed 215 people and had eight salespeople based in Auckland. It produced about 600 tonnes (80,000 m2) of glass per week and exported 40% of its production to Australia, Japan and the Pacific.

"Glass production stopped at New Zealand Window Glass on 14 February 1991… The machinery was sold to Gunge Glass of Pakistan. So after 18 years of New Zealand production, window glass once again needed to be imported." [17]

Pilkington Automotive

In the meantime, Pilkington Automotive Limited continued to provide for the needs of the local vehicle assembly industry from its Lower Hutt factory.

In September 1971, the company advertised:

"All glass in the new Chrysler Valiant is supplied by Pilkington Brothers (New Zealand) Limited…" [18]

However, by 1977, the Lower Hutt factory struggled to service the many vehicle models assembled by the industry — as reported by the Christchurch Press in September that year:

"A glass manufacturer blamed the big increase in available car models for a decline in furnace productivity. Mr R Robinson, managing director of Pilkington Brothers Ltd, said that the proliferation of vehicle models had had a detrimental effect on his company's production costs.

"The increased model range meant smaller production runs resulting in a loss of efficiency and a poor use of labour and plant. Mr Robinson told the commission of inquiry into the distribution of motor vehicle parts that his company was supplying glass for 90 models compared with 46 in 1968. The company was using 544 sets of tools for assembly requirements and was holding 815 sets for vehicles no longer in production…

"Because of the highly competitive nature of the vehicle market, franchise holders were continually introducing new and additional models to penetrate the market. Motor manufacturers should be given an incentive to reduce the number of models on the New Zealand market, Mr Robinson said. They should concentrate on selected models to give economies of scale which could be shared with the consumer. There was a need for the Government to formulate a long-term plan for the motor-vehicle industry in order to give vehicle and component manufacturers the opportunity to plan for future growth." [19]

But, not only did the factory have to deal with an increasing number of model variations, but also with the varying standard of windscreen glass required — as reported by the Christchurch Press in November 1981:

"Laminated glass windscreens now account for more than 15 per cent of the 90,000 or so windscreens fitted as original equipment on New Zealand-assembled motor vehicles. Laminated windscreens have been used extensively, overseas for more than 20 years, and became readily available in New Zealand when Pilkington Brothers (NZ) Ltd started to make them about a year ago.

"Pilkington's have also tooled up to make laminated windscreens for a number of models originally fitted with toughened glass. Mr R A Fowler, Pilkington's marketing manager, says that the recognition by assemblers of the benefits of laminated windscreens was a welcome move which justified the nearly $1.5 million spent in establishing the manufacturing plant.

"Top of the range models in the Holden and Mitsubishi stables have 'Bondlite' laminated glass windscreens as standard and Mr Fowler expects that more assemblers will change soon." [20]

Toughened safety glass was also needed by the vehicle assembly industry and plans for its manufacture at a new Pilkington factory in Ellerslie were announced in May 1982:

"More than $1.4M will be spent by Pilkington Brothers (NZ) Ltd on new plant and equipment to make toughened safety glass. It is expected to be commissioned early next year. The managing-director of Pilkington Brothers (Mr R G Cambie) said the new plant, at the company's factory in Ellerslie, would meet most of the country's demand for flat toughened glass for the next few years at least." [21]

By February 1984, Pilkington were able to report:

"Laminated glass windscreens are now fitted to 40 per cent of the new passenger cars assembled in New Zealand. Three years ago only 12 per cent of locally assembled cars were fitted with laminated screens.

"Laminated screens are manufactured locally by Pilkington Brothers (NZ) Ltd and the marketing manager, Mr R A Fowler, says that some assemblers have converted each new model to Bondlite laminated windscreens as it has been introduced.

"All Toyotas are fitted with laminated screens, including the about-to-be-launched front-wheel-drive Corolla. They are also fitted to the Ford Falcon, Mazda 626 and latest Talbot Alpine.

"However, some assemblers fit laminated screens to their top-of-the-line models only. Some Holden Commodores have laminated screens, but others are fitted with toughened glass. The same applies in the case of Todd Motors with its Mitsubishi Mirage, Cordia, Sigma and Tredia models, Ford with its Laser and Mazda with its 323. Subaru, Nissan, Suzuki and Honda cars are fitted with toughened glass screens." [22]

Laminated windscreens became a legal requirement for new cars sold in New Zealand after 1 July 1985:

"All new cars and vans sold in New Zealand after July 1 next year will have to be fitted with laminated windscreens, the Minister of Transport, Mr Gair, has said.

"The decision would reduce accident costs, both in monetary terms and in terms of human suffering, Mr Gair said…Pilkington Brothers already produce laminated screens in New Zealand and last year more than a third of New Zealand assembled cars were fitted with them.

"'This year the figure is expected to be about two-thirds and there should be no problem in meeting all New Zealand's requirements by the July 1, 1985, deadline,' he said." [23]

Pilkington Automotive continued to manufacture automobile glass until the vehicle assembly industry came to an end in 1989 and then switched to manufacturing for export during the 1990s. [24]

However, the end finally came in 2003 — as reported by The New Zealand Herald:

"Lower Hutt windscreen manufacturer Pilkington Automotive Ltd will close in September this year putting 130 people out of work, the company said today. General manager Timo Rautarinta said the Taita-based automotive glass plant, a subsidiary of Pilkington (New Zealand) Ltd, would close on September 30…

"At the April 30 meeting staff were also told that several years of difficult trading conditions had led management to consider closing the operation…Mr Rautarinta said: 'Continuing competitive pressure from other countries with lower cost structures and the recent appreciation of the New Zealand dollar have made closure inevitable.'

"Aside from closure, the British-owned company had considered selling the plant, or continuing on if better profitability could be achieved. It currently has annual sales of about $31 million, and its efforts to resist fluctuations within international markets included a $15 million capital investment…" [25]

Electronics
Joseph Lucas

Joseph Lucas Limited was founded by Joseph Lucas who established a factory at Birmingham, England in 1897 for the manufacture of ships' lanterns and photographic lamps. By the 1930s, he and his son, Harry, were manufacturing all kinds of cycle accessories, including what would become the world-famous 'King of the Road' bicycle lamp. [26]

A description of a visit to the Joseph Lucas factory by an English reporter, syndicated and published by the Evening Post in July 1922, marvelled at the level of mass production engaged in by its workers:

"…one had an opportunity of seeing the famous bicycle lamps being turned out by mass production. There are 4000 employees. Most of the light processes of manufacture are done by girls, and in the making of a lamp it is surprising to find how many processes there are involved from the pressing of the metals to the laying on of the ebony blacking or nickel plate." [27]

"Later, the firm began to make dynamo lighting sets and motor accessories and [by 1934] had become "…the biggest motor, motor-cycle, and cycle accessory manufacturing concern in England…supplying the electrical equipment for 98 per cent of British cars…" [28]

Joseph Lucas had a presence in New Zealand at least as early as June 1926 when L M Silver and Co of Wellington, "Specialists in Dynamo and Motor Repair. Armature Rewinding, Magnetos, etc…" advertised that they were the agents for Joseph Lucas with "Large Stocks of Magnetos and Parts, Lucas Spares for English Cars, Dynamos and Batteries." [29]

The continuing success of the automotive components produced by Joseph Lucas was demonstrated by the number of innovative products available to New Zealand motorists and reported by the press between 1927 and 1933:

"The confidence of this firm in its own products is well evidenced by the fact that all Lucas magnetos are now guaranteed for a period of two years against mechanical and electrical breakdown, and also the burning of contact breaker points and ordinary wear and tear." [30]

"On one of the largest stands [at the International Cycle and Motor Cycle Show, Olympia, London] the various products of Messrs Joseph Lucas were displayed. The new headlamp marketed by this firm has a gas-filled bulb with two filaments; one gives a brilliant driving light and the other an alternative dipped beam the change-over being effected by a neat switch on the handle bar.

"Another exhibit to attract attention was their racing magneto, every one of which is tested before leaving the works at a speed corresponding to 200 m.p.h., and guaranteed for two years against electrical and mechanical breakdown." [31]

"Among new electrical equipment, a novel design of dual arm windscreen wiper by Joseph Lucas Ltd, possesses noteworthy features. In this new type the electric motor and mechanism are mounted on the engine side of the dash, where they are hidden from sight and are inaudible in action. The wipers themselves are carried on short shafts and the drive is by an oscillating shaft and roller chain. As the wipers are mounted below the screen the drive is concealed by the scuttle rail, and when the arms are not wiping they are entirely hidden." [32]

The company's New Zealand presence was completed by the establishment of Joseph Lucas New Zealand Limited, incorporated on 31 January 1936 with a Capital of £5000. The first Shareholders were named as Joseph Lucas Australia with 4999 shares and H E Barrowclough with one share. [33]

By May 1936, Joseph Lucas had established a service centre at Beach Road, Auckland:

"Famed throughout the entire world for Lighting, Starting and Ignition Equipments, the English firm of Joseph Lucas have pleasure in announcing that they have opened a New Zealand branch and service depot at 75-77 Beach Road, Auckland…

"Here the owners of British, Lucas-equipped vehicles are assured of prompt, efficient, courteous service by Lucas-trained experts using the very latest Lucas equipment for testing and repairs. A full range of all Lucas King of the Road products, including parts will be carried. A cordial invitation is extended to all motorists to visit this modern electrical service depot…" [34]

By 1975, the product offering of Joseph Lucas New Zealand Limited had expanded to include a lot more than just auto-electrical parts and accessories — as advertised in the Christchurch Press:

"…our big spares department is ready with all auto-electrical parts and accessories for cars, caravans, trailers . . .Lucas wiper arms and blades....Lucas Pacesetter batteries…Girling and Lockheed braking systems...Girling shock absorbers...Zenith, Solex and Stromberg carburettors...C.A.V. and Simms diesel injection parts and service..." [35]

The name of Joseph Lucas New Zealand Limited was changed to Lucas Industries Limited on 28 November 1975 and to JRA (NZ) Limited on 18 April 1988. [36]

The latter name change resulted from the acquisition of the Australian and New Zealand Lucas service operations from the British parent by the Australia-based automotive product supplier and manufacturer, JRA Limited.

In March 1989, JRA (NZ) Limited "…announced the formation of a joint venture company 50 per cent owned by JRA and 50 per cent owned by Yuasa Battery Company, of Japan.

"The joint venture company, to be known as Yuasa JRA Batteries Ltd, has purchased JRA's Battery Manufacturing Division at Te Papapa, Auckland. The new company will manufacture Lucas-branded batteries under a long-term supply agreement and will have access to Yuasa and other brand names for the further development of market share in New Zealand." [37]

In February 2001, Lucas Industries Limited was place into voluntary liquidation and struck from the companies register on 16 August 2005. [38]

The Chloride Electrical Storage Company

"The Chloride Electrical Storage Syndicate Ltd was incorporated on the 12 December 1891. The company had been established to adopt a provisional agreement dated the 30 November 1891 and made between The Electric Storage Battery Company and The United Gas Improvement Company on one part and John Arnold Einem Hickson to exploit patents belonging to The Electric Storage Battery Co of New Jersey, United States of America.

"At an Extraordinary General Meeting of the Syndicate held on the 6 May 1902 a Special Resolution was passed and amongst the business of the day was the changing of the company name to The Chloride Electrical Storage Co Ltd. The company expanded as a result of the many batteries it developed and the applications they were used for. From 1909 it began developing relationships with other companies producing batteries." [39]

One of the first Chloride batteries produced at Manchester, England was of the lead-acid type branded Exide and one of the earliest references to its use in New Zealand was in September 1911when the cars for a new tramway service to be commissioned at Wanganui were to be equipped with 'Hycap Exide' batteries. [40]

Long before the Exide Battery became an essential component for the motor car powered by an internal combustion engine, it played an important part in the early development of the electric car — as reported by the Evening Star in November 1917:

"The New Zealand Express Company have just imported…an 'Orwell' electric motor vehicle, the first of its kind seen in Dunedin. It is of two-and-a-half ton capacity, is fitted with an ironclad Exide battery, and is capable of running 45 miles on one charge." [41]

By 1924, Hope Gibbons Limited of Wellington, Auckland, and Christchurch had been appointed the New Zealand agent for the Exide Battery, by now very much used to fire up the country's increasing numbers of internal combustion engines.

In an advertisement, published by the Otago Witness in December 1924, Hope Gibbons not only promoted the Exide Battery but also the customer's ability to service the product at the company's Exide Battery Service Stations, one of which was trading from 293 Princes Street South, Dunedin. [42]

In September 1926, the Exide Long-Life Battery was also advertised as a source for house lighting the power requirements for which were, of course, far less in those days. [43]

But it was the motor car and its incorporation of an increasing number of electrical gadgets that really demanded an efficient battery system — as reported by the Waikato Times in May 1927:

"Battery service is of the utmost importance to all car owners, as all the moving parts depend on the battery to set them in motion. Just what battery service means is demonstrated by Mr Carrick Nisbet, the principal of the Exide Service Station.

"Battery repair is a speciality with this firm, not a side-line, and therein lies the secret of a competent Battery Service Station. The practical experience gained by many years of specialisation in all battery matters is at the disposal of all motorists at any time. The Exide agent this year is displaying batteries for every make of car, and the makers of these efficient batteries have given years of study to this product in order that every user of an Exide can travel with security, knowing that he can depend entirely on his battery seeing him through." [44]

The supply of batteries to New Zealand was to come a step closer in 1928 with the announcement:

"The Exide Batteries Co Ltd has decided to build a factory in Australia. Mr H V Schofield, export manager for the company, has been in Australia making the necessary arrangements." [45]

And the business of selling Chloride batteries was booming by 1930:

"At the annual meeting of the Chloride Electrical Storage Company Ltd held at Clifton Junction, near Manchester, on May 29, the chairman reported a continuance of development and prosperity...

"'We have the largest storage battery factory in the British Empire, and one which has grown from a very small beginning nearly 40 years ago...Abroad our sales organisation is widespread. We have representatives and offices throughout the British Empire, and we are obtaining important business in the highly protected Continental countries.'" [46]

One of the most important reasons for the company's success was reported by the Poverty Bay Herald in July 1932:

"Mr H Boon (Exide Batteries) told at length 'How we made the public buy our batteries,' which (in addition to the quality of the product) was due to boldness in advertising in newspapers. Last year his firm increased newspaper advertising by 40 per cent.

"All the spaces, he said, were of large sizes, and it was estimated that each series of advertisements would reach a reader public of no less than 10,000,000. Their experience had led them to believe that large spaces gave the essentials of prestige and the general idea of a big company with something very important to say." [47]

In 1939, the Chloride Electrical Storage Company established Exide Batteries of NZ Limited, registered at Wellington with a Capital of £20,000. The initial subscribers were named as D P Dunne & C M Mills of Manchester with 19,999 shares and J E Salmon of Wellington with one share. [48]

A year later, an advertisement published by the Waikato Times promoted the merits of Exide Batteries, particularly those produced at the Lower Hutt factory:

"There are more Exide Batteries in use in the world than any other make of battery. The Exide Factory in England is the largest battery factory in the British Empire. The world-wide Exide organisation has over fifty years' experience in the manufacture of batteries. The New Zealand Exide product is backed by this experience. The Exide factory is the only complete battery plant in the Dominion, manufacturing all component parts for the Exide battery in its own factory.

"The first car ignition battery was an Exide. The first car lighting battery was an Exide. The first car starting battery was an Exide. The first S.O.S. wireless call was made with the aid of an Exide Battery. Exide Batteries are made by the largest battery manufacturing organisation in the world, with factories in England, Canada, Italy, United States, Australia and New Zealand. Exide makes a battery to suit every make and model of car..." [49]

And for many youths, battery manufacturing was a good opportunity:

"Boys Wanted, 16-19. Positions are now available for a number of Youths to be trained in Accumulator Manufacture. Good working conditions, with definite prospects for suitable lads. Wages average 10s per week above award. Works Engineer, Exide Batteries of NZ Ltd, Hutt Park Road, Lower Hutt." [50]

Chloride Batteries New Zealand (1)

The first Chloride Batteries (NZ) Limited (W 1954/176) was registered at Wellington in May 1954 as part of the British Chloride Group and the company was granted a wholesale licence on 1 June of that year. [51]

However, following the merger of Exide Batteries of New Zealand with Battery Makers of New Zealand in 1967, as later described, the name of the original Chloride Batteries New Zealand was also changed to Battery Makers as of 16 April 1973. [52]

Battery Makers of New Zealand

As of 13 November 1967, the name, Exide Batteries of New Zealand Limited (W 1939/26), was changed to Battery Makers of New Zealand Limited [53] with a wholesale licence granted in December of that year. [54]

However, despite this change, the company remained a wholly-owned subsidiary of the British Chloride Group, [55] as advertised by the Christchurch Press in July 1970:

"An opportunity exists for the appointment of a Branch Manager for our Dunedin-based operations. Battery Makers of New Zealand Limited, New Zealand's largest manufacturer and distributor of automotive batteries, is a member of an international Group of Companies. The leading Exide, Vesta and Rokfire brands are marketed nationally through Company Branches and Distributors…Battery Makers Of New Zealand Ltd…Lower Hutt." [56]

With new technology came the need for extra factory space — as reported by the Christchurch Press in October 1972:

"More power and easier topping-up are said to be the main advantages of a new design of a car battery now being made in New Zealand. The new red battery, which has a polypropylene case, is being made by Battery Makers of New Zealand Ltd and will replace about three-quarters of the company's present Exide, Vesta and Rokfire ranges.

"The company says the easy-filling device moulded into the battery top makes sure each cell is topped-up correctly, and prevents overfilling. Larger cell cavities within the casing contain more electrolyte and give the battery more power than others of the same size, and the case design is said to give extra strength.

"The company has built 20,000 sq. ft of extra factory space at Gracefield for the manufacture of the new battery. The firm is a member of the Chloride Group of London, one of the three biggest battery-making groups in the world.

"The group employs 15,700 people in 19 countries. There are only two other battery-makers in New Zealand: Joseph Lucas Ltd and Amalgamated Batteries Ltd. At present Battery Makers supply about half the replacement car batteries bought in New Zealand, the other two companies supplying the rest in approximately equal shares." [57]

Another change of company name occurred in April 1973:

"Battery Makers of New Zealand Ltd the Lower Hutt-based manufacturers of Exide, Vesta, Rokfire and Chloride lead acid batteries, has changed its name from April 1 to Chloride Batteries New Zealand Ltd. No change in management or company structure is involved." [58]

Chloride Batteries New Zealand (2)

By December 1976, the Lower Hutt factory of the former Battery Makers of New Zealand, now Chloride Batteries New Zealand, had well and truly expanded into the export business:

"New Zealand-made car batteries will be on sale soon in Greece. Chloride Batteries, New Zealand Ltd has an export order for a trial consignment, and the batteries are awaiting shipment. This is the first substantial export order to Europe by a New Zealand battery manufacturer, although Chloride also exports to Fiji and the Pacific." [59]

The overseas markets continued to grow for batteries manufactured by Chloride — as reported by the Christchurch Press in September 1977:

"Chloride Batteries NZ Ltd which has been exporting in a minor way for many years, has recently built up substantial sales in such diverse markets as Kuwait, Nigeria, Greece, Gibraltar, Tripoli, Mauritius, Bahrain, and even England.

"During the first five months of its financial year the company exported 10,000 auto batteries and industrial cells for forklift trucks valued at $270,000, compared with $36,000 during the comparable period a year ago…In terms of quality and price New Zealand-made batteries are fully competitive with any produced overseas." [60]

The company's exporting success continued into 1979:

"Chloride Batteries New Zealand Ltd will start next week on production of 5100 standard batteries worth more than $100,000 which it will ship out late next month to a Los Angeles trucking firm with retail outlets throughout California…The American sale follows another secured for Chloride by the New Zealand Export Import Corporation in Venezuela last year for more than 2000 car batteries." [61]

However, by December 1982, Chloride's overseas sales were not matched by those at home:

"In Wellington, Chloride Batteries dismissed 11 workers at the Seaview plant on Tuesday afternoon. Confirming the lay-offs yesterday, a spokesman for the company said that Chloride Batteries, like the rest of the car components industry, was feeling the effects of the severe motor industry downturn. The plant employed about 120 workers up to the dismissals." [62]

In September 1985, the Christchurch Press reported that a new global entity was to acquire ownership of the Lower Hutt factory:

"Dunlop Olympic Ltd will acquire the international battery manufacturing operations of the United Kingdom-based Chloride Group PLC on October 1 under an Australian $69 million…agreement approved by Chloride shareholders last night.

"Dunlop Olympic's managing director, Mr John Gough, said that approval by Chloride shareholders at a meeting in London was the final step in clearing the way for Dunlop Olympic to become one of the world's largest producers of automotive, traction, and stationary batteries.

"The acquisition includes Chloride Inc which operates five factories in the United States and one in Vancouver, Canada; the 49 per cent Chloride interest in Monterrey Chloride of Mexico; Chloride Batteries New Zealand which has a plant at Lower Hutt; and Chloride Batteries Australia Ltd which has plants at Padstow in New South Wales and Elizabeth in South Australia.

"The company planned to use the Chloride operations to form a new international battery division, with 13 factories world-wide and about 3000 employees." [63]

Dunlop Olympic

As recorded by Greg Bell of the Australian National University Archives:

"In 1888, John Boyd Dunlop invented the pneumatic bicycle tyre, forming the Dunlop Pneumatic Tyre Company in Dublin in 1889. In 1893, the Company opened a branch office and factory in Melbourne's Chinatown district. In 1899, a Canadian syndicate purchased the Australasian rights from the UK Company and floated the Dunlop Pneumatic Tyre Company of Australasia Limited in Victoria on 30 August 1899.

"In 1905 the Company purchased its main rival Barnet Glass & Sons Proprietary Limited. In 1908, Barnet Glass created another public company, Barnet Glass Rubber Company Limited which also merged with Dunlop in 1929, being fully absorbed in 1937.

"On 16 August 1920 the company changed its name to the Dunlop Rubber Company of Australia Limited and became a listed public company on the Melbourne Stock Exchange, and since then has remained the parent company of the group.

"After merging with the Perdriau Rubber Company in 1929, the company adopted the name Dunlop Perdriau Limited, which changed to Dunlop Australia Limited in 1967. In 1980, the company acquired Olympic Consolidated Industries and a half-share in Olex Cables (which became a wholly-owned subsidiary in 1981). To reflect this merger, the name of the company was changed to Dunlop Olympic Limited." [64]

With its 1985 acquisition, Dunlop Olympic Limited retained Chloride Batteries New Zealand as a subsidiary operating from the Lower Hutt factory.

In February 1988, another reorganisation of the New Zealand battery industry occurred with the transfer of brand names to Chloride Batteries from a struggling Amalgamated Batteries of Christchurch.

"Pacific Dunlop has announced that the brand names of Amalgamated Batteries, the Christchurch firm, would be transferred to its subsidiary, Chloride Batteries New Zealand. As reported, 78 workers were laid off at Amalgamated Batteries' Woolston factory earlier this month, because it was no longer considered viable. Marketing operations, senior staff, and Amalgamated's branch network would all continue unchanged, Pacific Dunlop said." [65]

Battery Equipment Manufacturers

Battery Equipment Manufacturers Limited was registered at Auckland in May 1937 — established as:

"…manufacturers of and dealers in electric storage batteries with a Capital of £10,000.

"Original shareholders were: G C W Reid, H W Shore, F W L Michie, R M Hacket, W H McCorkindale." [66]

A year later, the Auckland Star reported:

"The modern trend in factory design is fully reflected in the imposing building recently completed in Broadway, Newmarket for Battery Equipment Manufacturers Ltd, a New Zealand company formed early in 1937 to manufacture in the Dominion the well-known Erg battery and battery parts generally.

"This enterprising company early decided to make its factory second to none for its purpose in New Zealand. To this end the construction of the building was undertaken in collaboration with the health authorities to ensure that operatives would work under the best possible conditions. Overseas experts and technicians were co-opted to ensure that the plant installed was the latest in storage battery manufacture.

"Experts were also brought from Australia to establish the factory and train New Zealanders who will comprise the future operatives of the company. The firm acquired the New Zealand manufacturing rights of Erg Batteries Ltd, Sydney, and is fortunate in its arrangements with this overseas concern, which has made such notable progress over the last decade.

"In order to ensure that the past high standard of Erg batteries will be maintained in the New Zealand product, Battery Equipment Manufacturers Ltd have secured the services of Mr J Pryor, one of Australasia's leading battery experts, who for the past 10 years has been directing the manufacture of Erg batteries in Australia…" [67]

Following completion of the new factory, the ERG Battery was widely advertised:

"Battery Equipment Manufacturers Ltd — New premises at 436 Broadway, Newmarket — The famous ERG Battery now manufactured by New Zealanders for New Zealand conditions." [68]

And an innovative service was introduced by May 1939:

"Something entirely new is being introduced for the convenience of Auckland motorists by the modern firm of Battery Equipment Manufacturers Ltd of Broadway, Newmarket, makers of the well-known ERG battery. Any motorist may call at their up-to-date service station and receive prompt, courteous battery inspection and service. This service is available at all times, to all motorists, is entirely free and places no obligation on the motorist." [69]

Amalgamated Batteries

Vega Batteries Limited and Amalgamated Batteries Limited were both registered at Christchurch in 1935 and 1936, respectively. [70]

By December 1940, with war constraints limiting the fortunes of motor vehicle and parts selling, Vega Batteries, Battery Equipment Manufacturers, and Amalgamated Batteries amalgamated to form Amalgamated Batteries Limited, based at Garlands Road, Woolston, Christchurch. [71]

Nevertheless, the Woolston plant was kept very busy supplying the war effort:

"The South Island's sole battery producing plant is a factory in Woolston, Amalgamated Batteries Ltd, which during World War II supplied more than 50,000 units to forces in the Pacific…" [72]

A 1960 Christchurch Press report provided an update on the progress of Amalgamated Batteries:

"The company has been operating in Christchurch since 1936 and has a range of 40 sizes, the biggest being a 12-volt, 25-plate battery for a large diesel earthmoving machine. A change noticed by the plant is a trend in the motor vehicle industry's requirements towards 12-volt electrical systems. Six-volt batteries now only account for about half the production for vehicles. Batteries are also produced for caravans, fishing boats, fire alarm circuits, holiday bach power, and emergency installations for hospitals and other public buildings." [73]

In April 1961, Amalgamated Batteries acquired another battery company — as reported by the Christchurch Press:

"Amalgamated Batteries Ltd, Christchurch, and Solarc Storage Battery Co Ltd, Wellington, have amalgamated. The amalgamation took effect as from April 1. This brings together two of the oldest battery manufacturing companies in New Zealand. The management of both companies will remain unchanged but the merchandising policies will be considerably extended by the manufacturer of other lines associated with the motor industry in particular.

"The merger brings Solarc Storage Battery Co into the group of Amalgamated Batteries subsidiaries — Phoenix Metal Co, Battery Supplies Ltd, and Auto Electrics Ltd. Mr R. Carruthers, managing director of Solarc, will join the board of Amalgamated Batteries." [74]

Solarc Storage Battery Company

As early as August 1933, "full-life, fresh Solarc Storage Batteries" were being advertised by SIMMS Motor Units (NZ) Ltd, Lower Taranaki St, Wellington [75]

However, the Solarc Storage Battery Company Limited was not incorporated at Wellington until 7 June 1934 [76] with a "Capital of £1000. Original subscribers were named as Robert Carruthers, Thelma D Carruthers, and Alice M Carruthers. Objects: To carry on business of electrical storage battery manufacturers and retailers and general incidental." [77]

The Solarc Storage Battery Company operated from a factory at 80 Tory Street, Wellington. [78]

In June 1939, the company had applied to the Bureau of Industry for a licence to manufacture storage battery plates for the Besco Battery Equipment Company Limited. [79]

Following the merger of Solarc Storage Batteries with Amalgamated Batteries, the latter company suffered a profit downturn — as reported by the Christchurch Press in December 1962:

"Steep Fall In Net Profit — The consolidated net profit of Amalgamated Batteries. Ltd., Christchurch, fell to £8607 from £18,793 the year before. In his report, the chairman (Mr H W Shove) says the result for the year has been disappointing.

"'It was confidently hoped that the amalgamation with the Solarc Storage Battery Company Ltd would result in improved trading figures being shown this year, but unfortunately considerably increased competition has been experienced which has offset the anticipated improvement.'" [80]

However, by 1970 and 1971, the financial position had improved:

"The net profit of Amalgamated Batteries Ltd, Christchurch — at $101,227 — slightly exceeded the estimate made by the directors in August. This result represents an increase of 66 per cent on last year's profit.

"The export trade had again been buoyant, and the market in New Zealand, particularly for batteries, had shown a substantial increase, said the chairman (Mr R G Compton) in the directors' report.

"'The rise in costs had been covered by the increased turnover…A new building has already been completed which provides additional manufacturing space, as well as a large area for the storage of raw materials,' Mr Compton said." [81]

"Production and sales of Amalgamated Batteries Ltd for the six months to February 28 [1971] have again exceeded any previous corresponding period, the directors say in their midyear report. The extension to the factory buildings at Christchurch is now in use and with the new plant installed therein production is proceeding at an accelerated rate." [82]

By March 1979, it was the turn of Amalgamated Batteries to be absorbed by a larger entity:

"The Cable Price Downer Ltd offer for Amalgamated Batteries Ltd has been declared unconditional. A substantial majority of Amalgamated Batteries shareholders had accepted the offer, and C.P.D. expected to reach 90 per cent before it closed yesterday." [83] CPD paid $1.7 million for Amalgamated Batteries. [84]

But the writing was on the wall for New Zealand's motor industry by 1988 — as reported by the Christchurch Press in February that year:

"Seventy-eight workers at Amalgamated Batteries, Ltd factory in Woolston were laid off yesterday without warning…

"'We have tried every avenue to secure profitable business, including an export drive into Australia and the Pacific. But the impact of high exchange rates, the depressed state of the car assembly industry, local discounting, and competition from low-cost Asian imports have all contributed to a decision to close the plant,' [the general manager, Mr John Goffin,] said…

"'There is now no prospect that the plant can be made viable and the situation can only deteriorate with the impending removal of import licence protection during 1988…'

"'Chloride Batteries NZ Ltd has acquired the rights to Amalgamated Batteries' name and range of automotive products. Chloride intended to market A.B.L. batteries so that customer services and arrangements would be unchanged,' said Mr Goffin.

"The secretary of the Canterbury branch of the Engineers' Union, Mr Bob Todd, said the impact of the closing would be 'quite horrendous.'

"'It was another sad day for manufacturing in Canterbury,' he said.

"'The reasons advanced by the company, Cable Price Downer, for the closing need to be questioned as the notice of such large corporate bodies is not always that which it appears on the surface,' he said.

"'Another question that must again be addressed is the morality of allowing countries where the labour market is exploited and health regulations are non-existent to freely import car batteries or any other commodity into our country at the expense of New Zealand workers' jobs,' said Mr Todd

"Amalgamated Batteries has about 25 other staff in Christchurch and 60 at branches throughout New Zealand." [85]

By July 1988, Cable Price Downer had closed the factory doors at Amalgamated Batteries:

"During the latest year [1988] CPD [Cable Price Downer] sold off Neeco and closed other firms, including Amalgamated Batteries of Christchurch. Amalgamated Batteries had the lowest battery market share in New Zealand — about 25 per cent — and was further away from the market — Auckland — than any of its competitors…

"Exports were becoming unprofitable because of the high New Zealand dollar and imports were becoming a problem. The last nail in the coffin was when the parent firm of a rival manufacturer [Chloride] bought the firm from which Amalgamated Batteries bought its technology rights." [86]

The Willard Battery

"The Willard Storage Battery Company, an early leader in the development and manufacture of automobile batteries, was founded by Theodore A Willard as the Willard Electric & Battery Co [of Cleveland, USA] in 1896…

"Willard reorganized the company as the Willard Storage Battery Company in 1902. The company produced batteries for use by dentists and physicians, in Edison phonographs, and for lighting railroad cars, and made its first battery for automobile ignition in 1908.

"Beginning in 1910 Willard produced batteries and electric lighting accessories and sold them directly to individual automobile owners, unable to convince the manufacturers of their viability until 1912. Business then grew quickly; the company built a 15-acre plant…in 1915 and had contracts to supply batteries to 85% of the automobile factories in the U.S. by 1918.

"The company grew with the automobile industry…In November 1930 Willard had more than 2,500 employees, additional plants in Toronto and Los Angeles, and distributors in 89 countries. The company produced batteries for submarines during World War II and was a pioneer in the development of small, hand-sized batteries…" [87]

As early as August 1917, Willard Storage Batteries were offered for sale in New Zealand by service stations represented by Thomas Ballinger & Company of Wellington [88] and, in 1918, by A & T Burt of the South Island. [89]

Whereas many early batteries used various insulation materials such as wood in their construction, Willard Batteries were unique in their use of threaded rubber — as reported by the Gisborne Times in June 1920:

"T H stands for 'Threaded Rubber'…the insulation found only Willard batteries with the red trade mark. The insulation that lasts as long as the plates, so that 90 per cent of those that buy the red trade-marked Willard have no re-insulation bills to pay." [90]

By December 1920, the British entity, The Electric Construction Company, had established a presence in New Zealand as the Auckland district agents for Willard Batteries — as reported by the Auckland Star:

"The Electric Construction Company of New Zealand, Auckland district agents for the famous Willard storage battery for motor cars have now opened a large new service station at the High Street corner of Victoria Street.

"Over 75 per cent of the American cars are fitted with Willard batteries and the demand for this make of accumulator, together with the free testing and attention which go with it has grown to such an extent that the original service station premises were much too small…" [91]

Of course, 'British was Best' during the 1920s so a British version of the Willard Battery was a welcome development:

"British Starter Batteries—The British C.A.V. Willard Batteries have been expected on this market for some time. These have now arrived. The C.A.V. Co. has the patent rights for the Willard Threaded Rubber Insulators for the British Empire. The name C.A.V. on electrical goods has always stood for quality. These British Starter Batteries are being sold at remarkably low prices…" [92]

By October 1923, the Electric Construction Company of New Zealand had premises at both Auckland and Hamilton:

"Whatever your car — Willard has the right battery for it, of the right size, capacity and voltage. That's because Willard has installed more batteries on more makes of cars than anybody else. We don't guess, we know what your car requires. Electric Construction Co of NZ, Electric House, 52 Fort St, Auckland and at Collingwood Street, Hamilton. Representing Willard Batteries (Threaded Rubber Insulation) and CW Batteries (Wood Separators)" [93]

As reported by the Waikato Times in September 1928 and June 1929, the Electric Construction Company was manufacturing Willard Batteries at its Collingwood, Hamilton factory:

"68 per cent of car manufacturers fit Willard Batteries as standard equipment. The Electric Construction Co, Collingwood Street, maintains an efficient plant and employs a Willard expert of many years' experience in the actual manufacture of storage batteries." [94]

"The test of experience has proved to many car and radio owners that Willard batteries are the most reliable and economical. Leading men, explorers, aviators, and others endorse these remarks because they have used Willard batteries and found them to stand for all that is claimed of them. Full stocks of Willard Batteries are held by the Electric Construction Company of New Zealand, Collingwood Street. Here also are full supplies of Delco-Remy and Auto-Lite fittings and parts." [95]

Again, in May 1939, the Waikato Times advertised the manufacture of Willard Batteries at Hamilton:

"The Electric Construction Company, whose head office is in Auckland, have a large branch office, workshops and showrooms in Collingwood Street, Hamilton…Adjoining the showroom, this company have their own battery service station and workshop where the famous Willard Batteries are sold and serviced by experts…" [96]

Electric Construction Company

Long before it had become agents for the Willard Battery, the Electric Construction Company of London and Wolverhampton had established a presence in New Zealand as the providers of battery power for the country's new electric trams:

"The [Wellington] City Council has accepted the tender of McArtney, McIlroy and Co, England, for the erection of the City Electric Tramway, the amount being £112,884. The tender of the Electric Construction Co was accepted for the power house, at £26,353. [97]

Since 1890, the Electric Construction Company had been providing such services to England's first electric trams — as reported by the New Zealand Times:

"The advantages of electricity as a motive power on tramway lines seem to have been satisfactorily demonstrated by the arrangement entered into between the North Metropolitan Tramway Company and the Electric Traction Company…

"The motors used by the Electric Traction Company are those of Mosers Immisch and Co and the batteries those manufactured by the Electric Construction Company. The cost of an accumulator car is not more than that of an ordinary car with its complement of 10 horses…" [98]

As early as May 1893, the Electric Construction Company had representation for its products in New Zealand:

"Persons wishing to secure the latest and most improved machinery could not do better than purchase it from Messrs John Chambers and Son, whose show-rooms are at Fort-street, Auckland, and Stuart-street, Dunedin. This firm are the sole authorised vendors of the machinery manufactured by…the Electric Construction Corporation (Limited). The firm's Fort-street show-room is a credit to them in the matter of general arrangements. The machinery displayed here is in the finest order and of the greatest variety..." [99]

The Electric Construction Company became a formal New Zealand entity in 1905:

"…for the purpose of constructing the Christchurch electric tramways — up to that time the largest single engineering contract placed in New Zealand (£260,000)." [100]

By 1911, the Electric Construction Company of New Zealand had established a head office in High Street, Auckland — as recorded by a New Zealand Herald advertisement:

"Lithanode Accumulators For Ignition and Lighting. Red Seal Dry Cells; Metallic Filament Lamps all voltages and candle-power; Electric Motors, Lifts, and Dynamos; Watchmen's Portable Electric Lamps; Electric Novelties of all kinds. Electric Construction Company of NZ. 38 and 40, High Street…" [101]

As the market for electrical goods grew, so did the line of products sold by the Electric Construction Company — as reported by the Auckland Star in December 1921:

"The extent to which electricity has proved its worth as an important adjunct to national progress is to be seen in its universal use and demand as a modern facility for power for all purposes…For some years past the Electric Construction Company of New Zealand, with its head office at Auckland, has given a fine lead. At the large premises in High Street the smallest item to the largest in the electrical line may be obtained or arranged for on a business efficiency basis satisfactory to all customers…" [102]

The 'largest in the electrical line' was to include electric elevators — as reported by The New Zealand Herald in October 1923:

"A predominant position in all matters connected with the installation and maintenance of modern electric lifts is being maintained in Auckland by the Electric Construction Company of New Zealand. This up-to-date firm is furnishing lift appliances in most of the important new buildings at present in course of erection in the city, and is responsible for some of the largest pieces of work of this kind in the Dominion…

"Among the more notable contracts now being executed by the Electric Construction Company is the installation of a complete electric elevator system consisting of seven lifts in the huge new premises erected for Messrs Milne and Choyce Ltd in Queen Street." [103]

Some sixty years later, in 1984, the Electric Construction Company Limited was referred to as one of the main New Zealand installers of lifts and escalators. [104]

The Electric Construction Company of NZ Limited (52837), registered as a limited liability company from 12 August1955, having ceased to operate, was placed into liquidation on the 8th day of March 2004 [105] and the company was removed from the Companies Office Register on 23 June 2006. [106]

Young Brothers

Another New Zealand manufacturer and retailer of Exide and Willard Batteries, and other electrical components celebrated seventy years in the automotive spare parts business with the opening of another showroom at Blenheim Road, Christchurch — as reported by the Christchurch Press in June 1988:

"It was 70 years ago when Young Brothers first set up their business in Timaru. The original Young brothers, Percy and Jim, recognised the demands being created by the growing automobile industry for batteries, electrical services and replacement parts. They began importing batteries and assembling them in their Timaru workshops.

"Contacts with overseas suppliers built up, and in 1925 Young Brothers moved into a new two-storey building in Timaru. In the early 1930s Mr P G Young travelled overseas to negotiate agencies with the well-known suppliers. This was soon followed by the establishment of Young Brothers branches in the main centres, and the setting up of the Willard Battery Service network.

"In these early years, a close relationship was formed with General Motors, and Young Brothers today are the largest New Zealand distributors of many General Motors products…

"Throughout the next three decades Young Brothers continued as an importer and wholesaler of automotive spare parts, dealing also direct with the public as retailers of parts and accessories.

"In 1968 they opened yet another new building in Timaru, and in 1975 another branch in Christchurch…To add to their two Christchurch branches and the ones in Timaru, Dunedin and Gore, Young Brothers took over a Wellington company in 1987 and created branches in Hamilton, Nelson and Blenheim Road [Christchurch] this year.

"In 1980 they began using a computer system, and have extended their product base to offer a wider range of parts and accessories, while continuing to hold the largest stocks of A.C. Delco, Bella, VDO and other well-known products in the South Island. The Agip oil range, a new product recommended by the most prestigious car manufacturers in the world, is one of the new ranges Young Brothers now stock…" [107]

"They believe that their success is due, at least in part, to the experience of their staff. Many have been with Young Brothers for over 30 years, and have come to know their trade and their customers backwards. Another factor contributing to their stability is their shareholding. After 70 years, Young Brothers is still a private company with only 19 shareholders — the Young family and the members of the company's staff. Although the Blenheim Road building is the latest step in Young Brothers' programme of expansion, it is not the last. The company intends to continue its progress and enlarge its share of the New Zealand automotive spare parts market." [108]

In celebration of the opening of their latest retail premises at 55 Blenheim Road in June 1988, Young Brothers advertised some of the products then for sale, including:

"Hella Driving Lights, stereo cassettes, car speakers, car care products, car seat covers, Agip oil, AC Delco oil filters, and the Willard Battery…" [109]

In April 1993, Young Brothers registered Willard Batteries (NZ) Limited but the company traded as such only until 1995. [110]

Hella New Zealand

"Hella, the lighting and accessory manufacturer to the motor industry was established in Germany in June 1899 as the Westphalia Metals Industry Limited and began operations supplying lanterns and horns to the developing German motor industry.

"After World War II, Hella became the original equipment supplier for the Volkswagen Beetle and in the 1950s also supplied many of Ford Germany's models.

"Hella was the first manufacturer to receive European type approval for the asymmetric dipped beam headlight in 1957. The company was in the forefront of halogen headlights which were introduced in 1962, auxiliary brake lights in the '70s, plastic lenses during the '80s and, most recently [1999], xenon gas discharge headlights…

"Hella New Zealand Limited was established in East Tamaki in [March] 1973 and shifted to…Pakuranga premises in 1980. Before the demise of the local motor vehicle assembly industry, Hella New Zealand had changed its focus from being a supplier to the local industry to exporting…" [111]

General Electric Company

Osram automobile lamps, supplied by the General Electric Company, were fitted to many vehicle models assembled in New Zealand.

"General Electric Company (GE), a multinational conglomerate headquartered in Boston, Massachusetts, was incorporated in 1892 following a series of mergers between various companies owned and operated by Thomas Alva Edison and the Thomson-Houston Electric Company.

"For well over a century, General Electric was one of the largest and most diversified corporations in the world, spanning a wide range of sectors and industries." [112]

General Electric was established as the New Zealand General Electric Co Limited at Wellington in June 1936 with a Capital of £500. The majority shareholder was listed as British General Electric Co Limited, 498 shares; J L Griffin & J W R Saunders, 1 share each…" [113]

The New Zealand General Electric Co Limited was registered until struck off in May 1991. [114]

Osram

Meanwhile, the Osram light bulb was first registered as a trade mark in Berlin in 1906 and Osram as a company (Osram Werke G.m.b.H. KG) was formed when Auergesellschaft, S&H and AEG merged their lamp production facilities in Berlin in 1919.

In 1925, Osram produced the two-filament headlight lamp, the Bilux, which enabled high and low beam in one light for the first time and, in 1929, General Electric became a shareholder in OSRAM Werke G.m.b.H. KG.

Osram halogen lamps were produced in 1967 and the first coloured LED was introduced to automotive dashboards in 1974.

In 1978, Siemens AG became the sole shareholder of Osram GmbH. [115]

Lawrence & Hanson

Some of the first Osram lamps were offered to the New Zealand public by Lawrence & Hanson — as advertised by the Dominion in July 1909:

"Lawrence & Hanson, Electrical Engineers & Importers, 45 And 47 Cuba Street, Head Office, Sydney. Also At Melbourne. Sole Agents for the General Electric Co Ltd, England. Also For Osram Lamps. Wholesale Suppliers of All Classes Of Electric Appliances…" [116]

These advertisements were followed a few months later by a warning:

"Public are Warned against So-called 'Improved' Osram Lamps. All genuine Osram Lamps are marked on the globe as 'Osram Patent G.E.C.' — Sole Agents for Australasia: Lawrence & Hanson, Electrical Importers, Cuba Street, Wellington." [117]

Lawrence & Hanson was established as a New Zealand-registered company in 1916 and by the 1920s Lawrence & Hanson Electrical Co Limited traded from branches at Auckland, New Plymouth, Hastings, Christchurch, and Dunedin — also selling electric lamps of the Philips brand. By 1927, the company also traded exclusively as wholesalers of a range of electronic products. The company was deregistered in February 1939. [118]

Champion Spark Plugs

The first Champion Spark Plug was made by Albert Champion at Toledo, Ohio in 1905. However, Albert Champion soon sold his interest in the Champion Spark Plug factory to fellow shareholders, the Stranahan family, and later set up a rival factory at Flint Michigan making AC spark plugs — as described later. [119]

In the meantime, by 1916, the Champion Spark Plug had been improved — as reported by the North Otago Times:

"The Champion Spark Plug Co in the United States, have announced the issue of a new type of priming plug called the All-in-one Champion. It is of the pet-cock type and, the makers claim, will start any motor on a single turn." [120]

The number of spark plugs produced reflected the world's increasing number of motor vehicles using them by 1925:

"The Champion Spark Plug Company produced 40,000,000 plugs in 1925. The capacity of the plant is now 75,000,000 a year… [121] The company Is the largest of its kind in the world, supplying more than two-thirds of all spark plugs used." [122]

That use continued through to 1936:

"Advice has been received from Canada that the Chrysler organisation has adopted Champion spark plugs as standard equipment. This means that Champions are now furnished as original equipment to every motor car manufacturer on the American Continent where the spark plug contract is open to competition. In addition to the Chrysler organisation, seventeen of the largest motor car firms in America have adopted the Champion spark plug." [123]

In the meantime, the Australasian market was keeping pace with the worldwide demand, necessitating a new factory closer to the market — as reported by the Evening Star in 1930:

"The Champion Spark Plug Company is to open a large factory in Sydney shortly from where it is planned to supply the New Zealand market." [124]

As the New Zealand vehicle assembly industry continued to churn out more vehicles, a local spark plug factory was also needed — as reported by the Christchurch Press in April 1965:

"A factory to be established near Auckland this year will manufacture a complete line of automotive and marine spark plugs. The Champion Spark Plug Company of the United States, and Fisher and Paykel Ltd will be associated in the new factory to produce Champion spark plugs which have been sold in New Zealand since 1921.

"The president of the American company, Mr R A Stranahan, said yesterday that the decision to begin manufacture in New Zealand had been prompted by the long association with the Dominion, the prosperous state of the New Zealand economy and a significant increase in vehicle registration." [125]

Accordingly, Champion Spark Plug NZ Limited was incorporated on 21 February 1966 with Champion Spark Plug Company, Toledo, Ohio as the majority shareholder and Fisher and Paykel Limited with a 33.3 per cent holding. [126]

In 1988, a consolidation of Champion's manufacturing activities resulted in the end of its partnership with Fisher & Paykel:

"Fisher and Paykel Industries Ltd has announced the end of its 22year partnership with Champion Spark Plug New Zealand Ltd. Mr Don Rowlands, group chief executive of Fisher and Paykel Industries, said that as a result of Champion's wish to restructure its Australasian activities, his company has sold its 33.3 per cent shareholding of the New Zealand company to Champion.

"Mr David M Wilson, managing director of Champion Spark Plug Co, Australasia, explained that the move to consolidate Champion's activities and corporate structure, in the Pacific Region is a positive step. Since the partnership began in February, 1966, more than 100 million Champion Spark Plugs have been manufactured and sold in New Zealand." [127]

The sale of its interest in Champion resulted in a profit increase for the company to 30 September 1988:

"Fisher and Paykel Industries, Auckland-based whiteware manufacturer, increased its total profit 13 per cent to $17,544,000 in the six months to September 30…an extraordinary profit of $723,000 ($1.1M) came from the selling of the group's 33.3 per cent interest in Champion Spark Plug New Zealand and a surplus building." [128]

In 1989, Champion was incorporated into the Cooper Industries Group, a Texas-based electrical products manufacturer. [129]

AC Spark Plugs

As previously noted, after selling his interest in the original business making Champion Spark Plugs, Albert Champion moved to Flint, Michigan where he started another company called "The Champion Ignition Company" making, of course, spark plugs.

"He was a major supplier to General Motors (GM) and expanded his business through WWI. In 1922, Albert Champion renamed the company 'AC Spark Plug Company' (the AC standing for Albert Champion).

"He was making a quality product and in 1927 his spark plugs were in the engine that flew Lindbergh from New York to Paris.

"After Mr Champion died in 1927, GM purchased the stock of his company and in 1933 AC Spark Plug became a Division of GM. By then the products being made by AC Spark Plug included: Spark Plugs, Speedometers, Air Cleaners, Oil Filters and Gasoline Filters, and dashboard Gauges." [130]

AC Delco

"AC Delco is an American automotive parts brand owned by General Motors… Factory parts for vehicles manufactured by GM are consolidated under the ACDelco brand, which also offers aftermarket parts for non-GM vehicles.

"It began with William Durant and his United Motors Corporation, which acquired dozens of smaller parts manufacturers, including Dayton Engineering Laboratories Company (DELCO). When General Motors came along, the United Motors Corporation name was changed to United Motors Service [in 1918] and adding AC Spark Plug to the roster…United Motors Service became a fully integrated division of General Motors in 1944

"In the 1950s, United Motors Service branched out, and began providing sales, service and training for AC rebuilt fuel pumps, DELCO batteries, and DELCO radio service parts…Eventually, AC Spark Plug and DELCO were united by General Motors to form ACDelco." [131]

"ACDelco now provides a wide range of quality products for the automotive replacement parts industry, including batteries, spark plugs, oil filters, air filters, wiper blades, and brake components. ACDelco also offers a comprehensive range of oils, fluids and cleaners. [132]

"In 1964, an AC spark plug and oil filter manufacturing facility was opened by General Motors NZ in Petone" [133]

Auto Electrical Wiring
Hamal Industries

It is thought that Hamish Robert McLean founded Robt McLean Limited at Christchurch in November 1960 and Robt. McLean (Mfg.) Limited as a subsidiary in 1965. [134] The latter company, trading from 353 St Asaph Street, Christchurch from at least September 1966, became Hamal Products Limited as of 2 April 1969. [135]

In July of 1969, Hamal Products advertised:

"Auto Electrical Wiring Factory" seeking a "…Young man 17-19 years required for general factory duties. Good wages and prospects to successful applicant. Apply in person to: Factory Manager, Hamal Products, 353 St Asaph Street, Christchurch." [136]

However, by September 1970, the St Asaph Street premises became too small for the business, occupied by the Robt McLean Limited factory and its trading subsidiary, Hamal Products, and a move was made to a much larger building at 105-109 Victoria Street — described by a Christchurch Press advertisement as:

"…A Complete Automotive Electrical Centre, Elaborate Fully Equipped Workshop, experienced engineers…" [137]

A second advertisement described the company as:

"…Manufacturers of Automotive and Marine Wiring Harness, Battery and Earth Straps, Auto Electrical Accessories….a completely new industry to New Zealand…" [138]

A news item on the same page noted:

"…this company now employs a staff of 22 manufacturing a wide range of electrical components and dealing directly with wholesalers, motor assembly plants and home appliance manufacturers." [139]

In 1971, Hamal Products Limited was bought by Christchurch businessman, Bruce Reynolds Guyon Carey — as described by a profile of him and the company published in 2017 by the New Zealand Rolls-Royce & Bentley Club Inc:

"Hamal Products later became Hamal Industries Ltd [April 1976], [140] manufacturing and supplying electrical cabling, terminals, and other products to the motor assembly plants in Porirua, where Todd Motors built mainly French designs before settling upon Mitsubishis, and the factory then building British Motor Corporation products in Nelson. ["One of the cars assembled by Todd Motors, with Hamal components, was the Talbot, remembered as a thoroughly competent car with excellent handling qualities."]

"It is perhaps forgotten that Triumphs, Jaguars, Land Rovers, and the Leyland P76s were built there, along with the Honda Accord, and Hamal were closely linked with building components for this factory.

"In the days before the arrival of used cars from Japan, there were at one time twelve car assembly plants in New Zealand, employing 6,000 staff, and Hamal supplied parts for Holden, Mitsubishi, Toyota, Mazda, Suzuki and Subaru.

"During the mid-1990s everything changed, although the expertise built up made the company well able to further diversify, to provide cabling to many New Zealand manufacturers, fibre optic cables to telecommunication companies, and some terminals to British companies, including Jaguar.

"Bruce retired in 1995 from the day to day running of Hamal, in favour of his elder son Mike, but remained Chairman of the Board until the company was bought by Tyco Electronics in 2001." [141]

A New Zealand business mentoring and consulting firm, Blue Gum Consulting Limited, once described Hamal Industries Limited as:

"A privately owned manufacturing company…built on the core skills of a wire harness manufacturing company, diversifying into manufacture of wire harness and cable assemblies for industries requiring cable assemblies and wire harnessing for power, data, radio frequency, fibre optics, and a combination of these used to provide assemblies to the aerospace and defence industry, to the point where the company was sold following nine years of strong growth.

"A multinational company, Tyco Electronics, purchased Hamal Industries, in which the market development functions within the aerospace and defence industries were continued for a further seven years." [142]

As a result of its sale to Tyco Electronics, an entity ultimately owned by European interests, the name of Hamal Industries Limited was changed to Harecroft Holdings Limited in May 2001. [143]

Standard Telephones and Cables

Standard Telephones and Cables was incorporated as a British company in 1910 manufacturing and selling United States-designed telephones and exchanges. [144]

In February 1927, Standard Telephones and Cables (Australasia) Limited had established itself in New Zealand with headquarters at 156 Lambton Quay, Wellington [145] and then 24-26 Balance Street, Wellington from 13 May 1927. [146]

As the Christchurch Press reported in June 1930, Standard Telephones and Cables (Australasia) was responsible for the first traffic lights to be installed in Christchurch. The report also described how the traffic was to be controlled by this innovation:

"'What people do not understand is that the automatic system of traffic control regulates all traffic, whether motor, bicycle, or pedestrian,' said Cr. H T J Thacker yesterday, referring to the system to be installed on trial at the intersection of Colombo and Cashel streets. The equipment has already been ordered from Standard Telephones and Cables (Australasia) Ltd…

"Cr. Thacker explained…'There was a red light on top of the apparatus, an amber light in the centre, and a green light at the bottom. The red light showing meant that traffic should stop. When the amber light shone it was a sign that all traffic should get ready to move; when the green light flashed it should move.'

"'All users of the street at this intersection would have to abide by these signs. Cyclists and pedestrians could not go on at their own sweet will in opposition to the signs from the lights…'" [147]

A New Zealand subsidiary of Standard Telephones & Cables, Standard Telephones & Cables (New Zealand) Limited was registered in November 1967. [148] By early 1973, the company had opened a plant at Martinborough, manufacturing communications and data transmission equipment, and then another at Masterton later that year:

"Standard Telephones and Cables (NZ) Ltd, which opened a plant in Martinborough earlier this year, will expand to Masterton next May with a staff of 50 to assemble electrical products. The Martinborough plant, which has 24 workers on the same task, will continue operations. [149]

In 1974, "Standard Telephones and Cables NZ Limited started making wiring looms…for Todd Motors' Hillman Hunters…By the eighties, ST&C was manufacturing wiring looms for New Zealand-built Toyotas, Nissans, Hondas, Mitsubishis, Fords…and for Britax Australia to export to the US…" [150]

However, by November 1982, the downturn in car sales affected the production of wiring looms at Masterton:

"Masterton's Standard Telephones and Cables (NZ) Ltd, which produces wiring looms for cars, will lay off 36 of its 160 workers on November 30 according to the company's product line manager, Mr M J Gates. The lay-offs resulted from a dramatic reduction in orders, caused by the downturn in new car sales, he said, and further staff might have to be laid off." [151]

By August 1991, Standard Telephones & Cables (New Zealand) Limited had been acquired by the French telecommunications company, Alcatel New Zealand Limited, [152] and although car sales had by then improved, the closure of New Zealand's assembly plants inevitably led to the demise of component manufacturers such as Standard Telephones and Cables/Alcatel — as described by Mark Webster in his book, Assembly — A History of New Zealand Car Production 1921-1998:

"Mitsubishi Motor Corporation was always the biggest client, and after the last Mitsubishi was assembled in New Zealand [in 1998], the Masterton factory closed." [153]

Pan Pacific Auto Electronics

When Pan Pacific Auto Electronics Limited opened its Christchurch branch in 1989, the Christchurch Press described the company's history:

"Pan Pacific Auto Electronics Ltd imports and distributes auto electrical products. Since 1979 it has grown from a truly 'back yard' operation to market challenger within a clearly defined market niche.
The company started making a small range of voltage regulators. Sales were made by one of the founders, Danny Inglis, from the boot of a car. Storage was provided and manufacture conducted in a 60 square metre shed at the back of the family home in Auckland.

"In 1981 a mobile warehouse was introduced to service the Auckland region and the 'family shed' was abandoned for a 500 sq metre warehouse…

"The stock market crash during October 1987 and subsequent impact on the economic climate presented growth opportunities for Pan Pacific. Branches were opened in South Auckland, Hamilton and Palmerston North. Since 1986 sales revenue has increased at an annual compounding rate in excess of 40 per cent…

"Pan Pacific acts as the New Zealand distributor of products from about 67 manufacturers including Robert Bosch, Hella, Wilson (Canada), New Era (Japan), Motorolla (United States) Leece Neville (United States), Mitsubishi (Japan), Hitachi (Japan), Nikko (Japan), Wehrle (Germany), Gates (United States)." [154]

Pan Pacific Auto Electronics continued to prosper, as reported in August 2009:

"PPAEL [Pan Pacific Auto Electronics Limited] began as a family business employing four people in 1979 and operating out of a garage in Henderson. It now employs around 50 people operating from eight branches around New Zealand. Its business is importing and distributing auto electrical products including alternators, starters, cable, lighting, air-conditioning products, and car audio systems." [155]

As of 2024, Pan Pacific Auto Electronics describes itself as "New Zealand's leading distributor of Auto Electrical products" with branches at Auckland, Hamilton, Tauranga, Palmerston North, Wellington, Christchurch, and Dunedin. [156]

The company's current directors and majority shareholders are: David John Edward Cunningham, Heather Gay Cunningham, and John Lindsay Cunningham. [157]

Brake & Clutch Parts

Don Agencies

Don Agencies was first registered as a private company at 79 Tuam Street, Christchurch on 10 December 1936 with a Capital of £1000. The initial shareholders were Sydney Gill and M C Gill of New Brighton, and H L Gill of Dunedin. The company was formed to "Purchase business of agents and importers of Central Trading and Agency Company together with assets, property, and effects." [158]

By September 1937, Don Agencies Limited was advertising itself as the "Factory Wholesale Importers" of "Fully Guaranteed Don Brake Linings" [159] and in January 1949, the company advertised itself as the "Canterbury Distributors of India Super Tyres…" [160]

For its Christchurch workshop at 196 St Asaph Street, Don Agencies advertised for a: "Mechanic for brake shoe relining and Bowden brake cable swaging. Up-to-date equipment and well heated workshop…" in July 1951. [161]

By February 1955, Don Agencies had increased its Capital to £19,500 [162] and to £100,000 in July 1963. [163]

A new headquarters building for Don Agencies was completed at Durham Street, Christchurch in August 1965 — as reported by the Christchurch Press:

"In Christchurch, and all over New Zealand, motoring is growing rapidly. More persons have cars, and they are travelling further. More cars mean more vehicles requiring service and when brake and clutch linings and parts are required the call often goes to a long-established Christchurch firm that now has 10 branches all over New Zealand — Don Agencies Ltd.

"Don Agencies, which has just gone into a new building, has its head office in Christchurch. A wholesale firm, it makes and distributes clutch and brake linings and distributes brake parts, and it is the firm's proud boast that there are very few cars in New Zealand for which it cannot immediately provide brake parts…

"Now a plant in the Durham street building carries out all the finishing processes on the brake linings, for instance fitting linings to brake shoes and drilling for rivets. In the early days all the lining material was woven, but today much of it is moulded. Another new process, and one which the firm was instrumental in introducing to this country, is the bonded lining, which is bonded to the brake shoe instead of being riveted on…

"In the 1950s the firm established branches in most parts of the North Island. Branches were later formed at Hastings and New Plymouth…In addition to brake parts Don Agencies stocks seat belts and air and oil filters. Hydraulic hoses and cylinders are, of course, kept in stock, and the firm makes its own brake cables…" [164]

However, by June 1976 the original family shareholders had either died or retired and the corporate wolves were circling:

"Andrews and Beaven Ltd has received the consent of the Minister of Trade and Industry…for its take-over offer for Don Agencies Ltd. The offer is now declared unconditional without any proviso. A. and B. has now received acceptances for 413,917 shares, or 77.6 per cent, of Don's capital." [165]

The takeover naturally resulted in a new direction for Don Agencies:

"New branch facilities are being established for Don Agencies in Wellington, and plans have been initiated to increase production at the Christchurch plant." [166]

In May 1979, a new General Manager was sought — as advertised by the Christchurch Press:

"Don Agencies Limited has been widely recognised for over 40 years in the motor trade and allied industries as New Zealand's leading manufacturer and importer of Brake Linings and associated Brake and Clutch Parts. The Company, with its Head Office based in Christchurch operates the largest friction material manufacturing and processing Factory in New Zealand and distributes its widely known 'Don' products through its national spread of modern warehouses and brake service depots." [167]

A more comprehensive takeover of Don Agencies Limited occurred in 1983 with the merger of Andrews and Beaven, MSI Corporation Limited, and Repco New Zealand Limited to create a new company, Repco Corporation (NZ) Limited. Repco Corporation of Australia retained a 60 per cent interest in the new company then described as "…one of the largest manufacturing and distribution groups in New Zealand." [168]

However, it was the beginning of the end for Don Agencies — as reported by the Christchurch Press on 5 November 1985:

"The 16 workers employed by Don Agencies Ltd, part of the big Australian-based Repco Corporation, were given one month's notice of redundancy yesterday.

"Repco's New Zealand managing director, Mr Lionel Evans…said from Auckland yesterday that it was sad that the old-established firm of Don Agencies would no longer make brake pads, but it was a question of survival for the corporation.

"A recent report by the Industries Development Commission had forced the corporation to rationalise. The corporation had therefore bought the Auckland firm of Eady's which produces brake pads and would now work towards making the plant more efficient to compete against the expected influx of imports from places such as Southeast Asia, Canada and the United States.

"Mr Evans said it was regrettable that Christchurch would lose its brake pad production and jobs associated with it, but the biggest market in New Zealand was Auckland and it would not make sense to make the pads in Christchurch and freight them north.

"Repco formerly held a 70 per cent interest in Don Agencies but bought it out completely last year. Repco also bought out the Christchurch firm of Andrews and Beaven, and moved its head office to Auckland…Don Agencies would continue as a business entity, and Christchurch would become the centre for making some automotive parts other than brake pads [Mr Evans] said.

"The secretary of the Canterbury branch of the Engineers' Union, Mr Bob Todd, said he had a sneaking suspicion that the corporation would have gone ahead with its plans to rationalise irrespective of the I.D.C. report or Government policy…Another angle was that the union had had a running battle with the company over working conditions, especially over asbestos, used in brake linings. The company had promised to renovate the factory, at a cost of about $30,000, said Mr Todd." [169]

Interior Trim & Fittings
Brugger Industries
    The Brugger Group was founded in New Zealand as Brugger Holdings Limited at Petone, Wellington in November 1947 by Austrian, Frank Brugger. [170]
    By October 1959, Brugger Metalcraft Limited had been established as manufacturers of various metal products including garages. However, as Brugger Industries Limited, the business soon began the more lucrative production of car-seat frames for the car assembly industry — as reported by the Christchurch Press in February 1973:
    "Production of the millionth car-seat frame at the Wainuiomata factory of Brugger Industries Ltd, Wellington, was marked by a ceremony at the factory yesterday. This production figure has been reached in 14 years, and the firm now makes 172 different seats for 60 different vehicles. Some are exported.
    "The company was founded at Petone in 1959 by Mr F Brugger, an Austrian migrant. Within 12 months six men were employed (the present payroll is 200) and seats were being delivered to the Gracefield assembly plant of the Ford Motor Company.
    "That year, 3820 seats were made, and the growth of the business forced the company to move to larger premises in Nelson Street, Petone. The move to larger premises at Wainuiomata took place in 1970. This provided 50,000 sq ft of factory space, and in 1972 a further 24,000 sq ft was added.
    "In December last year, work began on a new 9000 sq ft despatch area, which will be completed in April. The company plans to deliver more than 250,000 seat frames to New Zealand and overseas customers this year. It has also designed a reclining mechanism for car seats which has been accepted by two local vehicle assemblers in preference to overseas products.
    "The company now supplies seats to every motor assembly plant in the country, and since 1968 it has earned $325,000 from the export of collapsible containers (used for shipping automotive components, and carbon black for the rubber industry) and a further $126,000 from the export of car seats and sun visors. The company has designed and developed much of the machinery it uses, including a paint oven." [171]
    With some Government assistance, Brugger Industries had expanded its factory enterprise to the South Island by 1976:
    "The Cabinet had recently approved regional development assistance for Brugger Industries Ltd in Dunedin, the Prime Minister (Mr Muldoon) announced. He told a meeting of the Otago Chamber of Commerce that the company would be making automobile component parts with a high degree of regional content.

"Brugger had been attracted to Dunedin because of the regional development incentives available, the strong engineering base there, and the excellent shipping facilities providing an avenue for exporting to Australia. The concern will make frames and other parts of car seats in a new factory now under construction." [172]

However, just as the 1980s would prove to be the beginning of the end for New Zealand's vehicle assembly industry, so the decade proved to be for its ancillary industries also facing the reduction of tariffs that allowed for cheaper access to the New Zealand market by overseas manufacturers.

One of the first indications of difficulty was reported in October 1982:

"More than 120 workers at three motor-vehicle component factories in Auckland and Wellington will lose their jobs as a result of a reduction in new car sales. The Auckland firm, Brugger Automotive Ltd, which supplies seating to the Ford Motor Company and Nissan Datsun Ltd will lay off 88 employees, half of its work-force.

"The general manager of Brugger, Mr N E Stent, has said that his company, a branch of Brugger Industries, Ltd, had suffered a drop in production of more than 50 per cent since August.

"'We work exclusively with the motor industry and although August was a record month for us, production since then has dropped rapidly,' Mr Stent said." [173]

The following month proved to be even worse for redundancies:

"About 200 more Hutt Valley and Wainuiomata car industry workers face the prospect of Christmas dole queues, after receiving redundancy notices yesterday. The three Wellington companies that announced layoffs blamed the severe slump in the new car market, which has already led to dismissals, extended Christmas shutdowns, and voluntary redundancies.

"In Wainuiomata, redundancies at a car component firm, Brugger Industries, totalled 100; in Petone, 71 New Zealand Motor Corporation workers were laid off; and in Upper Hutt, 18 Repco employees were made redundant. Repco, a component manufacturer, also announced 14 lay-offs at its Panmure plant in Auckland.

"Brugger's managing director, Mr Frank Brugger, said the possibility of more redundancies was high if the slump became worse…Brugger Industries has been in Wainuiomata for 12 years and is one of the town's biggest employers.

"When 71 of NZMC's 258 Petone staff were made redundant yesterday, the plant manager, Mr R Bartlam, said that the company had explored every way to avoid the dismissals. It had investigated and negotiated for the assembly of additional brands entirely new to the Petone plant, but the proposals had not come to fruition. With the market slump and increased stocks, the company had no option but to reduce production, he said." [174]

A year later some improvement had occurred — as reported by the Christchurch Press in November 1983:

"Brugger Industries Ltd, the biggest employer in Wainuiomata…has rehired 120 workers it was forced to lay off last December. The managing director, Mr Frank Brugger, said yesterday that an upturn in the car industry had boosted his firm, which makes mainly car components, furniture and heaters." [175]

In April 1984…"General Motors New Zealand Ltd announced the sale of its plant and land at Petone and part of the plant was let…to Brugger Industries Limited to commence manufacture, including of automotive components, from early 1985." [176]

However, in July 1985, the Brugger Group was acquired by an Owens Group subsidiary:

"Wenrich Investments Ltd completed its acquisition of shares in the Brugger Group yesterday. Wenrich said that it now held all shares in the group except for the 22 per cent interest in Brugger Industries Ltd held by the Australian company of Hendersons Federal Spring Works Pty Ltd." [177]

By March 1988, Brugger Industries Limited remained a subsidiary of the Owens Group but had been renamed Kenson Industries Limited which traded as such until November 1998. [178]

The Component Industry 111

Fabco Industries

Fabco Industries Limited was first established at Auckland K D Plastic Fashions Limited (A 1947/218) in May 1947 and the name of the company was changed to Kaydee Footwear Limited in October 1957. [179]

At that time, the company manufactured and sold plastic sandals and, by 1960, had become an associate company of Plastic Products Limited of Hamilton. [180]

The Kaydee Footwear Limited name was changed to Fabco Industries Limited on 15 January 1970 [181] and, as such, the company was reinvented as a component maker for the motor vehicle industry in April of that year — as reported by the Christchurch Press:

"New Zealand Forest Products Ltd, Bing Harris and Company Ltd, and Williamson Jeffrey Ltd are partners in a new company which will make components for the motor industry. It is named Fabco Industries Ltd and amalgamates the plastics division of Rainster (NZ) Ltd with H A D Jannse Ltd and Board Fabricators Ltd.

"Rainster is a subsidiary of Bing Harris and H A D Jannse is owned by Williamson Jeffrey. New Zealand Forest Products and Sebelin and Duncan Ltd of Palmerston North jointly own Board Fabricators. Forest Products has a further interest in the venture through its holding of 18 per cent of Williamson Jeffrey's ordinary capital." [182]

By October 1980, Fabco Industries was well established as a manufacturer of automotive trim componentry:

"Fabco Industries Limited, East Tamaki Road, Otara, Auckland...Manufacturers of Fine Quality Automotive Trim Componentry...Luxurious Cloth or Vinyl Seats, Door Trim Panels, Sun visors, Headlinings and Many Other Interior Panels and Sound Deadeners...

"Fabco Industries and their subsidiary companies, NZ Tool & Gauge Co (Nelson) Ltd and Raudon Plastics Ltd are constantly seeking better ways to make your car safer, more comfortable and better value.

"Fabco Group products are designed to meet international safety standards and tested to ensure they provide maximum performance and durability. We are pleased to be associated with the development of components for the new Datsun Bluebird and congratulate Nissan on another fine product." [183]

However, Fabco Industries was also affected by the automotive industry downturn of 1982 — as reported on 29 October of that year:

"Another Auckland company, Fabco Ltd, which also makes seating and door panels for the motor industry, will lay off 36 people; 27 from its East Tamaki plant and nine at its Upper Hutt factory near Wellington. The moves follow recent acceptance of voluntary redundancy by more than 200 workers at several Auckland motor-vehicle assembly companies because of the decline in sales...Fabco employed a total of 400 workers, said its general manager, Mr Graham Astley, yesterday." [184]

Nor was 1985 a good year for employment at Fabco Industries' Wellington factory:

"About 90 per cent of the contents of Fabco Industries' factory in Trentham was destroyed on Friday evening [26 April 1985] in one of the worst industrial fires in Hutt Valley for some years...The factory makes vehicle interior fittings and door panels..." [185]

Following its acquisition of the Brugger Group in 1985, the Owens Group subsidiary, Wenrich Investments Limited, sought control of Fabco Industries in May 1986:

"Wenrich Investments Ltd is at an advanced stage of negotiations with NZ Forest Products Ltd to acquire control of manufacturer Fabco Industries Ltd, Wenrich's chairman, Mr J T F Francis, said yesterday. Fabco, a subsidiary of NZFP, manufactures interior trim for locally-assembled motor-vehicles and owns the seat frame manufacturer, New Zealand Tool and Gauge Co (Nelson) Ltd, and the polyurethane foam pad manufacturing company, Raudon Plastics Ltd.

"Wenrich is the parent company of Brugger Industries Ltd which is the largest vehicle trim manufacturer in New Zealand. Mr Francis said that the amalgamation of Brugger Industries and

Fabco Industries operations would provide long term opportunities for rationalisation. It was in line with other changes to achieve a more internationally competitive vehicle assembly industry in New Zealand.

"This was envisaged under the motor-vehicle industry plan, under which assembly companies have increased access to imported componentry at reduced tariffs. Both companies produce much the same range of products." [186]

By August 1986, the acquisition of Fabco Industries was complete:

"Brugger Industries, which mainly produces car accessory components for the domestic market, has had to cope with a depressed market and the restructuring of the industry to allow greater foreign access. The company has purchased a 60 per cent share in Fabco Industries Ltd which was the main competitor. Mr Jim Francis [chairman of Wenrich Investments] said that the end result would be a company that was more cost effective and able to provide a better service." [187]

But that cost-effectiveness was not reflected in the profitability of Wenrich Investments which, by late 1987, sought to rid itself of the combined Brugger and Fabco Industries — as reported by the Christchurch Press in November 1987:

"Rationalisation had restored Wenrich Investments to profitability, 'albeit as a much smaller company,' the chairman, Mr Bob Owens, told shareholders at the company's annual meeting in Auckland yesterday….After Owens Investments took over the company the manufacturing plant of Brugger Exports based in Wainuiomata had been mothballed and its operations curtailed…Agreement in principle had been reached with a major overseas company to form a joint venture company which would acquire Brugger Industries assets at market value subject to shareholders' approval." [188]

As the last vehicle assembler was about to close, Brugger Industries found itself with much less to do by March 1988:

"About 20 workers will lose their jobs at Brugger Industries in Wainuiomata because of falling sales…The company makes interior trim for vehicles. The special projects manager, Wieke Stoks, said the fall in new car sales had meant the company was not producing the volume it had been. The great increase in fully assembled car numbers had also affected the company's work…" [189]

Exhaust Systems
<u>Southward Engineering</u>

The Southward Engineering Company Limited and its sole shareholder, NZ Tube Mills Limited, were both established at Wellington by Leonard Southward in December 1955.

While the Southward Engineering Company retained its original name until its deregistration in October 2006, NZ Tube Mills Limited became Atlas Specialty Metals Limited in January 2015, and then NZTB Melting Limited in June 2015, before deregistration in November that year. [190]

In February 1958, the original Southward Engineering Company factory at Gracefield, Lower Hutt was consumed by fire:

"Mr L Southward of the Southward Engineering Company who sustained losses of at least £100,000 in the fire, said any estimate above that figure could not be known as he was able to salvage some of his machinery. Today, he had two mobile cranes employed in salvaging work. Machinery saved will be taken to a new factory almost completed in Seaview, not far from Gracefield. Mr Southward said there would be no unemployment in his firm because of the fire. His factory employed 70 persons." [191]

In January 1959, NZ Tube Mills Limited (incorporating Southward Engineering Co) advertised that they were "…Makers of Lesco New Zealand Products, Rear Vision Mirrors, Lesco Pour-a-Can…" [192]

At the time, a 'Lesco Pour-a-Can' was a very popular petrol and oil can with a metal pouring spout attached.

By the 1970s, the Southward Engineering Company was also manufacturing exhaust systems for New Zealand-assembled motor vehicles — as advertised by the Christchurch Press in January 1973:

"We appreciate being associated with the Toyota Crown in supplying the Exhaust System and Interior Rear Vision Mirror, as original equipment. New Zealand Tube Mills Ltd — Sales Division Of Southward Engineering Co Ltd..." [193] and again in October 1978:

"New Zealand Tube Mills Ltd — Manufacturers of Lesco Pour A Cans, Lesco Car Stands, Lesco Rear Vision Mirrors, Steel Exhaust Tubing..." [194]

Bicycle makers also obtained parts from the Leonard Southward companies:

"...New Zealand Tube Mills Ltd, Manufacturers and suppliers of: The special AISI1010 and AISI1021 cycle Tubing used in the Healing Cycles..." [195]

It was no doubt because of such diversification, that the Southward companies were able to weather the automotive industry downturn in 1982:

"A unique plan agreed on by workers and management at the Wellington car components plant of Southward Engineering Company Ltd has averted lay-offs which seemed almost inevitable. Early in the New Year some 30 Southward Engineering workers will be available to work on major projects organised by charitable organisations while still being paid by the company...

"Southward's general manager, Mr Roy Southward, said that most of the work-force of 280 would continue working at the plant, while some gangs would work on the building and others would be available for community work. Southward Engineering said yesterday that its business was 15 per cent down on the usual figures for this time of year. The company makes exhaust systems and replacement parts for cars." [196]

Despite the downturn, the Southward Engineering Company Limited was still advertising itself as:

"...manufacturers of Stainless Steel and Mild Steel Tube..." in August 1985. [197]

Campion and Bolton

Campion and Bolton Limited was a firm of Waitara engineers that evolved as manufacturers of automotive components, mainly mufflers and tailpipes.

The company was granted a wholesalers licence on 1 August 1951 [198] and was licensed as a manufacturing retailer on 7 October 1953. [199]

Amalgamated Batteries purchased the whole of the ordinary shares in Campion and Bolton in 1962 [200] and Motor Holdings Limited acquired a majority shareholding in the company in January 1966 — as reported by the Christchurch Press:

"Motor Holdings Ltd, Auckland, holding company for the New Zealand Volkswagen companies, has bought a 75 per cent interest in Campion and Bolton Ltd, Waitara manufacturer of automotive components...Campion and Bolton's main products are mufflers and tailpipes. The company will continue to supply existing customers, but now also manufacture for Volkswagen. This will double the output. It is planned to expand the range of products." [201]

On 19 June 1967, the name, Campion and Bolton Limited, was changed to Motor Components Limited [202] and, later that year, the firm "...transferred to an improved factory of 15,000 square feet. However, the change-over and installation of equipment seriously hampered production and resulted in a loss." [203]

While the manufacture of automotive parts continued in the new factory, it was soon to become a much larger enterprise — as reported by the Christchurch Press in August 1973:

"The Government has given the green light for the assembly of motor-cars at Waitara in Taranaki, and the reequipping and extension of Motor Components Ltd plant in the town will start next year.

"This was announced by Mr B P Hopkins, the chairman of the Auckland-based Motor Holdings Ltd, of which Motor Components Ltd is a wholly-owned subsidiary. Production is due to start no later than next April and 10 cars a day will eventually come off the assembly line." [204]

Four years later, the car assembly operation at Waitara was in full swing:

"Compared with most car assembly plants in New Zealand, the Subaru plant at Waitara is relatively small, covering only 53,000 sq ft. Another company in the Motor Holdings group, Motor Components Ltd, also occupies a portion of the factory. The relatively small scale of the Waitara operation has advantages, according to the company…

"Through its subsidiary, Motor Components, Motor Holdings has a long connection with the town. The necessary skilled tradesmen were available and most of the installation of assembly line equipment was done by existing Motor Components staff.

"The 30 spot-welding machines at the Waitara plant were made in the Motor Components machine shop, the only bought-in parts being transformers and electronic timers. Motor Components staff also made the 'body grip' hoists, and the various stillages racks and trolleys used in the plant. This policy allowed the company to build up a core of staff before the first cars were assembled in December 1974…

"More than 4500 cars and station waggons have been assembled at Waitara for companies in the Motor Holdings Group and under contract to other importers." [205]

However, while Motor Components Limited continued making both original and replacement vehicle parts at the Waitara factory, the Subaru assembly plant ceased operating during the recession in the motor industry in the second-half of 1977 until September 1979. [206]

The assembly of Subaru at Waitara ceased altogether in 1987. [207]

Paint

<u>British Australian Lead Manufacturers</u> (BALM)

What were described as "…the leading white lead manufacturers of the United Kingdom…" established British Australian Lead Manufacturers Pty Limited in Australia to manufacture white lead, mixed paints, etc., in the Commonwealth…" [208]

The new company began construction of a £100,000 factory at Sydney in January 1920 "…to manufacture white lead from Broken Hill metallic lead." [209]

In June 1935, British Australian Lead Manufacturers (NZ) Ltd was incorporated at Wellington with a Capital of £10,000. Subscribers: H J Barncastle 9990 shares and H D Guthrie 10 shares, both of Sydney. [210]

(H D Guthrie was Hugh Douglas Guthrie who "…joined his brothers and Mr G Bowron in the firm of Guthrie, Bowron and Company Limited. He came to Auckland in 1916 to open a branch of the firm and remained as manager until 1935. In 1938 he went to Lower Hutt, where the company [British Australian Lead Manufacturers (NZ)] built Its first factory. He remained there as general manager until he retired in 1951.") [211]

Guthrie, Bowron & Co represented British Australian Lead Manufacturers in New Zealand until the latter company's establishment in June 1935, when it was announced in all the country's major newspapers:

"British Australian Lead Manufacturers Pty Ltd (Melbourne, Sydney and Adelaide), the sole proprietors in the Commonwealth of Australia and Dominion of New Zealand of the manufacturing processes of the well-known 'DUCO' Lacquers and 'DULUX' Finishes, beg to announce that they have opened branches at Auckland, Wellington, Christchurch and Dunedin, under the name of British Australian Lead Manufacturers (NZ) Ltd to undertake the sale of the above-mentioned products in New Zealand…" [212]

By August 1937, plans were afoot for the establishment of a paint factory in New Zealand — as reported by the Evening Post:

"Details of the premises which the British Australian Lead Manufacturers (NZ) Ltd are to erect for the manufacture of Dulux and Duco finishes…will contain special features necessary in the manufacture of these products, the New Zealand supplies of which at present come from Australia…

"The directors in Australia have now decided that the time has arrived for the erection of plant in this country in order to keep abreast of the growing market in the Dominion hence the acquisition of the land in the Hutt Valley. The five and a half acres which the company has purchased lie behind the Ford Motor Works…" [213]

The new factory at Lower Hutt, described as the "…manufacturers of paints, white lead, duco lacquers and dulux finishes…" attracted a good deal of publicity following a visit by the Prime Minister, Michael Joseph Savage, in February 1939. [214]

However, by then, Imperial Chemical Industries of Australia and New Zealand Limited (ICI) had become a major shareholder in the British Australian Lead Manufacturing Group — as reported by the Evening Post in February 1940:

"A bonus share issue of £50,000 is being made by British Australian Lead Manufacturers Pty Ltd of Melbourne. Sanction has been granted by the Treasury to the capitalisation of £50,000 of undivided profits. Issued capital will now stand at £500,000. The largest shareholding in the company is held by Imperial Chemical Industries of Australia and New Zealand Ltd." [215]

The name of British Australian Lead Manufacturers (NZ) Limited was changed to BALM Paints (NZ) Limited on 12 January 1955 [216] and the company opened a second factory at Auckland in 1956. [217]

Great marketing emphasis was placed on the company's employment of scientists at its factories:

"Balm Paints have two modern laboratories covering an area of 8,600 square feet. One at Gracefield, Lower Hutt, and the other at Tamaki, Auckland. These are staffed by over 40 scientists and laboratory technicians." [218]

The concept of continuous improvement was referred to in December 1959:

"Continuous improvements are going on in the manufacture of paint, said Mr D P Wines, commercial director of the BALM Paints organisation in Australia and New Zealand, in an interview yesterday

"Imperial Chemical Industries of Australia and New Zealand held a 70 per cent holding in the company, said Mr Wines…

"When the Du Pont company developed Duco after the First World War, that was the first revolutionary change in paint. Had it not been for the quick drying qualities of that paint there could not have been the mass production of motor-cars in the present volume. An important new development in paint was the greatly improved finish on cars in the United States. This would hold its gloss for very much longer than other types of finish, said Mr Wines." [219]

In 1960, BALM Paints celebrated 25 years of selling paint in New Zealand:

"The biggest supplier of paint in New Zealand is BALM Paints (NZ) Ltd…In 25 years since it began selling paint in New Zealand, the company has developed to the stage where it has large factories in Auckland and Lower Hutt, producing an immense range of products for distribution through the length and breadth of the Dominion…" [220]

An expansion programme to meet the growing needs of the car assembly industry was announced in March 1962:

"A £250,000 expansion programme which would include new plant at the Mount Wellington factory would be carried out by Balm Paints over the next two years, Mr E P Sanford, operations director of Balm Paints Pty Ltd…said in Auckland.

"The expansion plans in New Zealand included production of the latest overseas finishes for the rapidly growing automotive assembly trade, continued Mr Sanford. It was expected that this would save the country overseas exchange. Mr Sandford said that work was expected to begin on additions to the Mount Wellington factory by August this year. The new plant should be in operation about the middle of next year. [221]

By November 1965, ICI New Zealand, considered to be one of the country's largest companies, owned 70.3 per cent of BALM Paints (NZ) Limited which was then referred to as subsidiary of ICI. [222]

"Taking its cue from survey evidence that the Australian public had no idea what BALM Paints was, but that everyone knew Dulux, [BALM Paints Australia] changed its name in 1971 to Dulux Australia…[223]

BALM Paints (NZ) Limited followed suit with a change of name to Dulux New Zealand Limited on 21 September 1971. [224]

"Until 1997, Dulux Australia [and Dulux New Zealand] was a key player in the ICI Paints World Group, after which ICI informed ICI Australia of its intention to sell its 62% share in the company…" [225]

"When parent company ICI Plc divested its major shareholding in ICI Australia in 1997, a new independent Australasian company was formed…on 2 February 1998…known as Orica…" [226]

"In Australia and New Zealand, Dulux was wholly owned by Orica until July 2010, when Dulux Group was spun off as a separate company on the Australian Securities Exchange." [227]

ICI Paints & Dulux New Zealand

Imperial Chemical Industries founded ICI Paints in the United Kingdom in 1926 and the brand, Dulux, "derived from the words, Durable and Luxury, was introduced in 1931." [228]

As early as December 1931, tenders were invited at Auckland "…For the Painting of the Entire Atta Cab Fleet in Dulux…" [229] and, in February 1932, a Christchurch Star advertisement placed by L Philpott of Victoria Street announced: "Cars Ducoed or Enamelled with the latest Dulux Enamel, the next best to Duco." [230]

("Duco was a trade name for a product line of automotive lacquer developed by the Du Pont Company in the 1920s.") [231]

Dulux New Zealand Limited was registered at Lower Hutt in May 1935 [232] and the popular use of Dulux paint for motor vehicles was soon evident — as illustrated by a New Zealand Herald image published in December 1935:

"The latest 40-seater diesel motor-bus, finished with Dulux paint, which has been built locally by the Passenger Transport Company Limited." [233]

Nearly forty years later, the Dulux brand continued to be used to protect New Zealand's motor vehicles — as reported by the Christchurch Press in January 1973:

"The Jewel of the Orient Crowned with Dulux Acrylic Enamel — the magnificent new Toyota Crowns are painted in Dulux Acrylic Enamel to put a sparkling finish to a jewel of a car! Dulux was chosen because it is long lasting, gives a hard, high-gloss surface and resists oxidisation. Dulux brings to the automotive industry a superb range of high quality enamels and lacquers suitable for a variety of applications including repair and refinishing jobs." [234]

Dulux remains represented in New Zealand as an overseas-registered company, Dulux Group (New Zealand) Pty Limited which was incorporated on 30 October 2009. [235]

However, "On 21 August 2019 a Scheme of Arrangement was implemented under which Nippon Paint Holdings Co Ltd, a Japanese paint manufacturing company, acquired 100% of Dulux Group shares." [236]

Tyres

As more and more vehicles were driven greater distances, often over inadequate road surfaces during the early years of motoring, a ready supply of inner tubes and tyres soon became as essential to the motorist as the petrol and air needed to provide their engine's internal combustion. And, just like the inevitable bang of that combustion or a tyre blowout, there has always been a New Zealand businessman with the will and tenacity to satisfy a need.

Early Tyre Importers & Retailers
Some of the earliest tyre importers and retailers and their advertisements included:
Spencer Moulton (April 1916)
"Haydock and Spragg Central Garage, Wakefield Street — "Motorists! About Your Tyres. Are you getting a fair mileage from your tyres? If not, try the Spencer Moulton All British High-Grade Tyres. Moderate prices. Owing to the great demand at Home we have only a limited consignment, and orders must be booked early to avoid disappointment. Agents wanted in every centre north of Rotorua…"
Harrison and Gash, Carriage and Motor Works, Newmarket — "Motorists why not do your own vulcanising? Buy one of our small Outfits with full directions and enough material to do 20 repairs. Price 30s post free…"
Spragg's Auckland Garage, Cor. Lorne and Wellesley Streets — "Large Stocks of Tyres and All Requisites for Motors…"
Gaulois Tyres (April 1916)
"R Bieleski, 9 Hill Street, Newmarket — Gaulois Tyres. High-Grade French Manufacture. All Sizes now in Stock. Motorists if you wish to obtain Best Value in Motor Tyres, apply direct…"
Gilmour, Joll and Williams (April 1916)
"Carriage Builders and Motor-body Specialists, Symonds Street — Is Your Business Motor Spick and Span? Does it look the part? Is it a good advertisement for you? Is the sign on it fresh and attractive? Look to these things; they mean better business. We can do the work promptly and well. Ask us for advice and quote…" [237]

Michelin (December 1916)
"Wherever there are motors, there are Michelin car tyres, for Michelin was the first to fit pneumatic tyres to any motor car. At that time no manufacturer could be induced to fit them — the suggestion was regarded as a madman's fantasy. To demonstrate that it was not, Michelin bad to build three cars of his own. Until Michelin in 1895 drove his car fitted with pneumatic tyres, no one had ever given the idea of pneumatic car tyres a single thought.

"Michelin Motor Tyres wore first in 1895, and they have been foremost ever since, because they are made in one Quality only—The Best; and Michelins are the only car tyres that have not advanced during the war. The reason for this is that Michelin grow their own rubber, and therefore are not affected by the fluctuation of the rubber market.

"Motorists are assured of receiving Michelin Tyres in perfect condition, as they come direct from the Factory to P H Vickery, who represents Messrs Michelin Ltd of Paris and London. For motorists demanding a non-skid all rubber tyre, the 'Firestone' is the original All Rubber Non-Skid Tread for safety and saving." [238]

Moseley Tyres and Tubes (August 1917)
"M C Farrington, Repairs and All Accessories, 10 Gore Street — Moseley Tyres and Tubes — All British. I have been appointed Auckland Agent for the above, and have good stock of all sizes. These are the Tyres for mileage, and they can be thoroughly recommended for Price and Durability…" [239]

Cousins and Aitken (August 1917)
"Stanley Street — Enamelling Motorcars — We have just erected special room and plant, and are using the finest enamel in the world. Enamel wears better than varnish; easier cleaned…" [240]

Mephan's Motor Garage (August 1917)
"Opp. Mount Eden Station — Mephan's New and Up-to-date Fireproof Motor Garage is now open and if you wanted your Car overhauled, repaired, or repainted in a first-class style, at a reasonable cost, give us a call or phone…for an estimate before going elsewhere…" [241]

The New Zealand Tyre and Rubber Company (May 1919)
"The New Zealand Tyre and Rubber Co Ltd Office: Dominion Buildings, Cathedral Square, Christchurch. Registered as a private company May 12 [1919]. Capital: $50,000 into 50,000 shares of £1 each. Subscribers: Christchurch — W S Newburgh 25,001; W E Best 24,997; Sarah E Best 1; Rose I Newburgh 1. Objects: To deal in rubber products, motor-cars, and general." [242]

Goodrich (August 1919)
"Forde And Co, The Goodrich People, Queen Street — Talisman. Purchase At Once Our 5-Finger Specially Reinforced 30 by 3-1/2 Black Safety Tread Goodrich Tyre. Something You Have Not Seen Before. You Will Never Regret It. Eight Plies Of Fabric. The Best Para Rubber. Recognised Out On Its Own. Now Don't Be Silly. Try This Tyre And Then Give Us Your Opinion…" [243]

Nobby Tread Tyres (November 1919)
"The exhibit [at the Show Grounds] of the United States Tyre Company — the biggest rubber company in America — attracted a great deal of attention. In a tasteful manner their famous 'Nobby Tread' Tyres were displayed. These tyres are easily the most popular in the Dominion to-day. Their durability is saving money daily for a host of motor-car owners. The big feature of this company's tyres is that they are scientifically designed and built to fit a particular requirement of motoring.

"Among the five you will find exactly the tyres you need, whether your car is large and heavy, or small and light—whether the roads you travel are rough or smooth, hilly or level, hard or soft. No other tyre manufacturer provides so complete a line from which to choose, with which to make the most of your car…

"These tyres are sold by all garages throughout the Dominion, and your dealer will gladly help you to select the right tread for your car, and you owe it to yourself to learn why United States Tyres are reducing the cost of motoring in all parts of New Zealand.

"An idea of the esteem in which these tyres are held by motorists in all parts of the world can be gained from the record output of the combined factories of the company of 24,000 tyres in one working day of eight hours.

"In addition to motor tyres, the exhibit displayed vulcanising rubber and solution, both of which are held in high esteem by all qualified to judge. Messrs Magnus, Sanderson and Co, Wellington and Dunedin, are the sole agents for New Zealand…" [244]

Para Rubber Co Limited (July 1920)
"Victoria Street, Hamilton — Motor Tyres and Accessories…Dodge Tubes…" [245]

Wright Stephenson (December 1933)
"Motorists! You can't buy TIRES better anywhere than at Wright Stephenson's 97 Taranaki Street — The Cheapest place for TIRES in Wellington." [246]

India Tyres (December 1933)
"India Tyres — The Super Quality Tyre giving Superior Service — Manufactured in Scotland by British Workmen — British Capital — India Tyres give High Mileage, Safety, Economy — The three important essentials for motor vehicle owners…Murray, Roberts & Co Ltd." [247]

The Later Tyre Importers & Retailers
Dunlop New Zealand
Philip Proctor (later Sir Philip Proctor) "…who was born in Melbourne, set up Dunlop in New Zealand in 1936, and became the first chairman and managing director of Dunlop New

Zealand in 1946… He was credited with convincing Dunlop to build a tyre factory at Upper Hutt in the post-war years, against some opposition from Dunlop's English head office." [248]

Dunlop New Zealand Limited was incorporated on 5 July 1946, [249] as reported by the Otago Daily Times:

"A new public company, with a capital of £1,500,000, Dunlop New Zealand, Ltd., has been registered in Wellington. The company was one of three which were granted licences last August to manufacture motor tyres and tubes in the Dominion. The capital, which is in £1 shares, is divided into 500,000 4½ per cent, cumulative preference shares and 1,000,000 ordinary shares. So far only one share each has been allotted to seven subscribers.

"A tyre factory is being built by the company on a 40-acre site in the Hutt Valley, 20 miles from Wellington. The company also owns and operates a general rubber goods plant in Christchurch, and both factories are expected to employ about 500 persons.

"In addition to manufacturing its own products, the company has made an arrangement to manufacture tyres for the Goodyear Tyre and Rubber Company (New Zealand) Ltd.

"The seven subscribers who have been allotted one share each are Messrs H. R. H. Chalmers, F. H. Bass, G. M. Murch, G. P. Proctor, W. R. Birks, A. E. Tunley and F. T. Clere, all of Wellington. The objects of the company are described as tyre manufacturing and incidental.

"The other two companies which were granted tyre manufacturing licences were Reid New Zealand Rubber Mills Ltd., Auckland, and the Firestone Tyre and Rubber Company of New Zealand Ltd., which will operate in Christchurch." [250]

"The company…took over the assets and liabilities of the businesses formerly carried on by the Dunlop Rubber Company (N.Z.), Ltd., and the Barnet Glass Perdriau Rubber Company of New Zealand, Ltd." [251]

"Production at the Upper Hutt factory commenced during the year [1949], but the task of building up to volume production has been hampered by the labour supply situation. A further reduction in tyre prices ordered by the Price Tribunal had an adverse effect on trading results The landed cost of many of the imported articles increased during 1949, and since devaluation of sterling, further increases had been advised by the company's overseas suppliers." [252]

By 1952, the tyre business was hardly thriving with "Dunlop New Zealand Limited incurring a net loss of £NZ6191 in the year to December 31 of that year compared with a record net profit of £ 61,438 in the 1951 year…The directors state that last year's trade recession in New Zealand was 'especially severe in the tyre business.' The Upper Hutt factory was working well below capacity for most of the year." [253]

Toward the end of the decade, the tyre manufacturing business continued to struggle against both the cost and lack of raw materials, as reported by the Christchurch Press on 2 May 1958:

"Though Dunlop New Zealand Ltd. had not yet obtained all the raw materials it needed to maintain production at both factories on the planned output basis, the directors were satisfied, by promises already made, that adequate import licences would be forthcoming for the rest of the year…

"Mr Proctor said that the Board of Trade last year concluded a long and detailed inquiry into the New Zealand tariff structure, and the report was now in the hands of the Minister of Customs.

"It was to be hoped that the Minister would carefully consider the vulnerability of industries lacking adequate tariff safeguards and give effect to a policy of reasonable tariff protection where circumstances justified it. Progress of the rubber industry could be checked if it could not continue to rely on adequate safeguards against overseas competition." [254]

The economic outlook had improved by 1963, however, with Dunlop New Zealand reporting "After record output of tyres at the Upper Hutt factory, consolidated net profit…rose 28.8 per cent in the year ended December 31 [1963].

"The managing director (Mr P Proctor) said in his report that all industry benefited from the upsurge in business activity last year, not least the tyre section of the rubber industry. Output in this sector was still further increased by the Government decision to remedy the new car shortage by allowing greater imports.

"As a result, industry output figures showed a growth in car tyres from 622,000 to 731,000. Mr Proctor said Dunlop had secured a satisfactory share of this growth. He also announced that competitive developments had obliged the company to enter the field of wholesale retreading of car and truck tyres. Retreading factories had been bought at Wellington and Palmerston North." [255]

Dunlop expanded its retreading business in 1965:

"Dunlop New Zealand…which went into tyre retreading a few years ago, has expanded this field to Auckland by the acquisition of Ridge Tyre Remoulding Company, believed to be the oldest retreading firm in the country. The company will also soon open a retreading business in Hamilton, the chairman (Mr A. Hamilton) said today. Consideration in the Ridge take-over is an undisclosed sum in cash. The take-over takes effect as from July 1 [1965]." [256]

By 1971, more cars on New Zealand roads meant more tyres needed, as reported by the Christchurch Press on 3 April 1972:

"The demand for new car tyres increased significantly over the previous year, the managing director of Dunlop New Zealand, Ltd (Mr J. E. S. Hammond), said in the annual report for the year to December 31[1971].

"This reflected the greater number of cars on New Zealand roads and an increasing consciousness of the risks from using badly worn tyres, he said. The demand for tyres from the New Zealand car assembly plants also remained buoyant, the company's tyre sales to this market being satisfactory.

"Mr Hammond said that the company's radial-ply tyres were becoming increasingly popular. Throughout the year, the company had to make maximum efforts to meet rising demand.

"In contrast with the car tyre market, the demand for truck tyres had been depressed, and towards the end of the year the company had to curtail production because transport fleets were not working at their full capacity and their tyre use had fallen significantly, Mr Hammond said." [257]

Toward the end of the 1970s, there was even newer tyre technology to be adopted by New Zealand manufacturers:

"Dunlop New Zealand, Ltd, has announced a range of steel-belted radial tyres for cars, buses and trucks which, although more expensive than conventional tyres, offer the promise of better road-holding and longer life. Steel radials have been popular in Europe for years and are expected to be offered as original equipment on a number of New Zealand-assembled cars now that both Dunlop and Firestone are making them here.

"The advantages of steel-belted radial tyres for cars — longer tread life, improved road-holding, more responsive steering, better braking and better fuel economy — have been well documented overseas. But a further benefit, high puncture resistance, is the key to their use on trucks and buses." [258]

Poor economic conditions during 1981 resulted in a 'static market' for tyre sales and this was reflected by the profit fall announced by Dunlop New Zealand in February 1982 — as reported by the firm's chairman and managing director, W B C Evans:

"In tyres, although the level of turnover kept pace with inflation, profits fell noticeably compared with 1980 and the second half in particular failed to repeat the successful pattern of recent years. This was in spite of the continued strength of the retread market and of the vehicle assembly business — to which Dunlop supplies a high share of tyres. Along with other New Zealand tyre manufacturers Dunlop felt the effects of significant changes in the replacement market, especially in trunk tyres where imports have increased rapidly." [259]

However, in anticipation of the Industries Development Commission's pronouncement 'that change must occur in the industry', and despite its earlier profit fall, Dunlop New Zealand bought the Feltex company's Reidrubber division in March 1983.

"In a deal involving a $1.5 million Government loan…The six Reidrubber retread factories and 31 sales branches will be taken over as going concerns, with new tyres and retread material supplied from Dunlop's factory at Upper Hutt. The 340 staff in these Reidrubber units will transfer to Dunlop with no break in employment. However, the Reidrubber tyre factory at Penrose, Auckland, will close on June 17 with the loss of 440 jobs.

"The restructuring will consolidate Dunlop's position as New Zealand's leading tyre producer. Dunlop's managing director, Mr Bill Evans, said it would not be the end of changes in the tyre industry. 'Technical improvements in tyre design and production methods are not only reducing the car tyre market by about six per cent every year, but are putting pressure on manufacturers to use new equipment in place of the heavily manual methods of the past.'

"Labour's trade and industry spokesman, Mr D F Caygill, called on the Government to find alternative work for the 440 workers. 'Another unfortunate aspect of the closing is that the two remaining tyre manufacturers, Dunlop and Firestone, are both foreign owned. We have just lost the New Zealand-owned tyre company.'" [260]

Industry restructuring continued in 1984 with the full takeover of Dunlop New Zealand by the Australian Dunlop Olympic Limited which reportedly "…suggested big gains in tyre production efficiency. Rationalisation moves would include a $10M investment of modernising New Zealand plant and the movement of some tyre production from Australia." [261]

"Dunlop's main production in New Zealand was then centred in Upper Hutt where the company made tyres, tubes, flaps, and retread rubber…the Australian firm had paid $25 million to take over the New Zealand business." [262]

From 1 January 1986 the name of Dunlop New Zealand was changed to Pacific Dunlop. [263]

Restructuring and consolidation of the tyre manufacturing industry continued with another merging of industry heavyweights — as reported by the Christchurch Press on 9 December 1986:

"The Goodyear Tire and Rubber Company and Pacific Dunlop plan to merge their tyre manufacturing, marketing and retailing activities to New Zealand and Australia in a drive to lift their international competitiveness.

"The two companies say they will invest $260 million in new facilities in the region over the next five years to boost efficiency and to fight off import competition on local markets.

"Goodyear and Dunlop plan to invest up to $1300 million on their New Zealand distribution network and the one manufacturing plant they will own in this country — the Dunlop factory at Upper Hutt…

"Goodyear and Dunlop would be equal partners in the company, which would continue to face local competition from Firestone in New Zealand and Bridgestone in Australia." [264]

Dunlop New Zealand Limited was cleared by the Commerce Commission "…to merge its tyre business with that of Goodyear New Zealand Limited" in March 1987. [265]

From 30 March 1987, the new company became known as South Pacific Tyres N.Z. Limited — "…an Australasian joint venture between Pacific Dunlop, which owns the Dunlop and Olympic brands among others in this region, and the Goodyear Tire and Rubber Company." [266]

Tyre Manufacturing in New Zealand

During the post-war years, while markets and factories struggled to recover their former productivity, there were many shortages of all types of goods, particularly in the far-off regions of the Antipodes where the first solution seemed to be local manufacturing — as described by Allan Dick in the Motor Trade Association Centenary Publication of 2017:

"In 1946, suggestions that the shortage of tyres could be overcome by making tyres in New Zealand were at first greeted warmly, but then with dismay as it looked like the government was considering setting up a state-controlled, monopoly tyre factory in Christchurch. Eventually this came to nothing, but tyre companies did set up manufacturing plants themselves." [267]

One of those companies was the Firestone Tire and Rubber Company of New Zealand:

Firestone New Zealand
The Firestone Tire and Rubber Company of New Zealand Limited existed for some seventy years following the incorporation of the company on 1 June 1928. [268]

In the beginning, Firestone was an importer of its American-made tyres to New Zealand and Australia but, in December 1947, the Bay of Plenty Times reported that Harvey S Firestone Junior, then president of the American Firestone Tyre and Rubber Company, was planning to establish tyre manufacturing plants at Christchurch and Adelaide.

These new factories were said to complement others outside the United States in Canada, Brazil, Argentina, England, Switzerland, Sweden, Spain, Union of South Africa, and India.

"Horace G Miller, managing director of the Firestone New Zealand Company, whose plant is now under construction, handled negotiations with the Australian government and will supervise activities in both countries." [269]

By February 1955, Firestone New Zealand advertised that its Papanui, Christchurch factory had "…now produced over 1,000,000 tyres…This is more than any two brands manufactured by any other factory…" [270]

A second Firestone entity, Firestone N.Z. Limited, was incorporated on 31 July 1973 [271] amid a decade of increased demand for its products — as reported by the Christchurch Press in January 1975:

"Firestone New Zealand, Ltd increased sales 14 per cent to a record level, but a combination of labour, production and pricing problems led to much higher costs — with the result that profit showed a sharp decline…The chairman (Mr C W Campbell) says in his annual report that the selling price of tyres and tubes was increased during the 1974 year — the first increase since 1956.

"Commenting on operations, he says that the buoyant trading climate set the stage for a keen demand for tyres and tubes. Supplies from the factory were at times uncertain and considerable quantities of tyres were imported from Firestone plants in Britain, Australia, Switzerland and Spain.

"As usual vehicle assembly plants were steady buyers and sales to this market increased. Supplies of raw materials were maintained throughout the year and the disruption threatened by the oil crisis was averted." [272]

Toward the end of the 1970s, Government intervention and the demand for cheaper retreads, led to some uncertainty for the tyre industry:

"'It is as yet unclear what effect the Government's recent relaxation of the regulations covering new car sales will have on local [assemblies,' the chairman of Firestone New Zealand, Ltd (Mr C W Campbell) said at the annual meeting in Christchurch.

"'The assembly plants ran into increasing problems toward the end of last year, with the result that 61,824 new car sales represented the lowest level since 1969.

"'There has, however, been a stronger demand for retreads as new tyre prices have risen, but production in this area has been limited by the availability of sound casings. Surveys carried out by Firestone indicated that motorists were tending to run their tyres past the legal 1/16 inch minimum skid depth,' said Mr Campbell." [273]

Although Firestone's profit margin had increased by 1982, the competition posed by imported tyres without some import licensing protection remained an uncertain hurdle:

Meanwhile, Firestone New Zealand reported "…a group net profit rise of 43.1 per cent in the year to 31 October 1982, on sales 21.8 per cent higher to a record $74.6 million.

Referring to Firestone's submissions to the Industries Development Commission, company chairman, R L Deal, commented:

"The tyre manufacturing industry was not large enough to stand against the major low-cost manufacturing countries without import licence protection, because tariffs alone would be inadequate. Already, more than 10 per cent of all replacement tyres were imported and sold in competition with the local product. At the same time, the I.C.D.'s [Industries Development Commission's] motor vehicle study was important because a significant portion of the locally made tyres were fitted to vehicles assembled in New Zealand, and this business was needed to ensure the continuing economic volume of factory output." [274]

When the Government introduced its 'tyre industry plan' in April 1983, [275] the intention was that a tyre tariff level for 1989 onwards was to be settled in 1986 with a progressive reduction in tariffs on tyres from 40 per cent to 25 per cent beforehand. However, by the time of the Firestone annual meeting in February 1987, the tariff issue remained uncertain, as outlined by the company's chairman, Mr R. L. Deal:

"'…the company's management had met with Government officials for six hours to deal with the tariff issue. It's kinda like swimming up Niagara Falls. You get tired of it,' he said.

"'Firestone had spent more than $13 million in the last five years buying and installing equipment to improve productivity and efficiency so that Firestone's New Zealand made tyres could compete with imported products. Factory workers had agreed to a productivity deal to assist in ensuring that the company's tyre factory survived,' he said." [276]

Both the assemblers of new vehicles and the providers of components such as Firestone had to adjust to the importation of used vehicles, mainly from Japan, from the mid-1980s. Indeed, by 1990, used imports had overtaken new car sales with 53.4 per cent of total new New Zealand registrations that year: [277]

"Firestone New Zealand profit for the half-year ended April 30 [1989] has fallen sharply on the previous corresponding half-year. The pre-tax profit is down 40 per cent at $2,507,000 but sales are down only 1.5 per cent…

"Mr J B Millar, the chairman and managing director of Firestone New Zealand since April, said the importing of used cars affected component makers such as Firestone as well as the makers of new vehicles. In April, 6400 used vehicles were imported.

"Firestone's sales and market share in the replacement market increased in spite of the market remaining weak and in the face of intense price competition. Export sales declined, compared with the same period last year, but this was considered to be temporary and would be reversed." [278]

Despite the adoption of 'New Zealand' in their titles, the majority shareholdings (83 per cent in 1980) [279] of Firestone New Zealand Limited and Firestone Tire and Rubber Company of New Zealand Limited were owned by American interests.

In May 1988, Firestone and Bridgestone merged their American production and this was followed by the merger of Firestone New Zealand Limited and Firestone Tire and Rubber Company of New Zealand Limited with Bridgestone Tyres (NZ) Limited to form Bridgestone/Firestone New Zealand Limited on 1 September 1998. [280]

"In 2009 Firestone still manufactured tyres for the domestic market and exported to Australia and the Pacific — by then it had made over 35 million tyres." [281]

Bridgestone New Zealand

The Bridgestone Tire Company had its origins in Japan where it made its first tyre in 1931. The company established the Bridgestone Tire Company of America in 1967 and purchased a plant for manufacturing tyres and diversified products in Australia in 1980. The Bridgestone plant at Wacol, Queensland now manufactures retreads and commercial tyres for both Australia and New Zealand. [282]

Bridgestone (NZ) Limited, incorporated as Bridgestone Tyres (1965) Limited on 25 May 1965, [283] never established a manufacturing facility in New Zealand but continues to represent the brand as a retailer and wholesaler.

Tyre Industry Study

The Industries Development Commission's 1981 tyre industry study, a forerunner of a review of the general automotive industry, "…required it to take specific account of the potential of the tyre industry to contribute to the economic growth of New Zealand, and to recommend a development plan for the future." [284]

The study, which included the manufacture and importation of tyres, tubes and retreads, was completed and its recommendations with trade and industry officials for consideration by April 1982. [285]

The Commission found "…some form of continuing support for the domestic tyre industry was deserved…but not necessarily in its present form…" stating it believed "…that change must occur in the industry because it has considerable excess productive capacity and the current market is fairly static, because of technological improvements giving longer tyre life."

"The commission did not suggest what form the change would take. It did, however, recommend a detailed development plan, designed to encourage the development of a stronger tyre industry. The essential feature of the plan was the gradual replacement of import licensing by tariffs and the controlled liberalisation of import licensing through tendering, with a view to encouraging the industry to restructure and rationalise its production." [286]

General Parts Distributors

Motor Specialties

Celebrating Motor Specialties' fifty years in business "As one of New Zealand's leading motor parts companies…" the Christchurch Press published a brief history of the company in September 1969:

"…Motor Specialties Limited was registered in Auckland as a private company with a capital of $5316 on September 3, 1919…The founding directors of the company were James Johnston and Charles Edward Tomlinson. Both were engineers, and they had previously bought the engineering business of Holland and Gillett, cylinder-grinders and gearcutters. This was subsequently sold.

"The new firm began selling and importing spare parts from premises in Fort Street, Auckland, and its early catalogues feature vehicles virtually unknown today except to vintage enthusiasts: Anderson, Briscoe, Chalmers, Cleveland, Dort, Durant, Gray, Jewett, Maxwell, Moon, Oakland, Paige, Reo, Saxon and Velie, for example.

"Many of these cars used Continental, Lycoming, Northway, Rutenber or Waukesha engines. British cars did not appear in quantity until about 1924. The first were Austin and Morris, and they were followed by the Bean, Clyno and Star, and then such Continental makes as Renault, Panhard and Minerva…" [287]

A New Zealand Herald advertisement, published in April 1921, alerted "Garagemen and Dealers" to the availability from Motor Specialties Limited, now trading from 3 Fort Street, Auckland, of "High-Grade Replacement Parts for Ford Cars." [288]

Later that year, Motor Specialties was advertising their distributorship of "B and W All-Brass Radiators of Exceptional Efficiency for Ford, Dodge, Chevrolet…" [289]

"The years after the First World War were boom years for the motor trade, but they were followed immediately by times of anxiety and rigid economy. In 1926, however, the company moved to Emily Place, Auckland, for it had outgrown its premises.

"Two years later a five-storey warehouse was built in Anzac Avenue — the 18,000 sq. ft building, complete with electric lift, cost $18,096. In 1937 a similar building was built alongside, and these two buildings now house the company's head office.

"The first branch was opened at New Plymouth in 1935, and after this another branch was opened at Hamilton. South Island Operations were conducted through agents until, through mergers, branches were started in Christchurch, Timaru, Dunedin, and Invercargill.

"In 1948 the company was registered as a public company. Progress was rapid in the 1950s and many more branches were opened throughout New Zealand. Three new warehouses were also built.

"A subsidiary company, India Tyre Distributors Ltd, was formed in 1957, and Highway Industries, a manufacturing subsidiary was formed in 1958. In 1959 a joint company was established with the Wix Corporation of Canada to make oil filters and mufflers.

In the 1960s other companies have been acquired, Paykel Brothers Ltd, Engine Rebores Ltd and Watson Steele and Ganley Ltd. In 1961 Glacier Bearings NZ Ltd was established in conjunction with the Glacier Metal Company of London, and in 1964 this company became a joint operation with Repco Ltd, of Melbourne.

"The Motor Specialties group now [1969] also works in the fields of heavy transport equipment, industrial engines and manufacturing and exporting to several Pacific countries." [290]

MSI Corporation

The name of Motor Specialties Limited was changed to Motor Specialties Industries Limited in September 1969 — as reported by the Christchurch Press:

"In a circular to shareholders, the directors say the name change is proposed because of the present anomalous situation which has arisen as a result of having one company as both parent and major trading company in the group. This, they say, is not desirable, and internal structural reorganisation will be undertaken.

"Since 1964, when Paykel Bros was taken over, the group has diversified well outside its original activities. As well as the chain of 14 engine reconditioners throughout the North Island the group is active in the production of various motor components and items of garage equipment. It is also involved in electrical distribution and brake servicing." [291]

The steady expansion of Motor Specialties Industries continued in 1971:

"Motor Specialties Industries Ltd has acquired the Meteor Manufacturing and Engineering Company Ltd of Auckland, the chairman (Mr W D Barclay) has announced.

"Meteor is a well-established engineering company with a highly-developed and well-equipped precision machine shop. Its acquisition will allow Motor Specialties Industries to manufacture a wider range of automotive and industrial components and equipment. It will also enable the company to manufacture fully many products at present partly produced by the group.

"It will work as a separate section of MSI Manufacturing, which is the division responsible for the control of all manufacturing and rebuilding in the group. It is planned that the facilities of Meteor will be expanded in due course." [292]

By December 1971, the growth of the company was enhanced by a joint venture with another established motor parts company, Andrews and Beaven Limited — as reported by the Christchurch Press:

"A new company, Bearing Service Company Ltd, has been formed as an equally owned joint venture between Motor Specialties Industries Ltd and Andrews and Beaven Ltd, the managing director of Motor Specialties (Mr T A Gibbs) and the managing director of Andrews and Beaven (Mr W B Barnes) have announced. The new company will handle a wide range of bearings, related products, and transmission units. Motor Specialties and Andrews and Beaven, acting as stockists for the Bearing Service Company, will provide more than 100 distribution points throughout New Zealand." [293]

Further expansion included the acquisition of The Dominion Oil Refining Company and its subsidiaries in December 1971:

"Motor Specialties Industries Ltd, Auckland, has acquired a 95 per cent shareholding in the Dominion Oil Refining Company, Ltd for $378,000 in shares and cash. Dominion Oil and its subsidiaries, Premoil Ltd, and Apex Ltd, were established at Onehunga in 1934 to undertake the re-refining of motor oils.

"The company provides products reconstituted out of waste from garages and similar sources. Announcing the acquisition, Motor Specialties says that the take-over fits in closely with the group's plans to diversify and develop its industrial range." [294]

However, by late 1976, the rapid diversification of its interests required another change for Motor Specialties:

"Motor Specialties Industries Ltd has begun the current year well, with both sales and profit ahead compared with the corresponding months of last year, says the managing director (Mr T A Gibbs) in the annual report…The slow-down in imports of new capital plant and vehicles was likely to increase sales of the maintenance and component supply companies within the group.

"At the annual meeting the directors would propose to change the company's name to M.S.I. Corporation Ltd which would more adequately reflect the wide base of activities…

"Mr Gibbs says that both domestic and export sales increased, and further development of exports was expected this year. The market for manufactured and remanufactured products was buoyant, while excellent growth was experienced by the recycling industries…

"Trading in the automotive parts after-market was buoyant, and high demand continued for garage equipment and machinery. The merchandising division now has 28 branches. There was a considerable increase in the market for heavy truck and trailer components, but many sales were of maintenance components because of deferred replacement…

"Engine Rebuilders, with 14 branches, had a record year because of high demand for rebuilt engines and the introduction of new lines. Swedish Motors faced a decline in heavy-duty truck sales, but this situation is expected to improve soon. Wix greatly expanded exports of oil and air filters…" [295]

The corporation's activities attracted some Government recognition in March 1978:

"An Auckland-based firm which is saving New Zealand millions of dollars by resurrecting cars and recycling engine oil has won Government recognition. The Minister of Trade and Industry (Mr Adams-Schneider) has presented a conservation award to the M.S.I. Corporation Ltd for making an outstanding contribution to the saving of the nation's resources.

"The company won the award for its development of an industry which remanufactures all types of engines, clutch covers, driveshafts and other automotive parts. A separate subsidiary recycles used lubricating oils.

"M.S.I. had its beginning in the era of the Model T Ford in 1919 with the formation of Motor Specialties Ltd but in the past 58 years it has grown to include more than 20 related companies. The company had developed an assembly-line technique for remanufacturing engines, driveshafts, brake shoes and clutch plates at its 2200 square metre factory in Takapuna.

"Much of the equipment used in the remanufacturing process was designed and built in Auckland and the company also has 16 smaller plants scattered throughout the country. Discarded engine parts made of steel, aluminium and other metals are sold as scrap for recycling and the company is looking into the possibility of restoring motor vehicle bodies. [296]

However, despite the diversification of M.S.I. Corporation's business, the downturn in the automotive industry in the early 1980s required some retrenchment — as reported by the Christchurch Press in September 1981:

"One of Auckland's largest companies, MSI Corporation Ltd, faces a major shake-up in which a number of staff will be transferred or laid off. The corporation, holding company for such firms as Motor Specialties Ltd, employs about 1200 people and the changes will affect everyone from top management level down.

"The company's secretary, Mr W T Choy, said the MSI directors had been forced to look at restructuring because of major changes in the vehicle wholesaling industry. The recent joining of forces by MSI's major competitors, Andrews and Beaven Ltd of Christchurch and Motor Traders (NZ) Ltd of Auckland had forced the corporation to look at itself closely, Mr Choy said. The Australian manufacturer, Repco Ltd had bought a 24.9 per cent holding in MSI to protect itself against the new bigger rival…" [297]

Little had changed by April 1982:

"About 50 people have been made redundant by Motor Specialties Ltd, the main trading subsidiary of MSI Corporation Ltd, said the group's managing director, M F Lionel Evans. The redundancies were part of a major restructuring of the company aimed at reducing its overheads and increasing its sales, he said.

"Most of the people involved had worked at Motor Specialties' head office. Motor Specialties was not the company it was a week ago, he said. Major changes had been made to its management structure aimed at greater responsibilities at the regional level and increased sales representation." [298]

Meanwhile, foreign competition circled — as the Christchurch Press reported in June 1982:

"Repco Corporation Ltd of Australia has raised its stake in MSI Corporation Ltd…from 40 per cent to 60 per cent…" [299]

Repco Corporation

Repco Corporation Pty Limited was established in Australia in late 1981 — as reported by the Christchurch Press:

"Two major Australian manufacturing companies have announced plans for huge corporate restructuring aimed at overseas expansion. Australian Consolidated Industries and Repco Ltd, two of the biggest Australian manufacturers and both with extensive overseas operations will undertake schemes of arrangement aimed at internationalising the groups' management and financial structures…Both companies gain new names, Repco will become Repco Corporation and ACI's new holding company will be called ACI International…" [300]

By May 1983, Repco Corporation had continued with its plans to expand overseas with the absorption of its long-established New Zealand competition:

"The end of the 105-year-old Christchurch-based firm, Andrews and Beaven Ltd, as an independent entity will come about with a proposed merger. Last month, after a takeover bid, the firm became a subsidiary of the big Australian firm, Repco Corporation Ltd.

Yesterday, the boards of directors of Andrews and Beaven and two other Repco firms, the M.S.I. Corporation Ltd (based in Auckland), and Repco New Zealand (based at Upper Hutt) announced that they would recommend a merger of the firms to shareholders.

"The companies will apply to the High Court for the merger under section 205 of the Companies Act. Meetings of shareholders will then have to be called, and their approval obtained. The boards plan to merge on July 1, a new holding company, Repco Corporation NZ Ltd, acquiring all the capital of the merging firms…" [301]

Andrews and Beaven

One of the earliest advertisements placed by Andrews and Beaven was published by the Lyttelton Times on 18 March 1879:

"Agricultural Engineers & Importers, Opposite Railway Station, Christchurch. The inspection of Farmers, Chaff Merchants, Batchers, and others requiring steam power is invited to the Cheapest Portable Engines Ever imported into Canterbury. A two-horsepower engine at about the cost of one good horse. Before purchasing horse gears this engine ought to be examined as it is the more economical power." [302]

Some 56 years later, Andrews and Beaven continued to prosper — as reported by the Christchurch Press in May 1936:

"Mr Arthur Ward Beaven, chairman of directors of the firm of Andrews and Beaven Ltd and one of the most prominent members of the senior generation of Canterbury business men, will celebrate his eightieth birthday on Monday…He was associated with Mr [William] Andrews in the establishment of the agricultural implement and manufacturing business of Andrews and Beaven, now a limited liability company [as of March 1906]. [303]

"From its early days the firm enjoyed remarkable success throughout New Zealand, much of which was due to the ingenuity of Mr Beaven in designing farm machinery particularly suited to the needs of colonial farming. One of the first great achievements of the firm was the winning of the highest award for chaff-cutters at the Sydney Centennial Show in 1888." [304]

By 1959, Andrews and Beaven had added road-making machinery to its agricultural manufacturing business:

"Roading contractors throughout the Dominion today are using crushing, screening, compacting and sealing equipment manufactured in Christchurch. Tractors, graders, mechanical shovels, screening and crushing plant, road rollers, bitumen-spraying plant and other equipment is manufactured or assembled by the firm of Andrews and Beaven Limited, started 80 years ago by Messrs William Andrews and Arthur Beaven.

"Restrictions in the supply of specialised machinery caused by the import restrictions have not meant a lessening of output, but a higher gearing for local production of the same items. Machinery that was previously imported is now manufactured to a much greater extent in the city or Middleton shops of the firm." [305]

Indeed, by December 1960, Andrews and Beaven had plans to build additional workshops to meet the demand:

"A 50 per cent, increase in manufacturing capacity is planned by Andrews and Beaven Ltd, Christchurch engineers. A contract has just been let for the construction of additional workshops on the company's four-acre site at Middleton, said the chairman and managing director (Mr M W Beaven) yesterday.

"The new workshops will be in use quite early next year. In deciding to expand, the directors have taken into account the need for New Zealand to conserve overseas funds, said Mr Beaven. The firm intends to increase the percentage of New Zealand-made components in the machinery it already partially manufactures and also to introduce more lines for partial manufacture at Middleton." [306]

More space meant more production as reported by the Christchurch Press in November 1961:

"Referring to the Middleton works, the deputy-chairman (Mr E T Beaven) says that a large increase in floor space has made it possible to assemble more industrial and agricultural equipment. New assembly lines have been laid down, and this year it is planned to increase the output of fork trucks and side loaders by 50 per cent." [307]

The expansion of Andrews and Beaven included more than just its Christchurch factories in October 1965:

"Andrews and Beaven has assumed control of John Chambers and Son of Auckland." [308]

(As referred to earlier in this chapter, John Chambers and Son was another long-established company that distributed the British Electric Construction Company's 'latest and most improved machinery' from its Auckland and Dunedin premises as early as 1893.)

As a result of the acquisition of John Chambers and Son, Andrews and Beaven also acquired an automotive division as per its advertisement for staff in September 1968:

"We require the services of an Intermediate/Senior man for our Automotive Division handling a comprehensive range of spare parts, accessories and garage equipment…in our new modern warehouse in Bath Street…" [309]

A year later, another acquisition, that of the General Accessory Company Limited, resulted in an even greater involvement of Andrews and Beaven with the automotive industry — as reported by the Christchurch Press in November 1969:

"Andrews and Beaven is set to double its size in six short months, and to become a potent force in the motor parts industry…" [310]

As a result of its acquisition of John Chambers and Son, the General Accessory Company, and a good deal of restructuring, Andrews and Beaven reported record sales levels in October 1973:

"The automotive and merchandising division, now re-established in Christchurch, recorded increasing sales each month. The agricultural division, which increased sales 30 per cent, could have returned much higher figures had it not been for serious supply problems. However, a number of important shipments have recently been received. The construction equipment division increased sales 48 per cent, while materials handling sales were also higher…The clutch and brake bonding plant moved into full production, as did the engine services and plant service divisions…" [311]

However, the 1980s heralded a new era with the incursion into New Zealand of the Australian Repco Corporation in March 1983:

"The 105-year-old Canterbury firm, Andrews and Beaven Ltd is now officially a subsidiary of the big Australian firm, Repco Corporation Ltd. The Stock Exchange has been advised that, after off-market purchases, Repco is now the beneficial owner of 52.16 per cent of the issued capital of Andrews and Beaven.

Later that year, additional mergers and quickly-changing market conditions resulted in a dramatic downsizing of Andrews and Beaven — as reported by the Christchurch Press in September 1983:

"Two hundred and fifty employees of Andrews and Beaven, Ltd, the 106-year-old Christchurch-based engineering firm, have been told this week that they will be made redundant between now and the end of the year. Of these, 180 in the company's 29 branches will leave the company immediately and receive a month's pay in lieu of notice. The redundancies are additional to 100 in the Christchurch head office who will be either made redundant or transferred to Auckland in accordance with an earlier decision, after the merger with MSI Corporation and Repco New Zealand Ltd in July…

"Mr Beaven said that as a national distributor of heavy industrial machinery, automotive and agricultural equipment, the company had battled a sustained contraction within the New Zealand market for the last two years. During the last financial year our position reached an abnormally low level and the company suffered a 75 per cent drop in profitability…

"Competition among manufacturers had become tougher. In the automotive parts sector the company had been affected by the large influx of new Japanese cars. They tended to last longer and with the present state of the roads did not need replacement parts so frequently. New models were coming out each year and with some parts that meant that new designs replaced old parts, which become obsolete and unsaleable…" [312]

General Accessory Company

A brief history of the General Accessory Company Limited was published by the Christchurch Press in November 1969:

"From a single wholesale automotive warehouse supplying the motor trade in Otago with a restricted range of replacement parts and accessories, the General Accessory Company Ltd has grown since 1953 to a nationwide organisation servicing many industries.

"Branches or wholly-owned subsidiaries have been established in most main cities of New Zealand, providing a strong chain of distribution for overseas and local manufacturers. As a consequence, many agency arrangements have been established to enable the company to provide full services to the transport industry.

"To provide alternatives for imports, the company has established its own specialised factories for the re-manufacture of widely used components and this policy is continuing. In addition, these factories process a wide range of friction materials for automotive and industrial use.

"The company has, as a wholly-owned subsidiary, Metalspray (Dunedin) Ltd, tool and die maker and automotive parts rebuilder…

"In addition to the engine service plants, and the tool and die making company, the group comprises 12 fully-stocked warehouses at Auckland, Hamilton, Rotorua, New Plymouth,

Hastings, Palmerston North, Wellington, Nelson, Christchurch, Timaru, Dunedin, and Invercargill, and two remanufacturing factories at Dunedin. Almost all the land and buildings in use are company owned, and the staff exceeded 600.

"The directors of G.A.C. Ltd say they believe that the decision to merge with Andrews and Beaven Ltd will result in a company of greater strength with unparalleled manufacturing and distributing facilities to service the industry of New Zealand." [313]

Schofield and Denton

As early as January 1914, the engineering firm of Schofield and Denton was operating from premises at Newmarket, Auckland — as reported by The New Zealand Herald in January of that year:

"Our 10-ton Weighbridge has been re-erected by Messrs. Schofield and Denton, Engineers, in front of their premises in Victoria Crescent, Newmarket…and they will in future weigh all loads on our behalf. J H M Carpenter Ltd, Coal Merchants and Carriers." [314]

By 1915, trading as the Globe Engineering Works, Ernest James Schofield and Harold Denton were soon reconditioning and selling automobiles:

"Cycle-Car, English make, beautifully sprung, new tyres, will do 34 miles per gal. Five-Seater Buick, just been thoroughly overhauled, take £150 cash. Six-Seater 40-H.P. Car, in excellent condition, electric lighting all through, dual ignition. This is a splendid riding car and honestly worth £375. Inspection invited. No reasonable offer refused. Schofield and Denton." [315]

In October 1918, tenders were called for the enlargement of Schofield and Denton's Newmarket premises needed to accommodate the firm's business growth. [316]

However, on 17 October 1919, the partnership of Schofield and Denton was dissolved with Harold Denton announcing in the Auckland Star that he "…will discharge all liabilities of the partnership and is entitled to receive all accounts." [317]

In 1920, E J Schofield was selling Hupmobiles and other motor vehicles from Broadway, Newmarket [318] and established Schofield & Co Limited on 11 February 1925. [319]

Meanwhile, Harold Denton continued to trade from the Victoria Crescent, Newmarket premises as H Denton and Co (sometimes also known as just Denton and Co), motor engineers.

H Denton and Co

One of the firm's specialities was the fitting of truck tipping gear — as described by 'Sparkwell' in the Auckland Star in August 1923:

"During my peregrinations around the city it is surprising to find the number of heavy transport vehicles which are fitted with tipping gear for all kinds of heavy cartage work and especially in relation to building and hauling contracts.

"Tip-gear making for motor wagons has been responsible for quite a useful local industry, to wit, the manufacture of tip lorry equipment at the engineering workshops of Messrs. H Denton and Co at Newmarket.

"This firm claims to have an improved patented tip gear which is foolproof. Already some of the largest transport firms are utilising it with advantage. It will be realised that such a line involves very skilled work in engineering processes, and, no doubt, as time goes on, this industry will develop in common with motor development." [320]

H Denton and Co also designed and manufactured hydraulic hoist equipment for trucks — described by The New Zealand Herald in February 1924 as "…absolutely fool proof and perfectly reliable." [321]

H Denton and Co was incorporated as a limited liability company on 21 February 1946 [322] and traded as such until the name of the company was changed to Transport Enterprises Limited on 15 July 1960 and then to Jack Tidd-Ross Todd Limited on 17 April 1967. [323]

The company continues to trade from its head office at Hamilton and branches at Auckland, Christchurch, and Brisbane as Tidd Ross Todd (TRT) Limited. The company's key areas of business are a more modern version of that started by Harold Denton in the 1920s — "…manufacturing, design and engineering, truck and trailer parts, truck and trailer mechanical service and repair, crane sales, service and parts, trailer sales, and heavy transport and equipment design and manufacture." [324]

Motor Traders (NZ)

Motor Traders (NZ) Limited was registered on 11 June 1926 [325] "…to acquire the business of importer and agent for manufacturers of motor parts carried on by H Denton at Newmarket…Capital, £7500. Subscribers: Harold Denton, motor engineer, Newmarket, 5998 shares; Motor Traders Ltd 1500 shares; Jane Ingram Wood, Sydney, and Ethel Catherine Denton, Auckland, married women, one share each." [326]

By 1938, Motor Traders (NZ) was trading as a "…motor accessory warehouse" from Cook Street, Auckland [327] and later, from August 1940, as a "…motor replacement and accessory warehouse." [328]

Motor Traders (NZ) had opened wholesale motor parts outlets at Hamilton by September 1943 [329] and then at Palmerston North by January 1944. [330]

At a time of increasing use of vehicles in New Zealand, the business of Motor Traders (NZ) could only prosper — as reported by the Christchurch Press in October 1958:

"After record sales in the year ended July 31 [1958], net profit of Motor Traders (NZ) Ltd…expanded by £5528 to a record of £73,992. The previous record was £68,545 earned in 1954-55." [331]

In August 1958, the "Spare Parts Specialists" advertised for "Experienced Parts Men…for their new Christchurch Branch…being constructed on the Corner of Durham and Bath Sts." [332]

The Christchurch branch opened on 26 January 1959:

"The official opening last evening of the new warehouse of Motor Traders (NZ) Ltd at the corner of Durham and Bath streets, marked one of the most significant steps in the company's progress since it was established more than 32 years ago…Until now the company's operations have been confined solely to the North Island, where it already has five warehouses…

"As the wholesale distributors for four large overseas motor manufacturing groups, the company stocks more than 12,000 individual lines at each of its warehouses. Like the other North Island branches, the Christchurch warehouse carries a complete range of spare parts for 28 English American and Australian cars, trucks, vans and tractors. It also supplies a big range of miscellaneous accessories, and is the sole New Zealand agent for the most widely-used shock absorber systems and universal joints.

"Motor Traders (New Zealand) Ltd is a public company with a paid capital of £250,000 and assets of more than £485,000. It has a head office at Auckland and branches at Otahuhu, Hamilton, Rotorua, Palmerston North, and now Christchurch.

"Established in 1926 at Newmarket…the company has grown from a small spare parts shop into an organisation which supplies components for a big proportion of the Dominion's motor industry. As the business expanded, larger premises became necessary and in 1931 the company moved nearer Auckland. A new warehouse was established at Palmerston North in 1936, followed by the opening of branches at Hamilton, Otahuhu, and Rotorua. In 1948 the company moved into its headquarters in Cook street, Auckland." [333]

Although the number of vehicles on New Zealand roads continued to steadily increase, import controls and the diversity of vehicle makes and models proved to be a problem for those companies supplying spare parts:

"The range of makes of motor vehicles on New Zealand roads created problems which were greatly accentuated by import licensing, said Mr W K Michael, chairman of Motor Traders (NZ) Ltd, at the annual meeting yesterday [28 November 1962]. It was difficult to carry adequate stocks to serve the motor repair industry.

"Although local manufacturers were supplying a continually increasing range, the need to import the majority of spare parts would remain for many years. Between 1956 and 1961, a total of 60 different trademarks of cars were imported, with 40 different makes of commercial vehicles.

"On March 31 [1962], the vehicle population, excluding trailers and motor-cycles, totalled 782,961, of which nearly 400,000 were more than five years old. Of this total, 200,000 were more than 10 years old." [334]

Nevertheless, Motor Traders (NZ) managed to cope with the trading conditions — as reported by the Christchurch Press in November 1965:

"The continued growth of the motor industry and the company's increasing capacity to serve it enabled Motor Traders (NZ) Auckland to achieve a record turn-over in the year to July 31 [1965] the chairman, Mr W K Michael, says in the annual report. The accounts show net profit…of £96,044, an increase of £16,153, or 20.2 per cent…" [335]

The acquisition of various manufacturers and distributors also improved the company's prospects by November 1971:

"The scale of the business had enlarged materially with the addition of operating companies providing a comprehensive range of goods and services. The board believed these new dimensions enhanced the group's security and future prospects.

"As announced, the net profit jumped $168,317, or 72 per cent, to $401,667 after the acquisition of E W Pidgeon and Company Ltd, distributor of Ace tyres and specialised products, and New Zealand Silencers, which makes silencers, exhaust systems and tail pipes.

"The results of these new subsidiaries were for 13 months and nine months, respectively. The distribution of spare parts and accessories showed marked growth. Prospects were good, but increasing costs eroded the profit element. A selective emphasis would be placed on those product areas where the gross profit margin was adequate under current conditions.

"Branches recently established in Wellington, Tauranga and Hastings traded satisfactorily; the increased volume attracted by the new Hamilton warehouse confirmed the advantage of the new location.

"The output of exchange clutches by the engineering division was increased to meet the demand, including the supply contracts with plants, particularly General Motors and Ford….

"Since the agency for Ferodo friction materials was acquired there had been a marked increase in activity; non-recurring start-up expenses eroded profit.

"The processing and bonding plant at Otahuhu worked to capacity and additions were now under way. New Better Brake stations were opened at New Lynn and Wellington. The company had formed an export division and market surveys of the South Pacific and Singapore were encouraging. The future in the export field was regarded with confidence." [336]

However, as with most long-established and particularly-profitable companies, takeovers are inevitable and Motor Traders (NZ) was no exception — as reported by the Christchurch Press in August 1981:

"The directors of Motor Traders (NZ) Ltd are recommending to shareholders that they accept an offer from H W Smith Ltd…[a majority shareholder of Andrews and Beaven Limited]

"It is now apparent that for the year ended July 31 [1981] the company's trading profit will be minimal. Although some sections of our group — notably manufacturing — are trading well, others are not and it is clear that some major restructuring will be necessary in any event…Accordingly, we recommend that the remaining shares be sold to H W Smith in order that this company, which in a very short time has built up an enviable record in positive company restructuring, might move towards rationalising some of our activities with those of the Christchurch-based manufacturer and national distributor, Andrews and Beaven Ltd…" [337]

A Notice by the Examiner of Commercial Practices of Consent to a Merger and Takeover Proposal, dated 4 September 1981, stated:

"(a) H W Smith Limited may acquire all the issued capital of Motor Traders (NZ) Limited; and

"(b) Andrews and Beaven Limited to acquire from Motor Traders (NZ) Limited certain assets of ACE Traders Limited and MTL Manufacturing Limited." [338]

Following the acquisition of Motor Traders (NZ), the managing director of Andrews and Beaven, W B Beaven, stated in his annual report for 1982:

"The decision in August 1981 to buy the automotive activities of Motor Traders (NZ) Ltd was an additional challenge to the company, and the integration was expected to be completed this month, giving Andrews and Beaven a much improved branch structure.

"The company gained three new branches in Auckland, one in Wanganui, a brake bonding factory (Auckland), and a muffler factory at Porirua. Considerable costs were involved in the rapid transfer of facilities and staff. In the case of engine reconditioning and remanufacture, four plants were closed down.

"Mr Beaven said. "In spite of the abnormally high integration expenses, the automotive section of the company's operation still traded at a satisfactory profit." [339]

As previously noted, by March 1983, Andrews and Beaven and Motor Traders (NZ) had, in turn been acquired by the Australian firm, Repco Corporation.

Inquiry into the Distribution of Motor Vehicle Parts

In April 1977, the Government appointed a Commission of Inquiry into the Distribution of Motor Vehicle Parts. The Commission comprised Michael James Moriarty, Alexander Campbell Begg, John Alexander Connolly, and Keith Robert Congreve. However, Keith Congreve resigned because of ill health in June 1977. The Commission reported its findings on 30 November 1977. [340]

The Commission was charged with making inquiries "…into the source of supply, distribution, and pricing of motor vehicle parts…distributed in New Zealand."

Motor vehicle parts were defined as including agricultural or horticultural machinery but not second-hand component parts, tyres or tubes, or accessories.

In its overview of the motor vehicle parts industry, the Commission outlined the distribution chain of component parts then operating in New Zealand, as per the diagram included on the following page:

DISTRIBUTION CHAIN DIAGRAM

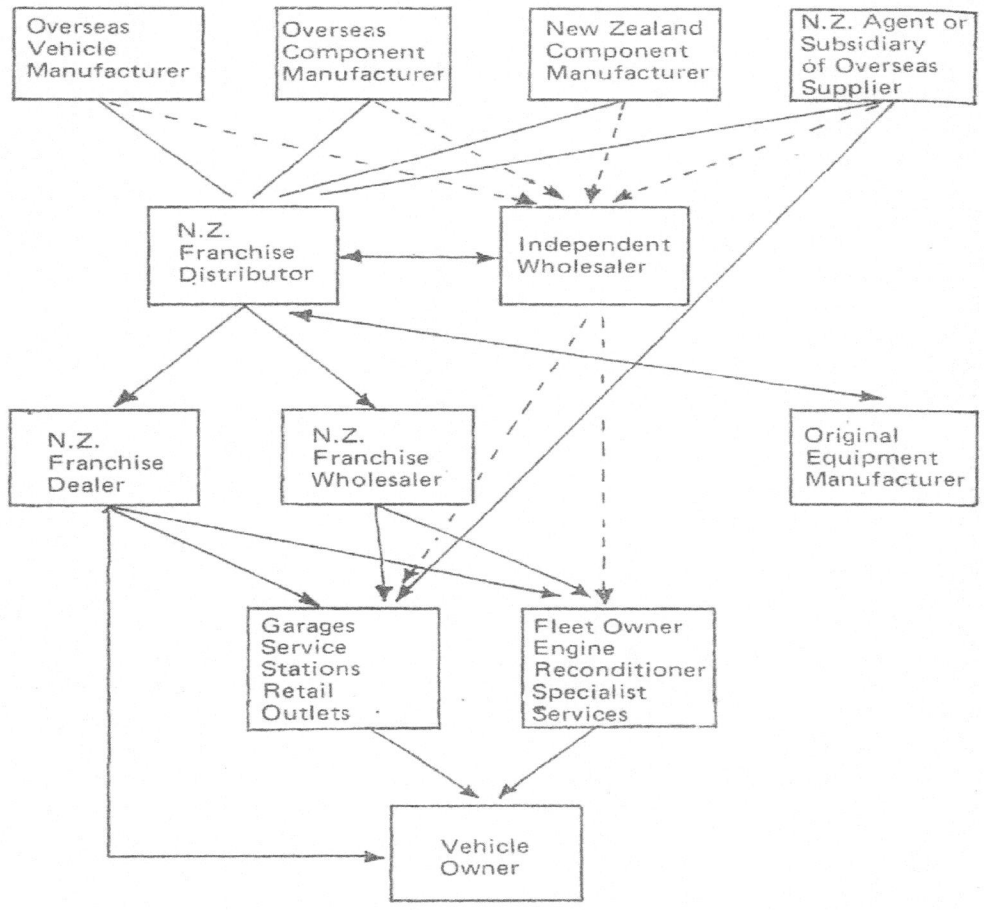

In its abridged profile of the parts industry, the Commission observed:

"A number of witnesses drew attention to the age of the vehicle population. It is clear that a high proportion of vehicles are over 10 years old and that the demand for spare parts for such vehicles requires that more lines have to be stocked with consequent costs arising from storage and financing, as well as costs incurred in identifying parts needed for the repair of vehicles long out of production...

"Another factor which has added to the difficulties of maintaining an efficient, moderate cost industry, has undoubtedly been the proliferation of models imported into this country. There may be some commonality of parts as between models coming from the same overseas manufacturers, but this advantage can be offset by modifications to parts during the assembly period of the model.

"The Commission was not specifically asked to examine the question of model proliferation but this problem was raised by a number of witnesses although none claimed to have a solution. The question is relevant to this inquiry in so far as the entry of a new model or models to the market requires the expenditure of overseas funds for an initial stock of spare parts, some of which may not be needed for many years. Overall this must add to the total cost of servicing the motor vehicle industry…"

With regard to recent price increases, the Commission noted:

"There have been very large increases in prices for replacement parts in the years from 1973 to 1977…

"An analysis of prices through this period shows that the following factors were common to all increases but varying in degree largely related to the overseas source.

"The common factors are:

"(a) Increased prices in the country of supply;

"(b) Increased freight costs from source of supply to New Zealand;

"(c) Changes in currency values adverse to New Zealand;

"(d) Increased import duties applying to parts of United Kingdom origin;

"(e) The imposition of sales tax in 1976 on many parts and again in 1977 on the remaining spare parts items…

"Evidence tendered to the Commission on the supply of replacement parts indicated that, due to the large number of different makes and models of vehicles marketed in New Zealand, the parts also were derived from a wide variety of sources.

"Ford New Zealand listed 33 New Zealand companies and a further 33 overseas suppliers in 7 countries, in addition to their parent company in Canada and Ford affiliates in Australia, Britain, Belgium, Germany, and the United States. General Motors (NZ) Ltd obtain supplies from 75 overseas sources in addition to 65 New Zealand suppliers...

"Other important sources of replacement parts are the New Zealand agents or representatives of overseas component manufacturers. Lucas Industries Ltd, supplying electrical and other equipment, and the representatives of such specialist manufacturers as S.K.F. and Timken, are typical examples.

"The importance of the New Zealand manufacturers in this field cannot be overlooked, since a wide variety of replacement parts as well as original equipment is required to be produced locally, e.g., automotive glass, muffler assemblies, spark plugs, batteries, etc. One franchised distributor indicated that, of the total revenue from the sale of replacement parts, 31.8 percent was from sales of parts made in New Zealand, and this appears to be the general pattern..."

Some additional comments contained in the Commission's report include:

"Within recent years there have been major changes within the industry in the methods of stock control, and in the geographical distribution of the bulk stockholdings. This has resulted in the centralisation of the main stock warehouses in a few centres, usually in the Auckland or Wellington regions.

"The main factors influencing this change have been:

"(a) The introduction of computer control;

"(b) The increasing cost of replacement parts;

"(c) The increasing costs of warehousing, administrative overheads, and distribution;

"(d) The need for better stock control, including more sophisticated projection of future demand and ordering;

"(e) Better control of pricing with the advent of price control...

"The New Zealand market for motor vehicles, and consequentially for replacement parts, is remarkable in that while it is too small to be other than of marginal importance to the overseas vehicle manufacturers (with the exception of Australia), it has such a wide variety of makes and models available to the public.

"While this wide freedom of choice is obviously valued by the public, it involves very substantial costs which are less welcome. The stocking and marketing of the necessary replacement parts for so many makes and models adds substantially to the annual costs of vehicle ownership…

"The vehicle owner has eventually to pay for the cost of obsolescence in the price of the parts which are sold. It is not practicable or economic to stock every part, but the closer the stockholding is to 100 percent, the higher the obsolescence provision becomes. Some balance must be struck which provides a satisfactory level of service with an acceptable level of price.

"There has been some criticism of the number of links in the chain of distribution of replacement parts, and of the effects of the mark-ups applied at each point on the price to the retail buyer, and it has been sufficiently demonstrated in the evidence supplied to the Commission that the elimination of one or more of these links has a substantial effect on the price.

"Lucas parts for example are supplied to British Leyland and thence to New Zealand Motor Corporation, but the same parts are obtainable through Lucas Industries in New Zealand which imports direct from the United Kingdom manufacturer, and thus eliminates British Leyland from the chain...

"Concern has been expressed to the Commission on the length of the distribution chain and the high mark-ups being applied at the various points along the chain...In dealing with the question of the reasonableness of mark-ups being obtained it should be emphasised that the question taken in isolation is meaningless. The level of mark-ups should be examined in relation to both the stock turn and return on investment being achieved by the individual company. Taken in this context margins which at first sight appear excessive ran be viewed more dispassionately...

"It is reported that the modern motor vehicle contains some 10,000 parts, of which about 600 are critical to its operation. How many of these should be stocked? The franchised distributors clearly recognise their obligation to provide a service and this is demonstrated by the very large inventories carried of which some 20 to 40 percent are over 3 years old. Three franchised distributors each list over 100,000 line items pertaining to their particular vehicles, and one carries over 85,000 different line items in the warehouse...

"The motor vehicle industry (including agricultural and contracting machinery) has been subject to Government controls of varying degrees of severity for many years. This applies also to the supply, distribution, and pricing of parts. So far as replacement parts are concerned the influence of Government policy [includes]: Import licensing; Industrial development; Customs duties; Sales tax; Price control; Overall Government policy...

"Price control over spare parts of motor vehicles was removed in 1965 but reimposed on 12 November 1970 by the Price Freeze Regulations 1970. Since then spare parts have been under continuous control in one form or another.

"Some 6000 firms are engaged in the sale of spare parts ranging from major manufacturers (the assemblers) to medium to small component manufacturers; large and small dealerships and above 4600 repair garages, service stations, and panelbeaters, many employing less than 10 persons...

"A number of organisations stated that the spare parts side of the motor vehicle industry could not be looked at in isolation from other parts of the industry, viz, assembly, distribution, and selling of new and second-hand vehicles; the manufacture of component parts in New Zealand; and the servicing of the fleet whether by service garages, engine reconditioners, or panelbeaters...

"The major user organisations in their submissions criticised almost exclusively the escalation in prices of replacement parts and little mention was made of supply problems or of the lack of service or efficiency in the distribution system...

"The Commission has concluded that the efficiency of supply and distribution and the quality of the service provided are satisfactory and has no recommendations on these matters...

"The Commission's investigations have not disclosed any basis for allegations of profiteering in the supply of motor vehicle parts. Indeed it appears that some sections of the industry are experiencing difficult trading conditions with a low level of profit, and that at all levels where substantial stocks of replacement parts are maintained, the escalating costs of replacing stocks is causing severe liquidity problems.

"The industry has suffered with all others from the general effects of inflation on costs of operation, and in addition three successive devaluations of the New Zealand dollar and other international currency changes have had a major impact on parts prices. The effects of these influences have been accentuated by the extension of sales tax to all motor vehicle parts in the Budgets of 1976 and 1977...

Conclusions

"The Commission regards the competition between franchise dealers and independent wholesalers as desirable and conducive to efficiency and to the maintenance of a satisfactory level of service and prices.

"The Commission is satisfied that the protection accorded to local manufacturers of replacement parts has not been misused.

"The Commission has concluded that the efficiency of supply and distribution and the quality of the service provided are satisfactory and has no recommendations on these matters." [340]

Chapter Six

The Assemblers Disassemble

A Brief History of New Zealand Tariffs

New Zealand has never been a particularly wealthy country — almost always dependent on export sales of primary produce and import controls to survive in the commercial world. The importation of luxury goods, including motor vehicles and accessories, has always been subject to Government-imposed restriction and regulation.

Nevertheless, as William B Sutch wrote in his 1969 revised history, *poverty and progress*, from the day New Zealand was founded:

"The prevailing economic philosophy was, of course, that of free trade…underlined by the fact that Parliament predominantly represented the farming community." [1]

It is only since the advent of manufacturing industries that tariffs, import licensing, and other trade restrictions have become an important means of protecting New Zealand's commercial enterprises and their workers from overseas products.

Poverty and progress continues:

"As the population grew and railways widened the markets of the main centres, it was possible to establish more industries to compete with imports. In the [18] forties the main industries had sprung up to supply local needs: ship-building, brick-making, flax cutting and rope-making, soap- and candle-making, sawmilling, brewing, blacksmithing, leather-working, coopering, fencing, flourmilling, printing.

"By 1870, manufacturing establishments had expanded to make biscuits, soft drinks, malt, lime, bone-manure, joinery, coaches, and scouring wool.

"Perhaps most important of all were the iron and brass foundries and engineering workshops; and there were, of course, goldmining and coal mining. Gasworks had been built in Auckland in 1862, in Christchurch and Dunedin in 1863, and Wellington in 1869…

"By 1896 there were nine woollen mills in New Zealand. This industry, as with most New Zealand industries at the time, began without tariff protection. Until 1888 the only product of significance to be protected was soap made from tallow, the product of the boiling-down works. Aided by a duty in 1869 it established itself on the New Zealand market… [2]

"…against the wishes of the free traders [Prime Minister, Harry Atkinson] put through in 1888 the first major tariff measure which would raise money from taxing imports and at the same time help industries — boot-manufacturers, garment-makers, machinery-makers, woollen millers, and the metal-working industry. The duty was 20 per cent… [3]

"…customs duties continued as the main revenue producer (three-quarters of it) throughout the [18]nineties. The average tariff rate on items taxed was 25 per cent but those on the imported necessities of life remained higher: sugar, 30; tea, 40; rice, 42; salt, 48; kerosene (for lighting and some cooking), 90 per cent…In 1895 there had been some lightening of customs duties on grocery items; in 1900 the duty on kerosene was removed, but it was not until 1907, after trade union agitation, that there were substantial reductions of duties on household items… [4]

"In New Zealand, unlike many other countries, the number of items which were admitted duty free kept on increasing and there was thus less possibility of the growth of industries. The percentage was 31 in 1894, 32 in 1896, 38 in 1906 and 50 in 1908. In Australia, on the other hand, frequent changes were made to the tariff to give greater protection to more infant industries… [5]

"…Britain and other industrial trading nations…preferred import duties, for, if any strong industrialists from abroad thought it worthwhile, they could surmount a tariff, unless it were prohibitive, by temporarily lowering their prices to force the domestic industry out or stop it growing and thereby maintain their goods in the New Zealand market. With import selection this undercutting had its limits, for if the New Zealand industry were producing satisfactorily and supplying its share of the market, the amount of imports permitted could be made complementary." [6]

The Twentieth Century View

During the first years of the twentieth century, the rights and wrongs of import controls were again subject to much debate in New Zealand, particularly with regard to imports from the country's chief export markets of Britain, the rest of the Commonwealth, and America.

In 1907, it was proving difficult to negotiate a tariff agreement with Britain, then a particularly important recipient of New Zealand's meat and dairy produce. Yet agreements reached with other countries were more successful — as reported by The Thames Star on 18 January 1907:

"New Zealand is entering into reciprocal tariffs with the Commonwealth of Australia, with South Africa, Canada, and America — in fact it is carrying, out a policy of fiscal reform and advancement with other countries, while the Motherland foolishly stands aloof." [7]

Eventually, a British preferential tariff regime with New Zealand would be settled, much to the regret of those in favour of trade free of regulation of any sort:

"Freetraders have never denied that nations could prosper under a protective tariff. They have simply pointed out the error of supposing that the prosperity was in any way due to the influence of a protective tariff. They also consider that the restriction of trade produced by high tariffs prevents nations reaping the full benefit of the rising tide of prosperity and accentuates the difficulties produced by a period of loss of confidence when prices are low and money tight." [8]

In his speech to the Auckland Chamber of Commerce Members' Annual Dinner in June 1907, Ivor Evans outlined the preferences of many of his business colleagues when it came to the results they expected from tariff protection soon to be subject to Parliamentary debate:

"The very means of existence of many people depended largely on this question, and, therefore, the revision of the tariff should be from a broad statesmanlike standpoint. While endeavouring to cheapen the cost of living to every citizen, Parliament must at the same time consider the need of assisting local industries — and do nothing in either case to impoverish the revenue.

"Everything in the shape of a luxury was fair game for revenue purposes. The true aim of any Government was not the building up of large surpluses, while the cost of living continued abnormally high. The tariff should afford a fair and reasonable assistance to industries and manufactures established, and capable of being started with fair assistance from a tariff. No raw material, not produced in the colony, should be taxed.

"What they wanted was local industries to employ local labour in manufacturing the complete article. The manufacturers should have such protection, as to be on a slightly better footing than the over-sea shipper, but the amount should not be such as to become a subsidy, as well as protection.

"Opportunity should not be given to any individual or set of individuals to exploit their fellow men. High tariffs tended to produce both millionaires and paupers, and any parliament that placed on the Statute Books an act which conduces to the unequal distribution of wealth was betraying its trust.

"What was wanted, was a just and also a simple tariff, and not one which only experts could understand. Complicated tariffs were an inducement to fraud. In the present tariff were many anomalies which, they hoped, would be swept away." [9]

The Tariff Act 1907

The month of September 1907 was particularly notable for two reasons.

First of all, by royal proclamation of King Edward, "…on and after the twenty-sixth day of September, one thousand nine hundred and seven, the said Colony of New Zealand and the territory belonging thereto shall be called and known by the title of the Dominion of New Zealand.." [10]

Secondly, on 25 September of that year, Parliament enacted the Tariff Act 1907 — "An Act to impose Duties of Customs and Excise and to amend the Law relating thereto." [11]

The Act comprised various Schedules of goods subject to duty or, as in the case of Schedule B, none. Those Schedules listing motor vehicles and parts included:

Schedule A (Class XIII) — "Motor vehicles, motor car bodies, or bodies for motor busses (sic), whether attached or unattached — rate of duty (tariff) 20 per cent ad valorem (in proportion to the value)"

Schedule B (Class XIII) — exempt from duties of Customs if…entered for home consumption — "Material for the manufacture of carriages, carts, drays, and wagons, motor vehicles, and railway cars or wagons — viz., springs, truck pedestals, mountings, trimmings…rubber tyres, pneumatic rubber tyres…inner tubes; also iron or metal fittings…for the manufacture of carriages, carts, drays, wagons, and motor vehicles…" [12]

Motor Vehicles

During the Parliamentary debate on the 1907 Tariff Bill, "Mr Massey said '…there should be higher duties on motor cars, which at present were undeniably the toy of the rich.'" [13]

Not everyone agreed and the initial response to the Tariff Act was one of general acceptance — as per the Auckland Star editorial of 25 November 1907:

"The new Tariff Act, in spite of its complexity and the wide range of interest it involves, already seems to have justified its claim to produce the maximum increase in revenue and security for our industries, with a minimum of disturbance or injury to trade; and it confirms our fiscal policy on the sound basis of moderate Protectionism." [14]

As Daniel A Witt outlined in his 1985 Institute of Economic Research study, 'The New Zealand Motor Car Industry After The Plan':

"From the conception of the motor car industry in New Zealand, there has been a high degree of Government imposed regulation. Over the years the regulation has been in various forms and in a constant state of change. Initially the protection was indigenous to New Zealand as a result of its location. Therefore, distance that translated into high shipping costs of CBUs was the stimulus to engage in local assembly and protect it in the early years. Successive tariffs followed and supplemented the natural protection.

"Motor vehicles first appeared in a tariff item in 1907. Duty for CBUs was 20% and local vehicle body builders (the means by which vehicles were assembled which evolved from coachbuilding prior to the mass production assembly line introduced in New Zealand by General Motors in 1926) were provided free entry of chassis and materials, thereby providing them protection.

"From the onset, the removal and reinstatement of protective tariffs occurred. In 1915, the war tariff removed the protection previously provided to the local builder and substituted a flat 10% tariff. In 1921 protection was reinstated with an additional tariff of £15 pounds for CBUs.

"The protective tariff is cited as being largely responsible for allowing motor vehicle assembling to get a firm start in New Zealand. A 1924 trade journal indicated, 'The busy times of the industry can be credited to a measure of tariff protection, for which the manufacturers are grateful…' The production figures clearly illustrate this." [15]

In his New Zealand Institute of Economic Research Paper, 'Development Options in the New Zealand Motor Car Assembly Industry', published in 1971, William Rose commented on the history of the tariff and licensing situation that first influenced the unassembled and assembled vehicle industry:

"The motor assembly industry, like any other, operates in a commercial environment substantially modified by government intervention designed to change the shape of the industry consistently with public policy." [16]

"In 1907 a new tariff itemized motor vehicles for the first time and drew a pattern which, in its essentials, has persisted. Assembled motor vehicles were to be dutiable at an ordinary rate of 20 per cent but a schedule of exemptions provided for the free entry of chassis whether attached to a vehicle or not. Effectively the local body building industry could import its materials free and enjoyed protection on body building. The war tariff of 1915 remove this protection and substituted a flat 10 per cent tariff on body and chassis, but protection was reintroduced in 1921 when an additional variable specific duty was imposed on assembled bodies…" [17]

Customs Amendment Act 1921

The Customs Amendment Act 1921, an amendment to the principal Customs Act 1913, included motor vehicles and parts thereof as Class XI. The British Preferential Tariff remained at 10 per cent for assembled vehicles with rates of 20 and 25 per cent levied on vehicles from North America and elsewhere. Motor vehicle bodies attracted the same tariffs plus an additional duty ranging from £15 (British Preferential) to £22 10s. Tyres (then spelt as tires) and inner tubes were subject to the same tariff duty as assembled vehicles. [18]

Customs Amendment Act 1926

"The dominance of North American cars on the New Zealand market (in 1929 19,000 of the 23,000 passenger vehicles and chassis imported came from North America) occasioned criticism from a number of sources on the ground that it prejudiced New Zealand's trading relationship with Britain." [19]

"In 1926 — a record year for NZ car sales — British cars had accounted for only 11% of New Zealand's market, but the percentage rose to 19% in 1927…" [20]

This increase followed the passage of the Customs Amendment Act 1926 which retained the 10 per cent British Preferential Tariff for assembled vehicles but increased the Intermediate and General Tariff for such vehicles to 25 and 35 per cent, respectively. [21]

"…the specific duty on bodies was replaced by an ad valorem duty of 10 per cent on the first £200 by value of the whole car in an attempt to reduce the effective duty on smaller, particularly British, cars." [22]

As defined in the 1926 Act:

"(1.) When any body of a motor-vehicle suited or designed for carrying passengers is imported by itself or otherwise than as set out above, body duty shall be payable, and the Minister shall determine the amount of such body duty. The body duty so payable shall, as nearly as may be, be equal to the amount of body duty that would have been payable if such body had been imported as part of and attached to a motor-vehicle manufactured in the same country as the body.

"(2.) Where the Minister is of opinion that any body duty is being or is likely to be evaded or avoided by the importation of any motor-vehicles without engines, tires, or other component parts which, in the ordinary course of business, are usually imported therewith, the Minister may, at his discretion, require that body duty shall be paid as if such engines, tires, or other component parts had been imported with such vehicles." [23]

Customs Amendment Act 1927

"The NZ government revised the tariff system in August 1927 to promote the smaller British cars. British chassis could be landed, then bodied and sold at an advantage to American ones, as a new duty of 10% had now to be paid on the whole value of any car valued at £200 or over, but this was perceived as a failure by the industry in Britain…

"Smaller motor body builders in Christchurch and Wellington objected, but in 1927, New Zealand assembled cars were given a further 5% advantage over CBU [completely-built-up] imports by the Reform Party Government of Joseph Coates…The government was beginning to see motor assembly as an essential industry…" [24]

Motor-Vehicle Assemblers v Motor-Body Builders

The Customs Amendment Acts of 1926 and 1927 went some way to protect the motor vehicle assembly industry by ensuring that the importation of (particularly British) built-up vehicles was far more expensive than the separate importation of chassis and body for assembly in New Zealand.

However, this protection for the assembly industry did nothing for those of the country's original coach builders who had progressed to the construction of New Zealand-made vehicle bodies for fitting to imported chassis — as reported by the Christchurch Press on 15 September 1927:

"The effect of the new tariff proposals is viewed with alarm by local motor-body builders and is likely to lead to the dismissal of a large number of employees. 'It means the-ruin of the industry,' said the manager of one concern yesterday who went on to state that his firm was dismissing 35 men this week, and had taken the step of cancelling by cable orders for material of a value of over £1000.

"Besides this, he said, it had been found necessary to cancel an order for some £200 worth of Southland timber. 'The only people who will benefit from the tariff,' he said, 'are motor assembly concerns who assemble cars manufactured in outside countries.'

"'In the past, bodies of cars which were not assembled had been imported on the same basis of duty as assembled bodies, but now these were reduced by five per cent. Formerly local body builders were accorded some little measure of protection; now, however, the position was altered, and the industry had to face a very bad outlook.'

"Mr Vivian Grant, secretary of the New Zealand Coach and Motor-body Builders' Association, said that the new tariff was of no benefit to the local body-builders. They had requested the Government to admit to the Dominion British motor chassis duty free, but the appeal had been ignored.

"A 20 per cent, instead of the 35 per cent, duty on foreign chassis had been asked for, in response to which the Government had left the duty as it was, in consequence of which the body-builders received no benefit. Yet in the face of this, preference was given to knocked-down bodies for assembly in New Zealand.

"British manufacturers were penalised because American material coming into the Dominion through Canada with 50 per cent British manufacture in it could be landed at the same rate of duty as bodies from England.

"No English manufacturer was at present in the position of being able to export bodies unassembled, in consequence of which all the preference went to such American lines as were imported via Canada. It had to be remembered, too, that all the work of assembly in the Dominion was carried on by unskilled labour, in addition to which all the material was foreign, not a particle of it being made in New Zealand.

"From another source, it was learned that thousands of pounds had been expended by local firms in Christchurch in extending their premises, which it is claimed are as modern and as up-to-date as any in the matter of equipment. Builders after going to so much expense in this connexion now discovered that their outlay was rendered superfluous by the tariff proposals.

"Mr Pryce, of the firm of Cooper and Pryce, said that if the proposals were made operative, it would mean that all the machinery he had installed recently would become idle. It seemed to him that the Government had endeavoured to assist the motor-body builders, apart from chassis, by increasing the duty on such raw materials as paints, white leads, and varnishes. Another point touched on by Mr Pryce was that his firm had 16 apprentices, who had to be taught the trade. He wondered what was to become of them. They could not be turned over to car-assembling, which was not a trade, but was purely for unskilled or partly-skilled labour.

"As a result of the action of the Government, his firm would have no option but to dismiss several of its men, and thus add to the ranks of the unemployed. He also stated that a large quantity of Southland beech, which he had ordered for motor-bodies, was drying in stacks, so that the tariff was a direct setback to the industry.

"Mr R. J. Jay, manager of the Christchurch Motors; Ltd., said that the tariff was a blow to the English car manufacturer, and it appeared as though the Government was assisting the Americans." [25]

Anxious to save the livelihoods of its members, the Wellington Coach and Motor Body Builders' Association appealed for public support by means of newspaper advertisements:

"BUY NEW ZEALAND MOTOR BODIES! Every time you purchase a NEW ZEALAND-MADE ARTICLE you help to keep your fellow workers employed. Too much of our money goes abroad; keep it in your own country. If we must spend money on IMPORTED MOTOR-CARS, a wise Government would place a prohibitive duty on motor bodies so that only chassis would be imported, and the body work done here, as is done in Australia." [26] and:

"BUY NEW ZEALAND MOTOR BODIES! The folly of extravagant importing has now been exposed, and the time has come for New Zealand to help itself instead of following the old stupid policy of helping alien manufacturers who are benefiting at the expense of every employed and unemployed New Zealander. The public can, for the present, do no better than follow the advice of the Dominion's political leaders, who have at last realised that New Zealand can no longer expect prosperity if economic reliance is placed solely upon the prices that can be obtained overseas for the produce of the land." [27]

Railways Protection

Criticism of the new tariffs on vehicle imports also came from motorists and others suspicious of an ulterior motive:

"The Reform Party (May 1925 - December 1928) had incurred the ire of the Kiwi motorist through raising customs on automobiles twice in a short period in what was seen as an attempt to promote the use of the railways, a government department." [28]

This suspicion of Government protection for rail had existed for some time and was more overtly demonstrated as road-user charges — as explained in a Letter to the Editor of the Hawke's Bay Tribune published 12 November 1926:

"Sir, —Heavy transport in our Dominion is being heavily handicapped by the extreme measures of the Reform Government, whose slogan during the last electioneering campaign was 'More business in Government and less Government in business.'

"The policy adopted to protect railways is seriously affecting the large amount of capital outlay expended by private, enterprise, in that the restriction with regard to weight allowed to be carried over roads, whether served by rail or not, together with heavy traffic licenses, which have become so heavy is making the carriage of goods impossible for farmers and small townships to procure excepting at very heavy expenditure…

"Sir Joseph Ward, when speaking on the question last session, strongly urged the Government to concentrate their capital expenditure upon the completion of main trunk lines and their energies upon the carriage of freight and passengers over long distances. He uttered a warning note against entering into competition with motor transport, controlled by private capital…F G Smith, Napier" [29]

A Time of Poverty

By May 1930, the Reform Government had been replaced by the United Party with George Forbes as Prime Minister. However, it was time for another Depression, a really big one this time —

"Export prices had fallen catastrophically as a result of the world economic crisis. New Zealand could no longer borrow abroad, the overseas banks operating in New Zealand refused help, and the Bank of New Zealand agreed with them. Government revenue fell away. Public works were virtually stopped and unemployment went up by scores of thousands annually.

"The only solution that the Forbes Government could propose was to cut wages, reduce the number of jobs, reduce all Government activity, and abolish some of it. Early in 1931 civil service wages were cut 10 per cent and private firms were asked to follow suit." [30]

The nation's businessmen recommended cuts to every possible item of expenditure while economists advised that adjustments had to be made to the economic system.

"Until…January 1933, the advice of the businessmen was followed. Instead of trying to devise ways of maintaining production and incomes and reducing imports of goods which New Zealand could produce (and which was done half a dozen years later…), the businessmen advised drastic deflation which reduced public works and the production of goods and made unemployment worse.

"The people least able to bear the burden were, in 1931 and 1932, those asked by the Government to bear it: the pensioner, the hospital patient, the schoolchild, the widow, the family man…" [31]

Joseph Gordon Coates

Following the 1931 general election, a coalition of the United and Reform Parties retained power with George Forbes as Prime Minister. Joseph (Gordon) Coates subsequently became Minister of Finance desperate to stem the continuous rise in unemployment and to improve the country's foreign exchange position.

In the vehicle assembly and motor body building industries that meant further restrictions on the importation of fully-assembled vehicles. Of course, ever mindful of the need to encourage New Zealand's reciprocal meat and dairy trade with Britain, the British Preferential Tariff was retained:

"In 1932 the Right Honourable Coates…devised a tariff that further distinguished between assembled and non-assembled vehicles: fully-assembled vehicles from Britain were to be charged a duty of 15% and English Completely Knocked Down (CKD) cars 5%, but for importers of American and European cars the tariff was substantial – 50% for US CKD and 60% for Completely Built Up (imported, finished) cars." [32]

The Customs Tariff Commission 1934

The Customs Tariff Commission, consisting of George Craig, Comptroller of Customs; James Burman Gow, settler of Whakatane; Bernard Edward Murphy, Professor of Economics, Victoria University College; and George Augustus Pascoe, Christchurch Company Director, was appointed by the Governor General on 9 May 1933.

The Commission's purpose: "To inquire into the Customs Tariff of New Zealand, and to recommend for consideration by the Government any alterations therein, having regard to existing trade agreements to which New Zealand is a party and particularly to the agreement concluded at Ottawa in 1932 between His Majesty's Governments in the United Kingdom and in New Zealand; to the financial, economic, and industrial conditions in the Dominion; to the reasonable requirements of local industries which are being conducted in an efficient manner and are economically justifiable; and to all other relevant considerations." [33]

In his later summation of the Commission's findings, Joseph Coates, then Minister of Customs, explained the need for the tariff inquiry:

"Under the Ottawa Agreement of 1932 New Zealand, in common with the other Dominions, was committed to hold an inquiry into the tariff, and, if necessary, to revise it in accordance with certain explicitly stated principles. Our undertaking was that protection against United Kingdom products should be afforded only to industries which are 'reasonably assured of sound opportunities for success' and, further, that protection should be on a level to enable the United Kingdom producer to compete on the basis of the relative cost of economical and efficient production…" [34]

The Commission's original reporting date of 30 September 1933 was extended to 31 January 1934, then to 28 February 1934. After interviewing no fewer than 682 witnesses and visiting some sixty-two establishments, the Tariff Commission finally submitted its report to Parliament on 29 March 1934. [35]

In his address to Parliament of 10 July 1934, outlining the Tariff Commission's proposals and his Government's intended course of action, Joseph Coates commented:

"New Zealand, although a country with a relatively small population, has a very large external trade, upon which it is vitally dependent to discharge its external obligations and to carry on its national life. The tariff, therefore, must be considered not only from the point of view of encouraging production for local consumption, but also of developing markets abroad for our exportable surplus. Another and very important matter which must be borne in mind when our tariff is under review is the revenue required to carry on the Government of the country...

"The policy of the Government with reference to the tariff may be stated as:

"Development of local industry:—

(1) To accord protection only to those industries regarded as suitable to New Zealand;

(2) To grant protection only to the extent necessary to enable local industries to function efficiently;

(3) To give effect to the Ottawa Agreement so far as it relates to the New Zealand tariff;

(4) To give employment to our people;

(5) To keep down costs of living and costs of production;

(6) To admit raw materials for primary and secondary industries at as low a rate as possible.

"It does not seem likely that in the near future any considerable market will be found outside New Zealand for the products of our secondary industries. Hence, generally speaking, the market will be limited to the local demand. It is obvious that where there is only a small demand for an article it would not, except in very exceptional cases, be economic to assist the manufacture of such an article by a protective duty.

"Motor-vehicles

"As an item in the tariff schedule motor-vehicles have a number of special features:

"The Customs taxation derived from them is of importance from the viewpoint of revenue; they are a class of manufacture in which we give an especial degree of British preference. In passing, it may be mentioned that of the number of our motor-vehicles imported the percentage from United Kingdom in 1929 was 15 per cent; in 1930, 21 per cent; in 1931, 65 per cent; in 1932, 83 per cent; in 1933, 75 per cent.

"Although they are not made in New Zealand, we are concerned in the question of body-building and also in the more substantial question of assembling cars. All of these considerations have been borne in mind in reviewing the tariff, and, in addition, the aim has been to simplify the tariff for administration, and, as in other items, to reduce it to the advantage of users and consumers.

"The Tariff Commission's recommendations, not all of which the Government propose to adopt in full, cover the following points:

"(1) Abolition of the differential duty between the complete vehicle and the chassis. This was intended to encourage the building of motor-bodies in New Zealand. It has not succeeded.

"(2) Imposition of a flat rate duty of 15 per cent on all motor-vehicles entered under the British Preferential Tariff. This would have the effect of reducing the advantage in duty obtained on vehicles imported in parts — completely knocked down — for assembling in New Zealand.

"(3) Increase of the duty on motor-cycles, under the British Preferential Tariff, from the present 10 per cent, to 15 per cent.

"From these recommendations the Government's decision departs in two respects:

"Firstly, with regard to the assembly of cars in New Zealand, the Commission were of opinion that the industry was one suited to the conditions in the Dominion. They found from figures produced to them that, owing to freight and other savings, the industry could be economically carried on without special protection.

"Information obtained, however, since the Commission reported, with respect to the more recent types of cars which have come upon the market shows that some concession in the rate of duty is necessary if the industry of assembling cars in New Zealand is to be carried on satisfactorily.

"The Government have therefore decided to depart from the recommendations of the Commission in this respect. Having regard to the desirability of encouraging the assembly of cars in New Zealand, we propose that completely knocked down cars should be admitted at lower rates than those on cars completely set up.

"Honourable members and others who are familiar with conditions in the motor trade are aware of the value of the employment provided in assembling here in New Zealand the cars of some of the principal British and American manufacturers. We do not propose to disturb this condition, but, on the contrary, the aim is to encourage other manufacturers to assemble their cars in New Zealand and utilize New Zealand labour and material.

"The other variation from the Commission's recommendation that we have made is in maintaining motor-cycles at their former low rate. In so doing we sacrifice the advantage of simplicity that would be given by charging motor-cycles at the same rate as motor-vehicles; but this advantage to the Government is foregone rather than increase the cost of motor-cycles which are a form of transport popular amongst the less affluent in the community." [36]

Customs Acts Amendment Act 1934
"Thus in 1934, to encourage British trade and local assembly, the Coates' Tariff was introduced. This tariff regime allowed preferential treatment to British sourced cars and distinguished between C.B.U. [completely built up] and C.K.D. cars." [37]

The Coates' Tariff was subsequently legislated for with the passage of the Customs Acts Amendment Act 1934 of which Tariff item 389 (a) defined:

"Motor-vehicles unassembled or completely knocked down (c.k.d.) — Up to and including 31st December, 1934 – British Preferential Tariff 10 per cent and General Tariff 55 per cent.

"On and after 1st January, 1935 — British Preferential Tariff 5 per cent and General Tariff 50 per cent."

The British Preferential Tariff for assembled motor vehicles, imported on or after 1 January 1935, was listed as 15 per cent and for non-British vehicles, 60 per cent. [38]

Section 16(1) of the 1934 Customs Act also stated:

"The Minister shall from time to time, by notice in the *Gazette* determine the goods which may be entered under Tariff item 389(a) as motor-vehicles unassembled or completely knocked down, and may in like manner determine the conditions under which such goods shall be imported into and used in New Zealand and the purposes for which those goods shall be so used." [39]

First Determination
The first such determination defining the composition of a CKD was published by Joseph Coates, as Minister of Customs, in the New Zealand Gazette of 18 October 1934. This determination described the CKD car (Class I) as consisting separately of:

"(i)(a) Chassis frame, engine, and gearbox; (b) Scuttle, wind-shield assembly, mud-guards, valances, running boards and other parts of chassis; (ii) Bodies consisting of (a) metal panels and framework (b) Other parts of body excluding upholstery, seat springs, and cushions (in any form whatever)

"Motor vehicles being omnibuses, commercial trucks, or delivery vans (Class II): Chassis" [40]

"The [1934] determination defined a c.k.d. car as one in which the chassis frame was assembled and the engine and gearbox, but no other parts, attached. Other elements such as the scuttle and windscreen assembly, and the body shell, could be assembled and primed. Upholstery materials could be cut to shape but not sewn. There was no restriction on the range of components that could be imported as part of the c.k.d. pack, the determination dealing solely with the degree of assembly that could be undertaken.

"The Customs determination, the agreement with the United Kingdom companies, and recovery from the depression led to a rapid expansion of the New Zealand industry…" [41]

The Canadian Anomaly

As outlined in a previous chapter, by 1922, Model T Fords were being assembled in New Zealand by the Colonial Motor Company with components shipped from the Ford factory in Canada. As a fellow Commonwealth country, these imports from Canada were entitled to receive preferential tariff consideration.

However, as reported by The Dominion on 22 August 1930, that consideration had been described as somewhat of a cheap back door for American vehicles, first complained of in 1926:

"Allegations that as a result of Canada being used as an exporting point for the United States of America interests, the New Zealand Government was losing not less than a quarter of a million pounds annually in Custom duties on motor vehicles alone, and that the English manufacturer was not receiving the preference which Parliament intended, were made by a deputation which waited upon the Prime Minister, Hon. G. W. Forbes, yesterday.

"The deputation consisted of representatives of the British (U.K.) Manufacturers' Association of New Zealand. Mr. G. H. Scott, president of the association, who was the spokesman, said that the increased rates of duty imposed by Parliament even in 1926, which aimed at giving a preference to the manufacturers of the United Kingdom, had not been collected in regard to the majority of cars bearing the names of manufacturers in the United States…

"'I put it to you, sir,' continued Mr. Scott, 'is it fair to our English manufacturers that a change in your tariff in New Zealand, which aimed at collecting higher duties from American vehicles, should be capable of evasion by the fact that the preference certificate leaves the gate wide open simply because it does not go far enough to give adequate protection and brings about a serious, but avoidable, condition of affairs?'

"'It may surprise you to learn that out of 27 cars bearing American names and trade marks now being imported into New Zealand only about five of them are paying the American rate of duty which Parliament provided and expected they would have to pay from 1926 onwards.'

"'As an example,' said Mr. Scott, 'take a car of a well-known American make selling in the United States retail at 875 dollars, equalling £175. If imported through Canada the duty payable is approximately £34/4/10. If imported to New Zealand direct from the United States the duty payable under to-day's tariff is £95/15/7, showing a difference of £60/10/9.'

"Mr. Scott said that between 1926 and 1929 the imports of tires from Canada were very little short of doubling, whereas the imports from the United States had dwindled to almost one-third. These changes in volume did not show any corresponding change in regard to the trade marks or names (and the same remarks could be applied in regard to motor vehicles).

"'Obviously this Dominion's, highway fund was losing a large portion of revenue which the community would require to make up in some other form of taxation. Tire companies of the United Kingdom were suffering because such competition was not fair to them.'

"The Prime Minister, in his reply, said it was the desire of the Government that as much assistance should be given to the Homeland as was possible. That policy was evidenced in the tariff, and it was only right that the people whom the Legislature intended to benefit should benefit. He intended to go into the question of the proportion of preference granted to Canada while he was abroad." [42]

The Coates' Tariff Schedule eventually recognised the Ford anomaly with a Gazette Notice published on 21 November 1935 stipulating:

"As of 1 May 1936, modified duty on CKD motor-vehicles imported into New Zealand produced or manufactured in Canada and subject to the British Preferential Tariff:
— when local production [in Canada] is not less than 75 per cent — Tariff 10 per cent
— when local production [in Canada] is not less than 65 per cent — Tariff 12½ per cent
— when local production [in Canada] is less than 65 per cent — Tariff 50 per cent" [43]

Following the introduction of the 'local production' requirement for CKDs from Canada, Ford incorporated the Ford Motor Company of New Zealand Limited in January 1936 and established its own assembly plant at Seaview, Lower Hutt in April 1937. In doing so, Ford took over the distribution of Ford products in New Zealand and was able to benefit from more favourable import tariffs as a local manufacturer.

Customs Determination Amended

"In 1939 the Customs determination was amended so that hide leathers, upholstery textiles and flock, and other kinds of upholstery padding could no longer be imported as part of a c.k.d. pack. Batteries were also to be excluded. At the same time the permitted degree of overseas assembly was reduced. Welded panels could no longer be soldered, filled or trimmed, and body shells could not be painted." [44]

"The exclusion of specific items prompted the development of the componentry industry, as assemblers were forced to source vehicle components locally. These items were called the mandatory deletion items...The effect of this policy was to force local assemblers to use domestically-sourced components, or else pay a tariff, depending on where the componentry was sourced." [45]

Some of the mandatory deletion items also included various hoses and cables, springs, driveshafts, exhaust systems (successfully manufactured by Campbell Motors at Thames), floor coverings, curved or flat glass, rubber tyres and tubes, radiator assemblies, spark plugs, radios, wiring looms or harnesses, some alloy wheels... [46]

Import Restrictions

The first Labour Government was re-elected for a second term in November 1938 at a time when a large proportion of overseas loans, some dating from 1889, were due for repayment to Britain. As described by William Sutch in his book, Poverty and Progress in New Zealand:

"...in the eight years 1939 to 1947, debt amounting to £96 million, a very large sum in those days, was due to be repaid by New Zealand...The date of 1 January 1940 was a most important one for the future of New Zealand's social welfare and economic development, for on that day New Zealand had to repay in London over £17 million." [47]

New Zealand's financial situation was referred to in a 'Financial News' article published in London — as reported by the Grey River Argus on 14 November 1938:

"London — Mr H. H. V. Hodson, editor of 'The Round Table' has an article in 'The Financial News' referring to New Zealand's future under Labour. He draws attention, firstly, to a strain on its financial capacity which he considers likely to result in regard to overseas exchange and, secondly, to the flow of imports having been in excess of the Dominion's current means of payment. He adds: 'Outsiders, viewing New Zealand's affairs need not fear socialism as such, as the real cause of anxiety lies in the chances of internal inflation in a country which is dependent, as few others are, on external trade for finance.'" [48]

"In such circumstances the Labour party proposed that a central authority would ration the overseas funds and confine imports to the necessary consumer goods, raw materials, and equipment that could not be provided from New Zealand's own production." [49]

Import Licensing

Instead of increasing tariffs to restrict imports, the Government chose licensing — as reported by The New Zealand Herald on 8 December 1938:

"Within a few days it is expected that the Customs Department will be supplied with details of the general policy to be pursued in the licensing of imports into New Zealand. Such a statement will be necessary in order to ensure uniformity throughout the Dominion, and until this information is available, importers are in the dark on many important aspects of the scheme.

"Regulations issued in Wellington on Tuesday, and received in Auckland yesterday, together with forms required by the department, afford some information of procedure. Mr. F. N. Abercrombie, Collector of Customs, explained that importers must make application on forms under the regulations to import goods at a particular port over a period from December 31 next.

"The form of application requires the importer to give a full description of goods, but by that, a broad classification only would be required. It would be further necessary to state the country of origin of the goods and the c.i.f. value in New Zealand currency.

"Under the regulations licences would be granted to import various classes of goods, based on the application. Such licences would probably cover a period of six months." [50]

Dangerous Bureaucracy

Expressing some alarm, The New Zealand Herald took up the cause of the country's laissez-faire liberals with a warning to its readers:

"The Minister for Customs, the Hon. W. Nash, in his explanation of the system of import licensing, has said that applications for licences must be made to the Collector of Customs, at the proposed port of entry. There is no indication in his statement that this procedure is a provisional one only, and none is given of the authority by whom the applications will be considered and dealt with. It may be presumed, therefore, that the Minister regards this procedure as permanent and that the authority will be the Customs Department.

"The presumption is disturbing. It is obvious that the control so suddenly set up signifies the subjection of the Dominion's import trade both to quantitative limits and to selective limits. Moreover, Mr Nash has implied that the Prime Minister has expressly stated that the Government is not resorting to a temporary expedient but establishing a policy...

"Unless the Government is still to announce changes of plan, the information so far given means that the Customs Department will determine the quantities and classes of goods that may be imported from time to time and distribute the trade in them, under licence, in such proportions and to such individuals or companies as it chooses.

"It need hardly be said that, while the import licensing system is by definition and in intent an instrument of governmental interference with private trade, this application of it runs almost to the extreme of bureaucratic method and is correspondingly dangerous." [51]

New & Used Car Import Licences

By early 1939, licences were being granted for the importation of new and used cars based on the number of vehicles imported by individual dealers during the previous year — as reported by The New Zealand Herald on 5 January 1939:

"Licences to import motor vehicles for six months to the same value of the import figures for the first six months of last year have been granted to motor importers in Auckland. According to those who received licences yesterday, no restriction was placed on foreign car products in favour of British products. Most importers, anticipating increased business in the sale of new cars, accordingly raised their import estimates for the first half of the current year.

"Those granted licences found that no provision was allowed for increased business, but that the same figure, which they stated as their import total for January-June period of last year, was the fixed quota for this year's imports...

"It was evident that imports would be based solely on the total value of vehicles, as there was no direction that the number of units should be reduced. Importers agreed that it might be necessary to readjust orders for smaller and cheaper cars in preference to larger and more expensive makes, in order to spread their imports to meet the greatest demand. It was appreciated that there would continue to be some market for heavy cars, but it would be difficult to place orders…

"An importer of completely-assembled American cars said he was not disappointed with his licence, but rather experienced a pleasant surprise that his imports would not be drastically reduced.

"An executive of another import firm said no advice or licence had yet been granted in respect of unassembled cars imported last year from America, which would in future be imported from the Canadian factory. The same company found that its licence, covering the import of British cars completely assembled, showed some reduction, but it would be impossible to state the true position until the licences for all branches of the firm's imports had been obtained.

"Licences have also been granted for six months for the importation of used cars ordered from abroad before the restrictions started on December 5. The licences were stated to be very vague, making no mention that future importation of used cars would be prevented, but stating that it would be necessary to procure special licences for vehicles ordered after December 5. One prominent dealer said he was not disappointed, and had decided, as others had also done, to concentrate on dealing in the local used car market." [52]

War Restrictions

The start of World War II naturally affected all trade to some extent and the motor vehicle industry was no exception. New Zealand's 1939 import restrictions, only a precursor to what was to come, were easy to justify by July 1940:

"Defending the [import control] measures taken, Mr Nash said that in its endeavours to conserve overseas funds, the Government had found it necessary to restrict imports of some goods and equipment which were previously major items. Motor vehicles were amongst them, and the restriction of vehicles from the United States of America was particularly important because of the dollar funds involved. Dealing with petrol restrictions, Mr Nash said it was important to build up reserve stocks in New Zealand in case of emergency and to economise in the use of overseas funds, and he considered that the present war situation was adequate justification for the action taken." [53]

A year after the start of the war, Customs returns showed a sharp decline in the importation of all vehicles, parts, and motor spirits — as reported by the Evening Post on 21 November 1940:

"Returns of motor vehicle imports for the nine months ended in September last [1940] show a very substantial decline. The figures, as furnished by the Government Statistician from Customs returns, are as follows:

"Value of imports:

"9 mos. 1939 — Motor vehicles £4,070,432 Motor-cycles £47,100 Motor tyres £706,449 Materials and parts £271,994 — Total: 5,095,975

"9 mos. 1940 — Motor vehicles £932,363 Motor-cycles £19,613 Motor tyres £649,611 Materials and parts £235,945 — Total £1,837,532

"Motor spirit 9 mos. 1939 — £1,474,036 and 9 mos. 1940 — £1,723,586

"In gallons, the imports of motor spirit for the first nine months of this year were 71,383,349; but for the 1939 period they amounted to 78,603,370 gallons — more spirit for less money." [54]

By April 1941, motor vehicle imports had taken a steep dive:

"The imports of motor vehicles for the first three months of the current year [1941] were of the value of £16,848, against £164,617 for the first three months of 1940." [55]

Post-War Restrictions

As the war came to an end, motor vehicle industry leaders and motorists considered the future with a somewhat jaundiced eye — as reported by the Christchurch Press on 29 December 1945:

"The prospects for a new car are not bright for 1946 if it is assumed that at least the 80,000 motorists whose cars are 10 years old or more want to replace them urgently. The existing import licences will allow for the importation of between 7000 and 8000 British cars in 1946. Dealers will be allowed to import up to 75 per cent of their quota for 1938 when 28,000 cars were landed in New Zealand.

"The licences are, however, based on value, and the landed cost is likely to be double that of 1938. The British 10 horse-power car will sell at around £600.

"At present, 43.25 per cent of New Zealand's 192,624 cars are 10 years old or more, nearly 51 per cent of light trucks are the same age, and 16.53 per cent of the heavy trucks. The number of commercial vehicles likely to be imported, as the position now stands, is about 900.

"Here, the sales tax has risen 40 per cent compared with 1938, but that increase will now be applying to motor vehicles being landed here at twice their pre-war cost. A car which was landed here in 1938 at £300 would carry 5 per cent or £15 in sales tax. The same car landed here to-day at £600 would bear £120 sales tax.

"The question of import licences for American motor vehicles has still to be decided and is dependent on the dollar position and Government policy. American vehicles formed 38 per cent of all motor vehicle imports in 1938. American vehicles are stated to be in production at a much cheaper cost than Britain.

"Reduced importations of motor vehicles for assembly in New Zealand must mean that the industry here will be unable to absorb anything like the labour it did before the war. Outside the motor-vehicle plants come others who are dependent on the industry, and the public use of motor vehicles — salesmen, service station proprietors and employees, tyre dealers, mechanics and so on." [56]

Licence Quota for 1946

While import restrictions remained, the end of the war saw some relaxation of the number of imports allowed, as announced on 28 January 1946:

"The announcement by the Minister of Customs, Mr Walter Nash, of additional permits for the importation of motor vehicles is to be welcomed as a concession to a general need, albeit it is an inadequate one.

"The importation of motor vehicles into this country was first considerably reduced in July, 1939, and from July of the following year it was completely banned. Therefore, not only normal needs should be allowed for, but also the accumulated needs of nearly six years.

"It can be admitted that there may not be justification for the complete removal of restrictions in so far as pleasure motoring needs are concerned, but the need of business vehicles, including commercial trucks, should receive more consideration.

"Mr Nash announced that the new permits would enable 150 per cent in value of the 1938 importation of commercial vehicle chassis to be imported from the United Kingdom during the year.

"As, however, it is estimated that the increase in costs since 1938 is 50 per cent, the real position is that approximately the same number of chassis will be allowed into the country. This will not go far towards remedying the position even in its most essential aspect.

"The other increases of United Kingdom imports are 110 per cent for unassembled motor cars, and 100 per cent for assembled vehicles. [57]

Nevertheless, any increase of the import quota was never going to be enough for the New Zealand Motor Vehicle Importers' Association — as reported by the Christchurch Press on 7 September 1946:

"Disappointment at the extent of restrictions placed on the importation of commercial and passenger vehicles in 1947, and grave concern at the effect this will have on the motor transport system of the country, was expressed in a resolution passed by the New Zealand Motor Vehicle Importers' Association at a meeting recently.

"It was considered that six war years of non-supply of new vehicles was causing increased difficulty in the motor trade in keeping private transport, much of it essential, in roadworthy condition, and that the inordinately high prices now being asked for used vehicles were a direct outcome of the extreme shortage of new vehicles.

"The lack of new vehicles was shown by the inability of grocers, butchers, bakers, and other tradesmen to resume pre-war delivery of goods, continued the resolution." [58]

Licence Quota for 1947

"The importation of vehicles for 1947 granted under licence show that from Canada and the United States only one passenger vehicle is allowed for every six imported in 1938, and only one motor-truck for every four trucks imported in 1938.

"In the case of the United Kingdom the corresponding figures are:—passenger vehicles: three in 1947 for every five in 1938; motor trucks: four in 1947 for every five in 1938.

"It was considered that the number allowed to be imported was totally inadequate for requirements." [59]

In answer to a Parliamentary question regarding the new import controls on motor vehicles for 1947, Mr Nash replied:

"...licences for assembled motor-cars for 1947 were issued for 150 per cent of the value of 1938 imports from Britain and for unassembled cars for 160 percent. Additional licences, particularly for motor-vans, were also granted in a number of instances where it could be shown that the vehicles were actually available.

"Mr Nash said that in all circumstances it was considered very generous provision had been made for imports of motor vehicles from the United Kingdom. A greater value of cars was exported from the United Kingdom to New Zealand in 1946 than to any other country." [60]

Licence Quota Reduced for 1948

The 1948 vehicle import quota was considerably less than for 1947 — as reported by the Gisborne Herald on 20 October 1948:

"The 1948 import schedules gave the United Kingdom licenses for motorcars valued at £NZ 3,000,000 or just over 9000 units compared with a value of £4,340,000 in 1947 which was estimated to cover 14,000 units.

"For Canadian cars the value was £426,000 representing 1416 units compared with just over £1,000,000 or 3250 cars in 1947.

"For commercial vehicles, the 1948 schedule gave a value of £500,000 to the United Kingdom or approximately 1000 units compared with £840,000 or 1800 units in 1947. The Canadian value was £181,000 or 600 units against £900,000 or 3000 units in 1947.

"The overall total value of cars under the 1948 schedule was £3,370,532 representing 10,000 units compared with £5,741,926 or 18,000 units in 1947. For commercial vehicles the value was £685.430 or 1700 units in 1948 and the 1947 figures were £2,057,975 or 5673 units."

Naturally, the 1948 import restrictions did nothing to please the New Zealand Retail Motor Trade Association which predicted:

"...there would be a serious dislocation of transport in New Zealand if the restrictions on the import of new motor vehicles were not lifted or eased immediately..." [61]

This prediction, made by the President of the Association's Otago branch, Mr G T Clarke, was reported by the Otago Daily Times on 2 September 1949 and followed the publication of a booklet presented to the Minister of Finance and Customs by the New Zealand Motor Vehicles Importers' Association.

The booklet informed the Minister: "More than 100,000 new motor cars would be required to meet the normal demand for new cars, but a minimum of 30,000 cars is required to function normally and efficiently.

"With an increase in population of 240,000 in the decade 1938/48, and with more than double an export income, the number of cars per head of population has declined. In the meanwhile the cost of running and maintaining old cars imposes a heavy charge upon the whole transport industry.

"The great majority of the cars in use (68 per cent) are more than 10 years old, requiring excessive repairs with greater petrol and oil consumption and long 'off-the-road' periods. Efficient and economical transport is a necessity to modern communal life, as also to industry and commerce. There is an unanswerable case for increased car importations." [62]

In a closing comment to the Otago Daily Times, Mr Clarke pointed out that:

"In 1936-38, when our national export income averaged £60,000,000 a year, the public voluntarily spent 7 per cent of that on new cars. To-day, when our national export income is likely to be £130,00,000, only 3 per cent of that amount is allotted for the importation of new cars." [63]

Unassembled Cars Given Priority

The 1949 import licences were not only increased but preference for unassembled cars from Britain were given priority with a view to encouraging the New Zealand assembly industry — as reported by the Grey River Argus on 9 May 1949:

"An increase in the existing allocations for the importation of unassembled motor vehicles and bicycles from the United Kingdom has been announced by the Minister of Customs, Rt. Hon. W Nash. 'It is the desire of the Government', said Mr Nash, 'that the fullest possible provision be made for the transport requirements of the community, and to this end, a very careful examination of the existing position in regard to the country's income and expenditure has recently been carried out.

"'As a result of this examination, it has been found possible to grant additional licences for the importation of unassembled commercial vehicles and unassembled motor cars from the United Kingdom to the extent of 50 per cent, and 25 per cent, respectively, of the amounts of the 1948 period licences granted in respect of similar goods from the same source...

"As supplies of unassembled cars are now freely available from the United Kingdom in quantities well in excess of those for the importation of which vehicles can at present be granted, it has been decided that all future imports of cars must be in that condition. 'It is appreciated that this decision may cause a certain amount of hardship to some firms, but it is felt that, under the existing conditions, the Government's chief concern should be to provide for the importation of the greatest possible number of cars with the funds available.

"Some regard must also be had to the fact that several local industries have been created for the purpose of assembling motor vehicles in New Zealand, and these industries are entitled to a measure of assistance. Liberal provision has been made, and will continue to be made, for the importation of service parts of all types of vehicles, and every endeavour will be made to ensure that the vehicles at present in use are not immobilised through lack of the necessary spare parts". [64]

The post-war situation experienced by the motor vehicle industry was described by William Dennis Rose in his NZ Institute of Economic Research paper of 1971:

"During the five years 1946-50 imports of motor cars averaged 13,000 units a year, significantly less than the 24,000 average during the five boom years at the end of the 1930's. Slow recovery of the industry overseas, and local production and balance of payments problems, kept imports down. At the same time the dollar shortage meant that import licences were restricted in the main to British sources and this furthered the change in sourcing from American to British c.k.d. packs that had been encouraged by the tariff.

"Import licences were limited to use for c.k.d. imports but provision was made for dispensation in special cases. Such dispensations were widespread at first, but by 1949 more than 90 per cent of imports were for assembly in New Zealand…

"The imposition of import licensing was not without its problems and led to widespread allegations of inequity. In November 1950 the Import Licensing Committee appointed by the newly elected Holland administration reported that 'it was impossible to identify any general principle or principles which had been followed over the years in the case of licences issued to the 'Big Five'. This lack of uniformity was especially apparent in the establishment of basic licences.

"…in May 1950, the government had announced that no-remittance licences would be issued for imports which the applicant could finance out of his own overseas funds." [65]

No-Remittance Licences

The Labour Government had been replaced by the First National Government in late 1949 and, according to a Reserve Bank Bulletin of March 1981, this political change

"…resulted in a significant relaxation in the level of import controls as a large number of commodities were exempted from licensing requirements. The National Government believed that the system of import controls which had been developed by the previous Government contributed to rising costs and inefficiency.

"The Import Advisory Committee was established to overhaul the import licensing system and its administration. This resulted in changes which made the licensing regulations more consistent in their application to goods coming from the 'sterling area' and other countries. The changes included the reclassification of a large number of items into categories which were exempt from licensing.

"A further area of change was in the introduction of non-remittance licensing where licences could be issued to persons wishing to import goods, using for payment their own personally held foreign funds. Abuses of the scheme later resulted in it being modified to permit people to import only goods for their own use and subsequently the scheme was phased out." [66]

What was described as: "The first of a number of prosecutions against people with overseas funds who have imported cars into New Zealand for people without the necessary overseas funds…" was published by the Christchurch Press on 6 February 1970:

"…brought before the Auckland Magistrate's Court today…

"Christine Rose Willie was charged that in June, 1968, she made a false declaration when obtaining an import licence for a $2845 Ford Cortina that the car was for her personal use. She pleaded guilty. She also pleaded guilty to selling a 1967 Ford Falcon sedan worth $2346, between March and May, 1967, which under its import licence should not have been sold within one year of importation.

"Jack Willie, a clerk, of Titirangi, was charged that in September, 1968, he made a false declaration when obtaining an import licence for a 1968 Ford Zephyr sedan worth $3460 that the car was for his personal use. He pleaded guilty.

"Prosecuting for the Customs Department, Mr W D Baragwanath said the prosecutions followed investigations which revealed that people with overseas funds had used their funds to import cars under the no-remittance import licence scheme for delivery to third parties who did not possess the necessary funds…

"Both accused were convicted on the charges. Mrs Willie was fined $100 with court costs on each charge. [Jack] Willie was fined $250 with court costs $5." [67]

A common invitation to New Zealanders with funds in Britain was advertised in Salient, An Organ of Student Opinion at Victoria College, Wellington. Published on 3 September 1953, on behalf of Todd Motors, English Car Sales, Kearney's Service Station, and S M Motors, the ad promised immediate delivery of the "…very latest model Hillman Minx or Humber Ten if you have a no-remittance licence and suitable overseas funds or securities. A sterling deposit of only £254 is required, the balance to be paid in New Zealand..." [68]

Following the cancellation of the no-remittance import scheme in the 1971 Budget, licence applications were no longer received by the Customs Department after 28 February 1972. [69]

In its editorial review of the Budget announcement, the Christchurch Press commented:

"The end of the no-remittance scheme, which enabled a privileged minority to import new motorcars, is a cause for congratulation. The increased allocation of licences to import completely-knocked-down vehicles will largely offset the loss of no-remittance imports; and the extra new cars available in New Zealand should give motor distributors a much-needed incentive to compete for sales in a market which has for too long been under-supplied. The Government is to be congratulated, too, on its reiteration of the principle that local industry should be protected by tariffs rather than by import controls." [70]

Off Again — On Again

"In February 1951 [because of a surplus balance of payments] motor car imports were freed from control along with about 700 other items. The reaction was spectacular. Imports of assembled cars rose from 2,700 in 1950 to 14,100 in 1951, and 21,400 in 1952, as importers hurried to supply a starved market.

"At the same time imports of unassembled vehicles fell slightly from 13,000 in 1950 to 12,800 in 1951, and then rose sharply to 17,800 in 1952.

"The surge in overseas expenditure on motor cars (from $15 million in 1950 to $27 million in 1951, and $37 million in 1952) and the reduced level of c.k.d. imports in 1951, led to an early change in policy.

"As from March 1952 no built up cars could be imported and in June of the same year import licences were again required for unassembled vehicles...

"The 1951-52 experience showed that the backlog of demand for cars was large and could be expensive to fill, and also that the existing tariff differentials were not so great as to inhibit imports of assembled cars during a transition to open importing in a period of high demand." [71]

An illustration of that high demand was described by a Te Awamutu Courier report published in June 1950:

"The unsatisfied demand for cars in Wellington at present was emphasised when two modern cars were put up for auction. An American car which had done 12,000 miles was offered, and the bidding started at £900, which is £21 more than the price at which such models were selling new last year. It was finally sold for £1700. Bidding on a late model English car started at £800. These cars sell new at £870 and this model had done 12,000 miles. The car was knocked down at £1040." [72]

Import Quotas For 1952

By 1952, vehicle import licensing continued to favour the importation of CKDs destined for New Zealand's assembly plants — as reported by the Christchurch Press on 14 June of that year:

"New Zealand's expenditure on motor-vehicles this year will exceed £19,000,000, and imports will total about 32,000 vehicles...comprising between 18,000 and 19,000 built-up vehicles and the balance locally assembled...

"The Minister of Industries and Commerce (Mr J T Watts) announced this to-day. The Minister said the Government had confirmed its decision not to issue licences for built-up motor-vehicles for the balance of 1952, except in certain circumstances.

"Provision had been made, however, for imports of completely knocked-down motor-vehicles for the balance of the 1952 licensing period. These vehicles would go to assembly works to enable them to maintain employment. Mr Watts said import licences were being granted for the very heavy type of truck chassis, commercial bus chassis, and electrically-propelled chassis, covered by firm orders from local bodies and licensed operators..." [73]

Board of Trade Review

While the Customs Department still allocated the import licences for entry at each port, by 1952, the Board of Trade was providing an overview of what imports were needed and could be sustained by the country — as explained in the same Christchurch Press report:

"The Board of Trade had completed its review of vehicle imports because of the already large proportion of this year's over-all import expenditure which motor-vehicles would involve…The board had recommended imports for the assembly works to enable them to maintain employment…

"The Minister said the Board of Trade would examine the position for 1953 about next August, and the question of licences for both completely knocked-down and built-up units would then be examined in the light of the prospective overseas exchange position for next year." [74]

Supply and Demand

As usual, there was a large discrepancy between the 'official' assessment of what the country could afford and what was needed by the consumer — as reported by the Christchurch Press on 6 May 1953:

"It was a pity there were no more licences for built-up cars in 1953, said Mr A W Hamilton Brown, representative of the Society of Motor Manufacturers and Traders, today. About 30 importers depended on them he said. There was a steady demand for some of the less common makes and they could not be obtained knocked down. He hoped that that aspect might yet be reviewed…

"There was a big demand for motor-vehicles, not only for the public, but also to keep the assembly plants going, but the announcement, coming so late, might not affect the number of motor-vehicles that could be assembled and sold this year.

"It took several months for the cars to be processed overseas, shipped, and reassembled here. Mr Hamilton Brown said of the decision to exempt heavy motor-vehicles from import licensing that it was a big advantage to have any items unlicensed, but it would not involve a large number of vehicles. More than 60 per cent, of commercial vehicles sold in New Zealand were under one ton and there was still a big unfilled demand for these lighter vehicles." [75]

A year later, in August 1954, the president of the New Zealand Retail Motor Trade Association, Mr W A Christiansen, also complained of both shipping and local assembly delays:

"'The New Zealand public may not get all the 45,000 new vehicles promised this year…If I thought we would get the 45,000 vehicles then I would say that that would reasonably take care of our requirements, but I don't believe for a moment that we will get that many.'

"'New Zealand was a long way from the source of supply of motor vehicles. There is the question of shipping and the question of labour in the assembly plants,' Mr Christiansen said.

"'The turn-round of shipping was now better than it was during the big flood of vehicle imports two years ago but he seriously doubted whether the Dominion's assembly plants could cope with this year's importations, even if all the vehicles were received in the country in time…'" [76]

An Important Industry

Indeed, New Zealand's vehicle assemblers had a number of physical and government-imposed hurdles to overcome before they could successfully produce motor vehicles from parts received from overseas manufacturers. Nevertheless, as reported by the Christchurch Press on 2 March 1955:

"The assembly of motor vehicles is now firmly established as one of New Zealand's important industries. In the last eight years, according to the latest figures…New Zealand has imported some 233,000 vehicles, of which 167,000 – more than 70 per cent – were in c.k.d. (completely knocked down) form.

"Tariffs on motor vehicles imported from Britain are 5 per cent on c.k.d. vehicles and 15 per cent on assembled vehicles. With this 10 per cent protection the New Zealand assembly firms turn out a product comparable in price with – and in some cases cheaper than – the imported model...

"There are 12 motor assembly works in New Zealand...The bodywork, motors, fittings and wheels — but not tyres, for New Zealand-made tyres are used on c.k.d. vehicles — arrive in New Zealand in huge crates, weighing as much as 2¾ tons." [77]

While New Zealand's twelve motor assembly works enjoyed that 10 per cent protection and received 70 per cent of imports, their output was unable to provide for all of the consumers' needs. There remained some popular vehicle models in short supply — as reported by the Christchurch Press on 17 May 1955:

"Motor-vehicle imports this year will remain restricted to 50,000, plus a carry-over from last year of about 5000. The total of 55,000 is a record number. The Board of Trade had refused to increase its 1955 allocation of £21,500, the president of the Associated Motor Importers of New Zealand (Mr P E Coutts) said today.

"'Although this year's imports will be a record, some of our members wanted an increase in their allocation because they feel they can sell more cars of their makes,' Mr Coutts said. He felt, however, that on the whole more cars were entering the country than the assembly factories could handle. An indication of this was the large number of built-up cars that were being imported." [78]

An Unfair Imposition

"The cut in motor-vehicle import licences was an unfair imposition, and would result in the running and maintenance of uneconomic vehicles, said Mr G. W. Fairweather at the annual meeting of the New Zealand Retail Motor Trade Association in Christchurch.

"Registrations in June had shown that 37 per cent, of cars on the New Zealand roads were pre-war models. They were uneconomic and unsafe, he said.

New Zealand had a trade deficit of £35,000,000, but the motor trade had not contributed to this, Mr Fairweather said. There had been a spending orgy in luxury goods, many of which could be manufactured in New Zealand...

"'The licences granted for the importation of motor vehicles from non-scheduled countries were substantially increased for 1955 and, if all vehicles are imported, the new vehicles registered for 1955 will constitute a record,' he said.

"'Licences for the importation of vehicles from North American sources were issued and it is estimated that during the current year approximately 3000 vehicles from North American sources will enter the country. At June 30, the number of licensed motor-vehicles, excluding trailer and dealer plates, was 585,795; this includes 369,421 motor-cars.'

"'New Zealand is rapidly approaching the United States in the number of motor-vehicles to population. The latest figures available for the United States are one motor-vehicle for every 3.4 of the population, and for New Zealand 3.8,' said Mr Fairweather." [79]

Some Licence Relaxation

After some lobbying from representatives of various industries, including the Master Builders' Federation, [80] for light trucks and vans to be more readily available, such vehicles were exempt from licensing control on 17 August 1957:

"Commercial motor-vehicles, unassembled, would from tomorrow be free from licensing control when imported from non-scheduled countries, said the Minister of Customs (Mr E H Halstead) today...

"The Minister said that although the overseas funds position did not permit the removal of all motor vehicles from control, the Board of Trade had come to the conclusion that the freeing of unassembled commercial vehicles would not cause any excessive demand on overseas funds.

"Mr Halstead added that the Government had decided on a total 1958 expenditure of £17,500,000 on motor-vehicles, including the commercial vehicles now to be freed from licence. This figure would still be well below the 1955 figure, but would be higher than those for 1956 and 1957…

"Provision made for the import of vehicles from dollar sources in 1958, continued Mr Halstead, would be similar to that for 1957. [81]

Hello Australia

At the same time, the Minister of Customs announced that vehicle dealers could also consider the importation of Australian models:

"Most of the motor-vehicle imports into New Zealand would undoubtedly continue to come from the United Kingdom. However, more vehicles were becoming available from other sources, and some opportunity must be given to prove the worth of new makes and models. Under the decisions now made, Australia would have every opportunity of competing for business…" [82]

The Black Budget

However, "…towards the end of 1957 New Zealand's balance of payments deteriorated seriously…The newly-elected Nash administration reimposed comprehensive import controls and replaced the previously published 1958 licensing schedule with one much more stringent.

"Whereas the original schedule had provided for some increase in motor car imports above the record level of 1957, the new schedule cut allocations to 75 per cent of 1957 imports for c.k.d. packs and to 50 per cent for built up cars…" [83]

"The most famous balance of payments crisis in the second half of the 20th century occurred in late 1957. Arnold Nordmeyer was the minister of finance in the recently elected Labour government. He attempted to deal with the crisis by reducing demand for overseas goods through imposing additional taxes on cars, alcohol and tobacco. In a strict economic sense this was a logical response to the situation, but politically it was a disaster and the Labour Party was saddled with the memory of Nordmeyer's 'black budget' for the next decade…" [84]

Customs Acts Amendment Act 1958

Nordmeyer's 'black budget' was legislated for by means of the Customs Acts Amendment Act 1958, passed 25 September 1958, the Second Schedule of which provided for a "…sales tax at the rate of forty per cent of their sale value (for) motor vehicles, including trailers therefor (sic) but excluding motor cycles." [85]

By early 1958, the motor vehicle assembly industry feared job losses would result from the cuts to imports and the taxes imposed on car sales:

"There have been no dismissals from the staff of Motor Assemblies Ltd Christchurch since the Government's announcement of a 25 per cent reduction in imports of knocked-down cars but all overtime has been stopped.

"On the surface, the cut imposed…appears to be 25 per cent, but when all matters are taken into consideration it is about 40 per cent, [said Mr A R Cutler, general manager of the company]." [86]

Shortage of Imports

A comprehensive study of the effect of a shortage of imported vehicles during the period 1948 to 1963 was undertaken by New Zealand economist, Stephen J Turnovsky. His paper, published by The Economic Record in June 1966, explained the supply and demand effects of the New Zealand Government's import restrictions:

"Apart from a few years in the mid-fifties, and also in 1963, cars have been subject to severe import restrictions and, in particular, the more popular models have been in almost incessant short supply, with the result that since the war the market has strongly favoured sellers.

"Thus the level of stock is related to the number of cars the country can afford to import and this in turn depends effectively on its purchasing power abroad. Stocks of cars are therefore determined by factors exogenous to the second-hand car market itself. This conclusion would not necessarily hold in a market experiencing equilibrium. In this instance, the number of cars imported and hence the stock of cars might well be responsive to changes in price and income. If income fell and demand declined, the dealers would respond by importing fewer cars and in this way demand determinants would influence the level of supply.

"Such has not been the situation in New Zealand over the years studied, for there has been such a constant shortage that dealers have always wished to import as many cars as possible and have only been limited in doing so by New Zealand's purchasing power abroad. Evidence of this is provided by the persistent waiting list for new cars which has been characteristic of the post-war period.

"In the market under consideration, therefore, supply is exogenously determined, with the result that prices become an endogenous variable and adjust in such a manner as to equilibrate demand with the available supply…that is, supply is determined and then prices adjust appropriately…

"With the acute shortage of motor vehicles in New Zealand over the post-war period and the market strongly favouring sellers, one can consider the second-hand car dealers as collectively forming a monopoly and theoretically expect that price elasticity should exceed unity as in fact was the case. The result need not hold in an equilibrated market where cars are more readily available. In this type of situation, one can no longer consider the car dealers collectively as monopolists, but should rather regard them as mutual competitors." [87]

Insufficient Industry

An overview of how much the motor industry influenced the industrial base of New Zealand to the 1960s was provided by William Sutch in his book, 'the quest for security in New Zealand 1840 to 1966':

"It is worth noting that, during the Second World War and post-war years, the country did not develop many new industries or expand those that had been established. Consequently, most manufactured goods had to be imported, paid for by overseas borrowing to satisfy the needs of war-weary consumers eager to participate in a new era of consumption. That consumption naturally included motor vehicles with imports from Commonwealth countries receiving preferential treatment.

"The problems of economic management facing New Zealand in the fifties as contrasted with the thirties were the result of the change from lower living standards and stagnation to high living standards, full employment, and expansion.

"In addition to the increased purchasing power that came from full employment and high farm incomes, the reasons for the high demand in New Zealand after World War II were the rapid increase in population and the need to build the physical assets of the country in addition to roads. These other assets had deteriorated in the depression years and, of necessity, could not be sufficiently expanded in the war years.

"…the industrial needs were made all the more difficult to meet by the sequestration of certain revenues for road building only…if there had been somewhat less road building and expenditure on cars and petrol, New Zealand could have built a stronger industrial base…it had given the car industry a unique place in New Zealand, in that its goods could come in on a no-remittance licence, as well as receive an allocation of funds under normal import licensing procedure; that is, a person with sufficient foreign exchange could use it once a year to import a car. In other countries such funds would have been put at the disposal of the central bank.

"Since 1950 New Zealand's Reserve Bank has been deprived of tens of millions of pounds of foreign exchange and individuals have exported capital (shares sold abroad) to increase the supply of cars. At the same time the attempt to have more car components made in New Zealand has been very half-hearted.

"The exchange transactions recording the reduction of private assets held abroad over the 10-year period ending 1965 were £38.4 million. Most of this went on cars, and most of it was built up from funds which would have gone to the Reserve Bank if there had been no no-remittance scheme for cars…

"The following figures are from the Customs Department's Reports.

"Import Of No-Remittance Cars:

    1955 — 1,998   1961 — 7,727
    1956 — 2,321   1962 — 6,584
    1957 — 2,291   1963 — 11,426
    1958 — 3,323   1964 — 12,606
    1959 — 2,983   1965 — 14,116" [88]
    1960 — 4,482

Licence Quota for 1961

As previously referred to, an amended Customs determination of 1939 had excluded certain 'mandatory deletion' items from imported CKD packs as a means of encouraging local assemblers to use domestically-sourced components. However, the only incentive then for assemblers to incorporate locally-made parts as part of the vehicles they built was the avoidance of the additional tariffs to be paid on imported parts — additional cost to be added to the finished vehicle. [89]

The 1961 import licensing allocation for motor vehicles announced by the Minister of Customs, Mr Boord, in October 1960, provided a different incentive for assemblers to incorporate local content:

"Provision for at least the same general level of imports of cars as in 1960, with additional licences up to 15 per cent more for assembly companies incorporating a greater element of New Zealand manufacture in their cars, are the main features of the 1961 import licensing allocation for motor vehicles announced today by the Minister of Customs (Mr Boord).

"With the exception of commercial vehicles over 10,000 lb gross weight, which will continue to be imported under the 'R' or replacement scheme in the import licensing schedule, all motor vehicle manufacturing companies will receive licences of not less value than those granted for 1960….

"In addition, an increase In licence entitlement will be granted to those companies which incorporate local content, or which give firm undertakings acceptable to the Customs and Industries and Commerce departments to incorporate local content within a specified time, significantly in excess of the average at present being achieved by all companies.

"The amount of the increase licence will be determined by the actual degree of local manufacture attained or to be achieved to the satisfaction of the departments." [90]

"…provision was made for additional issue of licences provided that specific levels of local content were achieved:

"If local content increased to: 35% by 30 June 1961 — 7½% increase in import licence allocation

"If local content increased to: 37½% by 30 June 1961 — 10% increase in import licence allocation

"If local content increased to: 40% by 31 December 1961 — 15% increase in import licence allocation

"Although the incentive scheme was seen mainly as an inducement to increase the local content of established models, provision was made for the issue of c.k.d. licences for assembly of limited numbers of cars for other franchise holders. This scheme provided the basis for what was to become known as the '300 club', under which licences sufficient for 300 units could be issued for manufacturing proposals embodying a sufficiently high local content, with the prospect of larger allocations if higher content was achieved…

"The most noticeable effect of the 300 club has been an increase in the number of assembly plants and in the number of models produced. Most of the new assembly operations are at the minimum level envisaged under the scheme and in general assemblers have found it cheaper to multiply the range of models assembled rather than to increase the depth of manufacture.

"Although the 300 club had little effect upon the level of New Zealand content incorporated in the average car, it did increase the level of motor car production…" [91]

Boom, Bust and Boom Again

The importation of both unassembled and assembled motor vehicles continued to be regulated according to the political will and fortunes of the New Zealand Government during the 1960s and early 1970s — as described by William Rose in his Institute of Economic Research paper of 1971:

"In total, motor car imports increased by 74 per cent from 38,000 to 66,000, between 1962 and the peak year 1965. The Government did not, however, satisfy the demand for cars. Despite the large increase in imports demand still outran supply, and then, as balance of payments pressures again became evident, allocations for motor cars were cut successively in the 1966-67 and 1967-68 licensing schedules.

"The motor car boom of the early sixties was over. Retrenchment also led to the cessation of approval for new projects under the 300 club, which had been modified in 1965 so that manufacturers, to qualify under the scheme, had to include a specified list of components rather than achieve a particular percentage of local content.

"As New Zealand recovered from the exchange crisis of the late 1960's import licence allocations for motor cars were increased, by 15 per cent in 1968-69, and by 5 per cent in 1969-70. Then, in 1970, the Government, with a buoyant balance of payments behind it, once again set out to match the demand for cars. Substantial increases in import licences were announced so that imports were expected to rise to 80,000 units during 1970-71 as compared with an estimated 60,000 units in 1969-70…" [92]

Industry Overview

In contemplation of how the motor vehicle assembly industry and the consumer would be affected by the increases in import licences proposed by the Government for 1970, the Christchurch Press editorial of 19 February 1970 commented:

"For 30 years New Zealand's imports of motorcars have been regulated by licensing, at first to protect the country's meagre overseas reserves, but increasingly with the effect of protecting employment and capital invested in motor assembly plants. The Cabinet's approval of greatly increased import licences for cars next licensing year — possibly as a prelude to the abolition of licensing of car imports — may change all this. The significance of these proposals may not be widely appreciated, particularly among motorists under the age of 50 who have never bought or sold a car except in the artificial market of the last 30 years.

"Under the umbrella of import controls, vehicle assembly in New Zealand has expanded threefold, although it was not until the early 1950s that the 1938 figure of 19,000 cars was exceeded. The record year for imports was 1963-64, when nearly 62,000 'completely knocked down' cars and more than 7000 fully-assembled cars were imported.

"Last year, because of reduced import licences, only 49,000 c.k.d. and 4000 assembled cars were imported. For the last 30 years this has been a sellers' market; seldom if ever has the ordinary motorist had a choice of new cars of popular makes unless he has been prepared to wait months for delivery — or to sell his used car to a franchise holder at a discount.

"One of the effects of this perennial shortage of new cars has been to inflate the market value of used cars. It is by no means uncommon for a car two years old with 20,000 miles on the odometer to change hands within 10 per cent of its showroom price; in other motoring countries these cars might fetch half their showroom price.

"The first effect of a more plentiful supply of new cars is therefore likely to be a fall in the price of used cars. The reduced prices for used cars offered as trade-ins for new cars would soon eliminate the queues of buyers for new cars, and the 'shortage' of new cars would be eliminated.

"The Government's first concern in deciding whether to liberate the car market must be the effect on the balance of payments and overseas reserves…The present state of the country's external reserves and balance of payments allows the Government the rare luxury of contemplating with equanimity the expenditure of an extra $30 million of overseas funds in one year, especially as this figure may be regarded as a generous estimate. In the first instance, vehicle assembly plants would be unlikely to achieve a 50 per cent increase in through-put in a year, and many of the buyers of the extra new cars would restrict their spending on other commodities, including imports.

"Whether the extra expenditure turns out to be $25 million or $40 million, whether the increased rate of importing levels off after one year or two, the figures look small enough beside last year's foreign exchange statistics…The price is small indeed if it puts an end to the inefficient, costly, and frustrating business of licensing of vehicle imports." [93]

Economies of Scale

The 1971 New Zealand Institute of Economic Research paper by William Rose, referred to earlier, reviewed the economic activity of the motor car assembly industry to that date, commenting:

"The motor car assembly industry, which is one of the larger manufacturing industries, comprises nine companies, three of which are subsidiaries of overseas companies. One company [Austin] assembles cars in two plants, the rest each have one plant. Three quarters of the cars produced are assembled in factories in the Hutt Valley, and most of the others are assembled in Auckland…

"The motor assembly companies achieve considerable savings in freight and duty by assembling in New Zealand. Together these savings more than offset the higher assembly costs incurred in New Zealand plants. On the basis of data supplied by seven of the assembly companies it appears that the New Zealand wholesale price of an overseas assembled car is about 8 per cent more than that of one assembled locally. In the absence of the protective duty the New Zealand wholesale price of an overseas assembled car would be about 3 per cent less than that of its locally assembled equivalent…

"Economies of scale continue to far higher levels in motor car manufacture than in assembly. Estimates vary but, at a minimum, an annual volume of 200,000 units is necessary to secure the major economies in conventional car production...

"Tentative estimates were made which suggested:

"1. That a reduction, from 34 to 15, in the number of models assembled would, by lowering direct wage costs, lower the ex-factory cost of the average car by 1-1½ per cent.

"2. That a reduction in the number of assembly plants, to two of equal size, would, by reducing operating costs, lower the ex-factory cost of cars by about 3 per cent." [94]

The concept of economising the scale of motor vehicle production suggested as an alternative by the New Zealand Institute of Economic Research paper was taken up by the Minister of Trade and Industry, Mr Freer, on 20 December 1972:

"Fewer car models must be assembled in New Zealand, but savings through longer production runs must be passed on to car buyers, said the Minister of Trade and Industry (Mr

Freer) today. Mr Freer was speaking at the opening of a new head office building at Otahuhu for Mazda Motors of New Zealand, Ltd.

"The Government would seek to stabilise local vehicle assembly, with fewer models assembled but each vehicle containing more New Zealand components, he said. It would limit the range of models of built-up cars coming into the country and, although it was not intended to abolish such imports, review the size of entitlements for such cars. This first review would be early in the New Year, as would be clarification of proposed changes in tariffs on motor vehicles from different parts of the world...

"Mr Freer said that like many New Zealand industries, the motor trade had been subjected to many changes in Government policy in recent years. Therefore, one of the first objectives of the new Government will be to give planned stability to the whole of the industry. The Government did not want changes placing heavy demands for capital equipment and expansion on assembly plants one year, and labour displaced and idle plant the next...

"Mr Freer said the first aim was to establish a stable production plan for the assembly plants. This must be linked to the absorption of a steadily increasing level of local components. The large number of makes and models now available to New Zealanders had made it increasingly difficult to expand the use of local components. With, for instance, 172 types of car-seat made in New Zealand, the small production runs were far from being as economic as they should be, said Mr Freer. Accordingly, there will need to be some rationalisation of assembly runs...

"We must concentrate on longer runs with fewer models through the plants. Only in this way can we expect to obtain the maximum economies in production—economies which must, and I repeat must, be passed on to the car buyer...

"Mr Freer said the Government believed it was possible for assembly plants to gain economies with longer production runs, while imported c.b.u. [completely built-up] cars could give the public a choice.

"The present substantial overseas reserves could easily fall to a figure lower than the Government would like to see. We reserve the right to review from time to time the size of the entitlement for c.b.u. cars, so there is not likely to be any further extension of the number of cars so imported...

"At the same time, he assured the many people in the industry who had made large investments in the c.b.u. field that the Government did not intend to endanger either their profitability or that of any company which in the last two to three years had entered this field. But it is not our intention to allow the range of vehicles so imported to expand unless there are special circumstances...

"Mr Freer said he believed the motor industry in New Zealand would go forward in strength because it had recently suddenly had to look within itself. It has been too easy for some assembly plants and for some dealers in recent years. Both are now facing real competition, more than some of them expected or desired. But competition is here to stay in this industry...The shake-up in the last year—and which might be expected in the coming year or 18 months—was desirable..." [95]

That resulting competition was later commented on by journalist, Peter Greenslade, published by the Christchurch Press on 21 April 1989:

"I can recall the good old days of no-remittance motor business when a Holden dealer smiled only when a customer strolled into the empty showroom with Australian share scrip deforming an otherwise well-tailored suit.

"The deal involved realisation of shares in offshore...companies to furnish the required foreign currency (usually Australian) to buy Holden. Of course, in those days one purchased a Holden with overseas funds, drove it around for a couple of years and then flogged it off to anyone who had about twice the Australian currency cost price to spare — and there were plenty of those people about.

"Some pretty smart deals were put together, but Holden dealers and some of the others who looked to no-remittance business for their cakes and ale did not adjust easily to a much freer market and, to some extent at least, there is evidence to suggest that all General Motors dealers have not entirely recovered from their no-remittance hangovers." [96]

In the meantime, the registration of new cars continued apace during 1973 according to a Christchurch Press report of March 1974:

"New cars and utility vehicles registered in New Zealand last year totalled 100,348, a 14 per cent increase on the 1972 figures, and the first time the New Zealand new-car market for one year has exceeded 100,000 units. The only two major firms to increase their share of the market were Todd Motors (18,500 registrations, an increase in share to 18.4 per cent) and Nissan (market share now 6 per cent). Ford, General Motors, Toyota, and the New Zealand Motor Corporation all increased their sales, but had smaller shares of the over-all market than in 1972." [97]

Car Dealers On Notice

As well as the vehicle assemblers and importers, the retailers of new and used vehicles were also on notice to downsize or face the consequences — as reported by the Christchurch Press on 22 October 1977:

"The Prime Minister (Mr Muldoon) says there are too many car dealers, especially used-car dealers, in New Zealand. Some of them must be having increasing difficulty meeting their overheads, he said, in an address at the opening of the New Zealand Motor Show in Auckland. Some rationalisation is called for and economic circumstances may compel it, said Mr Muldoon.

"Earlier in the day, officially opening the Nissan Datsun Holdings assembly complex at Wiri, Mr Muldoon said that according to a car price list there were 228 different models or sizes of cars available in New Zealand, although not all were locally manufactured.

"He also repeated his comments about the proliferation of car dealers...A count in the Yellow Pages shows, for example, 23 car-sales firms in Hastings, 16 in Napier, 20 in Rotorua, 34 in Tauranga, 12 in Whakatane, and 23 in Timaru...These are both new-car and used-car firms. [A similar count in Christchurch gives at least 144 car sales.]

"Many of these firms must have mushroomed during the boom period, and I feel economic realities will compel readjustment...I have no evidence that the abundance of used-car lots, or for that matter of used cars in new-car dealers' rooms, is being reflected in lower prices to the public...Mr Muldoon said last evening.

"It seemed that many dealers were overstocked with cars in the over $4000 range. They might consider whether it would be in their long-term interests to knock off a few hundred dollars, and save themselves the overheads involved in carrying slow-moving stock. Not the least of the overheads, in some cases, would be advances from lending institutions...

"I recognise, at the same time, that to promote sales, holders of new-car franchises might give too favourable trade-ins and, in the process of recovering the amount involved, keep used cars at artificially high levels, and out of reach of the average working man...

"The motor industry was not an export earner, except modestly in parts, and was a heavy consumer of overseas exchange. In the 12 months to June this year, imports of motor-vehicles, excluding buses, cost more than $123M, of which almost $108M was for unassembled vehicles. Trucks and vans added another $61M — a grand total of $184M. Petroleum products directly related to motor vehicles cost about $365M, said Mr Muldoon.

"Vehicles and petroleum products together therefore accounted for about $550M in overseas funds. This is almost $100M more than we earn in overseas funds from dairy products, the third-largest source of overseas exchange earnings." [98]

Customs Duty Remains High

While Prime Minister Muldoon complained of the country's spending on motor vehicles and petroleum products, Government income received from the importation of these items, by way of Customs duty during the 1970s, remained high — as reported by the Christchurch Press on 23 August 1975:

"Customs duty on imported cars is assessed on the country of origin. Built-up cars from Japan carry a 55 per cent duty. Those from the United Kingdom have a 20 per cent duty. Japanese cars assembled in New Zealand carry a 45 per cent duty while British cars carry a 6¼ per cent duty.

"Australian duty rates vary because of the New Zealand-Australia Free Trade Agreement, and various agreements between car companies and the Government, but they are generally aligned with the British rates. Ford and General Motors have special agreements with the New Zealand Government for importing cars from Australia in return for manufacturing transmission units, and household whiteware in New Zealand...The rates giving a big advantage to British cars were made when more than 90 per cent of New Zealand's trade was with Great Britain." [99]

Industries Development Commission

First there was the Board of Trade, established in 1950, then the Tariff and Development Board which was founded in 1961 to report to Ministers about various matters regarding Customs duties, tariffs, import licensing, and "Any other matter affecting the protection or development of industry or the development of overseas trade..." [100]

A more modern version of the Tariff and Development Board was established in 1975 as the Industries Development Commission, administered by the Department of Trade and Industry. [101] During the second reading of the Amendment Bill in Parliament, then Minister of Trade and Industry, Warren Freer, "...said that the Bill emphasised the development of industry rather than simply its protection." [102]

Indeed, the establishment of the Commission was in line with the Labour Government's earlier-stated intention to undertake a comprehensive review of tariffs and a programme of industry studies as the first stage of what it called 'an economic strategy for New Zealand'..."to set the scene for significant improvements in the operation of individual industries and the structure of the whole economy." [103]

Many of the Commission's proposals were criticised by the workers employed in the industries studied. For instance, when the Commission proposed the closing of one of three tyre factories in its draft report on the tyre industry in November 1981, "...the Rubber Workers' Union proposed the Commission adopt a general principle of postponing changes where they would produce unemployment...Workers cannot understand the efficiency argument which rewards with unemployment those who have a recognised contribution to make to the well-being of New Zealand." [104]

In reply to the workers' concerns, then Minister of Trade and Industry, Mr Adams-Schneider, replied:

"...the Government had no intention of sacrificing jobs for the sake of international competitiveness and that it would ensure high quality tyres at reasonable prices to the motorist, reasonable returns on investment to the manufacturer, production at reasonable cost in New Zealand terms, and secure jobs for workers.

"He said the commission was an advisory body only, and that its draft report was subject to public submissions, rewriting into a final report, study by Government officials, recommendations by these officials to the Minister of Trade and Industry, and consultation by the Minister with companies and unions and all involved parties on the viability and possible effects of the final development plan. Then the Government would make its decision. Mr Adams-Schneider said there was ample opportunity for public participation at every stage of the process." [105]

Commission's Draft Report

The Industries Development Commission released its draft report on the motor industry on 10 September 1982. Described by the Commission as a discussion document only, its main proposals were reported by the Christchurch Press on 11 September 1982, including:

"…greater efficiency through competition with imports combined with tax and tariff changes…

"…the end of price controls on motor vehicles, hire purchase regulations, business-car depreciation limits, and car-hire regulations…

"…replacement of sales tax related to engine size with a standard 20 per cent tax, and an energy tax based on engine capacity…

"…gradual change so that a balance between knocked-down vehicle assembly and built-up vehicle imports improves the supply to private and commercial users…to do this it plans that the New Zealand assembly industry provides 75 per cent of the future car market and the same proportion of the commercial market over the next three years…

"…the balance of the annual market for cars to be open to competition between assemblers and a limited number of built-up cars paying protective duty…

"…wants the component manufacturing industry to supply the original equipment requirements of the assembly industry, provided the prices are not excessive…the component industry to have 90 per cent of the market for replacements to be secured for at least the first three years of the plan…

"…assemblers should have the option of getting components from overseas where New Zealand product costs are excessive…

"…duty on CKD packs cut to the lowest rate consistent with international obligations…

"Any of the 13,500 assembly-industry workers displaced because the assembly and component industries are unable to hold their share of the market will have to seek new jobs outside the industry, says the report.

"However, the commission strongly recommends that such workers be given Government-sponsored retraining if they want it, while being paid emergency unemployment benefit, first home-buyer status with the Housing Corporation, and relocation allowances.

"The Government will also lose on any restructuring. Based on 1981 figures, the commission said the Government would lose $50 million in lost taxes and tariffs, and recommends this be made up by increases in the cost of petrol and vehicle-licensing fees." [106]

Industry Response

Despite the Commission's assurances that its plan for the motor vehicle industry was a discussion document only, and that it would be some time before any final decisions would be made by the Government, the report nevertheless "…had a major effect on the industry," according to the chairman of Repco New Zealand Limited, Mr Frank Parkin:

"It is inevitable when a document such as this is released in such a manner that people will form their own conclusions, based mainly on emotional headlines, he told the company's annual meeting in Auckland. Unfounded predictions of cheaper cars must have a detrimental effect on the car market, with far-reaching consequences on the component industry and other suppliers to the motor industry…

"Mr Parkin said he was concerned that the IDC had adopted an 'economics text-book' approach to the car component industry. Implementation of the IDC report during a time of economic downturn would have grave social results…

"If one is undertaking a study of academic economics, that might be all very well, but economic textbooks will provide little consolation to our shareholders, and even less to employees who lose their jobs. Restructuring involved a process which has major impacts upon the lives of people and postulates great changes to a system which has been built up over decades of compliance with the policies of successive governments, he said." [107]

The reaction by some that the Commission's findings would lead to an imminent and substantial drop in new car prices was quickly denied by the Motor Vehicle Dealers Institute.

As reported by the Christchurch Press on 9 October 1982, the Institute's executive director, Colin Stone, denied the rumour and informed that a final plan would not be submitted to the Government for its consideration well into the following year.

"'New vehicle prices would continue to rise because of the increasing prices of overseas-sourced vehicle assembly packs,' he said…

"Motor industry officials believed the suggestions of lower-priced cars had had a marked effect in the market. They believed these suggestions have fuelled the recent fall in new car sales as motorists postponed buying in the belief they would soon be able to get cheaper cars." [108]

Indeed, the findings of the Commission's draft report, together with other financial restrictions, such as a price and credit freeze then in place, resulted in a substantial drop in car sales "…with September sales down about 30 per cent on those in June…" [109]

It did not take long for the assembly industry to react to the downturn in sales and the industry's uncertain future:

"Redundancy talks will continue today [21 October 1982] at the Auckland car-assembly plants where 65 workers are facing lay-offs. The redundancies, 55 at the Wiri works and 10 at Otahuhu, had already been selected on a last-on, first-off basis…

"Already 66 workers at the Nissan plants have volunteered to go…65 further reductions would be made on a section, basis within each plant and every section would lose some personnel. The Ford works in Auckland at which 110 workers volunteered to leave, is thought to be seeking about 40 more redundancies…" [110]

Motor Vehicle Hire Purchase

While many New Zealanders no doubt free-wheeled in horse-drawn carriages partly owned by the bank, it wasn't until the promotion of the horseless carriage as a need-to-have that hire purchase really came into its own as a selling aid. One of the first providers of hire purchase credit was described by the Otago Daily Times in November 1922:

"Credit Sales Of Motors. The New Zealand Guarantee Corporation Ltd will presently come before the public. It has been promoted by a strong financial group, and names identified with the company include:

"Sir Joseph Ward, Major Fraser (Dunedin) Messrs S Kircaldie, K Duncan, G W Magnus; Eric Johnson, S Wilson, A T Traversi, F H Taylor, E O Hales, and Colonel Hunter (Wellington), Mr R J Gilmour (Invercargill), and Mr F H Claxton (Thames).

"The capital is to be £200,000; the object, the financing of credit sales of commercial motor vehicles. The scheme was first tried in America and later in England. Similar corporations have been established in Sydney and Melbourne, with, it is claimed, so much success that it has become imperative for facilities which they provide being made available in New Zealand.

"The new corporation has been thoroughly considered by the New Zealand Motor Trade Association. At the recent conference of that body in Dunedin it was decided to accord it the active and whole-hearted support of the association as long as the interests of the trade were conserved and the public received a fair deal.

"It was recognised at the Dunedin conference of the trade that credit sales present a real difficulty to the average motor trader whose capital is soon locked up if he undertakes this class of business.

"In many cases, it was understood, business from reliable sources had had to be declined because of the inability of the motor trader to give the credit required. The establishment of the corporation would, it was realised, go a long way toward removing this difficulty, and credit sales made that would be impossible under present conditions. For the present the corporation will confine its business to commercial vehicles." [111]

Hire Purchase and Credit Sales Stabilisation Regulations 1955

In time, credit sales would be extended to include all manner of new and used motor vehicles and motorcycles but on very strict terms governed by various versions of the Hire Purchase and Credit Sales Stabilisation Regulations, first introduced by the Government in 1955:

"In addition to prescribing minimum credit under hire-purchase agreements and credit sale agreements, the regulations also prescribe the maximum amounts and maximum periods for the repayment of any loan made by a seller or by a person carrying on the business of money-lending on the security of goods purchased by the borrower, where any part of the price of the goods is paid out of the loan.

"This does not apply if a loan is fully secured on other goods, or is secured wholly or partly by a mortgage on land…The regulations describe a credit sale agreement as one under which instalments of purchase money for goods are payable over a period of nine months or longer." [112]

Subsequent Amendments

The 1955 regulations excluded motor vehicles but this category was added in 1957:

"The Hire Purchase and Credit Sales Stabilisation Regulations, 1957 applied only to cars, on which the minimum deposit was 50 per cent, and the maximum period of credit 18 months, and to motor trucks, buses and motor-cycles, for which the minimum deposit was 33 1-3 per cent and the maximum period of credit 24 months." [113]

A 1964 amendment to the regulations included hire purchase regulations for the purchase of used cars:

"An amendment to the Hire Purchase and Credit Sales Stabilisation Regulations 1957, forbids a seller or a lender from making an unsecured loan of more than 33 1-3 per cent of the value of a new car or more than 50 per cent of the value of a used car. Borrowers are required to repay these loans in full within 12 months in the case of a new car or within 18 months in the case of a used car. This regulation does not apply to cars for farm use or for use principally in a manufacturing or construction business." [114]

Another amendment, pertaining to motor vehicle deposits, was published in May 1968:

"The minimum hire-purchase deposit on second-hand motor-cars, light trucks and all motor-cycles will be reduced tomorrow. The deposit on second-hand cars and light trucks will be reduced from 66 2/3 per cent to 50 per cent. The minimum deposit for all motor-cycles will be lowered from 50 per cent to 33 1/3 per cent. The maximum credit period for all three types of vehicle will be extended from 12 to 18 months.

"The Licensed Motor Dealers' Association was gratified that the Government had considered its representation fully and decided to ease restrictions on the terms of sale…The recent survey by the Transport Department has revealed that the inability of the average citizen to replace his older vehicle has resulted in a very grave situation and danger to the public generally…" [115]

The Government's use of hire purchase regulations to limit consumer demand obviously influenced the New Zealand assembly industry — as reported by the Christchurch Press in September 1972:

"Some Austin and Morris cars rose in price today. The increases range between 2 per cent and 3.5 per cent. Overseas price increases and a lower throughput in New Zealand assembly plants had caused the rises, said a New Zealand Motor Corporation spokesman. Lower production from local assembly plants had been intensified lately because of New Zealand's 'stiff' hire-purchase regulations making it difficult for purchasers to find the ready cash to buy new cars." [116]

As a result of a deteriorating economic situation, in September 1974, the Government implemented another amendment to the Hire Purchase and Credit Sales Stabilisation Regulations to reduce the demand for consumer goods:

"Deposits for cars and light trucks had been increased from 50 per cent to 60 per cent and the period for credit reduced, in the case of new cars from 24 months to 12, and for second-hand cars from 24 months to 18…" [117]

By September 1976, demand had certainly fallen away:

"Sales of new cars last month fell by 50 per cent on the previous August, while total car sales during the month were 5319, compared with 10,500 in August last year. The fall in sales is blamed by motor manufacturers on more stringent hire-purchase regulations, the poor economic climate, and the fact that devaluation of the New Zealand dollar sent sales soaring last August as customers rushed to buy cars before the prices rose." [118]

Industry Plea

Following still more stringent hire purchase regulation, the motor vehicle industry called for some relief in August 1977:

"Unless the Government revises car hire-purchase regulations soon, motor vehicle retailers are likely to be forced to lay off staff. This is the prediction of the chairman of the Canterbury branch of the Motor Vehicle Dealers' Institute (Mr D A H Brown).

"'Motor-vehicle assembly plants throughout the country are not working to capacity, and I know of one plant where the staff are down to a four-day working week,' Mr Brown said yesterday.

"'It's not just the car dealers who will be affected by the depressed car market: the assembly plants and all associated industries and suppliers will feel the pinch,' he said. The institute has been making representations to the Government on the present hire-purchase regulations, brought in about 18 months ago in a successful attempt to reduce car sales throughout New Zealand.

"The regulations demand a 60 per cent deposit — with one year to pay the balance — on a used car, and full cash price for a new car.

"'I think we are the only country in the Western world where the full cash price has to be paid on a new car,' Mr Brown said. 'Although there has been a slight increase in car sales this month, sales will have to rise dramatically before they can get anywhere near the levels of 18 months to two years ago.'" [119]

The hire purchase regulations were finally relaxed in an economic package announced by the Government on 2 February 1978:

"The hire-purchase regulations, affecting the sales of both new and used motor cars, were relaxed from midnight yesterday. The Prime Minister (Mr Muldoon) said that the minimum deposit on new cars would be reduced from 100 per cent to 60 per cent, and a maximum repayment period of 12 months would be allowed. The 60 per cent minimum deposit on used cars is to remain but the maximum repayment period will be increased from 12 months to 18 months.

"Mr Muldoon said that the action had been taken in the light of the recent survey of the automotive assembly industry by departmental officials which revealed very serious problems of overstocking and excess assembly capacity." [120]

The change quickly resulted in an increase in car sales — as reported by the Christchurch Press:

"Motorists have wasted little time in taking advantage of the relaxed hire-purchase regulations for new cars. New-car sales in February were 25 per cent higher than in January, when the new-car market fell to its lowest level for eight years." [121]

"Christchurch car dealers have noticed a good response to the easing of the hire-purchase regulations on new and used cars. Although it has not been dramatic, sales have increased this month, especially of used cars in the $5000 to $8000 price range.

"The easing of the hire purchase regulations had restored public confidence in buying cars, said the chairman of the Canterbury branch of the Motor Vehicle Dealers' Institute…Now that the Government has made a firm decision, people are able to buy a car without thinking there will be another change in the regulations round the corner…He suggested increasing the repayment term for used cars to two years, rather than the 18-month term.

"A spokesman for Tench Bros Ltd said sales were excellent at the moment for both new and used cars. He said that people were now able to afford more expensive used cars, but he did not expect the regulations to have much effect on sales of new cars. Another dealer reported a similar situation, with increased sales of used cars, but not much response to new cars." [122]

Despite the easing of hire purchase regulations in 1978, the motor vehicle industry struggled to sell its vehicles to eager, but cash-strapped, motorists and continued to call for the Government to abolish its economy-regulating tool — as reported by the Christchurch Press in August 1981 and February 1982:

"The Government has rejected an Automobile Association plea to abolish hire-purchase controls on all car buying. The association's secretary…said his organisation had received 'a nil response' from the Deputy Minister of Finance…The association had asked for the abolition of hire purchase controls. It wanted financing arrangements for car buying to be left to assemblers, dealers, and the finance industry.

"…the Automobile Association felt the hire-purchase regulations, which require a 60 per cent deposit and the balance within a year on new cars, forced people to retain older and less economic cars. The regulations had also led to people financing cars by mortgages on houses and property. This was an expensive and untidy system." [123]

"Hire-purchase regulations on new motor vehicles were discriminatory, economically ineffective, and superfluous, the Finance Houses Association told the Industries Development Commission at hearings on the motor industry, in Wellington this week.

"On Tuesday the Automobile Association told the commission that the regulations should be scrapped. The regulations were brought in in 1978 to dampen demand for new cars and drains on overseas funds, by requiring a deposit of 60 per cent and payment of the balance over a 12-month period. This had failed because other means of financing the purchase of motor vehicles were in use — the numbers of leased vehicles had doubled, and personal loans had increased significantly…

"'Although car registrations were at record levels and imports of motor vehicles up, the number of new hire purchase agreements had not increased much over the same period. Although the Government had been trying to restrain demand for imported vehicles, other means of financing purchases had kept demand up and had been permitted by the Government,' the finance houses said.

"As they stood, the regulations discriminated against buyers without property or some large form of chattel security that would secure them a loan. Buyers were paying more than the cost of the vehicle in special arrangements to get round the regulations." [124]

<u>The Industries Development Commission Draft Proposal</u>

As detailed earlier, the Industries Development Commission released its draft report on the motor industry on 10 September 1982. One of the report's main proposals included: "…the end of price controls on motor vehicles, hire purchase regulations…"

These proposals were obviously welcomed by the motor industry but soon quashed by the Government in March 1983:

"The Government's decision not to ease hire-purchase regulations governing the sale of motor vehicles will be a blow to car assembly firms and their workers. From the arguments that the firms have put forward, a relaxation of the regulations would appear the only salvation available to the troubled industry…Existing hire-purchase restrictions on the sales of motor vehicles are recognised as a curb on the development of the motor industry in New Zealand…

"The Industries Development Commission, in its draft report for a motor industry development plan last year, recommended that the restrictions be abolished. Support for abolishing, or at least easing the restrictions has come subsequently from such diverse groups as the Automobile Association, the Engineers' Union, and the Motor Vehicle Dealers' Institute. Motor assembly firms, and their workers, naturally support such a move in the face of large stockpiles of unsold cars and widespread lay-offs throughout the industry.

"Hire-purchase regulations covering motor vehicles are the most stringent credit regulations applied to consumer goods. For new cars, 60 per cent of the price must be paid in deposit and the balance must be paid within 12 months. For used cars, the deposit is the same but the balance may be spread out in payments up to 18 months from the date of purchase.

"When the economy tightens, such limitations are a powerful disincentive to car purchases; easing them would have encouraged more people to buy cars, or exchange their present vehicles for newer ones. The number of unsold vehicles would still have taken some months to clear, but relaxed hire-purchase regulations would have given assembly firms some confidence of stability in the industry.

"A problem for the Government is that the hire-purchase regulations are only part of the motor industry's troubles. The Industries Development Commission report identified many other steps that could or should be taken towards comprehensive development. Relaxing the hire-purchase requirements would bring an immediate stimulus to the industry, but it would be a palliative and not a cure for the industry's ills.

"The main beneficiaries from eased hire-purchase regulations would not have been the industry, but the public, and the prospect of a buying spree would not have endeared the proposal to the Government. Nevertheless, the preservation of jobs is a persuasive argument. Hundreds in the industry have been laid off already; hundreds more seem likely to follow without the stimulus to car sales that easier hire-purchase regulations would have brought." [125]

Hire Purchase Controls Abolished

After some 26 years of Government control, hire purchase restrictions on all motor vehicle purchases were finally abolished on 8 September 1983:

"The dropping of hire-purchase controls on cars and motor-cycles was welcomed by the trade yesterday…The Prime Minister, Mr Muldoon, said after the Government caucus met yesterday that controls would be dropped. Regulations bringing the change into effect immediately were approved by the Executive Council yesterday. Until yesterday, buyers had to front up with 60 per cent of a car purchase price, with the balance for new cars over a year and for used cars over 18 months.

"In recent times, however, car sales firms have been able to get round the regulations because of what the Motor-Vehicle Dealers' Institute…described as grey areas in the law. Mortgages on property or other possessions often enabled sales to be made under terms not included in the regulations…that is one of the prime reasons the Government has abolished the regulations…" [126]

By June 1984, car sales had certainly improved:

"The increase in some vehicle hire purchase follows the Government's lifting of restrictions of regulations on minimum deposits and maximum credit periods…The Reserve Bank survey noted strong growth in new car sales since last August and attributed much of the overall recovery in spending to growth in this sector." [127]

The Preliminary Motor Vehicle Industry Plan

What was expected to be Government's 'final development plan' for the country's motor vehicle industry was completed in July 1984. However, the plan's proposed tariff reductions soon attracted a good deal of criticism from one of the country's closest trading partners, Australia:

"New Zealand has brought the potential row on with its car industry plan, released in July which mainly aims at cutting the cost of vehicle imports.

"Under the scheme, tariffs on Australian and British cars will be cut from about 15 per cent to zero, while those on cars from other sources, principally Japan, will be cut from 45 per cent to 15 per cent. That effectively would halve the Australians' margin of preference from 30 per cent over its rivals and threatens its already troubled motor vehicle industry and its exports to New Zealand which were worth about $A100,000 last financial year.

"New Zealand is Australia's biggest export market, although it is building up sales of four-cylinder engines to Europe. Officials are irritated that New Zealand has made the move in spite of the aims of the Closer Economic Relations agreement to promote trade.

"However, the Australians have a bargaining counter of their own, because one of the other main aims of the New Zealand car plan is to encourage the export of vehicle components. New Zealand is anxious to see Australia include these parts in their cars, in spite of the fact that the industry is facing wholesale reorganisation under the Australians' own car industry plan produced earlier this year...

"What the Australians want is to see the tariffs on their international rivals reduced by a lesser amount or more slowly in return for greater access to the market for New Zealand auto components. According to a recent report from Wellington, the Minister of Trade and Industry, Mr David Caygill, has ordered a review of the New Zealand industry plan...

"Several meetings have been held on the matter, but so far they have only refined the countries' respective positions. The latest talks last week in Canberra involved a New Zealand team headed by the Assistant Secretary of Trade and Industry, Mr Richard Fraser, and included representatives of the Treasury and the Customs and Trade and Industry departments.

"A senior Australian official said that the three days of meetings had seen the positions of both sides restated and ideas tossed around. We have two different car industry plans and what we are going to have to do is get them wedded together, he said." [128]

The Revised Motor Vehicle Industry Plan

After long talks to accommodate the industry needs of both countries, a revised New Zealand Motor Vehicle Industry Plan was completed in December 1984 — as reported by the Christchurch Press:

"Under the new plan, access to Australia for New Zealand-made vehicle components has been doubled from the present $26 million a year and they will compete with the local product on an equal footing because for tariff and regulatory purposes they will be regarded as being locally made.

"In return for what will be a big boost to the New Zealand industry, which will now be able to push harder into the lucrative spare-parts market, New Zealand has made what sources in Sydney consider to be significant concessions to the Australian industry.

"The first is that Australia's margin of tariff preference will be reduced over five years instead of four, giving the Australian industry longer to adjust to impending international competition in its biggest market; a second is the change in sales tax based on engine size; a third is in the component industry while there has also been a small but significant rise in the number of built-up cars...

"The New Zealand market is now opening up to competition...the biggest plus, said a senior trade official involved in the negotiations, is the opening up of the market generally..." [129]

Car Dealers Welcome Plan

"The national president of the Motor-Vehicle Dealers' Institute, Mr G. F. McIver, of Dunedin, welcomed the motor-vehicle industry plan but said the greatest advantages would accrue to a small part of the market...The market will be freer and people will be able to buy the car they actually need...Our attitude is that we believe this plan will reduce stock inventories and will help the consumer, said Mr McIver.

"The Government's plan created an environment where Japanese vehicle franchises would be become even more dominant in the New Zealand market, said Motor Holdings, Ltd, at Wellington yesterday. The company is a principal shareholder in Mazda Motors of New Zealand, Ltd, which assembles and markets the Subaru range and also assembles Daihatsu models under contract.

"The company's chairman, Mr Lloyd Brown, said the Government was to be applauded for an industry plan which preserved the local assembly industry, ensured a wider choice of cars for the New Zealand motorist, and enabled prices to be held or even reduced. Mr Brown said Mazda and Subaru would be importing more overseas assembled sporting and luxury vehicles to complement locally assembled ranges.

"The managing director of Motor Holdings, Mr Peter Turner, said the plan encouraged local assemblers to become more efficient and rationalise the number of models assembled locally." [130]

Market Shares

In October 1985, the New Zealand Institute of Economic Research Incorporated published a Working Paper, 'The New Zealand Motor Car Industry After The Plan', by Daniel A Witt. As the title suggests, the paper examined the effects of the Government's December 1984 Motor Industry Plan on the country's vehicle assemblers, importers, dealers, and buyers:

"It is apparent that The Plan, as far reaching and liberalising as parts are, will have a significant impact on the assembly sector of the industry. The likely effects of The Plan, which are consistent with the objectives set forth by the Industries Development Commission in its proposal to the Government, fall into four areas:

"1. Encourage competition by altering the competitive environment;

"2. Reduce the unit cost of New Zealand assembled vehicles;

"3. Liberalise the market place;

"4. Establish the appropriate levels of protection for domestically assembled vehicles." [131]

As a result of Daniel Witt's interviews of various principals of the assembly plants operating in 1984, he was informed that each plant's market share for that year was:

"Daihatsu	2.15%
"Ford Motors	23%
"General Motors	12.5%
"Mazda Motors	7.0%
"Motor Holdings Ltd	2.5%
"NZ Motor Corporation	11.4%
"Nissan Datsun	10.2%
"Suzuki	1.5%
"Todd Motors	17%
"Toyota NZ	16.5%" [132]

In 1984, some 92,292 vehicles (93%) were imported as CKD and 7,364 (7%) as completely built up. [133]

Import Tender Scheme

Following its announcement in the 1979 Budget:

"A limited system of tendering for additional import licences was introduced in 1980. The objective of this system is to increase flexibility, encourage efficiency and to create a more competitive environment among the manufacturing industries.

"This [tendering] scheme is the first move towards a more comprehensive restructuring of import licensing in New Zealand. Under this scheme licences additional to those available under the existing scheme are made available by tender. Each tenderer offers to pay a premium above the face value of the licence and the extra licences go to the highest bidder." [134]

The Christchurch Press of 27 February 1985 published examples of the premiums to be paid by various new vehicle importers during that year:

"Bids by Ford, General Motors, Todd Motors and Motor Holdings have all missed out in the first round of import tenders for new fully built-up motor-vehicles announced by the Department of Trade and Industry. Their major competitors, Mazda, Emco (NZMC), and Nissan have won the lion's share of tenders to import new vehicles, but at a substantial cost.

"Last month the department invited tenders for the import licences for 17,143 new cars worth $34.4 million. When tenders closed there were bids for eight times that number with bidders offering to pay up to $2300 for each unit.

"The lowest successful bid was for $542. Emco obtained 3000 units but must pay more than $2 million to the Government as a premium. Mazda obtained the right to 2690 units at a premium of $1.8 million, Nissan 2200 units at a premium of $2 million, Toyota 2887 units at a premium of $800,000, BMW obtained 1200 units at a premium of $800,000, and Moller Holdings 1200 units at a premium of $500,000.

"The major companies that submitted bids which were too low were Ford' (which sought 8256 units), Todd Motors (2422), Motor Holdings (1673), General Motors (3092), and Cable Price (1561).

"A spokesman for Ford said yesterday that its failure to win any licences was no tragedy. A second round of licences will be up for tender later this year. Aside from that, Ford had the right to import fully built-up vehicles under a system of rationalisation licences and in exchange for its very successful export trade in alloy wheels…" [135]

The Beginning of the End

The Government's tariff protection and import licensing measures that had cocooned the country's vehicle assembly industry since 1907 were progressively reduced by late 1987. The first indication that the beginning of the end for the assembly plants was nigh was announced by the Minister of Trade and Industry, Mr Caygill, in October of that year:

"New Zealand car prices have traditionally been higher than those of other countries. This has been due both to high levels of protection for the New Zealand industry and taxation policies pursued by successive Governments. The present Government has introduced policies to increase the efficiency of this sector and ultimately reduce the level of prices currently paid by consumers.

"In 1984, the graduated sales tax was replaced by a uniform 30 per cent. This was, in turn, replaced by an excise tax of 25 per cent at the time that GST was introduced. On July 1 this reduced to 20 per cent and it will reduce by a further 5 per cent at the same time next year.

"It is the Government's intention to remove excise tax from motor vehicles completely as and when fiscal policy allows. In addition, the motor vehicle industry plan under which the industry operates is being reviewed. The objective of this review is to continue seeking structural change and greater efficiency from the local industry. It is intended that this review be completed by the end of the year.

"These policies are already having an effect. In June this year a number of assemblers announced significant price reductions on a range of vehicles. I am confident that New Zealand assemblers will continue to pass on savings to the consumer as they adapt to the changes being demanded of them." [136]

The Reviewed Motor Vehicle Industry Plan

By December of 1987, the Government's review of the motor vehicle industry plan was complete and the outcome announced:

"Existing tariffs on automotive products would be phased down, the Minister of Trade and Industry, Mr Caygill, announced. He said the Customs Tariff already provided for reductions in the normal rate of duty on knocked-down car packs in 1988 and 1989. From January 1, 1990, the normal rate would be reduced to zero.

"At present, the normal rate of duty on cars and other vehicles up to 3500 kg is 55 per cent. It will be reduced to 45 per cent on January 1, 1989, and to 35 per cent on January 1, 1990. For commercial vehicles between 3501 and 10,500 kg, special purpose vehicles and omnibuses, the rate will be reduced from 30 per cent to 25 per cent in January, 1989, and to 20 per cent in January, 1990. For commercial vehicles over 10,500 kg, the rate will be reduced from 30 per cent to 15 per cent in January, 1989, and to zero by January, 1990.

"The future of the preferential rates now applying to Australian and British imports would be the subject of consultations with those overseas governments.

"From January 1, 1989, the normal tariff rates on nominated components for use in motor vehicle assembly would be aligned with the rates for built-up vehicles. For nominated components identical to all vehicle classes, the rate would be the one applying to cars and other vehicles not exceeding 3500 kg gross weight. For motor vehicle spare parts and accessories of types manufactured or reconditioned locally, the normal rates of duty will be gradually reduced to 20 per cent by January 1, 1992.

"From January, 1993, the standard tariff reduction programme will apply to these goods. Those automotive products already subjected to rate reductions under the standard tariff programme (gaskets, shell bearings and bushings, oil and fuel filters), will remain within that programme for further rate reductions…

"'The Government's decisions on the review of the Motor Vehicle Industry Plan provide a package of measures which will help induce greater economic efficiency overall and reduce costs in the vital transport sector. Export producers must benefit from these changes…" [137]

Price Cuts

Following the announcement in May 1988 that further tariff cuts would take effect from 1 July of that year, New Zealand's car manufacturers scrambled to cut their prices for new cars by thousands of dollars — as reported by the Christchurch Press on 6 May 1988:

"Mitsubishi and Toyota cut car prices within hours of the announcement and Ford followed with prices falling as much as 9.4 per cent. The New Zealand Motor Corporation has promised to match the average price cuts of 7 and 8 per cent.

"Mazda Motors of New Zealand has announced cuts averaging 7.6 per cent. The firm's general manager, Mr Peter Aitken, said he welcomed the Government's announcement to abolish the 25 per cent tariff on completely knocked down (c.k.d.) components from Japan. But the flood of cheap used-car imports from Japan was still concerning assemblers and dealers. The Government should act decisively to eradicate these imports, he said." [138]

The Japanese Invasion

It was during the 1960s that the makers of Japanese cars suggested that their products could economically supplement New Zealand's shortfall of British, American, and Australian models — as reported by the Christchurch Press on 21 October 1966:

"New Zealand was denying itself the chance to help to overcome its car shortage by importing more Japanese cars, the managing-director of the Nissan Motor Company, Ltd., Mr M. Okuma, said in Auckland.

"He said Japanese industry was competitive and, in spite of a 32.5 per cent import duty [in 1966], was able to match prices of British cars in New Zealand. New Zealand had a favourable trade balance of £6 million with Japan, and it was unfair that New Zealand's importing policy should not take more note of this. It was possible that the Japanese attitude to importing New Zealand produce could harden if the trade imbalance continued.

"New Zealand had a heavy trade deficit with Australia, yet continued to import many Australian-made cars. Taking more cars from Japan would help New Zealand correct the imbalance. Mr Okuma said it was scarcely economic for Japanese manufacturers to assemble cars in New Zealand when each maker was limited to an annual output of 300 units. Japanese manufacturers could be interested in eventually manufacturing in New Zealand if the local steel industry could provide the materials, but a maker would need to build between 20,000 and 30,000 units a year to make this economical." [139]

Indeed, only seven years later, cars from Japan were arriving in New Zealand in their hundreds — as reported by the Christchurch Press in November and December 1973, respectively:

"The 17,000-ton Kanagawa Maru will not be the first Nissan Motor Car Carrier Company ship to visit New Zealand: another Nissan car carrier, the Bluebird, is due to off-load 650 new Datsuns at Auckland in about 12 days. The Kanagawa Maru will bring a further 600 cars to New Zealand early in December, off-loading them by hydraulic lifts and ramps at Auckland and Lyttelton. The two shipments are worth a total of about $5 million.

"The Nissan company owns 11 car carriers, and the vessels which will visit New Zealand normally trade between Japan and North America. The company has a further 11 car carriers on order, most will be able to carry up to 3000 cars at once. The cars being brought to New Zealand are the first built-up vehicles to be imported under the extra $15m in car import licences allowed by the Government." [140]

"Nearly 800 new cars from Japan, worth $3m, will be discharged at Auckland and Timaru later this month from the car carrier Kanyoshi Maru. The cars, Datsun 140Js, are being brought to New Zealand under the Government's relaxation in built-up car imports.

"Announcing the delivery in Timaru, the sales manager for Nissan Motor Distributors (N.Z.), Ltd (Mr W. J. Broadbent), said 470 cars would be discharged in Auckland and 300 in Timaru. The ship is due in Auckland on December 15 and Timaru on December 21. All the cars have been sold." [141]

Import data as to the source of motor vehicles show that, by 1985, the comparative trickle of Japanese vehicles had become a deluge.

"Sources of NZ Motor Vehicles from 1975 through to August 1985:

	(1975)	(1985)
"Japan	24.9%	82.1%
"UK & Australia	68.9%	3.0% (UK) 8.6% (Australia)
"Other	6.2%	6.3%" [142]

By the late 1980s, the deluge continued — as reported by Craig Dowling of the Christchurch Press on 30 November 1989:

"The latest figures from the Customs Department show that used motor vehicle imports from Japan have sky-rocketed during 1989 — mainly through commercial dealers.

"In 1987 only 2541 second-hand cars were brought into New Zealand. But with the relaxation of import restrictions this figure jumped to a total of 21,280 Japanese cars in 1988.

"By October this year [1989] that figure had doubled again (to 48,190) and observers say the end of year figure should pass 60,000…

"Japanese used car imports got off to a bad start in New Zealand with back-up service and spare part supplies often lax. But these problems have been largely overcome by the large number of cars coming into the country, and the fact that dealers, having to offer warranties, have taken over the market from the private importers who blazed the trail. Though some dealers have been forced under in what essentially has been a rationalisation process, new car yards are still opening up." [143]

Assembly Plants Close

In 1985 New Zealand supported 14 assembly plants but with the reduction and removal of tariffs from the 1980s, plus the importation of second-hand Japanese cars, the entire local assembly industry had progressively closed by the end of 1998.

Those plant closures included:

"New Zealand Motor Corporation — closed its Newmarket plant in 1976, Petone plant in 1982, and Panmure plant in 1988.

General Motors — closed its Petone plant in August 1984 and its Trentham plant in November 1990.

Motor Industries International (Mazda) — closed its Otahuhu plant in 1987.

Ford — closed its Seaview plant in 1987.

Motor Holdings — closed its Waitara plant in June/July 1987.

Suzuki — closed its Wanganui plant in 1988.

Toyota — closed its Christchurch plant in 1996 and Thames plant in December 1998.

VANZ (Ford & Mazda) — closed its Sylvia Park plant in 1991 and its Wiri plant in March 1997.

Mitsubishi — closed its Porirua plant in June 1998.

Nissan — closed its Wiri plant in July 1998.

Honda — closed its Nelson plant in August 1998." [144]

Afterword

In his research paper, Development Options in the New Zealand Motor Car Assembly Industry, completed in 1971 for the NZ Institute of Economic Research, William Rose provided a general overview of the importation and assembly of the motor vehicle in New Zealand:

"In affluent societies the motor car is one of the commonest, and yet more expensive and prestigious of consumer durables. It forms an important part of the expenditure of the typical household and of society as a whole. At the same time motor car manufacture exhibits to an extraordinary degree the phenomenon of economies of scale; in general terms if we produce more cars we will produce them more cheaply. The same phenomenon is present in motor car assembly but to a lesser extent.

"These two characteristics have confronted smaller affluent nations such as New Zealand with an acute dilemma. They share the high per capita demand for cars but lack the scale necessary for their most economic production. To import cars is to incur a high cost in overseas exchange: to produce them locally may mean a wasteful use of local labour and capital which could more profitably be employed in other industries.

"In practice the dilemma has been resolved by cutting the car in two. Those parts which are more subject to economies of scale are imported from the major international motor car producers whilst other parts are produced locally and incorporated in the locally assembled car. Then as the scale of domestic industry increases, production is slowly extended to include more and more items that were previously imported...

"Historically, and apart from import licensing, the main incentive to assemble in New Zealand did not arise from any comparative manufacturing advantage. Rather a disadvantage on this account was offset by savings in freight costs and later by the effect of tariffs." [145]

Chapter Seven

Vehicle Importers & Dealers

While many of New Zealand's first motor vehicle builders and assemblers transitioned from the making of horse-drawn carriages and wagons, some of the country's first motor vehicle importers and sellers also progressed from another legacy form of transport — that of the bicycle:

Skeates and Bockaert

When Skeates and Bockaert Limited, trading as The Skeates Cycle Manufacturing Company, announced that it had moved to new premises at 58 Queen Street, Auckland, in December 1898, it described its new premises as: "…the most up to date and largest Cycle Factory in the North Island." [1]

As mentioned in a previous chapter, Skeates and Bockaert became agents for Auckland's first motor car, the Star, made by the Star Engineering Company of Wolverhampton, England and delivered in 1899. [2]

Percy Skeates and Emil Bockaert were soon promoting the De Dion and Darracq motor cars in Auckland and the provinces [3] having imported some 300 by December 1907. [4] The company also imported a number of 'Motosacoche' motor cycles [5] and became one of the first to provide motor cars for hire at the time. [6]

Also, "Mr Skeates travelled all over New Zealand and particularly in the Wairarapa, selling cars to wealthy station owners…" [7]

However, by June 1909, the business of Skeates and Bockaert Limited had reached its end, with many of its North Island branches sold and the company eventually placed in voluntary liquidation [8] and struck from the Companies Register on 12 January 1920. [9]

As of 30 June 1909, the motor vehicle business of Skeates and Bockaert had been sold to Percy Robert Skeates and George M White, trading as Skeates & White Limited. [10]

Skeates and White

The business of Skeates & White very nearly ended in tragedy when Percy Skeates and his mechanic, Bertie James Hanna, were both shot multiple times by a 19-year-old prospective car buyer during a test drive in March 1913. As later heard at the Police Court, "Hanna had several bullet wounds, but none dangerous…Skeates had two or three wounds in the head, one in the brow, one in the hand, and one in the side of the cheek." [11] Fortunately, the pair survived the ordeal and their assailant "…was sentenced to ten years' reformative treatment." [12]

As well as its early start as a motor vehicle dealer, Skeates and White continued with its bicycle and motor cycle business — as reported in August 1933:

"A fresh advertiser in our columns is Messrs Skeates & White Ltd. of 48 Fort St. Auckland. This firm has been in the bicycle and motor cycle business for over 40 years and specially caters for bicycle and motor cycle riders. They have a comprehensive stock of all accessories and parts and specialize in pistons for all makes of motor cycles. They also have a proficient repair staff both for bicycle and motor cycle work…" [13]

The success of the Skeates and White business was demonstrated by an article published by The New Zealand Herald on 22 December 1936:

"A presentation of a framed photograph of the 34 members of the staff of Skeates and White Limited was made to the two directors of the firm, Mr George White and Mr Percy Skeates, at a gathering of employees. Mr E Hughes, an employee of 27 years' standing, voiced the appreciation of the staff of the directors' policy of maintaining the staff during the years of depression and referred to their good treatment as conditions improved." [14]

From the 1940s, Skeates and White also sold all manner of goods including tyres, motor oils, and even revolving clothes lines. [15] The company was also the New Zealand agents for BSA Bicycles and Motor Cycles for many years. [16]

Magnus Motors Limited

Godfrey William Magnus, sometimes referred to as 'George' Magnus by the press, is another who transitioned easily from cycle to motor power during the early 1900s.

"The Massey-Harris Company, which is represented in Wellington by Mr George Magnus, finding its premises in Willis-street too small for its increased business, has leased the building further up the street so long in the occupation of Messrs J Myers & Co., and has fitted it up in first-class style for the purposes of its bicycle trade. The new premises were opened to-day with a fine display of the company's own bicycles and accessories." [17]

In 1901, Godfrey Magnus (1879?-1952) remained the New Zealand Manager for the Canada Cycle and Motor Company, then the manufacturer of the very popular Massey Harris bicycle. [18]

However, with the advent of the motor car, he also became one of New Zealand's first motor vehicle dealers with the establishment of Magnus Motors Limited in October 1907. At that time, Godfrey Magnus also became a senior partner of Magnus, Sanderson and Co Limited, an original cycle manufacturer and importer and an early importer of motor vehicles. [19]

As reported by The Dominion in 1908:

"The Post and Telegraph Department has placed an order for a handy motor delivery van for the collection of mail matter from the Wellington pillar boxes with Messrs. Magnus, Sanderson and Co., of this city. A Russell car, manufactured by the Canada Cycle and Motor Company of Toronto, has been selected, and is expected to arrive here some time during July. The Department has also been inquiring into the, utility of larger motor vans for the. removal of bulk mails from steamers and trains, but nothing definite on this point has been decided." [20]

Magnus Motors was also quick to establish itself as an important motor vehicle importer and dealer with Godfrey Magnus taking an early interest in overseas developments that could be incorporated in New Zealand — such as improved roads — as reported by the Nelson Evening Mail in July 1917:

"Concrete roads are the roads of the future, says Mr Godfrey Magnus, who has just returned from the United States…There such roads are being laid down in all parts of the country to meet the demands of the ever-growing motor traffic. He had the great pleasure of travelling over the 500-mile concrete road that joins San Francisco to Los Angeles. 'It is perfect travelling at last,' says Mr Magnus. 'The action of the car is so smooth that you could imagine you were travelling on silk.'" [21]

By 1923, Magnus Motors had acquired the rights to import vehicles of some prestige — as reported by the Hawke's Bay Tribune in May of that year:

"Although the name of 'Rolls Royce' is of world-wide renown amongst motorists, only a very limited number of these famous cars have, in the past, been imported into the Dominion. The motoring public will be interested to learn that Messrs Magnus Motors Ltd Wellington, have been appointed agents for the Rolls Royce and will shortly have one of the new 20 h.p. models on exhibition at their Hawke's Bay branch, which they have just opened in…Hastings…" [22]

By 1934, Magnus Motors was also the agent for America's Dodge motor vehicles and the 'Direct Factory Distributors' for the British Austin, then described as 'Britain's Dependable Car'. [23]

Magnus Motors Limited continued to trade profitably until it and other dealerships, including Dominion Motors, Seabrook Fowlds, David Crozier, and P H Vickery, together engaged in the assembly and master distribution of Morris, Austin, and Wolseley vehicles. The group eventually merged with the New Zealand Motor Corporation in 1970. [24]

J S Hawkes & Co

As early as February 1908, J S Hawkes & Co was advertising itself as sole agents for the British-made Siddeley Autocar obtainable from its Royal Garage in Gloucester Street, Christchurch. [25] The garage was aptly named because it was advertised that the Siddeley 'Bears the Seal of Royal Approval — By Special Appointment to The Queen [Victoria]'. [26]

By June 1919, J S Hawkes & Co was also importing Dodge Brothers Cars from America and by 1920 had moved to larger premises:

"Altogether, over 16,000 square feet of floor space is comprised in the modern garage of J. S. Hawkes and Co., in Durham Street, between Gloucester and Armagh Streets. There Mr L. Treleaven presides as manager, and it is to his foresight and confidence in the future of the industry that the company owes its present large premises, which, even now, are scarcely big enough to meet the growing demands made upon them. Extensions are contemplated. He has over 12 years' motoring experience.

"The firm was established in Gloucester Street until four years ago. The company's workshop accords in every detail with what is meant by the word modern; the most improved appliances are provided, and manipulated by eight mechanics with years of experience behind them. Of course, there are assistants, too, but the boy element has been eliminated.

"The workshop is run on the service station principle, special attention being given to those cars for which the company has the agency. In the garage three double pits are provided, together with the latest car-washing arrangement. There is also a Bowser petrol and oil plant, and the latest air-compressor. It is the intention of the company to make a specialty of accessories.

"The whole building is fire-proof, being built in brick, with concrete floor; there is only one support, and that is in the centre. Cool, well-ventilated, and lighted by day and night, the garage is a model of its kind.

"The agencies held by J. S. Hawkes and Co. are: Hood tyres, Dodge Brothers, Sunbeam, and D.F.P. (French) cars." [27]

Blackwell Motors Group

First, there was a company called Buick Sales Limited of Oxford Terrace, Christchurch, and later Ashburton, which advertised itself as sole agents for the Buick Six in December 1915. [28]

The company was run by Charles James Jones who found himself in financial difficulties by 27 April 1923 when the National Bank of New Zealand appointed a Receiver to manage the affairs of Buick Sales and recover some £18,000 owed to it.

In August 1923, Blackwell Motors Limited was incorporated with the sole purpose of purchasing the stock-in-trade, plant, book debts…and other assets of Buick Sales from the Receiver. On paper, the transaction also included Blackwell Motors inheriting any ongoing or future litigation against Buick Sales, known then as 'choses in action'.

Blackwell Motors paid the Receiver nearly £18,000 thereby satisfying the debt owed to the bank but there remained a number of unpaid, unsecured creditors who were subsequently represented by a liquidator.

During Supreme Court proceedings to set aside the sale of Buick Sales to Blackwell Motors, the liquidator argued that "…the sale was devised by [Charles] Jones in peril of just such proceedings as the present ones, with a view to placing the property out of reach of his creditors." [29]

The liquidator argued further "…that the shareholders in the new company [Blackwell Motors] were connected with Buick Sales and Jones guaranteed the new company up to £2000.

"The new company was coerced by the National Bank to make an offer to purchase the assets of Buick Sales Ltd on pretty hard terms. The total purchase money was £18,000 and the debt to the bank was £17,000…" [30] A Supreme Court decision went against Jones "…in respect of alleged acts of misfeasance" but he appealed and the Appeal Court subsequently found in his favour in October 1925. [31]

Blackwell Motors, with the Directors named as Walter F Blackwell, J B Johns, W Stewart, and G W Fairweather, and a capital of £7500, started trading from the 1919 Durham Street, Christchurch premises of the former Buick Sales Limited.

"Originally the company was agent for Buick and Itala cars, and boasted a staff of 13. In 1927 Blackwell Motors obtained the Chevrolet franchise — the company has dealt with General Motors products almost throughout its time, and has handled most of the General Motors trademarks over the years.

"The biggest change came in 1954, when the Holden franchise was secured. Although the Holden was first announced in Australia in 1948, it was six years before the cars appeared in this country. During the 1930s, the company had branches at Ashburton and Culverden, but these were later closed."

By 1971, nearly 50 years after its establishment, Blackwell Motors was referred to as the Blackwell Motors Group comprising six subsidiary companies in and around the Christchurch district, namely: Blackwell Motors (Sydenham) Limited, Horrells Motors Limited, Gibson's Motors (Darfield) Limited, Arthur Burke Limited, Blackwell Distributors Limited, and Adams Limited. [32]

[As an aside, in August 1929, The New Zealand Herald reported:

"Founder of the Buick Motor-Car Company, David Buick, died penniless in a Detroit hospital on March 5. Buick missed great fortune just when it appeared to be well within his grasp. He gave his name to the well-known American car but at a time of financial stringency Mr W C Durant, took over the concern and organised General Motors. Mr. Buick later went to California where he failed in an oil venture, and again in real estate in Florida."] [33]

Horrells Motors Limited

"Horrells Motors Limited started in 1940, when Messrs E. Ryde and L. A. Schluter set up in partnership with a staff of four. A Chevrolet agency was obtained in 1944, and International Harvester and Standard car agencies followed in 1947. In 1955, the company became a sub-dealer to Blackwell Motors for Holden cars, and the same year it opened a Waikari branch. A new paint and panel department was opened this year [1971], and the company's staff now numbers 23." [34]

Gibson's Motors (Darfield) Limited — the origins of which were described by a Christchurch Press article published in October 1962:

"The original garage was built in 1927 by Mr R. McMillan, and in 1929 it was sold to Mr M. Johnston. Mr Gibson went to work for Mr Johnston as a mechanic in 1937 and bought the garage in 1942. In 1946 Mr Gibson formed the business into a limited liability company, and the same year the garage was doubled in size and the staff was increased to seven.

"The managing director of the firm is Mr R. R. Gibson, president of the Canterbury branch of the Retail Motor Trade Association; and one of the directors is Mr P. M. Hoare, the well-known Canterbury racing driver…The company is an agent for farm machinery and does much repair work on such equipment. It also sells used machinery and recently has started to sell television sets. Sewing machines and refrigerators are also sold." [35] Gibson's Motors (Darfield) Limited merged with Blackwell Motors in 1966. [36]

Arthur Burke Limited

"Arthur Burke Limited started in 1935, when Mr Burke bought out Frews Motors, Ltd. At that time the company had a staff of five, and a total stock comprising a Model T Ford truck, a Morris 10, and a Teraplane. In 1936 the company became Austin and Chevrolet sub-dealers, and in 1938 it became an agent for Massey Harris combines, tractors and implements. The firm was appointed a sub-dealer for Chevrolet and Vauxhall cars in 1954, and terminated its Austin sub-dealership that same year. In 1956, the Holden sub-dealership was obtained." [37] "In 1968 Arthur Burke Limited…merged with Blackwell Motors." [38]

Blackwell Distributors Limited was first registered as Honda Empisal Distributors (NZ) Limited in 1965 and licensed as a wholesaler in Christchurch on 6 September 1965. [39]
 As reported by the Christchurch Press in February 1967:
 "…Honda Empisal Distributors (N.Z.), Ltd., has the agency for Honda sports cars in open and coupe versions. This company hopes to arrange the assembly of Honda's half-ton utility truck in Christchurch." [40]
 In 1970 Honda Empisal Distributors became part of the Blackwell Group and the name of the company was changed to Blackwell Distributors Limited on 12 May of that year. [41]

Adams Limited
 "Adams Limited was established in 1889, and was involved in the making and marketing of bicycles and later motor-cycles. It was managed by Messrs F N and H T Adams. The firm imported its first car, a single-cylinder Panhard Levassor, in 1900, and it later established branches throughout New Zealand.
 "From 1906 to 1940 the firm imported Studebaker vehicles, but over the years it also imported such makes as Erskine, Napier, Renault, Continental, Nash, Hudson, Rambler, Triumph, Talbot, Standard-Vanguard and Daimler.
 "Mr R. M. Adams controlled the business until 1970 when it was taken over by Mr B D Blogg. In December, 1970, it was bought by Blackwell Motors, Ltd, who are building new premises at Northlands to carry on the name of one of the oldest established motor firms in the country.
 "All the company's branches outside Christchurch were closed in the 1930s. At one stage during the 1920s, the company had a staff of 200 and sold about 700 Studebakers a year." [42]

John Andrew Ford
 What later became known as John Andrew Ford, founded by John Watson Andrew, a Papatoetoe-born engineer, started as one of Colonial's three key Ford franchises in Auckland in 1917.
 "Following its merger with the Colonial Motor Company's subsidiary, the Universal Motor Company, in 1927, what was then John W Andrew & Sons acquired complete control of the Ford franchise in Auckland for many years. In 1983, John Andrew Ford was acquired by Neville Alexander Crichton who subsequently sold the business to Nelson-born car dealer, Stuart Waring Bowater in 1987 for more than $11 million.
 "The John Andrew Ford business has been owned by the Ford Motor Company of New Zealand since the premature death of Stuart Bowater in 1998." [43]

Tench Brothers Limited
 Following the dissolution of the Christchurch motor repair and importing partnership, Hamlet (Joseph Hamlet) and Tench, in early 1917, George William Tench and his brother, John (Bert) Tench, entered into a new partnership on 29 January of that year — and "…carried on the repairing part of the original Hamlet and Tench business." [44]
 However, in May 1917, George Tench was called before the First Canterbury Military Service Board for the second time to appeal his call-up to military service. [45]
 During his hearing, which was "…further adjourned for inquiry…The board declined to accept the theory that motor-cars were not a luxury, and an expensive luxury at that. It intimated that a very big pruning knife would have to be put into the motor business when motor-men were called up…" [46]

A final Military Service Board hearing for George Tench was held on 21 June 1917 during which the motor vehicle industry was further disparaged by the Board and his appeal dismissed:

"The chairman said that it was not an essential business, and some of these non-essential businesses might have to go out. The question was whether appellant's should be the first to go out. After deliberation, the chairman said that the board considered it was not an essential industry, and appellant would have to go before any of the Second Division was called up. The appeal would be dismissed, but time until August 20 would be allowed." [47]

Not surprisingly, the following notice was published by NZ Truth on 25 August 1917:

"On Active Service — Tench Brothers, in order to safeguard their interests while on Active Service, have decided to suspend their Motor business from August 1st till their return from the War.

"In making this announcement they wish to heartily thank the PUBLIC for their generous support, and hope for a continuance of it on their return from the Front, when they will re-open in new premises…" [48]

After the war, George Tench restarted the business together with his brother, John (Bert) Tench.

"In 1920, two other brothers, Jack B Tench and Anthony (Tony) D Tench were also taken into partnership. On 8 February 1921, the partnership was incorporated as Tench Bros. Limited with a capital of $5000." [49]

By February 1928, Tench Brothers were the Christchurch agents for the British Talbot car [50] but, by late 1929, George Tench had fallen out of favour with his brothers and sued for the winding up of the company. [51]

After severing his connection with Tench Bros., George Tench then joined forces with another motor engineer, Ken England, and the two set up what was described as a "modern garage and workshop" in Christchurch.

"Petrol, oils, tyres and all motor accessories will be stocked, and a special display will be made in the up-to-date showrooms of all model Rover cars, for which the firm has the agency." An accompanying image shows that the new firm was also agents for Austin and Chevrolet at the time. [52] George Tench died in 1966. [53]

In the meantime, Tench Bros. Limited remained trading, offering a number of new and used cars for sale (Ford, Morris, Bedford, Singer) from its Cambridge Terrace premises in September 1953. [54]

Tench Brothers became part of Dominion Motors Limited in 1956 [55] and, subsequently, a subsidiary of the New Zealand Motor Corporation by 1971. [56]

Having sold and serviced Singer cars in Christchurch from at least 1924, the model eventually disappeared after it was absorbed by Chrysler in 1970. [57]

"At that time they [Tench Brothers] were the longest standing Singer franchise holders anywhere in the Commonwealth." [58]

After losing Singer, Tench Brothers sought a new franchise which came with an announcement by the New Zealand Motor Corporation on 10 April 1972:

"Tench Brothers Ltd had been appointed franchise dealer for Nissan Datsun cars and light commercial vehicles…an N.Z.M.C. spokesman said that the vehicles would not be handled by corporation dealers elsewhere in New Zealand." [59]

However, Tench Brothers, trading as Tench-Datsun, relinquished its Nissan franchise to Carthy Motors Limited on 1 December 1983 and was to close its doors soon after — as reported by the Christchurch Press:

"Tench-Datsun was Nissan New Zealand, Ltd's top South Island dealer, but it has relinquished the franchise because N.Z.M.C., Ltd, the automotive arm of the EMCO Group, which owns the company, is also the distributor for the Honda Motor Company in New Zealand." [60]

Tench Brothers Limited was removed from the Companies Office register on 1 May 1991. Carthy Motors of Christchurch was incorporated as a motor vehicle dealer on 26 March 1954. The company remains registered after its name was changed to Scott Adams Limited on 20 July 1992. [61]

Neal Motors (1)

As early as September 1922, W F Neal was named as the Taneatua (Bay of Plenty) agent for the American Overland motor vehicles. [62]

By August 1926, he was trading as Neal Motors from Barton Street, Hamilton selling General Motors' cars, particularly the 'Oakland Six'. [63]

In November 1928, the business, now known as Neal Motors Limited, had outgrown its Hamilton premises and moved to Auckland — as reported by the Waikato Times:

"Messrs Neal Motors Ltd announce that they have been appointed Sole Distributors for Buick, Oldsmobile, and Vauxhall Cars, also G.M C. Trucks, for the Auckland City and Suburbs and have disposed of their Hamilton Business to Messrs Ebbett Motors Ltd who will handle the same lines as Neal Motors…have in the past…" [64]

As mentioned in previous chapters, the advertising of all models of motor cars and the advantages of owing one have been with us since the early 1900s. Not many ads are very innovative but this, reported in October 1928, could be an exception:

"As a novel means of introducing to the public the silver anniversary model Buick cars, Neal Motors, Limited, Auckland distributors of Buick cars, presented a playette entitled 'When Better Cars are Built' at their premises last evening.

"The scheme was evolved at short notice and gives an adequate idea of the speed with which expression is given to business ideas in these days when every minute counts. The play was suggested on Wednesday, written and rehearsed on Thursday, and was ready for production last evening. Mr W F Neal, manager, was responsible for its authorship, and was assisted by a number of Auckland amateurs in its production.

"As the idea was novel, so was the presentation. A country squire, the possessor of a daughter and a car, finds his estate mortgaged to the hilt. On the day of his daughter's 25th birthday (of especial significance, as the Buick factory was established 25 years ago), he decides that all he can present her with is the car.

"It is driven on the stage, a magnificent anniversary model Buick, glittering before the footlights, its graceful lines reflecting to the fullest, extent the industrial enterprise of its makers. Great is the jubilation, and the final scene finds audience and players participating in the birthday celebrations, and forming an admiring throng about the new model." [65]

While there is no mention of the play making it to Broadway, Neal Motors Limited was firmly established in Auckland by early 1929 — as reported by The New Zealand Herald:

"Although newcomers to Auckland City, Neal Motors Ltd are by no means new to the motor trade, Mr. W F Neal, the director, having been in the trade all his life at Auckland, the Bay of Plenty and Hamilton.

"Mr Neal was a Buick distributor from 1917 to 1926, and since then handled a lighter range of General Motors cars. Knowing that a new Buick was soon coming on the market, he made investigations and found that the new Buick was just the car he wanted. He therefore secured the franchise for Buick and Oldsmobile cars, and to present adequately a full range to a discerning market, the Vauxhall was added." [66]

However, for reasons difficult to establish, W F Neal decided not to continue as per the Company resolution passed on 26 January 1930:

"…Neal Motors Limited to be voluntarily wound up as it intends to cease carrying on business and W F Neal is hereby appointed liquidator" [67]

There followed a series of newspaper advertisements through to March 1931:

"Neal Motors Ltd in voluntary liquidation, top of Symonds Street —all stock must go urgently…" [68] and "Neal Motors have moved to corner of Lorne and Wellesley Streets for the purpose of selling off our complete stock of quality used cars, service plant, and genuine Buick, Oldsmobile and Vauxhall parts…We are definitely winding up business and have allowed only a limited period for finality…" [69] "Neal Motors, 42 Lorne Street — Giving up business — closing doors in seven days…" [70] "Auction of Used Cars, Accessories, Tyres, machinery and tools, Lorne Street…" [71]

Neal Motors (2)

However, while the first Neal Motors Limited did not survive, another rose from the ashes, incorporated in October 1938 with a "Capital of £5000 — Subscribers W F Neal 4999 shares and R S McMillan 1 share." [72]

By 8 December 1938, the new business was trading from garages at the corner of Great South and Gordon Roads, Otahuhu and West Street Pukekohe advertising itself as "Master distributors of Vauxhall cars and Bedford Trucks for Otahuhu, Franklin and Raglan districts." [73]

A New Zealand Gazette notice of November 1940 recorded that Neal Motors Limited was approved to issue Warrants of Fitness as of 12 November 1940 at Otahuhu. [74]

But, again, the business faltered, with Companies Office de-registration warnings issued in October 1942 [75] and May 1943. [76] Neal Motors Limited (1938/233) was eventually struck off as of 13 August 1943. [77]

Ebbett Motors

Ebbett Motors Limited was established as a motor garage proprietor at Hamilton in November 1928 with a Capital of £2000 in £1 shares. The Subscribers were Alfred William Ebbett, 1908 shares; Robert Grant Anderson and Ronald Ebbett, one share each." [78]

This followed an announcement placed in the Waikato Times on 17 November 1928:

"Mr Alf Ebbett, of Messrs Ebbett Motors Ltd, Hood Street, Hamilton, begs to intimate to his numerous friends and the public generally that he has severed his connection with Dominion Motors and has taken over the Waikato Agency for the Chevrolet, Pontiac, Oakland and Vauxhall cars, and Chevrolet and G.M.C. Trucks, from Messrs Neal Motors…

"A feature of the business will be the Used Car Department, which will be personally supervised by Mr Ebbett himself. All used cars will be inspected and passed by Mr Ebbett and used car buyers are assured of a genuine deal. A wide range of accessories and spare parts is available…" [79]

According to the website of Ebbett Waikato Limited, which continues to trade:

"Ebbett Motors…was originally sandwiched between a Chinese laundry and a gunsmith's shop in Hood Street." [80]

In 1937, Ebbett Motors Limited recapitalised with an additional £7000 beyond what was then a registered capital of £3000. [81]

"When General Motors decided to separate its two product lines in 1938, Waikato Motors Limited was formed to operate the Vauxhall/Bedford franchise from the original Hood Street premises, while Ebbett Motors moved to a newly built dealership on the corner of Hood and Anglesea Streets to represent the Oakland, Pontiac and Chevrolet brands." [82]

Indeed, as reported by the Waikato Times, the new showrooms were opened on 29 July 1938:

"A pleasant function was held in Messrs Ebbett Motors Limited's new showrooms last evening when, as an opening ceremony, the managing director, Mr A. W. Ebbett, tendered a social evening for the staff…Keen interest was taken in the new rooms which, embodying the latest features of American motor showrooms, are the most modern of their kind in New Zealand." [83]

"Founder of the company, Alf Ebbett, dies at a young age in 1951. Holden and Ebbett formed a strong partnership in 1952; the same year Holden was first imported into New

Zealand. Ebbett's trucking business sourced and supplied some of the first milk tankers in the Waikato region." [84]

Because of the volatility of trading conditions affecting the motor trade during the 1970s, consolidation of the Ebbett business was necessary — as reported by the Christchurch Press on 22 November 1973:

"Two well-known Waikato motor dealers — Waikato Motors, Ltd, and Ebbett Motors, Ltd, — have merged. A holding company has been formed which acquires all shares of both companies, as well as a third concern, Waikato Holdings, Ltd. The new holding company will be known as Ebbett Waikato Group Ltd and has applied for listing on the New Zealand stock exchange as a public company." [85]

Government regulation did little to help the motor industry — as the Ebbett Group Annual Report to 31 July 1976 indicated:

"The restrictions on new and used car markets slowed the sales growth of Ebbett Waikato Group Ltd and sales revenue rose only 2.5 per cent to $15.4M in the year to July 31. After taking inflation into account, this represents a drop in unit sales and the 11.2 per cent increase in net profit to $223,265 was also less than the inflation rate.

"Restrictions imposed by the Government regulations turned new-car buying into a cash-only transaction, and deposit requirements for used cars and light commercials were raised to 60 per cent, and repayment limited to one year.

"'This dampened-down almost overnight the sales of these vehicles, and coupled with inflation and increases in every avenue of expense, the situation presented a very real challenge,' the chairman (Mr R. Ebbett) says in the annual report.

"Ebbett's sales of new cars dropped as the cash requirement put a new vehicle beyond the reach of many would-be buyers. Hire-purchase restrictions had a detrimental effect on used vehicle sales..." [86]

A new decade and although Government regulation had eased, there came the crash:

"A roller-coaster decade. The business was privatised and then expanded rapidly (opening new dealerships in Greenlane and Milford). Even more rapid contraction followed with the 1987 share market crash, leading to a withdrawal to just one dealership – Hamilton Holden." [87]

Nevertheless, the Ebbett Group has survived for nearly one hundred years and current dealerships, as listed at it website, include:

Auckland — Ebbett MG Pop-up East Auckland & Ebbett Pukekohe

Hamilton — Duncan & Ebbett, Ebbett Audi, Ebbett Hamilton, Ebbett Skoda, Ebbett Toyota Hamilton, Ebbett Toyota Morrinsville, Ebbett Toyota Te Awamutu, Ebbett Volkswagen Hamilton, & Lexus of Hamilton

Tauranga — BYD Tauranga, Ebbett Prestige Tauranga (2), Ebbett Tauranga & Lexus of Tauranga

Central North Island — Ebbett Rotorua & Ebbett Taupo

Hawke's Bay — Ebbett Hawke's Bay Napier Kia & Hawke's Bay Service Centre

Wellington — Johnston Ebbett Wellington & Johnston Ebbett Porirua [88]

Moller Group

Henry H Moller was a well-known motorcycle racer from 1921 to 1927. In September 1924, he was also employed by Hatrick and Company as a motor salesman [89] and then Lightband and Wann Limited until March 1926 when he left to race overseas. [90]

He had returned to race in New Zealand by December 1926 and had opened a garage, Moller's Kiwi Service, in New Plymouth by late 1929. [91]

The garage was advertised as the "First petrol station entering New Plymouth Ten pumps, oils, greasing..." [92]

Moller Motors Limited, incorporated on 23 September 1932, [93] first traded as H H Moller Limited from Egmont Motor Company's Garage in New Plymouth offering "Better used cars and trucks — Splendid range of late models…Essex, Ford, Chevrolet, Whippet, Austin, Morris, sedans and roadsters…" [94]

Moller Motors eventually became part of Moller Holdings Limited which had started as Cowan & Moller Limited, incorporated on 21 October 1937. [95] The name of the latter company was changed to H H Moller (Hawera) Limited on 13 October 1947. [96]

In November 1969, Moller Motors became part of a syndicate, with "…Shorters Car Distributors Limited (Auckland), Independent Motor Sales Limited (Wellington), and Archibald's Garage Limited (Christchurch)…solely responsible for importing and distributing Jaguar cars throughout New Zealand." [97]

By March 1975, Moller Holdings was describing itself as "…the New Plymouth holding company for a New Zealand-wide group of marine and motor vehicle importers, wholesalers and retailers…" [98]

As noted in a previous chapter, in 1975, Moller Holdings joined forces with New Zealand Motor Bodies which then assembled cars and manufactured omnibus, trolley-bus, and coach bodies at its Christchurch, Petone, and Auckland plants.

By September 1982, Moller Holdings extended its dealer network in Dunedin — as reported by the Christchurch Press:

"BWH Group and Moller Holdings have agreed to merge their Dunedin motor interests — Holland and Bell Moller Motors. The directors of both companies said the merger would give better working opportunities for the management and staff because of the combined franchises and increased use of existing facilities. Holland and Bell has the Dunedin franchise for Mercedes Benz, Mazda, and Fiat cars and Suzuki motorcycles. Moller Motors is the Dunedin agent for Daihatsu, Citroen, Volvo, and Alfa Romeo cars, and Yamaha motor-cycles." [99]

BWH Group

The BWH Group had been in business since 1958 with its head office in Dunedin. As well as its motor vehicle interests, the Group comprised investment (Commercial Advances & Securities) and real estate (Holland & Bell Real Estate) companies. [100]

Although the BWH Group was placed in Receivership in December 1984, Holland and Bell Moller Motors, then the Dunedin agent for Mazda vehicles, was unaffected and continued to trade. [101]

The relatives and descendants of Henry Moller who subsequently became the principals of the Moller Group include: John Russell Moller, Peter John Moller, Ross Earle Moller, Russell Ian Moller, Peter William Moller, and Norton Ross Moller. [102] The Rich List of August 1987 placed the Moller Family as the fourth richest family on the list with an estimated minimum wealth of $100 million. [103]

South Auckland Motors (1)

The original business of the South Auckland Motor Company was established in 1920 at Te Awamutu by proprietor, Hudson Taylor Salter [104] — as reported by the Waipa Post:

"Te Awamutu has attracted yet another firm who will be establishing in business as soon as the erection of premises is arranged. The South Auckland Motor Co., who have direct agencies for the popular Dort, Buick and Hudson motor cars are to establish in business here. Yesterday the firm purchased the section at the junction of Alexandra and Mutu Streets and are now negotiating for the erection of suitable premises. Te Awamutu will become their headquarters, for the Southern Waikato and King Country districts." [105]

By June 1921, the business had expanded to the sale of fuel:

"South Auckland Motor Company, Corner of Alexandra and Mutu Streets (New Premises in Course of Erection), Offer for Immediate Delivery 1000 Cases of Benzine, All Standard Brands. Price in Store at Te Awamutu, in Large or Small Lots, from 32/- per case Net Cash with Order." [106]

In January 1922, Hudson Salter was joined by accountant, John Cheverton Kersey, and the name of the business was changed to H T Salter & Co. As well as advertising itself as the sole district agents for Buick, Hudson, and Dort motor cars, the business stocked "Republic Trucks, Parrett Tractors, and United States Nobby Tread and Michelin Cord Tyres." [107]

The business also provided a Motor AARD Service carrying mail and providing a general taxi service in the Waikato. [108] By November 1923, H T Salter & Co had become a Ford agent "…specialising in Ford overhauls and repairs…with a complete assortment of Ford spares on hand always…" [109]

The Ford agency for the district was followed by that of the Overland Cars in January 1925. [110]

However, by 1927, Hudson Salter had had enough of the garage business — as reported by the Waipa Post:

"Messrs Tew and Hanna wish to inform the public that they have taken over the business of H T Salter & Co. as from the 1st of September, 1927. The business will be continued under the name of H T Salter & Co., and, as Mr Tew has had many years' experience in the motor engineering business, both in England and the colonies, clients may feel assured of the best advice and services at all times." [111]

Hudson Salter moved with his wife to Allenby Road, Papatoetoe from where he started a road transport business later known as Salter's Transport and Storage Limited. [112]

Messrs Tew and Hanna formed a limited liability company in June 1928:

"Tew and Hanna, Ltd. Objects: To acquire business of motor agents, etc., now carried on at Te Awamutu under style of H. T. Salter and Co. Capital, £2000. Subscribers: Albert Ithiel Tew and James Hanna, 1000 shares each." [113]

However, the party was soon over with Tew and Hanna Limited going into voluntary liquidation on 28 June 1928. [114]

A clearing sale of garage plant, cars, accessories…full stocks of tyres, oils, cycle parts, car springs, car accessories were auctioned at the Te Awamutu garage on 7 February 1929. [115]

South Auckland Motors (2)

The Colonial Motor Company acquired the Otahuhu site of John W Andrew and Sons in 1954 and renamed the dealership South Auckland Motors… [116]

South Auckland Motors Limited (2) was registered on 1 September 1954 as a subsidiary of the Colonial Motor Company Limited. [117] The company now describes itself as "Auckland's only New Zealand owned Ford dealership…with five branches; Manukau, Botany, Takanini, Airport and Pukekohe." [118]

Auckland Motors (1)

In November 1915, the Auckland Motor Company was advertising an almost-new three-seater Talbot Car, nickel finish with electric light, spare wheel, and all tools and accessories for sale at its Wyndham Street premises. [119]

The business had been started by Frederick George Farrell and his brother who were both at the front during the First World War…During that time, the business was carried on by their father, Fred J Farrell, and a mechanic by the name of John White. [120]

After the war, the firm continued to specialised in the importation, selling and service of Standard Light Cars. [121]

In May 1923, Frederick G Farrell, on behalf of the Auckland Motor Company, purchased a property on the corner of Albert and Federal Streets. "The Auckland Motor Company proposed erecting a brick building on the property with a floor space for 100 cars." [122]

"The demolition of one of the oldest brick houses in Auckland is involved in the sale of the property…erected about 65 years ago of hand-made bricks…" [123]

The new Auckland Motor Company garage and showroom at 87 Albert Street was opened in December 1923 — as reported by The New Zealand Herald:

"An interesting event in the Auckland motor world this month is the opening of the new modern garage erected for the Auckland Motor Company in Albert Street. Mr F G Farrell, who has been an energetic figure in Auckland motoring circles for a number of years, may well claim to possess in this fine structure the most modern garage equipment in the city.

"The huge arched roof, the centre portion of which is in glass, covers 10,000 ft. of floor space, without the intervention of a single supporting column. The result is an interior and exterior design of handsome appearance that justly entitles it to be described as a garage deluxe.

"Of importance to city and suburban motorists is the proximity of the new garage to Queen Street. It is only two minutes distance from His Majesty's Theatre, and in this respect will prove a boon to theatre-goers. A locker system installed in the building ensures perfect safety for the personal effects of car owners, motorists being supplied with keys which give access to their belongings at any time.

"A ladies' room, daintily equipped for the convenience of lady motorists, is another feature which will undoubtedly make a notable appeal. The latest free air and water standards are stationed on the kerb-stone outside the garage, the apparatus supplying air at a continuous pressure of 150lb to the square inch. Petrol is supplied from a Bowser kerb-stone pump.

"Inside the building is an up-to-date washing rack on which two cars may be washed at a time. After the New Year it is expected that a man will be employed continually at this rack. To complete the modern appliances installed in this garage is a turntable let into the concrete floor, thus enabling cars to leave the building without the awkward necessity of backing out.

"In the handsome show-window, will shortly be displayed the latest 1924 models of British Standard and Dort cars, for which the Auckland Motor Company is the Auckland provincial distributor." [124]

The Dort was a particularly popular car promoted by the company:

"The Auckland Motor Company is featuring the new model 'Dort' car, well and favorably known in all parts of New Zealand. It is a six-cylinder car fitted with overhead valves, and the lubricating throughout is done under pressure. It is an excellent hill-climber, and can do 22 miles on a gallon of petrol." [125]

By August 1930, the used car models offered for sale by Auckland Motors from its Albert Street premises included Dodge, Pontiac, Essex, and Standard. [126]

However, by June 1932, the estate of Frederick George Farrell, trading as the Auckland Motor Company, had been assigned to George W Hutchison [public accountant, secretary of the Auckland Automobile Association, & Auckland Mayor] of Durham Street East, Auckland and creditors were required to lodge their claims with him. [127]

The reasons for the assignment are unclear but may have been done to allow Frederick Farrell to pursue public office. By April 1941, he had put himself forward for a seat on the Auckland City Council [128] which he won, and was again elected in June 1944. [129]

Frederick Farrell was also President of the Automobile Association (Auckland) from October 1936 to 1946 [130] and then from October 1948. [131]

Nevertheless, by September of 1932, it was business as usual for the Auckland Motor Company, advertising that it stocked "…A full range of genuine Standard spare parts, all models from 1914 to 1932…" obtainable from its Albert Street premises. [132]

The Hillman Minx was an addition to the company's new-car range, as advertised in September 1933 [133] and in July 1937, the Auckland Motor Company Limited was advertised as the Auckland sub-dealer for the British Fargo truck. [134]

In September 1933, the Auckland Motor Company was registered as a limited liability company (1933/194) with a Capital of £300. The equal shareholders were named as N C Witcombe (former manager at Canadian-Knight and Whippet Motor Co.) and F E Farrell. [135] (The latter name is thought to be a misprint and is actually meant to be Frederick George Farrell)

The Auckland Motor Company Limited advertised itself as an authorised Hillman, De Soto and Plymouth dealer with more than 30 used cars for sale from its 87-91 Albert Street premises in June 1937. [136]

Auckland Motor Company Limited (1933/194) registered a change of name to Auckland Motor Company (Albert Street) Limited on 7 September 1972 [137] and registered another name change to Rent-A-Bomb Limited on 14 September 1981. [138]

Auckland Motors (2)

Another Auckland Motors business began as the Auckland Motor Company (Great North Road) Limited (1952/570), incorporated on 1 October 1952. [139] A subsequent change of name to Auckland Motor Company Limited was registered on 7 September 1972. [140]

By October 1973, the Auckland Motor Company Limited, together with Allied Finance and Investments Limited and Collingwood Holdings Limited, had become part of the Allied Group Limited which was then floated as a New Zealand public company. [141]

In March 1974, the Director and part owner of an established motor dealer took over the management of the Auckland Motor Company — as reported by the Christchurch Press:

"Mr J R [John Henry] Henderson, a director and, with Mr D W [David Willis] Cooper, owner of Henderson Motors Ltd, who has accepted the position of managing director of The Auckland Motor Company Limited. Auckland Motor is a Chrysler, Hillman, Mitsubishi distributor in metropolitan Auckland, and is a member of Allied Finance Group Ltd. Mr Henderson retains his shareholding and directorship of Cooper Henderson Motors." [142]

The performance of the Auckland Motor Company as an Allied Group company was reported by the Christchurch Press in August 1974:

"Auckland Motor Company, Ltd, like most vehicle dealers, experienced a period of difficult trading during December, January and February. The decision to change the balance of six- and eight-cylinder used car stock to four-cylinder vehicles was well worthwhile, as by March, the company was again trading profitably when others were feeling the pinch of price reductions in the bigger range. The ratio of new to used, cars sold during the year was 1:1.03…Spare parts sales increased from $870,000 to $1,130,000. The company's over-all turnover rose from $12.8 million to $16.8 million." [143]

The name of the Auckland Motor Company Limited (1952/570) was changed to Auckland Motors Limited on 13 August 1975 [144] and by September 1977, the business continued to prosper:

"Auckland Motors Limited…had kept profitable under very difficult trading conditions. Mr Griffiths [Chairman Allied Group] remarked: 'Car prices are higher than almost anywhere else in the free world, and relative earnings lower.'" [145]

However, some modification to trading activity was required by September 1978:

"A reduction has been made in the scale of activities of Auckland Motors Ltd, by a reduction in the number of branches, and efficiency improved. This company is also trading satisfactorily." [146]

A reconstruction of the Allied Group resulted in Auckland Motors becoming a subsidiary of Collingwood Holdings Limited of which Peter Hanbury Masfen (Newmans Group), Bryan William Mogridge (also a Director of Coachwork International and Newmans Coach Lines), and Barry George Neville-White (Newmans and Montana Group) were Directors and Shareholders (as Tytus Holding Limited, then a part of the Montana Group). [147]

The following year, 1979, also brought changes to Auckland Motors' operations:

"Auckland Motors…experienced buoyant trading. The dealership at Manurewa was sold, but a branch was opened on North Shore." [148]

Auckland Motors Limited was removed from the Companies Office register on 23 January 1998. [149]

Tappenden Motors Limited

As the proprietor of the Hamilton Used Car Sales Depot, Reginald (Reg) G Tappenden advertised the sale of "good used cars and motorcycles" from at least December 1925 [150] and by November 1926, the Hamilton Used Car Depot was advertising itself as "…the only Used Car Specialists in the Waikato…" [151] In May 1928, Tappenden Bros. was named as "district agents for Austin cars." [152]

E W Tappenden and Sons Limited

Newspaper advertising in 1927 also promoted the proprietors of the Hamilton Used Car Sales Depot as "Tappenden Bros". [153] The brothers were Reg Tappenden and Edward (Ted) W Tappenden.

The latter brother acquired the Tauranga Ford dealership of F N Christian and Co Limited in 1957 and renamed the company E W Tappenden and Sons Limited (HN1935/228) on 29 April of that year. [154] A December 1962 image of the business shows E W Tappenden and Sons Limited advertising cars, trucks, and tractors for sale. [155]

E W Tappenden and Sons Limited was removed from the Companies Office register in June 1978. [156]

In the meantime, by 1934, the Tappenden Bros business had become a limited liability company with Reginald Tappenden as its Managing Director and the company name was subsequently changed to Tappenden Motors Limited on 27 August 1934. [157]

The first Auckland motor vehicle dealer trading as Tappenden Motors Limited offered a "Range of six models and colours" of Vauxhalls from its 39 Beach Road premises in July 1934. [158]

Later that year, salesman, George Campbell, was offering a commission of £1 to anyone who provided a prospective buyer's name and address. [159]

By July 1935, Tappenden Motors was also selling Bedford trucks as well as various used models [160] and in order to meet the needs of increased business, "Capital [was] increased by [the] addition of £3000 beyond registered capital of £5000." [161]

A second company, Automotive Industries Limited, motor garage proprietors and dealers, was established in 1939 with a "…Capital of £5500, in shares of £1 each. Subscribers: Tappenden Motors, Limited, 3000 shares; R. G. Tappenden, 1500 shares; W. W. King, 1000 shares." [162]

In 1952, Tappenden Motors Limited took over George Fraser and Sons Ltd, engineering works, Stanley Street, Auckland:

"George Fraser and Sons was founded in 1862 and was for 90 years one of the foremost organisations of its kind in New Zealand. It began as a small engineering workshop on the site now occupied by the Auckland railway station. Among machinery turned out in its early days were several hundred gold ore stamping batteries for the Thames goldfields, and numerous marine engines for coastal steamers. About 1872 the firm moved to Stanley street and remained there until it went out of business in 1952." [163]

By this time, Tappenden Motors was the proprietor of Hall Service Station at Hall Avenue, Otahuhu as Tappenden Motors (Otahuhu) Limited but this business changed hands in 1953 and became Davie Motors Holden: [164]

"Davie Motors Holden was founded in 1953, when Ron Davie bought the company from Reg Tappenden during a game of golf! Both men accepted the terms of the agreement on the strength of their word and a handshake. The company was originally based in Otahuhu and was franchised to sell Vauxhall and Holden cars and Bedford trucks." [165]

As reported by the Christchurch Press in September 1957, Tappenden Motors Ltd became a public company:

"Tappenden Motors, Ltd., Auckland, is making a private placement of ordinary 10s shares at a sale price of 22s 6d. It is understood that approximately 120,000 shares will be available for sale.

"The company, which recently converted to a public concern, has an authorised and issued capital of £150,000 in ordinary 10s shares. It owns all the shares in Automotive Industries Ltd and George Fraser and Sons Ltd which are both property-owning companies. Net profit in the financial year ended March 31 [1957] was £48,087, compared with £63,917 in the previous year." [166]

Following its public float, Tappenden Motors Limited expanded its business to the engineering and manufacturing industry with first a takeover of Morris, Black and Matheson Limited:

"It is intended that both companies will be run and operated as individual and separate businesses under their present managements. The chairman of directors of Morris, Black and Matheson, Mr L Wilson, has been invited to join the board of directors of Tappenden Motors Ltd." [167]

Secondly, a takeover of P F Mann Limited:

"Tappenden Motors Ltd, has purchased the Christchurch firm of P. F. Mann, Ltd, engineers' supply merchants, in a takeover worth £55,000 at present market prices…P. F. Mann, Ltd which was established in 1924, will continue to operate as a separate company and will retain the present management and staff." [168]

Not long after, on 3 March 1961, the name of P. F. Mann Ltd (1928/34) was changed to Morris, Black and Matheson (S I) Limited [169] as a result of a merger with another engineering firm:

"George Guild and Sons, Christchurch, engineers' merchants, will be merged with P. F. Mann Ltd in a new firm, Morris, Black and Matheson (South Island) Ltd. The new firm will be a subsidiary of Morris, Black and Matheson, Ltd, Auckland, which was taken over last year by Tappenden Motors, Ltd.

"The take-over of P. F. Mann by Tappenden was reported on February 4. Shareholders in P. F. Mann (a private company) and in George Guild (a partnership) will accept Tappenden Motors shares in payment for their businesses.

"Morris Black and Matheson and P. F. Mann have distributed Behr-Manning coated abrasives for some years. George Guild and Sons and Morris Black and Matheson have distributed Alfred Herbert machine tools. Both Christchurch firms were established in the mid-1920s." [170]

Additional acquisitions by Tappenden Motors followed buoyant trading in 1964:

"Group sales of Tappenden Motors Ltd, Auckland car and truck distributors, rose 19.1 per cent to a record level in the year ended March 31 [1964]. As a result, group profit increased by £22,331 or 28.2 per cent, to a peak £101,614…At the end of March all the shares in Hall Service Station Ltd, and its associate company Jackson and Guinivere Ltd, service station proprietors of Pt. Chevalier, were bought for cash, the report says." [171]

And acquisitions continued in July and October 1965:

"The old-established Auckland machinery and engineering supplies merchant, Charles Palmer and Company Ltd, has merged into Tappenden Motors, Auckland Vauxhall and Bedford distributor, the directors of the two companies announced today…This integration will complement and strengthen Tappenden's subsidiary, the Morris Black and Matheson group, which operates in a somewhat similar field, Mr C H T Palmer and Mr W W King, say in a joint statement. Charles Palmer and Company will continue to operate under its own name from the present Hobson street premises." [172]

"Tappenden Motors, Auckland motor vehicle distributor, has bought all the shares in Peter Findlay Motors of Henderson and bought land and buildings tenanted by the company." [173]

As a result, Peter Findlay Motors Limited became Tappenden Motors (Henderson) Limited (055852) on 2 March 1966. [174]

Reg Tappenden was still in control of the Tappenden Group when he delivered an interim report on the Group's affairs in December 1967:

"Used car prices are becoming more stable, with trading at a reduced level, Mr R. G. Tappenden, chairman of Tappenden Motors Ltd says in his interim report. Further substantial stock losses were not expected and there appeared to be more confidence in the future than hitherto.

"The 27 per cent drop in tax-paid profit in the first half of the current year, reported last month, was entirely because of lower earnings by the parent company. As announced, directors expected to maintain the dividend at 121 per cent, but profits for the year would be down, and the pattern of future trading could not be forecast because of confused conditions.

"The reduction in profit in the first half was because of unfavourable trading conditions common to the motor trade. The introduction of stringent hire purchase terms had reduced the demand for used cars with a consequent depression of used car values. As a result, substantial losses on stocks were unavoidable. Other departments produced slightly lower but satisfactory returns." [175]

However, in a few years, the under-performing Tappenden companies were taken over by New Zealand's richest businessman, Alan Gibbs, and others:

"Through a private investment company, Tappenden Holdings, [Alan] Gibbs also linked up with…transport operator Trevor Farmer — a connection originating from the 1979 acquisition of Auckland's ailing Tappenden Motors by Gibbs…John Fernyhough and car dealer-turned sharebroker Warren Paine…" [176]

By 1981, much of the Tappenden Motors business had been inherited by more contemporary interests and a time-honoured tradition of the motor trade, first started in the 1920s, had ended:

"Mr C J Giltrap, of Auckland, has extended his motor business interests by the purchase of the Takapuna and Stanley Street branches of Tappenden Motors Ltd. The consideration has not been disclosed.

"Mr Giltrap said he planned to open a further branch in Great North Road, Auckland, and expected to become the largest General Motors dealer in New Zealand. His motor business interests already included Westbay Motor Company of Tauranga, Giltrap Mazda and Gulf Mazda of Auckland, and Wellington companies which held Datsun, Mazda, General Motors, Volkswagen, and Fiat franchises." [177]

Premier Motors

Premier Motors Limited was incorporated on 19 March 1928 with a capital of £3500. The initial Shareholders were named as H M Griffiths (840 shares); R J Giles, L E MacQueen, and W A Giles (800 shares each); R W G Wallace and R A Denny (100 shares each); F C Musker (20 shares); R D Boyes, H W Segar, P J H Munro and T J Perry (10 shares each). [178]

Trading from 77 Beach Road, Auckland, the new company advertised that it had "…leased the well-known premises latterly occupied by Messrs Skeates and White Ltd conjointly with taking over the Oakland Pontiac franchise formerly held by that firm…

"The new Company will concentrate on the sale of OAKLAND and PONTIAC CARS, and on giving the finest service possible to the present owners and future purchasers of these famous General Motors products throughout the territory. It is the intention of Premier Motors Ltd to continue their operations in the premises previously occupied by Messrs Skeates & White…and to extend their equipment so as to give even greater service than has been enjoyed by clients in the past." [179]

However, by the end of 1929, demand for General Motors' vehicles had obviously exceeded supply, necessitating some help from a competitor:

"A special fast freight train, carrying 49 Chevrolet, Pontiac, Oldsmobile and Buick cars, arrived at Auckland on Sunday from Wellington and by this morning the whole consignment had been delivered to the various distributing agents in and around the city.

"The trainload of cars, dispatched to the order of Premier Motors Limited, Auckland, was the first of its kind in New Zealand. Distributors, having reported an acute shortage of cars, it was decided to meet the demand by ordering a special train.

"The 49 cars were consigned by General Motors Limited, and the Railway Department made most efficient and smooth-working arrangements. Ordinary coal trucks, equipped with tarpaulins, were used for the transportation of the vehicles." [180]

In September 1930, Premier Motors Limited was "…appointed direct factory distributors for Chevrolet cars and trucks." [181]

By the 1940s, Premier Motors was trading from Auckland's Albert Street…unfortunately:

"During the past few weeks safe-breakers have been operating in large business premises in Albert Street. On Thursday night the burglars were again busy in this street when they broke into the office of Premier Motors Limited, 142 Albert Street, to gain the richest haul of cash in the present series of crimes.

"They entered by forcing the front door of the garage, and in the office they placed a charge of gelignite in the safe and blew it open. A large sum of money, as well as papers and documents, was stolen." [182]

"After forcing a skylight in the garage and showrooms of Premier Motors Limited, 142, Albert Street, thieves last night entered the premises and ransacked the office, stealing a small sum of money. They also stole a quantity of tools and motor accessories valued at over £100 and took a five-seater sedan which they drove through the main doors. The car, which is almost new, is valued at £400…" [183]

Premier Motors Limited had a change of name to Premier Group Limited on 7 May 1963 and, in August 1974, Allied Group Limited announced that it had "…agreed to buy Premier Motors Limited, Auckland motor dealer, for an undisclosed cash sum. The Allied Group chairman (Mr K M Griffiths), says that the added volume of sales of both vehicles and spare parts will be beneficial to the Group's business." [184]

Thus, by August 1974, Premier Motors had joined the Auckland Motor Company as part of the Allied Group of companies.

Manthel Motors

Manthel Motors Limited, garage proprietors was incorporated at Wellington on 18 November 1933 with a capital of £3000. The Shareholders were then Maurice Noel Manthel and A F Read. [185]

When advertising for staff, the company promoted itself as "…the new Chevrolet Distributors for Wellington…" [186] and as "Chevrolet's New Home…sales, parts and service…" [187]

Manthel Motors… "was the original distributor of Holden when this was introduced to New Zealand in 1954 by General Motors (NZ) Limited." [188]

By July 1984, Manthel Motors, "…the Wellington franchise holder for GM-Holden, Nissan, Daihatsu, and Subaru Vehicles, announced a one-for-five bonus issue after posting a 164 per cent higher profit at $579,000…" [189]

Indeed, despite a poor economic outlook for the country as a whole, motor vehicle sales remained steady so that dealers such as Manthel Motors remained profitable — as reported to shareholders by then Chairman, Roger Manthel, on 14 August 1986:

"The directors feel obliged to advise shareholders that the real worth of the company is now very much higher than the balance sheet reflects and the share asset backing is grossly undervalued…" [190]

The relatives and descendants of Maurice Noel Manthel who subsequently became the principals of the Manthel group of companies included: Neil Franklin Manthel, Simon Roger Manthel, Roger Arthur Manthel, Maurice Noel Manthel, and Richard Neil Manthel. [191]

Spencer Allen Motors

James Spencer Allen was born in England on 11 July 1909. [192] He was employed in New Zealand by Colonial Motors prior to July 1932 and had been elected President of the Gisborne branch of NZ Retail Motor Traders' Association by January 1947. [193] He was also chairman of the Garage Proprietors' Association in March 1948. [194]

Later that year, James Spencer Allen responded to the opportunity to invest in his own garage at Manurewa, Spencer Allen Motors — as reported by the Gisborne Herald:

"Mr J Spencer Allen, late of the firm of Allen Bros and Johnstone Limited [Gisborne motor dealers] left recently to take over a garage business in Manurewa, Auckland. Mr. Allen has been connected with the motor business throughout his adult life, and has taken an active part in organisations dealing with sales and petrol distribution. Formerly prominent in sport, he was a representative oarsman and took up aviation as a hobby, surviving a crash in the South Island while flying a club aircraft. He served in the R.N.Z.A.F. during the war. [195]

The business began with the selling of front-end loaders and tractors:

"Third-Yard 'Dozerscoop' Hydraulic Front-end Loaders, £225 for all tractors. Write Spencer Allen Motors Ltd Manurewa." [196]

In 1956, Spencer Allen Motors had expanded to include another dealership, Spencer Allen Motors (Papakura) Limited. In 1957, James Spencer Allen established a second company, Spencer Allen Products Limited, to promote the sale of British caravans and dealerships — as published by the Christchurch Press in August of that year:

"English Caravan Franchise. The Franchise for the Canterbury Provincial Territory covering the complete range of the world-famous Sprite Caravans is available to an approved dealer. An attractive trade discount is allowed on this fast-selling caravan. For further details, apply: Spencer Allen Products Limited, Manurewa" [197]

As Spencer Allen Motors, the business advertised its new and used vehicles widely:

"Humber Imperial — Unique opportunity to secure this outstanding 1 owner limousine in sparkling black, genuine 10,000 miles only, seats 8, a luxury car at £975. Spencer Allen Motors Ltd, Licensed Motor-Vehicle Dealers, Manurewa" [198]

When advertising for a spare parts assistant in May 1962, Spencer Allen Motors Limited was promoting itself as a "…progressive firm…Humber, Plymouth, and Commer dealers…in the fast growing South Auckland area of Manurewa." [199]

In April 1965, Spencer Allen Motors advertised for a sales manager:

"We require the services of a Salesman with ability to take charge of our Sales Department. A good knowledge of all car and truck dealing is essential and a particular knowledge of the Rootes and Chrysler franchise would be an advantage…" [200]

By that time, the motor business had taken over Howick Motors Limited and registered a change of its name to Spencer Allen Motors (Howick) Limited on 18 March 1965. [201]

The Howick business included a body shop, as advertised in March 1971:

"Panel Shop Manager Applications are invited from experienced panelbeaters with ability and ambition to take full charge of the established body shop attached to a progressive Chrysler Franchise at Howick…Apply to Manager, Spencer Allen Motors Howick Ltd…" [202]

The Spencer Allen Motors business also continued at Papakura:

"Tractor Sales Manager Applications are invited from experienced tractor men for a responsible position selling…used tractors in a South Auckland David Brown dealership…Apply: Manager, Spencer Allen Motors (Papakura) Ltd, 182 Great South Road, Papakura…." [203]

In the meantime, James Spencer Allen had once again crashed an Auckland Aero Club plane on a flight from Gisborne to Taupo on 16 June 1970. This time, he did not survive. [204]

By 1973, the Spencer Allen Motors businesses at Manurewa, Howick, and Papakura had been merged into the Auckland Motors Limited group of motor dealers and garages.

Spencer Allen Motors Limited (1949/353) registered a name change to Neville Caravan and Commercial Centre Limited on 19 June 1978. [205]

Spencer Allen Motors (Howick) Limited (1957/1069) was removed from the Companies Office register on 28 November 1980. [206]

Spencer Allen Motors Papakura Limited (1956/1033) registered a change of name to Auckland Motor Auctions Limited (054283) on 19 February 1975 [207] and Auckland Motor Auctions Limited (054283) was removed from the Companies Office register in August 1992, as was Spencer Allen Products Limited. [208]

Schofield & Co

Following the dissolution of his partnership with Harold Denton in 1919, Ernest James Schofield started selling Hupmobiles and other motor vehicles from Broadway, Newmarket [209] and, by 1925, as Schofield & Co, he was selling and servicing Chevrolet cars and trucks from the same premises. [210]

The business was registered as Schofield & Co Limited, motor car vendors and garage proprietors, on 11 February 1925 [211] with a Capital of £9000. The original shareholders were Ernest James Schofield 8999 shares and Irene W Schofield 1 share. [212]

In December 1926:

"General Motors (NZ) held a competition for Chevrolet salesmen…and the award went to an Invercargill salesman with 21 deals recorded. A Wellington salesman was second with 15 sales for the month. A member of the staff of Schofield and Co, Newmarket, was third with 13 sales." [213]

By December 1928, the garage services of Schofield and Co were also proving successful — as reported by the Auckland Sun:

"A new slogan for the sale of motor spirit will shortly be known in Auckland in 'Look for the Silver Pump'. This will be the slogan of Schofield and Company Ltd, Newmarket, who are regular importers of a new motor spirit. The spirit will be known as the '1929 model motor spirit' or 'Frisk', and is a super-grade spirit, selling for less than the standard rates.

"Frisk is said to be remarkable for not burning valves, and also easy starting and absence of knock. Schofields import direct from the American refineries, receive shipments every 28 days and always have ample stocks on hand. The sole distributing station is at Used Cars Ltd, Newmarket." [214]

Used Cars Limited had been registered in Auckland on 28 April 1926 by Ernest James Schofield and his wife, Irene W Schofield, with a Capital of £1250. [215]

A September 1928 advertorial published by The New Zealand Herald promoted the Schofield firm as a responsible used car dealer:

"Used Cars Ltd — Without reliability, the used car is a liability, and unless the reputation of the vendor can be relied on, the purchaser may find that first cost is trivial compared with maintenance. Reliability is claimed for the large variety of vehicles stocked by Used Cars Ltd and nothing is offered at an inflated price. The selection covers cars at all prices, the cost in every case being proportional to the amount of service still in the vehicle. Specialisation in this class of business has earned the firm a reputation throughout the province for giving value in used and reconditioned cars." [216]

By 1941, Schofield and Co had also established a dealership at Morrinsville:

"We Pay Cash for Suitable Used Cars & Trucks. Good-quality Late Models. Full Particulars to Schofield and Co Ltd, Chevrolet Distributors Studholme Street, Morrinsville." [217]

In the meantime, both the new and used-car dealership continued trading from Newmarket:

"Although Schofield and Co Ltd, Newmarket, pay the highest cash prices for any Late Model Used Cars, they still sell them on easy terms if required." [218]

Ernest James Schofield died on 16 May 1958. [219]

By 1968, Schofield and Co had become a public company paying a dividend of 12½ per cent that year. [220] Schofield and Co Limited, Newmarket was acquired by the Giltrap Group in the early 1980s.

Giltrap Group Holdings

Sir Colin Giltrap was inducted into the New Zealand Business Hall of Fame in 2013, the website of which describes his start in the motor industry:

"Sir Colin Giltrap's passion for cars began at a young age, and he bought and sold Morris Minors cars as a teenager before opening his first car dealership, Monaco Motors, in Hamilton in 1966. Sir Colin's empire extended through the Waikato to Auckland and then across the Tasman and into the United Kingdom." [221]

By means of Giltrap Group Holdings Limited, incorporated in October 1966, Colin Giltrap progressively acquired substantial dealerships selling a great number of motor vehicle brands.

According to the chronological history recorded at the Giltrap Group website, those acquisitions included:

"1960-1974 —

"Monaco Motors, Matamata Motors, and P Coutts of Great North Road (Daimler, Triumph and Rover); Mazda Dealership set up at 444 Great North Road, a dealership that also sold Audi. Colin Giltrap acquires the distributor right to Porsche in New Zealand.

"1977 —

"European Motor Distributors Limited is formed. This acquires distributorship rights for Volkswagen and later, Audi.

"1982-1985 —

"Acquisition of Schofields of Newmarket…Coutts Cars becomes a standalone BMW dealership: Coutts BMW at 150 Great North Road, with Giltrap North Shore, also hosting BMW, Audi, VW, Porsche, Rolls Royce and Bentley. Move to 101 Great North Road, under a new dealership called 'Giltrap Prestige'. This dealership also retailed GM products and later, Nissan.

"A 50% ownership of Archibald & Shorter in Greenlane, Auckland — a Jaguar dealership on a Joint Venture basis.

"1989 —

"Acquisition of a Toyota franchise for Auckland City. Giltrap City Toyota located at 101 Great North Road; Colin Giltrap becomes the Mercedes-Benz distributor for NZ, relinquishing the right to have both BMW dealerships- City and North Shore. Therefore Coutts BMW changes to Coutts Mercedes-Benz and moves to new premises in Newmarket

"An additional showroom was built at 100 Great North Road — a purpose-built prestige dealership, and Giltrap Motor Group is renamed as Giltrap Prestige.

"1993-1996 —

"Giltrap Prestige becomes the only Aston Martin dealership for New Zealand. The Giltrap Group acquires the distributor rights to Skoda in New Zealand

"2001—

Giltrap Prestige outgrows the building at 150 and creates a new purpose-built building with dedicated showrooms for Audi, Volkswagen and Porsche at 100 Great North Road. This is now also the new location for European Motor Distributors.

"2002-2009 —

"Giltrap Prestige becomes the only Lamborghini dealership for New Zealand. Coutts Mercedes-Benz and North Shore Mercedes-Benz are sold to the Ingham Group. Giltrap North Shore acquires the Kia franchise. Schofields of Newmarket acquires the Nissan franchise.

"2010-2012 —

"Lexus of Auckland City is split from Giltrap City Toyota and moves to its own purpose-built facility at 29 Great North Road. With Audi New Zealand expanding beyond expectations, the

Giltrap Group decided to construct a new Audi Terminal at…150 Great North Road. This was officially opened on July 15th, 2011. European Motor Distributors open a distributing centre in a purpose-built facility at the Airport Oaks.

"2013-2017 —

"McLaren Auckland opens marking a historic return to New Zealand. Giltrap City Toyota is sold after many years of being part of the Giltrap family. The Giltrap Group become 100% owners of Archibald & Shorter (Auckland) and Roverland (North Shore). Both dealerships retail Land Rover, Volvo and Jaguar. The Giltrap Group acquires the distributor rights to SEAT [Spanish manufacture] in New Zealand

"2017 —

Aston Martin, Lamborghini and Bentley move into a new bespoke premises at 119 Great North Road along with Giltrap Group Head Office.

"2018 — SEAT New Zealand open their first dealership in Newmarket…" [222]

Current (as of September 2023) vehicle dealer subsidiaries of Giltrap Group Holdings Limited include:

- Giltrap Prestige Christchurch Limited — since 2022
- North Star Motors Limited — since 2021
- Archibald & Shorter North Shore Limited — since 2020
- Archibald & Shorter Roverland Limited — since at least 2016
- European Distributors Limited — since at least 2006
- Motorcorp Distributors Limited — since at least 2005
- Adserve Limited — since at least 2004
- British Vehicle Importers Limited — since at least 2002
- European Motor Distributors Limited — since at least 2002
- Schofield & Co Limited — since at least 2002
- German Motor Distributors Limited — since at least 2001
- Great Auckland Motors Limited — since at least 2001
- P Coutts & Co Limited — since at least 2001
- Quattro Motors Limited — since at least 2001
- Independent Motor Distributors Limited — since at least 2000
- Giltrap Motor Group Limited — since at least 1983 [223]

The May 2000 edition of the National Business Review, The Rich List, records Colin John Giltrap (born 1940) as the then eighth richest New Zealander, with an estimated minimum wealth of $213 million. [224] Colin Giltrap died in April 2024 at the age of 84.

Neville Alexander Crichton

Neville Alexander Crichton opened his first car dealership with Colin Giltrap in 1972 and subsequently started importing vehicles into New Zealand. In the early 1980s, he emigrated to Sydney and began importing high-performance cars such as Ferrari, Maserati, Alfa Romeo, and Citroen as well as the cheaper, Chinese-made Great Wall and Chery vehicles into Australia and New Zealand as the Ateco Group.

A subsidiary of Balverona Pty Limited, the Ateco Group describes itself at its website, as of March 2019, as "…the largest Australasia-owned independent automotive distribution company…" [225]

The motor vehicle import and distribution companies operated in New Zealand by Neville Crichton included:

Crichton Imports Limited incorporated in November 1973 (Balverona Properties Limited since April 2013)

Ateco Automotive N.Z. Limited (incorporated September 2000)

Team Alfa Limited (incorporated October 2001)

Maxus Automotive Limited (incorporated November 2001 as Kiwi Alloy Yachts Limited then Citroen Drive Europe Limited from December 2012 to February 2020)

Torino Motors Limited T/A Maserati Auckland or Lotus Auckland (incorporated May 2002)

Chery Automobile New Zealand Limited (incorporated May 2006)

Dodge Ram NZ Limited (formerly GWM New Zealand Limited, incorporated May 2008)

Ramerican Limited (incorporated August 2008 as Great Wall Motors New Zealand Limited then American Special Vehicles Limited, Dodge Ram NZ Limited, & GWM New Zealand Limited)

Ateco Group NZ Limited (incorporated as Fiat Chrysler NZ Limited January 2013 then CFNZ Limited from July 2013, then Auto Distributors Asia Pacific Limited until July 2015) [226]

As The New Zealand Herald reported in 2012, "His success in the automotive business has made him [Neville Crichton] wealthy. The 2011 National Business Review Rich List valued him at $165 million." [227]

The 2017 "…NBR Rich List put Crichton's fortune at $130 million after he made a considerable amount dealing in luxury cars." [228]

Chapter Eight

Oil Exploration

Overseas Oil Discovery & Refining

While the process of distilling crude oil to produce various flammable products had been known for centuries, a petroleum industry, as such, did not eventuate until the production of kerosene from coal, and then from oil, was developed during the 1840s and 1850s.

"In the United States, the petroleum industry began in 1859 when Edwin Drake found oil near Titusville, Pennsylvania. The industry grew slowly in the 1800s, primarily producing kerosene for oil lamps..." [1]

While kerosene was first used as a lighting source, benzine (later known as gasoline or petrol) was developed as an industrial chemical, a solvent, and as a precursor to the production of gasoline and various chemicals, as described by the Daily Southern Cross with a republication of 'Extracts From The Scientific American' published on 18 May 1863:

"Benzine...is the product of the naptha of distilled coal tar, and its uses were first most clearly described in a patent granted in 1853 to Frederick Crace Calvert, the eminent English chemist...Benzine is useful for the removal of spots and stains caused by fatty or oily matter, tar, paint, wax or resin from cotton, woollen, silk, and other fabrics; and owing to its great volatility no mark or permanent odour remains on the fabrics operated upon..." [2]

In 1862, New Zealand insurance companies became concerned about the risk of storing petroleum products in any great quantity. This prompted the Wellington Independent to explain to its readers the danger posed by the crude and refined oil products then available:

"The crude coal oil, as obtained from the wells, is according to all accounts a most dangerous article but when properly refined its storage is perfectly safe. If a spoonful of the crude coal oil is poured into a saucer of Water it will ignite when a lighted match is brought to within an inch and a half; but if you put a light into a saucerful of the oil produced from it by refining [meaning kerosene], no ignition will take place...

"The destructive property of this substance has been known for ages. An old Italian writer, in a curious treatise on metals, relates that a mason having to repair the sides of a well in which, at a considerable depth, petroleum was collected, took down with him a lantern, in order that he might see to do his work. Unfortunately for him there were holes in its sides, and the gas coming thus in contact with fire exploded with a report louder than that of a cannon, and rushing up the shaft, blew the man to pieces...

"The oil when deprived of its dangerous properties is expected to find its way as a substitute for coal wherever gas is used, and entirely to supersede coal for that purpose. Meanwhile that which at present more immediately concerns us is that our merchants should exercise the greatest care with reference to the storage, and that consumers should try before they buy.

"The crude well oils, with which the inflammable horrors above described are chiefly connected will of course not find their way to these colonies; but the badly refined, and therefore, more or less dangerous oils of the kerosene class will be sure to reach us both from England and Australia...

"The Lancet informs us that nearly one half of the kerosene sold in London is of this character, and the official report by Dr. Macadam of Melbourne...states that out of twenty one samples purchased in shops in Melbourne, only eleven were found to be safe, five being dangerous, and five highly so. Much of these latter qualities will be sure to be shipped here, if only to get it out of the way and consumers will best consult their own welfare..." [3]

An importer of kerosene and benzine, Henry Brooks of Dunedin and Melbourne, advertised his wares in the Otago Daily Times as early as November 1863. However, at that time, the solvents were sold as cleaning agents or for use by those in the painting and decorating industries. [4]

A shipping report of November 1876 listed the cargo, including kerosene and turpentine, destined to arrive at various New Zealand ports from the United States:

"The Josephine…cleared from New York for Wellington, Dunedin, and Canterbury on August 11 [1876]. Cargo for Wellington as follows: 2250 cases kerosene oil, 20 cases turpentine, 43 cases drugs, 154 cases axes and hatchets, 75 cases clocks, 53 cases handles, 2 cases brooms…" [5]

New Zealand's Oil Exploration

As in America and elsewhere around the world, crude oil had always seeped from the ground in particular areas of New Zealand. As per The Report on the Management of the Petroleum Resource, published by the Waitangi Tribunal in 2011:

"…although Māori knew of the existence and the combustible nature of petroleum, they had neither the technological knowledge nor the immediate cultural imperative to extract and exploit the resource." [6]

However, in the course of time, boosted by what would become the insatiable needs of the automobile, the acquisition and refinement of this oil in great quantities became the overwhelming obsession of a number of prospectors and drillers — more often than not, with limited success.

In the early days of oil exploration in New Zealand, individuals and companies had first to enter into contracts with the owners of the land showing promise, usually with an agreement to share any profit in the form of royalties.

Petroleum Act 1937

However, the Government decided to become involved in the process by the 1930s and that involvement resulted in the Petroleum Act of 1937 which came into force on 1 January 1938.

The ramifications of the Act were explained by the Christchurch Press:

"Under the Petroleum Act 1937, the holder of a prospecting licence (as distinct from a mining licence) must be approved by the Minister of Mines and have the necessary financial and mining qualifications.

"One prospecting licence cannot cover an area greater than 200 square miles but the same licence holder can take out more than one licence. Each year, the holder must pay to the Mines Department 50c for each square mile of land in his area. Because all oil and natural gas belong to the Crown, a royalty of at least 5 per cent must be paid on the selling value at the well-head on petroleum, casinghead spirit, and natural gas. The royalty paid for the natural gas from the Kapuni field is 5 per cent.

"Mining Licence — If the holder of the prospecting licence wants to mine petroleum, he must apply for a mining licence which cannot cover an area greater than 100 square miles. But again, the prospecting licence holder has the right to take out more than one mining licence. Also, the holder has to pay $40 a square mile for his licence area held each year.

"The Petroleum Act, its amendments, and the Petroleum Regulations place considerable control by the Government over mining and petroleum exploration work in New Zealand. Deposits have to be made with the Mines Department by prospecting licence holders who also have to justify their holding the licence by drilling at least one well within three years of taking up the licence, and otherwise prospecting diligently.

"The Petroleum Act and the Regulations arose from the rash of oil strikes that occurred in the 1930s, causing share prices to rise and fall at each report. All of these strikes were insignificant but considerable amounts of money were won or lost on the rise and fall in share prices." [7]

By means of the Petroleum Act 1937, "…the Crown [effectively] nationalised the petroleum resource without paying compensation to landowners and without making provision for the ongoing payment of royalties to them." [8]

Specific clauses of the Act include:

"3. (1) …all petroleum existing in its natural condition on or below the surface of any land within the territorial limits of New Zealand, whether the land has been alienated from the Crown or not, is hereby declared to be the property of the Crown.

"4. (1) cannot prospect or mine for petroleum without a licence

"5. (1) licence granted by the Minister for each specified area

"6. (1) a deposit of one thousand pounds required for each licence

"7. Annual fee payable of five shillings for every square mile or part thereof comprised in the licence

"12. (1) licensee to pay to the Crown a royalty computed at the rate specified in the licence on the selling value of all crude petroleum, casinghead spirit, and natural gas that is produced from the land comprised in the licence (3) royalty to be fixed by Minister when granting licence but no less than five per centum

"13. No crude petroleum produced in New Zealand or any products derived from shall be exported except under authority of regulations" [9]

The 2011 Waitangi Tribunal Report on the Management of the Petroleum Resource, referred to earlier, described the Government's takeover of the country's petroleum resources as: "…a further breach of the treaty [of Waitangi]. They argued that these major deficiencies in the manner by which the Crown came to own the petroleum resource meant that they had enduring rights in petroleum that were being ignored by the Crown." [10]

The following is a brief overview of the oil exploration and refining that occurred in New Zealand:

North Island

"New Zealand's first petroleum exploration well, named 'Alpha', was dug near the Moturoa seeps in Taranaki in 1865, following the verification of oil samples taken from the area by a local politician, Edward Metcalf Smith…" [11]

The progress of the Alpha well was reported by The New Zealand Herald in March 1866:

"In the neighbouring Province of Taranaki petroleum oil has been found. Boring has been made to the depth of some 60 feet, and the oil welled out in very considerable quantities. The men engaged in the operation believe that after piercing the stone to which they have at present bored, they will tap a petroleum well which will yield enormous quantities of oil. A Melbourne firm has offered £10,000 for the ground and well, but the offer has not been accepted." [12]

The Sugar Loaf Islands are a collection of five small islands near Port Taranaki, the largest of which is Moturoa. The Taranaki Herald described a subsequent visit to the area by the Superintendent and members of the Provincial Council:

"We ought not to omit that from the top of Moturoa patches of petroleum could be seen floating about all round, and in pulling about among the Sugarloaves, not only were many of these patches passed through by the boat, but the bubbles of it were in many places seen coming up.

"In returning, the Superintendent and party visited the petroleum works of Messrs. Carter and Co. who were putting the necessary pipe down to commence boring — so that the motto on their sign-board 'To Oil or London' is still animating them. There is about thirty feet of water in their well, which to anyone looking down, looks as if it were boiling from the quantity of gas bubbling up; and all about there was a rich or, as some enthusiastic gentlemen expressed it, a delicious, scent of kerosine." [13]

In April 1866, the Provincial Council subsequently granted (Josiah) Carter and Co a nine-year lease of the property on which they were drilling at the Sugar Loaves. [14]

Of course, Carter and Co were not destined to have the oil all to themselves — as reported by the Otago Daily Times on 28 April 1866:

"A private meeting of the Provincial Council of Taranaki was held on Tuesday the 17th inst. to hear the explanations of the agents of the companies that had made application for leases for the purpose of sinking for petroleum. The first application was that of William Johnston, who with some others asked for a nine years' lease of five acres of land adjoining Carter and Co.'s section; capital £500.

"The second application was by Chilman and 26 others for the remaining portion of the Sugar Loaves Reserve and three of the neighbouring islands.

"And there was also the proposition of Bates, Sise and Co. of San Francisco and Dunedin, for a nine years' lease of the remaining portion of the Sugar Loaf Reserve and three of the adjacent islands.

"The last application received was for fifteen acres, by a Company called the 'People's Petroleum Company' represented by Richard Rundle and six others. It stated the capital proposed was £1000, to be raised in shares of £1 each; no subscriber to hold more than 20 shares. 340 shares had been subscribed." [15]

While its petroleum processing connection to American expertise and finance was seen to benefit the lease application of Bates, Sise and Co., unlike the other applicants, the company was not prepared to establish an entity that included local shareholders. As a result, in what is probably one of the first instances of protection of a national resource from international interests, the Bates Sise application was denied. [16]

Carter and Co

Carter and Co "…was the first of more than 50 companies, most of them in New Plymouth, formed specifically to exploit oil, between 1865 and 1950. Many failed to raise sufficient interest or capital to acquire the necessary equipment; most of them drilled holes which were either dry or yielded more sea water than oil; a very few were moderately successful. In all 48 wells were driven in New Plymouth, most of them in the Moturoa area." [17]

In the 1860s, a time of limited testing facilities, the small quantity of oil first obtained from Carter and Co's Sugar Loaf Alpha Well was of uncertain quality. Nevertheless, the newspaper reports of the day remained optimistic:

"Our readers have been made aware recently that petroleum has been discovered at the Sugar Loaves, in the Province of Taranaki, and that every prospect exists that no difficulty whatever will be experienced in working this great source of wealth on a most extensive scale.

"Mr John Martin, of this city, has had forwarded to him by Captain Gardyne, of the s s. Phoebe, a phial containing a sample of this valuable product, which the latter gentleman had obtained fresh from the well of the petroleum works of Messrs Carter and Co. at the Sugar Loaves, and he has kindly forwarded the specimen to our office, where it can be seen by any person calling for that purpose.

"The oil in its unrefined or rough state is of a dark-brownish color, and smells very similar to the kerosene used for ordinary purposes. Mr. Martin informs us that this specimen was obtained at a depth of sixty feet, and that the supply is said to be inexhaustible. When used in its present state the oil shows a light of great brilliancy, but it is much too powerful, and therefore consumes the wick as it burns." [18]

However, the means by which the oil could be accessed 'in payable quantities' at that time proved even less reliable and even more troublesome — as described by The Taranaki Herald in May 1867:

"In recording the shipment of the first barrel of petroleum, the produce of the Alpha Well, we take the opportunity of giving a slight sketch of the proceedings which have resulted in what we trust will be the commencement of a new and flourishing industry which, if fully developed, may prove as great a source of wealth to this Province especially, and to the Colony generally, as the oil fields of America are to that country.

"To Messrs Carter and Co belongs the credit of being the first to take practical means to ascertain whether or not the oil could be obtained in payable quantities. Nearly two years since they commenced boring operations at the Alpha Well, and the history of their proceedings is the usual record of most new undertakings, being a succession of disasters and disappointments which would have effectually discouraged less energetic and sanguine men.

"With a very slight practical knowledge of boring operations, they commenced drilling in what even to an experienced hand would have been a difficult field of operations, and the result was that after getting down about 30 feet the chisel broke and they were unable to extricate it. Not discouraged by this, another attempt was made and with the same result — the second hole being stopped at a depth of between 30 and 40 feet by the chisel breaking.

"These two accidents would have daunted most men and induced them to abandon the enterprise, but Messrs Carter and Co resolved to persevere, and having been twice beaten in boring they determined to sink a shaft, which they did to the depth of between 50 and 60 feet, when the water came in too fast and the gas became so overpowering that one man nearly lost his life by it.

"Boring was again resorted to and between 70 and 80 feet in depth the first oil vein was struck and samples of the oil sent to His Excellency the Governor, Dr. Sidney Gibbons, of Melbourne, and other parties…

"Thus encouraged, the Company persevered and after surmounting numberless difficulties, owing in some measure to the want of proper appliances, they got down to the depth of 170 feet where another, and they believe a larger vein of oil was struck; their further progress was stopped by losing the sand bucket in the hole and being unable to get it up.

"With an amount of energy and determination deserving of better success, Messrs Carter and Co still persevered, and endeavoured to pump the well by hand power, being sanguine of getting oil if they could master the water, but finding the attempt useless and being unable to purchase a steam-engine, and their capital and doubtless their patience being by this time exhausted, they parted with the Alpha Well and two acres of the adjoining land to the Taranaki Petroleum Company, who have lately commenced pumping, and have succeeded with a very imperfect pump in obtaining about 90 gallons of oil from it…we trust, that a larger supply only awaits a better means of extracting it.

"As Messrs Carter and Co obtained a lease of 50 acres of land from the Government and have retained an interest in the Alpha Well, they have still 48 acres to operate upon themselves or put into the market, so that we hope and believe they will still be handsomely rewarded for their perseverance; at all events they deserve all honor as the pioneers of this undertaking." [19]

The First Taranaki Petroleum Company

By 28 April 1866, the Taranaki Petroleum Company had issued a prospectus following its incorporation as a limited company with "…a Capital of £10,000 with power to increase to £100,000, in 1,000 shares of £10 each…"Provisional Directors: Richard Chilman, Warwick Weston, Thomas King, Charles Brown, J C Sharland…This Company is formed for the purpose of sinking for Petroleum on a portion of the Harbour Reserve at the Sugar-loaves, where, from the indications, there is every reason to believe that an extensive oil field exists.

"An application has been made to the Provincial Government for a lease of the land, which has been favourably entertained by the Provincial Council. If oil should not be obtained in paying quantities after the expenditure of £3,000, a meeting of the shareholders will be called to determine whether the enterprise shall be proceeded with…" [20]

Optimism for the successful recovery of oil from the Alpha Well remained high according to a Taranaki Herald comment in February 1867:

"The Directors of the Taranaki Petroleum Company having purchased the Alpha Well from Messrs. Carter and Co together with two acres of the adjoining land, work has been resumed there. The well has been deepened about six feet, and the obstruction caused by a portion of the pump being at the bottom of the hole, has been removed. It being necessary to take up the tubing from the shaft, some of the water was bailed out when the gas found a vent and strongly agitated the water in the shaft, bringing up with it a small portion of oil.

"The rods also when drawn up from the bore hole were coated with oil, although before any of the water was bailed out of the shaft, they did not show any signs of it, which would seem to prove that it is only the pressure of water in the shaft which prevents the oil from coming up…

"…the company will soon be able to test whether or not the Alpha is a productive well. From the facts above stated, there is every reason to believe that the result will be favourable, and a satisfactory answer given to the question as to whether a profitable oil-field exists in Taranaki." [21]

Unfortunately, the Alpha well did not live up to expectations:

"In 1867 the Alpha well yielded from 50 to 60 gallons a week, but it fell off to a few gallons only a day, and after much discouragement, in the form of lost boring tools and the rapid falling off of what were at first very copious flows, the then Taranaki Petroleum Company was wound up in 1868, after spending £4000, and boring one well to 684 ft. and two others to 310 ft. and 318 ft. and sinking two shafts of 60 ft. each." [22]

The Moturoa Petroleum Company and the Second Taranaki Petroleum Company

Shares in the second Taranaki oil exploration company, to be established as The Taranaki Petroleum Company Limited, were issued in June 1906 — as reported by Wairarapa Daily Times:

"This Company is being formed to acquire from the Moturoa Company Ltd its plant, machinery and exceptionally valuable boring rights, extending over about 6000 acres of land in Taranaki. As is well known, during the past few months the Moturoa Company has proved, by the splendid results obtained from the present bore, that an oil field, which has been found to be most extensive, awaits development in that part of the colony…The public is asked to subscribe 61,000 shares…" [23]

The Moturoa Company referred to had originated as an Adelaide-based company, New Zealand Oil Wells Proprietary (no liability) Company — managed by George Charles Fair, said to be an 'oil expert' having worked at Canadian, Persian, and European oilfields. The company applied in September 1903 for drilling rights at Moturoa and acquired about 5000 acres of boring leases in 1904.

By July 1905, the plant of the Adelaide Company had been taken over by a new entity, The Moturoa Petroleum Company, [24] as per a shareholders meeting reported by the Taranaki Daily News:

"A general meeting of shareholders in the Moturoa Petroleum Company was held at the Council Chambers on Monday afternoon. Mr S Teed (chairman of provisional directors) presided over an attendance of fully fifty shareholders. The Chairman remarked that…he did not think they could desire better prospects than had been met with to date.

"There had been a continuous flow of oil ever since it was struck some weeks ago. Since Saturday morning up to Monday morning 220 gallons had been tanked. This was a splendid indication of there being a good profitable prospect for the shareholders.

"The balance-sheet was read, as follows: Assets: Cash in hand, £12 10s, bank £547 0s 8d, due on shares £117 10s, Government subsidy £300, total £977 0s 8d. Liabilities: Estimated liabilities £63 17s, cost of pumping plant to arrive £200, total £263 17s, leaving an estimated credit at the present time of £713 3s 8d…

"The Chairman considered it would not be advisable to get to work on another bore. The credit balance was only £713 and if such a course were decided upon, there would be a considerable amount of money necessary for floating a new company. The manager (Mr Fair) said…Their first work was to get the present bore thoroughly tested." [25]

That lack of capital, a situation repeated so often in the case of the Taranaki oilfields, was to again prove the downfall of the Moturoa Petroleum Company by May 1906:

At a special meeting of about seventy shareholders of the Moturoa Petroleum Company at New Plymouth, chairman of directors, J B Roy, spoke of the lack of capital to continue:

"…financing the concern had proved no easy matter. There was a big weekly outlay. The directors realised there was need for more money in order to carry on the work of producing oil.

"The present company, said Mr Roy, would be liquidated, and the new concern registered in the course of a day or two, when the liquidator would transfer the whole undertaking to the new company…

"The Moturoa Petroleum Company Limited shall be voluntarily wound-up, a new Company having been formed (or about to be formed) under the name of The Taranaki Petroleum Company Limited." [26]

George Charles Fair was retained as the manager of The Taranaki Petroleum Company oilfield at Moturoa until his unexpected death from appendicitis and peritonitis on 26 November 1906.

The New Zealand Herald credited him with having succeeded to recover oil where others had failed:

"George Fair possessed wonderful patience which, added to his expert knowledge, enabled him to overcome all difficulties. To a sanguine disposition he added remarkable pluck and doggedness, without which his efforts to obtain oil at Moturoa would have been abandoned long ago…

"The pity is that he has not lived to see the complete fruition of his work. When, however, the oil industry of Taranaki becomes an established fact the name of George Fair will always be associated with the trials and vicissitudes of its history, and he will be regarded as the one man who above all others was instrumental in proving the existence and value of the field." [27]

However, as extracts from the 1906-1907 Taranaki Petroleum Company annual report illustrate, income from the sale of the oil procured was greatly exceeded by the cost of drilling for it:

"The annual report of the Taranaki Petroleum Company Ltd which is to be presented at the meeting to be held at New Plymouth on [4 November 1907] is to hand. The directors regret that so far no great success, such as was anticipated, has as yet rewarded their efforts, though the manager, Mr W A Simpson, reports that all the wells are to-day in a more satisfactory and sounder condition than they [have] ever been since the inception of the company…

"The balance-sheet shows that the bores have cost £10,357; casing £2030, and tools and casks £272. The working account shows that £77 5s 6d has been obtained from the sale of oil. Flotation expenses amount to £443; rents of boring leases, £216; offices and general expenses, £719." [28]

This point was not completely overlooked by at least one newspaper:

"According to the local [Taranaki] Herald, the Taranaki Petroleum Company is not a very flourishing concern. About £16,000 of the shareholders' money has already been spent, and there is very little to show for it. Of the five bores, of varying depths, which have been put down on the company's property, not one can be said to be on payable oil, while it is quite a speculation whether they are near to or far from that much-to-be-desired goal." [29]

By July 1908, with the price of company shares dropping, the directors of the Taranaki Petroleum Company found it necessary to issue a report of drilling progress. Unfortunately, it was not much of a positive statement, dwelling as it did on the struggle to eliminate the incursion of water — nevertheless:

"The directors would like to say that they have in no way lost heart, but believe in the ultimate success of the venture. None of the directors have sold any of their shares, nor would they advise shareholders to do so, for if the venture should turn out a success the reward will be great to all..." [30]

That anticipated reward seemed to recede further into the future after a New Zealand rail experiment failed to prove oil to be financially better than coal to power a locomotive — as reported by the Opunake Times in October 1909:

"Apparently the New Zealand Government hasn't any use for the petroleum so far saved by the Taranaki Petroleum Company. The Minister of Railways, who was asked to purchase the stock, replied stating that a locomotive was recently fitted with the necessary apparatus for using oil as fuel and was brought into service on the line between Christchurch and Lyttelton.

"The experiment has not, however, been successful as it is found in actual practice that the cost of using liquid fuel at the prices ruling in the Dominion makes it more expensive to use oil than to use coal. Under these circumstances Mr Miller regrets that the Government cannot see its way clear to purchase the oil." [31]

However, it helps to have a Member of Parliament as one of your directors. In this case, the MP for New Plymouth, Henry James Hobbs Okey (1857-1918), who addressed the House on 16 October 1909:

"Mr Okey, speaking on the Address-in-Reply, said the oil industry, which was of considerable importance to his district, had a perfect right to ask the Government's assistance.

"Sir Joseph Ward: By borrowing more money?

"No, said Mr. Okey; he did not want a big sum of money. All he asked was that the Government would purchase the crude oil at present in store at New Plymouth.

"'If you give us commercial value we will take it,' said the Hon. T Mackenzie.

"Mr. Okey accepted the offer, and called on the House to witness that it had been made." [32]

Accordingly, a deal was struck, as soon reported by the Evening Post:

"The Railway Department has agreed to purchase the Taranaki Petroleum Company's crude oil. The present stock is 25,000 to 30,000 gallons, and is being steadily increased." [33]

The outlook had improved according to the adjourned annual meeting of the Taranaki Petroleum Company held on 24 January 1910:

"The adjourned annual meeting of the Taranaki Petroleum Company, held to-day, was largely attended…The manager's report of the wells, read at the meeting, was considered very satisfactory, showing that deeper boring was being prosecuted with improving prospects. Oil is now being got at all three wells at which work is proceeding." [34]

Christopher Carter was elected to the board of the Taranaki Petroleum Company in March 1909 [35] and became chairman in January 1910. [36]

In February 1910, the Poverty Bay Herald reported:

"The company has now over 40,000 gallons of crude petroleum in stock, and is awaiting confirmation of an order for 500 barrels from the Government." [37]

While the flow of oil from the Taranaki wells continued, the market for the crude product remained limited. An increasing need to refine the oil for domestic use was necessary, at a time of intense competition from overseas suppliers — as reported by the Lyttelton Times in May 1911:

"Most people will be rather surprised to learn that the Taranaki Petroleum Company has earned a State bonus by producing more than 250,000 gallons of crude oil from the bores at New Plymouth. The figures look large and suggest that the day is approaching when the dominion will be able to use its own oil for the supply of power, light and heat.

"But the Minister of Mines, whom we do not doubt will redeem the Government's promise with very great pleasure, pointed to the problem still unsolved when he remarked that a refinery was required, in order that the petroleum might be prepared for sale. The erection of a refining plant is a very costly business and there is reason to fear that the company is going to encounter keen competition when it seeks a market for its products.

"Already there are rumours that New Zealand may feel the effects of the 'oil war' which is proceeding in other parts of the world. The Standard Oil Company has enjoyed a monopoly of our trade for very many years and has been able to adjust prices without much regard for the interests of the consumer.

"Now the British Imperial Oil Company, an immensely powerful corporation which has entered the field in open opposition to the older Trust, has a large shipment of oil on the water for the New Zealand market. In several parts of the world these big concerns are cutting prices against one another, and it does not seem likely that either of them will look with a kindly eye on local competition in this country.

"The men whose splendid courage and persistence have won oil from Nature's hidden reservoirs will not hesitate at the prospect of another struggle, but it may be that the bonus will not be the limit of the assistance they will require from the State before Taranaki's oil industry is firmly established." [38]

Despite the comparatively modest quantity of oil tapped from the Taranaki countryside, the Taranaki Petroleum Company remained conscious of the commercial power that could be wielded by the two oil conglomerates to stifle its future success. The Taranaki entity was particularly concerned that the New Zealand Government might not recognise the potential of its operations and fail to adequately protect it from foreign competition — as expressed by the company's Chairman of Directors, Mr Carter:

"What concerned the Taranaki Petroleum Company at present was not about any opposition that may be forthcoming, but how soon the company could satisfy people that they were in a position to supply the oil requirements, first of New Zealand, and then of Australia.

"He further pointed out that kerosene and benzine were the principal items affected by the oil war, whereas these products only formed about 50 per cent of the commercial articles they would realise when their crude oil was refined. There was also 24 per cent of spindle oil for lubrication purposes and 10.70 per cent of refined wax…

"Proceeding, Mr Carter said that if Taranaki or any other portion of New Zealand could satisfy the Government that it was in a position to supply the oil needs of the Dominion, he felt sure that, in the event of outside capital endeavouring to swamp a young industry, the Government would step in and protect the industry until it was sufficiently strong to stand by itself." [39]

Nevertheless, that 'outside capital' was essential to ensure the future of New Zealand's oil industry and remained attractive to English investors, in particular — as reported by The Taranaki Herald on 17 May 1911:

"According to 'Verax' who edits the financial page of John Bull, the oil market is ready to go ahead on the least encouragement…The New Zealand Oilfields is an important undertaking with 4000 shareholders, something in the neighbourhood of £50,000 working capital, owning oil concessions of about 230 square miles, and enjoying the sympathetic support of the New Zealand Government. The company's vast area is favourably situated for accessibility and transport, and the fact that the property is in British territory may weigh with investors." [40]

The following day, the report of a leaked cable message from London, addressed to the Taranaki Petroleum Company, was said to state: "negotiations for the sale of the Company's property and rights are on the eve of completion." [41]

Indeed, the sale of the Taranaki Petroleum Company interests was soon confirmed by The Taranaki Herald on 20 May 1911:

"The directors of the Taranaki Petroleum Company announce that a cable has been received this morning from Mr J D Henry, representing a powerful London syndicate, accepting the terms cabled by the directors on Wednesday night, for the sale of the company." [42]

The cable confirmed "…that the deposit of £2000 had been paid into the Bank of New Zealand in London. The agreed minimum price to be paid is £100,000, one-half to be paid in cash and one-half in fully paid-up shares in an approved company…

"The purchasers are the Oil Trust Limited, of which Mr H J [Henry John] Brown is managing director. It is a very wealthy concern, with large interests in other countries. Recently it acquired the control of a large oilfield in Central Ohio. The terms will mean a cash payment to the shareholders of the Taranaki Petroleum Company of just under 10s per share, and an equal interest in the new company to be formed." [43]

The business affairs of Henry John Brown were described as a biographical sketch by The Taranaki Herald in October 1911:

"He acquired an interest in the Petroleum World and engaged in many fortuitous speculations in the search for oil in Labrador, Newfoundland, Trinidad, New Zealand, Cuba, Nigeria, the Gold Coast, and elsewhere…He is managing director of that great concern, The Oil Trust Limited; chairman of the British Empire Oilfields Limited; chairman of the North Caucasian Oilfields Limited; and was, in addition to the promotion of the success of many subsidiary concerns, instrumental in opening up in Cuba one of the largest asphalt deposits in the world…" [44]

It was with some sense of relief that the Taranaki Daily News commented:

"The purchase by a wealthy British corporation of the Taranaki Petroleum Company's property marks an epoch in the history of this province. After years and years of pioneering work, at times almost heartbreaking, and the expenditure of large sums of money, the oil resources that have now been proved conclusively to exist here are to be developed on thorough comprehensive lines. The days of handicap are over. The oil expert, Mr Henry, who recently visited these parts, and did hot hide his satisfaction with the field and its prospects, was able to convince the British capitalists associated with him within a week after his return to London." [45]

By 11 May 1912, the days of the Taranaki Petroleum Company were numbered, as indicated by the following announcement:

"Matters in connection with the sale of the Taranaki Petroleum Company's undertaking to the Taranaki (New Zealand) Oil Wells Ltd are so far advanced as to enable the former company to take steps to go into voluntary liquidation. The Taranaki Herald understands that the date of meeting for that purpose is fixed for May 30." [46]

After they have left, the properties leased to the oil drillers naturally revert to the farmland they had once been and, where a breach of the lease agreement has occurred, the land owner had to seek court permission to re-enter — as reported by the New Zealand Gazette in January 1918:

"Application having been made to me by Thomas Inglis, of Mahoetahi, near Waitara, the registered proprietor of parts of Sections 53 and 58, Waitara West District…to register a re-entry by him under a deed granting rights to bore for and remove petroleum oil from above-described land, dated 13th day of October, 1903, registered in the Deeds Office at New Plymouth…made between John Rendall and Others and The New Zealand Oil-Wells Propriety (Adelaide), the said rights being vested in the Taranaki Petroleum Company (Limited), I hereby give notice that 1 will register the re-entry, as requested, after the expiration of one month from the 25th day of January, 1918. Dated this 21st day of January 1918 at the Lands Registry Office, New Plymouth. A V Sturtevant, District Land Registrar." [47]

The Taranaki (New Zealand) Oil Wells Company (1)

During the December 1911 annual meeting of The Taranaki Petroleum Company, the new part-owner of the company, Henry John Brown, addressed the company's shareholders covering a wide range of topics, including the establishment of the company to eventually replace the legacy company:

"Now I must turn to the subject matter of our meeting here to-day. The result of the negotiations as agreed between your directors and our directors is: A company is to be formed called 'The Taranaki (New Zealand) Oil Wells Limited' with a nominal capital of £400,000, of which sum £275,000 is to be issued for cash subscription, £50,000 is to be held in reserve, and

£50,000 is to be allotted to your company in fully paid shares, being part of the purchase consideration, and 25,000 shares go to British Empire Oilfields Limited." [48]

During the meeting, Henry Brown also commented on the new company's proposed refinery to be constructed at New Plymouth:

"While…drilling is proceeding, the final tests will have been made as to the refinery process most suitable, and one unit will be erected, to which can be added as many more as may be required for the oil we may have to refine, whatever the quantity.

"In the selection of a refinery plant there are many things to consider, the chief, from the shareholders' point of view, being the one that will give the largest returns. We must also consider that we may be asked to refine oils not produced by ourselves, and we must pay careful attention to the most valuable of by-products.

"One that comes into my mind at the moment is obtained from that which is left after the lighter and more valuable oils have been extracted, and more especially to oils having an asphaltum base. In one field in which my company are operating, the so-called residuum or considerably the larger part of it, is actually more valuable than the lighter oils, and there is a growing demand for the material I allude to.

"You will know that the question of road improvement is one that is absorbing the attention of road boards all over the civilised world, and it is a subject of which we also must have some little knowledge if we are to obtain the best results.

"The road boards want a road suitable for rather different traffic from that which our forefathers desired. Today we have the traction engine and motor car, both of which disintegrate the ordinary Macadam road, thereby creating dust. The action of these new vehicles destroys the foundations by allowing water to penetrate, thereby destroying the mud binder and creating dust. What the road board wants is a 'mackintosh sheet' in the form of a dustless, ductile, noiseless road.

"I have been connected with scores of tests and principles, but none of them will do unless oil is used in the form of an asphalt or bitumen as a binder. The road boards of London have been making tests lately, and a material made by a company of which we have the management, has produced a material which I believe will fill the bill, and the binder used is a natural asphalt, or oil from which the lighter parts have evaporated by Nature, and a residuum of oil from which man has extracted the lighter parts.

"I only mention this road question, as in future it will make large demands on oil refinery companies who are catering for the largest markets." [49]

Confirmation of the appointment of London Directors to the new company was received in New Zealand in January 1912:

"Jan. 8. A cable received from London states that the London Board of Directors of the Taranaki Oil Wells, Limited, has been fixed and comprises Lord Ranfurly (chairman), Messrs Joseph Brailsford (chairman of the Ebbwvale Steel, Iron, and Coal Company), Sir John [Lane] Harrington (chairman of the Oil Trust Limited which will act as Secretary for the new company), A [Andrew] L Horner KC, (Superintendent Director of South African Territories Limited), and Major [Dudley] Alexander (formerly private secretary to Lord Ranfurly). Probably Mr H. J. Brown, now in New Zealand, will join the Board later on." [50]

Announcing the imminent issue of a prospectus for the new company, the New Zealand Times, published 10 April 1912, also commented:

"The Taranaki NZ Oil Wells Company Ltd has been formed to acquire the oil rights over some 4800 acres of property at New Plymouth, from the Taranaki Petroleum Co. Ltd and on which there are already three flowing wells yielding about 15,000 gallons of oil per week.

There are, too, in the Company's tanks, now stored, some 310,000 gallons of oil awaiting the refinery which it is the intention of the directors to erect." [51]

By 20 April 1912, shares were said to be selling strongly with the issue expected to be over-subscribed:

"The brokers for the Taranaki (New Zealand) Oil Wells Ltd advise us that the following cablegram was received yesterday from London: 'People here are taking very great interest in issue...Shares are being purchased on the Stock Exchange at a premium of 3s 9d; anticipate rush for shares when list opens on Monday; market strong.'" [52]

However, due to many factors influencing the financial optimism of the British investor at the time, ranging from a national, coal-miners' strike and the loss of the Titanic, the company's share offering was not taken up by the numbers initially expected.

In fact, only 11,000 shares were purchased by British investors compared to 173,000 shares issued to some 5000 New Zealanders. The company was registered in London on 21 July 1912. [53]

Nevertheless, sufficient capital had been generated to install modern drilling equipment and to construct the much needed refinery at Moturoa — as reported by the Christchurch Press in June 1912:

"The order for the refinery was placed within a few hours of the flotation of the company, and the same enterprise is being shown in connection with the staff appointments and shipping of new drilling plant and machinery. What has been accomplished at a time of great market uncertainty cannot fail to have a beneficial influence on the colonial oil movement. The New Zealand subscription, large beyond expectation, has made a most favourable impression on the London market." [54]

New Zealand's First Oil Refinery (1)

By July 1912, the Evening Post was able to report:

"Confirmatory news came to hand yesterday in reference to a refinery for the Taranaki (New Zealand) Oil Wells Company Limited. Arrangements for its delivery had been completed, and it had been arranged that the first shipment should leave in June...A refinery manager has been engaged, and was himself going over the plant with the manufacturers prior to leaving for New Zealand. It is contemplated that all initial work, including preparation of the foundations, will be put in hand, so as to be ready to proceed at once with the erection of the refinery when it arrives.

"Preparations are also being made for pushing forward with all the expediency possible the sinking of new bores, in order to feed the refinery as soon as it is erected. The refinery ordered is thoroughly up-to-date and the wax plant has been considerably added to meet the requirements of the analysis of the Moturoa oil." [55]

A year later, in June 1913, the refinery was almost ready for full-time operation:

"The progress of the erection of the Taranaki (New Zealand) Oil Wells Company's refinery at Moturoa has sufficiently advanced to allow of the stills being fired, and this was done yesterday morning, the operation, which marks such an important step in the development of the oil industry, being performed by the chairman of the local board of directors, Mr C Carter.

"The underground connection from the stills to the big chimney stack worked most satisfactorily, but it is anticipated that at least a fortnight will be required to thoroughly dry the brickwork before the actual refining can commence. All that now remains to be done is to put the tinning plant, etc. in place, the whole of the building operations being finished." [56]

Indeed, "...The refinery had its own tin-making machinery, and a modern can-filling unit, in addition to the distilling process." [57]

"A new benzine extraction plant was erected at the refinery and gave every satisfaction, the benzine obtained being of good quality. For a period extending from January to August...the monthly sale averaged 1400 gallons and the spirit, which was chiefly used in motors in New Plymouth, was reported to compare favourably with any imported product. A demand was created for the company's crude oil as well as for the benzine, the average sale of the former for the year equalling 6980 gallons per month." [58]

The opening of the new refinery was certainly of interest, The New Zealand Herald reported, in August 1913:

"The Auckland Weekly News, on sale to-day, is a highly-interesting edition. The opening of the oil refinery at New Plymouth was an event of wide interest. The ceremony and numerous views of the works occupy a full double-page of illustrations. The refinery itself is claimed to be the first in the Southern Hemisphere, and is certainly the first in New Zealand. As oil-production may possibly become an industry of great importance in the Dominion these views of the pioneer refinery are doubly interesting." [59]

By November 1913, staff at the refinery was busy processing orders for its products:

"During the past week the staff at the refinery of the Taranaki (New Zealand) Oil Wells Company Ltd has been engaged in the export of orders for all classes of products which have been accumulating during the time that shipping has been held up. Large shipments have been sent to Wellington and others are awaiting shipment to Auckland. On Saturday the company received an order for 8000 gallons of fuel oil." [60]

Unfortunately, by November 1914, Government assistance was needed by the Taranaki (New Zealand) Oil Wells Company — as revealed during a Parliamentary debate of an Appropriations Bill:

"In reply to questions the Prime Minister stated that the proposal to advance money to assist oil refinery or development companies was brought forward to help an important prospective industry. A company which was at the end of its resources, had applied for assistance, which the Government would grant if the security was good enough. The company was the Taranaki (New Zealand) Oil Wells Company." [61]

Some opposition to what was described as a subsidy to only one of a number of private oil-exploration firms was expressed during the House of Representatives debate:

"The Prime Minister said the company concerned was in need of capital to keep it going. If it should shut down all the shareholders would lose their capital (about £100,000) and a promising industry would have to close.

"Mr. Wilford said that if the company could not keep going on private capital it was not the province of the Government to keep it going on public capital. Mr. Wilford put in a strong protest against the proposal in the Bill to expend £9000 in the development of the oil industry — the idea being, apparently, that the company concerned was the New Zealand Oil Wells Company, of which Sir George Clifford is chairman and in which Lord Ranfurly is interested...

"Mr Massey declared that the policy of the Government was to endeavour to conserve the oil industry of Taranaki by means of the subsidy proposed in the Bill, realising that if the refinery was not kept running the industry in the district would be ruined." [62]

The lack of working capital, evident from the company's inception, and a shortage of oil to refine, was revealed as the reason for the company's need of a Government subsidy. Its annual report for the year ended 30 April 1914 was reviewed by the Evening Post in January 1915:

"Throughout the report of the Taranaki (New Zealand) Oil Wells Company there is the plaint — lack of working capital. This, the public is told has seriously impeded operations in New Zealand during the year ending 30th April last. Repeated efforts have been made by the directors in London to secure the needed working capital, but in every case the terms required by the parties approached left the board no alternative but to refuse them.

"It is very deplorable that the company is so handicapped at this time when there is a keen and growing demand for all the products of the undertaking, and manifestly, unless some satisfactory arrangement can be made in the near future for the provision of additional working capital, it will be beyond the power of the company to carry on. The Government of New Zealand have been approached on the subject, and the matter is now under consideration...

"Although...output from the company's wells is less than with vigorous action and outlay was anticipated, it has shown a continuous steady production of oil, and demonstrates the existence of a genuine oilfield. From the first the directors looked to a goodly supply of oil for the company's refinery from a number of local drilling companies but, owing probably to want of capital, these concerns have not yet achieved their anticipations.

"With regard to the refinery, the working experience of the running of the same has been quite satisfactory, but owing to the shortage of oil it has not been constantly working, nor at any time at its full capacity, with the result that a loss has been sustained in obtaining the refined products. These, however, are of excellent quality and command a ready market. It is mentioned in the balance-sheet that no directors' fees have been paid since 1st August, 1913." [63]

At a subsequent meeting of shareholders reported by the Evening Post on 5 February 1915, company director, Andrew Horner, explained the lack of financial support for the company from Britain:

"Mr A L Homer, KC MP in seconding the adoption of the report and accounts, desired especially to impress through the press upon the shareholders in New Zealand that it was not impossible to raise capital in London for the enterprise. Capital could always be raised, and they could have raised any amount at a price. But it was at a price which the directors thought they were not justified in paying. And it was also at a price which would have struck at the independence of the company itself.

"It had been a dream of the directors that they should try and keep the company a British concern. His own dream had been to have oil within the Empire, and that was one of the reasons which governed the directors in their efforts to raise new capital…" [64]

While the oil continued to flow at Taranaki, the refinery remained a losing venture without further investment. Accordingly, the Southland Times reported its demise in January 1919:

"It is stated that the Taranaki (New Zealand) Oil Wells Company's refinery plant at Moturoa has been acquired by the Anglo-Persian Company — a concern in which the British Government is largely interested — and that the plant is to be dismantled and removed to the Persian Gulf." [65]

"A steamer has been specially chartered to ship the refinery plant recently owned by the Taranaki (New Zealand) Oil Wells from New Plymouth to the destination at which the Anglo-Persian Oil Company desire it…The vessel is the Orissa…due at New Plymouth on March 15." [66]

The question of collaboration with the Anglo-Persian Company was raised during a sitting in New Plymouth of a Parliamentary Industries Committee taking evidence on matters relating to the industries peculiar to the New Plymouth and Taranaki districts, in April 1919:

"Mr C Carter, representing the Taranaki (New Zealand) Oil Wells Company, after recounting the experiences of the company said they had spent about £150,000 on the project. The No. 5 well, which had been sealed for some time, would be re-drilled after Easter, and he was confident that oil would be found as before. He stated that none of the wells under the company's control had ever ceased to yield oil, except through defect of the mechanical means.

"He then referred to what the Government had done for the company, and further to the disposal of the refinery plant to the Anglo-Persian Company. He also explained that the Anglo-Persian Company, which was controlled largely by the British Government, had been negotiating with the New Zealand Government, and the representative of the company in the Dominion had said they were prepared to join with the New Zealand Government if the local oil fields warranted the step. He thought the Government should take the matter up.

"In reply to a question by Dr Newman as to the advisability of allowing an outside company to come in, develop and reap the profits from an industry which the country could develop, Mr Carter stated that he thought in the present case it would be a good proposition, as he understood that when the field was established the Anglo-Persian Company would be prepared to dispose of their interest." [67]

However, compared to its Persian Gulf prospects, the New Zealand oilfields held little attraction for the Anglo-Persian Oil Company, apart from its only refinery. Nor were the prospects of the Taranaki (New Zealand) Oil Wells considered to be worthy of further investment by its London backers — as reported by the Evening Post in October 1919:

"The Wellington Evening Post states that shareholders in the Taranaki Oil Wells Company have been advised by its London board that notwithstanding material financial assistance from the New Zealand Government (in the shape of loans at interest) in their persistent endeavour to test the oil field, without much larger capital at their disposal, it would be detrimental to the interests of the shareholders to continue further expenditure as, so far, oil in commercial quantities has not been obtained, certainly not at a cost that would show a profit…

"It proposes to circularise shareholders on the present state of the company's affairs, also upon the suggestion of the London board, that the company should be wound up and the undertaking sold to a new company if it is the desire of the New Zealand shareholders to continue exploitation of the oilfield." [68]

As of 22 January 1920, Taranaki (New Zealand) Oil Wells company, still registered in London, was in voluntary liquidation. [69]

Taranaki Oil Wells/Oil Fields Company (2)

Even though yet another oil explorer had run out of money, the prospect of a large oil discovery at Taranaki continued to entice prospective investors, including those from Australia, trading as Taranaki Oil Wells Limited (also referred to as Taranaki Oil Fields Limited in some press reports).

An initial inspection was undertaken in January 1924 — as reported by the Wairarapa Daily Times:

"An exhaustive study of and report on the oilfield of Taranaki is to be made by Dr Frederick G Clapp, of New York, who arrived in New Plymouth on Saturday night last. Dr Clapp, who is an eminent American geologist, and one of the world's highest authorities concerning oil lands, has been engaged by the syndicate which recently acquired the properties of the defunct Taranaki Oil Wells Company.

"He is accompanied by Mr A E Broue, of Sydney, and Mr A W Donald, of Auckland. A Daily News reporter was informed recently that if his report is favourable, the oil industry in Taranaki will be developed. Dr Clapp will afterwards visit the oil fields in Australia." [70]

The report was obviously 'favourable' because: "Taranaki Oil Wells/Fields Limited [incorporated in Victoria], was floated in July 1924 with a capital of £500,000 of which £150,000 was subscribed. Towards the end of 1925, the capital was increased to £800,000 and additional shares were issued realising £154,000. Altogether about £350,000 has been made available.

"A substantial proportion of the shares are in the hands of New Zealand investors, the balance being held in Australia. The Board of Directors includes two New Zealanders, and the office of the Company is located in Melbourne. This Company took over the property of the Taranaki Oil Development Company New Zealand, Limited [which was in voluntary Liquidation as of 9 September 1925 [71]]." [72]

By July 1924, preliminary work at the Taranaki oil fields was well under way — as reported by the Poverty Bay Herald:

"The new Taranaki Oil Wells Company, which has been formed to develop the Taranaki fields, has got off the mark quickly. It has completed the acquisition of all the boring rights required, besides entering into negotiations for a site for refineries, and it is hoped to start boring on the Tarata field early in September.

"By January or February some definite information should be available as to whether the Taranaki gushers will provide oil in sufficient quantities to make the proposition a payable one. The plant has already been ordered in New York, and it is ready for direct shipment to New Plymouth sometime this month…" [73]

"…in addition to acquiring the boring rights over 8000 acres in the Tarata district, it had taken over the interests of the liquidated Taranaki Oil Development Company in the neighbourhood of New Plymouth." [74]

The officers of the new company were keen to view their area of operation and travelled a long way to do so in September 1924:

"The party of directors and officers of Taranaki Oil Wells Ltd who arrived at Auckland from Sydney, travelled by train to Marton and came on to New Plymouth by motor yesterday afternoon. They are: Messrs Colin Fraser (Melbourne), chairman of directors; A E Broue (Sydney), director; E H Shackell (Melbourne), secretary; M B Hamer (Adelaide), stockbroker, one of the of the company; and Arthur H P Moline, who is to be general manager in Taranaki. They are accompanied by Mr. A W Donald (Auckland), director." [75]

Optimism remained high as drilling plans were revealed in December 1924:

"The search for oil in Taranaki is now entering upon an important stage. The Taranaki Oil Wells (Ltd) will commence drilling at Tarata in the course of a few days, and Dr Frederick Clapp, the eminent American geologist, on whose recommendation the company is exploiting the field, has now selected a site for the second bore. This is on the beach at the port of New Plymouth, near the original bore put down many years ago. Arrangements are also being made to select the site of a third bore. It is hoped that results at Tarata will be obtained by February." [76]

Not satisfied with their prospects at Taranaki, the Directors of Taranaki Oil Wells broadened their horizons to include New Zealand's east coast as well — as reported by the Auckland Star in July 1925:

"Interesting movements have taken place in connection with the Australian syndicate which is conducting investigations in this district in an endeavour to find oil in payable quantities. The Taranaki Oil Wells Ltd has now assumed a controlling interest in the Gisborne oil property, and the resources of the two companies will be available to carry out prospecting work. Most of the shareholders in the Taranaki company are also interested in the Gisborne oil proprietary, and include several wealthy Australians." [77]

Indeed, almost all the shares in Gisborne Oil Proprietary Ltd were acquired by Taranaki Oil Wells by July 1925:

"The secretary of Taranaki Oilfields Ltd, Mr Edward H Shackell, reports to the Melbourne Argus that the company has purchased practically all the shares in the capital of Gisborne Oil Proprietary Ltd, the purchase price being three shares in Taranaki Oilfields Ltd for each two shares in Gisborne Oil Proprietary Ltd." [78]

Further details about the Taranaki Oil Wells' joint exploration with the Gisborne Oil Proprietary Company at Gisborne were published in August 1925:

"The investigations being made by the Gisborne Oil Proprietary Company prospecting for oil in this district were detailed yesterday by Mr Fraser, one of the directors of the company, who with Mr A H Moline, manager of the Taranaki Oil Wells Company, have been inspecting parts of the district where the company holds leases.

"Up to the present, said Mr Fraser, the company had merely engaged in survey work, and it was not yet possible to make a statement as to the location of the trial bore...Recently the company had acquired the whole of the Waitangi oil area where attempts to bore have previously been carried out, and the geologists were now making detailed survey of that area...

"The company, which was now allied to and practically the same as the Taranaki company, now held leases over all the oil bearing localities in Poverty Bay." [79]

Once the first drill site had been decided, the transportation of construction materials to the remote location began in April 1926:

"The erection of a huge rig required in connection with oil boring operations is now proceeding at Ruatorea, the locality of the first well to be sunk in Poverty Bay by the Gisborne Oil Proprietary, which is a subsidiary company to the Taranaki Oilfields.

"More than three hundred tons of material were taken from Auckland to Tokomaru Bay by specially chartered vessels, and the whole of the heavy drilling plant was transported by road to the scene of the well.

"Carpenters in the district have been kept busy lately erecting accommodation houses, which will be required for employees when the boring has been commenced." [80]

In October 1927, the Evening Post reported on the drilling and exploration activities of the Gisborne Oil Proprietary Company (as a subsidiary of Taranaki Oil Wells Limited):

"This company's operations include the sinking of a well to over 5000 ft under specially engaged American drillers at Tarata, near Inglewood, Taranaki; drilling a well to 4630 ft at Moturoa, New Plymouth; drilling a well to 2540 ft at Ruatoria, Poverty Bay; and drilling a well now down to 2000 ft at Tokomaru Bay; another well is in progress near the Morere Hot Springs, some distance south of Gisborne.

"The company has also carried out geological surveys of extensive areas in the districts of Taranaki, Hawkes Bay, and Poverty Bay...It appears to be proceeding along its own lines, adopting methods markedly different from other companies which in the past have tried and failed to win oil in commercial quantities — where oil was found at all." [81]

Despite 'adopting methods markedly different from other companies', neither Taranaki Oil Wells nor Gisborne Oil Proprietary had achieved much success by January 1929:

"Boring to locate oil pools is very costly and a great deal of money has already been spent in the Dominion in the search for petroleum and success has not yet been achieved.

"The Taranaki Oil Wells Ltd, an Australian concern, has spent a huge sum of money in a scientific and systematic search for oil. But it is obvious that the company must spend a good deal more money and this fact is probably disheartening shareholders for it is now announced that the present limited liability company is to be converted into a no-liability organisation in which present shareholders will receive new shares of the denomination of 30s each. The scrip will be issued as paid up to 20s each, so that the Board will have a calling power of 10s a share. This will mean that all shares will have to contribute equally in future…" [82]

Nevertheless, optimism for a possible find remained high, reported the Feilding Star in August 1929:

"Progress in the development of the Morere oil wells, controlled by the Taranaki Oil Fields Company, is foreshadowed by Mr Arthur H P Moline, the general manager, who returned from Australia by the Niagara to-day.

"'Our new rotary drilling equipment is due to reach here tomorrow,' said Mr Moline. 'I am going on to Wellington to meet Mr S P Hart, an expert American driller who will be taking charge of our field operations. We will proceed to Morere in the Gisborne district, and hope to resume drilling in November.

"'I have always had confidence that we will get oil,' added Mr Moline, 'and although we have been looking for it for five years I was never more sanguine than I am to-day.'" [83]

But setbacks continued to March 1930:

"Gisborne No. 2 well — Operations again delayed by caving in below 3400 feet. Have taken additional steps to secure casing and now endeavouring to control caving in by application of high pressure. During the week ran tubing and swabbed well to test formations, penetrated to date. Gas pressure high but volume not sufficient to make well flow." [84]

While the company struggled on the oilfields, it also struggled with its finances:

"The profit and loss accounts of Taranaki Oilfields for the year ended April 30 1930 show a debit balance of £3,967. The company owed £5,388 to external creditors and held £764 in cash and deposits, shares in other companies, valued at £210,297, stores and tools valued at £14,786, also debtors' balances aggregating £67,741. The paid-up capital was £516,312 and calls unpaid totalled £2,458.

"The directors express the opinion that the company has good prospects of success with encouraging evidences of oil-gas seepages on Waitangi Hill where the next bore will be sunk. They point out that the Persian, Mexican and United States oilfields before reaching a producing stage, entailed more prolonged and more expensive prospecting operations than had been the case to date on the Taranaki fields." [85]

Defeat at its East Coast wells was finally acknowledged in October 1931:

"The management of the Taranaki Oil Wells Ltd regrets to report that continued difficulty has been met with in keeping the Waitangi No. 2 well open between 1960 feet and the lowest point reached, namely 2172 feet.

"The drilling superintendent and the field staff are now firmly of the opinion there is no reasonable prospect of carrying this well to the desired objective, namely a depth of approximately 4000 feet. It has therefore been decided to suspend drilling operations pending the review of the situation by the directors and staff. An announcement will shortly be made as to the company's future programme and in the meantime, the properties are being placed under a caretaker." [86]

Additional Taranaki Oil Exploration Companies

According to The New Zealand Herald, as of July 1924, there were [and had been] 14 to 15 additional oil exploration companies operating in Taranaki. [87]

Some of those, and subsequent companies, included:

The People's Petroleum Company

The People's Petroleum Company was founded in April 1866 with a capital of £1000 [88] and "…a lease over 2ha. Chairman was Julius Vogel (later Sir Julius Vogel, Prime Minister). Its well was christened 'Victoria' on the Queen's birthday…" [89]

However, it was tough going at the Victoria well: "This has, as yet, only reached the depth of about 17 feet, as the hardness of the strata makes the sinking very difficult." [90]

"No show of oil came, and in 1867 the Taranaki Petroleum Company took over its assets. This meant that much of the area in which oil in various quantities was found during the subsequent century was under control of [Christopher] Carter." [91]

New Zealand Petroleum and Iron Syndicate

Following his Parliamentary career, Sir Julius Vogel retained an interest in the Taranaki oilfields when, in 1889, he formed the London-based company, the New Zealand Petroleum and Iron Syndicate.

"The directors were Sir Julius Vogel and New Plymouth lawyer Oliver Samuel. In late 1890, with Canadian driller W E Booth in charge of operations, the company began drilling near the [Port Taranaki] breakwater.

"It produced 700 litres a day from a depth of 270m but did little to spark enthusiasm from its overseas investors, and even a hurried trip to England by Samuel only gained enough extra capital to repay debts.

"Gathering a group of local and Sydney-based backers, Samuel bought the plant and exploration rights, and attempted unsuccessfully to re-open the bore. Samuel and his backers drilled a further eight wells, the most successful of them being their No 3 well. Fire destroyed the derrick in its first year of operations but it was quickly replaced and produced oil for five years." [92]

Inglewood Oil Boring and Prospecting Company

The Inglewood Oil Boring And Prospecting Company Limited issued its first prospectus in June 1906, floating a capital of £5000 in £10 shares. [93]

By July 1906, the company had leased promising land — as reported by the Taranaki Herald:

"The Directors of the Inglewood Oil Boring Company have not been idle, and have secured to date about 2,000 acres of the most likely looking oil country in the Inglewood district. As soon as the weather moderates prospecting will be commenced for surface indications of oil which are known to exist." [94]

However, the initial drive for shareholding funds was not entirely successful by September 1906:

"Out of 500 shares in the Inglewood Oil Boring and Prospecting Company Taranaki investors took upwards of 400 at £10 each." [95]

Nevertheless, a start could be made that month:

"The driller engaged in Sydney on behalf of the Inglewood Oil Boring and Prospecting Company arrived in the district yesterday morning, and commenced boring at the company's property in the afternoon." [96]

But more funds were needed by November of 1906:

"At a shareholders' meeting of the Inglewood Oil Boring and Prospecting Co last night, the resolution increasing the capital from £5000 to £10,000 by the addition of 500 shares of £10 each, was confirmed." [97]

As usual, the initial optimism of 1906 had dissipated by September 1908 — as reported by the Hawera & Normanby Star:

"The Inglewood Oil Boring and Prospecting Company has ceased operations on Mr Burgess' property near the Norfolk road. All the men have been paid off and the works are being dismantled. The well had reached a depth of 2500 feet." [98]

At subsequent meetings in August 1909, the company's Directors and Shareholders retained some hope that efforts to raise capital in London and Paris might prove successful and so declined to sell plant in the meantime:

"An extraordinary general meeting of the Inglewood Oil Boring and Prospecting Company was held at the Town Hall, New Plymouth, last evening. Mr T Furlong, chairman of directors, presided, and stated that the object of the meeting was to give effect to the proposals recommended by the directors at last week's meeting of the shareholders. He explained that two inquiries had been received regarding the purchasing of the company's plant, one from Gisborne and the other from Dunedin. Prospects just now were particularly good, however, and he was averse to disposing of the plant. As to the question of the company going into liquidation, such an idea should not be entertained… it was resolved that the company's plant be stored pending further developments…" [99]

That hope remained in July 1910:

"The Inglewood Oil Boring Company has secured a renewal of boring rights for five years over a large area of country around Inglewood, also over 12,000 acres at Mokau, where coal, shale, sandstone and limestone outcrop. The directors intend to submit the whole to London financiers." [100]

With no London finance forthcoming, the inevitable end came in July 1917:

"An extraordinary general meeting of shareholders of the Inglewood Oil Boring and Prospecting Company Ltd was held at New Plymouth on Tuesday night…The resolutions adopted at a previous meeting to voluntarily wind up the company and place its affairs in the hands of a liquidator were formally confirmed…" [101]

The following year, shareholders were able to recover a very small portion of their losses:

"The Inglewood Oil Boring And Prospecting Company Ltd (In Liquidation). Notice To Shareholders. A Dividend of 2s 4d in the £ is now payable at the Office of the Company…" [102]

Taranaki Oil and Freehold Company

As early as March 1907, the Taranaki Oil and Freehold Company was ready to search for oil at Carrington Road, New Plymouth:

"The machinery on the property of the Taranaki Oil and Freehold Company, Carrington Road, is in position, and the shedding is now practically finished." [103]

However, initial drilling was to be a stop-start affair, reported the Taranaki Herald in May 1908:

"After a long enforced delay through one of those mishaps which seem to be inseparable from oil prospecting, the Taranaki Oil and Freehold Company is now able to resume progressive operations. About two months ago the bore caved — it is believed through an earthquake disturbance…

"Some special casing, 15 inches external diameter, was ordered in Wellington and it took some weeks to obtain delivery of it. This was lowered into the bore and on reaching the shingle the pump was got to work, the casing being gradually lowered and the bore cleared until it was possible to get hold of the buried tools.

"On Tuesday evening these were freed and withdrawn, and since then Mr Balloch has been engaged in lowering the special casing well below the shingle into the papa to prevent any further caving. The work has proved troublesome and tedious to a degree…Operations will now, it is hoped, proceed much more quickly." [104]

A year later, in June 1909, everything indicated a successful outcome:

"A meeting of the directors of the Taranaki Oil and Freehold Company was held this morning. The manager reported that the indications were of a very encouraging character, and that he considered it expedient to at once put in the 9-inch casing to the full depth of the present boring in order that a water-tight joint might be made before proceeding with the drilling. Excellent samples of oil have been obtained from recent pumpings. Applications for a number of shares were received and allotment made." [105]

However, despite the optimism, the money had run out by November 1909:

"The annual report of the Taranaki Oil and Freehold Company states that the bore is now down 1469 feet, and the excellent show of oil obtained justifies the expectation that payable results are near at hand. Funds, however, are exhausted, and it is necessary to consider whether additional money should be subscribed, or reconstruction faced. The company has 3000 unissued and forfeited shares, and land and plant costing nearly £6000, against which there are liabilities amounting to about £650." [106]

More than a year later, little had changed, as the chairman of the Taranaki Oil and Freehold Company, Mr F P Corkill, reported at the company's annual meeting of shareholders in December 1910:

"In moving the adoption of the report and accounts for the year the chairman shortly reviewed the year's business and said that early in the year the directors, in accordance with the authority given to them at the last general meeting, issued invitations to the shareholders to take up additional shares in the company but the response was not sufficiently ample to permit the resumption of boring operations.

"The directors then decided to close down the works for a time, paying off all hands except the manager, Mr Balloch [who subsequently travelled England].

"Mr W Balloch, writing on November 7, stated that he had had several interviews with the mining financiers [in London] who have been inquiring about the Taranaki Oil and Freehold Company's properties here. Mr. Balloch had furnished them with a considerable quantity of data, and he was hopeful that business might result." [107]

That 'business' did not eventuate, for a number of reasons outlined by Mr F P Corkill at the company's next shareholders' meeting in December 1911:

"Twelve months ago he thought that the negotiations which were going on would have led to the sale of the company to an English firm. This did not eventuate, although from the last cable advice from Home, it seemed that a company could have been floated. He hesitated, however, to do anything without first seeing the draft prospectus and meanwhile the bottom dropped out of the money market.

"This was followed by the Coronation, and that by wars and rumours of wars, so, acting on their own judgment, the directors decided to make all snug and wait awhile. They paid off their debts by raising a loan of £750 on their freehold property, and, except a small debt owing to their secretary, had no liabilities and they were in a position now to hold out for another year." [108]

By August 1916, the investment capital sought in England and from local shareholders since 1911 failed to materialise and "The Taranaki Oil and Freehold Company went into liquidation in March 1917 and the property was taken over by the mortgagees. There was not enough in the assets to pay the creditors of the company in full, much less the shareholders." [109]

By way of explanation, the acting chairman, G W Browne told shareholders:

"He was sorry that this stage had been reached because he could say without fear of contradiction that their bore was the only one outside of Moturoa where they got oil. They had twice cut seams and had put in 9-inch casing for 1300 feet. The last seam gave them six barrels of oil per week but, on the advice of their manager, they did not think it advisable to pull up and draw off the oil, but decided to push on with a view to obtaining a larger flow. Funds, however, had run out…" [110]

(F P Corkill had previously resigned the chairmanship and was ultimately declared bankrupt.)

The Bonithon Freehold and Petroleum Company

The Bonithon Freehold and Petroleum Company was registered on 25 July 1907 with a Member of Parliament, W H P Barber, as its Chairman of Directors.

In September 1906, the company then proposed was promoted as having certain advantages that set it apart from the run-of-the-mill oil prospectors:

"The advantages which appeal to investors in Bonithon oil shares and which distinguish it as an investment from most other ventures of the kind, are many. For instance, most oil companies only hold boring rights over other people's land. The Bonithon Freehold and Petroleum Company own the land which contains the oil…

"Then the Company do not need to bore for indications of oil. It is oozing from the soil. That the promoters of the Company have the greatest faith in the richness of their area is evidenced by the fact that they not only purchased the land, but have also subscribed the money for the purchase of a boring plant without awaiting the flotation of the Company." [111]

"The Bonithon property…consists of nearly thirteen acres of freehold under Land Transfer title, and is situated about midway between New Plymouth Post Office and the breakwater." [112]

Active boring operations were commenced by the Bonithon Petroleum Syndicate on 21 March 1907 [113] but, by October 1908, boring had been suspended, [114] presumably because of a shortage of capital necessitating a re-structuring:

"At a meeting of local shareholders in the Bonithon Petroleum Company, held last night [11 January 1909], it was decided to fall in with the Wellington and Wanganui shareholders in reconstructing the company with a capital of £25,000, none of which will be offered to the public. Operations will be resumed almost immediately." [115]

Indeed, by March 1909, the restructuring had entailed the dissolution of the company in favour of a new entity:

"Business connected with the winding up of the Bonithon Petroleum Company and the flotation of the Bonithon Extended Company has necessitated Mr William McLean of Wellington visiting New Plymouth. Mr McLean is the liquidator of the old concern and secretary of the new company." [116]

By June 1909, the Taranaki Herald reported:

"The Bonithon Petroleum Company has been re-formed in Wellington, principally among the original shareholders. It has been decided to continue boring another 500 feet, or probably more. Operations were re-started this week…" [117]

The re-formed company, now known as Bonithon Freehold Petroleum Company Extended Limited, retained W P Barber as Chairman of Directors and W McLean as secretary. [118]

By March 1912, the new company was prepared to invest in the latest rotary boring plant:

"The Bonithon Freehold Petroleum Company Extended Limited, having raised sufficient capital to secure a Rotary Boring Plant for Taranaki is prepared to receive applications for a limited number of shares, not exceeding 1000…" [119]

"The plant was considered to be an exceptionally good one, the latest design of the Parker-Mogul (1912), and was manufactured at Chattanooga, Tennessee, USA by the Southern Wells Works Company. It was capable of drilling 5000 feet, or with care 5200 feet could be penetrated." [120]

As reported by the Taranaki Herald in July 1913:

"A rotary drilling plant has been procured from America, and drilling started on July 24 to put down a new bore near the former well." [121]

However, despite the new equipment, a useful oil find proved elusive and, as previously noted, the Directors of the Bonithon Freehold Petroleum Company Extended Limited voted to sell its rotary boring plant to Percy Hadley in April 1915. [122]

The whole affair attracted a good deal of criticism from the shareholders of the Bonithon Freehold Petroleum Company Extended Limited, about which the NZ Truth columnist, Cambist, wrote in July 1915:

"Cambist has on more than one occasion sounded a note of warning to the deluded people who were trying to make fortunes out of the Taranaki alleged oilfields. He has warned investors to beware of the specious share-sharking individual that was to be met with in every town in the Dominion. The note he especially harped upon was this — If the people really wished to prospect the Taranaki petroleum oozes, and the gas exhalations of Moturoa let them do so, but let every penny raised for that purpose go into genuine prospecting…

"This company stands revealed as the…[illegible] of business ineptitude. It has lost nearly all of the shareholders' money. It has done nothing to forward the cause of sound prospecting methods, and to that extent it has dealt a hard blow at the future of Taranaki oil prospecting. The directors for the whole time of the company's existence have not issued a proper balance sheet and profit and loss account. By this means they have wittingly, or otherwise, kept the shareholders in the dark as to what was happening to their money. Had a profit and loss account been issued, assets could not have been sacrificed as they were…" [123]

Some five years later, the sale of the company's plant to Percy Hadley remained controversial, with a sequel at the Supreme Court in September 1920:

"In this dispute the Bonithon Freehold Petroleum Company had claimed from P A Hadley…the sum of £1200 damages for the wrongful conversion by Hadley of certain machinery to his own use. Hadley filed a counter claim for £1422, being the plaintiff company's share of expenses he had incurred in connection with the promotion of a company…

"His Honor found that the general purport of the agreement and negotiations between the parties was to the effect that the plant and machinery were to be held in common ownership with the intention of selling if to a new company to be formed, and the total proceeds to be derived from such sale were to be divided between the company and Hadley in the proportion of one-third to two-thirds. The promotion of the new company failed, and Hadley, without the consent of the company, sold the plant to a third party…" [124]

E Hadley Company (1)

By 1902, Percy Arthur Hadley had inherited his family's business, Hadley & Co, trading as mining and general machinery merchants from Albert Street, Auckland. However, Percy Hadley was adjudicated bankrupt in April 1904 [125] and the firm's stock and goodwill was subsequently purchased from the Official Assignee by J J Craig. [126]

During his court application hearing for discharge from bankruptcy in September 1913, Percy Hadley advised that, following his bankruptcy, he had taken a position as manager of a new firm, E Hadley Company, of which his wife was the shareholder. The E Hadley Company subsequently acquired three petroleum exploration concessions, one of which was a block at Carrington Road, New Plymouth. [127]

The first drilling undertaken by E Hadley Company was reported by the Taranaki Herald in December 1907:

"During the last few days boring operations have been commenced at the first bore of the Hadley Company situated on the Carrington Road. So far everything has worked smoothly, and the bore is already down to a depth of over fifty feet." [128]

By May 1908, drilling continued:

"The operations of the Hadley Company are proceeding smoothly. The installation of the electric light plant is complete. A second driller is expected to arrive from America during the week but in the meantime temporary arrangements have been made by which the Company is working a double shift." [129]

"Rapid progress has been made at the bore of the Hadley Company, Carrington Road, during the past three weeks, the formation being passed through having considerably improved." [130]

However, mainly because of drilling problems, by October that year:

"Operations at the bore of the Hadley Company on the Carrington Road have ceased indefinitely." [131]

Then, by March and July 1909, the Taranaki Herald was able to report:

"Encouraging news was received at this office yesterday afternoon regarding operations at the bore of the Hadley Company on the Carrington Road. A Herald reporter visited the well last night and found everything in full swing, work being carried on night and day. Mr O'Dowda, the manager, informed him that there had been excellent showings of oil during the past few days…" [132]

"…at the Hadley Company's bore, though there is no authentic information available to the public, the prospects are said to be so promising as to have determined the wealthy syndicate operating to carry on prospecting work on a much larger scale…Thus it will be seen that locally there is a good deal of quiet confidence in the ultimate success of the industry, and it is just as well that there is no excitement…" [133]

By September 1909, the E Hadley Company and its syndicate had entered into an agreement to sell its Carrington Road concession to the newly-incorporated Standard Oil Company of New Zealand Limited, [134] in which Percy Hadley retained both a shareholder interest and management role.

Standard Oil Company of New Zealand

The Standard Oil Company of New Zealand Limited became a New Zealand-registered company on 24 September 1909 with a capital of £200,000. The first shareholders, with 250 shares each, included Percy Arthur Hadley (Managing Director), Charles D Grey (Chairman & Auckland Mayor), A Carrick, J Coe, J C Colbeck, J D Jones, F Kneebone, J M Thomson, and R R Ross, all of Auckland. [135]

By August 1910, Percy Hadley was able to optimistically report some progress:

"The manager of the Standard Oil Company of New Zealand reports that drilling operations, which have been suspended for some time, are now progressing favourably. The well is down 3000 ft and in good oil-bearing country with, at times, a good show of oil and strong gas. He expects important developments any day." [136]

However, insufficient capital and a lack of any real oil finds again proved disastrous — as reported by the Taranaki Herald in March 1911:

"Yesterday afternoon the Standard Oil Company of New Zealand Ltd oil bore and plant on the Carrington Road were seized by the bailiff of the Magistrate's Court, under a warrant for immediate execution, issued in connection with the claims for wages by the company's employees. Judgment for these claims, by default, was given in the Magistrate's Court on Tuesday. The property seized is to be offered for sale next Thursday." [137]

Just prior to the seizure, the company had given up:

"The Standard Oil Company of New Zealand Limited — I hereby give notice that a special resolution was passed on the 22nd day of February 1911 and confirmed on the 21st day of March 1911, that the abovenamed Company be wound up voluntarily." [138]

In January 1913, the company's assets were for sale:

"Oil Boring Rights together with the Complete Boring Plant, Receiving Tanks, Buildings, and General Accessories, as they now stand on the property. The undersigned [auctioneers] have received instructions from Ernest Gerard acting as Liquidator of the Standard Oil Company of New Zealand Limited, to sell at their Salerooms…on Monday 20th day of January 1913…" [139]

E Hadley Company (2)

Not surprisingly, Percy Hadley and his original company were back for another go at Carrington Road — as the Taranaki Herald reported in April 1913:

"The E Hadley Company has purchased and taken possession of the property, plant, and assets of the Standard Oil Company Ltd and Mr P A Hadley is here making preliminary arrangements for re-starting work at the bore on the Carrington Road. When work ceased the well was down to a depth of 3246 ft and in good country. It is the intention of the company, Mr Hadley informed one of our representatives, to drill to at least 4000 ft but it is expected that a good well will be obtained after four to five hundred feet have been drilled. Everything at the bore is in perfect order, and work can be started immediately steam is got up." [140]

International Petroleum and Minerals Development Corporation

However, the Standard Oil Company property and plant was acquired by the E Hadley company working in conjunction with another, The International Petroleum and Minerals Development Corporation, a concern registered in Christchurch in June 1913…with a capital of £400,000. [141]

During the court application hearing for discharge from bankruptcy in September 1913, previously referred to, Percy Hadley successfully defended his living style, various company flotations, and share speculation as a bankrupt and was granted a discharge by the Court. [142]

Nevertheless, the NZ Truth commentator, 'Cambist', warned his readers against investing in the new consortium being established at Carrington Road:

"While the scheme, if ever it is carried through, looks good for the vendors and syndicate people, it certainly looks highly speculative for the contributing shareholders. Here is all that the latter have plainly in front of them: a certainty of having a lot of calls, and the great uncertainty of finding payable oil when the oil horizon is reached.

"It strikes 'Cambist' most forcibly that we have as yet never discovered in this country an oil horizon worth a row of pins. The facts are that up to the present, investors have suffered badly from the unpayable results of honest prospecting, i.e. in the real borings which been carried on for over 20 years past.

"It is therefore rather hard on the company…contributing shareholders to be saddled with so much 'watered' stock, so much debenture stock, and so much hard cash, all of which, or most of it, at any rate, is intended for the pockets of the cunning ones who are syndicators or vendors. Let our people be very careful in matters of this kind — let them not be led into 'wild cat' schemes which are more concerned with cash-grabbing than prospecting. Should oil ever be found in payable quantities, the results will be good enough to satisfy honest greed." [143]

As 'Cambist' had warned, by 1915, there was little return forthcoming for shareholders in the companies drilling at the Taranaki oilfields. Any promise of possible improvement in their fortunes was therefore welcomed:

"A meeting of shareholders of the Bonithon Petroleum Company was held to-day, Mr W H P Barber presiding. It was agreed to ratify and complete the directors' action in disposing of the company's new rotary boring plant to Mr P A Hadley of Auckland. It is understood that the plant will be erected on one of the properties comprising the Standard Oil Company of New Zealand Ltd. The transaction involves many thousands of pounds and it is believed it will infuse new life into the development of the Taranaki oilfields." [144]

It wasn't until January 1923 that Percy Hadley generated some interest again with the formation of yet another company — as reported by the Hawera & Normanby Star:

Taranaki Oil Development Company

"The development and production of oil in Taranaki is to receive a fresh impetus in the near future, according to Mr P A Hadley of the Taranaki Oil Development Company (NZ) Ltd who was in New Plymouth, yesterday.

"'The company is one with capital adequate to carry out the development of the oil industry in all its branches,' said Mr Hadley…That [Taranaki] property purchased by Hadley and Donald, Auckland, will be registered in Australia early in February, all preliminaries having now been completed." [145]

Percy Hadley's co-Directors included A W Donald and C G Macindoe.

However, by April 1924, Percy Hadley was again forced to declare himself bankrupt:

"The assets chiefly comprised Taranaki oil shares and interests in Taranaki oil lands and machinery. Mr Andrew Hanna, solicitor, who was the largest unsecured creditor, said that considerably over a year ago he obtained a writ of sale over the bankrupt's property, including a quantity of shares in various oil syndicates and a Benz motorcar. There were many delays before the sale was arranged, but it was eventually fixed for Friday last. Within ten minutes of the time fixed, however, Hadley lodged his petition in bankruptcy with the Supreme Court, and the sale had to be abandoned…

"Continuing, Mr Hanna said he understood that the Taranaki Oil Development Company, in which bankrupt held 65 £250 shares, was negotiating in Australia for the sale of its assets." [146]

"The complicated transactions of Percy Arthur Hadley in connection with his schemes for the flotation of oil development companies were further ventilated at an adjourned meeting of his creditors held yesterday…He said that in 1920 he entered into an agreement with Mr Herbert Thomson to acquire the Dominion assets of the Taranaki Oil Wells of New Zealand Ltd, an English company then in liquidation.

"After two and a half years' abortive flotation negotiations, Mr A W Donald bought out Mr Thomson's interest, and he and the bankrupt formed a private company, the Taranaki Oil Development Company of New Zealand Ltd, 160 shares of £250 each, each of them taking 80 shares." [147]

The fire sale of Percy Hadley's share assets by the Official Assignee was reported by the Christchurch Press in May 1924:

"The fifteen shares in the Taranaki Oil Development Company Ltd released for disposal were placed on offer…These shares, each have a nominal value of £250, were disposed of at £48 each. A further parcel of these shares were withdrawn from sale in keeping with the Official Assignee's undertaking, there being some uncertainty as to Hadley's title. Other shares in the Hadley estate, offered on behalf of the Official Assignee, were 10,875 fully paid up £1 shares in the Associated Oil Corporation Ltd which were disposed of at £5 for the lot. Another parcel of five shares in the same company brought 5s." [148]

Christchurch Oil Company/United Oil Company/The Consolidated Oilfields of Taranaki

The Christchurch Oil Company Limited was one of a number of New Zealand's oil prospecting companies whose Directors were more interested in profiting from share transactions with other companies than actually drilling for oil.

"The Christchurch Oil Company Ltd was registered on March 2 [1912] with a capital of £87,500 divided into 350,000 shares at 5s. The first subscribers are Messrs G B Ritchie, G Bowron, W Fox, M G Louisson, Percy Arthur Herman, and F M Warren, all of Christchurch.

The objects of the company are to carry on the business of producers, refiners, etc., of petroleum. The scene of their operations is at New Plymouth, the property known as Marfell's at Westown, having been purchased." [149]

However, by May 1916, the company's activities were shown to be something other than its stated objects — as reported by the Christchurch Sun:

"The operations of the Christchurch Oil Company Ltd occupied the attention of his Honour, Mr Justice Denniston, in the Supreme Court yesterday. Montague H Wynyard and others applied for an order for the winding-up of the company and the appointment of a provisional liquidator. Mr Alpers appeared for the petitioners...

"In the course of his opening statement to the Court, Mr Alpers said that the petition was based on two grounds, the first of which was that the company was unable to pay its debts, and the second that the substratum of the company was gone.

"Mr Alpers then went into details regarding the Christchurch Oil Company's connection with the United Oil Company, in which the former took 5500 shares and which subsequently ceased operations. Counsel also discussed the Christchurch Oil Company's transactions with the Consolidated Oilfields Company, which was working property 35 miles away from Marfell's freehold.

"Marfell's claim amounted to about £4000 and the petitioner's claim to £6000. Counsel argued that the substratum of the company was gone, firstly because the primary object was to work Marfell's freehold, and that had been abandoned, and secondly that in the construction of the memorandum of association the company's primary object was to produce oil, and in the three years and a half of its existence, the company had not produced, or attempted to produce, a gallon of oil..." [150]

Consequently, the Christchurch Oil Company Limited was in liquidation by January 1920:

"McKenzie and Willis — We have been favoured with instructions from Mr H P Bridge. Liquidator of the Christchurch Oil Co Ltd, Christchurch. to offer for sale by auction 5500 Ordinary Shares of One Pound each In the capital of £18,000 of the United Oil Co Ltd Christchurch... " [151]

United Oil Company

The United Oil Company Limited was registered in June 1913 with a capital of "£18,000...Subscribers (all of Christchurch) — S L P Free, F W Warren, A Freeman, J Morrison, W W Redmayne, A G Aldridge, and C C Morton..." [152]

The following August, the Lyttelton Times reported:

"In about a month, the United Oil Company would begin drilling out Waitara way. The plant, rig and derrick at present were stored in New Plymouth." [153]

Again, little oil was found and the drilling plant was up for sale by October 1922:

"Tenders will be received by the undersigned up to noon on Wednesday 1st November [1922] for the Oil Boring Plant and Buildings, the property of the United Oil Company Ltd located on Mr Sarten's property, Bertrand Road, Tikorangi. Tenders to be made separately for any item or the whole outfit..." [154]

The Consolidated Oilfields of Taranaki

The third Christchurch-registered company was established in 1912 — as reported by the Patea Mail in September of that year:

"...news has now been received that the Stratford district is to made the centre of boring operations by the Consolidated Oilfields of Taranaki Ltd, a company which has just been registered in Christchurch with a capital of £40,000. The company will probably offer a portion, but not a large proportion of the shares for subscription by the public.

"Whilst the situation of the first bore has not yet been fixed, it is probable that the derrick will be erected in the vicinity of Toko. The company has decided to import the very latest rotary plant with a view of quickly and thoroughly testing the actual producing capacity of the field…The territory over which the Consolidated Oilfields of Taranaki has rights includes a very large area lying around the Toko district and to the northward." [155]

By May 1913, preparation work had started:

"The Consolidated Oilfields Company is getting busy at Huiroa [inland Taranaki], and the Company's six men are busy erecting a boiler house and engine shed, as well as a workmen's cottage. An up-to-date rotary drilling machine, and other machinery required, arrived in Wellington…last week, and is now probably at New Plymouth." [156]

However, despite some assistance from the Christchurch Oil Company, drilling had halted by mid-1914:

"The Consolidated Oilfields Company, in which the Christchurch Oil Company, after the United Company ceased operations, invested £4800, was thirty-five miles distant from Marfell's freehold. The Consolidated Company's working capital was exhausted at the beginning of 1914; and increased capital amounting to £5000 was also, subsequently, exhausted. It attempted to raise £4000 by means of debentures on its plant, but the shareholders failed to take them up…" [157]

By January 1918, Consolidated Oilfields of Taranaki Limited had been dissolved. [158] When the company's leasehold interests and plant was advertised for sale by auction in December 1918, the auctioneer commented:

"The bore is near the Huiroa Station…is down nearly 5000 feet…The prospects when the bore was stopped by reason of a breakage were considered very favourable..." [159]

Blenheim Oil Company

The Blenheim Oil Company Limited (formerly the Taranaki Oil Lands Acquisition and Development Company Limited) [160] was floated by E Griffiths, R F Goulter, George McKay, and John Barry in December 1912 and began drilling next to the Taranaki New Zealand Oil Wells at Moturoa.

The Otago Witness reported in January 1914:

"The good prospects at the Blenheim Company's Moturoa bore still continue and it is now a highly payable well. On December 30 oil was struck at a depth of barely 300 ft. The first yield recorded after the well began to flow freely was 18 barrels, but on Saturday the yield was 50 barrels.

"If the flow of oil does not increase at all, which in the light of the present indications is most unlikely, the well even then will pay handsomely. The Blenheim well, as it is familiarly called, is the property of the Taranaki Oil Lands Acquisition and Development Company, in which both Christchurch and Blenheim capital is represented." [161]

As reported by the New Zealand Times, the yield had increased dramatically by 1915:

"Various bore-holes, in search of petroleum, had been drilled, or were in progress, the deepest being that of the Blenheim Oil Company, at Moturoa, which had attained a depth of over 5000 feet.

"Petroleum of good quality, but of limited quantity had been proved at Moturoa. The quantity of crude oil produced by this company amounted in March, 1915, to 776,161 statute gallons, of which 525,475 gallons were refined by the company. The product met with a ready sale at prices equal to the imported article." [162]

During a sitting of a Parliamentary Industries Committee taking evidence on matters relating to the industries peculiar to the New Plymouth and Taranaki districts in April 1919:

"Mr E Griffiths, chairman of the Blenheim Oil Company, stated that his company's well was now down to a depth of about 5300 feet. The plant was capable of drilling down to 6000 feet. The opinion of experts was that if oil was found it would be at a depth of about 5000 feet and the directors believed they were now approaching the main supply source.

"The company had spent about £20,000 on drilling and had received about £6000 on loan from the Government. The grant authorised was £9000, and the company was receiving £350 per month. The capital had all been locally subscribed, and there were no foreign shareholders. In the event of the company getting oil in a payable quantity the Government would not get a percentage of the profits, but merely the repayment of moneys loaned, with interest." [163]

However, the perennial problem of water ingress became too much to handle at the Blenheim well from about 1918 — as described by the New Zealand Herald:

"Unfortunately an accident happened to the casing between the 4000 ft. and 5000 ft. levels, which prevented the shutting off of the water…This accident really created the disaster which was never overcome, because the company finances were then too low.

"In 1918 the well was down 5200 ft. and was finally drilled to 5650 ft., or well over a mile. Blow-outs occurred and samples sent to the Government showed that the bit was undoubtedly in oil and that if the water was pumped out oil would be produced. Pumping, however, was of no avail against the flow of water, which entered as fast as it was taken out. Finally the well was abandoned." [164]

By 1921, the money had finally run out and, at an extraordinary general meeting held on 23 March that year, a resolution was passed to voluntarily wind the company up. [165]

Blenheim Oil Well Reclamation Company

"The Blenheim Oil Well Reclamation Company Limited…was formed in 1927 for the purpose of reclaiming the Blenheim well with a nominal capital of £20,000…The reclamation of the well consisted entirely of the elimination of the water trouble. The bore is located about half a mile from the port and was put down by the Blenheim Oil Company Limited…With the water effectively dealt with the well had then to be sunk past the water level down to the 2200-foot oil stratum, which has apparently again been reached and the present flow tapped." [166]

Despite continuing drilling difficulties, the Taranaki Daily News reported in August 1931:

"The company has in store at the present time about 50,000 gallons of crude oil, and the basis of the negotiations has been the sale by contract of the company's production up to five million gallons at 5d a gallon. It is understood that it is proposed to refine the oil and dispose of it to the New Zealand motoring public in the form of second grade petrol." [167]

Indeed, by late 1931, a Company had been set up to refine the Taranaki Oilfields crude:

"The refining of crude oil into benzine and other products is to be commenced at the New Plymouth oilfields in October. The trustees of the Refinery Company in the course of registration today signed an agreement with the Blenheim Oil Company to purchase crude oil up to 5,000,000 gallons at 5d a gallon." [168]

As described later, that company was New Zealand Oil Refineries Limited — "Registered as a private company October 16th 1931. Capital: £2500, in shares of £1 each. Subscribers — New Plymouth: W Fossey 625, H Williamson 313. Stratford: Union Foundries Ltd., 313, S Huston 313, A H Trotter 312. Wellington: E E Woodley 312. Masterton: S E Taylor 312. Objects: To carry into effect an agreement made with Blenheim Oil Well Reclamation Co Ltd for purchase of crude oil and carrying on business of refiners, oil merchants, etc." [169]

By November 1931, NZ Oil Refineries Limited was advertising that "Petrol, Power Kerosene, Diesel Oil and Fuel Oil refined at Moturoa, New Plymouth is now available." [170]

Unfortunately, the required crude oil output was not achieved and The Blenheim Oil Wells Reclamation Company Limited was placed into voluntary liquidation in May 1933:

"The Reclamation Company, working on the assumption that the main oil sands existed at a depth where the original production occurred, was successful early in 1929 in inducing a small flow, reports of which led to a considerable inflation in share values. These rose within a week to over £7 and fell almost as quickly.

"Further troubles led to a decision to abandon the old bore and sink a new one nearby. Although the new well was drilled to the required depth, a satisfactory flow was never obtained." [171]

Coal Oil (NZ)

Coal Oil (NZ) Limited was formed in Sydney in 1926 with a capital of £750,000 [172] to exploit coal areas at Westport and oil at Hawke's Bay. In 1930, the company drilled for oil at Omata, New Plymouth with the first modern rotary drilling plant in Taranaki. [173]

As reported by the Evening Post, an official opening of the drill site was held on 8 May 1930:

"The Honourable the Minister of Mines will officially declare Omata Open for Operation. The Directors of the Company…extend an invitation to all interested in Oil Development in New Zealand to attend the Ceremony, which will be held on the site at Omata.

"The plant, which commenced drilling on 24th April, is actually the largest and most comprehensive ever operated in either Australia or New Zealand and is capable of reaching a depth of 8000 feet. Its progress in drilling to date is unparalleled in this part of the world, and will be a source of interest to observers of modern methods." [174]

More than a year later, in June 1931, Coal Oil (NZ) had drilled to 3082 feet with no show of oil. [175]

However, in August 1931, after 18 months of drilling, the plant was closed… [176]

As reported by the Evening Post on 4 August 1931:

"On instructions by cablegram from the head office of the company in Sydney…drilling has been suspended at the Omata oil well, New Plymouth, the property of Coal Oil (NZ) Ltd. The well is drilled to 3400 ft…Recent drilling has been retarded by mechanical difficulties, always possible with deep drilling, but on the other hand, the drilling to date is reported as having shown exceedingly favourable oil evidences and it is expected that the present stoppage will be of a temporary nature only." [177]

But the stoppage was far from temporary as, by October that year, the company's debenture holder had called on a receiver to sell all assets:

"Under instructions from the receiver for the debenture holder, a resident of Sydney, tenders are being invited for the purchase of the whole of the property and assets of Coal Oil (NZ) Ltd.…" [178]

By January 1932, Coal Oil (NZ) Limited was in liquidation. [179]

"Over 60 shareholders of the Coal Oil (NZ) Ltd, now in liquidation, decided at a meeting at New Plymouth last night that a new company should be formed with a nominal capital of £175,000 to take over the plant and assets of the Coal Oil Company and develop the oilfield at Omata…" [180]

Moturoa Oilfields

Moturoa Oilfields Limited was formed in 1930 to rework the oil wells previously drilled but abandoned by Taranaki Oilfields Limited in 1919.

As reported by the Evening Post in January 1930:

"Although the new company is not yet incorporated, sufficient capital has been secured to ensure the sinking of the test well, and drilling machinery will arrive in New Plymouth next week. It is expected the plant will be erected and drilling commenced within the next two months." [181]

Indeed, drilling commenced on 1 April 1930 [182] and, by July of that year, the land had protested at the intrusion:

"Moturoa Oilfields Ltd's bore this morning blew out without warning, sending up great gushes of mud that coated the derrick and spread over a wide area. The bore was down 1740 ft, and the force of the gas blew the drilling gear up till it stuck in the debris gathered. Then the gas, gathering force, blew the gear clean out of the hole and up 80 ft, twisting the wire ropes and doing damage to the tackle. The gear came straight down like a huge spear, burying itself 20 ft in the ground. The blow continued for a quarter of an hour, and was followed by a continuous flow of inflammable gas." [183]

Nevertheless, despite the usual setbacks, oil production had stabilised somewhat by May 1933:

"Moturoa Oilfields Limited reports as follows for the week ended May 13 [1933]: — 'No. 2 well produced 110 barrels (3850 Imperial gallons) of oil. After exhaustive tests, No. 3 well failed to produce commercially. Removal of equipment to new location is now being considered.'" [184]

An update from Moturoa Oilfields Limited, published by the Otago Daily Times in May 1934, included:

"The No. 2 well is reported to be continuing its steady production, and up to the time of the last monthly report, which was issued on March 27 had produced 503,059 gallons, the whole of which had been bought by the refinery at New Plymouth and converted into petrol and other grades of commercial motor spirit." [185]

More than three years later, in November 1937, the future remained relatively optimistic despite a slight drop in production:

"The report of Moturoa Oilfields Ltd…for the year ended August 31 [1937], states that the sales for the year at £2671 show a reduction of £587 compared with the previous year, due to a decrease in the production of the wells….

"It is considered the future prospects of the company are brighter than at any stage of its existence. It is stated that the need for discovering oil in British countries has never been more urgent and, with the big advances that have been made in geological and drilling technique, New Zealand stands a good chance of having its potential oil resources thoroughly explored and developed." [186]

Steady, if modest, oil production at Moturoa continued throughout the war — as reported by the Greymouth Evening Star in April 1946:

"Moturoa Oilfields Ltd drilled four wells on its leases at Moturoa between 1931 and 1934. Three of the wells were producers and except for brief cessations have produced continuously ever since. The refinery at Moturoa in its peak year put through about 130,000 gallons of oil, and for the last two years the figures have been 84,000 and 90,000 gallons." [187]

However, as with previous drilling companies, operations were not profitable enough for the backers of Moturoa Oilfields Limited — as reported by the Wanganui Chronicle on 30 January 1947:

"An offer of purchase of rights of the oil wells, plant, equipment and stores of Moturoa Oilfields Ltd has been accepted by the board of directors, states a circular issued to the shareholders by the board. When the sale is completed there should be enough funds to return to preference shareholders a substantial amount of their share capital, plus accrued dividends. There will, however, not be a return on ordinary shares. During 16 years of its operation about two and a-half million gallons of oil has been taken from three of the four wells belonging to the company at New Plymouth." [188]

Surprisingly, the purchaser was an individual, according to the Otago Daily Times of February 1947:

"Further drilling for oil in the Moturoa field at New Plymouth is likely to be undertaken in the near future, but the intending purchaser of Moturoa Oilfields Ltd and New Zealand Oil Refineries Ltd, Mr F J Dobson of Kaitawa, declines to disclose the locality he has selected in which to put down the first bore…

"He is a deep-well drilling contractor and he has been doing that work for 15 years…The main source of the Moturoa oil supply had not yet been tapped, Mr Dobson said, and all the information available tended to prove that the present producers had a major supply feeding the bores that were in operation." [189]

By October 1947:

"The sale of the rights, oil wells plant, and equipment owned by Moturoa Oilfields Ltd has now been completed according to the directors' annual report to shareholders. The price received was £5250…

"It is regretted that no return of capital to ordinary shareholders is possible. After an ordinary general meeting of shareholders on November 7 an extraordinary meeting will be held to consider a resolution to wind up the company voluntarily." [190]

New Zealand Oil Refineries

While Moturoa Oilfields Limited ceased to exist, the new owner, Frederick John Dobson, assumed control of its oil wells and refinery as New Zealand Oil Refineries Limited, the company previously referred to as having been established in 1931 to refine the oil produced by the defunct Blenheim Oil Well Reclamation Company. [191]

By November 1948, drilling had resumed at Moturoa — as reported by the Bay of Plenty Times:

"Some petroleum gas and small shows of oil were passed through between 1200 ft and 1300 ft in the current drilling at Moturoa, New Plymouth, said the managing director of New Zealand Oil Refineries Ltd, Mr F J Dobson, today." [192]

By March 1949, the refinery had all it could manage:

"Formerly working only two days a week, the company's refinery, said Mr Dobson, was now working at its full capacity of 1000 gallons a day and was unable to cope with all the petroleum now available.

"Although the new bore was producing more than four times as much as the company's other three bores combined, Mr Dobson emphasised that its ultimate rate of flow would not be known until the second month." [193]

Indeed, the flow of oil was so great that expansion was necessary:

"Encouraged by the success of the oil well recently bored at Moturoa, New Plymouth, New Zealand Oil Refineries Ltd plans a new bore in the vicinity of the present well to explore the same field. The managing director of the company, Mr F J Dobson, said today that all plans had been made for the new well. In addition, an extension of the company's refinery was planned to cope with the increasing output from the present well. A contract had also been let for the construction of a 40,000 gallon storage tank." [194]

In the meantime, distribution of the refined product remained a major problem compounded by competition with the major overseas oil companies — as reported by the Ashburton Guardian in October 1949:

"Although motor spirit is rationed in New Zealand [after the Second World War], New Zealand Oil Refineries Ltd is having difficulty in selling the 10,000 gallons of first grade petrol now being refined every month at New Plymouth because of distribution problems.

"Before the Dobson No. 1 well was brought into production the plant at Moturoa was producing 1000 gallons of petrol a month from pumpings from the three old wells under the control of the company, but the output of the new well stepped the figure up to 10,000 gallons a month and this, it is reported, could be increased. Of this quantity, 2000 gallons a month has been sold at the refinery.

"Petrol resellers are licensed and the demand is restricted by the rationing of supplies to the motorist. The refinery itself is licensed to sell, but it is recognised that it alone is not an adequate agency for the sale of all the motor spirit now being refined. A further obstacle to the free offering of Taranaki petrol is the difficulty the refining company has in procuring pumps. It is not easy to make arrangements with established resellers who have pumps leased from importing companies. Sites, tanks, and pumps are all difficult to obtain." [195]

The absurdity of the situation was reported by a number of newspapers, including the Bay of Plenty Beacon in January 1950:

"It is unbelievable that New Zealand produced petrol of excellent quality is unsaleable and may have to be disposed of by burning. Petrol restrictions, which grind down the pleasure of so many motorists, are jibed at by the situation in New Plymouth where the NZ Oil Refineries Ltd are producing 10,000 gallons monthly and could double the quantity, but can sell only 2,000 gallons per month. The company can secure neither bowser nor storage. Whilst we moan for dollars to spend here, dollars could be saved by using the local supply of petrol." [196]

Egmont Oil Wells

The start of 1950 saw some changes with a separation of companies engaged in oil drilling and refining.

On 7 February 1950, the name of New Zealand Oil Refineries Limited was changed to Egmont Oil Wells Limited, a company that had operated since 16 October 1931. [197] Frederick John Dobson remained the company's field manager.

Following the merger, Egmont Oil Wells continued to expand its drilling programme — as reported by the Christchurch Press in January 1953:

"Three more oil bores are to be drilled in the Moturoa area, New Plymouth, by Egmont Oil Wells Ltd, according to an announcement today by the general manager of the company (Mr E J Wright). Mr Wright has just returned from the United States after an extensive oil study tour. Mr Wright said that the start of the new drilling programme now depended entirely on the availability of equipment and piping. When the new bores were sunk, the question of using natural gas from them would, no doubt, be considered. He expressed his confidence that oil would be found." [198]

By 1954, a use for natural gas, previously disregarded as a nuisance, had at been found — as reported by the Christchurch Press in August of that year:

"Natural gas from Egmont Oil Wells Ltd's new well at Bayly road, Moturoa, was drawn off recently for the first time and fed into the New Plymouth domestic supply. The quantity being taken off is not great, and it is not yet known how much is available from the new well. The New Plymouth Gas Company is already using natural gas from other Moturoa wells. The gas company manager, Mr A Blackman, said that, with the recent cold spell, gas consumption had risen and the company was taking off new taps meet the increased demand." [199]

In the meantime, oil exploration continued throughout New Zealand:

"'The year 1955 has seen a further acceleration in the tempo of petroleum exploration in New Zealand, after a period (1944-1954) in which little work was done,' says the district geologist in Christchurch (Mr B W Collins) in an article he has prepared on petroleum exploration in New Zealand in 1955…

"Egmont Oil Wells Ltd holds the only petroleum mining licence, over an area of 10 square miles at New Plymouth, on the west coast of the North Island. Crude oil recovered during 1954 amounted to 239,800 gallons from five wells (278,100 gallons in 1953) and for 1955 (to November 30) to 185,510 gallons…

"At the end of 1955, the total area covered by petroleum prospecting licences in New Zealand was 11,715 square miles, an increase of 3898 square miles on the previous year. Of this area 8901 square miles were in the North Island, and 2814 square miles in the South Island."

"Mr Collins says: 'The not unattractive features of prospective oil lands in this country — thick sedimentary sections, likely source beds, a few oil seepages, and very many gas seepages, and the strong probability of stratigraphic traps of various types on the flanks of the uplifts — will continue to offer chances for the venturesome.'" [200]

By September 1957, oil production reports remained optimistic:

"Egmont Oil Wells Ltd obtained 244,870 gallons of crude oil from the Moturoa field, near New Plymouth, last year [1956], according to the annual report of the Department of Mines. This was an increase of 45,360 gallons, or 23 per cent, on the production in 1955.

"The company's new oil refinery has been almost completed and will be used for refining the crude oil from the four producing wells. The interest in the search for oil in New Zealand has been maintained, according to the report. At present there are 141 petroleum licences, covering an area of 23,012 square miles, in existence.

"Licences are distributed as follows: Canterbury 11; Gisborne, Hawke's Bay and Wairarapa 75; Taranaki 33; Auckland 11; Bay of Plenty 1; Marlborough 2; Otago 1; Southland 2; and Westland 5." [201]

The following year, oil production had slowed but natural gas continued to flow strongly:

"Last year [1957] 205,210 gallons of crude oil were recovered by the Egmont Oil Wells Ltd from its three wells in the Moturoa field, says the annual mines statement tabled in the House of Representatives. This was a decrease of 39,660 gallons from the amount produced in 1956. From the same wells, 6,781,500 cubic feet of natural gas was supplied to the New Plymouth Gas Company for domestic and industrial purposes." [202]

In 1961, Shell BP and Todd Oil Services Limited bought a controlling interest in Egmont Oil Wells Limited and the company was placed into voluntary liquidation as of August 1983. [203]

New Zealand Oil Refineries (1949)

New Zealand Oil Refineries (1949) Limited was formed to manage the refining and selling of the oil produced by Egmont Oil Wells and others with an application "…to resell motor-spirit from one pump to be installed on premises at Paritutu Crescent, Moturoa, New Plymouth" granted as of 11 August 1952. [204]

While initially set up to refine the crude pumped from the ground by Egmont Oil Wells, the company was refining the product of others by 1959 — as reported by the Christchurch Press in September that year:

"About 20,000 gallons of condensate, extracted from the Kapuni No. 1 oil well of Shell-BP-Todd Oil Services Ltd will be refined in New Plymouth by New Zealand Oil Refineries Ltd, Moturoa, New Zealand's only oil refinery." [205]

"All the condensate obtained from the Kapuni No. 1 oil bore would eventually be processed by New Zealand Oil Refineries Ltd at New Plymouth, the chairman of directors of Shell-BP-Todd Oil Services Ltd (Mr J B Price) said in New Plymouth last night. Some of the condensate — it is estimated that about 20,000 gallons was obtained from the bore and transported to New Plymouth — had already been refined by the company." [206]

In 1961, Shell BP and Todd Oil Services Limited bought a controlling interest in Egmont Oil Wells Limited and New Zealand Oil Refineries (1949) Limited. [207]

As of 12 January 1962, the registers of both companies had been transferred from New Plymouth to Wellington. [208]

While ownership of the companies may have changed, prospecting, production, and refining continued at Moturoa and elsewhere during 1970 — as reported by the Christchurch Press in July 1971:

"There were 329 petroleum-prospecting licences covering 53,814 square miles of New Zealand and its territorial sea to the three mile limit at December 31, 1970, according to the annual report of the Mines Department tabled in Parliament on Friday. In addition, 32 licences covered a total of 381,922 square miles of the continental shelf. Three on-shore and seven off-shore wells were drilled during the year.

"Oil production during the year included 66,855 gallons of crude oil from Egmont Oil Wells Ltd at Moturoa, near New Plymouth. In addition to 71,500 gallons of condensate from Kapuni and 20,000 gallons of Kapuni condensate recovered from deballast tanks at Paritutu, the crude oil was fed to the company's refining plant during the year.

"Shell BP and Todd Oil Services Ltd reported 16,175,283 gallons of condensate sold at the Whangarei refinery making a total production of 16,266,783 gallons when the condensate refined at Moturoa is included. Kapuni sold 3766.5 million cubic feet of natural gas having a total thermal value of 1,985,202 million British thermal units, says the report." [209]

The 'Whangarei refinery' referred to was that operated by the New Zealand Refining Company Limited at Marsden Point which began production in May 1964 [210] and quickly made the New Plymouth plant redundant in terms of operational efficiency, capacity, and location.

The announcement by Shell, BP Todd, published by the Christchurch Press in July 1972, therefore came as no surprise:

"The Moturoa oilfield at New Plymouth — the second-oldest in the world — will stop production at the end of this month. As well, its production company, Egmont Oil Wells Ltd, will be wound up. The decision was announced today by Mr D H Tudhope, chairman of the Shell, BP Todd oil consortium, which owns Egmont Oil Wells Ltd.

"The Moturoa field has produced oil and gas since 1931. The first well was drilled in 1865. Mr Tudhope said the exploration and production licence held by Egmont Oil Wells would expire at the end of the month. The consortium would not apply for renewal because rapidly decreasing production has now reached a level that is no longer economic.

"The field now produces about 3000 gallons of crude oil a month, compared with 25,000 gallons a month in 1952, when the field's production was at its peak.

"Mr Tudhope said the consortium had no plans for further development drilling in the district. The production company would be wound up and its assets — the three wells, pumping equipment and the small oil refinery — would be taken over by the marketing company, Taranaki Oil and Gas Ltd. This company still processed some of the Shell, BP, Todd sludge which came from tankers' ballast and from the Paritutu oil tanks." [211]

East Coast Exploration

While Taranaki proved to be the most successful oil producing province in New Zealand, the East Coast of the North Island had shown some promise as early as 1874. However, as per the early days in Taranaki, the lack of serious investment in equipment often meant the abandonment of promising wells.

As well as Gisborne Oil Proprietary Company, previously described as a subsidiary of Taranaki Oil Wells Limited, a number of exploration companies drilled for oil on the East Coast of the North Island:

Kotuku Oil Fields Syndicate

The Kotuku Oil Fields Syndicate Limited, a company incorporated in England, began drilling two wells about 2000 yards apart in the Weber Survey District, about 23 miles from Dannevirke, Southern Hawkes Bay. Known as the Waipatiki oil well, it opened on 29 August 1912. [212]

The New Zealand Gazette records that the Kotuku Oil Fields Syndicate Limited was "…no longer carrying on business in New Zealand as of 12 December 1916." [213]

Certainly, the wells had closed by 1921, apparently with little oil discovered.

Poverty Bay Petroleum and Kerosene Company

"In 1874 the Poverty Bay Petroleum and Kerosene Company commenced operations on land known as the Pakaka-a-Whirikoka block with a driller to supervise the operations of an old-fashioned primitive plant.

"This company failed to locate payable wells, but it was later known that at the site chosen (about 1450 ft. above sea-level) there was, and probably still is, oil in considerable quantities. Indeed, over forty years ago [1890] a spring of oil was struck which yielded from eight to ten gallons a day, and this was obtained without striking the bed rock at all!" [214]

Minerva Petroleum Company

"…the Minerva Petroleum Company…started a well in 1888 on the bank of the Waipaoa river at Mangataikapua, near Whatatutu. This well raised, hopes of ultimate success, but finally it had to be abandoned, principally from mishaps to the bore through bad drilling.

"Where the gas flow was regulated, a continuously burning flame could be obtained over two feet in height from a pipe line sunk to a depth of about 700 feet. At 750 feet a brown shale impregnated with oil was met. Again the small diameter of casing at this depth prevented further sinking, though the prospects were considered highly satisfactory, but the needful capital was not forthcoming." [215]

South Pacific Petroleum Company

As reported by the Auckland Star in April 1880:

"Private advices from Sydney by this day's mail state that a Company with 60,000 shares at £1 each has been formed for working the petroleum springs at Whirekoha block, Poverty Bay. The directors are William Fleming, William Clarke, J Rossiter, G C Ewing, and F McNeil.

"The Company have a lease of a block, 6,054 acres for 36 years in consideration of giving the proprietors 15,000 fully paid-up shares.

The remaining 45,000 have been subscribed principally in Sydney, threepence per share being paid on application. It is anticipated that not more than one shilling per share will be required before oil is procured in paying quantities. It is not intended to enter into any heavy work till the oil is obtained.

"The machinery is already purchased at a fraction of its value. It is proposed to call for tenders to sink a bore with the old machinery, and Mr Clarke is expected here. The first-named directors were here two months ago, and after viewing ground leased it, and undertook the formation of the company, which is now named the South Pacific Petroleum Company." [216]

The quick buying of shares in the new company reflected the optimism of the time that oil riches were only a few feet away:

"A New Zealand telegram was received on the 11th instant by the promoters of the South Pacific Petroleum Company from the agent at Gisborne, New Zealand, the seat of the oil country, stating that 6200 shares had been disposed of.

"Over 15,000 have already been taken up in Sydney, and this encouraging report from New Zealand will give additional confidence to those who purpose to invest.

"The prospectus, which appears in the advertising columns of Sydney papers, fully explains the situation of the oil springs, the extent of the lease, the quality of the oil, and the general prospects of the company." [217]

However, by November 1880, a difference of opinion between the company's Sydney-based Board of Directors and the New Zealand-based Director, William Clarke, occurred — a dispute that resulted in some resentment directed toward the Australian shareholding influence on local decisions — as described by The Poverty Bay Herald:

"…That the local shareholders here will much longer submit to be ruled from Sydney we do not think likely. There are seventy shareholders here to thirty in Sydney. We know that the local shareholders have answered to the calls made upon them, but we do not know so much of the shareholders located in Sydney, and possibly may have our doubts.

"This is a matter which has to be enquired into. But when over twenty thousand shares are sent to Sydney as proxies are ignored, and received with a sort of contempt, it is high time the Poverty Bay shareholders looked to themselves. We have majority in number of shareholders, and we hold an equal number of shares; the workings are in Poverty Bay; the interests of the Bay are affected in many ways. If oil is obtained, it is Poverty Bay and not in Sydney it has been obtained…" [218]

'Looking to themselves' also involved the Maori land owners — as reported by the Ashburton Guardian in December 1880:

"Mr William Clarke, who floated the South Pacific Petroleum Oil Company, is at present negotiating with the natives of the East Coast, and has succeeded in obtaining the consent and signatures of a large number of the native owners to a deed of conveyance of a portion of the Rotokautuku Block to him for oil boring purposes." [219]

A year after the company was formed, a show at last:

"An important discovery of paraffine has been made on the South Pacific Petroleum Company's ground. It is very pure, and will turn out a very high per-centage. Seventy-one feet deep has been obtained with no bottom." [220]

"In 1884 the machinery was moved to a fresh location on the Wairangaromia river. Another bore was sunk, but owing to the primitive nature of the plant and the smallness of the casing the company only reached 1320 feet with a 4½-inch casing.

"It was at this wall in December 1887, that a blow-out of oil took place which burned down the derrick. The burning oil continued to play up and down like a fountain to a height of 24 feet for some days." [221]

By May 1890, the prospects of the South Pacific Petroleum Company were not looking too good:

"Gisborne 31 May 1890 — The local directors of the South Pacific Petroleum Company reported visiting the well, where the pipes are down a hole 1343 feet in depth. The bottom is slatey puna rock, without even the slightest sign or smell of petroleum." [222]

Indeed, as reported by The Poverty Bay Herald in August 1890:

"The following resolutions were passed at the meeting of shareholders of the South Pacific Petroleum Company held at Sydney on July 17th: — That considering the withdrawal of the larger shareholders and the small response made to the last calls, it is not possible for the Company to continue to meet its liabilities, and that it be therefore wound up, subject to the concurrence of the meetings of Gisborne and Christchurch shareholders held this day; that the Directors of the Company be empowered to appoint a liquidator to deal with the Company's estate." [223]

"All the available capital having been disposed of, the shareholders became dissatisfied and the plant was sold to meet liabilities." [224]

Southern Cross Petroleum Company

In December 1880, following his dispute with the Sydney-based Directors of the South Pacific Petroleum Company, William Clarke established a second oil prospecting entity, the Southern Cross Petroleum Company, with a "…capital of 48,000 shares of 20s each." [225]

By January 1881, the usual optimism for a shareholding in oil prospecting companies was shown by The New Zealand Herald:

"This morning's Herald announces with satisfaction that the Southern Cross Petroleum Co is being well subscribed to. The lists may close before advertised time." [226]

Unfortunately, that optimism did not last for long…

"In 1881 the Southern Cross Petroleum Company undertook boring operations in the Rotokautuku block, seventy miles north of Gisborne…Seven wells were drilled ranging from 150 feet to 1820 feet…but none of these wells reached more than a moderate depth on account of faulty drilling. In 1883, another position was selected to the north-east of the previous base of operations, and another feeble attempt was made.

"At about 400 feet a hard band of crystalline rock was encountered lying in a blue grey shale formation, followed by a mud vein at about 180 feet lower, which eventually caused the work in be discontinued.

"Another site was located on a river flat, a mile and three-quarters south west of the original workings, and the depth reached was 1820 feet. Gas was met at 170 feet and sand-stone with gas and oil at 1000 feet and 1200 feet. After reaching 1820 feet, however, the well was abandoned, although the indications were good. The trouble was again want of capital." [227]

The Southern Cross Petroleum Company Limited was wound up and dissolved as of 10 April 1891. [228]

The New Zealand Petroleum Company (1)

Not long after the establishment of the South Pacific Petroleum Company at Poverty Bay, a Christchurch syndicate also sought oil prospecting rights next door — as reported by the New Zealand Mail in December 1883:

"A Poverty Bay paper of a recent date says: — Mr Hooper, having been deputed by a syndicate in Christchurch to come here and inspect the oil deposits on the Waipaoa Block, owned by Muir and Co…a new company will immediately start, and lease 1000 acres from Muir and Co with a right of purchase, capital £60,000, in £1 shares, to be called the New Zealand Petroleum Company, and will be immediately put on the market on Mr Hooper's arrival at Christchurch.

"Fifteen thousand shares will be reserved for Gisborne, and the remainder will be taken up in Christchurch. Machinery will be immediately ordered from America, and it is expected that the works will be in active operation in three months." [229]

Indeed, by March 1884, the Christchurch Press was able to report:

"A number of gentlemen in Christchurch have succeeded in securing the lease of 1000 acres of land adjacent to the South Pacific [Petroleum] Company for the purpose of boring for oil. The surface indications are considered good. The land has been secured on very advantageous terms, and is only eighteen miles from Gisborne. At a meeting held at Mr Hooper's office it was agreed to issue a prospectus of a new company, to be called the New Zealand Petroleum Company." [230]

However, very little else is published as to the success or otherwise of the New Zealand Petroleum Company's efforts to produce oil at Gisborne until January 1899 when the Evening Post advised:

"Tenders are invited in another column for the purchase of the New Zealand Petroleum Company s properties." [231]

Brett's Option & New Zealand Oilfields

"In 1902-03 two bores were drilled at Totangi by an English syndicate [Brett's Option] in which Mr R Brett, of Auckland, was interested. Traces of oil and much gas were met with. During the years 1911-12 a concern with a large capital, the New Zealand Oilfields Ltd began operations at Totangi and Waihirere, but though indications of oil were met with, the concern, chiefly owing to limitations of capital and trouble with drilling, was compelled to cease operations." [232]

Gisborne Oil Company

"In 1909 the Gisborne Oil Company began boring on the Waitangi Hill [Gisborne], on a spot selected by the Geological survey. A light flow of oil equal to three barrels a day was struck at 655 feet. Drilling was continued to 1,478 feet when, principally owing to trouble with the casing, which was not strong enough to withstand the pressure of the caving ground, the bore was stopped.

"When the casing was being withdrawn the oil at 655 feet was again tapped and a flow of 10 barrels a day obtained until, chiefly owing, it is said, to mud blocking the holes in the casing, the flow was reduced to less than three barrels when pumping…and was abandoned." [233]

The New Zealand Petroleum Company (2)

By May 1938, a number of prospecting companies had decided to combine their resources in a search for oil on the East Coast of the North Island — as reported by the Northern Advocate:

"For the purpose of co-ordinating efforts to discover producing oilfields in New Zealand, a company called the New Zealand Petroleum Company Ltd with an initial capital of £250,600, was incorporated at Wellington yesterday [17 May 1938]. It is believed by the participating companies that there are good reasons to be optimistic about the results to be obtained from a well organised and well-directed attempt to find commercial oil as is proposed by the new company.

"The formation of New Zealand Petroleum Ltd is the result of lengthy negotiations which were initiated by Taranaki (New Zealand) Oilfields, No Liability, which is a large shareholder in Moturoa Oilfields Ltd. As a result, two major overseas oil companies agreed to become interested, through their subsidiaries, in the search for oil in New Zealand, in co-operation with certain important Australian mining companies which are large users of oil.

"Commenting on the preparations made by the new Petroleum Company Ltd to commence boring on the East Coast, the Minister of Mines, the Hon. P C Webb, said he personally was gratified that work would soon be put in hand. The search for oil was timely, and if the results reached the expectations of the company, a new industrial and economic era would dawn in the Dominion.

"The Minister also said that the Shell Company had been granted a license to operate over an area of 900 square miles, a little to the south of Napier. Other licenses would be granted during the next few weeks." [234]

"The New Zealand Petroleum Company Ltd has been granted four licenses for prospecting for oil covering 10 different areas [in the Gisborne District]. The interests behind the company are Taranaki (NZ) Oilfields, Gisborne (NZ) Oilfields Ltd, Waitanga (NZ) Oilfields Ltd, Waiapu (NZ) Oilfields Ltd, Moturoa Oilfields Ltd, the Vacuum Oil Company Proprietary Ltd, and Oil Search Ltd." [235]

However, despite the vast prospecting area available and the extensive drilling experience of its shareholders, the first well drilled by the New Zealand Petroleum Company Limited in 1938 proved unsuccessful:

"…commenced drilling at the Totangi Dome, about 20 miles inland from Gisborne. The well was drilled to 5700 feet without striking oil, and subsequently seven other wells were put down, ranging in depth from 1173 feet to 10,925 feet…" [236]

Indeed, that lack of success was to last for the next six years with the result that:

"The search for petroleum in New Zealand has now been abandoned by the New Zealand Petroleum Company Ltd after extensive operations extending over the past six years and the expenditure of nearly £1,000,000.

"Eight major and over 100 smaller bores were put down, and among the large bores were two which are the deepest yet drilled in the Southern hemisphere. The history of the investigations was outlined yesterday in a statement by Mr Wesley Ince of Melbourne, a director of the company.

"'It is with deep regret that the directors and management acknowledge that their hopes have not been realised, and that the results obtained do not justify further exploration,' said Mr Ince in his statement…

"The exploration work had been both extensive and exhaustive, involving comprehensive geological, gravity, and seismograph in both islands. After reaching basement rock at a depth of 6942 feet in Notown No. 1 bore, the exhaustive programme undertaken by the company had now been brought to a close.

"The exploration campaign had cost nearly £1,000,000, the whole of which had been provided by the company without financial help from any outside source. New Zealand Petroleum Co Ltd was financed solely by its three shareholding companies — Vacuum Oil Co Pty Ltd, California-Texas Investments Ltd, and Shale Oil Investigations Pty Ltd. The last-named company represented the Australian Metal Group's interest…

"At all times those associated with the formation of the company had been influenced by the economic and commercial advantages which would have been enjoyed by the Dominion and Australia had a nearer source of payable oil been discovered. Hope in attaining this desired goal and optimism and courage had stimulated and sustained a lively interest on the part of all those engaged in the company's activities." [237]

On 16 July 1951, the New Zealand Petroleum Company Limited was placed in voluntary liquidation. [238]

South Island

Just as it had in the province of Taranaki, oil and gas had seeped to the surface of a number of South Island districts for as long as could be remembered. It was only a matter of time, then, before drilling of those South Island prospects began. One of the first areas to be explored was Kotuku, about 35 km inland from Greymouth in Westland, and also Murchison, about 125 km south-west of Nelson in the Tasman District.

West Coast
Kotuku Oil Springs Association

Kotuku is described as a 'farming locality' situated about 35 kilometres south-east of Greymouth at the northern end of Lake Brunner. One of the first reports of an oil discovery at Kotuku was first published by the Grey River Argus in October 1900:

"It is now about three years since no little interest was created by the discovery of petroleum oozing out of the sandstone rock some half a mile distant from the railway station at Kotuku…A lease of a section of the oil country was applied for in due course but as the land was part of the Midland railway reserve in that neighborhood, no rights to take up the ground and prospect for the oil in a proper manner could be granted by the Government, though the prospecting rights of the discoverers, as prior applicants, were protected from being invaded by anyone else.

"Now, however, that the Midland Company have been declared to have forfeited all rights to the reserves, the land is open for selection for prospecting or settlement purposes. Consequently arrangements are being made to form a large company to first of all prospect the area applied for by the discoverers — that is one square mile…

"The work of floating the company has been entrusted to Mr Edmund Wickes, who has had some experience in boring for oil, as he was one of the principal shareholders in the Southern Cross Company, who prospected a considerable area of land in the Gisborne district…

"A receptacle has been cut out of the rock in which to catch and hold the oil as it exudes out of the soft sandstone. The oil is a splendid sample…" [239]

A prospectus for the Kotuku Oil Springs Association Limited, with a capital of £5000, was eventually published in October 1901:

"This Association is promoted for the purpose of acquiring two Mineral Licenses containing 570 acres, more or less, and to exploit the same by boring operations…There is ample evidence that oil exists in the vicinity, for in several places on the property it is exuding freely. Should the Association be successful in starting a flow, the profits to the founders will be incalculable." [240]

The Kotuku Oil Springs Association Limited did not have the whole area to itself, however:

"The information that all, or nearly all, the available land in the neighborhood of the oil springs, near Kotuku, has been pegged off on behalf of outside syndicates will come as a surprise to folk in this district.

"Yet such is the fact. Rumours have been afloat for the last week that a good deal of pegging out prospecting leases had been going on, and on enquiry it was found that a surveyor and assistants had been engaged in pegging off all the ground in the vicinity not already applied for. It appears that this move is mainly on behalf of an Auckland syndicate or two. For miles all around the prospectors' area and leases already taken up locally, the land has been pegged out for miles." [241]

By 1903, the Kotuku Oil Springs Association had started drilling but soon found that the process was not to be easy — as reported by the Grey River Argus in October of that year:

"Some little time ago the directors of the Kotuku Oil Syndicate sent to Australia for a tool called a rimer to enable them to continue their boring operations as work was brought to a standstill for the want of some such appliance. They found that after boring a certain distance they could not get the pipes down any further. They now find that a rimer is not to be obtained in Australia, and will have to send to the United States for one." [242]

There was some delay before the new tool arrived at the drilling site but, even then, it was tough going and some financial assistance was sought by August 1906:

"The Kotuku Oil Prospecting Association, which has put down four bores and intends putting down two or three more bores on its holding near Lake Brunner, applied to the Government for assistance towards prosecuting its search for petroleum. The association has been informed that after carefully considering the application the Minister of Mines regrets he cannot see his way to accede to the request for assistance." [243]

However, "…little came of the bores put down…" [244]

Kotuku Oil and Goldfields Company

Some 26 years after the attempts by the Kotuku Oil Prospecting Association, the promise of an oil find at Kotuku remained — as reported by the Grey River Argus in November 1932:

"The registration is announced of a new company, Kotuku Oil and Goldfields Ltd, with a capital of £25,000 divided into 25,000 shares of £1. The subscribers are A S Johnson, H J Page, G. Barltrop, H J Flatt, W G Frost, D E P Bradley, one share each. The objects of the company are to purchase from the Kotuku Oil Syndicate, mineral prospecting warrant granted over 1000 acres in Block II Brunner Survey District, and plant and machinery on the property. Also an option held by the syndicate's secretary (Mr H Milner) in respect of a special alluvial claim over 100 acres Block II Brunner S D, and plant and machinery suitable for oil well drilling, mining for oil, gold, silver and other ore, metal, mineral and incidental." [245]

"The Kotuku Oil and Gold Fields Ltd propose to recondition the existing bores on the property which, it is expected, will result in the yield of a considerable quantity of oil per day…" [246]

As usual, that was not to be and, by June 1934, the company was struggling to pay its debts culminating in the advertisement published by the Evening Post on 13 June 1934:

"Kotuku Oil And Goldfields Co Limited — Tenders are invited ,and will be received up to noon on the 2nd day of July, 1934, for the Purchase of the Plant, Equipment, Stock, and Mining Rights of the Kotuku Oil and Goldfields Co Limited. Schedule of equipment and full particulars, together with authority to inspect plant and property, may be obtained upon application to the undersigned…P S Boyes, Public Accountant, Receiver for Debenture-holders…" [247]

That month, the Greymouth Evening Star lamented the situation:

"The Kotuku Oil and Goldfields, which began with such a flourish, does not appear to be coming up to expectations. For some time an air of silent gloom has hung over the deserted derrick, and the work which was expected to absorb the unemployed, seems as far off as ever." [248]

As of 17 September 1934, Kotuku Oil and Goldfields Company Limited was placed in voluntary liquidation. [249]

The Maoriland Oil Fields

Maoriland Oil Fields Limited was registered as a private company at Nelson on 20 July 1934 with a capital of £1800. "Subscribers: Nelson—J Baird, B Trathen, Ada J Baird, G M Trathen, R V Trathen. Objects: To search for mineral oil and incidental." [250]

As reported by the Hokitika Guardian in July 1936:

"The Maoriland Oil [Fields] Company Ltd has taken over the Kotuku Oil and Goldfields Company's plant and property at Kotuku. An extensive exploration of the possibilities of the area is being carried out by the Brown Boring Company and excellent progress has been made; the first bore put down to a depth of 75 feet, producing approximately a barrel of oil a week.

"A number of scout bores are being put down to make a thorough test of the first oil horizon, and to see if a number of such bores will produce oil in sufficient quantities to make them a payable proposition, in the meantime. When the area has been thoroughly tested by scout bores, the best site will be chosen and the bores put down to a greater depth." [251]

However, despite the usual initial optimism, the Auckland Star reported in May 1938:

"According to official records mining and prospecting warrants formerly held in the vicinity by Kotuku Oil and Goldfields Limited (in liquidation) [and] Maoriland Oil Fields, Limited…no drilling has been done or oil production carried out. In 1935, 312 gallons of oil were collected from seepages and a much larger quantity must have been lost in the process. In 1936, 2188 gallons were collected from five shallow boreholes." [252]

Kotuku Oil Syndicate

Reefton is a small town on the west coast of the South Island, about 80 miles north-east of Greymouth.

"When 81 years of quartz mining at Reefton came to an end in 1951 the Reefton gold field had produced more than two million ounces of gold." However, between about 1882 and 1895, gold production experienced a slump until rejuvenated by a mining investor from South Africa, David Ziman, and his company, Consolidated Gold Fields of New Zealand Limited. [253]

He was also involved in other projects on the West Coast:

"…in 1909…David Ziman attracted the prestigious Royal Dutch Shell Company as the main investor in his oil venture spin-off, Kotuku Oil Syndicate Limited…[but] despite early promise and tantalising oil shows, the holes drilled by the Syndicate were unsuccessful." [254]

Kotuku District Overview

An overview of the oil exploration that had taken place in the Kotuku District was published by the Christchurch Press in February 1975, parts of which included:

"There are local tales of the exudations being used to grease machinery, and even to run a tractor. But all efforts to find payable quantities of oil in the area have failed, in spite of wells drilled to more than 5400 ft.

The first oil seepage at Kotuku was reported in 1897 by a Scandinavian, Nils Mortenson, in what became known as Petroleum Creek. The Kotuku Consolidated Oil Company drilled first in 1902, striking traces of oil and gas at 167 ft, and the Lake Brunner Oil Company had similar results in 11 wells drilled between 1902 and 1908.

In 1908 and 1909 the Kotuku Oil Association drilled six wells, the deepest being 448 ft but again only traces of oil and gas came to light. In 1911, the London-based Kotuku Oilfields Syndicate started drilling with similar results. In conjunction with Waipatiki Oil-Wells Ltd, the company drilled until about 1915, then again in 1921, going as deep as 3000 ft.

"Most of the company's bores were near Molloy Creek, beside the midland railway line, and at one site it reported obtaining 80 gallons of oil in 12 hours.

"As late as 1937, a contractor in the area was known to pump a 44-gallon drum of oil a day off the surface of a pond nearby. Traces of oil and gas, occasional gas 'blows', salt water — or nothing at all — were the only results recorded by the Kotuku Deep Creek Oil Syndicate (1915-; 1918), the Kotuku Petroleum Prospecting Company Ltd (1921-1923), Kotuku Oil and Goldfields, Ltd (1934), and the Superior Oil Company of New Zealand Ltd (1942 and 1943). The deepest of the Superior company's wells reached, about 5400 ft." [255]

The Superior Oil Company of New Zealand Limited (incorporated in California) was placed into voluntary liquidation as of 30 August 1946. [256]

Tasman District
The Murchison Oil Company

First there was the Murchison Oil Syndicate — as reported by The New Zealand Herald in December 1924:

"Advice has been received that applications for prospecting warrants made on behalf of the Murchison Oil Syndicate were granted by the warden at Murchison yesterday. Including rights already obtained by negotiation with private landowners, the syndicate has secured the exclusive right to bore for oil over areas in Murchison County aggregating 21,539 acres. It has expert advice that the prospects of obtaining petroleum in commercial quantities are exceptionally favourable." [257]

The syndicate soon became the Murchison Oil Company Limited, registered at Auckland in 1925 with a "…nominal capital of £30,000, in 30,000 shares of £1 each, of which 14,100 shares were offered to the public. The objects of the company were to take over from the vendors, the Murchison Oil Syndicate, a property of 21988 acres in the Tutaki, Matiri, Maruia, and Hope areas of the Nelson Provincial District…" [258]

The prospectus of the new company, published in June 1925, announced:

"…the Murchison Oil Company Ltd…has been formed to prove the commercial value of petroliferous areas near Murchison, Nelson Province. Prospecting and boring rights have been secured by the vendor syndicate over areas totalling 21,988 acres, and it is proposed to sink two or three test bores at sites selected by expert advisers. The present offer to the public is limited to 14,100 shares. Provisional arrangements have been made for the purchase of boring plant and the engagement of an experienced driller with a view to the commencement of active operations in the field immediately the company proceeds to allotment." [259]

The company's Directors were named as:

"Herbert James Duncan Robertson, Produce Broker, Auckland; John Bassett, Retired Mining Engineer, Hokitika; Edwin James Vallentine, Mining Engineer, Auckland; Rupert Alexander Maxwell Colyer, Company Manager, Auckland; and Harry Tinsley Goldie, Timber Merchant, Auckland.

"The Incorporation of this Company represents a serious and genuine effort by New Zealanders to find Oil in Commercial Quantities in their own Country." [260]

Preparations for the search for oil were underway by November 1925:

"Thirty tons of boring plant for the Murchison Oil Company were landed from the Opihi on Wednesday, and was sent on by rail to Glenhope. it is said that a considerable amount of the capital invested in the enterprise has been subscribed in the Nelson district." [261]

By the end of 1925, optimism of early success remained strong:

"The statutory meeting of the Murchison Oil Company was held yesterday. There was a good attendance of shareholders…The secretary reported that the drilling plant and other material had been delivered to the site selected for the first bore, and the head driller would arrive within a week, everything being in readiness for the commencement of active operations. Mr J Spencer, the company's consulting geologist, briefly discussed the company's prospects, expressing his complete confidence that the enterprise would prove the existence of a valuable oilfield." [262]

Drilling plant was also acquired from abandoned wells — as reported by the Greymouth Evening Star in April 1926:

"The Murchison Oil Coy which is commencing boring operations on an extensive scale, has purchased the plant of the Kotuku Oil Coy [at Greymouth]. At present, the plant is being transported to Murchison, and is expected to be ready for use shortly." [263]

Drilling progress was reported later that year, in August 1926:

"The latest report from the Murchison Oil Company's bore at Murchison is as follows:—The bore is down one thousand feet in sandstone and mudstone. The hole is standing up well. Work is being shut down to repair a drilling stem." [264]

A year later, in July 1927, the search for oil in the valley of the Mangles River continued:

"The Murchison Company reported on 8th July last [1927] that its bore had been drilled 2355 ft, and supplies of gas and oil had been received and submitted for analysis. The oil was a light brown colour, almost transparent, burning like benzine and leaving very little residue. The Murchison Company began boring on 29th March 1926 in the valley of the Mangles River, and has continued to do so without intermission." [265]

Although the company's annual report showed that a great deal of its working capital had been spent, the outlook remained optimistic:

"The annual report of the Murchison Oil Co for the year ended August 31 [1927] states that during the year the bore has been continued from 1494 ft to 3340 ft, and at various depths shows of gas and oil have occurred, proving that the company is operating in petroleum bearing strata. The latter at present consist of mudstone and sandstone of varying thicknesses. The presence of oil is evident in the balings. The indications are very promising, and it is hoped the drill will soon reveal the beds of porous sandstone which should prove to contain oil in quantity.

"The report states that, additional capital having been raised for the purpose, the directors purchased 3200 ft of 5-inch casing which has been delivered at the bore. A new drilling cable will arrive about the middle of November.

"The balance-sheet shows that capital to the amount of £14,737 has been paid up in cash. Plant, tools, and building have absorbed £7085; the cost of the bore has been £3744; general development amounts to £2663; deposits and other expenses, £753." [266]

Inevitably, without additional finance, the drilling had to end — as reported by the Nelson Evening Mail on 10 August 1928:

"The Murchison Oil Company has ceased operations owing to sufficient finance not being available to permit of continuance. An extraordinary meeting of shareholders is to be held at Auckland on 20th August to consider a proposal to go into voluntary liquidation to wind up the affairs of the company. The staff has been off the pay-roll since 7th August." [267]

But not quite yet:

"At an extraordinary general meeting of the Murchison Oil Company held at Auckland a resolution that the company go into voluntary liquidation was unanimously defeated. Subsequent to the meeting being called advice was received that a gas blow had been discovered on the company's area in the Blackwater Valley about 41 miles from the present bore, and it is considered to be an extremely favourable indication of the existence on the company's areas of petroleum-bearing strata.

"In the opinion of those present at the meeting the company's interests would not be adversely affected by delaying a decision as to future operations or otherwise until the annual meeting at the end of September.

"A tentative scheme for the reorganisation of the company has been suggested. A number of shareholders indicated their willingness to subscribe further sums to prosecute the search for oil provided sufficient capital was forthcoming to ensure that the job would be done thoroughly. The directors are now enquiring into the possibilities of the suggested scheme for reorganisation." [268]

By October 1928, drilling was resumed but then paused, waiting for more equipment:

"The Murchison Oil Co continued the sinking of its well at the Mangles River but was delayed a good deal waiting for casing, etc. For the year the bore was carried down a further 1,698 ft making a total depth of 3,461 ft. At about 2,300 ft gas came in freely, and from that depth down particles of white filtered oil were visible. On one occasion about 2 quarts of this was collected...

"Some of the gas from the well was tested at Canterbury College and is said to have shown helium. The white oil, analysed by Mr A J Parker F.C.S., of Auckland, gave 64.5 per cent motor spirit, 32 per cent kerosene, and 3.5 per cent heavy oil." [269]

Nevertheless, the obtaining of Murchison Oil Company's much needed investment capital remained an elusive hope — as reported by the Nelson Evening Mail in November 1930:

"Since the last annual meeting the directors have been actively engaged raising further capital to meet the Company's liabilities and consolidate the position pending a reconstruction. In February last our mineral prospecting warrants were due to expire, and Mr B Bassett made a trip through Nelson and Murchison explaining the position to shareholders and obtained substantial financial support. An appeal was also made to other shareholders by letter and altogether £1378 was subscribed. Application was then made for a renewal of our leases and the final grant has now been obtained, thus giving the Company rights for a further five years, subject to payment of rentals…

"In March the directors were invited to place a definite proposition before one of the leading English oil companies and full data, maps and proposals were sent to England. After a good deal of delay and several cables had been sent, advice was received from the English company mentioned that after full examination of our maps, reports, etc., their geologists were of the opinion that the area of the sedimentary rocks was too small to justify their interest…

"…since then, both in Australia and Canada, financial brokers have been approached. Unfortunately, considerable depression exists in both countries and the parties approached consider the present time quite unfavourable for raising further capital for any speculative enterprise…

"The directors take this opportunity of again proclaiming their unshakeable faith in the existence of a payable oil-field within the confines of the Company's holdings at Murchison." [270]

Another year, at the height of the Depression, and the financial outlook looked bleak while optimism for an oil strike remained strong:

"The annual report of the Murchison Oil Company for the year ended August 31st [1931] records further efforts by the directors to engage the interest of overseas concerns in the company's property but without positive results owing to the unfavourable world conditions. Though the directors can only show negative results to date, says the report, their faith in the prospects at Murchison is unshaken, and several other parties are at present being approached. A new lease of the Blackwater Valley area for five years has been obtained and sufficient funds are in hand to carry on other leases until the end of next year." [271]

By August 1932, the end was in sight for the Murchison Oil Company — as reported by the Auckland Star in November 1932:

"The annual report of the Murchison Oil Company Limited, for the year ended August 31 [1932], states that unceasing efforts to raise fresh capital have so far been unsuccessful. Proposals have been submitted to likely groups in Japan, America, England and Australia, but, although the overtures were in the main favourably received and commented upon, present world conditions stood in the way of completing arrangements. The directors state that fresh capital raised from the shareholders two years ago had been almost exhausted and the funds in hand amounted to only £42. The company's plant was unencumbered and other assets included £325 on deposit with the Government." [272]

Very little drilling activity seems to have occurred after 1932 and the end had come by December 1939:

"The annual report of the directors of the Murchison Oil Company Ltd to be presented at a general meeting of shareholders in Auckland this week is as follows:

"At the last annual meeting held in 1937, none being held last year, the shareholders present were strongly against liquidation until Mr J A Spencer had been given an opportunity of securing financial support overseas. Negotiations were carried on for several months without success.

"An agreement was then entered into with Mr C E Clarke, solicitor of Auckland, empowering him to offer the whole of the company's undertaking for sale on the best terms he could arrange. This agreement will expire towards the end of January 1940 and to date no success has been achieved.

"The company's prospecting warrant over 1,000 acres in the Blackwater Valley lapsed in consequence of new legislation during the past year, with the result that we have now no lease to offer any prospective purchaser, but merely an understanding with the Mines Department that the company shall have the prior right to a new lease, if and when £1,000 deposit is lodged and satisfactory evidence of sufficient capital to undertake active work is forthcoming.

"The directors, who are not prepared to assume further personal liability for expenses, see little chance of carrying on the company after the end of January and liquidation will be the only course open. In view of the fact that the only saleable asset, plant, is now obsolete and has had no maintenance, owing to lack of funds, for some years, the directors do not anticipate that shareholders will receive any return of capital on realisation." [273]

Exploration at Murchison Continues

While the Murchison Oil Company drillers had run out of money, there was no shortage of prospectors to take its place. In March 1929, oil was found while drilling for gold:

"Mr G Black, member for Motueka…has received the following wire from Mr John Spencer, field geologist: 'My drillers, engaged in boring for gold, passed through a black shale capping releasing a large quantity of rich oil. The location of the bore is near Warwick Junction…Warwick Junction is about fifteen miles from Murchison." [274]

"Mr John A Spencer, field geologist who made the recent oil strike at Murchison reports that the casing is now plugged but oil and gas are freely emanating from outside the casing. A syndicate composed of Auckland business men have filed applications for 1000 acres under the title of the Warwick River Oil Syndicate.

"Another syndicate of Australian businessmen have applied for a further 1000 acres in the name of J D Prophet, Civil Engineer, Sydney, the title of this syndicate being the Green Valley Oil Syndicate, Sydney. A further application has been filed on behalf of a Sydney syndicate for another 1000 acres. Mr Spencer has received instructions to make a comprehensive oil survey over the above areas and will commence operations immediately." [275]

Hackathorn Oil New Zealand

Some 40 years later, in 1968, American interests also became involved in the search for oil in the Murchison District:

"In spite of the wide publicity on the natural gas and oil indications in the Blackwell No. 1 well near Murchison, the potential of this area as an oil field will not be known for at least six months. Although the No. 1 well has apparently satisfied the American-owned Australian Oil Corporation, which is working in the area on a 'farm-out' basis with the holder of the prospecting licence, no further assessment can be made until the No. 2 well is drilled.

"The prospecting licence which covers the Blackwell field is held by an American company, Hackathorn Oil New Zealand Ltd, which holds other licences in the Murchison area and has done so for some years…

"Farming Out — The 'farm-out' arrangement with A.O.C. [Australian Oil Corporation] means that this company does the exploration work for the holder of the licence. It does not involve the assignment of title from the licence-holder or any interest in the licence which cannot be done without the approval of the Minister of Mines.

"A.O.C…has a paid-up capital of $US2,570,000 and has interests in Canada, Australia and the northern United States. The Hackathorne Company…has world-wide interests in oil exploration…" [276]

Those 'world-wide interests' attributed to Hackathorn also included the North Island where the company had been granted licences in September 1960 — according to the Christchurch Press:

"American oil-drillers are preparing a major oil search in the middle of the North Island. Ten licences, granting exclusive petroleum prospecting rights over 1872 square miles, have been granted by the Minister of Mines (Mr Hackett) to Hackathorn (New Zealand) Oil Ltd, a company incorporated in Wilmington, Delaware, on May 24.

"This company is backed by a larger oil-prospecting corporation, Kamon Petroleum Exploration, Ltd., of Cisco, Texas. The area to be prospected ranges from Shannon in the south to Turakina in the north, and reaches up the middle of the island almost to Waiouru. The licences also cover off-shore drilling rights over 115 miles of seabed up to the three-mile limit on the western coast.

"This is neither the first time an American oil firm has drilled in New Zealand, nor the first time the middle of the North Island has been tried. Between 1940 and 1944 the Superior Oil Company of California sank a 6837 ft well at Marton and a 3395 ft well at nearby Mount Stewart. Both were dry." [277]

New Zealand Petroleum Exploration

Another American-owned but New Zealand-registered company, New Zealand Petroleum Exploration Limited eventually concentrated its oil exploration efforts at Murchison. But first, the company explored the Waikato in 1962, and then Southland.

"A group of Texan 'wildcat' oil drillers plan to mount a big search for oil in the Waikato, in Southland, on the West Coast and along the East Coast of the South Island.

"Mr T Alexander of Dallas said today that he and associates were seeking registration of a company to be called New Zealand Petroleum Exploration Ltd with a nominal capital of £1 million. Mr A F Downer, a Wellington civil engineer and contractor, is believed to be associated with the enterprise.

"Mr Alexander said New Zealand investors would have the opportunity to hold half the shares in the company. Wellington stockbrokers were preparing an issue of 5s shares.

"Exclusive petroleum prospecting rights had been granted over about 1.75 million acres of land south of Auckland, about one million acres in Southland and about 1.4 million acres on the West Coast.

"The search would probably start in the Hamilton basin, which was regarded as promising territory…" [278]

Indeed, a prospectus was issued by the company in February 1962 offering 800,000 shares to New Zealand investors stating the objects of the enterprise as:

"To explore for oil and gas in areas totalling approximately 2765 square miles in North and South Auckland Land Districts, 2125 square miles in South Westland and 365 square miles in Canterbury, Otago and Southland. Prospects will be drilled by contract arrangements with overseas oil companies. Preliminary surveys indicate the possibility of likely oil structures within the concession areas." [279]

Despite the company's optimism, no oil finds could be reported by July 1964:

"The three oil wells drilled in the Hamilton area by New Zealand Petroleum Exploration Company Ltd cost about £107,150 say the directors in their annual report. No indication of oil or gas was found in any of the bores, the report says. The company considered the area had been properly tested…

"Discussing other prospective search areas, the directors say that two basins in Southland appeared encouraging and negotiations had begun with major oil companies for drilling the areas. Seismic surveys in Southland had cost about £170,000 so far. Gravity surveys only have been made in Westland and seismic work had been delayed pending further geological studies. No further work had been done in the company's areas on the east coast, South Island because it was felt they must be subordinate to the larger areas meanwhile." [280]

Unfortunately, the company's fortunes were not much better in Southland — as reported by the Christchurch Press on 2 February 1965:

"New Zealand Petroleum Exploration Company's Gap road, Winton, oil drilling site has had to be abandoned before testing of a possible oil bearing zone could be completed…

"Unfortunately, the tubing failed as the test tool was being lowered allowing the equipment and 800 ft of tail pipe to fall to the bottom of the hole…

"As a result, further testing at this site is considered to be impracticable and in the meantime the hole has been abandoned…The accident has come as quite a set back to the company. A statement issued by the company on January 11 led to speculation on the possibility of oil deposits being found at the site." [281]

Unlike exclusively-owned, New Zealand oil exploration companies which struggled to finance their drilling, the New Zealand Petroleum Exploration Company was able to call on their American associates for support — as they had to by October 1967:

"Recently Triton Oil and Gas Corp, Dallas, obtained a substantial interest in the company by purchasing both ordinary and vendors' shares from some shareholders and directors resident in Dallas, the consideration being an exchange of shares…

"In order to enable the company to meet its current administrative expenses, shareholders from Dallas, Texas, including the US directors of the company, advanced to the company $2562. Since balance date further moneys have been advanced to the company for the same purpose by Triton Oil and Gas Corp." [282]

By May 1968, the company had set its sights on the Murchison District:

"New Zealand Petroleum Exploration Company Ltd owns a 25 per cent interest in the Blackwater No. 1 well near Murchison and the 120,000 acres round the well, according to the International Energy Company Ltd of Texas, which has a 50 per cent interest in the well and 120,000 acres. As well, New Zealand Petroleum is believed to have an option of another quarter interest in the No. 2 well planned, and the 120,000 acres round it.

"The remaining 25 per cent interest in the No. 1 well and surrounding land is held by private investors. International Energy which operates in New Zealand under the Australian Oil Corporation, NZ Petroleum and the private Investors have a 'farm-out' agreement with the holder of the oil prospecting lease for the area, Hackathorn Oil New Zealand Ltd of the United States." [283]

Triton Oil and Gas also supported the Murchison venture — as reported by the Christchurch Press in May 1968:

"The Triton Oil and Gas Corporation, Dallas, which has about a third interest in N.Z. Petroleum, has made an unsecured loan of $US10,000 to the company to meet its cash commitment in the terms of the agreement." [284]

The search for oil at Murchison yielded little results as did the company's drilling in Canterbury — as reported by the Christchurch Press in October 1969:

"The search for oil in Canterbury ended at the week-end when the New Zealand Petroleum Exploration Company abandoned its bore at Newlands, near Ashburton, after striking hard rock strata more than a mile below the surface. The company is awaiting instructions from the United States before shifting the drilling rig to Kaikohe, North Auckland.

"In the last two months the exploration company has drilled two bores for oil in Canterbury under a farm-out contract to the BP-Shell-Todd consortium, which has an oil prospecting licence over an extensive area of the province…The bore cost about $130,000 to put down, averaging about $5500 a day." [285]

Little wonder then that, by February 1971, losses had been incurred:

"New Zealand Petroleum Exploration Company, Ltd, incurred a loss of $209,167 in the year to February 28 [1971], compared with $51,971 the year before." [286]

Nevertheless, after some years of inactivity, the New Zealand Petroleum Exploration Company was still ready to participate in further exploration opportunities — as reported by the Christchurch Press in January 1980:

"New Zealand Petroleum, a local exploration company, is trying to complete arrangements for a drilling venture off the West Coast along the lines of the recent oil-search agreement between Shell-BP-Todd and Petrocorp Exploration. New Zealand Petroleum, with the financial backing of some big United States oil explorers, would like to tap a structure south of Greymouth.

"This year presents a good opportunity as a deep-sea rig is being brought to New Zealand by Shell-BP-Todd for its three-well search off North Taranaki. But the company's American partners have yet to give their approval to the West Coast project and accept the Government's new oil exploration terms…Triton Oil, of Dallas, Texas, New Zealand Petroleum's principal shareholder, would be involved…

"New Zealand Petroleum last drilled for oil on the West Coast at Waiho Beach in 1972. Before then, the company drilled extensively around New Zealand in such areas as Northland, Southland, Canterbury and Waikato. It has blamed its eight-year lull in activity on 'unsatisfactory' Government exploration policies." [287]

The American response to the new venture was favourable, as the Christchurch Press reported in August 1980:

"'We like the look of this area [Westland] very much,' the spokesman (Mr Jake Goodson) told NZPA in a telephone interview from Dallas. He said that Triton — which had drilled a number of dry holes on shore in New Zealand before pulling out — had agreed to resume exploration after Government changes in the tax laws relating to oil ventures by overseas companies.

"'We couldn't live with the tax position as it was,' he said. 'The Government made it uneconomic for us to be there. Things now look very much better.'" [288]

Triton Oil NZ

Triton Oil NZ Limited was registered in New Zealand as a subsidiary of the American company, Triton Energy Corporation, on 3 July 1968. [289] As of 30 September 1984, Triton Oil NZ Limited had in turn become a subsidiary of New Zealand Petroleum Exploration Limited. [290]

By June 1989, New Zealand Petroleum Exploration was 63 per cent owned by Triton Energy Corporation [of Dallas] and 7 per cent by Petrocorp Exploration. [291]

Although somewhat discouraged by Government fees and taxes, the drilling of prospective wells, in conjunction with various partners, continued — as did losses — reported the Christchurch Press in October 1989:

"Increased exploration expenses saw working capital drop by $2.3M to $266,522 between May 31 and August 31 [1989]…And interest income would be significantly lower this financial year because of the need to realise short-term deposits and government stock. The directors were concerned that the proposed tax of petroleum explorers would see less interest in exploration investment development in New Zealand." [292]

As a result, overseas investment proved far more attractive:

"NZ Petroleum's subsidiary, Triton Oil, bought a 6 per cent interest in the Enim oil project in Indonesia during the year, and…production there had increased to 1600 barrels a day with 16,000 barrels expected in two or three years." [293]

Bounty Oil

In the meantime the search for oil at Murchison was also continued by another Australian concern in 1969 — as reported by the Christchurch Press in August of that year:

"A New South Wales company, Bounty Oil Ltd, is to drill an 8000 ft exploration well in a 120,000-acre area which includes the site of the Blackwater No. 1 well near Murchison, where traces of both gas and oil were found last year.

"The Minister of Mines (Mr Shand) announced today that he had approved an agreement allowing Bounty Oil to acquire a 57½ per cent working interest in the Nelson land district block, where petroleum prospecting licences are held by Hackathorn (New Zealand) Oil Ltd." [294]

Not satisfied with the prospects at Murchison, in 1970, Bounty Oil expanded its interests to include other parts of New Zealand as well:

"Bounty Oil Ltd has placed 30 million of its 10¢ shares with an institution to raise $4.2m to increase its oil and gas prospecting areas in New Zealand. It has acquired the leases from International Energy Company and Hackathorn Oil New Zealand — a group with which Bounty has previously arranged a farm-in deal. The leases, of about 3.2m acres, include substantial properties in the Taranaki, Wanganui and Canterbury basins. The vendors retain a 1¼ per cent interest in the areas…

"The chairman of Bounty (Mr J O Bovill) says that it was decided to purchase the leases because of the potential of the area indicated by recent discoveries. Bounty has already started a substantial seismic programme in the Taranaki-Wanganui basin, estimated to cost $US700,000 and it is expected a strong drilling programme will be undertaken shortly on targets indicated by the survey." [295]

But an oil find at Murchison proved elusive — as reported by the Christchurch Press in October 1970:

"The Bounty oil-drillers are moving out. The big rig which has been a feature of the Murchison district over the last five months, is being dismantled. Hopes that it would be used again immediately to drill another exploratory well in the district have been dashed — but most Murchison residents expect to see the drilling crew and its American executives again.

"…the general opinion among the Murchison business community tends to the view that another well will be sunk in the district some time. They believe that the results of Bounty No. 1, although far from conclusive, are too encouraging to be ignored by an oil-exploration company. Certainly, the drilling did not reach bedrock — estimated about 10,500 ft— beyond which there would be no hope of an oil strike.

"The rig was plagued with troubles over the last few weeks as the drillers struggled with problems presented by extremely hard rock at a depth close to two miles…The well did produce several shows of oil and one pocket of gas under high pressure." [296]

By June 1971, there seemed little chance that Bounty Oil would resume oil exploration in New Zealand:

"Bounty Oil Ltd of Sydney still has no definite plans for a return to New Zealand. The company drilled a well in the Murchison Valley late last year, but it was plugged and abandoned at 10,273 ft. Bounty also completed seismic surveys in the Wanganui basin and in Canterbury last year.

"A spokesman for Bounty said today that earlier plans to drill on-shore in Wanganui still stood, but we are not yet in a position to say when. The company also wanted to do more exploration work in the Murchison Valley, regarded as a very promising area, but again could not be more specific about timing. Bounty is still evaluating seismic survey results from New Zealand and will not work out its next step until this is completed." [297]

"Negotiations are in progress with a major United States oil company for a farm-out of Bounty's Wanganui concession. The Southland and Glenhope licences were abandoned to the nominal holder, Hackathorn NZ Oil." [298]

Australian Inquiry

Bounty Oil, which by March 1973 had become a no liability company, and its associated entities, were ordered to be wound up by the New South Wales Equity Court in December 1974. [299]

This followed the disappearance of the principals of the companies, Alexander Barton and his son Thomas Barton, after the call for an inquiry into their business affairs — as reported by the Christchurch Press in March 1973:

"The Australian Shareholders' Association [A.S.A.] want a public inquiry into the activities of the Alexander Barton group of companies, which names among its subsidiaries Harbourside Oil and Bounty Oil N.L. The association believes it is a matter of grave concern that since 1969 these companies have raised or taken control of cash assets in excess of $20m…Yet at June 30,

1972, accounts for just two of these companies, Harbourside Oil N.L. and Bounty Oil N.L., show accumulated losses totalling $13.7m.

"The statement says that Harbourside and Bounty accumulated cash resources of more than $16m according to their prospectuses and succeeding annual reports…The A.S.A. said that it was extremely disturbing that the annual reports of the group of companies had almost without exception been qualified by their auditors since 1970, the main points being the auditors' doubts as to the value of loans to and investments in associated and subsidiary companies.

"It is also clear from inspection of the individual company accounts that the major source of their loss of shareholders' funds have been these loans and investments, the association said. The association emphasises that the accounts of group companies in no way shows where the major portion of these public moneys came to rest, it said. The association said it believed that as an amount between $10m and $20m was involved, and thousands of small shareholders were affected, it was a question of major public importance for it to be ascertained where these missing millions had gone." [300]

Further news reports of April and November 1974 described the Australian Government's unsuccessful attempts to extradite the father and son from first Brazil and then Paraguay. In the latter country, they had been jailed for false declarations when applying for citizenship. [301]

Alexander Barton and Thomas Barton returned to Sydney on 5 January 1977, alleging that they had returned of their own accord to set the record straight:

"A few hours later they were in court facing a total of 28 charges alleging conspiracy and fraud arising from the crash of dozens of companies in the once-thriving 'Barton Empire' which led to the biggest corporate affairs investigation in Australian history. A Government prosecutor told the chief magistrate that the Bartons had obtained $Aust4.5M through the sale of shares in Bounty Oil Ltd. The money was to have been used to obtain a consideration from an American company, but instead it had been sent to Zurich, Switzerland, he alleged.

"What happened to the money is a matter for conjecture at this moment, the prosecutor added. He said that further conspiracy charges involving two million dollars of another oil company — Harbourside Oil — would be laid against the Bartons. It was also expected that there would be further charges…The magistrate remanded the Bartons…in custody for a further hearing." [302]

Some years after Bounty Oil had abandoned its drilling, new technology more precisely identified areas of promise in the Murchison area — as reported by the Christchurch Press in September 1985:

"The State-owned oil company Petrocorp, is to begin drilling for oil near Murchison in about five weeks. A 1600m exploration well is to be drilled in the Matiri Valley, 8km north of Murchison, near the Matiri Valley road.

"Petrocorp's public affairs co-ordinator, Mr Keith Fitzpatrick, said that an underground structure had been identified by surface geological mapping. 'It was subsequently confirmed by seismic acquisition work carried out last year,' he said…the area was well-known for gas and oil seeps.

"There had been three other wells drilled in the area, the nearest about 25km to the south-west of the Matiri-1 site. They were Murchison-1 in 1925, Blackwater-1 in 1968, and Bounty-1 in 1970. Petrocorp is the operator of the licence for the area, PPL 38044." [303]

By December 1985, the latest Murchison well, like all those before it, had failed to find the promised oil in sufficient quantity:

"Limited shows of hydrocarbons have been found in the Matiri-1 oil well near Murchison in the last week, Petrocorp reported yesterday. Their significance must await further evaluation…At 6 a.m. yesterday the well was at 1214m and drilling was continuing." [304]

The Petroleum Corporation of New Zealand (Petrocorp)
A brief history of Petrocorp is recorded by The Fletcher Trust Archives, part of which includes:

"The Petroleum Corporation of New Zealand Ltd (Petrocorp) was established on March 30 1978, when it was registered as a Ltd liability company responsible to the Government as its shareholder and with an authorised capital of $55 million.

"The company, known as Petrocorp, had three subsidiaries; Offshore Mining Company Ltd, Natural Gas of New Zealand Limed (NGC) and Petroleum Corporation of New Zealand (Exploration) Ltd. The companies (sic) charter was to assume the Government's commercial activities relating to the search for oil and gas and the use of known gas reserves which previously had been the responsibility of Government departments and their associated Government agencies.

"The Offshore Mining Company held a 50 percent joint venture interest in the Maui gas field and a corresponding interest in Maui Development Ltd. Its partners in the joint venture were Shell Petroleum Mining Company Ltd, BP Exploration Ltd and Todd Petroleum Mining Company Ltd...Petrocorp Exploration was responsible for the group's exploration…

"In March 1988 Petrocorp was purchased by Fletcher Challenge Ltd, the structure of the company was Corporate, Exploration & Production, Natural Gas, Petrochemicals…" [305]

By July 1979, the exploration arm of Petrocorp was advertising its willingness to enter into joint partnerships with any interested in off-shore drilling:

"A fresh hand has been dealt by the Petroleum Corporation (Petrocorp) in the search for New Zealand oil, opening up the exploration programme to bids from other companies for a share in new ventures. Petrocorp is prepared to work in partnership with other companies in off-shore fields where there are reasonable prospects, the chairman (Mr F W Orr) has said. The corporation is also prepared to go it alone, however, should other explorers fail to come to the party." [306]

Shell BP and Todd Oil Services
Originally incorporated as Shell-D'Arcy and Todd Oil Services Limited on 5 October 1955, the company began drilling at Palmer Rd, Kapuni, in South Taranaki in January 1959. [307]

However, from 22 November 1957 to 23 January 1991, Shell-D'Arcy and Todd Oil Services Limited joined with BP to form a consortium for joint-venture exploration as Shell BP and Todd Oil Services Limited. [308]

In September 1960, the Christchurch Press referred to the limited success of Egmont Oil Wells Limited:

"In Taranaki, Egmont Oil Wells Ltd has been producing relatively small quantities [of oil] for years. Its yearly output is up to 250,000 gallons of crude oil, most of which is sold locally, and between 5 and 10 million cubic feet of natural gas, most of which is fed into New Plymouth mains. [309]

Kapuni
It was therefore not totally unexpected that, as described at the Todd Energy website:

"The Kapuni natural gas-condensate field was discovered (Kapuni-1) in 1959 by a Joint Venture consisting of Shell (37.5%), BP (37.5%) and Todd (25%). Field appraisal took place in 1962-1963 with the drilling of three additional wells Kapuni-2 to -4.

"Twenty Kapuni field wells are [2024] distributed around the surrounding farmland on nine well sites, and natural gas, condensate and water production are fed by underground pipelines from these well sites to the Kapuni Production Station for processing." [310]

In 1961, Shell BP and Todd Oil Services Limited bought a controlling interest in Egmont Oil Wells Limited, thus acquiring the latter company's legacy success. [311]

Maui

"Demand generated off the back of the onshore Kapuni field spurred further exploration in the Taranaki area and led to the discovery of the offshore Maui natural gas and condensate field in 1969. The Crown acquired a 50% interest in the Maui field which led to its development to full production by 1979." [312]

That acquisition by the Crown was finalised in 1973:

"The year 1973 is significant for the agreement reached between the Government and the Shell-BP-Todd consortium to develop the Maui offshore gas field as a joint venture. Agreement in principle was reached between the two parties on 3 April 1973, with the Crown purchasing a 50 percent interest in the field for $30 million. Heads of agreement were signed in July 1973, and the detailed contract was signed in October 1973. The Maui field, which was initially discovered in 1969, is planned to be in production by 1978." [313]

The Shell BP and Todd Oil Services Limited consortium has changed ownership since July 2017 and rights to the Maui Gas Field are now owned by OMV New Zealand Limited whose ultimate holding company is OMV Exploration and Production GMBH, Vienna, Austria.

As described by an 'Offshore Technology' profile in November 2023:

"OMV New Zealand Ltd…is an oil and natural gas exploration and production company…OMV NZ has been in search of additional oil and gas reserves in New Zealand and currently holds interests in nine exploration permits, and in three offshore production licenses or petroleum mining permits. It produces liquid hydrocarbons and natural gas. The company has operations across Europe, the UAE, Australia, and Pakistan. OMV NZ is headquartered in Wellington." [314]

As of March 2022: "According to the most up-to-date fact sheet on OMV's website, the company produces [from the Maui field] 35,000 barrels of oil equivalent per day, comprised of 70 percent gas and 30 percent condensate and oil." [315]

In 2018, with the spectre of climate change looming, the Government banned further offshore petroleum exploration but, as it has always been with the political management of New Zealand, such monumental decisions are always subject to reversal by new governments — as was reported in June 2024:

"The Government will reverse its ban on oil and gas exploration, Minister for Resources Shane Jones has confirmed. Jones said New Zealand's natural gas reserves were declining and sustainable sources like wind, solar and hydro were too inconsistent…

Jones said…'Offshore petroleum exploration was banned…by the previous government…it not only halted the exploration needed to identify new sources, but it also shrank investment in further development of our unknown gas fields which sustain our current levels of use…'

"'The government is tipping oil and gas on the climate crisis fire, lining the pockets of fossil fuel companies, while everyone else will pick up the bill,' Green Party co-leader Chloe Swarbrick said in a statement. Swarbrick said New Zealand could have a more sustainable and efficient economy by prioritising clean energy that works with the environment and not against it…" [316]

New Zealand's First Oil Refinery (2)

Many of the early New Zealand fields produced so little oil that its refining was given very little consideration. However, at wells that did produce modest flows, and where refineries were but a dream, the storage of the oil proved a very large problem — as reported by the Lyttelton Times in May 1911:

"Mr F P Corkill, chairman of the Taranaki Oil and Freehold Company…gave a reporter some interesting information regarding the progress of the oil industry in Taranaki.

"He said that there could be no doubt now as to the attainment of success, as the operations of the Taranaki Petroleum Company's wells at Moturoa, close to the breakwater and wharves, had resulted in the tapping of an apparently large supply of oil. The oil struck was of phenomenally rich quality, and was said to be about two and a half times as valuable as any other known oil...

"The position now was that since February 1910, the No. 2 well of the company had been yielding oil continuously day and night, at the rate of over 100 barrels per week...but the company had been seriously embarrassed by the question of the storage of the oil, and had therefore refrained from making any further attempt to develop the flow.

"Until a refinery was erected to deal with the oil it could only be stored in its crude state and as casks were not available the company had excavated a number of large tanks, which were filled, timbered over and covered with soil. The company had a very large quantity of oil stored in that way. The Moturoa oil coagulated as soon as it reached the surface, and in appearance resembled solidified treacle. It was phenomenally rich in wax...

"At the No. 2 well a miniature refinery was in operation and though primitive, it served to illustrate the method of refining the crude oil. By the simple application of heat at various temperatures, benzine, kerosene, light and heavy lubricating oils and wax were produced, and the benzine had been used in motorcars by the manager and others. The kerosene had been distributed and had been burned in lamps at shows in the district, and the experiments had proved very interesting..." [317]

As previously detailed, a more sophisticated oil refinery was operating at Moturoa as early as August 1913 — Indeed "...The refinery had its own tin-making machinery, and a modern can-filling unit, in addition to the distilling process." [318]

However, following the failure of its owner, Taranaki (New Zealand) Oil Wells, to provide the refinery with sufficient crude oil over a period of time, in 1918 "...it was acquired by the Anglo-Persian Company, dismantled, and removed to the Persian Gulf." [319]

New Zealand Refinery Company

As detailed in the next chapter, overseas oil companies took full advantage of New Zealand's lack of a refinery and shipped tens of thousands of tons of petrol and other refined products to its shores.

It wasn't until the 1960s that country again had its own refinery:

"Proposals to establish an oil refinery in New Zealand date back to the late 1950s. Shell Oil New Zealand Ltd entered into discussions with Government officials in December 1958, and submitted a project study in May 1959. Government approval was announced for the project on 20 May 1959.

"Subsequent developments led to modified proposals being put to Government in July 1959. The end result was that the international wholesalers operating in New Zealand, as well as Europa Refining New Zealand Ltd and members of the New Zealand public, took up shareholdings in The New Zealand Refining Co Ltd formed in 1961." [320]

In October 1962, the Christchurch Press reported details of the prospectus issued by New Zealand Refinery Company:

"The £9,770,000 oil refinery to be built at [Marsden Point] Whangarei by the New Zealand Refining Company Ltd is expected to come on stream early in 1964...

"[As well as] the public issue of 1,885,714 ordinary £1 shares...The 4,114,288 ordinary shares of £1 already issued have been subscribed by the following companies: BP (New Zealand) Ltd 905,143; California Texas Oil Corporation 514,286; Mobil Petroleum Company Inc. 1,152,000; Shell Oil New Zealand Ltd 1,028,571; Europa Refining Company Ltd 514,286...

"The refinery will be able to process up to 2,500,000 tons a year of suitable supplies of feedstocks, and is designed to produce the following products:—

"Motor gasolines 1,150,000 tons; gas oils 300,000 tons; diesel oils 190,000 tons; fuel oils 450,000 tons; bitumen 85,000 tons. These quantities are estimated to be the requirements of New Zealand in 1967.

"The refinery has been designed to all expansion [specifications] to meet estimated requirements for many years to come. Between 1951 and 1961 consumption of petroleum products in New Zealand increased by 60 per cent which is an annual cumulative increase of 4.8 per cent the prospectus says.

"The oil companies have undertaken to process annually at least 90 per cent of their 1964 requirements in the refinery…" [321]

As the Commission of Inquiry looking into 'The Distribution of Motor Spirits and Ancillary Products' reported in 1976:

"The refinery commenced production in May 1964…In 1974 the company employed 184 persons. The company's net profit after taxation was $2,675,000 for the year ended 31 December 1974." [322]

The Distribution of Motor Spirits and Ancillary Products

The Commission also reported that, as of 1976,

"There are…six wholesalers and 4131 licensed retailers involved in the distribution of motor spirits and ancillary products in New Zealand. The wholesalers are the Atlantic Union Oil Co (NZ) Ltd, BP New Zealand Ltd, Caltex Oil (NZ) Ltd, Europa Oil (NZ) Ltd, Mobil Oil New Zealand Ltd, and Shell Oil New Zealand Ltd.

"The companies are responsible for arranging:

"The ordering of crude and feedstocks from various overseas sources for shipment to the New Zealand Refinery Company…The coastal distribution of refined petroleum products…the ordering of refined petroleum products from overseas sources for shipment to main port bulk installations, and the inland distribution of refined petroleum products…to inland depots…to retail outlets, bulk consumers, farmers, and other users.

"The wholesalers operating in New Zealand are all owned and controlled by overseas interests although a minority shareholding of Europa Oil New Zealand Ltd still remains in New Zealand hands…" [323]

Expansion of Marsden Point Refinery

As the Christchurch Press reported in April 1983:

"By the end of this year, more than $583 million will have been spent on the Marsden Point refinery expansion, the chairman, Mr R A Broughton, says in his review, with the annual report.

"Construction of the pipeline from the refinery to the new terminal at Wiri, and a jet-fuel pipeline to the Auckland Airport are well advanced. Both the terminal, and the lines…will be completed by the end of next year…

"A breakdown in production, in thousands of tonnes, with the corresponding figures for 1981 in parentheses, is: motor gasoline 1154 (1262); automotive and diesel fuels 544 (678); light and heavy fuel oils 396 (562); bitumen 69 (90).

"The report lists the company's 10 leading shareholders. These, with their proportion of the total shareholding in parentheses, are: Mobil Oil (19.20), Shell New Zealand (17.14), BP Oil NZ (15.09), Caltex Oil NZ (8.57) Europa companies (8.57) Colonial Mutual Life Assurance (2.91), Triton Oil NZ (1.44); State Insurance (1.39), Commercial Union General Insurance (1.25); Government Life (1.18). Together, the top 10 hold 76.4 per cent of the shareholding." [324]

While the Marsden Point refinery was shut down, the country's need for petroleum products, including bitumen, continued — as reported in June 1985:

"The first bulk shipment of bitumen to be imported since the Marsden Point refinery came on stream in 1964 is due to arrive in Auckland late tomorrow. The cargo of 23,000 tonnes is in the tanker Paludina, one of a limited number of tankers available worldwide for carrying bulk bitumen, Shell New Zealand said yesterday.

"The bitumen, refined from Venezuelan crude oil, has been arranged to cover the shortfall of production at Marsden Point while the refinery is shut down for almost five months to enable the new refinery to be linked with the existing facilities. The company said the shipment would cover the needs of the roading market up to the next sealing contracting season, after which local bitumen production will be resumed at Marsden Point." [325]

Despite the Marsden Point refinery expansion completed in the mid-1980s, some doubt remained as to its future — as reported by the Christchurch Press in May 1989:

"A year ago, there was doubt that the New Zealand Refining Company could lick its Marsden Point refinery into shape to compete with the refiners of Singapore and Australia. This was even after the New Zealand Government had paid $1.2 billion to cancel the debt of the refinery.

"The main oil companies own 80 per cent of New Zealand Refining but they are free to go overseas for refining if they wish. Competitiveness with the oil refineries of Australia and Singapore is the key to the success of Marsden Point, even perhaps to its survival." [326]

Channel Infrastructure NZ

The name of the New Zealand Refinery Company Limited (also known as Refining NZ) was changed to Channel Infrastructure NZ Limited on 1 April 2022 with Mobil, BP, and Z Energy (formerly Shell) remaining its main shareholders. [327]

The new name reflected the change in activity from that of a refiner of crude oil to that of an importer only of refined petroleum products — as reported by the Post:

"Channel Infrastructure, then called Refining NZ, closed the refinery with the loss of 240 jobs in April last year [2022]. That was in keeping with the wishes of its fuel-company shareholders which argued it would be more cost-effective for them to switch to importing pre-refined fuels, such as petrol and diesel.

"Critics of the closure expressed concern it could reduce New Zealand's fuel security but that risk was played down by the former government which argued the country was already reliant on crude oil imports.

"A Cabinet paper revealed that former energy minister Megan Woods had floated the idea of saving the refinery by underwriting its operations for a period of up to 10 years but that the option did not get the support of her fellow ministers." [328]

Chapter Nine

The Petrol & Oil Suppliers

The Vacuum Oil Company/Mobil
"…the history of Mobil…stretches back to the discovery of kerosene. The cost-efficient lubricating oil made its debut in 1866, by accident, when an employee distilled crude oil in a vacuum. In order to produce and market the oil, Mobil formed a company, Vacuum Oil Company." [1]

"Vacuum Oil Co Pty Ltd was formed in Melbourne in February 1895 and a New Zealand branch established in 1896. Its products included Laurel kerosene and Flame benzene. Marketing continued through this branch office until 1952 when Vacuum Oil Co (NZ) Ltd was incorporated in Wellington." [2]

While there seems little doubt that Mobil was the first oil company to operate in New Zealand, there is some indication that the company actually started selling kerosene in New Zealand in the 1870s as the Colonial Oil Company. By September 1897, the Auckland Harbour Board had "…agreed that the Vacuum Oil Company be granted a trial of their lubricators and oil on dock machinery" [3]

By 1898, Vacuum Oil Company's oils were prominently displayed at the country's Agricultural shows, including the Marlborough Agricultural and Pastoral Association's Show held in December 1898. [4]

And, by January 1900, Tothill, Watson & Co., Wool, Grain and Seed Merchants, Gore was advertising itself as "Agents for Vacuum Oil Co., Rochester, N.Y. U.S.A. The Oldest and Largest Manufacturers of Petroleum Oils and Greases in the World, [including]:

"Vacuum Reaper and Binder Oil, Vacuum Plough Oil, Vacuum Engine and Thresher Oil, Vacuum Leather Oil, Vacuum '600W' Cylinder Oil, Vacuum Axle Grease, Vacuum Harness Belting Compound. In All Size Packages, large stocks of which are always kept at Gore. Vacuum Sight Feed Lubricators, Vacuum Locomotive Sight Feed Lubricators, Vacuum Automatic and Crank Pin Oilers." [5]

At Auckland, in 1911, a number of businesses took the opportunity to lease recently-reclaimed, Harbour Board land, to the west of the main port, at Freemans Bay. Both the Vacuum and British Imperial Oil Companies (Shell) were the first to erect storage facilities upon what would later become known as the Wynyard Tank Farm — as reported by The New Zealand Herald and the Auckland Star:

"The brick stores to be erected for the Vacuum Oil Company Limited in Beaumont-street, on the newly-reclaimed portion of Freeman's Bay, will be the largest of the kind in New Zealand, covering a total area of 315ft by 125ft. The whole of the structure — with the exception of a small portion…to be constructed in galvanised iron — will be erected in brick, and will have a steel span roof, thus rendering it completely fire-proof. The main portion…will be used for the storage of refined oil, the galvanised iron portion for storing lubricating oil, and the remainder for workshops and offices." [6]

"The 67 acres of the Freeman's Bay reclamation, which were recently leased by the Harbour Board, are fast being occupied…The British Imperial Oil Company (Shell), which has secured three allotments, intends to build a large store 113ft by 83ft, and a contract has been let to Messrs. J. T. Julian and Son for about £3000." [7]

"Ultimately, Standard Oil Company of New York (Socony) bought a controlling interest in Vacuum Oil. In 1931, the two companies formed Socony-Vacuum and, two years later, it merged with Standard Oil of New Jersey to form Standard-Vacuum Oil Company, known as Stanvac." [8]

The petrol brands marketed by the Vacuum Oil Company then included Pratt's, Voco Power, Plume, and Mobil.

"In 1955 the name of the company was changed to Standard-Vacuum Oil Co (NZ) Ltd [9] and, as a result of what became known as "…the biggest corporate dismemberment in business history", Standard Oil was no more, broken up into a number of independent companies.

"As a result, Standard Vacuum Oil (NZ) Limited, which markets a full range of oil products under the brand name 'Mobil'…became known as Mobil Oil New Zealand Limited from 3 April 1962." [10] "It [then became] a subsidiary of the Mobil Oil Corporation, New York, and markets under the Mobil brand." [11]

The British Imperial Oil Company/Shell

What became "…the worldwide group of companies known as Royal Dutch Shell…began life in London's East End in 1833 when Marcus Samuel opened a trading shop that dealt mostly in exotic shells. Under his son, Marcus Samuel junior (later Lord Bearsted) trading broadened to include Caspian Sea oil from the Black Sea port of Batum. Shell's first major success came in 1892 when Samuel won permission from the Suez Canal Company to transport oil in tankers through the Canal. Following this, Samuel and his nephews expanded the business [as The Shell Transport and Trading Company] by buying up land for tank installations for kerosene throughout Asia." [12]

"Meanwhile in 1890, another new oil company had been formed at the Hague in the Netherlands — the Royal Dutch Company for the Working of Petroleum Wells in the Netherlands Indies, commonly known as Royal Dutch. This company prospered too, under Henry Deterding, and soon Royal Dutch and Shell Transport and Trading had so many mutual interests in the Far East that an alliance of some kind became increasingly desirable to help them meet severe competition.

"In 1903 a joint company, The Asiatic Petroleum Company Limited, was formed to combine the sales and distribution organisations of Royal Dutch and Shell for their East Indies production. In 1907 complete integration of the two companies took place and it was from this merger that the present world-wide Royal Dutch/Shell Group of Companies came into being." [13]

Originally known in Australia as the Shell Transport and Trading Company Limited, the name of the entity was changed to the British Imperial Oil Company Limited in July 1905. [14]

In 1909, the company was importing oils and spirits into Australia from Singapore. [15]

By January 1911, The British Imperial Oil Company had committed to the importation of its products into New Zealand with the company seeking tenders and local council permission for the erection of brick stores at the country's main centres:

"The British Imperial Oil Company, or 'Shell' Co. handling Sumatra oil, is now building stores in Auckland, Christchurch, Dunedin, and Wellington. The kerosene, motor spirit, and benzine will not, however, appear on the market for at the least three months from date." [16]

Indeed, as reported by the Evening Post in April 1911:

"It is understood that a full cargo of 'shell' oil for The British Imperial Oil Co is on the water for the four chief New Zealand ports." [17]

Additional detail about the anticipated delivery was provided by the Evening Post in May 1911:

"A rival to the Standard Oil Company's specialties is shortly to come into the New Zealand market, and from America, the home of the Standard Company. The steamer John Hardie, which left Philadelphia for Fremantle and New Zealand on 12th March, is bringing a full cargo of kerosene in case for distribution in the four centres of New Zealand where new, large stores have been erected for its retention.

"The oil is being shipped by the 'Shell' Transport Co or, as it is known in Australasia, The British Imperial Oil Company, the avowed rival to the Standard Company.

"About the same time as the John Hardie a cargo of motor spirit and benzine from the Shell Company's works in Sumatra is expected to arrive in New Zealand. The Shell Company's oil-well interests are distributed all over the world — the United States, Egypt, Europe, Russia, and the Dutch East Indies. There is an abundant supply to draw upon. It is likely that Dunedin will be the first port of call in New Zealand for the John Hardie." [18]

As well as some competition to be generated as far as quantity was concerned, some discrimination as to the origin of the oil products was also anticipated, according to the Auckland Star:

"The British Imperial Oil Company is entering the New Zealand oil trade in competition with the Standard Oil Trust. The initial shipment of 100,000 cases of kerosene for the four principal ports of the Dominions arrives at Auckland by the steamer John Hardie about May 28. There is said to be no intention at present of cutting prices, as it is anticipated that sympathy for the British product will ensure business." [19]

However, some explanation as to the definition of 'British product' was later called for, as reported the next day by the Otago Daily Times:

"…that the oil was a 'British product'…This information is rather misleading, as although the company [British Imperial Oil Company] is controlled by British and Continental financiers the kerosene is obtained from the United States oilfields. The Shell motor spirit sold by the British Imperial Oil Company is obtained from Borneo…" [20]

As a further step to consolidate its presence in New Zealand, The British Imperial Oil Company (New Zealand) Limited was registered in London on 7 August 1912 with a Capital of £20,000. [21]

By December 1913, The British Imperial Oil Company Limited began trading in New Zealand as The British Imperial Oil Company (New Zealand (or N. Z.) Limited. [22]

As reported by the Bay of Plenty Times, the monthly meeting of the Tauranga County Council was held on 4 November 1913. Of particular interest from the aspect of the privacy laws in force today was a letter from the British Imperial Oil Company "…asking to be furnished with a list of owners of motor vehicles registered by the Council…" [23]

The same request was received at various times by a number of Councils throughout New Zealand. The Council's eventual response is not recorded but, in those more simpler times, it would not be hard to imagine that the list was provided.

It took some time to establish distribution for its Shell product throughout New Zealand but, by April 1922, distribution on the west coast of the South Island was finally settled — as reported by the Greymouth Evening Star:

"Messrs the British Imperial Oil Co. Ltd., have entered into an arrangement with the old-established firm of Messrs Dalgety and Co. Ltd, Greymouth, to act as distributors and stockists for Shell Motor Spirit and Oils on the Coast. Adequate supplies of Shell Motor Spirit and Oils will be always available in order to meet the requirements of the garage trade and motor-car owners. Shell Motor Spirit is noted for its uniform quality, easy starting and good mileage." [24]

Obviously, infrastructure was required, if only to keep pace with the major transition from tinned product to its bulk transport shipped across the world in tankers:

"Apparently Wellington is going to be the centre for crude oil storage in New Zealand, for now it is announced that the British Imperial Oil Company has bought 27½ acres of land, also at Miramar, for the purpose of erecting thereon extensive works for the handling of residual oil, petroleum spirit, lubricants, etc…

"Petroleum and residual oil will he brought to Wellington from the Sumatran fields in bulk in specially constructed tank boats, of which the company has several. The tankers would berth at the Miramar wharf, and the oil would be pumped to the works where it would be prepared for the market. In many instances it will be possible to distribute petrol to consumers without the necessity of supplying expensive tins." [25]

The British Imperial Oil Company (New Zealand) Limited had a change of name to The Shell Company of New Zealand Limited registered on 26 October 1927. [26]

Various changes of name ensued, including:

Shell New Zealand Limited from 18 June 1959 to 9 December 1992; Shell Oil New Zealand Limited to 6 April 2010; Greenstone Energy Limited to 11 May 2011; and then to the current name of Z Energy Limited. [27]

"The turnover of the Shell New Zealand Holding Company in 1982 was $735.8M, 14.8 per cent up on the 1981 total of $640.9M. The net profit was $39.5M, 13.8 per cent up on the 1981 profit of $34.7M.

"The 1982 profit was after providing $38.1M for taxation. The company sold 7.4 million barrels, of oil within New Zealand during 1982, 4 per cent less than in the previous year. The reduction was entirely in sales to international customers — airlines, and shipping or overseas fishing companies." [28]

A S Paterson & Co/Big Tree

A S Paterson & Co existed from at least September 1888 when it was reported that the firm had: "…loaded the Hauroto with 10,000 bags of oats for Melbourne, being the largest cargo of grain ever loaded at Dunedin wharf." [29]

The following month, it was announced that: "Messrs A S Paterson & Co have been advised by cable of the sailing of the Penpont for Dunedin with their first shipment of new season's sugar." [30]

In July 1890, A S Paterson & Co traded as attorneys and merchants from Rattray Street, Dunedin [31] and by August 1891, the firm had opened an office at Customhouse Quay, Wellington. [32]

Later that year, the business advertised that it had "…made Special and very Satisfactory Arrangements for the Disposal Of Frozen Meat, Dairy, And Other Produce In Liverpool, and can deal with Shipments to the best advantage…we offer our Services to Shippers desirous to avail themselves of this outlet, and will make Advances upon Consignments." [33]

In March 1898, A S Paterson & Co were appointed Auckland Province agents for the Royal Exchange Assurance Corporation of London [34] and the sole wholesale agents for Nirvana Ceylon Tea ("picked and packed under British supervision") in August 1900. [35]

By March 1902, A S Paterson & Co was advertising itself as: "Wholesale Import and Export Merchants…Buyers of Hemp, Butter, Cheese, and All Farm Produce…" [36]

A S Paterson & Co was incorporated as a limited liability company on 9 April 1912 and traded as such until its acquisition by the Goodman Group in June 1979. [37]

In 1912, the Evening Post reported that the company was established with a capital of £150,000…the object being to "…take over as a going concern the business of general merchants, commission agents, etc., heretofore carried on at Dunedin, Wellington and elsewhere in New Zealand by A S Paterson & Co." The initial shareholders were named as: "A S Paterson, C W Statham, T Thomson, J M R Galloway, G Shirtcliffe, W E Fussell, and F G Dalziell." [38]

In February 1949, A S Paterson and Co Limited had become a public company with its listing on the stock exchange — as reported by the Otago Daily Times:

"The name of A S Paterson and Co Ltd is familiar enough in Dunedin, as it is in northern centres; and in investment circles anyway considerably more interest will be evinced in the company by reason of its recent [Stock Exchange] listing. Capital at £279,000 tops the quarter-million mark…Born in this city [Dunedin], the company subsequently gravitated north, and the head office is now located in Wellington.

"The agency for Big Tree petrol was a mainstay in years gone by but to-day the company has wide import and export ramifications with the emphasis on primary produce. The export of seeds from Dunedin and hides and sheepskins from Canterbury are two profitable activities." [39]

Big Tree Motor Spirit

As reported by Wellington's Evening Post in January 1915:

"A new entrant into this market is the Big Tree kerosene from California, introduced by the Standard Oil Company (of California). There are now three competing lines in this market, where there was only one comparatively recently — viz., the Standard oil brands through the Vacuum Oil Company. Then came the Shell kerosene, at first from Philadelphia, and now coming direct from Sumatra for the first time in the Physa, due here about next Monday from Auckland. The Physa has 5000 cases of kerosene and 35,000 cases of motor spirit for this centre." [40]

The brand and logo, Big Tree, was derived from California's giant sequoia or redwood trees. Not only was Big Tree-branded kerosene available in New Zealand in 1915 but also the first benzine — as advertised in the King Country Chronicle in May of that year:

"Wanted Known, that Big Tree Benzine is the best, at Zainey's Motor Garage Company, 17s 6 per case, five cases lots at 17s cash, ex-store." [41]

Any doubts as to the quality of Big Tree benzine were soon eased by a Poverty Bay Herald report of July 1915:

"Advice has been received locally that the new quality Big Tree benzine was awarded the highest honours at the Panama-Pacific International Exposition in competition with all other benzines" [42]

Bay of Plenty land agents and wholesale merchants, Mountfort and Baker, were one of the first importers of Big Tree benzine in 1915 according to the Bay of Plenty Times:

"Messrs Mountfort and Baker Limited have on the water large supplies of [Big Tree] benzine which are due to arrive the first week in August." [43]

However, there appears to be no announcement of the shipment's arrival and its distribution by Mountfort and Baker. Instead, A S Paterson and Co is reported to be the distributor of Big Tree product in New Zealand — as reported by the Evening Post in September 1915:

"The Big Tree brand of kerosene and distillates is distributed by A S Paterson and Co. Mr G Shirtcliffe, the manager for the company, explained…that the company had no oil of its own in store. What was there was already sold. Oil was due that day, and it actually arrived by the Wairuna from San Francisco…" [44]

In anticipation of a large shipment, AS Paterson had advertised for staff in July 1915:

"Wanted, Stackers for Oil Store, about Six Men required; must be strong and active. Reply…A S Paterson & Co Ltd Oil Store, Hutt Road" [45]

According to subsequent news reports, A S Paterson & Co Ltd became the main New Zealand agents of the branded oil, with distribution branches around the country, and Big Tree benzine and oil quickly gained popularity due to its performance in motor races.

During an interview by N S Lawrence, published by NZ Truth in June 1929, Howard Henry Newton, General Sales Manager for Big Tree, stated:

"…for the whole of its life, Big Tree has been associated with A S Paterson Ltd…

"Big Tree Sales…have been steadily rising since its inception. You might call the rise spectacular during the last 3 years, for they have doubled in that period…[the reason]…

"Big Tree does not boast of any one outstanding feature. It is so perfectly balanced that all its features are outstanding. Easy Starting, Smooth Running, Hill Climbing and Power are all equally balanced in Big Tree. It is a perfect all round spirit." [46]

"In 1935 Shell took over the marketing of Big Tree petrol from A S Paterson and Company" [47] and its General Sales Manager, Howard Newton, continued to jointly promote the Big Tree and Shell brands of petroleum products until the Big Tree brand was eventually phased out in favour of Shell.

Nevertheless, for what the Christchurch Press described, in June 1960, as 'partly sentimental reasons', Big Tree petrol pumps remained for some years:

"The last Big Tree petrol pump has just disappeared from Auckland—although the brand has not been sold in New Zealand for nearly 30 years. The pump was at the Ferry Petrol Station in Quay street. One other—at the Carlton Service Station—was taken out about three weeks ago. There are still a number of the pale blue Big Tree pumps with the distinctive kauri (sic) tree trademark scattered about New Zealand. Some petrol stations have kept them for partly sentimental reasons — and by keeping a few pumps in service the brand name has been kept alive. But the petrol they contain is Shell — the company that bought out A S Paterson Ltd, the distributors of Big Tree petrol…" [48]

By 1976, A S Paterson & Co Limited remained a New Zealand wholesaler, not only for Shell, but also for Caltex and Mobil petroleum products. [49]

The Texas Company/Texaco

In 1910, the Texas Company was said to be:

"…probably the second largest oil concern in the United States, having extensive refining and pipe line capacity, besides owning a fleet of steamships. The company has never paid less than 12 per cent dividend and it is stated that the earnings this year promise to be the largest in the company's history." [50]

"The marketing of 'Texaco' products in New Zealand was undertaken by agents in the early 1900s and The Texas Company (Australasia) Ltd was formed in 1918 to undertake the marketing of these products in Australia and New Zealand." [51]

In May 1920, the Texas Company (Australasia) Limited advertised a proposal to carry on business from an office at Lambton Quay, Wellington [52] but the Texas Company (New Zealand) Limited wasn't established until March 1941 and existed as a New Zealand-registered, limited liability company until November 2012. [53]

From 1945, the company was owned by Caltex Oil (NZ) Ltd which had been established in January of that year. Subsequent names assumed by Caltex included Caltex New Zealand Limited from November 1996, Chevron New Zealand Limited from May 2006, and Z Energy 2015 Limited from June 2016. As of December 2023, the sole Shareholder of the latter company is Z Energy Limited, once better known as Shell Oil and owned by Ampol Limited of New South Wales. [54]

Prior to the marketing of its products in Australasia, the Texas Company experienced a bit of bad luck — as reported by the Poverty Bay Herald in October 1905:

"The biggest oil fire on record occurred recently at Humble, Texas, in the heart of the oil region. Lightning struck an oil tank of the Texas Company, igniting it and starting a conflagration which consumed the contents of 13 large earthen tanks, covering about 80 acres, and containing about 2,500,000 barrels of oil. Several hundred men fought the fire until the liquid began to boil over. A high barbed-wire fence checked the flight of the men, until by sheer force of numbers they broke it down. At least twelve men and forty mules were burnt to death. The company's loss amounted to something- like £200,000." [55]

In May 1920, the Poverty Bay Herald reported another disaster that involved Texas Company oil:

"In connection with the loss of the Commonwealth Government liner Carawa, the master has reported that the vessel struck a reef off Puerto Chica, on the Island of Chatham, in the Galapagos Group, on March 21, and foundered on March 24 in nine fathoms of water. A small portion of the cargo, consisting of case oil from Texas, consigned to the Texas Company of Australasia Ltd has been recovered." [56]

Of course, that loss was an exception and most Texas Company product destined for New Zealand did arrive — as advertised in The New Zealand Herald in April and May 1921:

"Now Unloading ex the S.S. Singapore Maru Texaco Motor Spirit Retail Price, 34/- Texaco Benzine Retail Price, 33/6 Texaco Light Of The Age Kerosene Retail Price, 22/. Texaco Power Kerosene Retail Price, 21/, Discount of 6d allowed for ex-ship delivery. Place your order with your Garage or Distributor To-day. The Star Oil Company Limited, Sole Distributor of Texaco Refined Products in NZ, Richards-Upton Building, 54 Customs Street East, Auckland…" [57]

"More Motor Mileage On Less Fuel. Yes, you can get Bigger mileage and better motoring When you get Texaco Motor Spirit! Every ounce of the spirit goes into power — Power that sends your car easily over hill and dale. Power that responds instantly to the spark, no matter what the climatic conditions may be! Every tin of Texaco is required to meet a 'Quality Test' before it leaves the refinery. Therefore it is always dependable. All garages and stores sell Texaco Motor Spirit. Wholesale: The Star Oil Co, Customhouse Quay, Wellington…" [58]

Star Oil Company/Caltex

As reported by the Waipawa Mail in August 1920:

"There is in process of formation the Star Oil Company, a private company, with a capital of £80,000. The objects are the handling and distribution in New Zealand of kerosene and petrol of the Texas Oil Company of United States of America. A site for a store has been secured at Kaiwarra [Wellington]…The company will handle case oil only." [59]

The original Shareholders of the Star Oil Company Limited were named as E V Riddiford, A de B. Brandon, C W Birch, of Wellington and D H V Riddiford of Featherston. [60]

Along with other oil product distributors, the Star Oil Company was quick to establish waterfront storage facilities:

"Sale Of Harbour Board Leases — Park, Reynolds (Ltd) offered at their rooms Harbour Board leases in block LXXV, adjoining Victoria wharf. Sections 35-40 were secured by the Vacuum Oil Proprietary Ltd; 41 and 42 by the Star Oil Company; 43 and 44 by A S Paterson and Co Ltd; 68 and 69 by A. S. Paterson and Co Ltd…" [61]

However, for reasons unknown, a New Zealand Gazette notice of 13 September 1923 records that the shareholders of the Star Oil Company Limited had resolved to voluntarily wind the company up and appointed a liquidator. [62] It was not until May 1937 that the liquidation of the Star Oil Company Limited was finally completed. [63]

Empire Oil Company

First known as the Producers' Refining Company, the Empire Refining Company site was "…located on approximately 200 acres of land, located northwest of the City of Gainesville in Cooke County, Texas. The site was owned and operated by Empire Oil Company from 1916 until the 1930s." [64]

The Empire Oil Company had a commercial presence, registered as a New Zealand company, from at least June 1909 when J H Gilchrist of Palmerston North advertised itself as the agent for a great number of goods, including:

"Empire Oil Company's Non-corrosive Paints, Lubricating & Gas Engine Oils, Oil Solvents, etc." [65]

The Marlborough Garage also stocked Empire Oil according to an advertisement published by the Marlborough Express in September 1910:

"It having come to my knowledge that some malicious persons have circulated a report that I am selling inferior lubricating oils, the sum of £100 will be paid to anyone proving that I have ever had in stock any oils except Price's Motorine C, which I sell at 4s 9d per gallon, Empire Oil at 3s 6d per gallon, and Salamander at 3s 6d per gallon. I get a fair and reasonable profit at these prices. They are the finest oils in New Zealand. George Birch, Marlborough Garage Blenheim." [66]

Many advertisements for Empire oil and paints were advertised during 1911 through to 1921:

"Motorists — Try Empire Cylinder Oil for water-cooled and air-cooled engines. Non-carbonising, economical. Empire Oil Co Ltd, Harris street, Wellington, sole proprietors." [67]

"Lubricating Oils and Greases — For Engineers, Sawmills, Factories, Freezing Works, Corporations, Dairy Factories, Stores, Farmers, etc. Red Hand brand Anti-corrosive Paints, ready mixed. For Harbour Boards, Corporations, Freezing Works, Painters, Farm Buildings, etc…Empire Oil Company Ltd, Harris Street, Wellington." [68]

By 1922 and 1923 the Empire Oil Company was importing American oil for important customers:

"Gisborne Borough Council have placed an order for 350 barrels of fuel oil with the Empire Oil Coy, for delivery about July, at a total cost of about £1100. [69]

"The Power Board — Empire Oil Company advised they would have a vessel discharging fuel oil at Napier in about 12 days and that there would be about 25 tons available, and enquiring whether the board was requiring a supply. The chairman reported that this matter had been gone carefully into, and he had ordered 20 tons." [70]

Sometimes, the title of 'Empire' used by this American company led customers into believing it to be a British entity. However, this September 1931 letter, addressed to the editor of the Dominion, revealed the writer to be unimpressed:

"We hear a great deal about the exploitation of the New Zealand market by American oil companies, and of their charges, but we have also an 'Empire' oil company, which admittedly gets most of its supplies from America. I suggest that the Associated Chambers of Commerce approach this company and press that in consideration of all the 'pickings' it gets in the expenditure of public money on bitumen and other oil products, it should give a lead in the reduction of prices to a reasonable level. I am, etc. New Zealander" [71]

The Empire Oil Company Limited company records were transferred to Dunedin from Wellington in September 1958 [72] and the company was in voluntary Liquidation from 23 February 1959. [73]

Demand Outstrips Supply

In August 1908, the Vacuum Oil Company also represented the American giant, Standard Oil Company and Trust, in New Zealand. When inquiries were made as to why the prices of oil products had remained high, particularly after a duty of 6d per gallon was removed from kerosene in August 1900, the manager of Vacuum Oil, also speaking for Standard Oil, remarked:

"…that owing to the loss of vessels at sea, or protracted voyages, the stocks of oil in New Zealand had run short, and it had been necessary to bring in supplies from Australia…The present price was due solely to the legitimate addition of the transport charges from Australia…The harbour dues, Government and local taxation, labour, cartage and office expenses have all involved a greater rate of expenditure.

"Simultaneously there has been a huge demand for petroleum products, such as naptha and benzine for motors, and that has left less kerosene available for domestic and other purposes." [74]

The issue of 'the loss of vessels at sea' was demonstrated by the later loss of a steamer, reported by The New Zealand Herald in September 1913:

"The steamer Burgermeister Hackman is in flames in the Long Island Channel. Three hundred thousand gallons of crude oil are burning, and the whole city is lit by the glare. Fire boats have been at work all night, hoping to sink the vessel before an explosion occurs…The Burgermeister Hackman was about to leave with a full cargo of case oil, consigned to the Vacuum Oil Company in New Zealand, for discharge at Auckland, Wellington, Lyttelton, and Dunedin…" [75]

The problem of 'protracted voyages' offered as a reason for the shortage of oil stocks can be appreciated from the shipping reports published by The New Zealand Herald in May 1909:

"The Vacuum Oil Company of Wellington advise that their chartered steamer Walkure left New York on May 3 for Wellington direct: She has on board 150,000 cases of various oils, and is expected to reach Wellington early in July…It is announced that the steamer Bannockburn will take the loading berth at New York for New Zealand early in July, and that the vessel will bring about 200,000 cases of various classes of oils." [76]

The shortage of petroleum products ascribed to greater consumption by 'motors', was aptly described by a Press Association article from Christchurch, entitled "Starving Motor Cars", published by The New Zealand Herald in May 1912:

"The 'petrol famine' is strongly felt in Christchurch. The price of petrol has risen, and now not a drop is to be obtained from the principal distributing agency, the Vacuum Oil Company. The garages in the city and some of the oil business firms have supplies for five weeks, but it is anticipated that the next two weeks will see a material reduction of the city's motor traffic.

"There are reports of fabulous prices being offered for petrol, even up to £3 a case. These, however, cannot be authenticated, though there is no doubt that as much as £1 15s has been paid for one case containing eight gallons...

"Quite a number of firms, and particularly those engaged in drapery and grocery business, have discarded horse delivery vans in favour of a motor delivery. Some of them are in the fortunate position of having stocks of petrol sufficient for a few weeks, but others have been left in the lurch...

"The firms engaged in motor and rubber business are rather pessimistic as to the effect the shortage of petrol will have on their operations. It seems to be certain that a large number of vehicles will be withdrawn from commission, and consequently there will be a decline in the demand for tyres and accessories, and a considerable falling off in repairs. The tyre turnover by one of the motor firms is enormous.

"The garage proprietors fear a fairly heavy loss if the famine continues. Every ordinary substitute for petrol has been bought up with the petrol. There are some cars which will run on kerosene, but a special engine is required for its efficient use. There are all sorts of rumours about various substitutes being tried, and an old story about a motor party coming in from Little River by feeding a bottle of whisky into their machine is being revived...

"The reasons for the present shortage are said to be that the chartered vessels had been delayed, and the demand for petrol had been extraordinary for this season of the year. Instead of sales falling off after January, as they usually do, they kept up and as much was sent out in March as in January." [77]

While the petrol shortage did not quite force New Zealanders to revert back to the horse and the bicycle, it did persuade resellers to look to alternative sources — as reported by The New Zealand Herald in June 1912:

"The acute stage of the petrol famine seems to have passed. The position is not exactly normal, but there are sufficient supplies in hand to enable garages to supply their clients at the normal price...The improvement was brought about to a large extent by the importation of motor spirit from Australia. For instance, some firms have imported shell benzine [British Imperial Oil Company] from Australia. This spirit is made in Sumatra by a British company, which, so far, has only supplied Australia. Importations of the British Australian Company's spirit, manufactured in Australia, are also being made.

"It is stated in trade circles that both the Sumatra and Australian motor spirits could find a ready market in New Zealand at any time, and that there is a probability of the companies concerned extending their operations to include New Zealand...

"The Dominion, so far, has been entirely dependent on the Vacuum Oil Company, and the trade is naturally anxious to have a second string to its bow. One garage owner stated that in the event of there being another shortage supplies could be got from Australia within a week. A shortage of the sort that had just been experienced could not happen in New Zealand again. He had just landed 100 cases of the Sumatra spirit and 100 cases of the Australian spirit..." [78]

However, despite some access to secondary sources, petrol supplies failed to fully satisfy demand through the war years to 1918 when Government control also influenced the supply and demand situation — as reported by the Christchurch Sun in April of that year:

"Petrol supplies have been short for some time, but the position has now reached its acutest stage, with the result that the trade has set itself sternly against unnecessary consumption, and supplies are being literally doled out. There is a strong suspicion that prices are only being kept from soaring to famine rates by a certain attitude taken up by the Government.

"Unfortunately this Government control is only directed against the wholesale trade, with the result that in such places as Auckland, petrol costing wholesale about 25/- per case, is being retailed from 35/- to 40/-.

"The position locally is that petrol is only being supplied in such limited quantities, and in most cases after investigation, that 'joyriding' is now almost a thing of yesterday…Most garages are only supplying regular customers, and in limited quantities…In many cases, the retailer is exploiting the consumer, although there are several concerns which are quitting at fair prices — sometimes 28/- per case…" [79]

Any exploitation of a shortage was promptly denied by the Motor Garage Proprietors' Association:

"To the Editor of The Sun. Sir, —With reference to your article headed 'Joyriding Tabooed', and statements bearing on the petrol question in Christchurch, and in view of the suggestion contained therein that the garage proprietors are exploiting the public, my association wish to state that they decided some time ago to prevent exploitation by fixing the retail price of petrol in so far as the garages are concerned, and as a result of this action I am in a position to state that no garage in Christchurch is charging more than 28/- per case.

"Furthermore, there is no serious shortage of petrol, and no real cause for alarm, providing the public are reasonably careful. — I am, etc., Thos. Newburgh, Secretary, the Motor Garage Proprietors' Association of New Zealand (Canterbury branch)." [80]

By January 1920, the supply situation had not appreciably improved, forcing the Prime Minister to personally intervene:

"Steps have been taken by the Prime Minister to abate the acute shortage of petrol which has been felt more or less all over the country, but particularly in the Auckland district and to relieve the dairy farmers in the Waikato who need petrol for milking machines.

"Arrangements have been made with the Vacuum Oil Company to rail to Auckland small supplies and larger supplies will be sent on by steamer later from Wellington. Mr Massey has also arranged to divert to New Zealand from the cargo of the Waihora, presently in Wellington, 6000 cases of petrol consigned to Melbourne.

"Part of this will be sent to Auckland and the distribution of this and the other supplies will now be controlled by the Board of Trade. Users of petrol are asked by the Board of Trade to limit their demands to immediate requirements, as it is anticipated that reasonable supplies will be available towards the end of the present month." [81]

A more active control of petrol distribution was needed by March 1920:

"In consequence of the shortage of petroleum products throughout the Dominion, the Government has decided to take control of the distribution, and for this purpose it has set up a Petrol Committee at Wellington to act in conjunction with the Board of Trade.

"Sub-committees have been appointed at Auckland Christchurch and Dunedin. These committees will deal with all inquiries relative to supplies, and, in order to conserve the benzine, the needs of essential users will receive preference.

"All orders in excess of five cases must receive the sanction of the Board of Trade's representatives in each centre. Every oil importer will be required to prepare a list of daily supplies and hand it to the Board of Trade's committees. Every distributor of 100 or more cases per week will be requested to supply a weekly list to the committees of persons whom he has actually supplied and the quantity.

"The Prime Minister states that the petrol regulation gazetted on July 12, 1918 as to the distribution of petrol, was still in force, and any breach of these regulations as to hoarding supplies, or any attempt to secure supplies except through the committees, would be dealt with as a breach for which heavy penalties were provided.

"The shortage was merely temporary, and stocks to arrive showed that the present rigid distribution would not be necessary a few weeks hence. There was enough petrol available at the present time to supply essential industries, and there was no need for anxiety on this account, but economy was essential and with a view to securing that, the present control of distribution was being instituted." [82]

Nevertheless, despite assurances to the contrary, those increasingly dependent on the internal combustion engine sought some certainty as to their future prospects — as reported by the Evening Post in October 1920:

"Alarming rumours of a world shortage of petrol have given some concern in the Dominion to motorists and motor traders as to how New Zealand is going to fare in the future. A reassuring reply was given by Mr. Hamilton, director of the Vacuum Oil Company, when he was in Wellington recently, to a deputation representing the local motor trade.

"Among them were: Messrs. H Rogers (Inglis Bros), A Hope Gibbons (Colonial Motor Company), G Magnus (Magnus, Sanderson, and Co), C. B. Norwood (Dominion Motor Vehicles), H. McKibbon (A Hatrick and Co), W Stuart Wilson, and J F Cousins, general secretary, Motor Garage Proprietors' Association.

"The case was put by Mr. Cousins, who laid stress on the vital importance of an adequate supply of benzine at the earliest possible moment. The idea of the deputation was to see what prospect there was of an increase of supplies, as the reports from America were not encouraging.

"Mr Hamilton, in reply, stated that Mr. Cornforth, managing director of the company, had recently returned from America, where he had made it his business to investigate all sources of supply to find if there was the particular grade of benzine suitable for this market.

"New Zealand and Australia used a higher grade of petrol than any other country in the world. If a lower grade could be accepted for part of the supplies, Mr. Cornforth had secured a grade suitable for better-class requirements. As a result, supplies should be adequate.

"The only difficulty was in securing tin plate. Increased supplies might be expected before long, and in the meantime there was enough in stock to carry on with.

"Meanwhile there has been another advance in the price of benzine. Last Monday week benzine could be secured at 35s a case, but to-day 37s 6d is about the minimum. The increases are not uniform. The Board of Trade has sanctioned the rise on the increase in cost to the importing firms, due to the adverse movement of the exchange rates.

"The average price to the consumer would work out at something more than 37s 6d a case, and on some grades a retail charge of 40s a case could be justified. The rise has caused some concern to private carrying firms, to whom it will mean a fairly substantial increase in running costs." [83]

Petrol Tins & Cases

Before the introduction of bulk transport and storage facilities, such as those now found at ports and modern service stations, blacksmiths, grocers, and stock and station agents sold petrol in 4-gallon (18-litre) tins with two tins in a case called 'flimsies'.

Tin plate was a necessary component in the manufacture of kerosene and benzine containers. Indeed, such was the importance of tin plate for these and other containers that English and American manufacturers thought it beneficial to amalgamate — as reported by the Lyttelton Times in December 1908: "The English and American tin plate manufacturers have formed a combine with a huge capital, practically controlling the tin plate industry of the world." [84]

Initially, the tins and wooden cases were manufactured in the exporting countries but some product received in barrels, such as lubricating oil, was also repackaged in manageable quantities to suit marketing and distribution demands throughout the country.

New Zealand already had its own tin plate manufacturers producing cans for agricultural produce, for instance. So it is not surprising that, as the bulk shipping of petroleum product increased in the 1920s, the same industry should be called upon to make petrol and kerosene tins — as reported by the Nelson Evening Mail in August 1932:

"In addition to the purchase of petrol and kerosene tins, the company [Vacuum Oil Co. Limited] has for many years past been large purchasers of locally made tins for packing lubricating oil in connection with their general trading. Orders for these are placed regularly with Messrs A. Harvey and Sons Ltd., Auckland, Messrs J. Gadsden and Co. Ltd., Wellington and Christchurch, and the New Zealand Canister Co. Ltd., Wellington. The amount of labour involved in the manufacturing of these cases and tins is the means of keeping in employment a large number of New Zealanders." [85]

That same month, probably as a result of employment disputes that had closed several large tin plate manufacturing plants in America, the Vacuum Oil Company placed a very substantial order with New Zealand firms:

"A contract for the supply of over half a million four-gallon petrol tins, involving the employment of approximately one hundred additional workers throughout New Zealand, has been let to the Christchurch firm of J Gadsden and Co. Ltd by the Vacuum Oil Company Ltd.

"'This has necessitated the extension of our plants in Wellington and here in Christchurch,' said Mr S W Gadsden, a director of the company to a Press representative yesterday. 'I am now in the middle of arrangements for establishing plants in Auckland and Dunedin. These should be in full operation within the next two months. Our Wellington plant has given additional employment to over forty unemployed men and youths since the contract has been let, and the Christchurch plant has within the last month employed fifteen additional workers.

"'It is quite safe to say,' he continued, 'that employment will be given to one hundred unemployed men and youths for more than twelve months at the least, and there is no reason why the demand for tins should not continue.

"'Our payroll will be increased for the year by at least £10,000. The contract is the first of such a size let to a New Zealand firm,' Mr Gadsden said, 'and in addition to establishing the two new factories in Dunedin and Auckland, it has been necessary to make extensive alterations to, and purchase additional plant for, our present factories. In all, more than half a million four-gallon tins will be produced.'

"'This development is quite recent, and in addition to creating employment for so many people the contract calls for British plate to be used in the manufacture. Before importation in bulk was decided upon by the oil companies, petrol was sent to New Zealand in tins, and these were of American manufacture, so there is a boost for British manufactures in this requirement,' he concluded." [86]

J Gadsden & Company

J (Jabez) Gadsden & Company Limited operated at Christchurch, [87] incorporated as a company for some sixty years, from 13 September 1922 to 19 August 1983. [88] Horace A Gadsen is recorded as having been a Director until his death in London in April 1936 and Stanley W Gadsen was a governing director based in Australia in March 1939.

Brownlee Manufacturing

Of course, wooden cases remained essential to safely contain the tins for transport and these were also ordered by the Vacuum Oil Company at the same time:

"It is understood that contracts have been placed in New Zealand for the manufacture of some hundreds of thousands of petrol and kerosene cases, with manufacturers at the four centres, namely: Mr William Casey, Auckland; Brownlee Ltd, Wellington; St. Leonard Sawmilling Co, Christchurch; and McLeod Bros, Dunedin.

"The conditions of the contract require that New Zealand timber be used, and each contractor has been provided with a set of dies, for printing the cases, these also being made in New Zealand. The effect of these activities will naturally be to resuscitate not only the boxmaking industry, but also the saw-milling business, since the timber required will keep a number of mills operating." [89]

Brownlee Manufacturing Limited operated from Kilbirnie, Wellington, incorporated as a company for some eighty years, from 19 January 1911 to 30 September 1991. [90]

Bulk Storage & Distribution

The delivery to New Zealand of petroleum products in tins and drums continued well into the 1920s simply because, before then, the country lacked the storage facilities large enough to receive the kind of bulk tanker deliveries that had been shipped around the world since 1892.

Indeed, the Shell Transport and Trading Company's Murex, was the first oil tanker to carry petrol in bulk to England from the East via the Cape of Good Hope in 1903. [91]

The uniqueness of the Murex (named after a shellfish, as all Shell tankers were) was explained by the New Zealand Times in February 1902:

"This steamer, the Murex, was built for the purpose of carrying petroleum in bulk, and is one of a fleet of thirty-eight steamers belonging to the Shell Transport and Trading Company (Limited) of London...

"While carrying oil or general cargoes, the Murex uses no coal, its boilers being fired entirely by liquid fuel, which is the residue of crude petroleum after all the lighter oils have been extracted. The steamer has been using this fuel for the last two years with remarkable success...The great economy resulting from the use of liquid fuel is so remarkable that there is no doubt that in the near future the major portion of the mercantile marine will discard coal in favour of the new fuel.

"The Murex is so fitted that general cargoes can be carried in the tanks, the system of cleaning and ventilating the tanks being so perfect that the steamers of the company have on various occasions carried the most delicate cargoes from the Far East, including tea, rice, etc." [92]

Reporting on the first arrival of the Murex at Brisbane in September 1911, the Evening Star commented:

"The Murex has been built to carry oil in bulk, and is fitted with all the latest appliances for the shipping and discharging of her liquid freight. She has a capacity for about 4,500 tons in bulk." [93]

Unfortunately, as reported by the Christchurch Press in January 1917:

"The Anglo-Saxon Petroleum Company's steamer Murex (3564 tons) has been sunk [in the Mediterranean], and some lives lost." [94]

Following the First World War, the Murex was replaced by another tanker of the same name, later to deliver New Zealand's first cargo of bulk motor spirit — as reported by the Evening Post in January 1926:

"On 21st January there may be expected at Wellington the British Oil tanker Murex, built in 1922 by His Majesty's Dockyard, Portsmouth, the Murex takes her place in the Shell Company's fleet of some 200 tankers. This vessel carries the first cargo of bulk motor spirit to New Zealand.

"The name Murex has more than a passing interest to Australasians. Built to the order of the Shell Transport and Trading Co, the original Murex, arriving in Sydney in August 1914, was despatched after discharge to Rabaul, and brought the first batch of German War Prisoners to Sydney for internment. Subsequently in war service she was torpedoed in the Mediterranean.

"The arrival of the new Murex at Wellington has a special significance in that it serves to forge a further link in the Shell policy of reducing petrol costs by bulk distribution. The huge installation at Miramar, which has taken almost twelve months to complete, will commence active operations on the 25th January, and reduced petrol prices will at once come into operation.

"The saving in tins and cases has represented a direct saving to motorists in Australia of £350,000 to £400,000 per annum, and the introduction of this method into New Zealand will, it is anticipated, mean a direct saving to consumers of over a quarter of a million pounds yearly.

"This saving is passed along to the country consumer by delivery from the installation in rail tank-cars to the country depots. In Australia, the innovation has meant an all-round reduction of approximately 4½d per gallon, and as similar works to the Wellington installation are being established at Auckland, the reduction will soon be felt all over the Dominion.

"The installations will comprise the most modern facilities and equipment for the handling of oil in bulk, and are giving employment to an army of local workers…" [95]

Freemans Bay Tank Farm

At Auckland, in 1925, the Inspector of Dangerous Goods recommended that an application to install bulk tanks be approved on reclaimed land leased from the Auckland Harbour Board at Freemans Bay, "…noting that precautions in applicable by-laws included embankments to prevent outflow in case of accident." [96]

The tanks at what was to become known as the Freemans Bay tank farm were used for the bulk storage of petroleum products and chemicals delivered by ship to the adjacent Wynyard Wharf for subsequent distribution to the Auckland region.

A description by J G McLean of the Freemans Bay facilities was published by the Auckland Sun in April 1928:

"Though bulk-oil depots are relatively new in New Zealand, the big storage tanks are already familiar objects. In Auckland the first tank was put up by the Vacuum Oil Company in 1926, and filled from a shipment brought by the tanker Lubrico. Subsequent shipments have made tankers quite familiar maritime visitors. Case oil is still landed, largely from the Union Company's trans-Pacific freighters…

"Space for storage in Auckland alone would hold several million gallons. One firm has three tanks, each capable of holding one million gallons. Others have tanks with an individual capacity of half a million gallons. The new tanks under construction for the Atlantic Union Oil Company are of the latter measure.

"Certain fire precautions are prescribed by Government regulation. Stores are set below street level or else have 3-feet sills round the storage area, to prevent the spread of blazing oil, and for the same reason, compounds in the outdoor installations are surrounded by sloping banks, the top of which can be seen, in one instance, above the outer fence. Dealing with these banks, a Government regulation stipulates that they must be high enough to enclose the maximum oil which the tanks are capable of storing, and 10 per cent more besides.

"In a typical installation the benzine is pumped from the ship to the tanks through mains under the streets, and from the main tanks to smaller working tanks, from which it is drawn off as required. Tank wagons rumble through the gateway dragging the 'static chains' which caused so much bewilderment at first, and caused so many kind-hearted people to cry out, 'Hey, mister! You're dragging your chain.'

"The idea, of course, is to provide an 'earth' for static electricity generated by the swilling of the fluid in the tank. Chains wear out rapidly, in two or three months, through the incessant dragging, and the worn piece is generally replaced by means of a shackle at ground level.

"The big tanks of the Shell Company have fixed roofs and are fitted with cooling devices, pouring water over the roof and sides, to reduce evaporation. The Vacuum Company's tanks, on the other hand, have floating roofs, which float on the surface of the petrol. They are very strongly braced and a close fit round the sides is obtained by means of a fabric joint or 'kearsage' pressed outward by strong hangers placed at intervals round the circumference. Walking on this type of roof, which is held to conserve stocks by reducing evaporation, one can feel the movement of the benzine underneath…" [97]

The history of the Freemans Bay tank farm was encapsulated in a New Zealand Court of Appeal judgment given in May 2015. The case, brought by Auckland Waterfront Development Agency against Mobil New Zealand, involved a claim for the cost of cleaning the contamination left at the tank farm by the oil companies after their departure in 2011. Judgment was entered against Mobil in the sum of $10 million.

However, as the Court of Appeal found:

"Mobil was not the only source of subsurface contamination. Contaminants could spread from other sites on the reclamation. In 1986 a neighbouring tenant, Shell Oil, experienced a major spillage of aviation fuel which is known to have added to accumulated contamination beneath the Mobil sites.

"It is now common ground that sometime during the 1970s the land became so polluted as to require complete remediation. The Judge described this as the tipping point…

"The historical record also includes reports by Mobil of spills and contamination after the original leases were granted. In 1935 an explosion occurred in a City Council pumping station, caused by leakage from oil company pipes finding its way through saturated ground into the sewers. There is evidence dating from 1963 of awareness, again on the part of the Council, that the reclaimed land was porous, so that spilled petroleum could reach the harbour." [98]

Wiri Oil Storage

Auckland received its supplies of bulk fuel via the Freemans Bay tank farm until the facility was replaced by a pipeline from the Marsden Point refinery near Whangarei to Wiri in south Auckland, commissioned by the oil companies.

"The Marsden Point to Wiri pipeline was in operation by May 1986. At about the same time a pipeline was constructed from Wiri to carry aviation fuel to Auckland Airport. These developments substantially reduced the need for bulk petroleum storage at Freemans Bay, which by 1999 was no longer used for petrol, aviation fuel or diesel…" [99]

The Wiri Terminal was constructed in 1982 and has been operating since 1983…originally serving the rural districts of South Auckland…but "…the terminals now store and distribute about 95% of the Auckland region's fuel supplies and about 40% of New Zealand's fuel supplies…"

"Last year [2022], WOSL [Wiri Oil Services Limited] was responsible for distributing around 9 million litres of fuel a day around New Zealand. It is now in operation 24 hours a day, 7 days a week, 365 days a year…

"WOSL manages the Marsden Point Terminal from its Wiri base…and is owned by New Zealand's four main oil companies, BP, Mobil, Z Energy [formerly Shell], and Z Energy 2015 (formerly Chevron)." [100]

Service Stations as Bulk Suppliers

"Until the mid-1920s blacksmiths, grocers, and stock and station agents sold petrol in 4-gallon (18-litre) tins and larger drums. Some of them also repaired the often unreliable early cars. In 1917 a Garage Proprietors Association was formed.

The first petrol pumps (bowsers) were installed in 1926 when the large petrol companies were setting up their bulk distribution networks. The petrol was drawn from underground tanks. The number of petrol stations expanded very rapidly, often offering motorists a choice of brands…" [101]

As the use and bulk storage of petroleum products in New Zealand grew, so did the need to regulate that use. Consequently, the Explosive and Dangerous Goods Amendment Act 1920 came into force on 1 April 1921. With regard to petroleum products, the Act defined:

"2.(1) Dangerous goods means any fuel oil when kept or stored in receptacles holding more than two hundred gallons, and any petroleum spirit and petroleum oil, and such other goods as the Governor-General by Order in Council declares to be dangerous goods:

"4. (1) (a) Dangerous goods shall be kept, stored, or used only (a) In premises licensed under this Act for the keeping, storing or using dangerous goods…

"(c) In such quantities and in such manner and subject to such conditions as to safety as may be prescribed by regulations under this Act:

"Provided that nothing in any such regulations shall authorize the keeping in unlicensed premises of more than three gallons at any one time of petroleum spirit used or intended for use in such premises in connection with any trade or business or any purpose incidental thereto." [102]

In other words, service stations had to be licensed and the dangerous goods sold had to be clearly marked as such:

"5. (1) No person shall keep, convey, sell, or expose for sale within New Zealand any dangerous goods unless the receptacle containing the same and any outer package containing such receptacle is marked with the trade-name of the goods, and such other markings as may be prescribed by regulations." [103]

That marking naturally included the familiar brand names found on the face of the gasoline pump, still referred to as a 'bowser' after the American, Sylvanus Bowser, who is said to have invented the first gasoline pump in 1885. Obviously pre-dating the automobile industry, Bowser's pump was commonly used to dispense the kerosene used in lamps and stoves.

"He later improved upon the pump by adding safety measures, and by adding a hose to directly dispense fuel into automobiles…The first gasoline pump was patented by Norwegian John J Tokheim in 1901." [104]

In New Zealand, service station petrol pumps were not functioning until the early 1920s and the first electric petrol pumps, or 'palometers', were made in New Zealand and designed by Estonian immigrant Karl Pallo in the 1930s. [105]

"From the early 1950s, petrol companies began to contract petrol stations to sell only their brand. Over time, fewer petrol stations included car repairs as part of the business – by the late 20th century on-site car repair was not common in major cities, but petrol stations had begun selling a much wider range of food items, and some were like mini supermarkets." [106]

Solus Trading

"The entry of BP into the New Zealand oil industry was achieved at a time when most service stations were 'multi-brand' — that is, service stations which sold each of the wholesalers' products in different coloured pumps...

"…late 1950 in New Zealand saw a change in marketing strategy by the oil companies in that they embarked upon a campaign to persuade retailers to sell only one brand of motor spirits. 'Solus trading' as it is known in the oil industry was achieved principally by the wholesaler approaching a selected service station and offering inducements if it would sell one particular brand of motor spirits.

"Inducements came in a variety of forms. Financial assistance was given by way of gift or large loans at low interest rates. Service stations were substantially rebuilt. Good-wills became inflated. High prices were paid for service stations as oil companies competed to ensure that a particular service station sold its products exclusively.

"For the oil company, solus trading achieved significant savings in distribution costs. Larger storage tanks could be provided at service stations to allow larger drops of petrol at less frequent intervals. A one-brand system meant that only one oil company representative called at any one brand service station, that only one petrol tanker needed to make deliveries, and that accounting records could be greatly simplified. Solus trading also enabled an oil company, by painting the service station, training service station attendants, providing advertising and window displays, to project a company and brand image from each one-brand service station.

"For the service station proprietor, solus trading meant a retailer might not have an effective choice of which wholesaler to deal with. Once inducements had been given, a service station owner would be tied to a particular wholesaler for a period.

"A further possible consequence of the change to solus trading was the danger of proliferation of retail outlets. In small towns where there might be only two service stations a change to one-brand stations would mean that four oil companies would find themselves unrepresented in that particular area, and would seek to establish new outlets…

"Throughout 1951 the New Zealand Retail Motor Trade Association, some wholesalers, not then participating in the one branding moves, and the Government were concerned about the developing situation within the oil industry in New Zealand. The Government's concern was not with solus trading *per se*. Rather, objections centred around the oil companies' possible control of retailers and the inflationary effects their acquisition of service stations was having on the price of retail outlets.

"Nevertheless, the wholesalers were able to proceed with the conversion of the New Zealand retailing sector to solus trading. By June 1952, it was estimated that there were some 630 one-brand service stations in New Zealand and that Vacuum (Mobil) had 99; Atlantic 66; BP 47; Shell 136; Caltex 116; and Europa 66." [107]

Motor Spirits Distribution Act 1953

"The petrol selling industry was already subject to control by way of licensing under the Industrial Efficiency Act 1936 but the current Government policy was to phase out the licensing of industries under this Act and to make specific legislative provision for the licensing of individual industries where this was considered desirable. The result was the Motor Spirits Distribution Act of 1953, which is defined in the preamble to the Act as:

"An Act to make provision for the establishment of a system of licensing of wholesalers and retail sellers of motor spirits for the purposes of encouraging independent traders and competitive trade in the motor spirits industry and maintain the economic welfare of those persons engaged in the motor spirits industry.

"More simply, the Motor Spirits Distribution Act was designed, as the Minister of Industries and Commerce told the House, 'to see that the public get the petrol of their choice…to see that the wholesalers have a reasonable opportunity to offer their brands of motor spirits to the public…and to see that the retailing of petrol as far as possible is in the hands of small independent retailers.'" [108]

"The Motor Spirits Distribution Act came into force on 10 March 1955 and superseded earlier licensing legislation and regulations relating to the industry. The Act…created the three-member Motor Spirits Licensing Authority (MSLA) and also a one-member Motor Spirits Licensing Appeal Authority.

"The Act also, *inter alia*, established procedures for the handling of licence applications, set out principles on which wholesale and retail licences would be granted by the authority and defined conditions which were required to be prescribed in retail licences issued by the authority." [109]

The Later Suppliers of New Zealand's Petroleum Products
Gilmore Oil Company/Gilmore Lion

The origins and growth of the Gilmore Oil Company are synonymous with those of corporate America at the turn of the twentieth century:

"The Gilmore Oil Company was an independent oil company in California which was founded by Arthur Fremont Gilmore after he struck oil on his dairy farm in the Fairfax district of Los Angeles around 1903. His son, Earl Bell Gilmore, took over the family business and expanded its distribution network which, at its peak, operated over three thousand gas stations on the West Coast. He promoted the company in a flamboyant style with much advertising, branding and sponsorship." [110]

"The Gilmore Oil Company Limited refined and marketed oil products in California, Oregon, and Washington and asphalt in Arizona…Overseas, they marketed oil products in China and New Zealand…" [111]

As per the newspaper advertisements of 1924 and 1926, Gilmore Motor Spirit was by then widely distributed throughout New Zealand:

"Gilmore Motor Spirit £1 per case; Wilshire Motor Spirit, 19s per case. Yes, but it is only for cash down with order that you can get it at this particular price from H Andrew & Sons [Te Awamutu]." [112]

"Gilmore Motor Spirit Gilmore Gasoline — Next direct, shipment arriving New Plymouth per 'Dewey' about December 20. Mr. Farmer — get a 7-case lot or more railed direct from boat to your nearest railway station. Gilmore was a farmer, who, many years ago, struck oil on his farm. Gilmore has been refining and marketing high-grade spirit ever since, and has now extended his market to New Zealand. You will be more than satisfied with Gilmore. Ring or Write — Hodder & Tolley Ltd, Hawera." [113]

The first company to be registered in New Zealand by the name of Gilmore Oil Company (New Zealand) Limited was incorporated in 1912, placed into voluntary liquidation on 31 March 1931 [114] and subsequently struck off on 10 December 1934. [115]

This first company, Gilmore Oil Company (New Zealand) Limited was immediately replaced by a second company of the same name, registered in New Zealand on the 15 April 1931. The new company acquired the business of the first company and carried on trading from its registered office, Quay Buildings, Quay Street, Auckland. [116]

The second incorporation of Gilmore Oil Company (New Zealand) Limited was reported by The Dominion on 24 April 1931:

"Gilmore Oil Co (N.Z.) Limited Private Company Capital £155,000 Subscribers: W A Ince of Melbourne [Chairman of Claude Neon Industries] 154,999 shares H M Rogerson of Auckland 1 share Objects: Deal in oils etc." [117]

In February 1933, the Capital of Gilmore Oil Company (New Zealand) "…was increased to £220,000 by creation of 65,000 shares of £1 each." [118]

Indeed, the size of the business carried out by the Gilmore Oil Company in New Zealand was demonstrated by the description of a storage tank erected on behalf of the company at Lyttelton — as reported by the Christchurch Star in April 1933:

"…the construction of bulk storage petrol tanks was the subject of an address delivered by Mr J H Beck of Anderson's Ltd at a meeting of the Canterbury College Engineering Society on Saturday evening. The speaker illustrated his remarks by reference to drawings and photographs of a 632,000 gallon tank recently erected at Lyttelton. This tank was designed by Mr H G Royds for the Gilmore Oil Co and the work of construction was carried out by Anderson's Ltd. The tank was cylindrical in shape, 72 ft in diameter and 30 ft high with a weight of 90 tons empty and 2700 tons when full…" [119]

However, some of the pricing-cutting practices employed by Gilmore Oil, despite the passage of the Motor-spirits (Regulation of Prices) Act the previous year, and the suspicion that the company was, in fact, controlled by Vacuum Oil, came up for discussion in New Zealand's Parliament in October 1934 — as reported by the Evening Star:

"Parliamentary Report of 30 October 1934 — Allegations of the existence of what he called 'a piratical oil company, formed for the purpose of price cutting,' were made in the House of Representatives by Mr Fraser, the Labour member for Wellington Central, and were supported in some respects by Mr J A Nash, the Government member for Palmerston North.

"The difficulties of the petrol resellers were under consideration, and Mr Fraser was making a plea that they should be helped to maintain good conditions for their employees by having a reasonable minimum retail price fixed by law…

"Mr Fraser…added that the difficulty was caused by a mysterious company known as the Gilmore Oil Company, registered in Delaware, USA so that nobody could get access to its records. New Zealand shareholders were Sir James Gunson [James Henry Gunson, Auckland Mayor from 1915 to 1925] and the Gilmore Oil Company of Australia.

"I am sure…that Sir James will not deny that the Gilmore Oil Company of New Zealand was sold to the Vacuum Oil Company of New York, and that if we were given access to the records, this would be proved. The Gilmore Oil Company was registered at Delaware obviously for the purpose of being used in various countries for piratical purposes. This is a factor in the disorganisation of the petrol reselling industry…

"Later in the debate, Mr Harris (Waitemata) said that, in fairness to the Gilmore Company, there had been no evidence of any practices on their part that could be questioned in the slightest way. When the Gilmore Company purchased the business of an aerial [Aerial motor spirit] company it had agreed to continue contracts to supply a certain number of pumps with petrol in bulk. There were still two or three contracts to be completed.

"The object of the company was to purchase petrol in bulk and sell it in drums to stock and station agents, farmers, and dairy companies, and it was not right to say that this concern was competing in the ordinary way with the petrol sellers.

"Replying to the debate, Mr McLeod (chairman of the Industries and Commerce Committee) said they were not entirely satisfied with the Gilmore Company. The general manager of that concern had been very frank, but the speaker did not think that the manager knew the whole history of that firm. The Gilmore Company imported only one-fortieth of the total petrol, and if that was so he did not think the company could play a very big part in the petrol business." [120]

During the Parliamentary debate, Mr J A Nash (Palmerston) stated:

"The Gilmore Oil Company operates in Palmerston North, and although there are petrol-bowsers all over the place, only four petrol-stations sell the Gilmore petrol at the cut rate of 2d. per gallon less than that charged by the major oil companies. I presume that that is substantially the position all over New Zealand. Some resellers are placed in an unfair position as a result." [121]

"By 1940, Socony-Vacuum Oil Company Inc had acquired 75.56% of the Gilmore Oil Company stock and Gilmore became a subsidiary of Socony-Vacuum whose trade name was Mobiloil.

"In 1942, the company started the transition of stations from Gilmore to Mobil, and by 1945 the task was completed. All leased stations and all 50 bulk plants, 3777 acres of oil property, and two remaining refineries became part of Socony-Vacuum Oil Company Inc which is now Mobil Oil Corporation." [122]

Oklahoma Trading Corporation/Meteor

The Oklahoma Trading Corporation and sister company, Nevada Oil Company Limited, were incorporated on 13 December 1920 as export and import companies at 2 Rector Street, Manhattan, New York, each with a Capital of $100,000. The original Directors of the companies were named as K Ress, H Gitlin, and J M Herzberg. [123]

The Oklahoma Trading Corporation applied to the United States Patent Office for the trade mark, USOL, for its illuminating [kerosene] and lubricating oils and greases in February 1922, claiming use since November 1921. [124]

By 1921, New Zealand was importing the Oklahoma Trading Corporation's 'Meteor' Oklahoma Motor Spirit in wooden crates containing 8 imperial gallons [125] — as advertised in the Northern Advocate during November of that year:

"Meteor Motor Spirit — It is a super-refined motor-spirit from the world-famous Oklahoma Oil Fields…Meteor is subjected to a special distillation to render it suitable to our New Zealand climatic conditions…Distributors for Auckland Province: A B Donald Ltd, Auckland." [126]

In February 1923 the assets and liabilities of the Oklahoma Trading Corporation were taken over by another American company, the Texas Foreign Trading Corporation. [127]

A B Donald

A B Donald Limited, the Auckland district distributors of Meteor Motor Spirit from about November 1921, was founded by Alexander Bell Donald who advertised his Queen Street business as ship chandler & sailmaker as early as 1869. He was trading very successfully by 1877 — according to a report published by The New Zealand Herald in February of that year:

"The contracts recently given out by the commanding officer of H.I.M.S. Hertha, for the refitting of the vessel, are rapidly approaching completion, and we are glad to record that those which are finished have met with the approval of the officers composing the commission…One of the largest contracts was that secured by Mr A B Donald, sailmaker, who tendered for a complete suit of sails for the ship, and we are informed that it is the largest job of the kind that has ever been executed in the colony…" [128]

By 1880, A B Donald Limited was advertising itself as ship chandler, sail, tent, and tarpaulin maker, corner of Fort and Queen Streets — suppliers of "…white and red leads, paints, varnish and linseed oil…" [129]

The business, which also traded as Donald & Edenborough, also owned several ships that principally traded between New Zealand and the Pacific Islands. [130]

Descendants of Alexander Donald continued the business as Donald Distributors Limited and A B Donald (Rotorua) Limited until their liquidation on 16 August 1965. [131]

Atlantic Union Oil Company/Atlantic

It was announced in September 1924 that yet another American company, the Union Oil Company of California, had provided the American automobile industry, the original Road Gang, with much hope for the future:

"In quest of the oil from which is produced gasoline which propels America's 13,000,000 automobiles, the Union Oil Company of California has accomplished the astounding feat of drilling a well with a rotary engine to a depth of almost a mile and a half. The world's record for oil well drilling has been accomplished in the Gardena No. 1 well of the Union Oil Company, located ten miles south of Los Angeles, states the San Francisco Chronicle.

"The automobile industry, which is marching hand in hand with the oil industry, owes much to the latter for such exploratory feats as this sinking of a well 7300 feet underground in search for oil. Cries that the country will face a shortage of gasoline can be answered by the assertion that so long as companies like the Union Oil let nothing stand in the way of the search for petroleum, even to drilling a mile and a half into the earth, automobiles may be driven with assurance of an indefinite supply of fuel." [132]

Following the amalgamation of Union Oil with the Atlantic Refining Company, the bulk transportation of Atlantic Union petroleum products to New Zealand was planned in 1927 — as reported by the Auckland Star and Poverty Bay Herald:

"Mr James Vandyke, chairman of the Atlantic Refining Company, has confirmed the agreement that his company made with the Union Oil Company of California. It is stated the two companies have agreed to incorporate an Australian company to be known as the Atlantic Union Oil Company Limited for the purpose of consolidation and expansion of their respective businesses in Australia and New Zealand.

"Mr. Vandyke said arrangements are now under way for the erection of modern ocean terminals at Sydney, Melbourne, Auckland and Wellington and internal distribution will be made from these terminals by tank car, tank wagon and service stations on a parallel, to a large degree, with the methods of delivery employed in the United States." [133]

"Interesting and important developments are taking place in connection with the oil and motor spirit supplies of the Dominion, the latest being the advent of the Atlantic Union Oil Co

Ltd which is putting in large installations for the storage and handling of its products at Wellington and Auckland.

"The Atlantic Union Oil Co Ltd has been registered in New Zealand to take over and expand the interests of the Union Oil Co of California, with headquarters at Los Angeles, and the Atlantic Refining Co. of Philadelphia, which are said to be two of the largest concerns in the petroleum industry of the United States.

"The Union Oil Co., with resources of £40,000,000 employs 9000 men, and has a fleet of 15 large oil tankers, two of which are over 8000 tons register. The Atlantic Refining Co with resources of £30,000,000, has over 10,000 employees and operates a fleet of 18 ships, the largest being a tanker of nearly 10,000 tons. The two companies are stated to have a daily output of 200,000 barrels of petroleum products…" [134]

"The Atlantic Union Oil Company is one of the largest petroleum organisations in the world…It refines 8,000,000 gallons daily in its nine refineries at Philadelphia…Its 3,500 motor tank waggons operate in 27 countries…" [135]

With so much oil and petroleum being produced, its transportation and storage remained a risky business but still insurable — as reported in April 1926:

"A message from San Luis states that with an area of three miles square burning fiercely, California's two great oil fires continue altogether beyond control, with a likelihood of 26 tanks all exploding and their contents being destroyed. The losses run to millions beyond the first estimates. Orange groves in the vicinity are flooded with boiling liquid, and a veritable river of oil has overflowed on to the nearby highways, blocking traffic. The Union Oil Company has issued a statement to the effect that the losses are fully covered by insurance…" [136]

And New Zealand was not immune to the danger — as reported by The New Zealand Herald in April 1928:

"Petrol and motor oils to the value of about £50,000 were destroyed yesterday when the burning of the oil store of Winstone Ltd in Freeman's Bay, provided the most spectacular fire in the history of Auckland.

"Discovered at half-past one in the afternoon the fire raged with unabated fury throughout the whole of the afternoon and night, and at an early hour this morning there was no sign of the flames subsiding.

"Expert opinion is that there is a possibility of the fire continuing for many hours, unless some unexpected development occurs. A similar fire, but one of smaller dimensions in Beach Road some years ago, burned for three days. The building was stored to the roof with almost 500,000 gallons of petrol in cases and 40 gallon drums, the last lot having been put into the store on Saturday morning.

"All that was saved of this large quantity of spirit was three cases of benzine, which were ultimately used to feed the fire brigade pumps. About 20,000 cases were stored on behalf of Messrs. H O Wiles Limited…

"Messrs Wright Stephenson Limited had about 5000 cases in the building, this stock being insured for about £3000…Messrs Robertson Bros also had about 5000 cases and 250 drums in store…

"The Dominion Trading Company also lost about 1000 cases and 100 drums…There were also various smaller lots stored by other firms." [137]

The loss of so much petroleum product was nevertheless soon replaced by a bulk shipment of Atlantic Union Oil Company petrol which arrived at Auckland in June 1928:

"The first shipment of petrol for the Atlantic Union Oil Company is being carried by the tanker Ranja, which is due at Auckland on Monday from Los Angeles. After unloading a quantity of bulk motor spirit into the company's tanks at Freeman's Bay she will sail for Wellington when she is due about the 10th of June to complete discharge…" [138]

By the 1930s, oil and petrol companies sought various ways to differentiate their brands from those of their competitors — as advertised by the Northern Advocate in November 1933:

"No one motor fuel possesses the attributes necessary to suit all types of motor vehicles. For example, the highly volatile spirit preferred by motorists for its easy starting properties and flashing acceleration cannot possibly meet the requirements of the truck driver, who wants a slower burning gas, generating more power, and giving greater mileage. Maximum motoring efficiency demands Two distinct fuels!

"The selection of the correct type of petrol for your particular motor purpose is made easy by these Two distinct fuels manufactured by the Atlantic Union Oil Company Ltd…Atlantic Petrol or Union White Flash…Both the same price - both super grades…" [139]

Surprisingly, regional expansion of the Atlantic Union Oil Company's services to the lower South Island didn't occur until September 1949:

"Advice has been received from Wellington that the Atlantic Union Oil Company, Limited (inc. in N.S.W.), has decided to extend its services to the southern half of the South Island and will, from next Monday, be ready to serve Otago and Southland in all the ways in which it has served the rest of New Zealand during the last 22 years.

"The Atlantic organisation is the New Zealand link in the world-wide (and world-famous) chain of Esso marketers. The renown of Esso products is too well known internationally to need mention, but less well known is the fact that there are now over eleven hundred petroleum products sold under the Esso banner— specialised fuels, lubricants, solvents, waxes and the like, of which Atlantic petrol and kerosene are in this country, the best known, and Essolube the most recent." [140]

Ten years later and the competitive edge of one brand over another continued to be promoted — this time by an advertisement in the Christchurch Press of December 1959:

"Fill your tank today with Atlantic VITANE the only petrol with the dynamic new power compound VITANE developed by Atlantic research laboratories…frees wasted octanes…adds power to your engine…reduces power-robbing deposits…breathes new life into your engine…" [141]

The Atlantic Union Oil Company formally became a New Zealand-registered company in December 1960:

"The Atlantic Union Oil Company Pty Ltd which formerly traded in New Zealand as a branch of the Atlantic Union Oil Company, Australia, was registered as a New Zealand company under the Companies Act on December 20. The company will be known in future as the Atlantic Union Oil Company (New Zealand) Ltd. The registration names the present New Zealand manager, Mr E J Melrose, as the sole director. Shareholders are E J Melrose and the Atlantic Union Oil Company Pty Ltd of Australia. Atlantic entered the New Zealand market in 1928. Since that time the constitution of the company in New Zealand has not been altered." [142]

By February 1980, no doubt to consolidate their market share, the Atlantic Union Oil Company and Mobil Petroleum (which had acquired the assets in New Zealand of the Standard Vacuum Oil Company in April 1962 and held a considerable shareholding in Atlantic Union) announced a consolidation of their marketing activities — as reported by the Christchurch Press:

"In a joint statement last evening, Mobil's chairman (Mr P W Marriott) and the general manager of Atlantic (Mr J A Hazlett) announced that the two companies would consolidate their activities to set up one marketing organisation. The shares of both companies are held by Mobil Petroleum Inc." [143]

Eventually, a full amalgamation occurred: Mobil New Zealand Finance Corporation Limited, Mobil Oil New Zealand Limited, and Atlantic Union Oil Co NZ Limited amalgamated to become Mobil Oil New Zealand Limited on 31 October 1998. [144]

H O Wiles

Harold Oliver Wiles (1884-1964) began his Auckland business career as a Chemist with shops at Queen Street and Great North Road, Grey Lynn from about 1905. Eventually, he branched out opening as a wholesale manufacturing chemist and indent merchant in Fort Street on 1 June 1912. [145]

H O Wiles Limited was registered on 15 January 1917 and the company existed under the care of descendants to 26 July 2007. [146]

By June 1920, H O Wiles had expanded its business to include the distribution of motor vehicles, motorcycles and associated ancillaries — as advertised in the Northern Advocate:

"The District Agency For The Well Known Paige Motor Cars [Jewett] and Trucks, James Motor Cycles, Old Oak Covers and Tubes, J.E.D. Fuel Economisers is open to be allotted.

"Live Firms will seize the opportunity of these representations. Attractive terms will be offered and full facilities given to develop sales. Write now for full particulars to H O Wiles Limited 65 Fort Street, Auckland." [147]

From at least 1921, H O Wiles Limited advertised itself as distributors of motor spirit for the Auckland Province and sole importers of "Power Benzine — Union Oil Company of California (UNOCO)." [148]

During the previously-referred-to fire at the Winstone's Store in April 1928, H O Wiles Limited lost about 20,000 cases of petroleum products. [149]

Nevertheless, not all eggs had been placed in one basket, Harold Wiles assured his customers:

"We wish to place on record our sincere thanks to our many valued clients for messages of sympathy on account of serious loss of petrol stocks at Winstone's Store. Fortunately we have sufficient stocks of all grades in our other stores to meet all current requirements. Orders faithfully and promptly attended to. Howdah Motor Spirit (Equivalent Unoco) Unoco Motor Spirit, Unoco Benzine. Howdah Kerosenes. H O Wiles Ltd - Harold O Wiles, Managing Director, Anzac Avenue." [150]

Not long after, in May 1928, H O Wiles Limited divested itself of the petroleum business but not so its managing director:

"The petroleum branch of the business carried on by Messrs H O Wiles Ltd, general importers, has been sold to an American firm, the Atlantic Union Oil Company Ltd. The purchase price, which is stated to be considerable, has not been disclosed. For some time past H O Wiles Ltd has been carrying the Union Oil products among their many lines. Now the American firm has determined to open a branch in New Zealand and has appointed Mr Wiles the Auckland manager..." [151]

Harold Wiles remained the Auckland manager of Atlantic Union Oil for some eighteen years, until his retirement in May 1946 — as reported by the Gisborne Herald:

"A large gathering of the staff of the Atlantic Union Oil Co Ltd farewelled Mr H O Wiles, retiring manager of the Auckland branch, at a smoke concert last week..." [152]

British International Oil Company/Aerial

One of the earliest advertisements for Aerial Motor Spirit was published by the Manawatu Standard in May 1928 with Combined Buyers Limited stated to be the sole importers of the brand:

"Aerial Motor Spirit is stocked by all Dairy Factories and by the Sole Importers, Combined Buyers Limited, Rangitikei Street, Palmerston North" [153]

Combined Buyers Limited, as described in a later chapter, was registered in August 1916 to carry on the business of merchants and importers of motors and motor vehicles. [154]

The business purchased a three-storied building at the corner of Dixon and Quinn Streets, Wellington, [155] and once wartime restrictions had eased, it imported and sold all manner of automotive accessories, operating as co-operative for the benefit of its shareholding members.

However, the Directors of the company quarrelled over the importation of motor spirits and other matters and liquidators were subsequently appointed on 18 January 1929. [156]

By June 1929, The British International Oil Company Limited was advertising Aerial motor spirit as a successor to Combined Buyers Limited:

"Aerial First Grade Motor Spirit 1/9 a Gallon — The British International Oil Co Ltd, Jackson Street [Masterton] (Late Combined Buyers Limited)" [157]

In subsequent advertisements, The British International Oil Company also offered a number of vehicles as "…the balance of Combined Buyers' Liquidation Stock…" [158]

The British International Oil Company Limited (Company No. 1927/209) was incorporated in 1927 with a capital of £250,000. The principals of the company included Robert Graham Buckleton as Managing Director and his younger brother, John Graham Buckleton. Both were the sons of Sir Henry Buckleton, the long-serving general manager of the Bank of New Zealand.

By January 1929, The British International Oil had adjusted its capitalisation — as reported by the Evening Post:

"British International Oil Co Ltd has reduced its capital from £250,000 to £25,000 by cancelling 199,894 preference shares of £1 each and 25,000 ordinary shares of £1 each." [159]

The company had also become a car dealer at Taranaki Street, Wellington, advertising for salesmen in the Evening Post in May and July 1929:

"Wanted, a smart youth, about 17, for our Used Car Department. One able to drive a car preferred. Apply British International Oil Company 81-89 Taranaki street." [160]

"Motor-Car Salesmen. We require Several Energetic Salesmen for our New and Used Cars. The British International Oil Co Ltd 91-99 Taranaki street, Wellington." [161]

In the meantime, The British International Oil Company continued to expand its sales of Aerial petrol and other automotive products in Wellington causing a price war, according to an Evening Post report of November 1930:

"Though it is a far call from Wall street, where investors stand and fall on the fluctuations of oil stock brought about by battles for markets, Wellington people can take a passing interest in price wars nearer home. There is a petrol price war on in Wellington at the present moment, which has been chiefly brought about by the entry into the retail field by the British International Oil Company, an independent New Zealand concern.

"With the opening of a new petrol and service station on up-to-date lines in Lower Tory street; by the British International people, the fourth move in the petrol price war in Wellington has been played. Developments will be watched with interest.

"The British International Oil Company opened a new Service Station on the Hutt road last July, and made an entry into the retail business. The increase in tariff was brought about in August, when the duty was raised from 4d to 6d a gallon. The major oil companies carried one-penny of this duty, and the British International Oil Company did likewise.

"In November, the associated service stations in Wellington reduced their prices by one penny, making the retail prices the same as those which ruled before the increase in tariff. This was followed by the independent New Zealand Company establishing a new Service Station in Lower Tory street, where petrol is being sold at even a lower price.

"While it would appear as though the local company, whose resources are comparatively small when compared with those of the big foreign vested interests controlling the petrol business in New Zealand, is up against a tough proposition, the competition has brought about a reduction in petrol prices by 2d a gallon, which amounts to an approximate saving to the motorists on the Wellington register £50,000 a year." [162]

However, price competition did not come without some criticism that demanded a response:

"It has come to the knowledge of The British International Oil Co Ltd, Importers and Distributors of Aerial Petroleum Products, that certain slanderous statements have been made concerning the quality and attributes of Aerial Motor Spirit And Gasoline. A reward will be given by the Company to any person giving information as to the statements made, and as to the names and addresses of any person or persons making any such statements.

"Aerial customers are assured that all shipments of Aerial Products are tested by a competent analyst before being sold, such certificates being available for inspection at either of our Stations on the Hutt Road or Lower Tory Street upon request. They, therefore, can rely upon the uniformity of grade and performance of Aerial Products. R G Buckleton, Managing Director." [163]

The British International Oil Company also sold Aerial Motor Spirit, Cases and Drums, and automotive accessories from Cashel Street, Christchurch but the company had closed this outlet by August 1930:

"The British International Oil Co Ltd…has closed down its Christchurch Office, and in future Aerial Products will be handled in the South Island by Messrs Kent and Co Ltd 157 Hereford Street, Christchurch." [164]

Nevertheless, its North Island operation continued with competitive tenders submitted to public organisations — such as that reported by the Pahiatua Herald in January 1931:

"Tenders were considered for the supply of motor spirit for the [Tararua Power] Board's Pahiatua vehicles for a period of 12 months (approximately 1,500 gallons) and that of the British International Oil Co for Aerial spirit first grade 2s per gallon and second grade 1s 11d was accepted." [165]

Cut-price incentives offered at The British International Oil Company's service stations continued later that year, as advertised extensively in the Wellington newspapers:

"Free Petrol — 10,000 gallons to be given away before 1st October 1931 at Aerial Service Stations Hutt Road & Lower Tory Street — with the cash purchase at our pumps of 8 gallons in one lot…one extra gallon will be given free on surrender of this coupon — British International Oil Co Ltd — Redeem this Coupon and receive the benefit of the temporary low prices in California." [166]

In 1932, the company opened a third service station on leased Railway Department land at the corner of Whitmore street and Waterloo Quay, Wellington. [167]

Buckleton Brothers Limited

By 1931, the importation of motor spirit in tins had been increasingly replaced by bulk shipments and storage in large oil tanks at the country's ports. As reported by The Dominion, in December 1931, the principals of The British International Oil Company were the innovators of the transition at Wellington:

"A good deal of interest is said to have been created in engineering and constructional circles in what is stated to be the first electrically-welded oil tank to be erected in New Zealand. It is also claimed for it that it is the first tank of its size to be entirely fabricated, and erected by New Zealand labour.

"It was recently built at Waiwetu, Lower Hutt, for Buckleton Bros. Ltd. Messrs R G and J G Buckleton, sons of Sir Henry Buckleton, general manager of the Bank of New Zealand, are the principal shareholders in the British International Oil Company Ltd and they have formed a subsidiary company, Buckleton Bros. Ltd for the purpose of the importation, storage, and distribution of Aerial motor spirit in bulk.

"They acquired property at Lower Hutt, and the first of a series of oil tanks has now been built. The erection of the tank has been a 100 per cent New Zealand job. All the material is British, and wherever possible everything made in New Zealand was used.

"The construction was done by W Cable and Co in the record time of nine weeks, and the tank, which has a capacity of approximately half a million gallons, is now under test. Riveted tanks are likely to be affected when empty, by heavy winds, and in this respect the new tank (which is welded) is unique. Its erection has shown that New Zealand engineers can fabricate and erect in record time such installations." [168]

Buckleton Brothers Limited was incorporated in December 1931 with a Capital of £500, R G Buckleton and J G Buckleton 200 shares each, J F Stewart 100 shares Objects: Business of importers, stores, distributors of and dealers in benzine, motor spirit, and petroleum products of all kinds." [169]

The tanks were soon used — as reported by The Dominion in January 1932:

"An event of considerable interest in the oil and motor-spirit trade of the Dominion was the arrival at Wellington yesterday of the big motor-tanker Bisca, from California, via Australia, with the first large bulk cargo of motor spirit for the first all New Zealand company [The British International Oil Company] to enter the business. The tanker brought one million gallons of motor spirit which is being distributed in equal quantities between the company's newly-constructed oil-tank installations at Wellington and Auckland…This company [Buckleton Brothers] is concerned purely with the bulk storage installations at Wellington and Auckland…

"The bulk storage tank installations…have been planned on the most up-to-date lines and include all the features designed for the rapid and economical handling of motor-spirit. Special mention must be made for the fact that the materials used are British throughout and have been fabricated wholly by New Zealand labour, which has also been employed throughout in the erection of the plants.

"The main storage tank, which has a capacity of over 500,000 gallons, was constructed by W Cable and Co Ltd from stock British steel plates. There is 54 tons of steel in the structure, which is novel in being all welded, not a rivet or a bolt being used in its construction. The tank installation is connected to the tanker wharf at Point Howard by a 6-inch pipe-line which is just under one mile in length. The pipeline, which is all welded throughout its length, was made and installed by Hume Steel Ltd…" [170]

The arrival of the Bisca was also reported by the Evening Post which again emphasised that the storage and distribution of the motor spirit was an all-New Zealand effort:

"An all-New Zealand enterprise, Messrs Buckleton Bros' petrol storage installation at Point Howard has been brought into operation. The first big shipment of petrol, 500,000 gallons, arrived yesterday by the 7000-ton motor tanker Bisca from San Diego, California, and a similar shipment will arrive about every eleven weeks…

"The present storage installations are at Wellington and Auckland and the petrol will be distributed by the British International Oil Company which will dispose of the shipments throughout the Dominion. Already there are some fifty distributing points for Aerial spirit." [171]

Indeed, The British International Oil Company and Buckleton Brothers were the first all-New Zealand importers and distributors of motor spirit (Aerial) in the country and not the Associated Motorists' Petrol Company, the importers of the Europa brand, which came later — as explained by a disclaimer published by The Dominion on 22 January 1932:

"In the report in yesterday's issue regarding the arrival of the tanker Bisca with supplies of petrol for the new bulk installation of Buckleton Bros. Ltd, it was incorrectly stated that the Wellington Automobile Club and the Canterbury Automobile Association would participate in the marketing of the petrol.

"The distribution is actually being carried out by the British International Oil Company, an organisation which is not to be confused with the former British Imperial Oil Company, now known as the Shell Company of New Zealand. There is no foundation for the association of either of the automobile clubs with negotiations with the companies previously mentioned, and no undertaking has been entered into with the new bulk company.

"Mr. E A Batt, chairman of the executive of the Wellington Automobile Club, confirmed this position last evening, and added that in fact members of automobile clubs throughout the Dominion were supporting the Associated Motorists' Petrol Company, which would shortly commence operations in New Zealand by the importation of petrol in bulk for distribution to motor users…" [172]

However, the companies' tenure as independent national entities was not to last for long — as reported by the Evening Post in May 1932:

"The businesses of the British International Oil Co Ltd of Wellington, and of Messrs Buckleton Bros. Ltd Wellington, have been acquired by the Gilmore Oil Co (NZ) Ltd Auckland. The first-named company was the marketing company for petrol and allied products and Messrs Buckleton Bros. Ltd undertook the storage and handling of the British International Company's goods. These two companies were owned and registered in New Zealand and furnished with New Zealand capital. Their Auckland district representative, Petrol Imports Ltd of Auckland, is also to be acquired by the Gilmore Oil Co and negotiations to that end are now approaching completion, to take over as from 1st June." [173]

Following their acquisition by the Gilmore Oil Company, both The British International Oil Company Limited and Buckleton Brothers Limited were placed into voluntary liquidation on 30 March 1933. [174]

Associated Motorists' Petrol Company/Europa

The involvement of the Todd family and the Todd Motor Corporation in the assembly and selling of vehicles has been referred to in a previous chapter.

As well as this activity, "…was the Todd's interest in the oil business — ultimately the greatest source of their wealth", according to Graeme Hunt in his book, The Rich List — Wealth and Enterprise in New Zealand 1820-2000.

Graeme Hunt's profile of Bryan Todd goes on to relate how he "…entered the petroleum industry after being denied supplies because of a price war in Christchurch in 1929. In 1931 he formed the Associated Motorists' Petrol Co (AMPC) with the help of friends, the New Zealand Farmers' Union…and car clubs." [175]

The company imported its first shipment from Russia with 7179 tons arriving in New Zealand aboard the tanker, Reliance, on 9 March 1933. [176]

"…the oil was christened 'Europa' to help disguise its communist origins — the brand went on sale nationwide in the same year…" [177]

"As the decade went on, the network grew, but not before Europa's arrival caused a price war. The price of motor spirit dropped eight times in 1933 alone, until the Government stepped in with price regulations that lasted in one form or another till 1988." [178]

"Europa Oil New Zealand Limited was established in 1954. In 1972, 60 percent of the capital of Europa was sold to BP New Zealand Limited. The transaction, which took place on 30 June 1972, was with Government approval but on the condition that the interests of the Europa group in mining and in petroleum exploration were transferred to companies owned by New Zealand citizens." [179]

BP "…also bought Europa's 26-strong service station network after deregulation of the industry in 1988." [180] However, the involvement of the Todd family in the oil industry did not end there. As detailed later, the family continued with investment as joint venture partners in NZ oil and gas exploration.

The British Petroleum Company/BP

"The British Petroleum Company of New Zealand Ltd was established in December 1946. Fifty-one percent of the company's shares were subscribed by the New Zealand Government; 49 percent by the Anglo-Iranian Oil Co Ltd of London. The Government's shareholding was transferred at par to the British Petroleum Co Ltd in 1955. The name of the New Zealand company was changed to BP New Zealand Ltd in 1957." [181]

"The experience of World War II, including New Zealand's dependence on Washington for the allocation of petroleum supplies and other material supplies and the uncertainty as to the future, together with certain reservations that Sir Walter Nash had concerning international companies, led to the Labour Government seeking an agreement with The Anglo-Iranian Company (BP) for the introduction of a new source of supply of petroleum products to New Zealand and the establishment of BP as an additional marketer within New Zealand.

"The New Zealand Government subscribed £1,275,000 of BP's initial capital of £2,500,000. Mr Nash said that it was the Government's intention to appoint some of the directors but to leave the company to manage its own affairs.

"BP's first cargo of motor spirits arrived on 15 April 1949 and within the space of 3 months there were 362 BP pumps distributed throughout New Zealand. By February 1951 BP New Zealand had 896 motor spirit pumps which represented some 8 percent of the total industry pumps." [182]

"There was concern about favouritism when BP arrived in New Zealand in 1946 because it was owned fifty per cent by the government. BP responded saying it only wanted fair trade…" [183]

In May 1989, the Christchurch Press reported:

"BP New Zealand Ltd, the unlisted subsidiary of the British international oil company, lifted its profit in spite of static sales in 1988. The company reports a group after-tax profit of $97,966,000 for the year ended December 31 on sales of $1.189 billion. This compares with a profit of $62.9M on sales of $1.180B in 1987…

"Downstream oil and gas business performed strongly, Mr Orange [John Orange, managing director] said. After deregulation, BP moved quickly to buy up its key service stations, including those owned by the Todd Group. It also bought Top Group and solo sites. Coro Trading New Zealand was set up to own and run most of the service stations bought, plus the 10 sites owned before deregulation.

"The company also bought Mobil's bitumen business, Emoleum, NZ Ltd, a minority interest in the road contracting company, McLoughlins Holdings, and bought the outstanding shares in Dominion Oil Refining." [184]

Gull Petroleum

Gull Petroleum was founded in Western Australia by Keith Mitchell, Mark Quackenbush, and Terry Lockwood in 1976. In 1978, a controlling interest in the business was acquired by Western Australia businessman, Frederick William Rae, who established Gull New Zealand in 1998. [185]

The Gull New Zealand website describes its New Zealand beginnings:

"Launched in 1998, with the building of its state-of-the-art terminal in Mount Maunganui…The terminal, with a total storage capacity of 90 million litres, is significantly larger than the other Mount Maunganui installations.

"Gull then made its first retail sale of petrol in 1999 and has grown its network to over 115 unmanned, manned and marina-branded sites around New Zealand, with Gull Norton Road [Frankton, Hamilton] appearing the North Island site in 1999, and Gull Maheno [State Highway 1, south of Oamaru], the inaugural South Island, twenty years later in 2019." [186]

In the meantime, the New Zealand company was acquired by Caltex Australia in 2017 as per the Australian Stock Exchange release of 26 June 2017:

"Caltex Australia Limited…welcomes the consent of the New Zealand Overseas Investment Office to its proposed acquisition of Gull New Zealand for a purchase price of NZ$340 million…Caltex anticipates completing the acquisition on Monday 3 July 2017." [187]

In May 2020, Caltex Australia officially changed its name and began to rebrand as Ampol with which it had been associated for many years. In March 2022, Ampol sold Gull New Zealand to the Australian private equity firm, Allegro Funds, for $572 million. [188]

Nevertheless, the Gull brand continues:

"These days Gull sells over 500 megalitres of fuel annually, representing an approximate 8% market share of New Zealand's liquid fuel volumes." [189]

Imports of Motor Spirits

New Zealand's gross importations of motor spirits between 1914 and 1935 are recorded in gallons by various Government annual reports and statements:

1914 — 6,799,625	1925 — 33,307,588
1915 — 7,171,965	1926 — 44,817,512
1916 — 9,214,524	1927 — 48,042,640
1917 — 8,259,404	1928 — 54,540,416
1918 — 10,725,149	1929 — 62,448,092 *[190]
1919 — 8,906,185	1930 — 68,300,000
1920 — 17,970,995	1931 — 61,800,000
1921 — 19,138,846	1932 — 58,400,000
1922 — 16,585,616	1933 — 55,400,000
1923 — 20,364,065	1934 — 64,600,000
1924 — 28,989,126	1935 — 65,300,000 **[191]

*[Transport Department Annual Report for Year Ending 31 March 1930]
**[Public Works Statement for Year Ending 31 March 1936]

Inquiry into the Distribution Of Motor Spirits and Ancillary Products

A Commission of Inquiry into the Distribution Of Motor Spirits and Ancillary Products, appointed 19 August 1974, recorded New Zealand's consumption of various petroleum products in the 1973 and 1974 calendar years (in millions of litres) as:

"Motor Gasoline 2265.25 & 2199.8
"Diesel 1180.13 & 1043.5
"Lubricants 65.46 & 85.3
"Bitumen 123.65 & 123.5" [192]

In 1975, the Individual Wholesaler's Market Shares of the New Zealand Motor Spirits Market included: "Shell 22.9%, BP 15%, Mobil 17.2% Atlantic 11.1%, Caltex 16.9%, and Europa 16.9%." [193]

Petrol Price Regulation

As previously noted, the independence of one of the first oil companies to sell motor spirit in New Zealand, the Gilmore Oil Company, allowed it to undercut the prices charged by Shell, Atlantic and Mobil. The later establishment of the Associated Motorists Petrol Company's Europa-branded petrol continued the potential for price competition in 1931 — as outlined by the Commission of Inquiry into the Distribution of Motor Spirits, which reported in 1976:

"The advent of a New Zealand-owned independent oil wholesaler in 1931 can be said to be the first incident which disturbed (beneficially) the equilibrium of the New Zealand motor spirits market. The early 1930s saw a price war amongst the oil wholesalers caused primarily by the fact that the newest and independent entrant into the oil wholesaling business, the Associated Motorists Petrol Co Limited (AMP), offered [Europa-branded] petrol for sale at substantially less than the other international oil companies...

"AMP was independent not only in the case of being a New Zealand-owned company but also by virtue of the fact that it obtained its source of supply from Russia.

"The international oil companies reacted by indulging in a retail price war. Retailers of motor spirits were particularly affected and, in 1932, a group of petrol resellers petitioned Parliament to pass legislation to control the price of petrol.

"In 1933, AMP as a New Zealand-owned wholesaler, also made representations to the Government seeking to safeguard its position, which was seriously threatened by the retaliatory price-cutting resorted to by the other internationally-owned oil companies and directed at crushing the new entrant to the market." [194]

AMP's representations resulted in a report completed by the Industries and Commerce Committee which was presented to Parliament on 5 December 1933.

The Committee's findings included:

"(1) that the recent progressive fall in prices was due mainly to the combination on the part of the major oil companies with the object of crushing the Associated Motorists Petrol Company Limited;

"(2) that present selling prices are uneconomic and unlikely to result in destroying competition among sellers, thus bringing about monopoly;

"(3) that such monopoly will probably result in substantially increasing prices to consumers;

"(4) that in the public interest the petitions should be referred to the Government for immediate and most favourable consideration, with a recommendation that special legislation should be enacted to control selling prices, or, in the alternative, that the powers provided in the Board of Trade Act 1919 be invoked for that purpose…" [195]

When presenting the Committee's report to Parliament, the Hon. Mr McLeod (Wairarapa) stated:

"The main evidence on behalf of the petitioners was given by Mr Todd, managing director of the Associated Motorists Petrol Company Limited. Full opportunity was given by the Committee for all other petrol companies trading in New Zealand to give evidence, but all courteously replied by letter declining to do so…

"Since the advent of Europa in March 1933, the wholesale price of petrol in New Zealand to consumers has been reduced by the major petrol companies by at least 6d per gallon, notwithstanding the addition to landed cost and 2d extra duty imposed in February.

"In his evidence in chief, Mr Todd also complained that the associated newspapers were discriminating as to advertising, to the disadvantage of his company, and to the advantage of major petrol companies…

"Mr Earle, as president of the Newspaper Proprietors' Association of New Zealand Incorporated, stated in evidence that in New Zealand his association followed the rules, adopted generally throughout the British Empire, of not permitting the insertion of advertisements by one competitor which reflected on a rival competitor…

"Re-examined, Mr Todd submitted evidence that his company (apart from other instances) had had an advertisement refused by the Newspaper Proprietors Association…pointing out that Europa had saved petrol consumers of New Zealand £2,250,000 over a year's consumption of petrol, while the association had permitted Big Tree to advertise that its petrol had a bigger mileage, better acceleration, bigger power, and had more economic value than any other first-grade spirit. Also that Big Tree was marketed in New Zealand by a New Zealand company with New Zealand capital.

"In addition to being a reflection on the quality of other petrols, Mr Todd stated that Big Tree was neither New Zealand nor British, but was owned and controlled by the Shell Company which paid the salaries and superannuation of Big Tree employees…

"While far from being unanimous as to the wisdom of fixing of prices generally, the Committee is unanimous – seeing the important part played by petrol in the industries of New Zealand – that price fixation of petrol should not be within the complete control of a trading monopoly." [196]

In reply, Mr Lee (Grey Lynn) commented:

"Sir, it is clear that the New Zealand is being run not by a Government but by external combines. American firms trading in New Zealand overcharge or adopt any tactics that will enable them to get a stranglehold on the business of the country…

"They introduce a petrol war for the purpose of undercutting prices; and everyone knows that the moment prices are undermined and the trade is concentrated in the wrong hands, up will go the price again…it is interesting to hear that a firm which was condemning Europa spirit on the ground that it was produced by godless community has been importing petrol from a godless country and selling it in this Dominion. It shows what little concern for ethical principles there is about these combines; all they are concerned about is the opportunity to make the maximum profit…

"...in New Zealand the Government has abdicated to the newspaper combine, or the oil combine, or the picture combine, or the banking combine; those combines call the tune and the people are compelled to march accordingly." [197]

In further reply, Mr Samuel (Thames) commented:

"There is no doubt that the foreign corporations are so powerful and so influential, and their resources, which they will use to the very last copper to squeeze out competition, so unlimited, that the Government has a tremendous responsibility...

"The motorists combined for the purpose of giving a cheap petrol supply to the users in New Zealand. They were not welcomed by the foreign corporations who eventually decided that they were to be squeezed out – they were to be suppressed at all costs.

"The trust [Standard/Vacuum Oil] immediately commenced to reduce their prices and by way of explanation, pointed out or stated definitely that they could reduce their prices on account of lowered costs. I think it was proved in the Committee...that that statement was altogether inaccurate — that instead of the landed costs in this country being lower they were greater than before." [198]

Captain Rushworth (Bay of Islands) commented:

"The fact is that benzine plays such a very important part in the cost of living of everybody in the Dominion. The position now is that the price-cutting war has developed but that was anticipated. The very first question that was raised when the company [Europa] was formed was what would be done in such a price cutting policy developed.

"Here is an oil combine [Standard/Vacuum Oil] that is world famous and is known to be fearfully unscrupulous and vindictive. Is there any possibility of putting up a successful fight against such a combine as that? We know what has happened in other parts of the world. That combine has been accused of resorting even to assassination to achieve its object. What chance would a small company here have in fighting such a combine as that? That was the question that was raised when the company was formed..." [199]

Mr Langstone (Waimarino) commented:

"Previously we had been told that the oil companies were making from £2,750,000 to £3,000,000 a year profit and that they were clearing from 9d per gallon to 1s per gallon; and the Government knew that people of this country were being exploited to that extent...

"But the Government dared not interfere with the trust and what the honourable member for Wellington Suburbs has said is true -– that the newspapers dare not say anything. They are hand in glove with the oil trust. The half-page and full-page advertisements of the big oil companies –- Big Tree, Voco, Shell, and so on — very effectually control the press...

"The independent company has saved the people of the Dominion £2,000,000 since it has been in operation, and that is naturally a very big thing for the oil trust. It has been shown in evidence that the trust has been buying Russian petrol and selling it as Big Tree, Shell, and so forth. It can be any old tree for all the trust cares..." [200]

Motor-spirits (Regulation of Prices) Act 1933

Further Parliamentary debate ultimately resulted in price regulation enforced by the Motor-spirits (Regulation of Prices) Act 1933 which became law on 22 December 1933.

The main part of the Act stipulated:

"3. (1) The Minister can fix maximum and minimum (wholesale and retail) prices at which motor-spirits can be sold by Order in Council 6. (1) It is an offence against the Act to sell above or below any maximum or minimum price fixed from time to time. 10. (1) Accurate accounts of transactions to be kept for inspection if required." [201]

Petrol price regulations "...lasted in one form or another till 1988." [202]

Motor-spirits Prices (North Canterbury) Regulations 1936

Later, district-specific regulations were introduced to define the classes of motor spirits for pricing purposes:

"1. These regulations may be cited as the Motor-spirits Prices (North Canterbury) Regulations, 1936.

"2. These regulations shall come into force on the day following the date of the publication thereof in the *Gazette*.

"3. For the purposes of these regulations there shall be two classes of motor-spirits, namely,- (*a*) Standard grade motor-spirits. (*b*) Premium grade motor-spirits.

"All motor-spirits sold at any time after the coming into force of these regulations under the following names, brands, or descriptions-namely, Power Chief, Texaco 400, Shell, Big Tree, Plume, Atlantic, and Europa are hereby declared to belong to the class of standard grade motor-spirits.

"All motor-spirits sold at any time after the coming into force of these regulations under the following names, brands, or descriptions-namely, Super Power Chief, Super Shell, Super Plume Ethyl, and Atlantic Ethyl-are hereby declared to belong to the class of premium grade motor-spirits." [203]

The Industrial Efficiency Act 1936

"The Industrial Efficiency Act of 1936 was, in itself, a landmark in the development of the oil industry in New Zealand in that for the first time it introduced a form of licensing for both wholesalers and retailers.

"The Act was a means of curbing the proliferation of both pumps and retail outlets. Any wholesaler or retailer of motor spirits who had been in business before 10 December 1936 was automatically entitled to the appropriate licence. However, anyone wishing to become a wholesaler or retailer of motor spirits after that date had to apply to the Bureau of Industry who was responsible for administering the Industrial Efficiency Act.

"In practice the bureau's permission was required for the establishment of a new selling point, a change of ownership, the transfer of pumps to a new site, and very substantial alteration of the existing retail premises, including a change of location of the pumps.

"Essentially, the bureau's criteria for the granting of new retail outlets were the efficiency of existing retail outlets and the potential demand. It is interesting to note that the bureau tended to accord applicants who intended to concentrate on the sale of petrol, a superior claim for a retail outlet, over and above applicants whose first business was in selling motor vehicles or in providing garage repair facilities." [204]

War Rationing

Obviously, oil and petroleum products became a restricted commodity during World War II and for some time afterwards — as reported by the Gisborne Herald in June 1950:

"First introduced as a war measure under the oil fuel emergency regulations in September 1939, the rationing system remained in force until May 30, 1946 when the controls were abolished.

"A modified scheme involving a 10 per cent, reduction in supplies to retailers only was reintroduced on November 4, 1947, but the scheme was unsuccessful and rationing reverted to the coupons and licensing system again on March 1, 1948. [205]

As usual, the country's balance of payments situation was always a consideration when paying for imports but petrol rationing ended on 1 June 1950:

"Petrol rationing ended tonight, and the necessary Order-in-Council will be gazetted immediately. Making an announcement to this effect today, the Prime Minister, Mr Holland, said that Cabinet had given full regard to the sterling position when examining the subject. Cabinet, he said, appreciated that the removal of rationing would involve additional demands on New

Zealand's sterling funds, but these had shown some improvement recently. It was considered that the extra burden involved in the purchase of additional quantities of motor spirit could be accepted." [206]

The Refining of Used Oil

In his address to the technological section of the Wellington Philosophical Society entitled 'Science to the Aid of the Motorist', given on 19 May 1937, Stuart H Wilson explained the two methods then being used to refine used oil:

"There are alternative methods of treating used oil — reconditioning and regeneration. The first seems to be preferred in England and America; the second on the Continent, particularly in Germany. Reconditioning aims not at regenerating an oil as good as new, but at removing only the most harmful impurities. Most of these can be removed by mechanical treatment. Suitable methods are settling, filtration and centrifuging...

"The second method aims at regeneration. The essential process is a fairly simple one of agitation with sulphuric acid, followed by filtration through fullers' earth. More plant is required; and regeneration and blending with new oil would need more expert control than the other process. This method would be more suitable to treatment of mixed oils of various grades...

"As all New Zealand's lubricating oils have to be imported, reclamation of used oil should be of particular interest to us. However, it is unlikely that there are users of amounts of oil large enough to justify going in for reconditioning or regeneration, although the outlook may change in the future..." [207]

That 'future' was as early as August 1940 when the number of sellers of used oil had so increased as to attract the attention of the Government, always eager to regulate:

"The refining of used oil for sale is declared a licensed industry by a notice in the Gazette issued last evening. For the purpose of the notice refining of used oil means the treatment of used lubricating or transformer oil in any way with the object of its preparation for use as a lubricant or in transformers, or for other purposes." [208]

This declaration was quickly followed with the following public notice:

"Industrial Efficiency Act, 1936. Refining of Used Oil. Notice is Hereby Given that pursuant to the provisions of the Industry Licensing (Used Oil Refining) Notice 1940, all persons who are engaged as principals in the industry of the refining of used oil are required to obtain licences from the Bureau of Industry to continue carrying on the industry as from 22nd August 1940.

"Applications in writing should be forwarded to the undersigned forthwith. The industry covered by the above notice is defined therein as follows: the treatment of used lubricating or transformer oil in any way with the object of its purification for use as a lubricant or in transformers or for other purposes. G L O'Halloran, Secretary, Bureau of Industry..." [209]

By early 1941, the Bureau of Industry had licensed a great number of entities throughout New Zealand to refine used oil. As well as oil importers such as the Vacuum and Shell Oil Companies, the licencees also included service stations and transport companies. [210]

However, by means of The Industry Licensing (Used Oil Refining) Revocation Notice 1942, dated 31 January 1942, the 1940 licensing regulation was revoked. [211]

The Dominion Oil Refining Company

The Dominion Oil Refining Company Limited was incorporated from 22 December 1933 to 22 December 2000 [212] and originally traded from 6 Stanley Street, Auckland.

The Company started with a Capital of £2000 and its first shareholders, both of Auckland, were J O Hailey 1999 shares and M E McChesney 1 share. [213]

In November 1934, the company's Capital was increased to £3000 with issue of another 1000 shares. [214]

In December 1938, it was reported that The Dominion Oil Refining Company Limited had applied for a patent for the refining of used oils. [215]

The patent application, entitled "A Process For Refining Of Used Lubricating Oils And The Like" was received by the New Zealand Patent Office on 27 April 1938. The application was filed on behalf of The Dominion Oil Refining Company Limited by Frederick Sedgewick Stevens, said to be the inventor of the process. His patent application included a detailed description of the refining process:

"This invention relates to a process for refining of oils especially lubricating oils that have been used and adulterated by friction and absorption of foreign matter thereby minimising the efficiency as a lubricating oil...

"The oil is put into a container and, if necessary, heated (but this is not essential), then intimately mixed with the oil from one quarter of one per cent… to 15 per cent by weight of sulphuric acid; the quantity varying according to the amount of adulteration and the nature of the oil. The sulphuric acid oxidizes the impurities which are precipitated in the form of a sludge settling.

"The treated oil is then drawn off and is mixed with a quantity of filtering earth or clay, the quantity varying from one per cent to 25 per cent by weight according to the amount of the impurities to be removed and the amount of sulphuric acid used and color required in the final product.

"The oil and clay mixture is then passed through a still when, by means of heating by steam or otherwise, or vacuum distillation, any volatile adulterates and light fractions are removed; the remaining oil is then passed through a filter or clarifier to remove the filtering earth and its absorbed impurities.

"This identical process can also be used for the production of lubricating oils from suitable crude oils." [216]

It is not known how unique to The Dominion Oil Refining Company this process was at the time of its application for a patent but, as previously noted, by 1941 the Bureau of Industry had licensed quite a few other entities throughout New Zealand to refine used oil.

With war-time savings a priority, advertisements were regularly placed in Auckland newspapers by The Dominion Oil Refining Company seeking used oil to refine:

"Do Not Waste — The Dominion Oil Refining Company Limited will buy all your used oil or refine it for you" [217]

As described in a previous chapter, Motor Specialties Industries acquired The Dominion Oil Refining Company and its subsidiaries, Premoil Limited and Apex Oil Products NZ Limited, as part of its diversification in 1971. [218]

The Dominion Oil Refining Company thrived as a subsidiary of Motor Specialties Industries (MSI) — as reported by the Christchurch Press in September 1973:

"Dominion Oil Refining Company Ltd, which completed its first full year of trading as a [Motor Specialties Industries] subsidiary company, had record sales and profits." [219]

'Record sales and profits' naturally encouraged further expansion in 1975 despite a lack of used oil:

"The Dominion Oil Refining Company Ltd commissioned new plant to increase production and widen the range of its products. Full advantage could not be taken of the new facilities because of the shortage of used oils which are being burnt as fuel or used for other purposes. Steps were being taken to overcome this problem." [220]

However, as well as a raw product shortage, the oil re-refining industry faced a new problem in 1976:

"The increased use of additives in car lubricating oils is causing concern to New Zealand's refiners of used oil. Because of these additives the process is fast becoming uneconomic, they say. It is possible for some oils to contain as much as 20 per cent of additives, and in the cleaning process these have to be removed. This is difficult and costly, and on top of this, it is not uncommon to recover only 50 per cent usable oil from every litre of dirty oil bought from service stations.

"The Minister of Energy Resources...said yesterday that he had received no approach from oil re-refiners on additives in oil but had held general discussions with the Auckland-based operators (Dominion Oil Refining Co Ltd) on the problems the industry faced. The industry was finding it increasingly difficult to show a reasonable profit because more and more people were using old oil themselves because it was so cheap, with the result that reduced quantities were available for collection, he said." [221]

Nevertheless, the Dominion Oil Refining Company was eventually able to solve the additive problem, according to the Motor Specialties' Annual Report published in October 1976:

"Dominion Oil Refining overcame problems with modern additives in oil and is working profitably at maximum capacity. Further plant was being installed." [222]

By 1977, New Zealand's economy was suffering yet another downturn with the Government looking to every industry to make savings — as reported by the Christchurch Press in May of that year:

"Recycling of lubricating oil is being encouraged to save overseas funds. New Zealand paid $13M during 1975-76 for nearly 17M gallons of lubricating oil for various industrial purposes. But with widespread recycling, millions of dollars of overseas funds could be saved.

"The Trade and Industry Department says 40 per cent of the 17M gallons was lost through combustion and other processes, but 55 per cent which was dumped, could have been recycled. A spokesman for the department said yesterday that 5 per cent of the used lubricant was being recycled at present...

"Four companies in New Zealand are now engaged in the business. They are: Chemicals Manufacturing Company, Wellington; Dominion Oil Refining Company, Auckland; Industrial Engineers Ltd, Christchurch; and Regent Oil Refining Company, Dunedin.

"In 1975 the New Zealand Oil Refiners' Association was formed to represent the four companies. It maintains there is no need to continue dumping used lubricant." [223]

The following year, BP New Zealand acquired a 50 per cent shareholding of Dominion Oil Refining Company Limited from MSI Corporation [224] and bought the outstanding shares in 1989. [225]

Advertising Standards Complaints Board

Following its full acquisition of The Dominion Oil Refining Company, BP New Zealand, as BP Environ Oil, faced a charge of false advertising with its claim "...that all of the waste oil was being re-refined..." when that was not the case.

A rehearing of the complaint against BP was heard by the Advertising Standards Complaints Board in January 1992 when BP described its re-refining-of-oil operation:

"1. BP Oil, through its subsidiary Dominion Oil, has a North Island waste oil collection network in place that encompasses workshops and service stations of all brands, together with local authority collection schemes. The number of outlets serviced is estimated to be in excess of one thousand. Our network in the South Island is not quite so extensive but collection takes place on BP's behalf in Canterbury, Otago and Southland.

"2. The retail network advised of 40 collection 'domes' in Auckland and 12 in Christchurch, refers only to BP service stations without waste oil tanks in those centres where publicised collection takes place. This network of collection 'domes' aimed at the DIY consumer is growing rapidly and should reach 100 by the end of 1991.

"We know that we are 'protecting the environment' by helping turn the tide of waste oil. We already process 7,000 - 8,000 tonnes and can process up to 15,000 tonnes if consumers join that recycling process and buy re-refined motor oils. The more re-refined oil used means more can be collected and processed.

"3. BP oil has taken the high ground on waste oil re-refining and collection. By doing so, we have been responsible for increasing consumer awareness that recycling oil does protect the environment. Our market research clearly demonstrates this."

However, for various reasons, some of the figures provided by BP were not substantiated:

"The Board reviewed the evidence and viewed the advertisement again. The Board recognised the efforts the Applicant was making to refine waste oil. However the central problem was whether the advertisement breached the Code.

"The advertisement says that 'B.P. is turning this tide of waste' rather than 'helping turn the tide of waste oil'…The Board reaffirmed that the meaning attributed to the claim in the advertisement is that all of the waste oil was being re-refined. Although more oil was being re-refined than originally thought by the Board it was still a long way short of all of the waste oil." [226]

The previous decision that BP was in breach of advertising standards was confirmed and the complaint upheld.

Chemicals Manufacturing Company

The original Chemicals Manufacturing Company Limited (C.M.C.) was incorporated at Wellington in May 1940 with a capital of £400 and the objects of "…producers, manufacturers and refiners of oils, fats, and greases, and incidental. The original shareholders were: H Halberstam, T Ranov, A Hirschbein, & O Hirschbein. [227]

Whether or not one of the original founders changed their name is not known but a later obituary notice of March 1982 recorded a founder of the company as Arthur Hilton:

"Mr Arthur Hilton, a pioneer of New Zealand's chemical manufacturing industry, died in Wellington on Saturday…He was born in Vienna and in 1939 emigrated to New Zealand, where he and his brother started the country's first grease-manufacturing plant, Chemicals Manufacturing Company Ltd.

"As a result of development work done by C.M.C., most greases used in New Zealand during World War II were 95 per cent of local raw materials.

"In 1942, the company was asked to investigate the feasibility of an oil refinery in New Zealand and in 1946 it was invited to manufacture grease for the newly formed BP (then called Anglo-Iranian Oil) company which was 50 per cent Government-owned. C.M.C. became one of the main industrial chemical industries in New Zealand and in 1970 was taken over by BP New Zealand Ltd with Mr Hilton as managing director…" [228]

In May 1955, the Chemicals Manufacturing Company Limited was named as the maker of a dishwashing liquid, BP Comprox — as promoted by newspaper advertisements. [229]

In September 1974, tragedy struck the company's factory — as reported by the Christchurch Press:

"Five men were killed when an explosion ravaged a chemical manufacturing factory at Gracefield, in the Hutt Valley today…The explosion occurred about 12.50 p.m. in the factory section of the Chemicals Manufacturing Company Ltd, described by its general manager (Mr B J O'Donoghue) as a subsidiary of BP (New Zealand) Ltd. In a second explosion, a 2000-gallon tank was hurled 50ft through the factory roof…" [230]

From 1 October 1985 to 15 May 1995, the Chemicals Manufacturing Company Limited was re-registered at Wellington as a BP Oil New Zealand Limited subsidiary.

Chapter Ten

Roads…Roads…Roads…

The Importance of Roads

An editorial published by The New Zealand Herald on 23 January 1865 emphasised the importance of roads to the Auckland province at that time:

"The importance of a net-work of roads, socially, commercially, and politically, can scarcely be over-rated in any country, and more especially is this the case in the Province of Auckland. We make no apology, therefore, for constantly alluding to this subject, and we are happy to see from the advertisements which have latterly appeared in the papers, asking for tenders for roadmaking in various districts, that the Superintendent and the Executive are paying considerable attention to the subject, and pushing forward road construction throughout the province. They are thus laying down the basis of its future prosperity by throwing open the country and encouraging the people to go and settle upon it, and subdue it, changing the desert into fruitful fields, and producing food for man and beast." [1]

Early Road Construction & Maintenance

Even before motorised traffic overwhelmed them, the country has needed roads and they have forever required rebuilding and maintenance.

In January 1865, the Auckland City engineer, Mr Wrigg, reported that Ponsonby Road was "…required to be repaired, re-formed and metalled…length 3300 feet at an estimated cost of £729 8s 10d." [2]

Even after that expense, which was an enormous amount then, parts of Ponsonby Road were so muddy that cart drivers found it easier to drive along what were supposed to be the footpaths — as reported by The Auckland Star in September 1870:

"C Duckinfield was charged with driving a cart on the footpath of Ponsonby Road…H Foreman deposed to having seen defendant committing the offence, and was cross-examined by Mr Hesketh as to the existence or appearance of the footpath in question.

"Stannus Jones deposed to the formation of the footpath and its separation by water courses.

"Henry Peckham, contractor for roads, called for the defence, swore that at this spot [on the day in question], the road was not passable for a horse and cart. The Court said that there was not sufficient evidence of the formation of the footpath, and dismissed the case.

"H Sully was charged with a similar offence on the same road. H Foreman deposed to having seen defendant driving a cart on the raised footpath on the east side of Ponsonby Road; and that at that place the path is raised a foot high, and marked off by posts; that he had passed inside the posts; and that the road is quite passable there…

"J Hogarth, called by Mr Hesketh for the defence, deposed to the impassable state of the road at that place, and to having had his own cart bogged to the axle on the day in question. J P Hatley corroborated the statement as to the impassable state of the road. The Court held that the footpath was clearly defined at this spot but, owing to the bad state of the road, the mitigated fine of 5s. was inflicted." [3]

Sometimes an attempt to remedy the muddy conditions proved dangerous – as reported by The Daily Southern Cross in May 1865:

"On Saturday as Mr Bacon of the Odd Fellows' Arms, was proceeding homeward on horseback along the Ponsonby Road, his horse stumbled and threw him heavily to the ground, but although much shaken he fortunately was not seriously injured. The cause of the accident was a deep drain recently cut at the head of Hepburn-street, and which crosses one part of the Ponsonby Road, neither the horse nor the rider observing the danger, owing to the darkness." [4]

Early Road Funding

After its establishment in 1870, the Government's Public Works Department supervised and controlled most of the nation's road construction, but a large proportion of the work within the boundaries governed by the Highway Boards was paid for by their respective local authorities. This funding was, of course, acquired from the rates imposed on 'local lands and the occupiers and owners thereof'.

However, by the time the Auckland City Council was created in April 1871, Auckland's street network was potentially a bottomless pit of expenditure and more roads were desperately needed. It is no wonder that, by October 1877, it was realised that, despite their revenue generating capacity, the Highway Boards and the provinces in general were struggling to maintain a national, road-building programme. [5]

According to a Bay of Plenty Times report of October 6, 1877:

"…Mr De Latour (for the Government) brought forward the motion – That in the opinion of this House, it being now established that the counties are unable to make provision for the construction and maintenance of the main arterial roads of the colony, it is imperative that immediate and permanent provision should be made by the Government for the gradual construction and maintenance of the same.

"As Mr De Latour truly said, unless some such motion be carried, traffic in the inland districts must inevitably be suspended during several months in the year, and the commerce of the country, from want of roads, severely handicapped." [6]

The South Island fared no better with the Provincial Council searching for some achievable means of funding the maintenance of its roads in February 1904:

"An inquiry regarding the apportionment of the cost of the maintenance of the Opawa Road was held at the Provincial Council Chambers yesterday…The Heathcote Road Board was represented by Mr Scott…[who] gave an explanation of the means which had been taken for the maintenance of the road.

"During recent years the traffic, he said, had increased considerably and the expense of keeping the thoroughfare in repair had increased proportionately. He considered the fairest means to provide for the maintenance of the road would be to increase the charge for building permits and by this means a considerable sum could be raised. He said the sand and shingle for a large building now in progress of erection in the city were being carted along the road in question and he thought it was unfair that people who did not contribute towards the rates should use the roads and leave the local ratepayers to find the cost of maintenance.

"A tally was kept from June 22 to June 29 1903 when it was found that 538 loads were carted into Christchurch, 26 to Woolston, and 84 to Heathcote. The loads carted to Christchurch included bricks 198 loads, metal 83, shingle 27, sand 32, rubble 99, and scoria 22. At least 80 per cent of the bricks carted along the road went to the city of Christchurch. Last year the Glenmore Brick and Tile Company produced about 3,300,000 bricks, and a large proportion of these was carted into the city along the Opawa Road…" [7]

Roads and Bridges Construction Act 1882

In order to provide some regular and secure funding for the construction and maintenance of the country's arterial network, the Government finally passed the Roads and Bridges Construction Act in September 1882.

Commencing on 1 April 1882, the Act provided for a 'Main Roads Account' to be credited with £100,000 from the Public Works Fund. Each financial year thereafter, the Main Roads Account was to receive a sum not exceeding £100,000 from the sale of Crown lands. Any residue was to be paid to the Public Works Fund. For the purposes of the Act, a 'Main Road' could only be designated as such following a resolution of Parliament.

With the permission of ratepayers, a Council could receive funding for a main road passing through its jurisdiction after submission of proper estimates of cost, plans, and specifications to the Minister for Public Works. One-fourth of the amount granted was then repayable within ten years.

Alternatively, a Council could pay one-quarter of the cost itself and receive funding for the balance needed. [8]

Paving the Way for the Motor

"The roads problem, like the poor, is always with us, but at no time during the history of our Dominion has it been more acute than at the present. Wherever we go, north or south, into the city or the backblocks, we find the cry: 'The more we pay, the worse are our roads' and 'Give us good roads!' And why is this…?

"Firstly, until very recent years, there has been no concerted action to either train men or seriously grapple with the problem; secondly, there has been an entire evolution of traffic and, thirdly, a mistake has been made in attempting to build roads to-day in the same manner and at the same cost as was done twenty to thirty years ago.

"In the past every road builder has struggled on independently, in his own tinpot way, knowing little and caring less what the rest of the world were doing, so long as his old standard could be kept up without increasing his levies. His ratepayers asked nothing, and expected nothing more. While the world progressed, road builders slumbered. The initial advent of pneumatic traffic was hailed as the natural solution — but what a rude awakening there was…

"Everything has been tried, starting with the old macadam rolled in water-bond to tar-concrete, tar-macadam, tarsealed macadam, Bituco, Tarvia, Kortfelt, and a dozen other patent and other methods, and, lastly, plain cement…" [9]

Motor Car the Enemy

By 1923, despite the funding provisions provided by the 1882 Act, meeting the cost of road construction and maintenance remained particularly difficult for the smaller towns and boroughs — as reported by the Ashburton Guardian in September of that year:

"…during the past seven years…the tidy sum of £10,000 in round figures has been paid out under the heading of streets which…covers maintenance, metalling, watering, asphalting, channelling, bridges and culverts and kerbing. On actual maintenance alone £5,305 has been expended…It is obvious the maintenance cost cannot decrease under existing conditions. What then is the explanation?

"Simply this: the streets here—and the experience is universal—have met a premature death. The years of usefulness have been shortened by the overwhelming advance of motor traffic. The avalanche, as it were, has moved onward so rapidly that many local bodies have been unable to turn a hand to check it. Numbers were caught without the slightest bit of modern machinery. It is true some boroughs and counties were quicker than others to realise the danger, but permanent roads did not make their appearance before great havoc was wrought on the old style of highway which was rather benefited than harmed by ordinary wheeled traffic…

"The motor car is the enemy of local bodies, yet the local bodies are in that peculiar position that they must comply with the car's demand for suitable roads. The car's modernity is lost, more or less, without an equally modern road. The motor lorry is a still greater enemy. Owing chiefly to the development of this vehicle as a convenient means of transferring heavy loads, a development largely helped by high railway rates forcing manufacturers to look in other directions for the carriage of goods, all classes of roads are now being used to an extent and by a type of vehicle hardly dreamt of when the roads were first built.

"We are thus faced with a network of roads the large majority of which are not suited for, and were not built for, modern traffic…on the successful solution of the problem of constructing roads to carry heavy and fast vehicles, at an outlay which will not be prohibitive either in first cost or in upkeep, the prosperity of industry, and therefore of the nation, depends to no small degree." [10]

Some five years later, the annual cost of maintaining what was then a relatively small number of highways and roads seemed sufficient to deal with the dramatic increase in motor vehicles — as reported by The New Zealand Herald in October 1928:

"Main road maintenance in New Zealand is costing an average of £119 18s a mile annually. This is more than double the expenditure obtaining before the Main Highways Board came into existence. The standard of maintenance can hardly be said to have increased in direct proportion to the expenditure per mile as the number of vehicles has increased about 70 per cent, with consequent increase in road usage and danger.

"Maintenance costs must rise as the number of transport units increases, but the assistance which local bodies have received from the Highways Board has made it possible to keep ahead of the increase in traffic, and generally improve conditions…

"Much money has been wasted in New Zealand through the expensive maintenance of roads which required total reconstruction. In roading, the first cost is never the last, but an ambitious programme is an assurance that future costs will be low. With 170,000 registered motor vehicles on less than 50,000 miles of highways and roads, New Zealand has a great deal of traffic damage to pay for and the maintenance of cheap roads is inevitably expensive." [11]

Early Road Construction
First Stone Quarries

The New Zealand landscape was blessed with an abundance of gravel and stone — most of it easily broken and crushed to form the metal needed to transform the muddiest road to a firm, fast highway. With the development of stone quarries, a crushing mechanism, and a reliable delivery system, there was no shortage of persons willing to provide what was soon to become an essential commodity — such an essential commodity that the Government of the day sought to protect it wherever possible — as demonstrated by Clause 20 of the Nelson Improvement Amendment Act of 1858:

"The Board shall also have full power and control over all pits or beds of gravel and all stone quarries situated on public land within the said town of Nelson; and any person who shall remove stone or gravel from any of the said pits, beds, or quarries without the consent of the Board shall be liable to penalty of not exceeding…to be recovered in a summary manner." [12]

As the need for stone and metal for buildings and roads increased, many additional quarry sites were developed throughout the country — as reported by The New Zealand Herald in January 1887 and September 1904:

"The Tamaki quarry stone is steadily growing in public favour. Already a large quantity has been supplied in the breastwork at the bastion fortification works, Kohimarama. The appliances at the quarry are so complete that the cranes which work the quarry can also load the barges. Every description of stone required for building and other purposes can be got at the shortest notice. There is also an engine and stone breaker on the ground and it is the intention of the proprietor to utilise both in the getting out of large quantities of broken metal…" [13]

"The Waihi Borough Council have just imported from Home a large stone-crusher, with engine, the plant having been landed at Paeroa. The crusher will operate at the several stone quarries breaking metal for the roads and also reducing stone to a sufficient fineness for footpaths. The plant is to be brought to Waihi at once, and erected for immediate use." [14]

The Stone Quarries Act 1910

Naturally the safety of workers became a concern after a number of deaths and injuries had occurred at many of the quarries, particularly as a result of blasting operations. The Stone Quarries Act 1910 was described as:

"…a distinctly a humane measure, framed chiefly to protect life in quarries. It provides that all managers or foremen in charge of blasting operations shall hold permits, and restrictions are placed on the storage and use of explosives and other appliances likely to endanger life and limb." [15]

The Act also provided for the appointment of inspectors and stipulated: "It shall not be lawful to renew the working of any quarry until notice has been given by the occupier to an inspector, and similar notice is required in the case of the discontinuance of the working of any quarry." [16]

By 1940, the Stone Quarries Act had been amended many times to keep pace as the newer explosives became available but the duties of quarry inspectors remained:

"Quarry Owner Fined — That many stone quarry owners in Northland failed to give the necessary notification to the department when opening or closing quarries was stated by the Inspector…who took a case as a warning at the Whangarei Police Court today. There were between 300 and 400 stone quarries in the district, he said, and if owners did not advise the department it caused a great deal of inconvenience and difficulty in making inspections…" [17]

Road Metal Shortages

Despite the great number of stone quarries available, only a few were equipped with crushing machinery and the relative remoteness of some sites made the transport of material to where it was needed very costly. As a result, local bodies such as the Wanganui Borough Council looked to modern technology to save it money:

"For the life of us we cannot understand why the Borough Council hesitate to purchase a motor waggon and the least that can be said is that it is a very nearsighted policy to adopt…If the Council had purchased a motor waggon when it was first advocated…it would by this time have saved the Borough more than double its cost and our City Fathers evidently still intend to fritter away the ratepayers' money by clinging to the old-fashioned method of carting metal.

"The Council's records contain the proof of the capabilities of motor waggons and the probable savings that would be effected if one of these modern conveniences were installed here. They are in use in Auckland, Wellington, and other places in the colony and the various bodies which have experimented with them are loud in their praise of the new machines.

"In Auckland…the motor waggon in use there effects a saving of not less than £28 per week as compared with the work done formerly by horses and drays. This machine…does the work of six two-horse drays which formerly cost £1 each per day, or £36 per week. It carries metal from the Mount Eden quarry to all parts of the city, the amount varying according to the distance traversed. It can take daily six loads of 5yds each to Ponsonby (2½ miles each way) and five loads of 5yds each a distance of 3½ miles each way. The cost of running is but £7 17s per week, or about 2d per ton per mile…

"The local bodies of Wanganui have to pay from 4s to 5s per yard for metal carted 2½ miles, and a good day's work for a horse and dray would be four such loads. The motor waggons, according to the Auckland figures, can deliver six loads of 5yds each per day — seven times as much as the ordinary dray, and the cost of running the former is certainly not twice as expensive as the latter.

"…within the next five years the Council will have to face the question of re-metalling all the streets in the borough, and that being the case the necessity for purchasing a motor waggon is all the more apparent. On the lowest basis, the Council should save £20 per week…by adopting the up-to-date and common-sense method of distributing the metal. It is therefore unreasonable, unbusinesslike, and unfair to the ratepayers to longer delay the purchase of a machine." [18]

The shortage of material and the competition for it forced the local bodies to seek alternative supplies where they could — as reported by The New Zealand Herald in May 1913:

"A special meeting of the [Hamilton] Borough Council [discussed]…The question of lack of road metal which is hampering the work of all the local bodies in the district…and the following resolutions were carried unanimously:

"That in view of the great difficulty experienced by local authorities in obtaining supplies of road metal, and owing to the fact of stone quarries being in the hands of private individuals and companies, local authorities, in order to obtain supplies, are compelled to compete with each other thereby increasing the cost to them of the material, the Government be asked to make arrangements for opening quarries in various parts of the district to supply local authorities with their requirements.

"That a copy of the above resolution be forwarded to all local authorities in the district and that they be asked to support it by approaching the Government in this direction, at the same time giving the Government an indication of the quantities that would be taken by each of them if a Government quarry were opened." [19]

The shortage also forced the Northland Roads Board to source its needed stone from further afield in 1914:

"Stone for Roads — It was decided to get all particulars of cost of stone at different Auckland quarries, and the possibility of an arrangement whereby the Board might get stone from Leigh was mooted…" [20]

Three years later, in October 1917, road metal was still in short supply in the Matamata District:

"Matamata County Council — The Piako County Council's circular letter dealing with the problem of providing metalled roads was considered at length. The letter suggested that as no local body in the district could attend to the matter by itself a co-operative company should be formed to acquire a quarry of its own, either by buying out some…existing concern or starting a new one…The Chairman: It's a matter we will have to consider.

"Cr. Barnett: It concerns all of us. It's a pity some portable crushers could not be obtained so that they could be transferred to the respective ridings. There is metal that seems suitable in various ridings. The chairman: I don't think the metal is suitable. It would be cheaper to get it by the railway…" [21]

By 1922, the supply of stone for the Piako County district had improved somewhat — as reported by the Waikato Times:

"Every year the cry is heard from local bodies for the need of stone quarries adequate to supply their needs, for the ever-growing motor traffic brings about never-ceasing thought regarding the requirements of roads. The Piako County Council, by adopting business methods, have, with the co-operation of its engineer…undertaken the erection of two stone quarries, one at Waiorongomai and the other at the Gordon Settlement.

"At Waiorongomai a large plant is now pounding large boulders of hard stone into road metal of suitable dimensions. Stone abounds here in countless thousands of yards…It is safe to predict that within five years the Piako County Council will possess the best roads in the Dominion." [22]

Auckland district supplies had also improved by 1926 with the opening of a quarry at Drury:

"The stone quarries at Drury which were opened up some few months ago are now in working order and metal is being carted out to fulfil orders. The Drury Basalt Company, under the management of Mr H R Baigent, of Patumahoe has installed an up-to-date plant, and is getting out a fine class of metal…

"Mr Baigent informed a Times reporter that several local body representatives had visited the quarry and spoke in high terms of the quality of the metal being crushed. The opening up of the quarry will give employment to a large number of men and with the carting operations several more will be in constant work." [23]

By December 1926, praise for the quality of the Drury quarry stone had not diminished:

"It is gratifying to know that, as far as Auckland is concerned, there is enough hard blue metal in the Drury quarry, the property of Messrs Darby Bros, to construct every highway and byway in the province and for the matter of that, practically every roadway in New Zealand.

"The Drury quarry, which is only now coming into prominence, is situated within a mile and a half of the Drury railway station on the main south line…There is a hill on the property of considerable dimensions which produces the finest blue metal to be found anywhere in the Dominion. Geologically it is a basalt hill, with millions of cubic yards of splendid metal. It has cost many thousands of pounds during the last few years to develop this quarry and eminent engineers who have been on the site have been loud in their praises of the quality of the stone…" [24]

Another quarry able to service Auckland's road needs was opened at Hunua on 16 December 1927:

"Before a gathering of Papakura residents, Mr E D McLennan, MP for Franklin, yesterday officially opened the Hunua quarry, three miles by metalled road from the Papakura railway station…

"Mr McLennan emphasised the tremendous value of the quarry to the whole of the Auckland district, especially as this was the age of motor traffic, demanding paved highways and well-maintained subsidiary roads. It was estimated there were three and a half million cubic yards of close-grained grey wacke metal in the quarry hill which towers for almost 300 ft. above the Hunua Stream…

"The owners of the quarry, the Guillard Blue Stone Quarry Company Limited…have taken advantage of every natural asset. As there is a plentiful supply of water near the quarry the whole output will be washed. This is an innovation so far as Auckland quarries are concerned. Metal absolutely free from dirt, with its consequent excellent aggregate for concrete, is in great demand for concrete roads and city buildings…

"The Franklin and Manukau County Councils had used the metal extensively for their recent road improvements. All the quarry machines are run by electricity supplied by the Franklin Power Board. The metal gravitates from the actual quarry face into a large washing screen. It passes on into a giant crusher and is reduced in size and then through a chip machine where it is broken into four different sizes. The metal is stored in bins 9ft. above the ground under which trucks enter to be loaded in two minutes." [25]

There were so many quarries operating by 1928 that an Auckland Quarry Owners' Association had been formed, members of which included:

"Messrs Morgan & Docherty, W Mcquoid & Sons, Winstone Limited, Ferguson & Kew, Wilson & Rothery, Mccarten Bros, J W Morgan, J J Craig Limited, and G J & T Picken." [26]

Naturally, not everyone was happy about the haphazard sitings of open-pit quarries that had blighted the Auckland landscape for some years — as reported by the Auckland Sun in April 1928:

"The question of damage by quarrying was before the executive of the Auckland Town Planning Association last evening. It was stated that a representative of the association had attended a conference last month to consider improvements in the organising of stone quarries in Auckland, and it had been decided that a committee of architects, surveyors and engineers should be set up to investigate. It had been felt that quarries had been commenced in several unnecessary places to the detriment of the scenic features…" [27]

The Mount Eden (Newmarket) Quarry

While access to quarries on public land at Nelson was restricted, such was not the case at Auckland where laissez-faire principles of commercial gain extended to the mining of the province's raw materials — as advertised by the New Zealander in June 1860:

"To Stonemasons and Quarrymen — Tenders will be received until Friday next, the 29th instant, from persons who may wish to work the Stone Quarries situated at Newmarket for 12 months, commencing July 2, 1860…" [28]

However, official Government control of the Mount Eden Quarry was affirmed by means of a public notification in the Provincial Government Gazette in August 1863:

"I Hereby notify for general information, that Mr. William Rowe is authorised by me to make arrangements for the proper working of the Mount Eden Quarry and is empowered to charge sixpence (6d.) for every load of Scori Ash or Gravel taken from the said Quarry. Robert Graham, Superintendent" [29]

By 1873, the Newmarket [Mount Eden] quarries were providing plenty of work and profit with the price per load having increased to 10d:

"The Newmarket stone quarries present a stirring scene to the spectator whose business or pleasure takes him in that direction at the present time. The process of excavating the stone for the silt basins at the foot of Queen street is now being pushed forward with commendable activity. Mr Taylor, the contractor, has between 20 and 30 men at work under the able superintendence of Mr Hill and as the substantial blocks of scoria are raised from their natural bed to the surface they are partly dressed and then carted by Messrs Winstone to the site of the Harbour Board operations…

"The Highway Board at Newmarket is, we are informed, enriched to the extent of tenpence per load for the stone taken from the quarries, and the circulation of ready money in the district in consequence of the expenditure now going on is a perceptible benefit." [30]

Of course, Newmarket also had a supply of unpaid quarry workers which would eventually destabilise the operations of the private suppliers, including the Auckland City Council which leased part of the quarry:

"Some changes and improvements have taken place lately at our Provincial Gaol. Since the stone wall has been built round the male criminal portion of the prison, the convicts and men sentenced to long terms of imprisonment have been employed within this section, while those who are undergoing light sentences, or whose terms of imprisonment are nearly expired, are employed in the stone quarries outside, under guard…" [31]

By 1912, the uncertainty of the City Council lease was restricting its further development of the quarry at a time when more investment was required:

"The discovery of excellent stone for road formation in the lower levels of the Mount Eden, quarry has relieved the City Council from the necessity of seeking further afield for metal supplies but its tenancy of the quarry is unsatisfactory since the lease may be terminated at three months' notice. With a view to securing an improvement in the terms of its tenancy, the Works Committee of the Council interviewed the Hon A M Myers (Minister for Railways)…

"The Mayor explained that the Council had leased from the Government access to the quarry for 15 years from October 1, 1901 but the lease was subject to cancellation at three months' notice.

"With a view to obtaining a more secure tenure, the Council interviewed the Minister of Justice in March of last year but its presentations had no result.

"The engineer had advised the Council that the lower levels of the quarry contained excellent stone but the Council had been delayed from erecting a modern plant in place of the existing inadequate machinery by the liability to ejectment. If it could obtain a satisfactory tenure, the Council would establish a permanent quarry on the site…plant costing £3000 or £4000 would be installed if a better tenure was given…" [32]

A more reliable lease was also important if the Council was to take full advantage of the new stone and advanced machinery to process it:

"Mount Eden Quarry will at last yield to the city engineer's department a quality of stone superior to that hitherto quarried for the making and maintenance of local roads. A few weeks ago the quarrymen, on reaching a lower level, found an excellent material commonly known as volcanic basalt. This stone extends right through the quarry and the supply will, therefore, last for many years to come…

"A Herald representative visited the quarry yesterday and saw the men taking out the new metal…In future, this new material will be almost entirely used for road construction in Auckland and district.

"Another interesting feature at the Mount Eden quarry is the rotary furnace, an ingenious device for heating the broken metal before passing it into large buckets, which are then dipped into tar, next screened, then emptied into carts to be taken away to the roads which are being made with this material.

"Park-Road, from the Grafton Bridge to Park Avenue, has been made with this metal, and Stanley-street is at present being laid with the same. The cost is almost double that of the ordinary plain metal, but in the opinion of all experts it is stated to be worth the expense. The new machine requires a little more adjustment before it will be thoroughly automatic." [33]

But not all were in favour of the use of the new machinery replacing manual work if a Letter to the Editor of The New Zealand Herald of April 1915 is to be believed:

"My experience is that you cannot find for miles around better metal for street purposes than that coming from the Mount Eden quarry. The trouble is not in the metal but in the crushing of it in the ponderous stone-crusher which crushes the resisting power out of it before it is put on to the road, and so you have a mass of disintegrated stuff that ought never to be called road metal. In my opinion the council would save thousands by breaking up the crusher and having all metal for the streets broken by hand. Many of the present councillors know that the hand-broken metal will last three times as long as the machine-crushed stuff. Ratepayer." [34]

However, "…the protest of Mount Eden ratepayers against the continuance of blasting operations in the City Council's quarries…" were more serious. [35]

So much so that in October 1919:

"The Mount Eden Borough Council decided last evening to oppose the extension of the lease of the Mount Eden quarry to the City Council. This lease has two years to run. The land being a prison reserve, the City Council applied to Parliament for an extension of the lease for 21 years.

"At last evening's meeting of the Mount Eden Borough Council a letter was received from the Parliamentary Petitions Committee asking for an expression of opinion upon the City Council's application, the reserve being in the borough and adjacent to the Mount Eden Domain.

"After discussion, a resolution was carried to the effect that the quarry was at present a danger to the people in the vicinity and to the considerable traffic to the Grammar School, the grounds of which adjoined the quarry, was a permanent disfigurement and further work would make matters worse. The council therefore opposed an extension of the term of lease." [36]

Probably as a result of the Mount Eden Borough Council decision, the extension of the City Council quarry lease was not a priority for Parliament and it became a non-issue in November 1920:

"In connection with the clause in the Washing-up Bill, by the deletion of which the City Council has lost the lease of the Mount Eden quarry, the Mayor, Mr J H Gunson, informed the council last evening that the chairman of the Works Committee and himself had done all possible to have the clause reinserted in the Bill but had failed…" [37]

Without the lease, City Council quarry operations had been limited by June 1921:

"On the recommendation of the Works Committee it was decided to accept the conditions laid down in a previous communication by the Minister for Justice under which the council may retain as much of the Mount Eden quarry area as may be necessary to house its metal crushing plant and equipment. These terms included the payment of a royalty of £37 10s a month, no stone to be taken out below the level at present being worked." [38]

However, the urgent need for road-making material for Auckland's roads meant that the Mount Eden quarry was operating at full capacity again by 1926:

"Another week will see the completion of the concrete road to Oakley Creek on the city boundary. For 14 months the City Council's forces have been engaged on this undertaking and the finished result is something that is unsurpassed in New Zealand. Undoubtedly the finest outlet from Auckland will be this new road to the North, which links up with the main northern highway…

"As to the features of the road, it is interesting to notice that provision has been made on the Point Chevalier Road for a tram track to be laid by concreting the two sides with strips each 18ft

7½in in width. From Gladstone Road to Oakley Creek the strip of concrete varies from 24ft to 18ft. It is laid in the centre of the road over this section and has metal shoulders three feet wide.

"The material for the two miles includes 1920 tons of cement, 7500 cubic yards of crushed metal and 3200 yards of sand. The metal was crushed at the City Council's quarry at Mount Eden, where a special plant was recently erected to provide what the engineers considered was an ideal aggregate for concrete.

"The sand was all taken off the beaches in the Manukau Harbour, brought to Onehunga wharf by barges and then transported on motor lorries to the work. Forty thousand square yards of concrete have been laid in making this portion of the road…" [39]

Three years later and work at the quarry continued at pace:

"At Mount Eden quarry, where the City Council is excavating rock at the rate of 40,000 tons a year, a sheer face of 70ft presents itself. Probably the basalt rocks on this part of Mount Eden would rank scientifically as coarsely crystalline, with a pale blue predominating. From parts of the face they stand out in bold masses, of the pentagonal shape so commonly attributed to basalt rocks…

"About the regular formation of the columns of rock there is a fine target for the quarryman. A charge of explosives set skilfully in the joints does its work in a simple manner, and a pile of rock weighing a ton or more is liable to be tumbled down in manageable pieces of a shape and size…In fact, the rock is of a type that seems common round Auckland, and was the lament of motorists in the days when concrete and tar-sealed roads were less extensive than they are to-day. Very sharp and dangerous-looking angles the little pieces have when they come in contact with a pneumatic tyre." [40]

Financial accounts for the City Council's Mount Eden quarry operations for 1937 were published in November of that year:

"Accounts of the…Mount Eden quarry and stone crusher, for the year ended March 31, were received from the city Treasurer…by the City Council last night. Sales of material from the quarry realised £14,226, a total considerably above that of the previous year (£9886). There was a revenue balance of £3010, compared with £2002 for 1936. This was directly attributable to additional works done under the £337,000 works loan. The net result of the year's operations showed a profit of £1532 against an estimate of £1300." [41]

Although the City Council was advertising for experienced quarrymen to work at the Mount Eden quarry in November 1945, [42] the quarry's proximity to residential areas was the main reason operations ceased at the quarry not long after.

Although Mount Eden Prison remains to this day (2024), its continued existence has not been without some controversy:

"In 1940, the Mayor of Auckland, Sir Ernest Davis, wanted it moved. 'Modern practice is to have prisons away from centres of population,' he told the Herald. Time was when the present site of Auckland's jail was on the outskirts of the city. Now it is on the inner approach to one of our finest residential suburbs. I think it should be removed to an outer area away from the busy town life.

"'If the jail were situated in open country it could be better-guarded, it could be made self-supporting and it would impart an isolation influence on its inmates which, in spite of lock and key, the jail in its present position does not give.'

"About the same time the Mt Eden Borough Council also wanted the prison moved. It said that if that was not possible the name should be changed, so that people as far south as Invercargill would not insist on calling it Mt Eden Prison. The Mayor of Mt Eden, Mr R J Mills, told a meeting: 'Here we have a beautiful suburb which has to bear the stigma of having a prison named after it.'" [43]

By that time, "…the shape of the mountain had been substantially altered. This old quarry was turned into a garden in 1985 by a group of volunteers." [44]

The Government v Private Enterprise

The advantage of using prison labour to produce the much-needed stone mined from the stone quarries adjacent to the Mount Eden Gaol, was illustrated by a report published by The New Zealand Herald in January 1875:

"In accordance with a resolution adopted at a meeting of the Public Buildings Commissioners…his Honor the Superintendent, accompanied by Mr Dignan, Mr Herapath (architect to the Commissioners), and Mr Allright, visited the Mount Eden Gaol with the view of ascertaining the resources of that establishment for supplying the stone required for the Hospital building.

"Having examined the quarry and finding that suitable stone could be obtained therefrom, an arrangement was made between Mr Allright, the architect, and the Governor of the Gaol for the supply of the stone required for the rubble work of the building from the Mount Eden quarry by prison labour. This will materially reduce the cost of erecting the Hospital." [45]

The administrators of Crown Lands were not at all keen to share the resource with whom they referred to as 'navvies' in 1875:

"A communication was received [by the Waste Lands Board] from the Under Secretary for Crown Lands…relating to the removal of stone from the vicinity of Mount Eden Gaol. The letter pointed out the inadvisability of allowing navvies to compete with the prisoners in breaking stones as that was the only remunerative work for which the prison labour could be utilised. The writer concluded by asking that a reserve of that part of Mount Eden to which he referred might be reserved for Gaol purposes. The Chairman said he did not think the Gaol authorities had a clear idea of the amount of land already reserved. It was no less an area than 21 acres 3 roods…" [46]

Nevertheless, the expanse of the Mount Eden quarry continued to provide plenty of room for the workings of both the prisoners and private enterprise.

The former (unpaid workers) were said to "…get up at half-past five o'clock in the morning and are in the quarries at work by seven; they work nine hours a-day (the eight hours system not having reached Mount Eden Gaol yet), and are to bed at eight o'clock at night and lights out, so that they form quite a model for more pretentious establishments in the city." [47]

The earnings of the private enterprise workers were debated in an editorial published by the Auckland Star in February 1884:

"Mr J C Jones, stonebreaker, has called upon us to contradict a statement…which appeared in last night's issue to the effect that practised stonebreakers can make 12s per day and the merest novice 5s. Mr Jones states that the best hand in Auckland cannot make more than 8s per day, working 12 hours, and it takes a very good man to break one yard of metal— 4s 6d worth — in eight hours. The average rate earned is not 5s per day of 10 hours, and this is at the Mount Eden quarry where there are excellent facilities for getting stone." [48]

The punishing labour must have been alleviated somewhat by the installation of a mechanical stone-breaker which was operating satisfactorily by June 1884. [49]

Meanwhile, the consistent output by the Mount Eden Gaol prisoners meant that, by the 1920s, competition with private enterprise had become a serious concern at the quarry — as reported by the Auckland Star in November 1921 and April 1922:

"The sale of metal quarried by prison labour was the subject of discussion at the executive meeting of the Auckland Industrial Association yesterday afternoon. A letter was received from a private firm of quarry owners stating that the gaol was selling metal to local bodies for and near at seriously cut rates, and the Morningside quarries, established for over 10 years, was now without an order.

"If this kind of thing went on much longer most private quarries must close and a famine for metal set in, particularly in country districts. No one could object if the Government sold at market rates and exercised no preference for trucks. It was decided to forward the letter to the Minister of Justice." [50]

"Recently, complaint was made by Mr J Wilson at a meeting of the Auckland Industrial Association that prison labour was being used to produce road metal at a cheaper cost than private enterprise and, in consequence of sales made by the department, quarry owners suffered considerably, owing to the lower price asked.

"The Industrial Association forwarded the complaint to the Minister in charge of the Prisons Department…and at yesterday's meeting of the association a reply was read stating that the matter had been thoroughly investigated…

"One of his [the Minister's] correspondents informed him that a private firm was practically ready to supply metal at the same price as the gaol, taking the size of the metal into consideration. In view of this testimony, which was from absolutely reliable sources, he could not see his way to add to the price charged local bodies for prison metal as had been suggested…

"Mr Wilson said that a local body that had been supplied with metal from the gaol for many years had tried 'to pull' a local producer into supplying metal at the same rate as the gaol. They, however, did not succeed…" [51]

The revenue earned from the Mount Eden quarry by the Prisons Department during the 1921-22 and 1922-23 financial years was disclosed in a report submitted to Parliament on 10 August 1923:

"At Auckland, states the report, where a few years ago £2000 was considered a fair amount by way of payment for road metal supplied to local bodies, 1921-22 produced a revenue of £12,000, while for the past year £15,000 had been the amount received.

"In addition to turning out metal to the above value, larger and more up-to-date crushing plant, with elevators and bins capable of holding 300 tons of metal products, have been installed. There are now two large jaw crushers available, and in addition a chip crushing machine for turning out chips for concrete making purposes.

"The air compressor plant is also being duplicated, which will permit of six pneumatic drills being operated at one and the same time if necessary, and an addition to the railway siding has been made. The whole of this plant will soon be completed and in full working order. Next year should therefore be a record year in metal production." [52]

Later in1923, the prison quarry began supplying the Hamilton Borough Council's £80,000 road improvement scheme — as reported by The New Zealand Herald:

"Large quantities of metal from the Mount Eden quarry are being laid on the streets. In a number of cases the streets have been graded prior to the metal being spread. As soon as there is a certainty of fine weather, a bituminous coating will be given." [53]

However, in December 1923, the delivery of road metal to Hamilton was suspended due to the requirements of railway excursionists:

"Shortage of railway trucks is given as the reason why the Auckland prison authorities found it necessary to suspend delivery of supplies of Mount Eden quarry metal required by the Hamilton Borough Council in connection with its roads improvement scheme. Work has been stopped on the roads and a large number of men have been diverted to other employment provided by the council. The shortage of trucks is considered to be due to the conversion of rolling stock into passenger-carrying waggons in preparation for the holiday traffic." [54]

In 1927, the competition from the prison continued despite the many complaints from the private quarry operators — as reported by the Auckland Sun in June 1927:

"There are some queer anomalies in our social system but the queerest of all is the cause of the sorry plight in which quarry workers in Auckland find themselves. Whenever quarry workers here ask for an improvement in wages or conditions the invariable retort from employers is: 'Sorry…but we can't possibly give you a rise owing to the competition of Mount Eden gaol'.

"That is a fact. Anyone who will provide for the carting can buy metal produced by free gaol labour against which the quarry owners have to compete and pay wages. The difference in rates for metal naturally resulting from this is a serious handicap to both owners and workers.

"If something does not happen soon, quarry workers will have to go to gaol to follow their line of toil. It is rather an oddity that folk incarcerated to prevent them being a menace to the community should so affect the living conditions of a class of workers from inside the gaol walls..." [55]

Another five years later, in April and September 1932, little had changed:

"Competition between the Prisons Department and private Auckland quarries in the supply of road and building metal was the subject of another pointed question in the House yesterday, when Mr A J Stallworthy (Coalition United, Eden) asked the Minister of Justice whether he was aware that the Prisons Department continued to undercut prices, and to state whether it was the Government's policy to cut the private quarries out of business.

"The Prisons Department, replied the Hon J G Cobbe, does not undercut private quarries in Auckland. In an effort to hold its regular customers, it has been obliged to follow the market in lowering prices. It is not the policy of the Government to interfere with the business of private quarries. The Mount Eden prison quarry is the oldest established quarry in Auckland and the sale of metal has long been recognised as essential to the economical administration of the Department. The Department contributes towards the maintenance of prisoners' dependents, consequently it is justified in marketing the produce of their labours to keep down the cost to the taxpayer." [56]

"Of course you realise that costs must come down to prices at which people can buy...The foregoing remarks were made by the Prime Minister, Rt Hon G W Forbes, this morning, when a deputation representing private quarry owners waited upon him and asked for support for a scheme to fix a scale of prices for metal, etc., from quarries.

"The contention of the deputation was that the price-cutting indulged in by the Prisons Department was proving ruinous to private quarry owners...The private quarry owners had been accused of trying to embarrass the Government, but that was not the position at all, and there was no objection to the prisons supplying metal, providing a fair and reasonable price was charged.

"Because of the price-cutting, one quarry in which there was £15,000 worth of plant might have to close down. Mr W H Terry [of the private quarry owners] said that the capital involved in the Auckland quarries was between £40,000 and £50,000 and there were about 200 employees..." [57]

Obviously anxious to retain its lucrative prison business, the objections of the private quarry owners continued to meet with opposition from the Government well into 1935 and 1936:

"The question of the sale of metal from prison quarries was raised by Mr W J Jordan (Labour—Manukau), who said quarry owners generally were alarmed at the competition from the department. The Minister of Justice, Hon J G Cobbe said...The sale of metal from prison quarries was another matter...but he had recently informed the quarry owners that as soon as they came to an agreement among themselves regarding prices he would be prepared to come to some arrangement with them." [58]

"A recent complaint made by the Auckland Builders, General and Other Labourers' Union that unfair competition was being resorted to by the Auckland prison in connection with metal supplies, is viewed with surprise by the Minister of Justice, the Hon H G R Mason. In a letter received by the union, the Minister said that the department did not cut prices and had been conforming strictly to a schedule of prices drawn up in collaboration with the Quarry Owners' Association.

"The Minister mentioned that as a result of shortened hours, costs of quarry materials and repairs had increased considerably. The matter of revising the prices to meet the higher costs was at present being discussed with the Quarry Owners' Association...the Minister added...The department's business has remained fairly static since the standard prices were agreed upon some time ago.

"Certain quarry firms had complained that their orders had dropped appreciably as a result of the alleged competition of the prison, said the secretary of the union, Mr T Stanley, yesterday. He added that there were members of the union out of work who had been employed until recently." [59]

Paradoxically, while the Mount Eden quarry had supplied stone for Auckland's roads for decades, it was the construction of a nearby motorway that resulted in its ultimate closure:

"And there was the curious position of Auckland Grammar School. Generations of pupils could watch through the barbed wire the prisoners working in the prison quarry. In 1948, after stone fragments from the quarry blasting narrowly missed a member of the school staff, the prison superintendent promised to double the strength of the blasting plates laid over the charges.

"And he asked the headmaster to notify him when parades or sports fixtures were being held in the school grounds. He would then delay blasting until the fixtures were over. (The school later acquired the quarry grounds for sports fields, compensation for land lost for adjacent motorway works.)…" [60]

J J Craig

The Craig family dynasty started with Joseph Craig, one of some 500 Scottish settlers who landed at Auckland from the Duchess of Argyle and Jane Gifford in October 1842. Joseph started out as a brick maker and his son, Joseph Craig junior, started business as a carrier in 1866.

In 1885, following the death of Joseph Craig junior, his son, Joseph James Craig, assumed control of the carrier business started by his father, delivering tons of coal, firewood, and building materials during the course of a year.

"On the death of his father, Joseph James Craig expanded the business to include shipping, haulage, mining, brickmaking, lime and cement interests. At one stage the company ran about 70 ships, most of them sailing vessels. Both coastal trading and later Trans-Tasman routes…" [61]

Trading as J J Craig, the firm also tendered its services for the improvement of the city's roads — as published by The New Zealand Herald in July 1885:

"Customs Street West — Tenders were opened for works in this street as follows: G. Knight, £284 5s 9d; William Smith, £239 15s; J J Craig, £226 10s; Thos Kneebone, £274 4s 3d ; Wm. Bolton, £229 10s 9d ; W and G Winstone, £256 18s 6d; Elias Pascoe and Co, £196 5s 1d; L Burke and Co, £286 7s; Conlan and Regan, £210. The Engineer's estimate was £250. The tender of Pascoe and Co was accepted…" [62]

By January 1886, J J Craig had also acquired an interest in part of the Mount Eden quarry, albeit a tenuous one:

"The continued disembowelment of Mount Eden for road metal has again engaged the attention of Mr D A Tole (Commissioner of Crown Lands), and further litigation is to be the result. In June last, Mr Tole applied for and obtained an injunction restraining Bernard McDonald from excavating his quarry on the eastern slope of the mountain. The consequence was that Mr McDonald disposed of all his interest in connection therewith to Mr J J Craig who seems to have resumed the excavation.

"The Commissioner of Crown Lands has, therefore, taken the necessary steps to apply for a fresh injunction. He alleges that the quarry is a source of danger, inasmuch as its eastern margin runs parallel with the Crown reserves, at a distance of only 7 feet, and that the face of the cliff is nearly perpendicular, while one portion of it actually overhangs its base. He contends that a landslip would do irreparable injury as the road skirting the brow of the mountain would thereby be rendered quite useless…" [63]

In September 1900, The New Zealand Herald published a profile of the business of J J Craig, parts of which included:

"No city in New Zealand can boast of such a vast enterprise as that controlled by Mr J J Craig in Auckland…The Government and every contractor of any note in the province freely admit that no more reliable bricks, lime, scoria, sand, etc., can be obtained in the colonies than from this firm's yards.

"Thousands of tons of sand, delivered at 4d per bushel, are supplied annually to the various contractors. The sand is brought to Auckland in the firm's vessels from different parts of the coast. Craig's hydraulic lime has a colonial reputation…

"At J J Craig's splendid brickworks at Avondale upwards of 80 men are constantly employed. The bricks are burned in Hoffman's patent kilns and the appliances used throughout are of the most modern invention. The bricks made are of first-class quality; they absorb the least amount of moisture of any in the market and they have a sterling reputation in New Zealand.

"The output amounts to about 6,000,000 bricks per annum. Drain pipes, ranging from three inches to two feet in diameter, are also made here in large numbers…

"One hundred vehicles of different kinds are in use, such as furniture waggons, timber trolleys, spring-carts, drays, etc., carrying various weights from one to 20 tons. Fine commodious stables are situated in Beach Road and cover two acres of land. One hundred and sixty powerful draught horses, magnificent animals, are fed and stabled here…" [64]

"When the transition from horse to horseless carriage was beginning, J J Craig Ltd was operating stables of 500 horses." [65]

J J Craig was registered as J J Craig Limited on 12 January 1903 [66] and, in 1906, the company occupied part of the building at 100 Queen Street. After the company purchased the building in 1951, it remained the company's head office until 1969. [67]

Joseph James Craig died on 12 July 1916. [68]

"At the time of his death the company operated 70 sailing ships and was the largest carrying concern in Auckland…his brother, Ernest Arthur Craig, became Chairman of the company until 1919, when he retired and was replaced by J J Craig's son [James Campbell Craig] as Chairman and Managing Director. James Craig retired in 1931 and the company was then administered by various boards…" [69]

A court proceeding of 1921 highlighted the business then carried out by J J Craig Limited:

"…in addition to the business of a transport and carrying company, and coal merchant and shipping agent, had carried on the business of a brick, lime, and cement manufacturer, and dealer, and machinery, bone dust, wool, flax, wood, and sand merchant, a shipowner and a general merchant…

"…carrying was the major part of the plaintiffs' business, the return from this source being about £12,000 a month. It owned over 200 horse vehicles, besides a number of motor vehicles, and employed nearly 150 horse drivers…" [70]

"In 1942 J A Gentles was the nominee of a group of business men who purchased the majority of shares from the J J Craig estate. The Winstone Ltd subsidiary company, NZ Wallbords Ltd, became a major shareholder subsequently becoming the sole owner through Winstone Ltd nominees. In February 1968 J J Craigs Ltd's trading activities were incorporated into Winstone Ltd." [71]

The retiring chairman of Winstone Limited, Mr E G Winstone, commented on the acquisition of J J Craig during the Winstone annual meeting of October 1968:

"During the past year to June 30, Winstone Ltd had placed emphasis on the consolidation of its activities rather than on expansion…Referring to the integration of the activities of J J Craig Ltd with those of the parent company, Mr Winstone said that results so far indicated that the merger was in the best interests of both shareholders and clients." [72]

The name of J J Craig Limited was eventually changed to Winstone (Auckland) Limited on 9 March 1976 and to Winstone Trading Limited on 4 April 1984. [73]

Winstone

The company now known as Winstone Aggregates is described as having had humble origins with its founder, William Winstone, arriving in Auckland from London in September 1859 as a sixteen-year-old.

At Auckland, William Winstone worked as a labourer until he could afford to buy his own horse and cart and started as a coal merchant and carrier, selling coal along the waterfront in 1864… [74]

As a general carter, William Winstone was not alone — as per an advertisement published by The New Zealand Herald in December 1863:

"The undersigned take this opportunity of informing their customers and the public generally, that their present prices for Carting are For all heavy Goods off the Wharf, 3s. per ton; For all other Goods, 3s. per load. For Carting in the lower parts of the Town, 2s. 6d. per load and for Carting to other parts of the Town, price according to distance. Robert Pollock, Joseph Harris, John Stewart, James Ballantine, William Winstone, James Boat, Robert Clifford, George Word, William Stirling, J Mcshane, P A Bonfield, W & F Rowe, P Coyle, James Quinn, Thomas Conlin, George Akers…" [75]

One of the first indications of the road-maintenance ambitions that would later become a mainstay of Winstone operations was published in March 1866:

"A letter was read from eight residents of William street calling attention to the condition of the street and stating that a carter named William Winstone had proffered to make the road passable for a cart or dray for £30; and to which sum the residents were willing to subscribe £15. They requested the Board would order the work to be commenced at once. The Chairman said the street was out of the jurisdiction of the Board." [76]

Indeed, a history of Mount Eden names Winstones as one of the first to access stone at the village quarry: "A quarry was established near Mt Eden Prison where prisoners extracted stone for prison buildings. Winstones opened three quarries on the mountain in the 1860s and others followed…" [77]

As told by Winstone Aggregates, the story of its origins continues:

"…When gold was discovered in Coromandel, transport demands lead to opportunities for William. In 1867 he temporarily transferred his cartage plant and some horses to Thames. Two years later he would be joined by his younger brother George.

"George had left home at 13 to work in his cousin's store in Queensland. By 21, his experience in retail combined with William's in transport, formed W and G Winstone.

"Together they worked from 5am to 9 at night, to ensure prompt service. By the 1870s, selling firewood, coal and operating cartage, William secured the contract to demolish Point Britomart, adding quarrying and excavation to business operations…" [78]

Advertisements at the time included:

"Wanted, Purchasers for best Newcastle Coal…Purchasers for Cut and Uncut Firewood delivered at lowest rates…W and G Winstone, Custom-house street…" [79]

"The business experienced rapid growth as the brothers' company became one of the first to offer water-borne cartage, allowing them to transport coal for gasworks and dairy factories to ports outside Auckland…" [80]

During the 1870s, the carting business was not without its rules and regulations — to be ignored at some cost:

"William Winstone, accused of omitting to have the number of his license painted on the off side of his cart in the manner prescribed by the regulations issued by the Board, was discharged on paying the costs, as he had but recently arrived in the colony, and seemed to labour under some difficulty in unravelling the maze of the City Board bye-laws and regulations." [81]

"George Winstone was charged with not having a sufficient light on a fence enclosing an excavation in Cook-street on the night of the 22nd inst. The defendant pleaded that the cutting was lighted by the moon on the night in question. This was not deemed sufficient by the Bench, and a penalty of 20s. and costs was inflicted." [82]

"William Winstone was charged with a breach of the Harbour Regulations by not walking at the head of his horse along the wharf on the 2nd instant…Mr. Winstone said, in order to save time, he would plead guilty. Had he been cautioned he should not have been in Court. His Worship said although the penalty was £10, he should only impose a fine of 10s. and costs, and he hoped it would be a warning to others." [83]

Coal and firewood was not the only commodity with which the Winstone brothers dealt in 1881:

"Messrs W and G Winstone have on sale a fine cargo of guano at very low quotations." [84]

And the reshaping of the Auckland's landscape by means of the horse and cart was gaining momentum by 1884:

"Tenders were received as follows for earth-cutting in Lower Hobson-street, and earth-filling in Patteson-street…W and G Winstone's tender was accepted." [85]

But while there was apparently plenty of work, thanks to the diversification of their goods and services, a profit was not easily achieved by the Winstone brothers who met with some objection in March 1890:

"Ten carters in the employ of W and G Winstone, coal merchants, one of the largest carrying firms in the city, went out on strike yesterday owing to the refusal of the firm to grant them an increase in wages. The men are paid 36s per week and seven days ago they asked for £2 per week but this demand was not granted. Messrs Winstone state that they could not grant the demand owing to the bad times, and they complain that the men have treated them unfairly in ceasing work without any warning. A movement is on foot among the men to form a branch of the New Zealand Federated Carters' Union." [86]

Six days later, it was reported:

"The carters' strike was finally settled today, when Winstone Bros yielded to the demand of their men and took four of them back into their employ at two guineas a week, beside raising the wages of those who had assisted them during the difficulty." [87]

W and G Winstone was registered at Auckland as the private, limited liability company of Winstone Limited on 5 August 1904 [Companies Office] with no shares offered to the public. [88]

The Winstone business continued to prosper despite many hard economic times suffered by the country from time to time. In 1912, a rising cost-of-living crisis necessitated an inquiry contributed to by George Winstone in June of that year:

"Interesting information in regard to the coal business was given before the Cost of Living Commission to-day by Mr George Winstone (of the firm of Winstone Ltd, coal merchants and carriers) who said that the business had been established over 40 years. The cost of distribution had increased considerably during the last 18 years owing to the price of labour and horses and an increase all round. Generally men worked harder twenty years ago than they did now. He was sure of that fact." [89]

As told by Winstone Aggregates, the story of its origins continues:

"In the 20th century the company expanded retail outlets and invested in the manufacture and importation of building products including plaster wallboard, bricks and tiles, updating equipment from agencies purchased and in 1914 developed a large supply yard in Nelson Street, selling cement, sand and shingle. Expansion included a metal quarry and scoria pit in Mount Eden which supplied the base for filling streets.

"Aggregate and cement were supplied to build Auckland's Grafton Bridge among other important New Zealand building projects shaping the country and creating a legacy…" [90]

In March 1924, Winstone celebrated its Diamond Jubilee — 60 years since the firm was established with one horse and one cart. The occasion was celebrated with a dinner to mark the occasion attended by the more than 300 then employed — as reported by the Auckland Star:

"Notwithstanding the fact that he has recently suffered an illness and that he is approaching his eighty-second birthday, the founder of the firm, Mr William Winstone, looked remarkably well…

"In 1809, within a few months of George joining his brother, William Winstone, when quarrying stone for the New Zealand Insurance Company's Building, known as the Auckland Stock Exchange, was severely injured by an explosion. This accident nearly cost him his life, and it was two years before he was able to return to business…

"In the early days the partnership was largely occupied in forming the main approaches to the city, cutting down and forming Hobson street and a portion of Fort Britomart. Under the able guidance of these two men, assisted by the late Mr Fred Winstone who was the highly esteemed manager of the company from 1904 until the time of his death in 1918, the company grew until to-day its staff consists of 400 employees, 288 of whom are on the permanent staff and to whom it paid an annual wages bill of over £100,000.

"The company…is one of the oldest established in its line in New Zealand, has its own brick and tile works, quarries, scoria, shingle and sand deposits, engineering, coachbuilding, blacksmith and harness establishments, a large fleet of coastal vessels, and employs daily some 200 horses and 24 motor trucks…" [91]

William Winstone died at his Mount Albert home on 23 June 1924 [92] and George Winstone died at the age of 84 on 1 May 1932. [93]

A legacy left by George Winstone was reported by The New Zealand Herald in April 1925:

"The upper part of the volcanic cone, Mount Roskill, has been donated by the owner, Mr George Winstone, to the public. The area is about 21 acres, while a further gift is a flat playing area of 12 acres for the purposes of a recreation ground and public park to be known as 'Winstone Park'." [94]

Winstone's Mount Roskill quarry was described by Andy Loader in a Quarry Mining Magazine of November 2017 as:

"One of the last quarries to stop operating was the Three Kings Quarry started by Winstones in 1922 when it purchased 27.5 acres on the Three Kings scoria hill in Mount Roskill (it was extended to nearly 40 acres in 1938)…"

Also…"Winstone set up the basalt quarry in Lunn Avenue, Mount Wellington in 1936 and it became the country's largest quarry with an annual output in excess of two million tonnes at its highest levels…" [95]

As told by Winstone Aggregates, the story of its origins continues:

"After a series of mergers and acquisitions the Winstone's story was not without challenges. One of these was the worldwide stock market crash of October 1987. Brierley [Investments Limited], which had increased its shareholding in Winstones throughout the early 1980s, was now overstretched, cash-strapped and vulnerable. It sold Winstone in 1988 to Winstone's then rival, Fletcher Challenge for $444 million.

"Fletcher Challenge boss Hugh Fletcher said, 'combining operations will bring synergistic benefits, enabling the companies concerned to offer more efficient services to customers.'" [96]

Eventually absorbed completely by Fletcher Challenge companies, Winstone Limited was struck from the Companies register on 31 March 2006. [97]

Remaining Quarries

"Two notable quarries that left a legacy were the Mt Smart quarries, initially run by three different quarrying companies till eventually they were all taken over by W Stevenson and Sons…

"The largest quarries left in the region are Drury Quarry and Hunua Quarry. Drury, owned by Stevenson, opened around 1939 and is now one of the largest and most technically advanced quarries in this country. It also incorporates a quarry based pugmill for producing modified aggregates.

"With its greywacke resource, Drury Quarry ranks amongst the biggest producers of aggregate in the Auckland region, employing 35 staff and supplying a large part of Auckland's requirements (currently approximately 2.5 million tonnes per year).

"As such, Drury Quarry is vital to the Auckland region's economy and its expanding infrastructure, providing an estimated economic benefit of around $40–$50 million per annum according to independent experts.

"Hunua Quarry began in the 1920s as a small business sourcing stone and aggregate from a rocky outcrop in the Hunua gorge. Winstone Aggregates recognised the quarry's potential to supply the rapidly growing South Auckland area and purchased the main Hunua block in 1955. The quarry is situated within a high quality greywacke rock resource.

"To provide for development, neighbouring property was purchased in 1958. This secured the Symonds Hill area for future extraction, and then in 1988 and 1990 adjoining rural land was acquired to 'buffer' the quarry zone from developments that may be sensitive to the effects of quarrying." [98]

Cement

Roman Cement

Various sources describe the development of what became known as Roman cement by Englishman, James Parker, in the 1780s. Described as one of the pioneering new cements, Parker's version was processed from extracting and burning "…nodules that are found in certain clay deposits…then ground to a fine powder. This product, made into a mortar with sand, set in 5 to 15 minutes. The success of Roman cement led other manufacturers to develop rival products by burning artificial mixtures of clay and chalk." [99]

Portland Cement

"Portland cement is the most common type of cement in general use around the world as a basic ingredient of concrete, mortar, stucco, and non-specialty grout. It was developed from other types of hydraulic lime in England in the early 19th century by Joseph Aspdin [an English bricklayer] and is usually made from limestone.

"It is a fine powder, produced by heating limestone and clay minerals in a kiln to form clinker, and then grinding the clinker with the addition of several percent (often around 5%) gypsum…

"Its name is derived from its resemblance to Portland stone which is quarried on the Isle of Portland in Dorset, England. It was named by Joseph Aspdin who obtained a patent for it in 1824. His son William Aspdin is regarded as the inventor of modern portland cement due to his developments in the 1840s." [100]

The hydraulic limestone from which cement was manufactured also became known as 'cement rock' — the American discovery of which was described by the Cromwell Argus in August 1925:

"1924 is the one-hundredth anniversary of the invention of Portland cement. Old records have been discovered showing that in 1850 deposits of rock needed for natural cement manufacture were found in Georgia and that cement was made in the state before the Civil War.

"The discovery of cement rock was made in 1850 at Cement, Georgia by the Rev Charles W Havard. In 1867 Colonel George Waring of Savannah took control of the plant and worked it as the Havard Hydraulic Cement Company." [101]

The New Zealand Gazette and Wellington Spectator advertised the sale of cement direct from the ship in 1841 and 1843, respectively:

"Public Sale. Messrs Bethune And Hunter will sell by public auction on Monday the 19th April ex the Bailey 20 casks cement…" [102]

"Roman cement in puncheons, barrels, and half barrels…" [103]

However, it was not long before canny New Zealand businessmen were manufacturing their own brand of Portland cement to satisfy the needs of a growing country.

John Wilson and Company

The manufacture of hydraulic lime was started in 1878 at Mahurangi by John Wilson and his brothers, Nathaniel and James, trading as John Wilson and Company.

"At first, John Wilson had great trouble to convince people that buildings made of concrete from hydraulic lime would be permanent. He met with much opposition and even put down water channels in Queen Street at his own cost to prove to the City Council that they would last. He built a residence for himself on Ponsonby Road out of concrete made with hydraulic lime…" It was his energy and persistence that eventually led to the great development in New Zealand of concrete buildings and roads. [104]

Some of the first advertisements for John Wilson and Company lime product appeared in The New Zealand Herald in November 1879:

"Messrs John Wilson and Co hydraulic ground roach lime; hydraulic ground roach lime for plastering purposes." [105]

And the company successfully tendered for a project involving concrete construction in September 1881:

"The tender of Messrs John Wilson and Co for concrete foundations for the factory of the Auckland Fibre Manufacturing Company Limited has been accepted by the directors. The erection of the works will be proceeded with at once." [106]

That same year, John Wilson and Co reminded the Auckland City Council of its presence:

"The fortnightly meeting of the City Council took place last night [20 October 1881]…Messrs John Wilson and Co. wrote making some representations with respect to the proposed conditions regarding the use of concrete and bricks in building, and suggesting that the new building regulations be advertised for public information, before being confirmed." [107]

However, the reputation of the John Wilson and Co product extended far beyond the Auckland district — as commented on by the Wanganui Chronicle in April 1883:

"The enormous quantity of cement imported into this colony continually suggests to thinking people how desirable it would be on every account if local industry and local material could combine to produce an article as good and as economical to the consumer as that for which year after year vast sums of money are sent out of this colony…

"Already cement is largely employed in the walls of our houses, the pavements of our streets and, as Wanganui increases, and the need of building regulations becomes forced upon the community here as in other large towns, concrete work will stand a good chance of being employed to a far greater extent than brick.

"This fact seems to have dawned upon Messrs Holcroft and Richards with such convincing force that they have determined to grapple with the cement supply and endeavour to substitute a sound article produced in New Zealand for the barrels of Portland cement which arrive here from the banks of the Thames [England].

"With that intention, therefore, the enterprising firm…has secured the appointment of sole agents on this coast for the hydraulic lime produced by Messrs John Wilson and Co of Auckland. This lime mixed with sand of a suitable character, such as can be procured in this district to an inexhaustible extent, makes the finest and most durable concrete in the world…

Messrs Wilson and Co's lime-kilns are on the Mahurangi River, north-east of Auckland, and they have risked a great deal of capital in erecting machinery to grind the lime. They started with two kilns and have now 10, and recently have had to enlarge and renew nearly the whole of the machinery.

We have before us…a score of testimonials from the Auckland City Council and business men in and around the northern capital, showing what has been done with the hydraulic lime in building and flooring of all descriptions. Messrs Wilson and Co…have erected nine concrete buildings one of them — Mr J C Firth's granary at the foot of Albert-street — being the largest of the kind in the colony…

"There is already a very great demand for Messrs Wilsons lime, but Messrs Holcroft and Richards are confident that, by means of small sailing vessels trading between here and Mahurangi…they can guarantee a constant supply for the settlers on this coast…" [108]

In 1885, John Wilson and Co

"…started making cement at Warkworth, burning the cement rock in the old fashioned upright brick kiln. That same year, one of their orders, and considered a large one at that time, was from the Auckland Harbour Board for cement for the building of the Rangitoto beacon.

"The beacon still stands today as a warning to those that go down to the sea in ships. It also stands as a monument to the quality of the Portland cement supplied by the Wilson brothers. It is evident that quality was their watchword and it has remained the watchword through all the vicissitudes of the intervening years. [109]

Wilsons cement was also first used in bridge construction in 1890 —

"…the attention of Highway Boards and County Councils [is called] to a new departure made by the Upper Mahurangi Road Board and a neighbouring Board, in the construction of the piers for the large bridge over Hepburn's Creek which are made of concrete from a formula adopted by Messrs John Wilson and Co with their hydraulic lime.

"It is notorious that all our bridges have been hitherto erected of wood which is more or less perishable in about…ten years. The concrete, if properly made, probably lasts ten times as long or more, and in the erection of such structures as bridges the permanency of the work should now demand the most serious consideration of all those having control of such works, more particularly when the expenditure of the public funds are involved." [110]

Nevertheless, cement and lime makers of the time had to prove that not only was their product reliable but also that it was the best:

"As more than one brand of Hydraulic Lime is being sold in Wellington and such maker of course claiming his is the best, those interested are requested to give our brand a fair trial, and not to condemn it because other limes may fail…Each bag of Wilsons Lime contains three bushels, and a printed slip bears the well-known star brand. And we claim quality (especially at a distance) is the first consideration and that the real value can only be gauged by the proportion of sand or gravel the lime carries.

"This Lime being a natural cement requires to be treated as ordinary cement, but is as easily worked as other limes, yet many have condemned it through want of care in using. If used for mortar in wet positions with wet bricks or in any wet place, it should be mixed as required; but for ordinary work it is better to make it up the day before and re-mix as used…John Wilson and Co, Auckland, Manufacturers of Wilsons Portland Cement and Hydraulic Lime." [111]

By 1893, the Wilson cement and lime business was manufacturing a trusted product:

"Messrs Wilson and Co of Warkworth employ about twenty men at their hydraulic lime and cement works. Their output is about 25 tons weekly. The industry is an important one to North Auckland and the quality of Wilsons Portland Cement has been fully established." [112]

That trust continued to win valuable customers — as reported by the South Canterbury Times in May 1897:

"The Hawke's Bay Harbour Engineer reported that Wilsons Portland cement, manufactured in Auckland, having been tested and found to be equal to and cheaper than the imported article, 1000 bags equal to 500 casks, have been ordered. The price was stated to be 5s 6d per bag." [113]

In 1898, John Wilson and Co displayed their lime and cement products at the Auckland Exhibition:

"Twenty years ago, John Wilson and Co erected the first machinery used in New Zealand to grind hydraulic lime. All the raw materials required for the firm's manufactures are obtained in the colony and so considerable is the demand for their lime and cement that the works give employment to about 80 men and work night and day. Messrs Wilson and Co were the first in the colony to produce Portland cement in marketable quantities, this branch of their business having been established in 1885." [114]

However, the country's demand for lime and cement soon required some investment:

"In 1900, no doubt after many anxious cogitations, John Wilson and Co decided to purchase modern revolving horizontal kilns and the latest grinding machinery. These arrived in the colony and in due course were erected. Unfortunately, the expense of this new plant considerably exceeded the estimates, as new plants do, and the Wilson brothers were compelled to seek outside financial assistance." [115]

By 1904, with their financial challenges met, John Wilson and Co had started an agricultural lime works at Te Kuiti [116] and also planned further expansion at Mahurangi:

"The extension of the business of Messrs John Wilson and Co Limited has necessitated the expenditure of about £20,000 in the purchase of new machinery and, in order to raise a portion of the new capital, 12,000 preference shares, carrying interest at six per cent, were placed upon the market and the whole were readily taken up within a few days." [117]

That new plant was described by the New Zealand Mail in January 1905:

"The firm of Messrs John Wilson and Co…have lately installed a new plant capable of turning out 25,000 tons of Portland cement a year. The company was the first in the colony to manufacture Portland cement. It commenced in 1885 and the business extended so rapidly that the plant is now believed to be the largest in Australasia.

"The cement has an excellent reputation and is guaranteed to pass all the recognised tests as to soundness, fineness and strength. Its suitability for sea work was early recognised, for it was in 1886 that the Rangitoto Beacon was constructed by the Auckland Harbour Board. Since then, the Napier and Wellington Harbour Boards have also used it…" [118]

At a company meeting in May 1907, the details of further expansion were discussed and a change of the company's name decided:

"At a meeting of John Wilson and Company Limited, the chairman said the plant and machinery account stood at £36,814. That was the cost price of the plant and machinery in actual operation, less amounts deducted for depreciation. Owing to the abnormal call for Portland cement and hydraulic lime all over New Zealand, their present plant had been quite unable to meet the demands made upon it, and whilst everything possible was being done to fulfil contracts, extensive orders offering at remunerative prices had to be refused.

"Some time ago, they decided to duplicate the plant at Mahurangi and, in order that the additions would be of very latest type, they sent their engineer to America, England and the Continent to select it and to superintend its manufacture.

"The order had been placed in America, the home of the rotary clinking kiln, and they had been advised that the first part was being shipped this month. They were at present making over 500 tons of cement and lime weekly. When the new plant was erected this quantity should be doubled. They turned out 4000 tons more last year than in the previous year. It was decided to alter the name to Wilsons Portland Cement Company Limited." [119]

Wilsons Portland Cement Company

A year later, in May 1908, John Wilson and Company held its first annual meeting as the newly-named, Wilsons Portland Cement Company Limited:

"The annual general meeting of the shareholders of the Wilsons Portland Cement Company Ltd was held…yesterday afternoon, Mr George Elliot (chairman of directors) presiding. The annual report and balance-sheet showed that the profit earned for the year, including the balance (£2130 11s 1d) brought forward, amounted to £16,188 18s 6d…he said that from a financial point of view this had been by far the most successful year in the company's existence, notwithstanding the fact that during the whole of the period they had been hampered by preparing for and erecting the very large additions to the plant at Mahurangi…

Roads…Roads…Roads…   313

"Owing to the increasingly large amount of cement sent out from the works, the directors considered it advisable that the company should not altogether be dependent on outside shipowners and during the year they had purchased two sailing vessels. These proved so satisfactory that a contract was let for building a steamer capable of carrying 200 tons, and it was successfully launched on the 19th of this month…" [120]

The company name may have changed but, by May 1910, the quality and reputation of the Wilson cement product remained the best:

"The Grafton Bridge was mentioned as a testimony to the good qualities of the Wilson cement. Additional land had been lately secured, and the stock of raw material available had been greatly increased." [121]

Availability of Raw Material

An abundance of raw material for the manufacture of cement and lime products did not just exist at the Wilson cement works at Mahurangi. Whangarei Harbour also proved to be a rich source — as reported by a New Zealand Herald correspondent in September 1910:

"I have already referred to the immense deposits of natural cement rock in Northern Auckland. Limestone Island in Whangarei Harbour is about as favourably constituted and situated for building up a great cement manufacturing industry as man could desire. Hydraulic lime, agricultural lime, building stone, plastic clays, fire clays are found in great abundance about Whangarei…" [122]

Reports of the resources available at Whangarei were published in 1911 by the Auckland Star and Northern Advocate, respectively:

"An interesting paper was read before the Institute of Mining Engineers by Mr F N Rhodes on 'New Zealand Cement Deposits'. He pointed out that with the exception of the deposits of the Milburn Cement Company near Dunedin, Wilsons Cement Company on the Mahurangi River, and those of the New Zealand Cement Company at Limestone Island, Whangarei, the cement resources of New Zealand remained practically undeveloped.

"After speaking of the many natural advantages Limestone Island possessed, both for shipping facility and handiness of all materials needed, he pointed out that the approximate quantity of cement rock at the island was 25,000,000 tons, yielding at least 15,000,000 tons of manufactured cement, and as the company's output is at present about 1700 tons a month, the life of the deposit could readily be appreciated…" [123]

"…the North New Zealand Coal and Cement Company's mine at Whangarei…Coal is not the only product of the mine and the full value and advantages of the Whangarei coal seams are only apparent when the inexhaustible deposits of cement rock in conjunction with them are taken into consideration.

"Cement is now the article most in demand, and no one will dispute the fact that the demand is increasing, but it cannot be produced without suitable coal. It exists in Whangarei, with the best of railway and deep-water shipping facilities, second to no place in the world.

"Only a little enterprise and capital is needed to make Whangarei the metropolis of the cement trade. What Newcastle has been made by the coal trade, it may be hoped that Whangarei will become, at a very early date, by the cement trade." [124]

The Dominion Portland Cement Company

By December 1912, others had appreciated the potential for making a profit from the Whangarei raw material:

"The first meeting of the Board of Directors of the Dominion Portland Cement Company Ltd with a capital of £250,000, was held to-day, when shares comprising the minimum subscriptions were allotted.

"Four additional directors were appointed: Messrs T Buxton, MP (Temuka), Robert McNab (Palmerston North), Vernon Reed, MP (Bay of Islands), and George Winstone (Auckland)." [125]

"The company proposes to operate on a cement rock deposit in Whangarei harbour where sufficient deposits are available to last for centuries. It is intended to at once put in hand the erection of a plant with a view to starting operations within 18 months. The works will be double the size of any cement works at present existing in New Zealand. The appointment of Mr W J Wilson (Auckland) as works manager was confirmed." [126]

"The Company is being formed for the purpose of…

"1. Acquiring from the vendors the freehold property known as Tikorangi, situated on the Whangarei Harbour, consisting of about 2,220 acres.

"2. Acquiring from the vendors the freehold property at Te Mata Point containing an additional deposit of White-Limestone.

"3. Taking advantage of an offer…by which the Company will have the right to receive hydro-electric power at a maximum price of £9 per h.p. per annum…

"Tikorangi is on the mainland and opposite to Limestone Island upon which are the works of the NZ Portland Cement Co Ltd…Tikorangi contains an almost unlimited supply of cement rock estimated at over 400,000,000 tons with only a few inches of overburthen of earth. The stone can be obtained by open quarrying and be carried down by gravitation to the works by means of a tramway.

"The cement is practically identical in composition with that on Limestone Island and at Mahurangi (Wilsons Portland Cement Co), is therefore proved to be of the first quality and capable of being manufactured into first quality Portland Cement…" [127]

As the Auckland Star reported in December 1921, the new cement industry at Whangarei resulted in the establishment of the town of Portland to accommodate its workers:

"The establishment of the Dominion Portland Cement Works at Portland, capable of an output of between 60,000 and 70,000 tons per year, has resulted in the growth of a township of cement workers on the shores of the Whangarei Harbour…

"When the late Mr Nathaniel Wilson started the cement industry in 1885 in the modest little works at Warkworth even those acquainted with the raw material resources of the Northern peninsula could scarcely have foreseen the development of the industry that was destined to take place when concrete became so important a feature of building and road construction…

"The resumption of building activities since the end of the war has created a steady demand for cement, but, apart from this, it is anticipated that a big fillip will be given to the industry when the end of the temporary financial stringency encourages the more extensive use of concrete roads." [128]

The New Zealand Portland Cement Company

As described by Engineering New Zealand's history of 'Limestone Island Cement':

"Ernest Schaw Rutherfurd produced what is thought to be the first cement made in the Southern Hemisphere at Limestone Island in 1881. However, it was not until 1895 that Rutherfurd and Company erected a cement works there and commenced manufacturing Portland cement.

"Rutherfurd's business was soon taken over by Alan Hall's new company, the New Zealand Portland Cement Company. The plant was able to produce 46 tonnes of cement and 61 tonnes of hydraulic lime per week. The island's wharf could take vessels of up to 3.3 metres draught, which brought over coal from nearby Kamo and Hikurangi and took away the manufactured cement and lime." [129]

Shares in the newly-formed New Zealand Portland Cement Company Limited were first offered to the public in July 1896 — as reported by the Evening Star:

"In this issue is published the abridged prospectus of the New Zealand Portland Cement Company with a capital of £10,000, in 10,000 shares. The vendors are to receive 4,000 shares and 4,000 are now offered to the public…" [130]

The objectives of the New Zealand Portland Cement Company were described by The New Zealand Herald in November 1897:

"This company, which has its headquarters at Dunedin, has been formed to work the large deposits of hydraulic lime at Limestone Island, Whangarei Harbour. The company have taken the island over from Messrs Rutherford and Co and have erected a new and up-to-date plant for the manufacture of Portland cement and hydraulic lime and have also considerably enlarged and renewed the mill buildings…

"Portland cement can be manufactured wherever a supply of its constituent parts can be obtained and, at Limestone Island, the company have everything suitable for its manufacture and in addition have cheap fuel and water carriage.

"As regards the process of manufacture, the material used is taken from a quarry of limestone (the quantity of which is practically unlimited)…The company have registered their trade mark as the 'Crown Brand' and all their manufactures will bear that brand…" [131]

The company's Crown brand of cement soon made a name for itself throughout the country:

"In our Supplement to day appears an advertisement in connection with the New Zealand Portland Cement Company's celebrated Crown brand of cement and hydraulic lime. The company have been in existence a considerable time in Auckland but have lately added a large plant of the most modern design which has enabled them to extend their operations to all parts of the colony. The cement and lime have been used by the Auckland Corporation and other local bodies and are especially favoured by builders generally. Very severe tests have been applied and compare most favorably with any other colonial or imported cement…" [132]

However, in what was the first of two fires, the fortunes of the company suffered a severe setback in September 1902:

"The New Zealand Portland Cement Company's works at Limestone Island were completely gutted by fire on Sunday morning. The plant was comparatively new and the damage is estimated at £20,000. About fifty people have been thrown out of work…" [133]

Nevertheless, the New Zealand Portland Cement Company soon recovered and, by February 1904, The New Zealand Herald reported:

"All building materials are in heavy demand. A good deal of the trade in cement is now taken by the New Zealand Portland Cement Company whose works on the Whangarei Harbour turn out hundreds of tons at a time…" [134]

And again in December 1905 and August 1906, respectively:

"The New Zealand Portland Cement Company have secured the contract for the supply of 1000 tons of their cement for the Makatote viaduct on the North Island Main Trunk line, and also for 300 tons for the Napier Harbour Board." [135]

"The scope of the operations of the New Zealand Portland Cement Company at Limestone Island is being rapidly enlarged. Last week the steamer Squall landed 80 tons of machinery, and there are still 50 tons to come. When the new plant is completed, it is estimated that the output will be doubled. The shipping facilities are excellent as vessels drawing from 18ft to 20ft can load at the island wharf at low tide.

"Last month the output was 1000 tons and vessels are taking away the cement as fast as it can be bagged by automatic machines working day and night." [136]

In January 1908, the Auckland Star reported:

"The New Zealand Portland Cement Company has secured the Government contracts for supplying cement to the railways at Auckland and Wellington. [137]

The New Zealand Portland Cement Company continued to profit from its activities — reported the Evening Post:

"The annual meeting of the New Zealand Portland Cement Company was held to-day…The directors reported that operations for the thirteen months ended 30th November [1911] showed that the net profits were £10,861 6s 9d while the balance brought forward from last year was £772 11s 3d…

"A third rotary kiln should be in running order by the end of the month when the output, it was expected, would be fully doubled. The chairman mentioned that the profit for the year had benefited considerably from the fact that the low price contracts entered into some time ago had been running out and more payable business had been substituted…" [138]

Unfortunately, as it had in 1902, the company suffered its second fire in January 1915. This time, because the company's manufacturing and storage capacity was so much greater, the effects were far more devastating:

"A big disaster befell the Limestone Island Cement Works, the property of the New Zealand Portland Cement Company, shortly after midnight, the most important parts of the works being totally destroyed by fire. The demolished portion covers over an acre and includes all the important machinery. Three reciprocating engines totalling 500 horse-power and a turbine engine of 500 horse-power were utterly ruined.

"The fire broke out between the engine room and the mill when an explosion appeared to occur on the engine-room wall. The destroyed buildings were all of wooden framework covered with corrugated iron and the whole place was immediately ablaze…

"There was a stock of 300 tons of coal on the island and this became ignited and will probably burn for days. The number of men employed at the works was about 130. Many of the men are married and have families so that the island community, which was solely dependent on the works, numbers probably over 200…

"A rough estimate of the damage is £80,000…A big shipment was being prepared for Queensland at the time of the fire…" [139]

Nevertheless, rebuilding was well under way by July 1915:

"The -works of the New Zealand Portland Cement Company…which were destroyed by fire some months ago, are being reconstructed as quickly as possible. Most of the machinery has been erected and the arrival of a small portion is being awaited. The company has been advised that it will arrive in time to enable operations to be recommenced on 1st October…" [140]

However, by 1917, the market for cement had been seriously affected by a number of factors that drastically affected the fortunes of the New Zealand Portland Cement Company:

"The directors of the New Zealand Portland Cement Company, in their report for the year ended November 30, 1917…The business of the company has been considerably affected both by war conditions resulting in a generally reduced demand for cement throughout New Zealand and by the fact that the cement manufacturers are at present in the throes of a 'rate war'. After making provision for debenture interest, bad and doubtful debts, repairs and maintenance, and other contingencies, the net profit for the year, in spite of the rate war, was £2810 18s 9d…" [141]

It is of little wonder then that, by March 1918, it was realised that for the North Island industry to survive, wholesale changes had to be made:

"It is understood that negotiations which have been proceeding for the past few weeks are approaching finality under which an amalgamation will be effected between the three cement companies in the Auckland province…

"Details are not available until everything has been finally settled and the agreement signed, but the effect will be to unite the businesses and assets of the Wilsons Portland Cement Company, the New Zealand Portland Cement Company, and the Dominion Cement Company.

"This will make a big combination of the old well-known business of Wilsons Company, with branches in the Waikato, for agricultural lime, the New Zealand Portland Cement Company's works at Limestone Island, Whangarei, and the Dominion Cement Company assets, also at Whangarei. The latter company put up a big plant and also has a dam for the supply of electrical power to the works." [142]

Wilsons (NZ) Portland Cement Company

By July 1918, the amalgamation of the three Auckland-district cement companies had been achieved — as reported by the Northern Advocate:

"The amalgamation of the Northern cement companies is now an accomplished fact. Negotiations have been in progress for some considerable time and their completion was announced in Auckland on Thursday.

"The new company, which will be known as Wilsons (NZ) Portland Cement Co Ltd has acquired the assets of the Wilson Portland Cement Company Ltd, the Dominion Portland Cement Company Ltd, and the New Zealand Portland Cement Company Ltd.

"The capital of the new concern is £600,000, in 600,000 shares of £1 each, which will be allotted to shareholders in the old companies...Mr George Elliott, who was chairman of directors of the Wilsons Portland Cement Company Ltd, has been appointed chairman of directors of the new company...

"Interviewed in Auckland, Mr Elliott stated that in the meantime the new company is running the Dominion Company's plant at Portland, Whangarei, and the plant at Warkworth. The existence of a contract entered into by the Dominion Company to supply Whangarei with electric light, apart from other reasons, practically forced the company to work the plant at Portland. It was possible that the plant at Warkworth would be closed down so far as the manufacture of cement was concerned, although it might still be used to manufacture hydraulic lime.

"Referring to the circumstances which brought about the amalgamation, Mr Elliott said it has been felt for some considerable time that the cost of running three separate plants by different companies to manufacture a quantity of cement which could be turned out by one mill, was not to the advantage of the industry as a whole.

"It was a fact that during the past year, owing to competition and war conditions, a considerable amount of money had been lost by certain of the companies. During the last 12 months especially, a large quantity of cement had been sold at a price much below that which it had cost to manufacture. The amalgamation of the companies had resulted in fixing the prices at the pre-war figure, plus the actual increase in the cost of bags, coal, and freight, which amounted to £1 a ton.

"The directors of the company were well known business men who would have nothing to do with any attempt to exploit the public and the price fixed was eminently fair, in view of the increased cost of production as the result of war conditions." [143]

It was not until November 1924 that the over-capacity of manufacturing operations led to the closure of the Warkworth plant:

"The decision to close the Warkworth plant, so far as the manufacture of cement is concerned, is announced by Wilsons (NZ) Portland Cement Ltd, the demand for cement having dropped to such an extent that the company is able to supply the existing demand from its Portland plants. Although the company finds it necessary to close the cement-making portion of the Warkworth plant, the making of hydraulic and other limes will be continued as formerly...

"At no time since 1914 has the demand in New Zealand reached anything like the output capacity of the existing works. It is true there was a shortage of cement during 1920, and for the first two months of 1921, during which period the Board of Trade assumed control of distribution. The shortage was due solely to the works being unable to secure adequate supplies of coal for cement manufacture owing to a go-slow policy in the coalmining industry...

"The year 1920 might be termed the boom year in cement, but the sudden collapse early in 1921 resulted in the closing of the Golden Bay plant for two years. During the last two years the plant at Limestone Island has been removed to the mainland and installed at Portland, and this plant is now actually in operation. The result is that Wilsons (NZ) Portland Cement Ltd has again its three plants in operation...Portland plant, Limestone Island plant re-erected at Portland, and Warkworth plant." [144]

By 1925, the cement industry was looking to resurrect its fortunes with an opportunity to supply local councils and the Road Boards with concrete with which to pave the country's roads as an alternative to the increasingly popular asphalt:

"…the New Zealand Portland Cement Company is so satisfied as to the practicability of laying a cement concrete roadway on the Great South Road at a cost which compares favourably with what is known as hot mix bituminous paving, that it has already made a definite offer to the local bodies concerned on that stretch of highway to construct the Great South Road, from Otahuhu to the Papakura Town Board boundary, in cement concrete.

"It must further be borne in mind that bituminous paving, in any form…means money for the purchase of the necessary asphalt leaving New Zealand, whereas the construction of concrete roadways means every penny piece expended thereon remaining in our country." [145]

Many of the country's roads were concreted at the time and they still exist today. However, as detailed later, bitumen was soon manufactured in New Zealand and quickly became the preferred road paving material.

In the meantime, free from wartime constraints and competition, the fortunes of the Wilson New Zealand Portland Cement Company had improved greatly by 1930:

"The Wilson New Zealand Portland Cement Company's nett profit for the year ended 31st March [1930] totalled £89,955, a record." [146]

However, such are the vagaries of New Zealand's commercial activity that, some two years later, the market for cement had stagnated:

"The works of Wilsons (New Zealand) Portland Cement Company Limited at Portland will close on December 23 and it is uncertain when they will reopen in the New Year…For some considerable time the position of the cement industry has been very unsatisfactory and the company has been compelled to close the works for varying periods during the year owing to lack of orders and the fact that all storage bins have been full. Although December is usually a slack month for cement orders, the position during the past fortnight has been exceptionally bad…" [147]

Construction work had picked up again by June 1941 when Wilsons (New Zealand) Portland Cement Company was able to announce a reduced but still significant profit:

"A net profit of £84,485 compared with £109,731 last year is shown in the accounts of Wilsons (New Zealand) Portland Cement Company." [148]

By July 1948, strikes by coal miners had taken their toll on many of New Zealand's industries, including cement manufacture:

"'There is at present an overall shortage of cement in New Zealand and the potential demand is far in excess of the existing New Zealand capacity,' said Mr G Winstone, chairman of Wilsons (NZ) Portland Cement Ltd in his annual address to shareholders…Costs were still rising in an ever-increasing spiral. The manager estimated that the loss of output last year, because of the shortage of coal, was approximately 30,000 tons, continued Mr Winstone.

"'There were only 52 days on which the mill operated at full capacity and the output was a little better than that of the previous year and sales slowed to an increase of 4446 tons. Had the company been able to make the 30,000 tons lost through lack of coal, there would have been little or no complaint of shortages in the areas supplied by the company.'" [149]

Nevertheless, the demand for cement continued unabated, for projects and developments small and large — such as at Tongariro, starting in 1965:

"Arrangements for the supply of about 250,000 tons of cement, which would be five years' needs for the Tongariro hydro-electric development, have been almost completed by the Government…The supply of cement to the project would be divided equally between the Golden Bay Cement Company Ltd and Wilsons (New Zealand) Portland Cement Company. Both companies were carrying out essential work to enable them to meet the commitment." [150]

On 15 August 2000, Wilsons (New Zealand) Portland Cement Company was amalgamated with a number of Fetcher Challenge companies to become Fletcher Concrete and Infrastructure Limited. [151]

The British Standard Portland Cement Company

Competition in a relatively small market resulted in the amalgamation of the three Northland cement companies to form Wilsons (NZ) Portland Cement Company in 1918. However, competition again reared its ugly head with the announcement in September 1926 that a new company with a lot of capital was soon to begin operations in the Whangarei area — as reported by the Northern Advocate:

"The prospectus of the British Standard Portland Cement Limited is now in circulation. This company proposes to purchase a coal mine, also an area of natural cement rock, both situated near to Whangarei, subsequently constructing an up-to-date cement mill which is expected to commence producing British standard quality of cement during the year 1928…" [152]

Additional information was provided by the Auckland Star and New Zealand Times in October and November 1926, respectively:

"The board or directors, of which Sir Joseph Ward is chairman, is composed of commercial men, and the vendors of the company are taking up £80,000 worth of contributing shares." [153]

"There is…a certain and steady market for the output of the new mills to be erected by The British Standard Portland Cement Ltd. This newly formed £350,000 undertaking has acquired a cement-producing area of an exceptional nature and estimates manufacturing 72,000 tons per annum with the most modern plant in New Zealand. The Company's properties contain, according to experts' reports, over 15,000,000 tons of cement rock and limestone, and over 1,000,000 tons suitable coal. It is believed that the demand for cement roads alone can absorb the whole of the Company's output…" [154]

A rather optimistic comment, no doubt designed to promote the buying of shares in the new company, was published by the Auckland Star in December 1926:

"This is the age of concrete, and it is only a matter of time when the main highways of New Zealand will be constructed of concrete, from the North Cape to the Bluff…." [155]

That concrete had a long way to go to compete with bitumen as a favoured road material in 1926 was demonstrated by figures published by the Southland Times:

"…out of approximately 64,000 road miles, New Zealand has only about 60 miles down in concrete whilst about 640 miles are down in imported bitumen or are tar sealed." [156]

In the meantime, the British Standard Portland Cement Company continued to expand the area of its proposed resources — as reported by the Auckland Star in June 1927:

"It is understood from a reliable authority that the British Standard Portland Cement Company have just completed the purchase from the trustees of the late Mr J J Craig of the whole of the limestone interests possessed by this estate at Urquhart's Bay in Whangarei harbour.

"A report furnished by the company prior to the purchase described the quality of stone as almost perfect for the manufacture of Portland cement. The British Standard Cement Company already has large interests at Urquhart's Bay and with the recent purchase it becomes the owner of practically the whole of an exceptionally high-grade deposit of limestone in this locality…" [157]

The company's expansion that year included the purchase of an established cement manufacturer:

"The British Standard Portland Cement Company Ltd has acquired a controlling interest in the shareholding of the Golden Bay Cement Company which has works at Tarakohe, Nelson." [158]

"The company had…purchased a controlling interest, for £40,000, in the Golden Bay cement works and was installing new machinery there. The capital of the venture was £500,000. The company would commence working the plant at Whangarei Heads as soon as the machinery had been installed…" [159]

However, despite all the hype projected by its 1926 prospectus, the British Standard Portland Cement Company had still not established a cement factory at Whangarei by December 1931, and the company's coal mine was proving to be unprofitable:

"The machinery is being removed today from the British Standard Portland Cement Company's mine at Whau Valley which is closing down on account of insufficient orders. The mine is one of the oldest in the district and the coal seams run for miles under the hill leading to Kamo….About four years ago it was purchased by the British Standard Portland Cement Company which at that time had under consideration the establishment of works on the Whangarei Harbour…" [160]

Golden Bay Cement Works

Golden Bay Cement Works Limited was established at Nelson in February 1907 with a capital of £25,000. [161]

In May of that year:

"A full meeting of directors of the recently registered Golden Bay Cement Works Limited was held at the office of Messrs Rout and Son. There were present Messrs E C E Mills, F W Hamilton, M M Webster, Geo London, I K Powell, T A Peterkin, Langley Adams and W Rout. It was resolved to visit the Company's properties at Terakohe and Pohara with a view to deciding site for the works and wharf and generally to make a thorough inspection of the resources of the district for cement making. The opinion of the directors is strongly in favour of establishing a thoroughly up to-date works and going in for the most modern plant." [162]

That subsequent visit to Golden Bay by the Directors also included:

"…the Cement Expert and a Danish Cement Engineer of wide experience…The prospects ahead of the Company, with a splendid property, a central situation, and a growing demand, are such as to render failure a very remote possibility…In addition to the constituents for cement making, the Company has a large area of coal upon the property." [163]

By April 1909, construction of the plant and the wharf at Terakohe had started and the resources needed for the manufacture of cement secured:

"The company has recently acquired the freehold of a limestone and clay property with upward of a mile frontage to navigable water in Golden Bay and together with other properties held under long lease, claims to hold control of the most accessible limestone clay and coal property in New Zealand. The present directors of the company are Messrs C Prendergast Knight, W M Hannay, George Wilson, Charles Stewart, Charles McArthur, and M W Webster." [164]

Production of the first batch of cement was ready for testing by September 1911:

"The first shipment of cement manufactured by the Golden Bay Cement Works has arrived in Wellington by the steamer Kaitoa. It weighed a ton and was brought over to Wellington for purposes of testing and analysis." [165]

And, by February 1912, full production was under way:

"The big works of the Golden Bay Cement Works Ltd at Tarakohe…are now turning out over 400 tons of cement per week. There is an inexhaustible supply of the finest material within easy reach and the plant is of the most up-to-date description." [166]

Just in time, it seems, to supply the needs of highway construction:

"At the opening ceremony in connection with the 'Victoria' bridge at Trentham on May 24 [1913], Councillor Galloway, chairman of the Hutt County, aptly remarked 'the day of the wooden structure is a thing of the past…'

"The Victoria bridge…is of reinforced concrete and of a total length of 240ft, divided into six spans of 40ft each — the roadway being 14ft wide…The cement used in this fine bridge was obtained from the Golden Bay Cement Works…which has been extensively used for bridge construction work in many other districts in both North and South Islands…" [167]

However, in circumstances that would later come under suspicion and be questioned in Parliament, the Directors of the Golden Bay Cement Works company engineered a sale of the company to another — as reported by the New Zealand Times in February 1920:

"At an extraordinary general meeting of the Golden Bay Cement Works Limited yesterday, Captain McArthur presiding, it was resolved to dispose of the company as a going concern to the Golden Bay Cement Company Limited…The resolution was passed unanimously." [168]

As a result, the original Golden Bay Cement Works Limited was no more:

"The Golden Bay Cement Works Ltd came to an official end yesterday [15 July 1920]…The company has been purchased by the Golden Bay Cement Co Ltd. The shareholders of the old company have become debenture holders in the new…" [169]

"Golden Bay Cement Works Limited, having sold its assets and undertakings to Golden Bay Cement Company Limited as of 18 November 1920, to be voluntarily wound up." [170]

Golden Bay Cement Company

However, the Golden Bay Cement Company had closed down its operations by May 1921, less than a year after the new company had been established:

"The Golden Bay cement works have been closed down owing to the market being overstocked." [171]

The reason for the plant's closure was reported by the Poverty Bay Herald in June 1921:

"The Golden Bay cement works which are now controlled from Christchurch, are still closed down owing to the lack of orders. A business man largely interested in the trade said the slackening off in orders was inevitable. When cement was short the price was raised and raised again, until consumers found that it would pay just as well or better to import so many thousands of tons of English and Canadian cement into New Zealand for the first time for a score of years… As it came for big jobs in most cases, local cement, when it became available, could not get in.

"Now the price of local cement has receded it would hardly pay to import from England or Canada so the depression will continue just as long as imported stocks last and the financial stringency continues. A great deal of building would be done if money were available at a reasonable rate, but as very little money is available for building under 7 per cent, people naturally hesitate at going on with the job." [172]

However, far more sinister reasons for the closure of the Golden Bay cement works were provided by the Stratford Member of Parliament, Robert Masters, in September 1921:

"Something in the nature of a sensation was caused in the House of Representatives when Mr R Masters…made grave allegations of commercial immorality involving certain cement companies and some individuals well-known throughout the Dominion. Mr Masters denounced in strong terms the operations of what he alleged to be a ring formed for the purpose of controlling and increasing the price of cement. He alleged that one company had been induced to close down its works and thus decrease the supply available, for which it received £15,000 per annum.

"Mr Masters stated that the price of cement had been increased from £2 3s 6d to £6 0s 6d per ton, and then — with the consent of the Government's Board of Trade — it had been increased another 30s per ton to £7 10s 6d. Mr Masters roundly denounced what he termed the operations of 'a syndicate of speculators' for the restraint of trade and laid the blame on the Government for its connivance…

"He was going to refer to the case of the Golden Bay cement works. He looked on this as one of the most criminal commercial things ever perpetrated in this country. The company had turned out to be one of the most successful enterprises in the Dominion. The point was, it was recently purchased by a syndicate of speculators. He did not blame the shareholders for selling. They were given to understand that the works would be developed, that fresh capital would be put into the concern, and that huge machinery was going into the works, and that, as a result, people would get cement cheaper…" [173]

Robert Masters also asserted:

"That monopoly methods have been introduced into New Zealand cement manufacture with the object of curtailing output and increasing prices was the allegation made by Mr Masters…in the House to-day. Mr Masters said that he was going to lay at the door of the Government the whole trouble of the want of competition and the high prices prevailing in the cement market, particularly with the closing down of the Golden Bay Cement Company's works…

"The company had started in a small way and after struggling against adverse conditions had developed into one of the most successful secondary industries of the Dominion. It was bought by a syndicate of speculators…Wilsons New Zealand Portland Cement Company and the Milburn Company…" [174]

Cement Industry Commission of Inquiry 1921

As a result of the allegations made by Robert Masters, a Cement Industry Commission of Inquiry was appointed by the Government on 14 October 1921:

"… for the purpose of inquiring into certain matters relating to the production, distribution, importation, and price of cement during the period from 1st January 1920, to 31st March 1921…" — a period during which: "…the price and distribution of cement of New Zealand manufacture was controlled by the Government through the Board of Trade…"

The inquiry was undertaken by Acting Chief Justice, William Alexander Sim, who was specifically charged with reporting as to:

"(1.) Whether the Board of Trade, in December, 1920, in sanctioning a maximum retail price of cement of New Zealand manufacture of £9 13s. 6d. per ton ex store Wellington, was guilty of any impropriety or of a grievous error of judgment.

"(2.) Whether the companies manufacturing cement in New Zealand during the period of acute shortage of cement, from 1st January 1920, and thereafter, took advantage of the excess of demand over supply to extort unreasonably high prices from the public.

"(3.) Whether the agreement dated 5th May 1921, set out in the schedule hereto, constituted an offence against the Commercial Trusts Act, 1910, or any other Act, or was in any way criminal or illegal.

"(4.) Whether the price for cement of New Zealand manufacture was directly or indirectly determined, controlled, or influenced by the parties to the agreement in such manner as to make the price unreasonably high.

"(5.) Whether the said agreement has in any manner operated detrimentally to the public interest.

"(6.) Whether the Board of Trade, being aware of such agreement, was lacking in any duty in taking no action with respect to such agreement."

The agreement of 5 May 1921, referred to in clause (3.), was the agreement that had been earlier condemned by Robert Masters in Parliament, the more salient parts of which included:

"An agreement made between the Golden Bay Cement Company (Limited) of the one part, Wilsons (New Zealand) Cement Company (Limited) of the second part, and the Milburn Lime and Cement Company (Limited) of the third part:

"Whereas the contracting parties are of opinion that the demand for cement in New Zealand is likely for some months to be considerably less than the supplies which are at present being manufactured by the contracting parties: And whereas the contracting parties desire to enter into an arrangement whereby the said parties may derive the most satisfactory results possible, and for this purpose have agreed to enter into this agreement:

"1. The Golden Bay Company shall close down the manufacture of its cement on the fourteenth day of May, one thousand nine hundred and twenty-one, or as near thereto as is possible, in order to clear out its present stock of clinker.

"2. The Golden Bay Company shall have a period of one month from the above date to sell the stock of cement which may be at its works or in the hands of its agents.

"3. From and after the fourteenth day of June, one thousand nine hundred and twenty-one, the Golden Bay Company shall not manufacture cement for a period of twelve months unless the other companies give notice of their intention to terminate this agreement under the power hereinafter contained…

"6. While this agreement shall be in force the Golden Bay Company shall take no steps towards reorganizing its capital or improving or reconstructing its works or machinery…

"8. As between the Milburn Company and Wilsons Company the selling percentage to which the said companies shall be entitled during the currency of this agreement shall be 22 per cent for the Milburn Company and 78 per cent for Wilsons Company…"

William Alexander Sim reported to the Government on 17 November 1921— a summary of which included:

"1. The Board of Trade in sanctioning in December, 1920, the increase of £1 16s. per ton ex store Wellington was not guilty of any impropriety or error of judgment.

"2. The increase was quite justified in the then state of the cement-market.

"3. The importation of cement into New Zealand was not in any way brought about by that increase, but was rendered necessary by the shortage of cement in the Dominion.

"4. The Board of Trade did not assist or permit the cement companies or any of them to fleece the public. On the contrary, the Board benefited the public, at the expense of the shareholders in the companies, by keeping the price of cement in New Zealand below its price in the world's markets, and by controlling the distribution of the cement.

"5. The companies did not obtain unreasonably high prices from the public at any time, and, if they had desired to take any unfair advantage of the acute shortage of cement, the action of the Board made it impossible for them to do so."

With regard to the May 1921 agreement between the cement companies, some of the Commissioner's findings included:

"1. The agreement does not constitute an offence under the Commercial Trusts Act, 1910, or under any other Act.

"2. It is not in any way criminal or illegal.

"3. It is in restraint of trade, but the restraint is reasonable having regard to the interests of the contracting parties and to the interests of the public, and is, therefore, not invalid.

"4. It was not made to prevent people from getting cement, or to stifle competition, or to increase the price of cement, and was not intended by the parties to operate to the detriment of the public in any way.

"5. It has not operated detrimentally to the interests of the public in general. The closing of the Golden Bay works has inflicted some hardship in individual cases in the way already specified, but the works probably would have been closed whether the agreement had been made or not…" [175]

Golden Bay Cement Company (Continued)

By July 1922, the cement supply and demand situation had not changed — as indicated by a Government Minister's comment:

"…the Minister of Industries and Commerce (the Hon E P Lee) said the Golden Bay cement works were closed down because there was almost a complete cessation of orders. Cement accumulated in the stores of the company until it was impossible to carry on any longer. The position has not materially altered. The two companies at present manufacturing can more than supply the demand and it cannot be expected that the Golden Bay Company could be induced to start again to work at a loss, much as they may sympathise with the men who may be out of work. There is over £120,000 worth of plant at present lying idle and it is safe to assume that it will not be allowed to continue idle for a single day longer than is necessary…" [176]

However, just over a year later, the vagaries of the New Zealand economy had again come full circle — as reported by the Evening Post in September 1923:

"The Golden Bay cement works, after a period of idleness of nearly two years, is once again in full swing at Tarakohe. The ever-increasing demand for cement in the erection of modern buildings finds the Dominion prepared with three payable deposits, one in the north, one in Otago, and the other at Golden Bay…" [177]

As previously noted, another cement entity, the British Standard Portland Cement Company Limited, was yet to establish a factory at its Whangarei property by 1927. Instead, the company invested some £500,000 to purchase a controlling interest in the Golden Bay Cement Works (for £40,000) and the installation of new machinery. [178]

But financial woes had once again descended on the country, and the world, by 1932:

"The directors of the Golden Bay Cement Company Ltd. report to shareholders as follows:

"The depression in the building trade has had the inevitable effect of diminishing the demand for cement, and this is reflected in the accounts which show a loss of £5,646 1s 10d, after providing for depreciation in the working plant…Owing to lack of demand it was found necessary to close down manufacturing on three occasions during the year." [179]

"…at the annual general meeting of shareholders of the British Standard Portland Cement Company Ltd…The accounts presented to the meeting for the year ended September 30 1932 showed a net profit of £368 16/8, as compared with £357 0/10 for the previous year. It was reported that the coal mine belonging to the company had been closed since December 1931 and that the main source of revenue was now from interest from the Golden Bay Cement Company Ltd, the interest being paid up to date…" [180]

Eventually, by the end of the Second World War, the financial prospects of both companies had improved:

"The British Standard Portland Cement Ltd which holds 66,625 £1 shares and £95,000 worth of debentures in the Golden Bay Cement Company, reported a net profit of £5,073 for the year ended June 30 [1945], against £5,400 in the 1944 year." [181]

"The accounts of the British Standard Portland Cement Company and its subsidiary, the Golden Bay Cement Company [for 1947] are now available. The British Standard Company returned a net profit of £7186 for the year, against £6490 the previous year…The net profit of the Golden Bay Company was £3714 against £9871 in the previous year…The directors report a substantial fall in turnover due to problems of distribution and of coal supply. They plan the introduction of bulk handling to solve distribution difficulties involving very considerable expenditure in the next three years." [182]

In 1950, a controlling interest in the Golden Bay Portland Cement Company was acquired by a British manufacturer — as reported by the Christchurch Press:

"A Reuter cable message from London stating that Associated Portland Cement Manufacturers Ltd [later known as Blue Circle Industries Limited] will own a controlling interest in the Golden Bay Portland Cement Company, as a result of negotiations practically completed, was confirmed by Mr D O Whyte, general manager of the Golden Bay Cement Company.

"Mr Whyte said that as a result of the merger, his company would be proceeding immediately with the installation of facilities for the bulk shipment of cement to eliminate transport difficulties which have limited deliveries from Tarakohe in recent years.

"The plant at Tarakohe would be expanded to produce more cement. Mr Whyte said the agreement with the British company would make available extensive technical experience of the biggest British manufacturers of cement and provide a large amount of capital required for the expansion of the Tarakohe works…" [183]

The results of this acquisition were evident by December 1954:

"At an extraordinary meeting in Wellington yesterday the company [Golden Bay Cement] decided to increase its nominal capital from £600,000 to £1,000,000 by the creation of 400,000 ordinary £1 shares.

"The issue will bring the subscribed capital to £750,000…British Standard Portland Cement Ltd has decided to take up its full quota of 53,025 shares in the new Golden Bay issue, bringing its total Golden Bay shareholding to 265,128 shares. It will then go into voluntary liquidation…" [184]

By April 1957, the British Standard Portland Cement Company was in voluntary liquidation. [185]

"In 1971 in association with Winstone Ltd the company [Golden Bay Cement Company] acquired 50% of Wilsons (NZ) Portland Cement Ltd (Winstone Ltd holding the other 50%). Golden Bay Cement Co Ltd became responsible for the management of Wilsons and allowed the integration of the two operations. [186]

On 26 August 1980, the Examiner of Commercial Practices consented to the Golden Bay Cement Company Limited acquiring Winstone Limited's 50 per cent holding in Wilsons (NZ) Portland Cement Limited. Blue Circle Industries Limited was also permitted to increase its 45.9 per cent holding in the Golden Bay Cement Company to 51 per cent. [187]

Accordingly, "…in October 1980 Wilsons (NZ) Portland Cement Ltd became a subsidiary company [of the Golden Bay Cement Company] and this transaction was completed on the 27th February 1981 with the purchase of the remaining 50% of Wilsons (NZ) Portland Cement Ltd from Winstone Limited…

"In 1982 major shareholder Blue Circle Industries PLC [known as Associated Portland Cement Manufacturers Limited prior to 1979] purchased the 20 percent shareholding held by Winstone Ltd in the Golden Bay Cement Company…

"In 1987 Winstones Ltd and Fletcher Challenge Ltd were granted authorization by the Commerce Commission to buy up to 100% of the Golden Bay shares. In May Blue Circle Industries Ltd sold its shareholding in The Golden Bay Cement Group to the Winstone Group. In October the Winstone Group sold 50% of its shareholding to Fletcher Challenge Ltd…The following year Golden Bay's head office was moved from Wellington to Auckland." [188]

In October 1992, the name of Golden Bay Cement Company Limited was changed to <u>The Golden Bay Cement Company Limited</u> [189] and the company was de-registered in August 2000 following its amalgamation with other Fletcher Challenge companies to become Fletcher Concrete and Infrastructure Limited. [190]

The Milburn Lime and Cement Company

The business that would eventually become known as the Milburn Lime and Cement Company Limited was started by James McDonald as Tokomairiro Lime Kilns at Milburn, Otago.

James McDonald was advertising his lime as early as September 1877:

"Important to Farmers and Builders — Lime Lime Lime — James McDonald Lime-Burner, Waihola Gorge has much pleasure in informing the Clutha farmers and Builders that he has succeeded in making special arrangements with the Government whereby his lime will in future be carried at the rate of tenpence per truck of five tons per mile which, added to 25s per ton at Milburn Station, enables him to deliver it at Balclutha for about 28s per ton…" [191]

In November that year, he expanded his business by leasing more land:

"Application by James McDonald for permission to lease section 20, block 5, Winton District, for the purpose of burning lime was granted at a rental of 1s per acre per year for five years, and for the remaining 9 years at 10s per acre per annum subject to a condition fixing the price of lime for farmers' use at 20s per ton; to commence operations within six months." [192]

He also sold his lime in smaller quantities:

"James McDonald, Tokomairiro Lime Kilns, Milburn, and Offices, Moray Place, Dunedin, Begs respectfully to announce that, in future, all Orders for Lime in small quantities must be accompanied by cash. Price 5s per Bag at the Railway Station." [193]

And, by December 1887, James McDonald had started to utilise his lime resources to manufacture cement and looked to expand his customer base:

"Timaru Harbour Board — Mr James McDonald wrote again asking for more accurate particulars respecting the tests of the cement manufactured by him in Dunedin. Left to the engineer to deal with." [194]

Finally, he had convinced a large customer, the Oamaru Harbour Board, to purchase his cement, delivered in February 1888:

"About 80 tons of cement has been delivered by Mr James McDonald under his contract with the Board, and the cement has been put through the usual tests with satisfactory results. It is finely ground, of good color, sets slowly, is cool in setting, weighs 117 to the striked bushel, and stands a tensile strain varying from 1500 to 1600 to the area of 2½ square inches." [195]

Unfortunately, James McDonald may have expanded his business too quickly. By May 1888, he was experiencing financial difficulties:

"A big failure is reported from Dunedin — that of Mr James McDonald the well-known lime merchant of Milburn, and ex-member for Bruce. His statement shows unsecured creditors £3837 secured, £7469. It is represented that the secured creditors hold property worth £33,200, but the debtor has no doubt taken an over sanguine view of his position. He values the Milburn property at £20,000 and that at Walton Park at £10,000." [196]

The business assets were advertised soon after:

"In Bankruptcy Estate Of James Mcdonald, Lime Merchant, Dunedin. Tenders will be received up to noon of the 29th June, at the office of the undersigned…separately for Lime Kilns situated on the Peninsula, with 19 Acres of Freehold Land, Lime Kilns near Winton, with 68 Acres of Land (leasehold), at a rental of £17 per annum; about 30 acres under grass….Deputy-Assignee, Invercargill." [197]

By July 1888, the business assets had been sold to what was then an unidentified syndicate:

"The properties in the estate of James McDonald, lime burner, Dunedin, were sold on Friday last. The Milburn lime works, together with freehold of 19 acres, and leaseholds of 155 acres, and the benefit of an agreement for occupation of about 120 acres more; the cement works at Walton Park, with plant and leaseholds of nearly 6 acres; the lime kilns on the Otago Peninsula, with 19 acres of freehold land and license to quarry for limestone on 95 acres; and the lime kilns near Winton, with 68 acres of land held under lease at a rent of £17 a year, were put up subject to mortgages, amounting in all to about £8100, and were knocked down to Mr J White for the sum of £3600, who bought as agent for a syndicate." [198]

At the same time, the following advertisement was published by the Otago Daily Times:

"Milburn Lime And Cement Company Limited — Having purchased the Properties of Mr James McDonald at Milburn, Walton Park, Peninsula, and Winton will carry on the works as usual and execute all orders." [199]

Tariff Commission 1895

On 26 January 1895, the Government appointed a Tariff Commission to inquire into the Customs and Excise Duties and Exemptions then operating in the Colony. The Commission reported on 31 May 1895, parts of which included a transcript of an interview of Frank Oakden, then Manager of the Milburn Lime and Cement Company.

Examined by the Chairman of the Commission:

"Mr F Oakden, Manager of the Milburn Lime and Cement Company carrying on business at Pelichet Bay, Dunedin — did not consider the present tariff of 2s per cask or 12s per ton as sufficient to protect or foster the cement industry in New Zealand. To protect the industry, the tariff should be 4s per cask.

"Present price of imported Portland cement is fixed by the quantity which arrives in the colony, by the state of the market…the ruling rates now are 12s to 13s per cask…our price is the same or slightly under…we have to cut a little below the imported price to make sales and get trade…even though our product is equal to the imported…

"…we have to sell for less because the trade generally is done through importing houses and contractors are supplied by these houses with a thousand and one things; and in getting orders these importing houses like to include the cement and we are placed somewhat at a disadvantage in that way…

"…selling for less is not because of the difference in quality but because of the trade customs that exist…when we went into cement-making six years ago, in 1889, the price of cement was then £5 1s a ton. It has now dropped to £3 14s 2d. Each consecutive half-year shows a depreciation in the price and shows an increase in output…

"We produce 50 to 60 tons per week…The importation in 1893 was about 10,000 tons…Supposing that about 15,000 tons were consumed altogether…local factories would provide about one-third and the other two-thirds imported…

"While the selling price has depreciated, wages have remained the same…we pay twice the amount in wages as the English cement makers and three times what they pay in Germany…In cement making, nearly 80 per cent of costs goes in labour…

"There is keen competition at home…The depreciation in price has been brought about through the shipping companies using cement for ballast so they don't pay freight as they used to… We are losing money. It is a very simple problem. We must either reduce the wages in the colony to a little more than they pay at Home, or have a protective duty; or we must close the works.

"You said 'Portland cement' is merely a term? — Yes, it is simply a name given to the admixture of chalk or carbonate of lime and clay. It has been stated, and generally supposed, that Portland cement can only be made at Home, but that is a mistake. Ours is equal to the cement imported from Home. We have had a certain amount of prejudice to overcome, and I think we have succeeded in doing it by showing that our returns have increased year by year, although the prices have fallen.

"What is the difference, if any, between the article called hydraulic lime and cement? — A vast difference. Hydraulic lime is very inferior to Portland cement — in strength, in the first instance, and it is not so reliable. It may be identical so far as chemical analysis is concerned but, in the case of Portland cement, it must be burnt to a clinker, and then ground to a powder.

"Did your company here supply the Napier Harbour Board with cement for the breakwater? — No. Did you tender? — No because the specification provided for casks. We wrote asking if they would accept bags, and they would not. That is one objection to our cement. It does not keep so well in bags as in casks. The local casks are too costly for us without a larger output…

"That matter of the want of casks is a serious drawback to you, I presume? — It is a serious drawback to us for export and West Coast trade. We have successfully tendered for the Wellington, Christchurch, and Dunedin Corporation works, and for the Oamaru Breakwater, and would have tendered for the Napier Breakwater, but they would not accept our cement in sacks.

"The Napier Harbour Board is a case in point. They require an immense amount of cement and it is rather hard on them to pay the duty. It is a public work, requiring a large quantity of cement. It is not like supplying cement for the building of a house — If the duty raises the price of imported cement we shall sell more of ours. The effect of raising the cost of imported cement will be to give us a larger trade and enable us to manufacture cement cheaper…" [200]

A few days later, Frank Oakden and a Milburn Lime and Cement Company Director, John White, again appeared before the Commission with news to substantiate their call for a higher duty on imported cement:

"Frank Oakden — the advertisement I now put in appeared in the Otago Daily Times of 2nd March, 1895: 'To builders and contractors and other consumers. Knight Bevan's and Sturge's Portland cement, 11s. per cask. We have a shipment in the Rangitiki, just arrived, of 4,500 casks Knight Bevan's cement — Arthur Briscoe and Co, ironmongers and iron-merchants, Princes,

Jetty, and Bond Streets, Dunedin.' — In this advertisement the price is still further reduced to £3 6s per ton…

"I think it would be possible for a powerful importing firm, in conjunction with large works at Home, to swamp this market with cement, and to so reduce the price that it could not be made profitably in New Zealand. The firm of Knight Bevan is one of the largest firms in the world and for them to send out here a few hundred casks of their surplus stock is a very small matter. They would not feel the loss of it while the final result, if they obtained the trade for themselves after crushing the local industry, would compensate amply for any temporary loss they might sustain…" [201]

However, not all the Commissioners agreed with an increase in the cement duty, going so far as to suggest that Harbour Boards and local bodies were entitled to import their needs free of such duty:

"They have also been asked to recommend an increased duty on cement; but they think that to raise the duty would tend to create a monopoly which would be prejudicial to the interests of consumers. They are of opinion that this view of the case will be justified by a perusal of the evidence.

"On the other hand, however, your Commissioners are of opinion that Harbour Boards and County Councils should be placed in the most favourable position to carry out the important public works devolving upon them by allowing cement imported for their purposes to be admitted free of duty." [202]

There was one dissenting opinion — by Commissioner, Thomas Mackenzie:

"Generally, I object to the recommendations of the Commissioners on the questions of tobacco license, inland charges, and the limitation of the number of local bodies who are recommended the privilege of cement duty-free." [203]

The Milburn Lime and Cement Company (Continued)

Despite its early trading difficulties, the Milburn Lime and Cement Company was ready for the new century and eager to demonstrate its success to the world — as reported by the Otago Witness in October 1901:

"The Milburn Lime and Cement Company arranged on Thursday for an inspection of their new plant by the architects, builders, and contractors of the city and a numbers of other influential business men…

"It had sprung from very small beginnings, its first year's output being only 10,000 bags. It was now 100,000 bags per annum. When the company commenced operations it had great difficulty in effecting the sale of its then small output, local architects and builders being slow to give the cement a trial. But this difficulty had long ago been surmounted, and their manufacture was now specified in nearly all Government and local contracts, and also in all public works and railway contracts…

"…it may be added that all the machinery at the cement works in Dunedin, both for grinding raw materials and finished product, is of the latest and most modern kind and the company have now a plant capable, if required, of producing 800 tons per month." [204]

The company's fortunes were further enhanced by the discovery of phosphate on its property —, reported in February 1903:

"The phosphate field is booming and the precious mineral is being unearthed in tons many and excellent. The Milburn Lime and Cement Co's deposits are opening out splendidly, thousands of tons being now laid bare. Over 100 tons per week are at present being sent away, the quality of the rock showing 70 per cent to 80 per cent grade." [205]

By June 1903, the Milburn Lime and Cement Company was also manufacturing concrete pipes and promoting their use to the local Councils for use in their drainage schemes:

"The Milburn Lime Coy wrote [to the Bruce Council] stating that some of its new manufacture of concrete pipes were on view at the Tokomairiro Show… [206]

In 1904, the company's concrete pipe manufacture had become a whole new industry:

"The Milburn Lime and Cement Company has secured the sole patent rights of the Keilberg machine — a machine that is capable of making high-class drain pipes of sand and cement without reinforcement. Tests of these pipes show their superiority over best vitrified pipes, both in strength and porosity…It is anticipated by the Milburn Company that the machine referred to will be the pioneer to a new industry — a cement-ware factory." [207]

However, the company's pipe-making branch was eventually sold to P McSkimming and Son of Dunedin in 1911. [208]

In the meantime, the cement produced by the Milburn Lime and Cement Company continued to be used for the construction of new civic infrastructure, including Dunedin's tramway system in 1903:

"The first outward indication the public had of the work of construction of the tramways was the start of operations on the permanent way…in some parts of Dunedin the ground is very bad…This has involved the use of a very large quantity of cement, the bulk of which has been turned out by the Milburn Lime and Cement Company and has proved eminently suitable for the work…" [209]

And Harbour works in 1905:

"The Milburn Lime and Cement Company has accepted the contract to supply half the cement required for the new dock at Port Chalmers…" [210]

Burnside Hydraulic Lime and Cement Company

In July 1903, the Timaru Herald described the discovery of marl at Burnside, Otago:

"Travellers by the south railway will have observed…about midway between Cattle Yards station and Burnside, a succession of hummocky hills and it is one of these which has now been discovered to be an entire mass of solid marl, very valuable for cement-making purposes consisting of upwards of 50 acres in area and to a proved depth of nearly 80ft…

"…in the course of examination it fell under the hands of Mr J Kelly who at once recognised that it contained a good proportion of the ingredients of Portland cement. For four years, he has been works manager for the Milburn Lime and Cement Company…With respect to the development of the find, we are informed that it is intended to proceed at once with the erection of works on a large scale, so that very shortly the Burnside cement will take its place among colonial products." [211]

The discovery eventually resulted in a company formed to exploit the resource — as reported by the Southland Times and the Evening Star in November 1905:

"About 12 or 18 months ago there was quite a mild form of excitement in business circles in Dunedin at the discovery of a deposit of marl at Burnside…a company was formed to thoroughly test its value for cement-making purposes and also to ascertain the extent of the deposit. It is now gratifying to be able to record that, after most exhausting tests, the marl has been proved to be most suitable for cement-making and the deposit has also been proved to be practically inexhaustible." [212]

"Abridged Prospectus of the Burnside Hydraulic Lime And Cement Company Limited…Capital £21,000. Divided into 4,200 Shares of £5 each…Directors: Mr Chas A Shiel of C & W Shiel, Brick Manufacturers, Dunedin; Mr George Clark, Builder, Dunedin; Mr John Watson, Messrs Crawford and Watson, Dunedin; Mr James Gray, Green Island; Mr James Jenkins, Green Island." [213]

However, it wasn't until 1907 that the company acquired the plant needed for cement manufacture:

"The Burnside Hydraulic Lime and Cement Company, who secured the freehold of the property in which [the Burnside marl] exists some years ago, are now taking steps to erect a complete plant on it. The plant was that used by the Wellington and Marlborough Cement, Lime, and Coal Company, a concern which, from various causes, got into difficulties and ceased work some time ago after running actively for a little over a year…Having examined the machinery, plant, etc, an offer was made for it, the result being that an agreement to purchase for £5,400 was entered into and a deposit paid…" [214]

The Burnside plant was finally opened on 28 January 1909:

"The works of the Burnside Hydraulic Lime and Cement Company Ltd…were officially opened yesterday afternoon in the presence of a large and representative assembly of the commercial community of Dunedin and its environs…" [215]

The first cement was ready for distribution in March 1909:

"The Burnside Hydraulic Lime And Cement Company Ltd have pleasure in notifying Builders and the Public generally that they are now in a position to Supply Cement Of The Highest Quality At The Lowest Prices. We guarantee our Cement Free from Adulteration…" [216]

However, in what would prove to be a contentious decision, in July 2010, shareholders were surprised to learn:

"Shareholders in the Burnside Hydraulic Lime and Cement Company met…last evening to discuss a circular from the directors calling for a meeting to pass a resolution to wind up the company. The directors' circular read: 'Your directors beg to report that they have arranged for the merger of this company in the Milburn Lime and Cement Company Ltd on an advantageous basis…'" [217]

Shareholders were quick to accuse the Directors of mismanagement of the company's affairs — as the Evening Star reported:

"The present Board of Directors, when they took office, had a credit balance of something like £500, £10,000 worth of uncalled capital, a complete plant, and since then there had been issued £10,000 worth of debentures. This meant that in the course of two years they had spent close on £21,000 and the present finances of the company were such that the sale to the Milburn Company was entered into…" [218]

Nevertheless, the sell-out to the Milburn Lime and Cement Company was eventually agreed to in August 1910:

"After a long debate last night, which had its bitter moments, the shareholders of the Burnside Hydraulic Lime and Cement Company accepted the merger arranged with the Milburn Lime and Cement Company, and also resolved to go into voluntary liquidation…" [219]

<u>The Milburn Lime and Cement Company</u> (Continued)

The Milburn Lime and Cement Company continued to manufacture cement at its Pelichet Bay works until March 1929 when it opened new, far-more-modern works at the Burnside site:

"…the enormous new works of the Milburn Lime and Cement Company at Burnside which will be officially opened by the Minister of Industries and Commerce (Mr J G Cobbe) to-day…A great and notable victory has been registered over enormous and unwieldy tools and costly methods for although there is no lack of big-bellied receptacles, heavy irresistible mills, and bulky machinery in the great concrete pile of buildings, everything depends on the small cogs of the powerful gearing and the hand switches and buttons that supply or withdraw the one motive power in use — electricity.

"Costly massed labour and slow functioning machines have had their day, at least as far as the Milburn Lime and Cement Company is concerned…One thousand tons of cement can be turned out weekly and 2100 horse-power and 40 tons of coal daily are required to keep the tremendous plant in motion…" [220]

Unlike its predecessor at the Burnside site, the financial position of the Milburn Lime and Cement Company remained a profitable enterprise — as shown by its 1947 accounts:

"A net profit of £12,141 against £15,286 last year, is reported in the annual accounts of the Milburn Lime and Cement Company Ltd. Provision for taxation was £24,119 (£25,368 in 1946).

Gross revenue including investment income but less expenses and depreciation, is stated at £36,860, which compares with the previous year's £41,254..." [221]

And extensive expansion was planned by September 1950:

"In proposing to lift paid-up capital from £200,000 to £500,000 the Milburn Lime and Cement Company will be embarking on the largest capital flotation ever undertaken in the city by a purely local industry publicly owned and listed on the Stock Exchange.

"Estimated to cost some £615,000, the duplication of the Burnside works is likewise one of the largest single asset creations ever undertaken locally...

"The long-awaited Milburn Lime and Cement Company issue beggared all expectations when it came at the beginning of the week. The importation of cement, particularly in the post-war years, has not been a creditable feature of our economy, but in fairness to the major Dominion manufacturers, Wilsons Portland Cement and the Milburn Company, it can be said that little time has been lost in taking up the slack between local production and consumption by vigorous and realistic expansion proposals..." [222]

Expansion and growth continued into the 1960s — as reported by the Christchurch Press in October 1963:

"After protracted negotiations, the directors of the Milburn Lime and Cement Company Ltd of Dunedin have arrived at a basis for a merger with the New Zealand Cement Company Ltd and have recommended the merger proposals to their shareholders. Arrangements for the merger provide that Milburn will become the holding company for the group. To reflect this, its name will be changed to New Zealand Cement Holdings Ltd. The present New Zealand Cement Company will become a fully-owned subsidiary of the holding company and its name will be changed to the Guardian Cement Company Ltd." [223]

New Zealand Cement Company & Guardian Cement Company

The New Zealand Cement Company Limited was incorporated at Wellington in 1955 (W1955/554) with the object of manufacturing cement at Cape Foulwind, some 11 km from Westport on the west coast of the South Island. [224]

On 12 September 1956, the company was given permission to erect power lines to its plant [223] which began operations in 1958 "...with one kiln and the next 12 years saw the introduction of two further kilns." [225]

Following its merger with the Milburn Lime and Cement Company, the name of the New Zealand Cement Company Limited was changed to the Guardian Cement Company Limited on 27 February 1964. [226]

"By 1970, the company had built two cement silos at Westport Harbour, each silo with a capacity of 2250 tonnes and was shipping cement from the port of Westport on a weekly basis using their bulk cement ships Milburn Carrier II and Westport. On an annual basis up to 430,000 tons of cement was shipped from the Port of Westport to Onehunga, Wellington, Lyttelton, New Plymouth, Nelson, Dunedin and Picton." [227]

The Guardian Cement Company plant was described by the Christchurch Press in June 1979:

"The Guardian Cement factory at Cape Foulwind provides employment for about 150 men and is the most modern plant of its type in New Zealand. Apart from the use of rail transport for distributing its product throughout the South Island, the company carries bulk cement to North Island ports in two company ships." [228]

New Zealand Cement Holdings/Holcim

In the meantime, the holding company of New Zealand Cement Holdings Limited recorded a record profit for the first year (1963-1964) since the merger:

"A net profit of £202,139 was earned by the New Zealand Cement Holdings Ltd group of companies in the year to July 31. This is shown in the first annual report of the company since the merger between Milburn Lime and Cement and the New Zealand Cement Company Ltd late last year. The result is almost a 40 per cent improvement on Milburn's figures for last year." [229]

This profit announcement followed a decision to increase its cement production earlier in the year:

"New Zealand Cement Holdings Ltd has decided to double the capacity of its plant at Westport. This decision, announced in Dunedin today, has been made after a careful study by the company of the prospects for the sale of cement within New Zealand…" [230]

Obviously, the ups and downs of New Zealand's construction industry influenced the fortunes of cement makers but sales were expected to improve by October 1968:

"New Zealand Cement Holdings Limited expects to increase sales this year after a 30,000 ton decline during the last two years…Referring to the group's drop in sales during the last two years…[the Chairman] said the Canterbury area had been hit hardest by the fall-off in building activity, and this was where the group had derived most of its sales." [231]

Declining demand for cement products resulted in some rationalisation of the industry in both the North and South Islands — as reported by the Christchurch Press in December 1969:

"The other important recent merger in the industry, which must be feeling the pinch of declining demand for its products, was the take-over of Southland Cement Company Ltd by New Zealand Cement Holdings Ltd, formerly Milburn Lime and Cement…" [232]

In 1971, the New Zealand industry soon attracted the attention of overseas interests:

"Australian and Kandos Cement Holdings Ltd has purchased 42 per cent of the total issued capital of New Zealand Cement Holdings Ltd in conjunction with Holderbank Financiere Glarus A.G. of Switzerland. New Zealand Cement has cement plants at Westport and Dunedin…" [233]

At the same time, in December 1971, New Zealand Cement Holdings expanded its local interests:

"New Zealand Cement Holdings Ltd has acquired a 26 per cent interest in McCallum Bros Ltd which deals in red aggregates, sand, barging, and in builders' and merchants' supplies in the Auckland province…" [234]

By June 1975, the company had become a major cement supplier:

"One of New Zealand's major cement suppliers today applied to the Price Tribunal for an increase of $15.50 a tonne in the price of cement. New Zealand Cement Holdings Ltd which produces 37 per cent of the nation's cement, and is the leading South Island supplier, wants, the rise to take effect in all areas except Auckland, Marlborough, and Nelson. If the increase is granted, the selling price of cement in the South Island would be $48.74. The Auckland price is $44.67…" [235]

Expansion continued through to the 1980s but, as reported by the Christchurch Press in March 1984, the demand for cement had again subsided:

"New Zealand's two strongly competing cement makers, weakened by fighting for the static market, announced yesterday that they are holding talks on restructuring the industry.

"Both New Zealand Cement Holdings Ltd and the Golden Bay Cement Company Ltd have been spending heavily on facilities and both have had poorer results in the last year or so. New Zealand Cement Holdings has recently undertaken a $10 million expansion, with development of the plant at Cape Foulwind and the setting up of several new depots throughout the country.

"Signs of strain have emerged with delays in announcing the date when the firm's planned $150 million plant at Oamaru will begin production. All planning approval by local bodies has been given to the company.

"Golden Bay has also pushed ahead with developments, such as new cement silos at Lyttelton and the spending of $47 million changing the process used at its Portland plant. With the country's low rate of economic growth, and a drop in public works of the type which use huge amounts of concrete, it has been clear for some time that the country's cement makers have been headed for trouble…" [236]

By November 1987, 72 per cent of New Zealand Cement Holdings was owned by an overseas cement maker:

"A Swiss cement maker, Holderbank Financiere Glaris, holds more than 62 per cent of the shares in New Zealand Cement and another Swiss company, Societe Suisse de Cement holds 9.75%. Trading results for the first three months of the current year were ahead of budget…They were ahead of sales for the corresponding quarter of last year. But sales for the five months ending December 31 would be lower than forecast because of industrial stoppages outside the cement industry during the wages round…

"Net profit after tax and before extraordinary items of $8,611,000 showed in percentage terms a satisfactory increase on the previous year's figure of $4,642,000 despite a taxation charge of $9,056,000 in 1987, compared with $2,264,000 in 1986…" [237]

In June 1988, New Zealand Cement Holdings Limited again became known as Milburn New Zealand Limited [238] and its Burnside Cement Works at Pelichet Bay were closed. [239]

In that year, a restructuring of the business also occurred:

"Christchurch-based Milburn New Zealand (formerly New Zealand Cement Holdings) has split its business activities into three main operating divisions as part of an organisational and management restructure. Mr Rodney Green has been appointed general manager of a cement division which will control the company's cement production, distribution and marketing…

"Former corporate marketing manager, Mr Rex Williams, has been appointed general manager of a new aggregate and concrete division. In recent years the company has purchased a number of quarries in the Wellington and Hawke's Bay area which supply aggregate for the ready-mix concrete and roading industries.

"The third operating division incorporates Milburn New Zealand's two lime manufacturing subsidiaries, wholly-owned Oamaru-based Taylor's Lime and 52 per cent owned Otorohanga-based McDonald's Lime…" [240]

"Christchurch-based Milburn New Zealand has acquired one of the North Island's largest concrete companies, Ready Mix Concrete. Purchase of the privately owned company, for an undisclosed sum, has been approved by the Commerce Commission. Hamilton-headquartered Ready Mix Concrete operates 11 plants and 65 trucks and delivers ready-mixed concrete throughout the northern half of the North Island…

"…the move was in line with the parent company Holderbank Financiere Glaris Ltd's strategy of becoming involved in complementary product areas. The Switzerland-based company, which is the world's largest cement manufacturer, has a majority shareholding in Milburn New Zealand." [241]

The name and brand of Milburn New Zealand Limited continued until after Holcim (New Zealand) Limited acquired a 100 per cent shareholding of New Zealand Cement Holdings Limited in 1999.

In September 2002, the Milburn label, "complete with yellow singleted man", was completely replaced on all products by that of its overseas parent, Holcim — a distinctive black H over a red C.

"Milburn, which employs 751 people and has a turnover of more than $200 million, will continue to source and process its New Zealand products locally under the new brand." [242]

However, that undertaking was not to last — as reported by The New Zealand Herald on 29 June 2016:

"The Cape Foulwind cement works closes at midday tomorrow, ending 58 years of cement production in Westport. Holcim signalled almost three years ago that it planned to close the works and import cement…The 80 or so remaining workers would leave at midday…Holcim employed about 120 in Westport before it started winding down." [243]

Additional information is provided by a Buller District Council history of Westport Harbour:

"In 2013 Holcim announced the closure of its Westport plant in favour of silo facilities in Timaru and Auckland taking imported cement from Japan. The MV Westport took the final load of Cape Foulwind cement from the port on the 29th of June 2016." [244]

Asphalt

A brief overview of the origin and uses of asphalt (then known as asphalte) was published by the Dunstan Times in February 1926 — parts of which included:

"Asphalte is, of course, a material known to antiquity, but it has been revived, as it were, and applied in a great diversity of ways, so that it may rightly be classed as a modern material. It requires no great expert knowledge to appreciate the enormously increasing use of this material in road construction, roofing work, waterproofing, insulating, and many other directions…

"Archaeologists have discovered ample proof that asphalte was known to the nations of antiquity. Bitumen, the basis of what is now termed asphalte, is found in various forms, and it was probably from seepages in various parts of the Near East that the bitumen was produced for the coating of ancient causeways which still exist in Baghdad, and which must have been laid centuries ago…

"Asphalte, as employed in modern construction, may be a natural rock or a composition consisting of bitumen mixed with suitable aggregates, such as clinker, limestone, or granite. The bitumen is found principally in three forms. There is the bitumen from the famous deposit in the island of Trinidad, known as Trinidad Lake bitumen; limestone rock naturally impregnated with bitumen and known as rock asphalte; and petroleum bitumen, which, as its name implies, is extracted from an asphaltic-base petroleum by a system of refining…

"In the group of materials available for modern road construction there is, in addition to the natural bitumens, bitumen which is the result of refining petroleum having an asphaltic base. High vacuum and steam stills are included in the plant by which the process is carried out and it is claimed that the final product of petroleum in fractional distillation is a high-grade bitumen practically 100 per cent pure, and of a uniform standardised quality.

"Although bitumen in this instance is the final product of petroleum distillation, it is somewhat of a misnomer to refer to it as a 'residual' for it is carefully refined to exact specifications both for road work and industrial purposes, an example being the now well-known mexphalte (manufactured by Shell Mex Ltd)…

"The miles and miles of asphalt roads along which the motorist can travel with ease testify to the remarkable qualities of the material as used for this purpose. Anyone who recalls the huge clouds of dust that heralded the advent of the motor vehicle must be struck by the contrast which these roads present, a result due to asphalte in the hands of the modern engineer…" [245]

"Contrasting asphalt and concrete road construction, [visiting American road-builder] Mr Warren mentioned that a big point in favour of the first-mentioned was the fact that there was no need to tear up an existing road, as a permanent coating of asphalt could be put down on any surface of an old road. He mentioned that since the war there had been a tremendous increase in the mileage of permanent roads laid down in the States, and hundreds of millions of dollars were being spent. The people were fully seized of the importance of good roads to the development of the country…" [246]

Neuchatel Asphalt Company

In October 1899, the Neuchatel Asphalt Company Limited of London wrote to the Auckland City Council "…with reference to the Council's approval of the proposal to lay a trial piece of asphalt slabs, and stated that the Board of the Company have given orders for a consignment of 20 tons of the slabs to the Council's address, and had instructed their representative at Capetown…to go to Auckland and lay the pavement. The Mayor explained that the Council had agreed to the asphalt being tried for 12 months, and if it were a success to pay the cost of laying down, namely, £35…" [247]

By 1901 the patience of the ratepayers had worn thin over the Council's inaction concerning upgrading the city roads. Since the 1880s, people had complained of the clouds of choking dust created by the two inch blue metal used in road repair. Only the lower part of Queen Street and some surrounding streets had been laid with asphalt coated blocks, but the arrival of horse trams forced the Council to upgrade inner city roads. Two pressure groups, The Auckland Cycle Roads League and the Auckland Good Roads League, continuously petitioned for smoother road surfaces. [248]

"Finally, the Council contracted the Neuchatel Asphalt Company to lay Auckland's first asphalt road surface in Queen Street at a cost of £27,492. When the task was completed a year later, the company claimed the new surface was 'non-absorbent, near-noiseless and easily-cleanable'." [249]

The composition and method of laying Neuchatel asphalt was described by the Christchurch Press in September 1903:

"Neuchatel asphalt was laid in Dunedin streets for the first time last week. The stuff was brought from the Val de Travers mine in Switzerland. It looks like chocolate-coloured garden soil; it is heated in open furnaces, thrown on with shovels, smoothed with the back of a rake, and then stamped and rolled until the necessary surface is obtained. This takes but a little while; in fact the roadway was practically ready for foot traffic almost at once." [250]

As more roads laid out, a number of road construction alternatives were tried:

"In 1902 Auckland possessed only one paved street; there are now [in 1922] thirty-three streets laid in either asphalt, wood blocks, or concrete, as well as a large number of macadamised roads. The failure of a supply of good road metal retarded Auckland's progress in road making, but the substitution of concrete has had successful results, and the Council has given authority for a large number of streets to be laid in this material, and the work is now being proceeded with." [251]

Nevertheless, whatever roading base was put down it was soon found that some form of coating was needed — as reported by The New Zealand Herald in December 1916:

"The various street works that are now being carried out by the City Council were inspected yesterday by the Mayor and the city engineer. The Mayor stated last evening that the eastern outlet scheme is being pushed on, and that after the holidays the work will be further expedited. All the other street work authorised last month is now in hand. The wood-blocking in Customs Street and Fort Street and the concrete roadway in Little Queen Street are being re-coated with union asphalt." [252]

Union Asphalt

When explaining the benefits of Union asphalt to various city and town Councils various spokespersons for Ellis and Co Ltd, Auckland, "…stated that the asphalt was not a tar production but was asphaltic bitumen, the product of the Union Oil Company of California." [253]

"The preparation, it was explained, is obtained by distillation from the crude Californian oil. After all the valuable oils have been extracted the residual is refined to so high a degree that 99.7 per cent of pure bitumen is obtained, the finished product being known as Union asphalt. The liquid which, in appearance, is so like tar, is in properties entirely different. The engineer was most emphatic on this point of discrimination, which he professionally considered a fatal mistake of all laymen and some engineers.

"The asphalt is heated to a temperature of 350 degrees F. and by means of a special machine is sprayed under pressure into the surface of the road which it firmly binds, its cementing qualities being almost as strong as cement. This class of roadway is cheap in construction, costing approximately one-third of concrete, while traffic can safely be allowed over the road ten minutes after finishing the work." [254]

As the Auckland Star reported in January 1917, the advantages of using union asphalt were many:

"The cost of coating the concrete with union asphalt had only been £40. The asphalt had not been applied to prevent crumbling, but to give horses a better footing…If a suitable covering could be applied to concrete it would give one of the best roads they could possibly get at half the cost. An experiment had been tried in Little Queen Street with union asphalt, which had been a success. The covering had two advantages — the street traffic was practically noiseless, and the strain on the eyes was greatly reduced." [255]

When reporting to the Taihape Borough Council on the proposed improvement of the Borough's Main Street in December 1920, consulting engineer, A G Walker, listed the suppliers of bitumen and asphalt then available:

"(1) Mexphalte Bitumen can be imported through Messrs Kidd Garrett Ltd, Little Queen St, Auckland. The manufacture and sale of this article is controlled by the Anglo-Mexican Products Co Ltd, London.

"There are two American Bitumens which are also in general use. (2) Union Asphalt from Messrs Ellis and Co, High Street, Auckland (3) Sogony (sic) Asphalt from Messrs John Chambers and Son Ltd, Auckland and Wellington.

"All the above are practically of the same quality and it is only necessary when obtaining quotes to mention the penetration required." [256]

At a similar meeting of the Waitoa riding ratepayers in December 1922, Mr T E Skitrop of the Union Asphalt Co recounted his experiences of road improvement and the methods adopted in laying down bituminous-coated roads and streets in various parts of the North Island since 1913:

"The best system for county work was to scarify the old road, add extra metal to ensure a good foundation and camber, and roll it thoroughly, then spray with Union asphalt under pressure, roll lightly again and allow traffic on it, next put a thin coating of asphalt on, add some metal dust, and spray again. This method, said Mr Skitrop, ensured a splendid lasting road…

"To the chairman, Mr Skitrop gave an assurance that his firm would supply given quantities of Union asphalt at a fixed price spread over a period. Payment would be made as shipments arrive, and any reduction in the dollar exchange rate would be beneficial to the local body. Shipping charges would not increase. The price was £9 10s per ton f.o.b. Auckland, and the asphalt was delivered in barrels…

"Mr Skitrop went on to give a good deal more information on roading problems. He said as long as there was a good firm foundation the road would carry any motor lorry traffic. There should be a depth of practically 9 inches of metal, the base of coarse spawls [stone fragments], and the top of finer metal. The asphalt would penetrate to a depth of two inches. Most people confuse asphalt with ordinary tar. The latter is not worth twopence per chain by comparison. What are really worthwhile are bituminous roads. They are more resilient than tarred roads and not so slippery as tar or concrete roads…" [257]

The agents for Union Asphalt, Ellis and Company, advertised their product throughout the country — an example of which was published by The New Zealand Herald in November 1923:

"Union Asphalt Highways Last Longer, Cost Less, Run Smoother! That's what Local Authorities are proving, and always will prove. The St. Heliers track is typical of Union Asphalt quality, not exceptional. Every road that is Union Asphalted will be as good. Down in Taranaki they thought no end of their roads— and they are good, without doubt. But Taranaki folk have found Union Asphalting better — why they're substituting Union Asphalt for the tarred highways. The prime cost is moderate, the cost of upkeep infinitesimal. While, as compared with concrete…Union Asphalt is only one-third the cost." [258]

Similar advertisements published by The New Zealand Herald and Auckland Star in 1921 and 1925, respectively, indicate the volume of Union asphalt then imported by Ellis and Co:

"Tenders…are invited up till noon, Thursday December 22 1921 for the delivery from time to time of Bitumen, in 50 ton lots, from ships' slings, Auckland Wharves, to trucks Auckland Railway Station. First consignment expected early in January. (Ellis and Co…)" [259]

"The Public Works Department has passed the following tenders…main highways, 260 tons of asphaltic road oil, £2364 15/ (Ellis and Co…)" [260]

Ellis and Company

As early as September 1859, the Auckland firm of Thomas Horace Ellis, trading as Ellis and Co, was importing such goods as tobacco, cigars, rum, and molasses. [261]

"In 1893, a group of businessmen took over the existing business of Ellis & Co…" [262] which was incorporated as a company on 28 May 1903. [263]

"Products in the early years were varied until 1920 when the company's foundation was laid in the supply of products in the electrical and engineering fields — a strategy which has contributed to the company's continued success with service and supply concentrated on Electrical & Engineering Manufacturers, Industries, Government Departments & Public Bodies. [264]

Described as "agents and importers" by The New Zealand Herald in 1910, [265] the company imported and advertised 'keystone water meters' from that time, and the aforementioned 'Union asphalt' from 1915.

In April 1917, Ellis and Co. wrote to a number of city and town councils proposing that the firm undertake "…all classes of road and street construction, particularly in bituminous works with Union asphalt…" [266]

However, the proposal was not a success, as epitomised by the response from the Waitotara County Council:

"The chairman moved that the Council procure plant of its own to do its own road-tarring work. He thought it would be money in pocket for the Council to have a sprayer of its own, and the material could be procured without difficulty. If the Council had its own sprayer, whatever work was necessary could be done at the most suitable time." [267]

Nevertheless, Ellis and Co soon diversified to other products that ensured its prosperity. In what was one of its first forays into the 'electrical and engineering fields', the company offered dry cell batteries to its customers from 1917 — as reported by the New Zealand Gazette in November of that year:

"Public Service Store Tenders Board — Accepted 30,000 Dry Cells for Telephones — Ellis and Co, Auckland £1859 7s 6d" [268]

And, as advertised from time to time in The New Zealand Herald from May 1917 to at least April 1935:

"Dry Cell…Columbia Batteries are all-round utility batteries which can be used for either heavy or light work. Columbia Batteries have higher voltage and amperage than wet cells… Designed to meet local conditions. They are durable and dependable…Catalogues & Terms from your dealer or from us: Ellis & Co, Auckland. National Carbon Co. Cleveland, Ohio, U.S.A…" [269]

While the products with which it now deals are vastly different from those of the early twentieth century, Ellis and Co remains an active trading company to this day. [270]

Mexphalte Bitumen

When reporting on the promotion of Mexphalte bitumen at the Manawatu Winter Show in June 1925, the Manawatu Standard explained:

"The product of The British Imperial Oil Co, Mexphalte, has been used in road construction in England, on the Continent, America — in fact in all parts of the world. This material does not come to New Zealand untried. It has been tested under all conditions and proves to make a permanent road. As far as New Zealand is concerned, Mexphalte has been used by many borough and city councils...The British Imperial Oil Co are also producers of Shell motor spirit and all Shell products." [271]

Mexphalte had one advantage over the previously-described Union product — it was of British origin — as reported by the Wanganui Chronicle in July 1931:

"Letter from Shell Co quoting for 24 tons 80-100 penetration mexphalte, f.o.r. [freight on road — no transport costs to client] Wellington, and letter from Atlantic Union Oil Co, quoting tor 24 tons Union bitumen 90-100 penetration, f.o.r. Marton. Referred to the Fire Board Committee with power to act, with a recommendation that the British firms be given preference." [272]

Kidd, Garret and Company

By 1920 Mexphalte Bitumen was imported by Messrs Kidd, Garrett Ltd, of Little Queen Street, Auckland — a business set up by Douglas Swanston Kidd and W Garrett.

In June 1920, Kidd, Garrett initiated one of many business acquisitions over the years that would see its operations grow to a nationwide organisation:

"Messrs A R Hislop Ltd of 37 Fort Street and Kidd Garrett Ltd of 24 Little Queen Street...have amalgamated...Their representation in this city includes many of the leading British manufacturers of Engineers' Requisites...The business of the new company will be conducted by Kid Garrett Limited..." [273]

There was certainly plenty of demand for its imports through the 1920s, such as November 1920:

"The Public Works Tenders Board have accepted tenders in connection with the Waikaremoana power scheme...three road rollers Kid Garrett and Co (Auckland) £1141 each." [274]

And March 1922:

"The One Tree Hill Road Board, in view of its decision to pave in concrete that part of Manukau Road lying within its boundaries, is preparing to relay the water mains, now under the roadway, beneath the footpaths, and has just received tenders for the supply and delivery of cast-iron pipes. Five tenders were received, and the lowest, that of Messrs Kidd Garrett Ltd of Auckland, for £899 12s 6d, has been accepted." [275]

And December 1923:

"The sound development of Auckland has brought in its train the establishment of businesses that are a big factor in handling the range of goods essential to the constructive and skilled trades and industry. Within a category of importance comes the merchant firm that links with engineering and important aspects of our huge dairying resources...

"Kidd, Garrett Ltd have demonstrated an intimate grip of their business and the up-to-date stocks, comprising all the highest grades of crucible and alloy steel, non-ferrous metals (from the Eyre Smelting Company), white metals and phosphor bronzes, together with a wide range of dairying requisites, and transmission lines including shafting, pulleys, belting and couplings, provide ample scope for meeting the varied needs of the trades concerned." [276]

By 1924, Kidd, Garett was also the Auckland agent for Oldfield Tires, distributed in New Zealand by the Anglo-American Tire Company Limited of Christchurch [277] and for Diabolo milk separators. [278]

In February 1964, Kidd, Garrett acquired another long-established engineering firm — as reported by the Christchurch Press:

"Kidd, Garrett Ltd, Auckland engineering merchant, has purchased the assets of Friar, Richards and Upton Ltd, Auckland. Friar, Richards and Upton Ltd, established in 1904, was one of the first engineering merchants in Auckland. It ceased operating on January 31." [279]

By 1966, Kidd Garrett had become Kidd Garrett Holdings Limited [280] with such a profitable business that it eventually attracted the attention of Brierley Investments and, in 1975, that of Jas. J. Niven which began its business as Niven Industries Limited in 1908: [281]

"Jas. J. Niven will acquire the total shareholding of Kidd Garrett Holdings, Ltd. Considerable benefits are expected from the rationalisation of the two companies, and the widened coverage of New Zealand's engineering requirements…

"Kidd Garrett Holdings is a wholly-owned subsidiary of Brierley Investments and it trades in engineering supplies. Jas. J. Niven is an engineer's merchant, and it also undertakes engineering, manufacturing, water treatment, and air conditioning work." [282]

Socony Asphalt

Often misspelt as 'Sogony' Socony Asphalt was a product of the Standard Oil Company of New York which merged with Vacuum Oil in 1931 to form the Socony-Vacuum Corporation. In 1955, the company became the Socony Mobil Oil Company, renamed Mobil Oil Corporation in 1966. [283]

As early as October 1910, Socony mineral turpentine was available to New Zealand consumers [284] and often sold as a Vacuum Oil product along with Pratt's motor spirit and kerosene. [285]

By 1921, Socony Asphalt was imported for the country's roads — as reported to the Hawera Borough Council in February of that year:

"The engineer (Mr J Sturrock) reported: The annual tarring of streets of the borough has been commenced. South road, High street…and part of Princes street have been coated with Socony asphaltum…This asphaltum is a similar preparation to the Union asphalt road binder, with which the test was made versus tar opposite Syme's mill. That test proved the asphaltum to stand for over two and a half years against one year for the tar.

"I decided to switch over to asphalt, and commenced with Glover road last year. Unfortunately the grade of asphalt was not quite suitable, and the surface was slippery. Last year, however, Mr Craven, the American representative of the Standard Oil Co's asphalt department, toured through New Zealand, and was wise enough to ascertain in every locality the character of the climate.

"From this he determined the class of asphalt suitable and as their price was best our last supply was obtained from that company. The stuff is more costly than tar, but is less costly when the wear is taken into account. I expect the roads asphalted this year will not require to be coated again for two or perhaps three years." [286]

The success of asphalt as a road material was illustrated by an Auckland Star comment of August 1923:

"In yesterday's issue we quoted a paragraph from the Dominion advising the arrival at Wellington of 200 tons of bitumen, which was claimed as probably a record shipment of bitumen in one vessel. Auckland, however, is not behind Wellington in this respect, as we are advised by John Chambers and Son, the agents for the Standard Oil Co, that they landed here for the Auckland tramway department 200 tons of Socony bitumen by the s.s. Hollywood in April, and 200 tons by the s.s. Hauraki in June." [287]

John Chambers and Son

Following his arrival in New Zealand from Britain in 1866, John Chambers unsuccessfully attempted to produce iron from the ironsands of Taranaki and Manukau Heads. A furnace built at Onehunga in 1883 eventually failed. Nevertheless, John Chambers started a business in 1892 with his son importing mining equipment and other products and incorporated John Chambers and Son Limited in 1898. [288]

John Chambers died in September 1903 but the business of John Chambers and Son continued with his son, John Moginie Chambers, at the helm, [289] with outlets at Auckland, Wellington and Dunedin by November 1903 supplying all manner of engineering and mining equipment.

In April 1904, the Auckland Star reported:

"Messrs John Chambers and Son have secured the order for the complete plant required for the power house and boiler room of the Christchurch electric tramway system." [290]

John Moginie Chambers died on 6 March 1918 [291] but the business continued with the guidance of a Board of Directors and senior managers, expanding into the motor vehicle parts industry later that year:

"The company entered the automotive parts and garage equipment business at the end of 1918. The then manager of the Dunedin branch visited America and from there he shipped parts back to Dunedin where the shipments were handled by Mr Henderson, who saw to the pricing and the preparations for distribution. Dunedin was the testing place for the automotive parts and garage equipment division of the company's activities and this division grew until it formed a large part of the business." [292]

Indeed, by 1957, John Chambers and Son Ltd was a wholesaler of motor parts and accessories for most motor vehicle makes and models. [293]

In October 1965, John Chambers and Son was acquired by Christchurch-based Andrews and Beaven Limited, [294] a company that had traded as agricultural engineers and importers since 1879. [295]

The Texas Company

As well Standard Oil Company sources, New Zealand's early imports from America of oil products, including bitumen, were sourced from The Texas Company, referred to in a previous chapter.

An early example of the approaches made to local councils desperate to provide good roads at minimum cost was reported by the Northern Advocate in August 1923:

"A letter from the Texas Company offering its services in connection with the company's supply of bitumen, brought on a long discussion at last night's meeting of the Whangarei Borough Council regarding the borough roads. Dissatisfaction with recent road work was frankly expressed, and the need for avoiding mistakes in the future was strongly insisted upon.

"The Texas Company referred to the success of its asphalt roads and the importance of the grade and quality of bitumen, also the quality of the aggregate and the disposition of drainage for carrying off surface water, as factors of vital importance in securing success.

"The company was ready, if it supplied bitumen, to give the Council the consulting services of its engineer, Mr A G Smith, to secure that the Whangarei Council's use of the bitumen was on the soundest possible lines.

"The Mayor said he did not think it was necessary for an advising expert to put in all his time. All that was required was to have expert guidance for about a week, until the proper methods were thoroughly grasped.

"In regard to the criticisms made, he recognised that mistakes had been made, in one case by overheating and in another by the pressure to secure penetration. These mistakes would not be repeated. He thought the calling of tenders was on the right lines, and saw no objection to firms tendering being asked to do what the Texas Company had offered. Councillor E G W Tibbits said the fact was they needed expert direction in this matter. They had not a man who was really qualified, with a thorough knowledge of what was required…" [296]

Tar Preparations

Once a base of metal or asphalt had been laid, a tar preparation of one sort or another was needed to seal the road surface and this was usually sprayed on. However, as with the metal and asphalt, the type and quality of the tar used made all the difference to the longevity of the road and its ongoing maintenance costs — all subject to uncertainty during the early years of road construction — as noted by newspaper articles of 1914:

"As to the tar and various preparations of it and the result obtained, most of them can be seen in Eltham and the vicinity. They are tar, de-hydrated tar, both used with sand, Soltar,

Tarvia, and Restar. Tar raw can be classed a failure. De-hydrated or properly boiled tar applied to a good road and sanded, is good while the weather is warm, but it quickly breaks up under lower temperature owing to it becoming too hard. Roads treated with it are, of course, immensely superior to ordinary good roads.

"Tarvia is a good English preparation but it is too costly to consider for county roads. Soltar is made in Auckland and is giving excellent results; this work may be seen on Taupo Quay near the Loan and Mercantile offices. Restar is the preparation made by Mr Basham and is, in his opinion, the very best for county roads and he has had more experience in dealing with tar on the county roads than anyone else in the Dominion.

"Comparing it with Soltar, it is very like it as both retain their resilient properties. Dig up a piece that has been down for some time and either is quite elastic, consequently the surfaces do not break up. Restar has the great advantage of being very much cheaper in this locality. It would not be much more than half the cost of Soltar." [297]

"Local New Zealand experiments have now fully demonstrated that the best road to withstand car traffic consistent with cost, is a thorough water-bound macadam road with a surface seal or roof of tar preparation such as Soltar, a dehydrated tar made in Auckland, or Restar, a new preparation patented and used so successfully by Mr Basham of Eltham and now being manufactured by the Restar Company of Wanganui.

"Road building of the future in county districts on these lines is going to be more costly initially but the maintenance will be greatly reduced. Ratepayers must shoulder a heavier responsibility in first cost of construction by loan and can reasonably expect, while enjoying a higher standard of road travelling, to pay less in annual maintenance." [298]

Restar
The final sentence of an otherwise unremarkable obituary published by the Christchurch Press on 6 February 1950 underscored a remarkable chapter in the long history of road construction that began in 1913:

"The death occurred to-day of Mr Frederick Basham, a civil engineer and surveyor. Mr Basham was born in London and took up sheep farming in Australia. Later he entered the service of the Tasmanian railways. He came to New Zealand and was appointed assistant engineer to the borough of New Plymouth.

"Next he became county engineer to the Hawera County Council and when Eltham was created a separate county, he accepted an appointment as county engineer to the new body. There he became widely known for his excellent roadmaking, laying down the first tar-sealed roads in New Zealand." [299]

It was in December 1913 that the Eltham County Council engineer, Frederick Basham, reported his early experiments with what he foresaw as a revolutionary form of road sealant — as reported by the Hawera & Normanby Star:

"From the manner in which the roads in the South riding have broken up in the last few weeks it is evident that more money must be spent on them than has been the case in recent years. As I have often pointed out in the past, the roads are wearing out faster than they are being renewed out of rates, and some greater expenditure on them is necessary…

"On the northern portion of the Mountain road I have, as proposed in my report of October 11 last, tried a new method which appears to be far ahead of the ordinary tar spraying. The first portion of the road treated, some 30 chains, has been done a month and it is possible to obtain some fair idea how the road is affected by traffic. The total distance treated is 70 chains and the cost was 26s per chain.

"The material used is a tar compound made in the Council's yard at a total cost of 7½d per gallon and is the result of experiments carried out by me during the past year. For the purpose of distinction and reference I have called it 'restar' and am registering that name and the formula.

"The average depth of the coat is from half-inch to 1 inch, and it is silent, resilient, and non-slippery. In my opinion it is very much ahead of the ordinary coat of tar and sand and is undoubtedly the best value of any work of this nature yet done in the county…

"In further explanation, Mr Basham said he first got the idea from the methods adopted on Essex roads by means of a preparation called 'Fluxphalte'. Also he had analysed several patent compositions and had others tested by the Government analyst, and guided by the information thus obtained, and as the result of experiments carried out at the county yards, he had been able to produce a material which he felt quite confident would fill the bill…He would probably be forming a small company for the sale of this preparation throughout New Zealand…" [300]

As with all experiments, the results had to stand the test of time — as reported by the Christchurch Press in January 1914:

"Experiments in tar-spraying of country roads in Taranaki have been going on for some time. The Rawhitiroa road in southern Taranaki was tar-sprayed with ordinary gasworks tar, but it has not proved very successful. A small section of the same road was treated with 'restar' which appears to be holding well.

"On another road 'soltar' was tried in the wheel-tracks and wherever there is a good foundation it is standing well. The Manaia road, which has had another top-dressing of tar, is reported, says the Hawera Star, to be in good condition. The 'restar' preparation, where tried on the Eltham-Stratford road, is maintaining a solid surface after three months' traffic." [301]

However, competition between tar manufacturers during those early days of uncertain results remained keen in the Eltham district:

"At last meeting of the Council a letter was read from the managing director of Soltar Ltd complaining of the Council's action in spending ratepayers' money on an unproved preparation such as restar.

In reply the clerk wrote…

"This Council comprises nine shrewd businessmen elected by the ratepayers to administer the affairs of the county. Many thousands of pounds are expended each year, provided by rates to which the councillors are contributors. None of them can be accused of squandering the ratepayers' money in experiments though they can be credited with introducing the most modern methods of road-making with results greatly in favour of their enterprise, the roads being considered by those in a position to judge, the best in the Dominion.

"Mr Basham's solution known as restar can be used at about half the cost of soltar, and the portion of the road first treated has certainly justified its use as, notwithstanding the large amount of traffic which the road has to carry, no evidence of wear is noticeable.

"To treat a road with Mr Basham's solution, restar, including labour and all requisite materials, does not exceed 26s per chain which is about equal to the cost of ordinary tarring and sanding.

"The Council has treated many miles of road with the latter process, and when an infinitely better system can be adopted at no greater cost or inconvenience there should be no cause for complaint. The ratepayers who find the money do not complain but on the contrary express their hearty appreciation with the improvement, and the outside public who use the road are struck with admiration." [302]

With Restar achieving such success, the company of Restar Limited was duly established — as reported by the Hawera & Normanby Star and the Wanganui Chronicle in April 1914:

"A letter was received from Mr J F Holloway, Wanganui, stating that a company was in process of formation to acquire the manufacturing rights of restar and also to manufacture any other tar preparation that may be desired for road-making purposes." [303]

"Another local industry fraught with great possibilities for this town and district has been successfully launched, namely, the Wanganui Restar Company. The Company has been promoted to convert crude tar into various marketable commodities, principally Restar, a tar-sealing composed for roads, the invention of Mr Basham, the well-known engineer of Eltham.

"Eltham County is regarded as the pioneer of tar-treated roads and Mr. Basham's preparation has stood all tests and is regarded by experts as the most suitable preparation for the economical and satisfactory treatment of road surfaces. At the initial meeting on Monday evening it was reported that the capital had been fully subscribed and a site near the Gas Works secured for the carrying on of the business…" [304]

By October 1914, the factory production of Restar had started:

"The first truck load of Restar was despatched from the local works yesterday to the order of the Patea County Council. The works are now in full swing and already a large number of extensive orders are in hand from local bodies all over this coast. Inquiries and orders have also been received from the East Coast and, as the quality of the material has been demonstrated beyond question, it is evident that Restar Ltd is destined to be one of our most prosperous and successful industries." [305]

The basic tar product prepared by Restar Ltd, Wanganui "…is generally known as 'British Road Board Specification No. 1' but this is again boiled up to 10 hours in County depot and tested and treated by addition of certain vegetable oils and delivered hot on to the job by motor lorry." [306]

In September 1917, The New Zealand Herald reported:

"The well-known firm of Restar Ltd, tar refiners, are opening up business in Auckland, and to that end are installing an up-to-date plant in Patteson Street, near the gasworks. This firm's products have a Dominion reputation and asphalters and local body engineers will be interested in this new local source of supply." [307]

The company's success and expansion was spoken of during an interview of J F Holloway, General Manager of Restar Limited, in October 1917:

"…Restar Ltd is now a household word in the local body world and it is wonderful how the Company's operations have grown and extended. Commencing three years ago in a modest way with a limited supply of raw material and a local body clientele unused to tarring methods, the demand for Restar has now reached such proportions that all the available tar in New Zealand would not suffice for the Company's business…

"You would hardly credit it, said Mr Holloway, but not less than a quarter of a million gallons of our tar are going into Taranaki alone this season and other districts in the Wellington and Wairarapa districts are absorbing large quantities…

"Restar came to the rescue at the opportune time and those local bodies suffering worst owing to the high price of metal, adopted the tarred road system — and the result has been a reasonable expenditure on maintenance and good roads for the general public and ratepayers.

"The experience of our [Wanganui] County Council is much the same as another and so dozens of them are now benefitting by the new system. Another reason was the supply of a standard article. Experience has proved that tars vary in quality as much as any commodity and because local bodies bought tar as tar —without reference to quality — some failures were very pronounced in the early stages.

"Restar has changed all this by supplying only standard articles produced by the latest machinery and up to certain recognised speculations as laid down by recognised British Engineering authorities. The result has been that where a standard article is used, the job has always proved successful…" [308]

By 1918, the Restar product was being used by the Railway Department in Taranaki and Wellington for station platforms and was promoted in Auckland by agents, Cruickshank, Miller and Co, as ideal for paths. [309]

But the main purpose of the product promoted by Restar remained the roads:

"Restar is carrying heavy road traffic in many parts of New Zealand…A Restar Concrete road is miles ahead of a cement concrete road for the reason that it is more resilient under heavy loads, does not work into pot holes, does not crack or creep and, in the case of a weak spot in the foundation, is repairable. Over 100 miles of Restar roads in Taranaki alone…" [310]

As the main product gained a reputation for consistent quality, the Restar company also expanded its manufacturing to include a number of by-products — as reported by the Wanganui Herald and Evening Post in June 1918:

"Mr J F Holloway, managing director of Restar Ltd, said Mr E Crow was in charge of the chemical and mechanical departments. This year the company had handled somewhere in the vicinity of 1,000,000 gallons of tar received from all directions. Mr Crow tested the tar received and supervised distilling operations and tested the prepared products before they were sent out to the various local authorities.

"Mr Crow was also in charge of the by-products manufacturing department, manufacturing articles from tar oil received in the course of distillation. Stains, disinfectants, various classes of paints, a fuel economiser, and a synthetic benzine were some of the products…The company also manufactured Diesel engine fuel and was under contract to supply a large quantity…" [311]

"No industry in Wanganui in recent years has grown as rapidly as the Restar Company, the manufacturers of the Standard Road Binder known as Restar. Its remarkable development reads almost like a romance, especially as the growth has been mainly during the war period.

"Four years ago it was a small concern, hesitating on the edge of an unknown field — today it is a force to be reckoned with amongst the principal industries of New Zealand. Its products go north, south, east, and west, and the volume of output far exceeds the most sanguine expectations. The company owes its success to many causes, but the chief lever has been the production of a sound standard article at practically pre-war prices…

"The Restar style of roading has come to stay as experience has proved its value. Thus it is that the output has reached huge proportions and is rapidly increasing. As an outcome of tar-distilling on a large scale, other industries involving the use of tar oils have followed in its wake with the result that today Restar Ltd have perhaps the largest bye-products plant south of the line, and are producing various articles — such as disinfectants, stains, paints, and various other products — many of which had to be imported prior to the advent of the company.

"The company have lately installed a complete plant in Auckland and indications point to that province comparing favourably in the matter of roads with Taranaki and Wellington in a few years' time…" [312]

By January 1920, Restar Limited was licensed under the Distillation Act 1908 to operate three stills at Wanganui and two at Auckland. [313]

In 1922, the company was also licensed to operate two stills at Wellington [314] with plans to extend their operations to Gisborne — as reported by the Poverty Bay Herald:

"Mr Ed Crow, engineer to the well-known firm of Restar Ltd, has just completed arrangements for the erection of a branch factory in Gisborne for his company. Mr Crow stated that this factory was decided upon after a careful study of the possibilities of the district and his directors are very sanguine about the future prospects, so much so, that a plant capable of producing 400,000 gallons of Restar per annum is being installed…

"Restar Ltd has factories in Wellington, Auckland, Wanganui and, in six weeks' time, will have one in Gisborne. The raw material is obtained from the local gasworks in the various centres, supplemented by direct shipments from Australia…" [315]

A year later, the Northland Age reported that Restar Limited had experienced record sales:

"The Restar Company, which is regarded as the pioneer of the good roads movement, report that the season just concluding has been the busiest on record, the demand being, at times, greater than the capacity to supply…Already orders are filed for next season's requirements, and indications are for yet another record as, in addition to the general demand, several large road loans have been authorised in different parts of the Dominion in which Restar is to be used exclusively." [316]

Local Taranaki roads were not neglected because of the company's expansion:

"Taranaki has the honour of possessing the best roads in the Dominion. This honour is awarded without question. Eleven years ago, when the Restar Company started to make and sell their now famous Restar Road Binder, the Taranaki roads were no better than any others.

"Since July 1913, 2,750,324 gallons of Restar Road Binder have been supplied to the local bodies contained in the Taranaki province. This is sufficient to carpet about 400 miles of road, 12 feet wide. This, with the intelligent co-operation of Taranaki road engineers, is the reason why Taranaki is famous for its roads.

"The Restar Company and its Road Binder are now household words throughout the Dominion, and from a modest beginning of one small plant in Wanganui, has now large manufacturing depots in Wellington, Auckland and Gisborne, whilst the output exceeds that of any similar concern south of the line.

"The secret of the remarkable success of Restar has been the fixed policy of the company to concentrate on the production of a high grade uniform article. In tar distillation there is a tendency to make the road binder the secondary consideration as compared with the other valuable bye-products obtained from tar. Restar Limited, on the other hand, whilst making good use of resultant bye-products, have made the road binder the main item. This policy has so appealed to road engineers that Restar is regarded as the standard binder in bituminous road construction…" [317]

By October 1929, Restar had expanded to the South Island with a new factory at Lyttelton:

"Wealth out of waste is the slogan of the coal tar products business which, with the help of the public, could be made a most profitable department of New Zealand's industrial life. From the waste of our big gas works can be made such widely different and useful articles as disinfectant, paint, creosote, flaked naphthalene and road binders.

"This industry, although first developed in Germany, has been strongly established in New Zealand by the firm of Restar Ltd and indirectly brings wealth to everyone in the community…

"Perhaps the greatest use of coal tar products is in road preparations such as tar-sealed roads, also for paths, tennis courts and so on. Tar Mac, a Restar product, is mixed asphalt tar and metal chips which can be put down by anyone as it requires no heat and no mixing. These varied products are only a few of the many lines produced by these wonderful processes. The Restar company are in a very large way in New Zealand, having five plants at Auckland, Gisborne, Wanganui, Wellington and Lyttelton." [318]

Indeed, the company was considered to be a huge New Zealand success by 1930:

"Now, at the end of 15 years, Restar Ltd is a household word throughout the Dominion for road materials and tar by-products. Every succeeding year from the beginning has been a record for output and Restar may now perhaps be ranked among the most successful industrial concerns in New Zealand.

"The secret of success no doubt has been quality and service — that is to say the aim has been to produce the best possible article of its kind and also to meet local body engineers' special needs in every respect…" [319]

Of course, as with all things, new technology and change is always just around the corner — as reported by the Hawera Star in December 1932:

"A new process for the treatment of the tar product of vertical gas retorts, to yield a form of road-surfacing material capable of standing up to the demands of modern traffic, has been evolved after years of research by the Metropolitan Gas Company Limited, Melbourne. The process has been patented and the New Zealand rights have been obtained by Restar Limited, which company has licensed a new company, Messrs J and S Tar Products Limited, to develop the process in Gisborne.

"The new road-surfacing material has been under exhaustive test by the highways authorities, it is stated, and has given full satisfaction so far as the tests have proceeded, with indications of complete success over the full test period.

"The new company to work on the tar product from the Gisborne Gas Company's vertical retort battery is a local development and it is anticipated that the re-modelled Restar works will yield some 300 tons of the new material per annum, this being the full capacity of the available supply of raw material from the gas works…" [320]

As one of the largest tar manufacturers in New Zealand, Restar Limited was the logical choice to transition to the new product, Bitural — as reported by the Dominion in December 1933:

"Bitural, the new tar substance which is being used for road-sealing in Wellington, is not a local product. It was the result of intensive research work carried out by Messrs. C F Broadhead and R S Andrews of the Metropolitan Gas Company, Melbourne, some years ago. The New Zealand rights were acquired from the patentees by Industrial Developments (NZ) Ltd which subsequently granted a sub-license to Restar Ltd.

"Under the terms of the license, Restar Ltd has been producing bitural at its works in Miramar. The bitural manufactured under the license is 99 per cent a New Zealand production." [321]

However, 1934 was to be a year of change for both Restar Limited and its founding principals — as reported by The New Zealand Herald and the Evening Post in June and July of that year:

"The following private company has been registered in Auckland: Restar (Auckland) Limited, dealers in bitumen and the by-products of coal and oil, and in road-making materials. Capital: £750 in £1 shares. Subscribers: John Ferguson Holloway, 500 shares; Austin Hamilton, 250 shares." [322]

"On the occasion of his retirement from his active executive position in the firm of Restar Limited, Mr E Crow of Wellington was recently farewelled by his colleagues…it being some twenty years ago when, in conjunction with two Wanganui business associates, Mr Crow pioneered the tar sealing of county roads and founded the now well-known firm. Mr Crow accepted the position of engineer to the firm which position he has held with distinction up to the date of his retirement." [323]

"Notice is hereby given that the tar by-product business hitherto carried on by Restar Ltd will in future be conducted by Restar (Auckland) Ltd. The New Offices and Warehouse are situated at 125 Albert Street…where all inquiries and orders will be promptly attended to J F Holloway, Manager." [324]

The original company, Restar Limited, was placed in voluntary liquidation on 16 October 1934. [325]

"An offer of the Wellington Gas Company to sell to the council the leasehold property of the Restar Works, including buildings and plant but excluding stocks, for the sum of £1,500, was not entertained." [326]

Restar (Auckland) Limited

Although its principal, John Ferguson Holloway, died at Auckland on 27 September 1937, [327] Restar (Auckland) Limited continued to manufacture refined tar products at Auckland — as per Christchurch Press reports of August 1947 and March 1953:

"Three workmen suffered burns when a 45-gallon drum of benzole caught fire in the factory of Restar (Auckland) Ltd, Hill street, Onehunga, this afternoon. Leslie Allen Bull, aged 30, of Grey Lynn, was admitted to the Green Lane Hospital suffering from burns to the arms and face, and two others Derrick Alfred Knight, aged 27, and Robert James Ross, aged 27, were treated for burns to the hands and face at the casualty department of the hospital and discharged…The three injured men, who, with the manager (Mr A E Knight), are joint owners of the business, were taken to hospital by ambulance." [328]

"A tar by-products factory in Hill street, Onehunga, was destroyed by fire this afternoon. Built of asbestos sheeting, the factory was controlled by Restar Auckland Ltd for the Laughton Trading Company. It was insured, but the sum was not available. The damage is estimated at £10,000…" [329]

Indeed Restar (Auckland) Limited continued to trade until the company was deregistered as of 4 September 1974. [330]

Restar (South Island) Limited
Following the demise of the original Restar company in 1934, Restar (South Island) Limited was registered at 16 Bedford Row, Christchurch on 14 November 1935 with a Capital of £15,000. The initial subscribers included: "L R C Macfarlane of Culverden and H Wright, J J Hurley, E E Roberts, L Watson, H S Smith, and P C Browne all of Christchurch. Objects: Manufacturers of coal tar, oils, and by-products of every description." [331] Restar (South Island) Limited was eventually placed into voluntary liquidation on 18 December 1973. [332]

Soltar
At about the same time that Restar was establishing its first factory at Wanganui in 1913, another tar refining entity, the Soltar Company Limited, was doing the same at Auckland — as reported by The New Zealand Herald in May of that year:

"A factory is to be erected at the corner of Patterson Street and Beaumont Street by the Soltar Company Limited for the manufacture of soltar which is a preparation of tar used for roadmaking purposes. The plans for the building have just been passed by the Auckland Harbour Board.

"The factory is to be built of corrugated iron with brick furnaces and a thoroughly up-to-date refining and condensing plant for the preparation of the tar. Arrangements have been made whereby the company may pump the tar required by it direct from the gasworks at Freeman's Bay and the tar will not be handled in any way until pumped out into tins in its prepared form. The area to be covered by the new factory will be 60ft by 35ft." [333]

The Soltar factory was officially opened on 3 July 1913:

"There was a large gathering of representatives of leading local bodies, engineers and others at the opening of the Soltar Company's works in Beaumont Street yesterday afternoon. The attendance numbered about one hundred, and the possibilities of soltar as the new roading material were demonstrated to the evident interest of those present. The visitors were conducted over the works by Mr H L Friend, managing director, and Mr R F Moore, the company's engineer...

"Mr H C Tewsley in proposing the toast of New Zealand Local Bodies, said he believed that it would at last be found that a satisfactory road-making material had been discovered. The commercial cheapness of Soltar would appeal to local bodies for it was ten times less expensive than most of the recognised materials at present in use...

"Mr C Bagley, vice-president of the Auckland Local Bodies' Association...said that if Soltar proved to be all that was claimed for it, local bodies faced with the ever-serious problem of road-making and maintenance, would welcome its advent...It gave a rubber-like, waterproof surface to roads and could be used five minutes after being put down..." [334]

Unfortunately, what had earlier been described as the factory's 'up-to-date refining and condensing plant for the preparation of the tar' did not meet safety standards, resulting in a terrible accident only three weeks after its opening:

"An explosion, followed by a fire, occurred at the Soltar Company's works in Beaumont Street yesterday afternoon. The employee in charge of the works at the time, William Massey, was thrown to the floor where he was terribly burned by the boiling soltar which rushed from two overturned tanks. He was conveyed to the hospital where he died at an early hour this morning." [335]

Obviously, some changes had to be made — as reported by the Auckland Star in August 1913:

"At a special meeting of the shareholders in the Soltar Company, a report on the work to date was read by the chairman of directors (Mr H Leslie Friend). He first mentioned the sad mishap that ended in the death of one of the company's engineers, and then referred to the erection of a new boiler which he stated would turn out a much larger quantity of soltar and in much shorter time than the old method.

"These alterations would not cost nearly as much as was at first anticipated and the directors expected to save the whole cost within a year. The sales and inquiries for Soltar were still keeping up wonderfully well and he believed that the company would have no trouble whatever in selling the whole of its summer output." [336]

By October 1913, the Soltar Company's product was beginning to make a name for itself throughout the country:

"Mr C Skitrop, New Plymouth Borough Engineer, writes to the Hawera Star as follows…

"If Soltar is put on a clean surface it will not lift or peel off. On the question of heavy traffic on County roads, I can only say that since Currie Street was treated, 14,000 tons of heavy traffic have passed over it without doing any injury, and I am quite sure that had Tarvia [an American-made tar preparation] been used in place of Soltar (and at the same cost per chain) it would have disappeared by now." [337]

Northland was also expecting an improvement in its road with the application of soltar in February 1915:

"A start was made this morning with the top-dressing of Cameron Street and already the work has been pushed well forward. The material which is being used is soltar of which the Borough Council has ordered 2000 gallons as an experiment. It is expected that this quantity will serve to do most of the street and, should it prove successful, other roads will probably be similarly treated next year. When finished, the surface should be of a springy nature, not unlike rubber, and the thickness of the dressing will be from three-quarters of an inch to an inch. It is confidently expected that the new surfacing will last four or five years without further attention." [338]

However, the refining of tar remained a precarious occupation, requiring new technology — as reported by the Taranaki Herald and Taranaki Daily News in January 1916:

"Referring to the two recent fires at the council's soltar depots, the [New Plymouth] borough engineer reported that the present method of boiling tar was primitive, expensive, and highly dangerous and he recommended that boiling tar by use of fire, as at present, be discontinued and that it be heated by steam by means of a high-pressure steam boiler." [339]

"The borough engineer was authorised to purchase a steam plant for heating soltar at an estimated cost not exceeding £30." [340]

In the meantime, to compete with the likes of Restar, it was necessary for the Soltar Company to promote its product far and wide:

"Mr H L Friend of Auckland is visiting Gisborne with the object of interviewing the Borough Council on the subject of the use of Soltar for roads. Mr Friend states that this preparation is coming very largely into use throughout New Zealand…the company, which has its works at Auckland, having contracts in hand for several million gallons on three and four year contracts.

"New Plymouth, after successful experiments, has undertaken to put down eight miles of roadway with soltar: it took 80,000 gallons last year and wants 110,000 gallons this year.

"The chief virtue of soltar is claimed to be its resiliency. Whilst other systems of tar treatment of roads crack, the soltar like a rubber surface does not break up. Mr Friend hopes to wait upon the Borough Council at its meeting to-morrow night to urge the suitability of his company's product for local conditions." [341]

However, Mr Friend's solicitations proved to be in vain for the shareholders of Soltar Limited voted for the company to be wound up voluntarily as of 13 December 1916. [342]

Nevertheless, the use of soltar continued to be favoured by borough and county councils seeking to improve their roads in the central North Island — as reported by the King Country Chronicle in February 1917:

"The roads as a whole are fairly good at present but shortage of funds will curtail local body expenditure…The preparation known as soltar laid down on Ralph's Hill [Matiere, Central North Island] has proved an unqualified success. About a sixth or eighth of the usual metal, screened to the size of a hazel nut, is mixed with heated soltar and laid down in a skin of about two inches, proper attention being given to underground springs by tile-draining and the whole dressed with loose, fine gravel, which the traffic embeds in the road surface.

"The resultant job is eminently satisfactory as to surface and wearing qualities and apparently needs little repair to maintain a first-rate solidity suitable to anything up to motor traffic." [343]

Although some setbacks were still being experienced just over a year later:

"The portion of Ralph's Hill laid down with soltar has stood the traffic remarkably well but portions have begun to break into potholes and as the mixture of gravel and soltar is only about two inches thick the holes will rapidly break down on the edges and should be repaired at once to prevent total destruction of a very fine piece of road." [344]

Soltar Limited was eventually deregistered in December 1919. [345]

Tarvia

The beginning of Tarvia as a paving for roads is described at the website of Barrett Industries:

"Road construction was far from Samuel E Barrett's mind when he began a small roofing business in Chicago, Illinois in 1854. As his operation expanded, Barrett realized that America's growing cities were literally getting stuck in the mud, and he saw the need for innovative solutions for the country's burgeoning road system. The demand for paved streets and sidewalks led Barrett to experiment with roofing tar as a treatment for brick, stone, and wooden block pavements. The concept was a success and Barrett Paving Materials was born…

"In 1903, the Barrett Manufacturing Company initiated experiments in Jackson, Tennessee which eventually led to the development of Tarvia. Tarviated roads were a cost-effective solution for creating and repairing the roads that Americans and their Model Ts so desperately needed.

"By combining Barrett coal tar with wooden blocks/bricks/stone, Barrett Paving Materials successfully created paved roads and thus a better and more economical way to finish roads and better prepare them for the future of the automobile.

"Barrett's advertising campaign, 'good roads at low cost', targeted American consumers and informed them of how Tarvia could improve not only their roads but also their lives. Tarvia drastically improved the nation's rural highways, contributing to the success of the automobile and unprecedented commerce between rural communities and distant cities." [346]

Prior to its use in New Zealand, a Christchurch Press article of August 1908 commented on the use of Tarvia in Yorkshire:

"Tarvia is a refined product of tar and an exceedingly cohesive cement, bituminous in character. Mixed with chippings, it is laid on the road to be treated, covered with stone and lightly rolled; then a top sealing of tarvia is applied, dry chippings are scattered over it, the whole rolled down, and the operations are at an end.

"In the result, it is claimed there is a road free from mud or dust, silent, non-slippery and sanitary and the cost, although varying in different districts, is about the same as the ordinary waterbind system whilst there is a distinct saving in that the maintenance is less." [347]

Tests of the Tarvia product had been carried out in New Zealand by November 1911 and were about to be continued in Taranaki:

"The experiment about to be made by the [Hawera] Borough Council in tarviating High street will be followed with a good deal of interest. Present operations are designed to reduce the crown of the road and prepare a bed for the application of a course of tarvia. Although the use of this material will be new to Taranaki, it has been tested in Christchurch under the observation of Mr Cameron, the borough foreman, and he found the results quite satisfactory for it has outlasted ordinary asphalte and the cost is not materially greater.

"In England and on the Continent results have been highly spoken of. The process is first to lay down a good bed, then spread a coating of tarvia and upon this put a comparatively thin coating of metal and roll it. The tarvia under this compression binds the metal and then another coating of the same material finishes off the road and gives a fine, hard surface.

"It is claimed that a road so constructed stands traffic very satisfactorily, is practically waterproof, and effectually provides against both wind and dust. The question of cost remains to be tested. Tarvia has to be imported from England and the freight charges will make it expensive, but it is calculated that the saving in time and labour laying down the road, together with the longer life of the road, will compensate largely." [348]

However, two years later and results were still uncertain — as reported by the Hawera & Normanby Star in March 1913:

"At Wednesday night's meeting of the Hawera Borough Council, a letter was received from the Hawera County Council asking for the cost of the South Road recently tarviated, and pointing out that from present appearances the work does not look lasting, possibly owing to the foundation being weak, and stating that the Council is of the opinion that a better foundation is required before proceeding further…" [349]

By December 1914, competition from other tar and asphalt preparations greatly influenced the choices made by Councils ever conscious of costs:

"Reporting on tarvia for roadmaking purposes to the Tauranga Borough Council, the engineers for street works state: As there are other preparations on the market now very similar to tarvia, we thought it advisable to obtain quotations for these before giving an order for same. We find there will be a considerable saving if Star asphaltum is used. This material is specially made for road surfaces and in composition is almost identical with tarvia, the difference in cost being largely due to its being shipped direct from the West Coast of America, instead of through Great Britain. We would recommend that this material be used, provided guarantees as to its chemical and physical properties are given." [350]

Tar preparations manufactured locally were particularly competitive because of the shorter delivery distances needed to get the product to the roads:

"For some time past efforts have been made to have an anomaly removed from the railway tariff in regard to the carriage of tar and tar preparations. Raw tar is carried at a specially reduced rate but tar preparations such as tarvia, restar, soltar, etc., have to pay a much higher rate. As tar preparations are now being generally used for road work in place of ordinary tar, it seems absurd that they should be penalised in the matter of railway charges. So far, efforts made to have this anomaly put right have failed but the [Hawera] Council decided to represent the matter to the various Taranaki MPs, asking their assistance." [351]

Road Contractors
Bituco Road-binder Company

The Bituco Road-binder Company was manufacturing its Bituco road binder at premises in Newmarket, Auckland from at least 1911. [352]

The business was established as a limited liability company in 1915 but was voluntarily wound up in June 1920 [353] after facing intense competition from the manufacturers of steadily-improving road-sealing products.

In the meantime, the Bituco Road-binder Company's early products met with the approval of local councils anxious to improve their road networks — as reported by the Auckland Star in March 1914:

"You can tell the man that asked you that question that there will soon be no dust at all in Newmarket, remarked the Mayor of Newmarket, Mr D Teed, last evening when Mr Fookes said he had been stuck up by a shopkeeper who wanted to know if the Council had sold its watering cart. The Tram Company's sprinkler has not been round that way lately, as there is difficulty in getting water during the road works now in progress, and there has been a little dust in Broadway.

"Mr Teed's remarks will soon be true as concerns the borough's fine main thoroughfare, as the last bit of old rubble road at the triangle near the foot of Khyber Pass Road is now being taken up and relaid in bituco, a bituminous macadam. The work is being done by the Council's own workmen, and the piece already laid gives promise of a solid even surface. This work when finished will make Broadway the finest suburban roadway in Auckland." [354]

The use of the Bituco Company's "…patent material for forming roadways…a bitumen emulsion product…" [355] was advertised widely throughout the country by means of local newspapers and circulars sent to council engineers promoting Bituco as a New Zealand-made product "…extensively used for permanent roadways." [356]

After the Bituco preparation was offered to the New Plymouth Borough Council, its deputy mayor and engineer visited Auckland to inspect the Newmarket road treated with the product. The engineer subsequently reported to the Council in July 1914, parts of which included:

"…that he is satisfied with the quality of the road he had inspected at Newmarket which had been treated with Bituco, both as a coating and as a foundation, but he was of the opinion he could lay it down at considerably less cost than was the case at Newmarket — viz. 5s 3d per square yard. He recommended the council to obtain one ton of the preparation for experimental purposes…" [357]

However, by June 1916, alternative road-making materials were starting to compete with those manufactured by the Bituco Road-binder Company — as reported at a Pukekohe Borough Council meeting:

"The Foreman of Works, Mr Clews, reported that the respective cost of experiments made in King street with Bituco and with tarred macadam, two chains each, was Bituco £113 6s 5d and tarred macadam £67." [358]

Nevertheless, price was not the only consideration — as reported by the Ohinemuri Gazette later in 1916:

"At the invitation of the Borough Council, Mr C Skiltrop, engineer to the Bituco Road Construction Company, visited Paeroa during last week for the purpose of estimating the cost of the reconstruction of the main street under his company's system. At the meeting of the Council on Thursday night Mr Skiltrop furnished the following report:—

"As instructed by the Bituco Road-binder Company I have this day gone carefully over your main street in order to ascertain the approximate cost of laying it down in bituminous surface-bound asphalt and beg to submit my report to your Council.

"My method would be to scarify the surface removing all bumps and irregularities, then spread a thin coat of clean metal which would be rolled to an even surface. The Bituco would then be sprayed into the road surface under pressure which penetrates from 2½ to 3 inches into the metal, binding it together and making a perfectly waterproof surface, which remains elastic and will not perish with time.

"I first communicated this method of road-making five years ago at New Plymouth, and they have stood extra heavy traffic without showing any signs of breaking…I have based my estimate with the intention of making a good job as it does not pay us to advocate cheap unsatisfactory work just for the purpose of getting rid of our material…" [359]

Unfortunately for manufacturers such as the Bituco Road-binder Company, by 1918, its product was being usurped by a 'more forward policy of road construction', cheaper and requiring less, transported raw material — as noted by the Waipa Borough Council:

"The great difficulty experienced in carrying the new formation in Alexandra Street to its present extent has naturally given rise to growing feeling in the Borough Council that there requires to be some re-modelling of policy before the continuance of the work through the town is attempted…

"…Borough Councillors are fully alive to the responsibility upon them to prepare, so far as they can in these difficult times, for a more forward policy of road construction next spring. That the task beset them is not an easy one cannot be questioned, particularly in the light of the experiences during the past few months.

"The great obstacle hampering the work is the uncertainty of metal supplies and the great difficulty of securing railway waggons for the carriage of such supplies as can be secured from the quarries. That being the case, the essential consideration in any future policy of work must be to devise a means of metal saving, and in this respect the concrete highway offers a distinct advantage, apart altogether from its being what is usually regarded as a distinctly preferable roadway…

"The concrete roadway has passed beyond the experimental stage. It is the adopted roadway of all the larger municipalities and may fairly be described as permanent. Prejudice may be forgotten when it is remembered that America, after years of research work, of costly experiment and most critical and trying examination, has adopted this construction for all its permanent roading. American cities and rural America are solidly for concrete; thousands of miles have already been put down, and it is not at all an indefinite future when a band of concrete will stretch across that great continent.

"In Europe the example of America has been copied with equally gratifying results; in England and on the Continent, concrete has been largely used in road construction.

"Even in New Zealand, in this very Provincial district, there is a steadily increasing acceptance of the same ideal. Only the other day, the Auckland City Council announced its adoption of concrete for permanent construction, and that, in the future, all city and suburban roadways would be put down on the American standard…

"Its application in New Zealand may well be encouraged if only from the fact that cement is a product of our own land, thus making the supply independent of shipping space…Once before, the concrete method was enquired into but proved more costly when in comparison with Bituco, but now that Bituco costs have increased by over thirty per cent the comparison may be reversed…" [360]

By the time Bituco Road-binder Company Limited was placed into voluntary liquidation in June 1920, councils such as the Te Awamutu Borough Council, still using bituco in their road construction, had to source their supplies from overseas:

"Several quotations for the supply of bituco were tabled. Two came from American firms and one from a British firm. The quotations were all approximately the same, but varied in the consideration of exchange rates. The English quotation at £13 per ton was accepted, forty tons to be obtained, for delivery in November." [361]

"The chairman [of the Tamahere Road Board] reported that the committee set up go into the question of ordering bituco had given the order to the Union Asphalt Co at £13 10s per ton ship's slings…" [362]

Of course, overseas suppliers were not quite as easy to communicate with as the Bituco Road-binder Company had been — as reported by the Waipa Post in January 1921:

"The Te Awamutu Borough Council held a special meeting yesterday forenoon to further consider the bituco trouble. The bituco is the material with which Alexandra Street was dressed some time ago…The Council, however, is now hindered in the further improvement of the streets by a hitch with the merchants from whom the last supplies were obtained over the quality of the bituco, the Council complaining that it is defective.

"Negotiations have been proceeding for many months past but one of the firms concerned is in England, and the correspondence has consequently been very tardy…During the discussion it was stated that Thames Valley County Council has 80 tons of the alleged defective bituco of which it refuses to take delivery." [363]

Bituco Road-binder Company Limited was struck off as of 22 January 1921. [364]

Emoleum NZ

Emoleum NZ Limited was registered at Auckland from 14 November 1929 to 28 August 1995. The company, described as manufacturers of bituminous road materials, started with a Capital of £5000, subscribed to by Henry Isherwood and Herbert Bellam, both of Auckland. [365]

As advertised in The New Zealand Herald in September 1934, Emoleum NZ sought to promote its bitumen product as suitable for more than roads:

"Emoleum (NZ) Limited wish to advise property owners when contemplating re-surfacing or making new drives and paths to always seek reliable information which is absolutely free on application to this office. Estimates free. Use Emoleum for Paths, Drives and Tennis Courts. No heating required, simple in application. Offices: 8 Winstone's Buildings Works: The Strand, Parnell…" [366]

By 1941, Emoleum NZ had expanded its services to the Waikato with its 'Seal of Quality' emulsified bitumen advertised in the Waikato Times:

"Reseal Your Roads, Footpaths, Tennis Courts, Paths And Drives, School Grounds, Etc. With Emoleum" [367]

In March 1966, Emoleum NZ Limited successfully tendered for a job much larger than the average tennis court — as reported by the Christchurch Press:

"A contract has been let for construction of Tauranga Airport. Accepted was the joint tender of Earthmovers (Waikato) Ltd and Emoleum (NZ) Ltd. The Minister of Civil Aviation (Mr McAlpine) said the contract figure was £305,977 8s which covered the construction and sealing of a single runway of 4200 ft by 150 ft of a strength to take Friendship aircraft, plus a grassed cross strip 2900 ft by 300 ft. The work also included construction of a connecting taxiway between the sealed runway and the terminal apron." [368]

However, by the late 1970s, Emoleum NZ, by then a subsidiary of Mobil Oil New Zealand, found that tenders were no longer so easy to win because of renewed competition and rising costs — as reported by the Christchurch Press in November 1979:

"Canterbury road-sealing contractors say they face a grim future, unable to sustain a price-cutting war with new competition backed by an oil company. A subsidiary of BP New Zealand Ltd, Road Developments Ltd, moved into the province in time for the present sealing season, bringing with it the highly competitive tendering which has erupted in the North Island between three contractors backed by oil companies.

"A newly formed associate company, Road Developments (South Island) Ltd, is expected to win 60 per cent of all road sealing offered this summer. Prices have dropped by as much as a half on tenders accepted a year ago and the three longstanding Canterbury contractors have had to drastically reduce their bids to keep a dwindling share of the market. This is in spite of a rise in July in the price of bitumen from $130 to $173 a tonne and rising labour and plant costs…

"An article in the October issue of the Contractors' Federation magazine, 'The Contractor', tells of fierce competition in the North Island between Road Developments, Emoleum NZ Ltd (controlled by Mobil Oil New Zealand Ltd), and Waikato Bitumen (which is 40 per cent owned by Shell Oil New Zealand Ltd).

"Smaller contractors are said to be on the verge of bankruptcy. Each of the four oil companies in New Zealand sells bitumen — a residual product from the heavy crude which each refines at Marsden Point. It is used predominantly for road sealing and different contractors buy from different companies which use Shell installations to bunker their bitumen at ports. Shell sells the largest share of an estimated 100,000 tonnes produced at Marsden Point each year…" [369]

Nevertheless, with the advantage of manufacturing much of its own asphalt, Emoleum NZ remained "…a leading Bituminous and Asphalt manufacturer and contracting Company, involved in pavement maintenance and allied construction in the North Island, with branches in Auckland and Rotorua." [370]

By June 1985, Emoleum NZ had expanded its operations to Gisborne after acquiring Bitumen Sprayers Limited.

Bitumen Sprayers

Bitumen Sprayers Limited was registered at Gisborne on 26 April 1949 with a Capital of £100. The original shareholders were recorded as D J Finnigan, K E Buscke, J D Finnigan, and J Newton. [371]

When advertising for a drainage manager in July 1982, Bitumen Sprayers Limited described itself as "…a Gisborne-based company operating in underground services, road sealing and paving, road construction and transport…" [372]

By June 1985, similar advertisements informed that Bitumen Sprayers Limited was then a subsidiary of Emoleum NZ Limited. [373]

By May 1989, BP Oil New Zealand Limited had bought Mobil's bitumen business, Emoleum NZ Limited and Bitumen Sprayers Limited. [374] The latter company was de-registered on 30 November 1989. [375]

Bitumix

Bitumix Limited, roading and paving contractors, sand, shingle and general merchants, agents, engineers and shipping proprietors was registered on 28 September 1937 with a Capital of £3000. The original shareholders were recorded as C F Farquharson, J B Brooke and R K Clemow. [376]

An early contract won by Bitumix in October 1939 was "…for metalling and sealing another four miles of the Paeroa-Pokeno State Highway…" [377]

Another important road project was assigned to Bitumix in April 1941:

"The Public Works Department, Paeroa, advised that the remaining section of the Paeroa-Auckland Main Highway has been let for reconstruction and sealing…The length to be done is the six miles between Waitakaruru and Maramarua and when completed the entire road to Auckland will be sealed…The successful tenderers were Messrs Bitumix Ltd, Auckland." [378]

Such contracts obviously led to investment in the company and further expansion — as reported by the Auckland Star in June 1942:

"An increase in the capital of Bitumix Ltd from £6000 to £22,000 has been registered at Auckland." [379]

It was also reported in December 1946 that Bitumix had been chosen to complete another major highway:

"A start has been made on the sealing of the Pirongia-Te Awamutu Main Highway, the contract for which was approved at the last meeting of the Waipa County Council. The project is being undertaken by the firm of Messrs Bitumix Ltd under a contract price of approximately £22,930." [380]

Bitumix was also involved in new road-making methods — as reported by the Christchurch Press in September 1959:

"Four miles of road in the Tauranga and Rotorua counties are to be experimentally reformed using a new process known as soil-cement stabilisation. Tenders have been called in Tauranga and work is expected to begin soon after tenders close in mid-October. The method involves mixing cement into the top five or six inches of soil on the roadway, making a hard waterproof surface. The surface is then sealed with a coat of bitumen. After about 12 months a second coat of bitumen and metal chips may be applied.

"Mr R K Clemow, managing director of Bitumix Ltd, Auckland, said yesterday he believed this was the first job of its kind in New Zealand. The method would have a wide application through the centre of the North Island where it was hard to obtain metal chips of the type used for road forming. The method is to dig up the top six inches of the road with a special machine and to mix 6 per cent cement into it. The mixture is then watered and rolled to a concrete-hard surface of clay which is then sealed with bitumen." [381]

As the pace of highway construction increased by the 1960s, so did the contract prices:

"A contract for £180,041 for building another nine-tenths of a mile of Auckland's southern motorway, between Green Lane east and Market road, had been let to Bitumix Ltd the Minister of Works and chairman of the National Roads Board (Mr Goosman) announced today." [382]

However, to survive the vagaries of highway construction tendering of the 1970s, road construction companies such as Bitumix had to amalgamate and diversify to land subdividing and development projects. [383]

By 1975, Bitumix Limited had become a subsidiary of Winstone Ltd which commented on the road-contracting situation at its annual meeting held in August that year:

"The present pattern of lower demand in the building industry would continue for the remainder of the financial year, the chairman of Winstone Ltd (Mr A H Winstone), said at the annual meeting…The level of activity for the road-contracting subsidiary, Bitumix Ltd, had been very satisfactory, but there were now signs that it was becoming more difficult to secure work at reasonable prices." [384]

On 1 April 1977, the name of Bitumix Limited was officially changed to Winstone Civil Construction Limited, a company that:

"…tenders in New Zealand for contracts in land development, reservoirs, motorway overpasses, drainage and sewerage schemes, and roading. Tenders have also been lodged in the Middle East and Papua-New Guinea." [385]

However, Winstone Limited did not retain Bitumix for long, selling it to Road Developments Limited in 1979:

"Winstone Ltd has sold its wholly-owned subsidiary Winstone Civil Construction Ltd to Auckland-based Road Developments Ltd for an undisclosed cash sum. The sale, which is conditional on the appropriate approvals, also includes Winstone Chemicals Ltd. The mainstream business of Winstone Civil was highway construction, associated civil engineering contracting, and the manufacture of asphalt and paving materials…Winstone chemicals manufactures bitumen emulsions and a range of chemical-based concrete mixtures and compounds…" [386]

Road Developments

Road Developments Limited was registered at Auckland on 17 March 1952 [387] and the company was trading as a manufacturing retailer at Onehunga and Whangarei from 1 February 1967. [388]

In December 1969, the New Zealand Gazette records that Road Developments Limited was awarded a tender by the Ministry of Works for "SH 1 Rodney and Waitemata County section: second-coat sealing and resealing — price $31,962." [389]

Further tenders awarded by the Ministry included:

1970 — State Highway 14 Racecourse — Dargaville section: strengthening and first coat sealing — $55,700.20. [390]

1972 — Northcote-Albany Motorway: second coat sealing — $34,611.80. [391]

1975 — Supply of bitumen emulsion to Ministry of Works Kaikohe Depot $27,400. [392]

1977 — State Highways 1, 12 and 14: Resealing Whangarei and Dargaville areas $281,519.36 [393]

By late 1979, Road Developments Limited had become a subsidiary of BP New Zealand Limited as well as a sister company, Road Developments South Island Limited which was registered on 21 August 1979. [394]

Following its incorporation, Road Developments South Island Limited soon made its presence known in the Canterbury region — as reported by the Christchurch Press:

"Road Developments had taken about 60 per cent of the business in Canterbury. British Pavements would have to withdraw from the sealing business before long if the competition remained. [The Managing Director of British Pavements] questioned whether was making a profit. He suggested that the company was getting cheap bitumen from BP. If a recent 30 per cent increase in the cost of bitumen was not passed on by BP, Road Developments would be able to undercut other contractors.

"[BP's General Manager] Mr K Rundon said Road Developments had the most modern equipment in New Zealand, had better methods, and was more efficient than its competitors. It could therefore keep its rates lower." [395]

Despite the criticism that it was creating a monopolistic business, BP continued to dominate the Canterbury road-building scene with a further acquisition in 1984:

"The Road Development Ltd group, a wholly-owned subsidiary of BP New Zealand Ltd, has purchased the assets and business of a well-known shingle producer in Christchurch, Ashby Bros Ltd. Ashby Bros was founded in 1930 by four brothers and, in recent years, owned and operated by John and Graeme Ashby.

"Canterbury Branch Bitumix Ltd (formerly Road Developments (SI) Ltd), now enjoys an interrelated package of business that includes bitumen sealing, general contracting, readymix concrete, and aggregate production. All staff formerly employed by Ashby Bros have been absorbed into Bitumix." [396]

W Stevenson and Sons

As the official Stevenson history tells it:

"In 1912, brothers William and Jim worked for their father (also named William) at his modest drainage business. These three pioneers would soon transform their small business into the large organisation that Stevenson is today…

"…by 1921 Stevenson & Sons branched out into construction. Armed with picks, shovels, a few wheelbarrows and a Model-T Ford, the Stevensons went out in search of work. Sons William and Jim took over the business when their father became ill, and were later joined by William's three sons [Bill, Jack and Ross]. They soon became one of the forerunners in the industry with their fleet of trucks, caterpillar tractors, and earthmoving machinery used to construct drainage tunnels, runways, dams, and motorways." [397]

A great number of tenders were won by W Stevenson and Sons during the 1920s, the details of which were published by The New Zealand Herald and the Auckland Star. Just a few of these included:

"The Mount Albert Borough Council met last evening…The tender of Messrs W Stevenson and Sons of £8986 for the sewerage of Reimers Avenue was accepted." [398]

"The engineer for the Northcote drainage scheme…last night informed the borough council that Messrs W Stevenson and Sons, to whom the contracts had been let for the various works connected with the drainage system, had started with the work…" [399]

"The One Tree Hill Road Board met last evening…W Stevenson and Sons' tender of £14,860 10s for the supply of concrete pipes in connection with the board's eastern area drainage scheme was the lowest tender and was accepted." [400]

"Somewhere under the hill between Orakei and Kohimarama the workmen who are tunnelling for the main intercepting sewer that is being provided by the Auckland and Suburban Drainage Board to connect with Tamaki, in the eastern part of its district, holed through on Tuesday. Work on the sewer was commenced last March and good progress has been made by the contractors, Messrs W Stevenson and Sons, in spite of the depth of the tunnel below the ground level, which has made it impossible to follow the usual method of sewer construction." [401]

"The tender of W Stevenson and Sons at £12,751 4s 6d, for the construction of branch sewer No. IB was accepted, being the lowest of eight alternative tenders submitted by four firms. It provided for the use of concrete pipes. This sewer will run from Lochiel Road, Green Lane, across the Ellerslie racecourse, to a point on Great South Road a little below the Harp of Erin. It will drain portions of the One Tree Hill, Ellerslie and Remuera districts." [402]

W Stevenson and Sons was registered as a limited liability company on 24 September 1931 [403] the establishment of which was recorded by The New Zealand Herald:

"The following private company has been registered in Auckland: W Stevenson and Sons Limited, to take over the business of W Stevenson and Sons, road-makers, drainers, contractors in all branches, plumbers, etc. Capital, £10,000 in £1 shares. Subscribers: William Stevenson, 4422 shares; William Alfred Stevenson and James Muir Stevenson, 2788 shares each." [404]

Not only had W Stevenson and Sons expanded its operations well beyond the borders of Auckland City by 1935, the company had also established itself as a reliable road maker — as reported by the Pahiatua Herald in April of that year:

"The monthly meeting of the Pahiatua County Council was held on Saturday…Reporting on the progress made by the contractors, Messrs W Stevenson and Sons, with the tar-sealing of the main road, the consulting engineers…stated: the sealing of the southern portion has been done…The reconstruction of the northern portion is nearly completed with the exception of drainage. About half a mile of sealing of this has been done…The contractor has been doing very well and we should be pleased if you were able to make the payment as asked by him." [405]

The company's road-construction services continued to improve North Island roads into 1938:

"The Franklin County Council this week approved the lowest tender received for the reconstruction and tarsealing of 5 miles 67 chains of the Runciman-Paerata road. It has recommended the acceptance of the tender to the Main Highways Board. The tender is from W Stevenson and Sons Limited of Hastings and the amount is approximately £15,000. The completion of the work will give a paved surface for the full 30 miles from Auckland to Pukekohe." [406]

The company history continues:

"In 1948 W Stevenson & Sons began the removal of overburden at the Kopuku opencast coal mine. This was a significant project which lasted over 39 years…By 1960 Stevenson & Sons had over 100 Caterpillar machines on the job, the largest privately-owned fleet of Caterpillars in the Southern hemisphere. The Kopuku opencast mine is still in operation today, producing 239,390 tonnes of sub-bituminous coal.

"United Concrete was established in the South Auckland suburb of Takanini in 1962. Stevenson partnered with United Concrete and owned 50% of the business. The following year, a plant was established in Gavin Street in Penrose, where our ready mixed concrete plant still operates today…By 1987, Stevenson had gained 100% of the United Concrete business.

"In 2018 Fulton Hogan acquired Stevenson Construction Materials, securing Drury quarry, four ready-mix concrete plants, transport, and a lab testing facility. Now fully owned by Fulton Hogan, Stevenson's concrete plants provide the Auckland region with high-quality ready-mix concrete, made from top quality aggregates sourced from the Drury quarry." [407]

Farrier-Waimak

Farrier-Waimak Limited started in 1919 as Farrier and Walker, "…carting coal and timber by horse and dray in the Christchurch district. Soon the business expanded into carting shingle out of the Waimakariri river." [408]

The firm was founded by Mr Henry Edward Farrier who died in January 1955. The business was subsequently taken over by his son, L E A Farrier.

Henry Farrier's Christchurch Press obituary read:

"Mr Henry Edward Farrier…founded one of the largest private contracting companies in New Zealand with a fleet of more than 70 vehicles. Mr Farrier was born in Wollongong, New South Wales in 1889 and came to Christchurch in 1906.

"Companies he controlled supplied many thousands of yards of shingle for the construction of many of Canterbury's country roads. He pioneered the use of the bulldozer for roading construction and clearing of building sites in Canterbury.

"Big contracts he carried out included the widening of the mouth of the Orari river and the supplying of thousands of yards of shingle for the construction of the Belfast-Woodend section of the Main North road. He also supplied shingle for the construction of many of Christchurch's largest buildings…

"He was the first contractor to set up a plant on the banks of the Waimakariri river to use river shingle for roading and building…In 1919 he founded the firm of Farrier and Walker Ltd which in 1931 became Farrier and Company Ltd.

"In 1944 the firm purchased Waimak Shingle and Sand Ltd and in 1952 acquired the controlling shares in F J Perham Ltd." [409]

As a result of this expansion, Farrier and Company Limited became known as Farrier-Waimak Limited, advertising the company as early as July 1955 as:

"Growing with Canterbury" and that it could "…do your job Faster, Cheaper and Better…" its "…Men and Machines Unmatched at "…Excavating Building Sites, Sub-Division Work, Roading Work and Sealing, Shingle Deliveries, Earth Moving, Section Levelling & Gorse Clearing…" and that the company had the "Largest Mobile Crushing and Screening Plant in NZ…weighs 23 Tons…Designed and Built by our own Engineers…" [410]

As a member of the Wellington Stock Exchange, Farrier-Waimak offered the public 50,000 ordinary shares of £1 each from 1 August 1955. [411]

By March 1960, Farrier-Waimak was able to report to its shareholders:

"Trading for the first six months of the present financial year has been satisfactory, directors report. The company has successfully tendered for sufficient Ministry of Works and county contracts to keep its plant fully occupied for the roading season. The shingle and bitumen plants at Coutts Island are also performing well, outputs being slightly up on the same period last year. Because of the seasonal nature of the business any forecasts of the year's results would be premature. However, present indications are that good progress is being made, the report says." [412]

Successful tenders in 1960 included:

"The tender of £11,240 by Farrier-Waimak Ltd was accepted by the City Council last evening for reconstruction of Westminster street. The contract includes sewer laterals and the Drainage Board concurred in the acceptance." [413]

And in April 1964:

"For reconstruction of Papanui road between Mays road and Paparoa street, the council accepted a tender of £25,958 by Farrier-Waimak Ltd. The tender was the lowest of three, and gave October 31 as the completion date." [414]

In November 1964, road construction and sealing competition encouraged Farrier-Waimak to look to additional profit-making opportunities:

"Farrier-Waimak is to manufacture concrete blocks and hopes to help satisfy the big demand in Christchurch…Shareholders were told about the company's block-making plans in a circular recently from the chairman (Mr C W Evans). Emphasising the need for diversification, Mr Evans said that Farrier-Waimak could not depend on the company's normal contracting work for profit because of 'fierce and unrelenting' competition…" [415]

Nevertheless, the production of bitumen and aggregates remained the company's core activity — as reported by the Christchurch Press in August 1965:

"…by the banks of the Waimakariri river, Farrier-Waimak Ltd have this year installed the South Island's biggest hot mix plant capable of turning out 60 tons of hot mix a day. Bitumen storage tanks at the plant hold more than 50,000 gallons and the giant crusher can produce more than 1000 tons of all grades of metal and sand daily." [416]

Although record profits were achieved, the Directors' Report of October 1972 sounded a note of concern for the road construction industry:

"Farrier-Waimak Ltd achieved its best ever result in the year to June 30. The net profit rose by 28 per cent to $45,245, the full accounts show…

"Mr Evans says that the higher turnover reflects increased sales of aggregates and ready-mixed concrete. Contract sales were slightly lower; contract activity with the company's own fleet and plant was about the same, but payments for hire and sub-contracts were less.

"The inadequacy of National Roads Board funds and the policy of many local authorities of doing much or all of their own road construction work, often uneconomically, we believe, indicate disturbing trends…" [417]

That concern for the road construction industry came to a head in Canterbury in November 1979:

"Because of declining sales of ready-mix concrete the future of Farrier-Waimak Ltd is largely dependent on how long BP New Zealand Ltd intends to sponsor the price-cutting war in the road-sealing industry in Canterbury. Farrier-Waimak's chairman (Mr C W Evans) told shareholders at the annual general meeting yesterday that the continued prosperity of Farriers is dependent on obtaining a reasonable share of road sealing work. A continuance of the price cutting tactics of BP through Road Developments Ltd will have far-reaching effects, he said…

"Mr. Evans said that the prices quoted by Road Developments were so low that Farrier-Waimak would not recover its direct costs if it performed work at that figure…This leads to the conclusion that BP is prepared to make contracting losses to win road sealing work for the bitumen content alone…

"However, the company is trying to ameliorate these effects by diversification. Recently Farrier-Waimak purchased the bituminous emulsion plant from Wright Stephenson. This manufactures the Coalfix brand of bituminous emulsion. Preparations are being made to move the plant to the Pound Road branch where it will be operated by the company's staff. Efforts will be made to encourage the Ministry of Works and local bodies to use emulsion for road sealing purposes as the process does not involve diesel and kerosene cut-back agents…" [418]

As predicted, Farrier-Waimak Ltd made a substantial loss in the six months to December 31 1979 — as reported by the Christchurch Press in March 1980:

"The chairman (Mr C W Evans) yesterday reported an unaudited loss of $140,919…Mr Evans says that the loss is largely the direct result of the loss of contract sales and lower prices caused by the entry of an international oil company into the road sealing industry in Canterbury.

In the annual report last year Mr. Evans said that the new competitor…had gained more than 60 per cent of the sealing work let out for tender so far this season. The company was subsequently identified as the subsidiary of BP New Zealand Ltd, Road Developments Ltd.

"In November Mr Evans told Farrier Waimak's annual meeting that the prices quoted by Road Developments were so low that Farrier-Waimak would not recover its direct costs if it performed work at that figure…'The prospects for the second half cannot be considered promising. Forward work for the contract division is minimal, and the continuing downward trend for aggregate and ready-mixed concrete sales gives no ground for optimism,' Mr Evans says." [419]

During 1979, Farrier-Waimak had "…taken over from Wrightson NMA Ltd and re-assembled at its Yaldhurst depot, the plant for the manufacture of bitumenous emulsion, selling under the 'Colfix' trade name…" [420]

In October 1980, the Farrier-Waimak chairman (Mr C W Evans) was able to report:

"The 'Colfix' plant was making a contribution to profits…In two years the price of bitumen had increased 132 per cent from $130 to $302 a tonne, doubling the oil company share of a normal road-sealing contract from about 22 per cent to 44 per cent…" [421]

Naturally, those paying for the cost of road construction and sealing by October 1982 were not that happy:

"Road-sealing prices have risen to a level above what is considered to be a 'fair and reasonable price', the Ministry of Works and Development resident engineer, Mr J O Ballantyne, reported with 'some distress' to a half-yearly meeting of the No. 13 District Roads Council at Cheviot. It would be fair to say that in many cases all tenders had been declined and the jobs readvertised on a different basis, said the District Commissioner of Works, Mr R D Grant, when asked to elaborate on the report…" [422]

The following year, in October 1983, the Christchurch Press reported:

"Farrier-Waimak Ltd has sold its road sealing and construction division to Pavroc Holdings Ltd the chairman, Mr H W Richardson, told shareholders at yesterday's annual meeting. Competition for the road sealing and construction work in the Canterbury region has been intense in the last four years and companies have been fighting hard for a market share ever since Road Developments Ltd, a BP New Zealand Ltd subsidiary, came on the scene.

"Mr Richardson said that the division was sold on October 31 and that it would enable Farrier-Waimak to concentrate on shingle and concrete production…

"Pavroc Holdings was formed from the merger of British Pavements (Canterbury) Ltd and Road Carpets Ltd in 1978. The firm was taken over by Fulton Hogan Holdings Ltd, the Dunedin-based roading and transport group, in 1981." [423]

Finally, after some 65 years, on 12 April 1984, Farrier-Waimak Limited was no more:

"Farrier-Waimak Ltd yesterday became New Zealand Equities Ltd as shareholders approved changes to the company's name, business, capital structure, and articles of association…

"The name, Farrier-Waimak, will not be lost in the Canterbury region. Farrier's chairman, Mr H W Richardson, and his family interests, have bought the business and the assets of the company, which will be now known as Farrier-Waimak (1984) Ltd without any loss of jobs." [424]

Fulton Hogan

"In Dunedin in 1933, Jules H Fulton and Robert (Bob) Hogan teamed up to start their own contracting business…" [425]

Fulton Hogan Limited was registered on 30 December 1935 with capital of £10,000 "…to carry on in New Zealand or elsewhere the business of practical and consulting engineers and contractors." [426]

It wasn't long before the new company found work on the West Coast — as reported by the Grey River Argus in February 1936:

"At a special meeting of the Westport Borough Council it was decided to accept the tender of Messrs Fulton Hogan Ltd, Dunedin for the tar sealing of the borough streets…" [427]

The contract price tendered was £11,538 13s 8d. [428]

As well as the tar sealing of streets and highways, Fulton Hogan was also acclaimed for the sealing of cycleways, arguably considered more important in December 1938 than they are today:

"Messrs Fulton Hogan of Dunedin, the well-known sealing contractors, have completed the sealing of the cycling track at Cass Square [Hokitika], and the members of the Club made a final inspection on Thursday evening and were well pleased with the work…" [429]

Meanwhile, tenders for road reconstruction and sealing continued to be accepted by the Public Works Department — as reported by the Otago Daily Times in December 1939:

"Rangitata-Geraldine main highway: Reconstruction and sealing—£13,191" and "Timaru-Cromwell and Milton-Queenstown State highways: Sealing—£10,331." [430]

Fulton Hogan was named as a co-founder with a 46 per cent shareholding of Fernhill Lime Company Limited, lime merchants and manufacturers, incorporated at Invercargill in October 1941. [431]

A second limestone manufacturing company, Totara Lime Works Limited, was founded at Oamaru in October 1945 with Fulton Hogan holding 73 per cent of the original shares issued. [432]

In 1950 Fulton Hogan acquired its first asphalt business, the Fairfield Asphalt Company Limited, [433] later described as: "A progressive company involved in road construction, paving and sealing in Otago and Southland…" [434]

In order to oversee its growing portfolio of subsidiary companies, Fulton Hogan Holdings Limited was incorporated at Dunedin on 24 April 1952 with a Capital of £150,000. Jules H Fulton and Robert (Bob) Hogan were the majority shareholders. [435]

As well as the many South Island road contracts undertaken by the Fulton Hogan Group, the construction and sealing of various airport runways was also carried out — as reported by the Christchurch Press in December 1967:

"Tenders for the sealing of the Queenstown Airport at Frankton have been accepted by the Ministry of Works, the district engineer (Mr F Unwin) said in Dunedin today. The successful tenderers were Fulton Hogan Ltd who will be responsible for the earthwork and metalling of the runway…" [436]

In 1970, Fulton Hogan expanded its operations outside of Otago and Southland for the first time with a 50% acquisition of Tasman Asphalt at Nelson. [437]

In the meantime, the Fulton Hogan Group continued to operate its bitumen plant at Fairfield, Dunedin — advertising for a plant manager in September 1976:

"Fulton Hogan Holdings, Limited Bitumen Plant Manager…Involves responsibility for the operating, maintenance and administration of the Group's subsidiary, Bitumen Sales Limited. Includes receiving of cargo from ocean tankers, blending and supply of bitumen product and the manufacture and supply of bitumen emulsions…" [438]

Another Fulton Hogan acquisition operating from Fairfield was Maxwell Bros Limited — a company that: "…operates a modern fleet of some 60 heavy vehicles, trailers and cars…operating throughout Otago..." [439]

Following Fulton Hogan's takeover of Pavroc Holdings Limited in May 1981, [440] Shell Oil acquired a 25 per cent holding in the Group. This shareholding was increased to 38 per cent in 1989. [441]

In April 1987, Daveys Concrete Limited, by then a subsidiary of Fulton Hogan Holdings, in turn acquired Unit Concrete Limited [442] and in September of that year:

"Owens Investments yesterday announced the sale of Burnett Construction Services to Fulton Hogan Holdings Ltd for an undisclosed sum…Burnett Construction comprises the road works, shingle operations and concrete services of the Burnett Transport Group which is a wholly owned subsidiary of Owens Investments." [443]

By January 1989, Fulton Hogan's Fairfield workshops had expanded considerably — as advertised by the Christchurch Press:

"Fulton Hogan Ltd — Engineering Manager — We Wish To Appoint a Senior person to the above position which Involves the management of our Maintenance/Engineering Division employing 40 staff.

"Trades include Automotive, Engineering, Hydraulics, Painting and Electrical. The Company is based at Fairfield, 12km south of Dunedin. The Division services a large fleet of company vehicles and plant from cars to earthmoving machinery. We also service outside clients and have Service Agencies for Fiat, Scania, Mercedes-Benz, Hitachi, Fiat Allis…" [444]

The year 1989 proved to be a turning point for Fulton Hogan's subsidiary, Pavroc Holdings:

"Three hundred thousand paving blocks have been individually picked up and put down by Pavroc's workmen to bring Stage Two of the redevelopment of the [Christchurch] City Mall to completion — and that is just on the surface. Beneath the new paving lie many man-hours of drainage and concrete work.

"Pavroc, which has now changed its name to Fulton Hogan Canterbury Ltd won the tender for the redevelopment and began work in mid-July…

"Fulton Hogan, a South Island-owned and based private company, is one of the biggest civil contractors in New Zealand and has owned Pavroc since 1981. It has a staff of 1200 throughout the country, 20 per cent of whom are shareholders, and it has a turnover of $140 million." [445]

In 1989, Fulton Hogan also extended its operations into the Auckland, Waikato and Northland regions with the acquisition of Reliable Roads Limited. [446]

Expansion continued — including the acquisition of four ready-mix plants, Drury Quarry, transport and laboratory business of W A Stevenson & Sons Limited in 2018.

"Today [2025], Fulton Hogan employs more than 7,800 people across New Zealand and Australia." [447]

Reliable Roads

Reliable Roads Limited was incorporated on 11 November 1947 [448] and soon earned a reputation for road construction and paving. By the 1970s, the company's tenders accepted for Ministry of Works and Development included such projects as:

"Mount Roskill - Wiri Motorway, Stage 1: Mahunga Drive connection — amount of tender accepted $33,223.64." [449]

"Government Stores Board: Sylvia Park Shipping Store, Auckland: asphaltic concrete paving and associated work — amount of tender accepted $27,829.40." [450]

However, by 1977, Reliable Roads Limited had become a subsidiary of Firth Industries Limited — as reported by the Christchurch Press in July 1978:

"Sales by Firth Industries Ltd in the three months to June, at $5,074,000, were running 33 per cent ahead of the corresponding previous quarter, the deputy chairman (Mr P R Blomkamp) told the annual meeting in Auckland. However, $1,294,000 or 25.5 per cent of the revenue was from subsidiaries acquired since last year…

"We want to reduce our dependency on the building industry and our entry into the road-paving and road-sealing business is proving successful. Both Waikato Bitumen and Reliable Roads are well managed, profitable businesses and their futures seem assured…

"Fletcher Holdings Ltd now owns about 33 per cent of the Firth capital but Fletcher involvement had not altered the direction Firth would take in the future, said Mr Blomkamp." [451]

By September 1988, Reliable Roads Limited had become part of Reliable Group Holdings Limited [452] consisting of several subsidiaries including:

Northland Roadbuilders Limited (originally registered 14 October 1957), Waikato Bitumen Company Limited (originally registered 30 August 1938), Allied Asphalt Limited (originally registered 16 April 1970), Associated Emulsions Limited (originally registered 12 March 1986), and Wilson Rothery Contractors Limited (originally registered 21 October 1983). [453]

As previously noted, Fulton Hogan extended its operations into the Auckland, Waikato and Northland regions with the acquisition of Reliable Roads Limited in 1989 and the company's name was subsequently changed to Fulton Hogan Contracting Limited on 31 March 1989. [454]

Wilson, Rothery

Originally called Wilson and Rothery Limited, the company was wound up and replaced by Wilson, Rothery Limited, registered in Auckland as carriers and contractors, on 2 October 1930 with a Capital of £5000. Initial Shareholders were: "Percy Rothery, Samuel John Finley Wilson, May Aubyre Wilson, Irene Rothery…" [455] The registered office of the new company was situated at the corner of Lunn Avenue and Panmure Road, Panmure… [456]

In March 1943, the share capital of Wilson Rothery Limited was increased from £5000 to £10,000 [457] and, by 1945, the company was operating a quarry at Ferndale Road, Mount Wellington.

By November 1969, Wilson Rothery Limited was one of the main contractors building additions to Auckland's LynnMall Shopping Centre [458] and, with a tender of $122,757.72, the company was chosen by the Ministry of Works and Development to develop the site for extensions to the Mount Albert Line Depot. [459]

The commercial activities of Wilson Rothery were not confined to the North Island — as reported by the Christchurch Press in August 1982:

"Preliminary site development work will begin at the Castle Hill Village mountain resort next month. [Castle Hill Village is located in the Canterbury high country 100km west of Christchurch.] A spokesman for the developer…said that the contract had been let to Wilson Rothery Ltd of Auckland, and that the company would begin work when it had finished a big contract in Nelson. The site would be landscaped and roading, sewerage, water, and storm water facilities installed…" [460]

By September 1982, Wilson Rothery Limited, as Civil Engineering Contractors, were advertising for:

"Operators And Pipelayers…" for their branches at Auckland, Nelson, and Christchurch. [461] As noted earlier, Wilson Rothery Limited later became part of the Reliable Group and subsequently Fulton Hogan Contracting in 1989.

Waikato Bitumen Company

The Waikato Bitumen Company Limited was incorporated at Auckland as bitumen manufacturers on 30 August 1938 with a capital of £4000. The original shareholders were J W Brown, C B Davis, J A Grinter, and F Grinter. [462]

By January 1939, the company had established itself at Clarence Street, Hamilton advertising itself as "Suppliers of Hot Bitumen and KoldSeal Emulsion. We deliver in bulk or drum lots, all complete with spraying outfits. Estimates given free of charge. For Paths, Tennis Courts, Drives, etc." [463]

In January 1946, the Hauraki Plains Gazette reported:

"Advice that the Main Highways Board had now given approval to the acceptance of the tender of the Waikato Bitumen Company for re-sealing of Orongo-Netherton, Ngatea-Turua and Pipiroa-Kopu main highways was received from the Paeroa Public works Department at the January meeting of the Hauraki Plains County Council." [464]

The company's continuing commercial success was demonstrated in 1976 when:

"Firth Industries (Hamilton) Ltd, through the issue of 315,700 ordinary shares, acquired a 50 per cent shareholding in Waikato Bitumen Company Ltd and a 10 per cent shareholding in the Auckland roading company, Reliable Roads Ltd. The investments represent an entry by Firth into the bitumen roading business which the directors consider give a measure of diversification to the company. Waikato Bitumen is already a large customer of the Firth-owned quarry at Karamu…" [465]

The following year, Firth's acquisition was shown to be a worthwhile investment — as reported by the Christchurch Press in June 1977:

"The profit increase of 32 per cent to $1,275,000 reported by Firth Industries Ltd last month was due, in part, to the contribution of Waikato Bitumen Company Ltd of which Firth secured a half-share during the year to March 26." [466]

By November 1979, Shell Oil New Zealand Limited also held a 40 per cent shareholding of Waikato Bitumen Limited [467] while the Fletcher Group had by then acquired all the shares in Firth Industries. [468]

Thus, Fletcher Construction also acquired roading interests with a 50 per cent ownership in Waikato Bitumen Company Limited and Reliable Roads Limited. [469]

Firth Industries

A description of its new subsidiary was published in the Fletcher Group Winter 1979 magazine, arrowhead — parts of which included:

"The name of Firth has been virtually synonymous with concrete and concrete products since the 1930s. Vibrabloc masonry, precast products, concrete tanks and readymix concrete are some of the products for which the Hamilton-based company is best known. Firth is also involved in mining Hinuera stone and three quarries are a source of metal chips and lime.

"The company's interest in roading, representing a sizeable percentage of its turnover, is manifested by majority holdings in Waikato Bitumen Co Ltd and Reliable Roads Ltd.

"The association between Fletchers and Firth dates back to 1973 when the latter purchased Decrapac, the Fletcher block-making facility in Auckland, with the Fletcher Group taking a 15 per cent holding in Firth as consideration.

"Following steady buying of Firth shares by Fletchers over the intervening years, the Examiner of Trade Practices approved in September 1977 an application by the Fletcher Group to increase its shareholding to 45 per cent. More recently, shareholders of Firth Industries accepted the Fletcher offer to take up all their shares.

"The company from which Firth Industries was to evolve was formed at Rangiriri, north of Hamilton, in May 1925. The Ironclad Products Company was formed by brothers E B (Ted) and G M (Tony) Firth to manufacture the Firth Ironclad Pumice Washing Boiler. It had been developed by their father in the backyard of the family's Auckland home.

"After the first six months in business the brothers began to broaden the range to include concrete troughs and other agricultural products. Growth was inevitably slow during the depression but, in 1932, seven years after the company was founded, it hired its first employee.

"By the late 1930s the country's public works programme was in full swing, bringing new opportunities for the company which by now had changed its name to the Firth Concrete Company…

"Throughout the fifties more factories were opened in the central North Island and in 1952 the Company began to make pipes. In 1959 the company appointed its first sales representative, Mr Peter Blomkamp, now managing director of the new concrete and aggregates group.

"During the sixties the company recorded a seven hundred per cent turnover increase. A large readymix concrete batch plant was established at Rotorua and the company's first Columbia block-making machine was purchased in 1960…

"Two metal quarries at New Plymouth and Karamu, near Hamilton, and the lime quarry at Hastings make up the Firth quarry division which supplies the aggregate used in concrete making…

"Operating subsidiaries of Firth are W T Trethewey & Sons Ltd, the Christchurch stone-processing firm, Waikato Bitumen Co Limited (60 per cent owned) and Reliable Roads Ltd (60 per cent owned)…

"Firth's new Wellington aggregate division also enjoys a high reputation among its many customers, including Vibrapac, because of its wide range of concrete aggregates and roading materials. Out of 40 different products it manufactures, 30 are produced to either New Zealand Standard Association specifications or National Roads Board standards…" [470]

The Pothole Prevention Fund

This chapter began with a brief overview of the need for good roads of an even and durable surface; and of how, as early as 1865, Auckland's Ponsonby Road required constant attention to maintain it in a safe condition. Some 160 years later, despite our progress from horse and carriage to the most modern vehicles, our streets and highways, including Ponsonby Road, still require constant repair.

Even accounting for the increased weight and number of vehicles that now rumble along these roads, it would seem that our road-construction methods and their composition have consistently failed, and continue to do so.

Hence the need for a Band-aid to protect the Road Gang's legacy and the billions of dollars already spent supporting it — as reported by The New Zealand Herald in June 2024:

"The Government will spend billions of dollars over the next three years fixing and preventing potholes on state highways and local roads nationwide. Auckland will get a $478 million boost in pothole funding; Waikato will get $214 million and Canterbury has been allocated $187 million in funding.

"Transport Minister Simeon Brown announced today $2.07 billion in funding would go towards state highway potholes and $1.9 billion for local road potholes…[Auckland Mayor] Brown claimed there were more than 62,000 potholes on State Highways that needed repairing and which have been causing damage to vehicles, disruption to travel and freight plans, and pose a risk to public safety…" [471]

In September 2024, Transport Minister, Simeon Brown, announced the establishment of a fleet of five 'Consistent Condition Data Collection' (CCDC) survey vans, each of which would patrol different sections of the country's roads "…hoovering up data to monitor the state of our roads and work out when they need maintenance." [472]

Such a modern innovation has come just a little too late for the injured Mr Bacon of the Odd Fellows' Arms whose horse stumbled on a poorly-maintained Ponsonby Road in 1865 but progress at last… [473]

Chapter Eleven

Consequences

Automobilism

For more than a century, the Road Gang, supported by its main beneficiaries, the politicians, has encouraged New Zealanders to purchase motor vehicles and to build roads to accommodate them. Consequently, access to reliable public transport has remained a secondary consideration for Auckland commuters since they lost their tramway service in 1956.

The flawed Auckland Master Transportation Plan of 1955 which prioritised the motor vehicle and roads over public transport systems actually predated America's decision to build the transcontinental highways on which New Zealand's motorways were modelled. Unfortunately, New Zealand lacked the funds to supplement the alternative transport systems that were also established in American cities.

It was in June 1956, that President Eisenhower signed the Federal Highway Act, which established America's Interstate Highway System:

"As a general during World War II, Eisenhower was impressed by Germany's autobahn system and he decided that the United States needed something comparable. After the war, the economy was booming and Eisenhower decided the time was right to push through the Interstate Highway System.

"It was the largest public works project in American history. It took longer than expected to build — 35 years instead of 12 — and it cost more than $100 billion, about three times the initial budget. But the first coast-to-coast interstate highway, I-80, was completed in 1986, running from New York City to San Francisco.

"It was a great boon for hotel and fast-food chains, which sprung up by interstate exits. It was also a boon for suburban living, since commuting was faster and easier than before. But it was not necessarily good for American literature. When John Steinbeck took a cross-country trip with his dog and wrote *Travels with Charley* (1962), he only travelled on the interstate for one section, on I-90 between Erie, Pennsylvania, and Chicago, Illinois.

"He wrote: 'These great roads are wonderful for moving goods but not for inspection of a countryside. You are bound to the wheel and your eyes to the car ahead and to the rear-view mirror for the car behind and at the same time you must read all the signs for fear you may miss some instructions or orders. No roadside stands selling squash juice, no antique stores, no farm products. When we get these thruways across the whole country, as we will and must, it will be possible to drive from New York to California without seeing a single thing.'" [1]

Headless Chicken Syndrome

As Hayden Donnell wrote in his 2022 New Zealand Geographic article, Streetscapes:

"It is tempting to see our cities as the product of forces beyond our control. But cities are a result of thousands of choices — decisions about who or what is important — and it's only relatively recently that cars took centre stage…set in motion in 1955, with the tabling of a dry report titled Master Transport Plan. It outlined a minor revolution in the city's transport system.

"At the time, Auckland's 387,000 residents were taking roughly 100 million public transport trips every year –— 258 each on average –— mostly thanks to the city's popular electric trams. The report's authors said Auckland was too sprawling for that to be feasible in the future. They suggested a different model: a state-of-the-art urban motorway system…

"Politicians were won over. In the coming years, Auckland's extensive tram network was ripped up. Bulldozers carved their way through Grafton Gully, demolishing whole neighbourhoods, and motorways began to hem the city centre." [2]

Details of the 'Master Transportation Plan for Metropolitan Auckland', included in a previous chapter, describe what soon became unsuccessful attempts to reverse, or at least modify, the effects wrought by the huge number of motor vehicles that eventually flooded the country.

The Plan superseded a number of public transport initiatives outlined in Part Two of Auckland's transport history, *Gas Pedal to Back Pedal*, including the promotion in the 1970s of a rapid transit network by Auckland's Mayor, Sir Dove-Myer Robinson. As always, the success of such an infrastructure scheme depended on Government support and finance — almost achieved prior to the November 1975 general election, but not quite.

Unfortunately, the Labour Government, which had tentatively promised to support the public transport project, was replaced by a National Government led by Robert Muldoon with whom Sir Dove-Myer had a testy relationship, to say the least.

This was one of many well-planned and almost-financed, Auckland infrastructure projects that have been cancelled or downgraded by newly-elected governments since the 1880s. The National Government's lack of support for Sir Dove-Myer Robinson's rapid transit scheme was the result of its conflicting support for the Road Gang and its motoring interests. The decision was therefore political and not one that fully considered Auckland's future transport needs.

In a New Zealand Herald article by Bernard Orsman, 'Auckland's train chaos highlights national infrastructure worries', published 15 February 2024, he quotes Infrastructure NZ chief executive, Nick Leggett, commenting on Auckland's suburban rail cancellations because of the hot weather then occurring:

"…this isn't the fault of one entity…It's long-term sweating of assets. There has not been enough investment over long periods of time in renewing and maintaining assets that really keep our country moving every day and keep us healthy and connected.

"…he believes independent project pipelines that take an overarching view of projects would be more beneficial, instead of new governments coming in and changing priorities every few years.

"It's bad for efficiency, and we don't get the best bang for our buck. So we've got to line this stuff up, depoliticise it, make sure that it goes on beyond the election cycle, and really accept that infrastructure shouldn't be politicised in the way that it has been…" [3]

In the meantime, despite the huge cost and time incurred in the planning, the custom continues, with the newly-elected National Government recently (February 2024) cancelling Auckland's light rail project, the planning of which has cost some $228 million over six years. [4]

A later New Zealand Herald article by Tom Dillane revealed that a Government Cabinet paper estimated that: "The disestablishment of the Ministry of Transport's work on the Auckland Light Rail project will likely cost millions of dollars spent over six months…" [5]

Similar transport projects, such as cycle lanes promised by the former Government, are also to be scrapped or downgraded, including the planning for any new harbour crossing which would now focus on the provision of extra lanes for traffic and not a light rail connection or the pedestrian access previously proposed. [6]

As might be expected, the thinking of New Zealand's National Party very much coincides with that of the United Kingdom's Conservative Party and that country's previous Prime Minister — as reported by Peter Walker of The Guardian in September 2023:

"Rishi Sunak, has pledged to end 'anti-car measures' as he set out a series of ideas to prioritise the needs of drivers at the likely expense of other road users such as bus passengers, cyclists and pedestrians.

"Outlining what he called a 'long-term plan to back drivers', the Prime Minister unveiled a clampdown on 20mph limits, bus lanes, low traffic neighbourhoods (LTNs), and the ability of councils to fine drivers who commit offences.

"The plan also pledges to stop councils implementing so-called 15-minute cities to 'prevent schemes which aggressively restrict where people can drive'…While much of the plan…is framed as a consultation, it marks a notable shift in transport policy, going against efforts by recent UK governments to try to ease congestion by making modes of travel other than the car more appealing." [7]

15-Minute Cities

"The idea of a 15-minute city is relatively new — first outlined in 2016 by Carlos Moreno of Pantheon-Sorbonne University in Paris — and none has arguably been created yet. But it is a concept that has gained significant prominence…

"At its heart, this is an urbanism concept, a framework rather than a specific plan: trying to gradually change cities so people tend to live relatively close to shops, workplaces and other amenities. With this comes an inevitable shift from car trips to walking, cycling and public transport." [8]

Of course, the concept of a 15-minute city poses a direct threat to New Zealand's Road Gang and the profits which it has enjoyed since acceptance of the Master Transportation Plan for Metropolitan Auckland by impressionable politicians and the public. The concept of an inner city utopia is also anathema to other Road Gang beneficiaries — the big-city property developers who have encouraged road users to drive down the motorway to purchase their suburban properties.

The long-anticipated start of the City Rail Link, planned for 2026, and general suburban rail improvements will encourage more to live in the greater city area with no need to own a motor vehicle — for decades, one of the main reasons for the Road Gang's opposition to any public transport system in Auckland and other cities.

However, those living in the outer suburbs, remote from railway services, will continue to rely on the motor vehicle for transport. Despite any proposed improvement by means of dedicated bus lanes, the intense competition for road space will undoubtedly remain.

Road Congestion

Congestion can be defined as a competition for road space, the need for one vehicle to take the place of the one in front as soon as possible — usually at a snail's pace during peak times — or when a huge number of vehicles congregate at a particular venue ill-served by road design.

The latter case occurred on a wet afternoon in November 2023 when the motorway adjacent to the Auckland borough of Newmarket became gridlocked. The flood of vehicles backed up to the roads adjacent to a shopping mall preventing egress from its carpark for hours — as reported by Radio New Zealand's Felix Walton:

"People just couldn't get out and some of that appears to be because of how the roads are configured around the mall…the traffic lights did not leave enough room for drivers to exit the car park at a reasonable pace…Newmarket would've seen upwards of 70,000 people visit the precinct…Historically, from research we've done, 60 per cent would be coming by car — so therein lies the problem." [9]

In Great Britain, motorway speed has taken on a new meaning — as reported by the International Express in March 2024:

"Traffic crawls along so slowly on stretches of Britain's motorways that it would be quicker to cycle, figures reveal. On congested parts of the network the average speed is so low, pedal power would be more beneficial to beat the jams. The slowest motorway is the M57 which circles Liverpool, where analysts have calculated the average speed to be 13.5mph. London's orbital, the M25, has sections where drivers fail to get above 20mph.

"And the Department of Transport figures, which are calculated over a 24-hour period, reveal there are five motorways which have at least one section where the average speed is below 30mph. Speeds during rush hour are considerably slower. Overall the M32 in the west of England had the slowest average speed over its entire length, at just 48.1mph…" [10]

Larger Vehicles

As New Zealand's roads have become increasingly congested, year by year, the build-up of motor vehicles vying for less space has been further compromised by the increasing size of those vehicles.

As Adrienne Bernhard of the BBC wrote in February 2024:

"Car shapes and sizes have steadily ballooned since the late 1970s. The reasons for this increase are various and complex. The addition of safety features like lateral and frontal airbags and 'crumple zones' require more space…The majority of vehicles in the UK used to be designed and produced in Britain with narrow English streets in mind. Now, vehicles in the UK (and the EU) tend to be larger imports designed to navigate the urban sprawl and looping freeways found elsewhere.

"In 2020, the average mass of new cars in the EU and the UK increased to 1.457 tonnes, 3% higher than in 2019 and 15% above 2001 levels.

"Even a stationary SUV can be a significant problem in a city that evolved around smaller cars. In 2023, Which? — an organisation that tests consumer products and services — found that 161 car models were too big for the average parking space in the UK. Twenty-seven of those models were so wide that it would be difficult to open the doors while constrained within a single parking bay…

"Cars fitted with electric batteries can also become weighty projectiles in the event of a crash…Battery electric SUVs often have batteries that are two to three times larger than small cars." [11]

The Congestion Question

In New Zealand, Parliament's Transport and Infrastructure Committee initiated an inquiry into congestion pricing [in Auckland] on 18 March 2021 and reported in August of that year.

A few of the Committee's recommendations included:

"…progress legislation to enable New Zealand cities to use congestion pricing as a tool in transport planning

"…implement a congestion pricing scheme in Auckland including:

"a region-wide strategic corridors scheme starting in the city centre

"an access charge that would apply once per journey in peak times

"the of use automatic number plate recognition (ANPR) technology to identify vehicles that incur a charge

"use any revenue raised by a congestion pricing scheme to:

"mitigate equity impacts

"reinvest in public and active transport in the region where the charge applies…" [12]

As of February 2024, the phasing in of congestion charges for Central Auckland from 2025, proposed by the Congestion Question report, had been superseded by an Auckland Transport timetable that proposed "…a congestion charging scheme be in place by the time the city rail link opens in 2026." [13]

By June 2024, the new National Coalition Government had decided that congestion charges would, indeed, be a fresh, modern method by which the motorist could pay for his and her privilege of congregating along Auckland's roads — roads already paid for by way of taxes since the early 1900s:

"The Government looks set to replace the Auckland Regional Fuel Tax with time-of-use congestion charges to help pay for its Roads of National Significance (Rons) programme…

"The 11.5c-a-litre fuel tax which has cost Auckland motorists $150 million a year since its introduction in 2018, ends tomorrow…In place of the fuel tax, the Government plans to introduce time-of-use charging to bill motorists at different times on sections of motorways during the morning and afternoon peak times. Councils will be able to do the same on arterial roads…

"…of the $868m raised from the fuel tax, $440m remained unspent and was ring-fenced by the Government for the Eastern Busway, City Rail Link trains and stabling and road improvements. Of the money that was spent, Auckland transport wasted it on many non-roading projects, including cycle lanes, red-light cameras, speed bumps, and speed limit reductions across the city…" [14]

Congestion Pricing a Reality?

Whether or not congestion pricing in New Zealand will become a reality can perhaps be best judged by the initial politically-influenced reversal of traffic congestion reform that occurred in New York — as reported by The Lever in June 2024:

"New York Gov. Kathy Hochul reversed course and blocked congestion pricing at the last minute — months after taking more than $30,000 from state auto dealers.

"Before her eleventh-hour decision to reverse course and 'indefinitely pause' a landmark plan to charge drivers higher prices for clogging up Manhattan streets, New York Gov. Kathy Hochul (D) received $36,000 from lobbyists for state automobile dealers. Half of that money came from a lobbying group that opposed congestion pricing, citing 'consequences for dealers and the thousands of people they employ…'

"Supporters of the plan hailed it as a major step forward for transit policy in the U.S., saying it could usher in a 'transportation revolution' and serve as a model for other cities looking to fund public transit and improve air quality…

"But auto dealers expressed apprehension about the consequences for dealerships, as the plan was estimated to reduce the number of cars entering the central business district by 17 percent, or 153,000 vehicles. In February, the Greater New York Automobile Dealers Association, a lobbying group for new car dealers in the New York metro area, noted in an email to subscribers that it had 'concerns that the plan could harm businesses and employees within the proposed pricing zone, where nearly all Manhattan [Greater New York Automobile Dealers Association] dealers are located…'

"Hochul has long been a major beneficiary of auto dealers. Since 2018, the Greater New York Automobile Dealers Association has donated a total of $92,700 to Hochul's campaigns, including a $47,100 donation in October 2021, according to campaign finance records. The Automobile Dealers of N.Y. political action committee has contributed almost $78,000 since 2018…

"Currently, air pollutants in the city cause 2,400 deaths per year, along with thousands of emergency department visits and hospitalizations because of asthma and other heart and lung problems, according to an analysis published by the New York City government…" [15]

Fortunately for many New Yorkers, sanity prevailed and the city's congestion pricing began on 5 January 2025. A month later, Metropolitan Transportation Authority reports have been "…undeniably positive with measurably reduced traffic (one million fewer vehicles) and more commuters choosing public transit, aboard buses that are now travelling more quickly across Manhattan." [16]

Early Vehicle Pollution

In 2020, Alexander Trapeznik of the University of Otago and Austin Gee, historian, published an article in the International Review of Environmental History entitled 'The Madding Wheels Of Brazen Chariots Rag'd; Dire Was The Noise': Motoring And The Environment In New Zealand Before The Second World War' — a study that chiefly concentrated on the environmental effects of the motor vehicle in New Zealand. A part of that article included:

"While today the impact of motoring on the environment is often seen in terms of emissions and congestion, in its early decades, concerns were different. Dust, noise and visual pollution resulting from the spread of motor vehicles were the main concerns; the fumes they gave off constituted far less of a problem. In cities, early motor vehicles joined a range of other polluting modes of transport: smoke from railways, noxious waste from horses, noise from trams.

"What attracted the attention of contemporaries was not so much the pollution caused by motor vehicles as what were seen as novel 'nuisances'. Unmuffled exhausts, for instance, attracted sustained criticism as they intruded in places and times when previously there had been an expectation of relative quiet. As early as 1904, a Canterbury newspaper complained 'the evil-smelling, evil-sounding machines are becoming an unmitigated nuisance…'

"Concerns regarding the noise of motor vehicles fitted into an international 'age-of-noise narrative' that formed part of a wider early twentieth-century 'anxiety about the progress of modernity'…" [17]

Alexander Trapeznik's study continues:

"Early motor vehicles entered an urban environment that already contained many other sources of air pollution. Virtually all businesses and private homes relied on coal, wood or oil for power and heating. In both urban and rural areas, dust was a significant problem in dry conditions. The dust 'nuisance' associated with motor vehicles was a development of an existing problem rather than an entirely new one.

"Wind-borne dust had been a nuisance from at least the mid-nineteenth century, especially in dry, windy regions such as Canterbury. The dust on urban roads was considered an important hazard to public health as it contained the dried, powdered residue of animal faeces. In the early 1900s, the 'poisonous bacilli' it contained were blamed for anything from quinsy to enteric catarrh.

"Overseas experience primed New Zealanders to anticipate a problem thrown up by the advent of motor vehicles. Horses' hooves, and the narrow, metal-rimmed wheels of the vehicles they drew, disturbed comparatively little dust. The wider, pneumatic rubber tyres of even the earliest, low-powered cars threw up a great deal more. Initially, the reasons for the difference were a mystery to contemporaries, but experimentation indicated the suction effect of the flexible tyre tread, combined with the movement of air around the car's bodywork, was responsible. At higher speeds, car tyres sucked out the fine binding material from a macadamised road surface, allowing the coarser metalled surface to break up…

"In contrast to the dust they disturbed, the emissions from motor vehicles were rarely considered a problem, except as a potential danger to their owners. Indeed, in the early years so little was known about the nature of motor fumes that they could be seen as a positive health benefit. In 1908, the popular science magazine *Progress* reprinted the opinion of an unnamed Harley Street specialist that the unpleasant smell of motor exhausts was 'a blessing in disguise'.

"'[It] is one of the finest disinfectants going. It clears the air of all germs and impurities. Partially-burnt, carbonised matter is a splendid antiseptic. The creosote vapours which come from a motor car are in reality a health tonic and a brace for the day…It would not do the city man any harm to have several good whiffs of this smell every morning…'

"Shortly before the First World War, several well-publicised cases spread awareness of the dangers of car exhausts in confined spaces, particularly private garages. The syndrome was briefly named 'motocide', but the significance of the colourless, odourless gas carbon monoxide was not widely recognised until the 1920s.

"The dangers of vehicle emissions in large cities overseas were widely reported in the New Zealand press, but with the assurance that there was no danger locally. The vastness of the atmosphere, together with the windiness of most New Zealand cities, was believed sufficient to remove any danger…

"Once the danger of carbon monoxide was generally recognised, concerns began to be expressed about the longer-term effects of vehicle emissions. The 'emission of smothering oil fumes and petrol gases that pollute the atmosphere and pollute human lungs' led one editorial writer in 1933 'to wonder how much longer, and how much more, the atmospheric envelope of the earth can absorb these noxious outpourings'". [18]

Ministry for the Environment Studies

That prescient, unnamed editorial writer would not have been surprised at the studies of air pollutants in New Zealand, undertaken by the Ministry for the Environment. The Ministry's most recent findings, published in July 2022, were updated from the earlier studies of 2007, 2012, & 2016 and included:

"This report summarises the updated health and air pollution in New Zealand 2016 (HAPINZ 3.0) study which evaluates the effects of air pollution on human health across New Zealand and the resulting social costs.

"The authors of the study (Kuschel et al) estimated anthropogenic (human-made) air pollution in New Zealand was responsible for approximately 3,300 premature deaths per year and social costs of $15.6 billion per year." [19]

For the first time, the 2022 update included the measure of pollution data from motor vehicles.

As reported by Kirsty Frame of Radio New Zealand:

"The new numbers were more substantial than previous records of air pollution — making car pollution more harmful than the damage household fires caused. Researchers said the extent of the nitrogen dioxide impacts were 'unexpected' and 'startling'. Nitrogen dioxide emission in New Zealand is almost exclusively from burning petrol and diesel…

"Previously, air pollution measured in the country had been largely from fine pollution particles which came from domestic fires, car brakes, and industry. That pollution caused an estimated 1300 deaths in adults per year. A closer look now showed that a further 2000 people were dying because of exposure to nitrogen dioxide." [20]

As the 2022 update reports, anthropogenic (human-made) air pollution sources included:
- "motor vehicles (exhaust and brake/tyre wear from on-road vehicles)
- "domestic fires (wood and coal burning for home heating)
- "windblown dust (construction, land use activities and road dust etc.)
- "Industry" [21]

Natural Resources Defense Council Studies

The causes of air pollution resulting from transport-related fossil fuel use was recently outlined by Jeff Turrentine of the Natural Resources Defense Council (NRDC), based in New York:

"The cars, trucks, ships, and planes that we use to transport ourselves and our goods are a major source of global greenhouse gas emissions. (In the United States, they actually constitute the single-largest source.)

"Burning petroleum-based fuel in combustion engines releases massive amounts of carbon dioxide into the atmosphere. Passenger cars account for 41 percent of those emissions, with the typical passenger vehicle emitting about 4.6 metric tons of carbon dioxide per year.

"And trucks are by far the worst polluters on the road. They run almost constantly and largely burn diesel fuel, which is why, despite accounting for just 4 percent of U.S. vehicles, trucks emit 23 percent of all greenhouse gas emissions from transportation…

"We can get these numbers down, but we need large-scale investments to get more zero-emission vehicles on the road and increase access to reliable public transit." [22]

Tyre Particle Pollution

The reference to 'brake/tyre wear from on-road vehicles' as a pollution source in the Ministry for the Environment-sponsored study referred to, is particularly relevant and echoes the findings of research undertaken by Imperial College London as part of its 'Transition to Zero Pollution' initiative.

The resulting report, authored by Tan Z, Berry A, Charalambides M, Mijic A, Pearse W, Porter A, Ryan MP, Shorten RN, Stettler MEJ, Tetley TD, Wright S, Masen MA, entitled 'Tyre wear particles are toxic for us and the environment', was published in 2023.

The report warns: "…that even though electric vehicles remove the problem of fuel emissions, we will continue to have a problem with particulate matter because of tyre wear.

"Six million tonnes of tyre wear particles are released globally each year, and in London alone, 2.6 million vehicles emit around nine thousand tonnes of tyre wear particles annually. Despite this, research on the environmental and health impacts of tyre wear has been neglected in comparison to the research and innovations dedicated to tackling fuel emissions…

"Tyre wear particles pollute the environment, the air we breathe, the water run-off from roads and has compounding effects on waterways and agriculture. Even if all our vehicles eventually become powered by electricity instead of fossil fuels, we will still have harmful pollution from vehicles because of tyre wear…

"As tyres break down they release a range of particles, from visible pieces of tyre rubber to nanoparticles. Large particles are carried from the road by rain into rivers, where they may leach toxic chemicals into the environment, whilst smaller particles become airborne and breathed in. They are small enough to reach into the deep lung.

"These particles may contain a range of toxic chemicals including polyaromatic hydrocarbons, benzothiazoles, isoprene, and heavy metals like zinc and lead…" [23]

The Imperial College research report was summarised by Ed Wiseman in an article published by The Telegraph on 25 July 2023, parts of which include:

"Having spent the past few decades fretting about tailpipe emissions (the carbon dioxide, nitrogen oxides, hydrocarbons and various other baddies emitted by internal combustion engines), we've largely ignored the vast clouds of toxic particles produced by every single car and truck whenever it moves…

"A 2020 study by independent testing organisation, Emissions Analytics, found that in normal driving conditions a family hatchback with new, correctly inflated tyres produces 5.8mg of particulates from its wheels per kilometre, compared to 4.5mg from its exhaust – an amount still considered harmful. Multiply this phenomenon by every single rubber-wheeled vehicle currently being used in the world right now, and you can understand why scientists are worried.

"Currently, electric vehicles seem to produce as much toxic tyre dust as conventional fossil fuel cars, so while there's no doubt that an EV's zero tailpipe emissions brings localised benefits for air quality, there's still a long way to go before EVs can be considered truly clean." [24]

The International Express of 6 March 2024 reported a recent study undertaken by scientists at Emory University, Atlanta that found a link between exposure to air pollution and Alzheimer's disease.

"Scientists examined 224 people who agreed to donate their bodies to furthering dementia research after they died. The team…counted the amyloid plaques and tau tangles found in their brains linked to Alzheimer's and compared it with the traffic-related air pollution exposure by their homes.

"Those with higher levels of pollution before death…had greater levels of amyloid plaques. The average level of exposure…was measured via fine particulate matter, which consists of pollutant particles of less than 2.5 microns in diameter.

"Study author Dr Anke Huels said: 'These results add to the evidence that fine particulate matter from traffic-related air pollution affects the amount of amyloid plaque in the brain.' She stressed however that this does not mean that air pollution causes more amyloid plaques and Alzheimer's. It only proves an association between the two…" [25]

A New Zealand Study

A recent study undertaken by University of Otago associate professor, Caroline Shaw, revealed that prioritising walking and cycling as part of New Zealand's transport plan "…would improve overall population health, save the health system money and reduce health inequities between Maori and non-Maori…"

Ms Shaw commented to Lauren Crimp of Radio New Zealand:

"…the Government was heading in the wrong direction. We are already killing thousands of people prematurely in this country every year because of air pollution, injury and physical inactivity from the transport system, and the policy settings we're looking to put in place will likely make that worse, as well as not actually reduce greenhouse gas emissions…" [26]

The Electric Vehicle Reincarnation

In an earlier chapter, it was related how the first horseless conveyances were propelled by steam, gas, and galvanic cell batteries long before the internal combustion engine powered by petrol came into being. By the 1890s, battery-powered vehicles were being built and, in fact, as recounted by Allan Dick in his history of the Motor Trade Association:

"The first World Land Speed Record was established on 18 December 1898, by Comte Gaston de Chasseloup-Laubat at 39.24 mph. He was driving a Jeantaud electric car powered by a single electric motor generating 36 bhp…But for almost all of last [20th] century, the electric car was consigned to being a mere curiosity, hampered by the need for bulky batteries that only provided sufficient storage capacity for a short distance…there was minimal advancement in battery technology and we are left asking, if the motor industry had collectively decided in 1898 to go electric rather than ICE [internal combustion engine], where would the motor vehicle be today?" [27]

Where indeed? While most of the Road Gang would still have made a profit regardless of the motive power ultimately decided upon to propel the horseless carriage, it is extremely unlikely that the world's all-powerful oil producers would have settled for just the production of kerosene, lubricants, and asphalt to make their fortunes.

The symbiotic relationship between oil producers and the internal combustion engine has made many fortunes since the beginning of the twentieth century. Consequently, the world's comparatively recent concerns about the effects of fossil-fuel use on climatic conditions have caused a good number of the Road Gang to scramble for alternative power sources — such as more up-to-date versions of the Jeantaud electric car of 1898 — anything to keep their vehicles on the road.

The Clean Car Discount

Pending the unlikely replacement of all vehicles powered by fossil fuel but, having to show willingness to the world to reduce its use in the meantime, the New Zealand Government introduced 'The Clean Car Discount' in July 2021.

As explained by Inland Revenue:

"…a Clean Car Discount was based on a vehicle's CO_2 (carbon dioxide) emissions. Vehicles with zero or low emissions qualified for a rebate and those with high emissions incurred a fee." [28]

Land Transport (Clean Vehicles) Amendment Act 2022

After the popularity of the Clean Car Discount subsidy proved unaffordable for the Government, the scheme was modified by means of the Land Transport Clean Vehicles Amendment Act 2022 which came into force in February 2022. As explained at the Ministry of Transport website:

"From 1 April 2022, charges will be imposed on high emitting vehicles, and rebates given to low-emitting ones. This will be done on a sliding scale…Charges on high emission vehicles act as a purchase disincentive and will fund rebates for zero and low emission vehicles. Vehicles with neither very low nor high emissions will not be subject to rebates nor charges…" [29]

However, by May 2023, the popularity of the electric vehicle subsidy had again proved unaffordable for the Government and had to be modified with changes to the level of rebates and charges:

"Due to the increased popularity of zero and low emission vehicles purchases, Clean Car Discount rebates and charges will change for vehicles registered from 1 July 2023. The changes will ensure that the scheme remains financially sustainable while also moving New Zealand's vehicle fleet towards zero emissions. Amounts and eligibility for rebates will reduce, and charges on high emission vehicles will increase." [30]

As Cameron Smith of The New Zealand Herald reported:

"The changes mean the maximum rebate for new 'clean' vehicles will decrease by about $1600. When first introduced, the clean car rebate took as much as $8625 off the price of a new clean vehicle. On the flipside, the maximum fee for vehicles that emit 150g of carbon dioxide per kilometre increased by about $1700.

"The scheme works by adding a fee onto the purchase of polluting cars to fund the purchase of 'clean' cars, either low-emission conventional vehicles, hybrids, or full electric EVs. Sales of electric vehicles have been surging since the Clean Car Discount came in…" [31]

Indeed, as reported by Justin Lester of The Spinoff:

"In July 2023, a whopping 55% of New Zealand new vehicle registrations were low emission, overtaking fossil fuel registrations for the first time in NZ's history. The trend continued into August and September. It's safe to say the paradigm shift taking place in New Zealand's automotive landscape is now undeniable.

"What the past three months has shown is that New Zealand is now at a tipping point for sustainable transportation. It's clear that low emission vehicles aren't just for greenies anymore; they're becoming mainstream, and the momentum is growing. This shift isn't just about cutting emissions, it's about rewriting the rules of New Zealand's automotive industry." [32]

Electric Vehicle Centre

Since the closure of the country's last vehicle assembler in 1998, it had been some time since a facility of any size had been established by a car manufacturer in New Zealand. The opening of a Tesla service centre was therefore of great importance, wrote Chris Keall for The New Zealand Herald in July 2023:

"Tesla is ramping up its local presence with the opening of a giant new facility in South Auckland. 'Tesla South' is 28,780sq m, or the size of three rugby fields. It features a showroom, a service centre, a delivery area, an area where cars are prepared before being handed over to customers and a huge parts warehouse…

"As owners raced to buy EVs before the Clean Car Discount was reduced on July 1, new vehicle registrations hit a record 23,560 for the month, according to Motor Industry Association stats.

"Of that total, a new high of 47.7 per cent or 8240 were electric-powered vehicles (2643 pure battery electric vehicles, 1318 plug-in hybrid EVs, and 4297 hybrids.) All up, electric vehicle sales were close to double that of June last year." [33]

The Electric Reality

Of course, the Government subsidy incentive to drive clean cars was not to last — particularly after the November 2023 election. As described time and again throughout this transport study, this three-yearly disruption to the best of well-laid plans almost always results in a new Government and a drastic change to previously-planned and -funded projects — particularly those affecting transport.

As expected, the 2023 election of a National Coalition Government meant that the representatives of the Road Gang were again in charge, with new plans for roads, roads, and more roads; and a greatly reduced pot of money for the improvement of public transport, cycling, and pedestrian incentives.

As reported by Chris Keall in The New Zealand Herald on 16 January 2024:

"Electric vehicles will lose their long-time exemption from road user charges on April 1 [2024], Transport Minister Simeon Brown confirmed this afternoon…

"EV owners will be charged $76 per 1000 km (the same rate applied to other non-petrol light vehicles; essentially diesel-powered cars), plus administration fees…when you pre-pay for a block of 1000km or more…" [34]

Land Transport (Clean Vehicles) Act Repealed

To facilitate the regime change, the new Government introduced the Land Transport (Clean Vehicle Discount Scheme Repeal) Amendment Act 2023 which was very quickly passed on 19 December 2023.

The Ministry of Transport commented:

"Repealing the scheme means that:
- charges end for all vehicles registered after 11.59 pm on 31 December 2023
- rebate applications will also close after 11.59 pm on 31 December 2023." [35]

The result was not surprising, and delightful news for the traditional Road Gang, as Chris Keall reported in January 2024:

"EV sales drove off a cliff in January, as expected, with a carrot gone and stick about to hit. At the same time, light commercial sales jumped 53 per cent with the abolition of the 'ute tax' and ICE [internal combustion engine] passenger vehicles sales surged.

"With the clean car discount gone, petrol and diesel vehicles — less than half the market during most months of 2023 — accounted for 96 per cent of new vehicle registrations in January 2024. There were just 244 new registrations of new battery electric light vehicles during the month compared to 3469 during December — when sales spiked in the final month of the CCD [clean car discount] — and 448 in January 2022." [36]

By June 2024, there had been little improvement in the sale of electric vehicles:

"Battery electric vehicle sales were 511 in June [2024] compared to 2595 in the same month of 2023. June sales for plug-in hybrid vehicles were 227 compared to the 1310 sold in June 2023." [37]

The Canadian Experience

A Canadian Press article by Sharif Hassan, first published 17 September 2024, reports that a leading battery manufacturer, the Belgian-based Umicore, which has operations in Asia, Europe and North America, has recently suspended the construction of a Canadian factory due to what it described as 'steeply-declined customer demand projections for its battery materials.'

At the same time, the Ford Motor Company "…has opted to delay its production of electric SUVs at its [Canadian] assembly plant. The American automaker now says it will produce 100,000 gas-powered Super Duty trucks at the plant, starting in 2026." [38]

The article quotes a McMaster University professor, Greig Mordue, as stating:

"'Many Canadian consumers aren't yet ready to transition to electric vehicles due to concerns that include range anxiety, lack of charging infrastructure and affordability…manufacturers outside China have struggled to build electric vehicles for prices people can pay…Consumers aren't as interested as the most optimistic prognosticators forecast two, three, five years ago…'" [39]

Toyota is another major vehicle manufacturer delaying its electric vehicle production — as reported by the BBC in October 2024:

"Toyota is pushing back the start date for electric vehicle production in the US, as global demand for battery-powered cars continues to soften…Toyota now expects to launch its EV operation at an unspecified time in 2026…" [40]

Policy Change Reaction

In New Zealand, the termination of the monetary incentive that favoured the purchase and running of electric vehicles prompted many to deplore a return to the bad old days with the traditional Road Gang again assuming full control of the country's transport industry.

As reported by Russell Palmer for Radio New Zealand on 4 March 2024, the Green Party Transport spokesperson, Julie Anne Genter, criticised the change:

"It's extreme, it's unbelievable. It's so backwards it's doubling down on the failed approach of last century and it will lead to more emissions, more congestion and higher transport costs for all of New Zealand…

"It looks like they're completely gutting walking and cycling, and buried in the detail it says that big roading projects cannot use their funding for walking and cycling improvements — which is a huge departure from even the last National government…That means people will be paying more, but they won't have the option to take public transport or to walk and cycle safely or to get a train somewhere…" [41]

The National Land Transport Programme

There were no surprises on 2 September 2024 when then Transport Minister, Simeon Brown, announced the Government's Land Transport Programme in conjunction with that of the New Zealand Transport Agency. The announcement confirmed the Minister's previous policy announcements, including:

"…the move away from prioritising public transport…with the new focus being put on 'economic growth and productivity'.

"The programme has $32.9 billion of investment, which has four key priorities:
- "Delivers on the coalition agreements to reintroduce the successful Roads of National Significance (RoNS) programme, with a pipeline of 17 RoNS across the country
- "Gets back to basics, focusing on maintenance and pothole prevention to reduce the number of potholes on our roads
- "Supports reliable public transport services and delivers four new major public transport projects to increase travel choices in our main cities
- "Ensures councils are doing the basics brilliantly, with increased pothole prevention, reduced funds for cycleways, and no funds for speed bumps

"Brown said $6.4b would be invested in completing and undertaking the following public transport and infrastructure projects.
- "Completion of the City Rail Link
- "Eastern Busway
- "Northwest Rapid Transit Corridor
- "Airport to Botany Busway
- "Lower North Island Rail Integrated Mobility

"In response to whether it was fair that walking and cycling funding had been halved, Brown said a lot of money had been spent on 'nice-to-haves' and the new programme was about 'getting back to basics' and focussing on road maintenance…" [42]

The National Land Transport Programme Reaction

Echoes of the past were evoked by the Government's National Land Transport Programme — as reported by Georgina Campbell in The New Zealand Herald:

"There's concern the Government's National Land Transport Programme (NLTP), which prioritises new roads, looks more like a budget from the 1960s and one that will lead to more congestion. The NLTP sets out where NZ Transport Agency Waka Kotahi spends the national transport budget…

"University of Auckland urban planning senior lecturer Tim Welch told *The Front Page* the Government has always been clear about its plan to prioritise roads. 'So, that's not unexpected but the level to which roads are funded at the expense of other modes is a bit of a surprise.'

"It was out of step with what most other countries were doing,' Welch said.

"'A lot of countries and cities are really focused on building up alternatives to driving, knowing that building one more road or one more highway isn't going to relieve congestion. It's only going to increase demand for more driving over the years and lead to further congestion,' he said.

"'The flow of budgeting in transportation across the globe has been to balance out other modes – public transport, walking and cycling – with road infrastructure. This budget looks like something that we would have budgeted for in the 1960s, 1950s.'" [43]

Continuing Road Gang Support

However, the reader need not cast his or her mind back to the 1950s and 1960s…when, as detailed in a previous chapter, such studies as those provided by Halcrow Thomas (March 1950) and De Leuw Cather (July 1965), emphasising a balanced approach to the provision of transport systems in Auckland, were ignored in favour of political decisions very much driven by vested [Road Gang] interests and by land speculation…resulting in sprawling subdivisions…

Indeed, as recently as December 2016, KiwiRail, the New Zealand Transport Agency, and Auckland Transport, in association with one of the world's leading engineering and professional service firms, WSP/Parsons Brinckerhoff, presented a business case to the Government for the improvement of rail freight movements in South Auckland.

Entitled 'Wiri to Westfield (W2W) — The Case for Investment' the business case presented ten options by which greater freight-carrying efficiency could be achieved along the Wiri to Westfield section of the North Island Main Trunk railway with a new 'Third Main' rail line as the best of 10 options — the worst alternative was to place greater reliance on road freight.

Following its completion in June 2016, KiwiRail refused to release the full business case — only a heavily-redacted version. After a good deal of public pressure, the unredacted study was finally released in July 2017 and, as asked by Ben Ross in his article, 'Finally revealed: report shows rail destroys roading for Auckland freight', published by the Spinoff on 27 July 2017:

"Why was the business case [initially] redacted? The answer is surely politics. It seems to come down to an attempt to protect the position taken by the government…

"Why does the government persist with the option of more roads for more road freight…?

"The government's continued support of the road freight industry in preference to expanding the role of rail, in the face of the data in this report, makes a complete mockery of its claim to prudent economic management. It makes, instead, a pretty good case for incompetence, or cronyism, or both…" [44]

Unsurprisingly, the Government referred to was a Road Gang favourite — the Fifth National-Party-led Government which governed New Zealand from 19 November 2008 to 26 October 2017.

Interislander Ferries

With the election of a National Coalition Government in October 2023, and with the 2016 Wiri to Westfield scandal hardly a distant memory, the same road versus rail conflict continued with the cancellation of the previous Labour Government's commitment to provide two rail-enabled, Cook Strait ferries to be delivered in 2025 and 2026.

As reported by Joel MacManus of The Bulletin on 12 December 2024:

By the time the National Party Coalition had assumed power, overall costs for the ferry project, including port upgrades to accommodate the larger ships, had substantially increased from an initial $775 million to an estimated $3.2 billion.

In December 2023, at substantial cost for breaking the contract with the South Korean ship builders, the National Coalition Government cancelled the project in favour of seeking a cheaper option — two smaller ferries that may, or may not be, rail-enabled. [45]

Ferries able to transport railway wagons are particularly important to the transfer of goods between the North and South Island rail termini — as reported by Thomas Coughlan in The New Zealand Herald of 25 September 2024:

"The managing director of one of New Zealand's largest logistics firms has warned that replacing the Interislander ferries with non-rail-enabled ships could mean longer, more expensive freight travel throughout New Zealand, putting further pressure on our pothole-riddled roads.

"Mainfreight managing director Don Braid told the *Herald* that his business had invested heavily in connecting its logistics hubs around the country to the rail network. It means that a container can be put on a rail wagon at Mainfreight's Penrose site in Auckland and seamlessly travel to another rail-connected site in Christchurch, thanks to the rail-enabled Arahura ferry, which currently sails the Cook Strait.

"KiwiRail itself warned that without rail on the new ferries, New Zealand's single rail network 'would be broken in two...with a separate network in the North and South Islands which could have a serious impact on rail's viability in the south.

"Braid said [that] adding additional time and cost to the crossing would make rail less competitive and see more freight shipped on road to the detriment of the nation's state highways, which might groan under the weight of more truck traffic…" [46]

More Echoes of the Past

This most recent instance of choosing a cheaper alternative is just the latest in a long history of such debacles, mostly politically-motivated to favour the Road Gang. Such short-sightedness has plagued the advancement of a modern, efficient transport system in New Zealand since the 1880s.

A prime example was the acceptance of a down-sized, Auckland Harbour Bridge in the 1950s. The resulting 'austerity' bridge omitted the previously-planned-for, public transport, cycling, and pedestrian access across the harbour in favour of road traffic only — the cheaper option that was to later cost so much more.

And then, despite the expense and advice of so many reports provided by independent experts advocating a complementary public transport system for Auckland, that advice was ignored in favour of what was falsely promoted by the Road Gang to be cheaper motorways — again an option that was not so cheap after all.

Time will tell, when this Government finally decides, if the cheaper option will include rail-enabled ferries to ply the Cook Strait. Whatever the outcome, the decision will no doubt favour the interests of the Road Gang, first and foremost, as it has for decades.

Afterword

As this study, and my previous volumes, Waka Paddle to Gas Pedal and Gas Pedal to Back-Pedal illustrate, the introduction into New Zealand of the motor vehicle as a new mode of travel was soon recognised as a good money-earner for a Road Gang which quickly flourished to satisfy the demand.

However, the original importers, dealers, and artisans soon found themselves competing with the government of the day and local authorities for the motorists' money. By way of import duties, taxation, registration, licensing, parking fees and fines, the lawmakers became the supreme leaders of the Road Gang while at the same time prospering from their mandate to make transport-related decisions that favoured the motor vehicle as a prime mover.

Unfortunately for the travelling public as a whole, many of those decisions were influenced by political-party ideology which resulted in unnecessary cancellations of a great number of plans for transport infrastructure and wasted countless millions of dollars and precious resources in the process.

As this three-volume study has shown, and as contradictory as it might at first seem, a permanent and politically-independent entity, with vision and sufficient experience and resources, would have been better suited to supervise the overall development of New Zealand's infrastructure — particularly transport.

In the meantime, the building of more and more roads with only a fraction of its budget for the provision of public transport systems continues to be a lucrative deal for the government but a poor investment in the future.

Transport and social advancement are joined at the hip.

References

Chapter One

1. Such, William B. (Revised Edition 1969). <u>Poverty and Progress in New Zealand - A Re-Assessment</u>. Wellington. A H & A W Reed. Pp. 84-85
2. Noonan, R. J. (1975). <u>By Design: A brief history of the Public Works Department, Ministry of Works 1870-1970</u>. Wellington, Government Printer. Pp. 36, 47, & 45
3. ibid. P. 48
4. Sinclair, Keith. (1969). <u>A History of New Zealand</u>. London. P. 163
5. Oliver, W. H. (1960). <u>The Story of New Zealand</u>. London, Faber. P. 118
6. Noonan, R. J. (1975). <u>By Design: A brief history of the Public Works Department, Ministry of Works 1870-1970</u>. Wellington, Government Printer. P. 48
7. (1871). The Kaipara Railway - Turning The First Sod. <u>Daily Southern Cross</u>. Auckland. Volume XXVII. Issue 4383 P. 3
8. (1879). Public Works Policy. <u>West Coast Times & Lyttelton Times</u>. Hokitika. Issue 3349 P. 2
9. Railway Commission. (1880). Report of the Railway Commission. Wellington: 26 July 1880. Pp. 3-4
10. Seddon, R. J. (1895). Public Works Statement 21 October 1895. Public Works. Wellington. Pp. iii-iv
11. Fraser, W. (1912). Statement to Parliament 18 October 1912. Ministry of Works. Wellington. P. i
12. Treasury (1911-1912). Expenditure of the Public Account. Treasury. Wellington: Pp. 597-601
13. Services, Public Works (1927-1928). Summary of Services Chargeable on the Public Works Fund. Public Works. Wellington: P. 43
14. Semple, R. (1948). Ministry of Works Statement 1948. Ministry of Works. Wellington, New Zealand Government. 31 March 1948. P. 10
15. Goosman, W. S. (1950). Ministry of Works Statement for the year ended 31 March 1950. Ministry of Works. Wellington. P. 4
16. (1947). Public Works Amendment Act. Statute No. 46. New Zealand. 25 November 1947. Section 4(2)
17. MacDonald, F. J. (2014). "Highlights From Primate City." <u>Griffith Review - Pacific Highways</u>. Volume 2 Issue 43. 29 January 2014
18. Demon. (1922) Cycling & Motor Notes. Otago Witness Issue 3542 31 January 1922 P. 4
19. Young, D. (1995). Review of Stephen B Goddard's 'Getting There'. <u>Chicago Tribune & Corpus Christi Caller Times</u>. Chicago & Corpus Christi. 22 January 1995. P. G14
20. Goddard, Stephen B. (1994). <u>Getting There</u>. New York, Basic Books. Pp. 57, 171, 58, 196, 193
21. Such, William B. (1966). <u>the quest for security in New Zealand 1840 to 1966</u>. Wellington, Oxford University Press. P. 220
22. (1919). Automobile Club. <u>Evening Post</u>. Wellington. Volume XCVII Issue 98. 28 April 1919. P. 11
23. ibid.
24. Works, Ministry of. (1946). The Shape of Things to Come. Ministry of Works. Wellington

25. Thomas, Halcrow. (1950). Halcrow & Partners Report. Auckland. 14 March 1950
26. De Leuw, Charles E. (1965). Summary Report On The Transit Plan For Metropolitan Auckland. Auckland, De Leuw, Cather & Company. 15 July 1965
27. Lee, Mike (2010). Sins of the Fathers: the fall and rise of rail transit in Auckland. Urban Rail Conference, Melbourne. 6 May 2010
28. KiwiRail, New Zealand Transport Agency, Auckland Transport, WSP/Parsons Brinckerhoff (2016) Wiri to Westfield (W2W) — The Case for Investment 7 December 2016 Pp. 5-6
29. Ross, Ben (2017) Finally revealed: report shows rail destroys roading for Auckland freight. The Spinoff 27 July 2017. https://thespinoff.co.nz/auckland/27-07-2017/finally-revealed-report-shows-rail-destroys-roading-for-auckland-freight

Chapter Two

1. Canada, General Motors. "The Story behind the Horseless Carriage." Retrieved 14 December, 2022, from: http://www.gm.ca/inm/gmcanada/english/about/OverviewHist/hist_timeline.html
2. Demon (1900). Otago Witness. Issue 2417. 12 July 1900. P. 49
3. Wilson, K. A. (2022). Worth the Watt: A Brief History of the Electric Car 1830 to Present. Car and Driver. 17 August 2022
4. Government, New Zealand (1904). Official Yearbook. Wellington, New Zealand Government
5. Dick, A. (2017). Motor Trade Association of New Zealand Centenary. Martinborough, RnR Publishing. Pp. 157-158
6. ibid.
7. History of the electric vehicle Retrieved 15 December 2022. Wikipedia. https://en.wikipedia.org/wiki/History_of_the_electric_vehicle
8. (1894) A Pleasure Yacht: A New Motor The New Zealand Herald. Auckland. Volume XXXI Issue 9664. 9 November 1894. P. 5
9. (1895) A Visit To Birkdale. The New Zealand Herald. Auckland. Volume XXXII Issue 9801. 23 April 1895 P. 6
10. (1903) Advertisements. The New Zealand Herald. Auckland. Volume XL Issue 12248. 18 April 1903 P. 8
11. (1905) News Of The Day. Christchurch Press. Christchurch. Volume LXII Issue 12279 24 August 1905. P. 6
12. (1905) News Of The Day. Christchurch Press. Christchurch. Volume LXII Issue 12297 14 September 1905. P. 6
13. (1905) Labour Day. Auckland Star. Auckland. Volume XXXVI Issue 243. 11 October 1905. P. 5
14. (1906) Advertisements. The New Zealand Herald. Auckland. Volume XLIII Issue 13247. 4 August 1906. P. 9
15. (1910) Southland Markets. Christchurch Press. Christchurch. Volume LXVI Issue 13703. 9 April 1910. P. 12
16. Hawkes, Graham (1990) On the Road - The Car In New Zealand. Wellington, GP Books. P. 10

17. (1898) General Assembly. <u>Temuka Leader</u>. Temuka. Issue 3310. 16 July 1898. P. 2
18. (1898) The McLean Motor-Car Act 1898. No.2 Preamble.
19. (1898) Motor Cars and Monopoly. <u>The New Zealand Times</u>. Volume LXVIII Issue 3487. 16 July 1898. P. 2
20. ibid.
21. (1900) Untitled. <u>Nelson Evening Mail</u>. Nelson. Volume XXXIV Issue 162. 12 July 1900. P. 3
22. Hawkes, Graham (1990) <u>On the Road - The Car In New Zealand</u>. Wellington, GP Books. P. 10
23. (1936) The First Car. <u>Manawatu Standard</u>. Palmerston North. Volume LVI Issue 37. 13 January 1936. P. 3
24. (1927) Now And Then. <u>Auckland Sun</u>. Auckland. Volume 1 Issue 118. 9 August 1927. P. 9
25. Gee, Austin & Trapeznik, Alexander. (2018) The Motoring Lobby in New Zealand, 1898-1930. Journal of New Zealand Studies NS27 (2018), Victoria University, Wellington Pp. 130-146. https://ojs.victoria.ac.nz/jnzs/article/view/5180
26. Hawkes, Graham (1990) <u>On the Road - The Car In New Zealand</u>. Wellington, GP Books. P. 19
27. Bush, G. (2014). <u>From Survival to Revival - Auckland's Public Transport since 1860</u>. Wellington, Grantham House Publishing. P. 94
28. (1921) Progress in Road-Making. <u>Nelson Evening Mail</u>. Nelson. Volume LIV. 3 February 1921. P. 6
29. (1921) Political Notes. <u>Evening Star</u>. Issue 17844. 15 December 1921. P. 11
30. This Day in Automotive History – The History of Auto Warranties — Cars & Copy Media, Spare Change Multimedia LLC https://automotivehistory.org/history-of-auto-warranties
31. (1924) Advertisements The Dominion Motors Ltd Evening Post Volume CVIII Issue 97 21 October 1924 P. 12
32. (1972) Criticism of car warranty cuts Christchurch Press Volume CXII Issue 32891 14 April 1972 P. 3
33. (1911) Advertisements. <u>The New Zealand Herald</u>. Auckland. Volume XLVIII Issue147679. 26 August 1911. P. 2
34. (1916) Advertisements. <u>Auckland Star</u>. Auckland. Volume XLVII Issue 244. 12 October 1916. P. 3
35. (1917) Advertisements. <u>Auckland Star</u>. Auckland. Volume XLVIII Issue 235. 2 October 1917. P. 1
36. (1920) Advertisements. <u>Auckland Star</u>. Auckland. Volume LI Issue 274. 16 November 1920 P. 10
37. (1916) Advertisements. <u>The New Zealand Herald</u>. Auckland. Volume LIII Issue 16240. 27 May 1916 P. 2
38. (1916) Advertisements. <u>The New Zealand Herald</u>. Auckland. Volume LIII Issue 16414. 16 December 1916. P. 2
39. (1915) Advertisements. <u>The New Zealand Herald</u>. Auckland. Volume LII Issue 16050. 16 October 1915. P. 2

40. (1916) Advertisements. The New Zealand Herald. Auckland. Volume LIII Issue 16210. 22 April 1916. P. 2
41. ibid.
42. (1916) Advertisements. Auckland Star. Auckland. Volume XLVII Issue 126. 27 May 1916. P. 3
43. (1919) Advertisements. Auckland Star. Auckland. Volume L Issue 224. 20 September 1919. P. 5
44. (1916) Advertisements. Auckland Star. Auckland. Volume XLVII Issue 126. 27 May 1916. P. 3
45. ibid.
46. ibid.
47. ibid.
48. (1917) Advertisements. The New Zealand Herald. Auckland. Volume LIV Issue 16609. 4 August 1917. P. 2
49. (1919) Advertisements. The New Zealand Herald. Auckland. Volume LVI Issue 17244. 21 August 1919. P. 2
50. ibid.
51. (1919) Advertisements. Auckland Star. Auckland. Volume L Issue 224. 20 September 1919. P. 5
52. Webster, Mark (2021). Assembly - A History of New Zealand Car Production 1921-1998. Sydney/Auckland, New Holland Publishers. P. 13
53. Archives, Fletcher. "Campbell Motors Limited." Retrieved 30 December 2022, from https://collection.fletcherarchives.co.nz/objects/1715/campbell-motors-ltd-company-records.
54. (1916) Advertisements. The New Zealand Herald. Auckland. Volume LIII Issue 16210. 22 April 1916. P. 2
55. (1916) Advertisements. Auckland Star. Auckland. Volume XLVII Issue 126. 27 May 1916. P. 3
56. (1919) Advertisements. Auckland Star. Auckland. Volume L Issue 224. 20 September 1919. P. 5
57. (1916) Advertisements. The New Zealand Herald. Auckland. Volume LIII Issue 16210. 22 April 1916. P. 2
58. (1916) Advertisements. Auckland Star. Auckland. Volume XLVII Issue 126. 27 May 1916. P. 3
59. (1918) Advertisements. The New Zealand Herald. Auckland. Volume LV Issue 17027. 7 December 1918. P. 2
60. The Distribution of Motor Spirits and Ancillary Products - Report of the Commission of Inquiry, Wellington 30 April 1976 P. 19
61. Dick, A. (2017). Motor Trade Association of New Zealand Centenary. Martinborough, RnR Publishing. P. 16
62. (1914) Local and General - Evening Post Volume LXXXVIII Issue 153 26 December 1914 P. 6
63. (1913) Motoring - The New Zealand Herald Volume L Issue 15369 2 August 1913 P. 11
64. (1914) Entertainments - Hawke's Bay Tribune Volume IV Issue 239 23 September 1914 P. 2

65. The British Museum & BBC - A History of the World at: https://www.bbc.co.uk/ahistoryoftheworld/objects/qPgTiS8fQ6SeIqZLvZVfXQ
66. (1915) Dominion Winter Show - Hawera & Normanby Star Volume LXIX Issue LXIX 5 July 1915 P. 7
67. (1915) Industrial Exhibits Hawera & Normanby Star Volume LXIX Issue LXIX 30 June 1915 P. 5
68. (1916) Supreme Court - The Dominion Volume 9 Issue 2823 14 July 1916 P. 9
69. (1916) News Of The Day - New Zealand Times Volume XLI Issue 9490 26 October 1916 P. 4
70. (1917) News Of The Day - New Zealand Times Volume XLII Issue 9624 2 April 1917 P. 4
71. The New Zealand Gazette No. 103 14 September 1916 P. 3026
72. (1916) New Companies Evening Post Volume XCII Issue 35 10 August 1916 P. 3
73. (1916) Advertisements Evening Post Volume XCII Issue 110 6 November 1916 P. 1
74. (1916) Local And General The Dominion Volume 10 Issue 2932 18 November 1916 P. 8
75. (1917) Combined Buyers Limited - NZ Truth Issue 632 21 July 1917 P. 5
76. (1917) Combined Buyers Limited - NZ Truth 22 December 1917 P. 4
77. (1918) Combined Buyers Limited - The Dominion Volume 11 Issue 152 16 March 1918 P. 10
78. (1918) Combined Buyers Limited - Lyttelton Times Volume CXVII Issue 17972 13 December 1918 P. 7
79. (1919) Advertisements - New Zealand Times Volume XLIV Issue 10232 19 March 1919 P. 8
80. (1919) Advertisements The Dominion Volume 13 Issue 61 5 December 1919 P. 1
81. (1925) Hear the Other Side - NZ Truth Issue 1023 4 July 1925 P. 5
82. (1925) Liquidation Refused The New Zealand Herald Volume LXII Issue 19079 25 July 1925 P. 10
83. (1928) Local and General - Waikato Times, Volume 104, Issue 17588, 18 December 1928, P. 4
84. The New Zealand Gazette No. 20 21 March 1929 P. 781
85. (1928) Local And General - Ashburton Guardian Volume 48 Issue 310 11 October 1928 P. 4
86. (1928) No Injunction Ashburton Guardian Volume 49 Issue 9 23 October 1928 P. 5
87. Mixed Petrol? Christchurch Press Volume LXIV Issue 19449 24 October 1928 P. 4
88. (1934) Unusual Practice Christchurch Star Volume LXVI Issue 20281 16 April 1934 P. 7
89. 1941) Advertisements - Evening Post Volume CXXXI Issue 38 14 February 1941 P. 2
90. New Private Companies - Evening Post Volume CXXVI Issue 75 26 September 1938 P. 12
91. (1932) New Companies Southern Registrations The New Zealand Herald Volume LXIX Issue 21315 17 October 1932 P. 5
92. New Zealand Gazette No. 28 27 April 1933 P. 811
93. New Zealand Gazette No. 32 13 May 1937 P. 1145
94. (1932) Wairarapa Show - Wairarapa Daily Times 27 October 1932 P. 6
95. Grace's Guide to British Industrial History at: https://www.gracesguide.co.uk/G._L._I._Co
96. New Zealand Gazette No. 24 6 May 1948 P. 497

97. (1942) Advertisements Auckland Star Volume LXXIII Issue 168 18 July 1942 P. 8
98. New Zealand Companies Office
99. (1943) Commercial Evening Post Volume CXXXV Issue 117 19 May 1943 P. 3
100. New Zealand Companies Office
101. (1948) Investment By State Questioned Christchurch Press Volume LXXXIV Issue 25546 14 July 1948 P. 6
102. (1948) Local And General Ashburton Guardian Volume 68 Issue 241 22 July 1948 P. 4
103. (1948) Tyre Retreaders Oppose State Work Monopoly Gisborne Herald Volume LXXV Issue 22809 2 December 1948 P. 6
104. New Zealand Parliamentary Debates Volume 288 30 September to 21 October 1949 Pp. 2784 – 2791
105. New Zealand Gazette No. 45 3 July 1952 P. 1168
106. New Zealand Gazette No. 57 30 September 1954 P. 1541
107. New Zealand Gazette No. 89 6 December 1951 P. 1818
108. New Zealand Gazette No. 68 3 November 1955 P. 1724
109. (1960) Advertisements Christchurch Press Volume XCIX Issue 29258 16 July 1960 P. 18
110. New Zealand Gazette No. 7 13 February 1964 P. 197
111. (1896) Advertisements Oxford Observer Volume VIII Issue VIII 7 November 1896 P. 2
112. (1915) Advertisements - Lyttelton Times Volume CXVI Issue 17043 18 December 1915 P. 3
113. (1926) Bus Services Christchurch Press Volume LXII Issue 18850 16 November 1926 P. 9
114. (1930) Bus Services - Christchurch Press Volume LXVI Issue 19962 24 June 1930 P. 12
115. (1933) The New Petrol Tax - Christchurch Press Volume LXIX Issue 20777 10 February 1933 P. 15
116. (1935) Banking - Christchurch Star Volume LXVI Issue 20616 17 May 1935 P. 9
117. (1935) Untitled Christchurch Star Volume LXVI Issue 20572 25 March 1935 P. 4
118. (1935) Bus Terminal Station Christchurch Press Volume LXXI Issue 21594 3 October 1935 P. 5
119. (1936) New Depot Christchurch Press Volume LXXII Issue 21708 15 February 1936 P. 20
120. (1938) Fifteenth Bus Put On Road Christchurch Press Volume LXXIV Issue 22424 10 June 1938 P. 19
121. Keith Laugesen drove his way into Canterbury history By Ken Coates Christchurch Press 9 December 1976 P. 21
122. (1948) Company Affairs Wanganui Chronicle 15 April 1948 P. 8
123. (1949) Company News Christchurch Press Volume LXXXV Issue 25814 27 May 1949 P. 11
124. (1955) Motor Transport Pioneer Retires Christchurch Press Volume XCI Issue 27668 26 May 1955 P. 11
125. (1966) Obituary Christchurch Press Volume CVI Issue 31075 2 June 1966 P. 14
126. (1967) Take-Overs By Midland Christchurch Press Volume CVII Issue 31494 7 October 1967 P. 18
127. (1969) Midland Purchases Auckland Company Christchurch Press Volume CIX Issue 31920 22 February 1969 P. 22
128. New Zealand Gazette No. 82 18 December 1969 P. 2667

129. (1976) Midland had only small beginning Christchurch Press 14 September 1976 P. 26
130. (1985) Firms that left the boards Christchurch Press 16 October 1985 P. 41
131. (1986) Mr L K Laugesen Christchurch Press 12 February 1986 P. 9
132. (1932) Advertisements Ashburton Guardian Volume 52 Issue 274 1 September 1932 P. 1
133. (1932) Advertisements Christchurch Star Volume XLIV Issue 621 26 November 1932 P. 3
134. (1933) Advertisements Ashburton Guardian Volume 53 Issue 152 8 April 1933 P. 1
135. (1933) Advertisements Christchurch Star Volume LXIV Issue 920 15 November 1933 P. 3
136. (1934) Advertisements Christchurch Press Volume LXX Issue 21294 13 October 1934 P. 1
137. (1935) Advertisements Christchurch Press Volume LXXI Issue 21436 30 March 1935 P. 1
138. (1937) Advertisements Ashburton Guardian Volume 57 Issue 180 13 May 1937 P. 1
139. (1949) Advertisements Christchurch Press Volume LXXXV Issue 25935 15 October 1949 P. 12]
140. (1950) Tyre Retreading Mould Christchurch Press Volume LXXXVI Issue 26075 30 March 1950 P. 3
141. (1961) Advertisements Christchurch Press Volume C Issue 29412 14 January 1961 P. 19
142. New Zealand Gazette No. 69 27 October 1960 P. 1696
143. Webster, Mark (2021). Assembly - A History of New Zealand Car Production 1921-1998. Sydney/Auckland, New Holland Publishers. P.20.
144. (1925) An Exhibitor's Record - 34 Years At The Show. Waikato Times. Hamilton. Volume 99 Issue 16654. 20 November 1925. P. 6
145. (1926) Motor Vehicle Imports. Evening Post. Wellington. Volume CXI Issue 79. 3 April 1926. P. 19
146. (1927) Dominion's Motor Cars. Waikato Times. Hamilton. Volume 102 Issue 17287. 24 December 1927. P. 6
147. Hawkes, Graham (1990) On the Road - The Car In New Zealand. Wellington, GP Books. P. 31
148. ibid. P. 95
149. (1921) Man Arrests His Friend. Christchurch Press. Christchurch. Volume LVII Issue 17162. 3 June 1921. P. 4
150. Hawkes, Graham (1990) On the Road - The Car In New Zealand. Wellington, GP Books. P. 48
151. ibid. P. 69
152. Sources of Cars 1914-1968. Accessed 2022 from The Encyclopedia of New Zealand: https://teara.govt.nz/en/photograph/22837/sources-of-cars-1914-1968.
153. (1953) Sales of Cars in New Zealand. Christchurch Press. Christchurch. Volume LXXXIX Issue 26945. 22 January 1953. P. 6
154. Hawkes, Graham (1990) On the Road - The Car In New Zealand. Wellington, GP Books. Pp. 93-94
155. ibid. P. 106
156. ibid. P. 111
157. The Colonial Motor Company Limited - History. Accessed 2022 from https://www.colmotor.co.nz/about/history/.
158. Hawkes, Graham (1990) On the Road - The Car In New Zealand. Wellington, GP Books P. 135

159. El Cheapo Cars. Accessed 2022 from The Encyclopedia of New Zealand: https://teara.govt.nz/en/photograph/22846/el-cheapo-cars.
160. The Colonial Motor Company Limited - History. Accessed 2022 from https://www.colmotor.co.nz/about/history/.
161. (1992). A Jalopy in Japan is a Kiwi's Cadillac. <u>The Christian Science Monitor</u>. Boston.
162. Wade, Harrison. (2024) Kiwis own the most cars per capita in the world, new data shows. New Zealand Autocar Magazine 23 February 2024

Chapter Three

1. (1990). People of Prominence. <u>Springdale School 75th Jubilee 1915-1990</u>. Springdale School. Matamata/Piako District. Pp. 34-35
2. (1925). The Te Aroha Bridge. <u>The New Zealand Herald</u>. Auckland. Volume LXII Issue 19102. 21 August 1925. P. 13
3. (1954). W S Goosman & Company Limited. <u>The New Zealand Gazette No. 28</u> Volume II. 1 May to 31 August 1954. P. 716
4. (1937). W S Goosman and Company Limited <u>The New Zealand Gazette No. 44</u>. 1 July 1937. Pp. 1554-1555.
5. Gustafson, B. (1986). <u>The First Fifty Years: A History of the New Zealand National Party</u>. Auckland, Reed Methuen
6. Laurenson, G. L. (1950). Annual Report of Transport Department Wellington, Transport Department. 20 July 1950. Pp. 8 & 36
7. Hawkes, Graham (1990) <u>On the Road - The Car In New Zealand</u>. Wellington, GP Books. Pp. 80-81
8. (1953). Report of the Roading Investigation Committee. Ministry of Works. Wellington. New Zealand Government
9. ibid.
10. ibid.
11. ibid.
12. (1953). National Roads Act 1953. New Zealand
13. (1955). Master Transportation Plan For Metropolitan Auckland - Report And Survey. Auckland, Auckland Regional Planning Authority. 8 July 1955. P. 3
14. ibid. P. 3
15. ibid. Pp. 16-17
16. ibid. Pp. 16-17
17. Goddard, S. B. (1994). <u>Getting There</u>. New York, Basic Books. P. 62
18. Mees, P. (2010). <u>Transport for Suburbia: Beyond the Automobile Age</u>. London, Sterling, VA: Earthscan
19. Nunns, P. (2014). Was Auckland's motorway network built on strategic misrepresentations? Retrieved 24 November 2014, from https://www.greaterauckland.org.nz/2014/11/24/
20. ibid.
21. (1955). Master Transportation Plan For Metropolitan Auckland - Report And Survey. Auckland, Auckland Regional Planning Authority. P. 28

22. ibid. Pp. 129-130
23. ibid. P. 28
24. Nunns, P. (2014). Was Auckland's motorway network built on strategic misrepresentations? Retrieved 24 November 2014, from https://www.greaterauckland.org.nz/2014/11/24/
25. Such, William B. (1966). the quest for security in New Zealand 1840 to 1966. Wellington, Oxford University Press P. 280
26. Hawkes, Graham (1990) On the Road - The Car In New Zealand. Wellington, GP Books P. 95

Chapter Four

1. (1901) The Minimum Wage Christchurch Press Volume LVIII Issue 11063 6 September 1901 P. 3
2. (1909) Department of Labour Report 1909 P. lvii
3. (1912) Coachbuilding Trade Evening Star Issue 14889 30 May 1912 P. 3
4. (1898) Evening Post Volume LVI Issue 13 15 July 1898 P. 4
5. (1898) The Motor Car Question Evening Post Volume LVI Issue 14 16 July 1898 P. 2
6. (1900) Nelson Evening Mail Volume XXXIV Issue 162 12 July 1900 P. 3
7. (1906) Patents Applied For Colonist Volume XLVIII Issue 11528 4 January 1906 P. 3
8. (1913) Late Locals Inangahua Times 13 March 1913 P. 1
9. (1910) Advertisements Column Oamaru Mail Volume XXXVIII Issue 10468 30 May 1910 P. 4
10. (1914) Waimate Show Timaru Herald Volume CI Issue 15497 6 November 1914 P. 9
11. (1924) Commercial Timaru Herald Volume XCVIII Issue 18084 24 September 1924 P. 10
12. (1926) Commercial Timaru Herald Volume CXXIII 7 September 1926 P. 8
13. History of Vehicle Dealers downloaded on 2 January 2023 from: https://www.theprow.org.nz/yourstory/vinings-in-the-motor-industry.
14. (1900) Advertisements Nelson Evening Mail Volume XXXIV Issue 69 24 March 1900 P. 3
15. (1907) Advertisements Nelson Evening Mail Volume XLII 12 June 1907 P. 4
16. (1913) Advertisements Colonist Volume LV Issue 13673 14 March 1913 P. 6
17. Automotive Industry in New Zealand. Wikipedia https://en.wikipedia.org/wiki/Automotive_industry_in_New_Zealand
18. (1927) Advertisements Nelson Evening Mail Volume LXI 1 October 1927 P. 1
19. (1945) Obituary Christchurch Press Volume LXXXI Issue 24536 9 April 1945 P. 6
20. (1963) Victoria St. Firm To Close, After 55 Years Christchurch Press Volume CII Issue 30167 26 June 1963 P. 6
21. (1914) An Up-To-Date Meat Van Christchurch Press Volume L Issue 14958 4 May 1914 P. 10
22. (1915) Steel Bros. Christchurch Sun Volume II Issue 548 11 November 1915 P. 11
23. (1963) Obituary Christchurch Press Volume CII Issue 30276 31 October 1963 P. 13
24. (1912) J Bett and Bayly, Ltd. Evening Post Volume LXXXIV Issue 106 31 October 1912 P. 17

25. (1912) National Dairy Show — Splendid Motors and Vehicles Manawatu Times Volume LXV Issue 1652 27 June 1912 P. 7
26. (1915) The Famous 'Buick' Car Manawatu Times Volume XL Issue 13101 21 May 1915 P. 3
27. (1915) Palmerston Industries Manawatu Times Volume XL Issue 13165 4 August 1915 P. 8
28. (1916) Advertising Memoranda Manawatu Times Volume XL Issue 13495 4 September 1916 P. 6
29. (1918) Personal Paragraphs Manawatu Times Volume XL Issue 13887 16 May 1918 P. 4
30. (1923) J Bett & Bayly Ltd The Dominion Volume 18, Issue 69, 15 December 1923, Page 13
31. (1923) The Old And The New Manawatu Times Volume XLVII Issue 3004 12 December 1923 P. 5
32. (1923) J Bett & Bayly Ltd The Dominion Volume 18, Issue 69, 15 December 1923, Page 13
33. (1924) The New Zealand Gazette No. 9 14 February 1924 P. 519
34. (1929) Obituary Manawatu Times Volume LIV Issue 6849 2 March 1929 P. 10
35. (1927) W Richardson Evening Post Volume CXIII Issue 138 15 June 1927 P. 22
36. (1877) Partnership Notices Lyttelton Times Volume XLVII Issue 5013 14 March 1877 P. 1
37. (1935) Obituary Christchurch Press Volume LXXI Issue 21472 14 May 1935 P. 12
38. (1894) Local & General Christchurch Star Issue 4938 30 April 1894 P. 3
39. (1898) Advertisements Christchurch Press Volume LV Issue 10180 29 October 1898 P. 10
40. (1898) The Metropolitan Show Lyttelton Times Volume C Issue 11734 11 November 1898 P. 5
41. (1912) Stevens and Sons Christchurch Press Volume XLVIII Issue 14506 7 November 1912 P. 8
42. (1925) Father Quarrels With His Sons Christchurch Star Issue 17680 29 October 1925 P. 7
43. (1920) Hawera Winter Show Wanganui Chronicle Volume LXXVI Issue 17915 8 July 1920 P. 2
44. (1936) FOB Transport In Ashburton Christchurch Press Volume LXXII Issue 21855 7 August 1936 P. 17
45. (1940) Men Out Of Work Gisborne Herald Volume LXVII Issue 20295 10 July 1940 P. 9
46. (1935) Untitled Poverty Bay Herald Volume LXII Issue 18714 24 May 1935 P. 4
47. Webster, Mark Assembly — A History of New Zealand Car Production 1921-1998 New Holland Publishers 2021 P. 13
48. (1922) Repute In Business Auckland Star Volume LIII Issue 296 14 December 1922 P. 9
49. (1935) Fire At Parnell — Auckland Star Volume LXVI Issue 296 14 December 1935 P. 10
50. (1936) New Factory Auckland Star Volume LXVII Issue 154 1 July 1936 P. 10
51. (1937) Down The Line Auckland Star Volume LXVIII Issue 260 2 November 1937 P. 18
52. Hunt, Graeme The Rich List — Wealth and Enterprise in New Zealand 1820-2000 Reed Books Auckland 2000 Pp. 173 & 201
53. (1965) Christchurch Press Volume CIV Issue 30928 8 December 1965 P. 27

54. (1966) Profit Rise For Seabrook Fowlds Christchurch Press Volume CVI Issue 31101 2 July 1966 p. 18
55. (1975) N.Z.M.C. leads market with 22.2 per cent — Christchurch Press Volume CXV Issue 33915 7 August 1975 P. 16
56. (1920) Commerce And Finance Lyttelton Times Volume CXVIII Issue 18561 13 November 1920 P. 10
57. (1921) Progress In Road-Making Nelson Evening Mail Volume LIV 3 February 1921 P. 6
58. (1921) Untitled Southland Times Issue 19057 16 February 1921 P. 6
59. (1923) Advertisements Christchurch Press Volume LIX Issue 17717 20 March 1923 P. 9
60. (1924) A Successful Test Ashburton Guardian Volume XLV Issue 10287 20 December 1924 P. 5
61. (1932) Untitled Poverty Bay Herald Volume LIX Issue 17875 3 September 1932 P. 6
62. The New Zealand Gazette No. 49 11 July 1935 P. 1917
63. (1935) Untitled Poverty Bay Herald Volume LXII Issue 18714 24 May 1935 P. 4
64. Webster, Mark Assembly — A History of New Zealand Car Production 1921-1998 New Holland Publishers 2021 P. 13
65. The New Zealand Gazette No. 111 23 September 1982 P. 3159
66. (1965) Long History Christchurch Press Volume CIV Issue 30875 7 October 1965 P. 13
67. New Zealand Companies Office
68. (1983) Amuri Motors debenture issue Christchurch Press 18 May 1983 P. 29
69. (1956) Companies Registered Christchurch Press Volume XCIII Issue 27876 26 January 1956 P. 16
70. (1983) Amuri Motors debenture issue Christchurch Press 18 May 1983 P. 29
71. (1985) Amuri shift only part of huge plans Christchurch Press 8 August 1985 P. 30
72. New Zealand Gazette No. 138 4 September 1986 P. 3742
73. (1989) Amuri gains Wellington GM franchise Christchurch Press 28 October 1989 P. 33
74. The Colonial Motor Company History https://www.colmotor.co.nz/about/history/
75. The Colonial Motor Company – The Encyclopedia of New Zealand https://teara.govt.nz/en/photograph/22840/car-assembly-at-the-colonial
76. Hawkes, Graham On the Road — The Car In New Zealand GP Books Wellington 1990 P. 23
77. The Colonial Motor Company History https://www.colmotor.co.nz/about/history/
78. Hunt, Graeme The Rich List — Wealth and Enterprise in New Zealand 1820-2000 Reed Books Auckland 2000 Pp. 173 & 221
79. Hawkes, Graham On the Road — The Car In New Zealand GP Books Wellington 1990 P. 32
80. (1929) New Zealand And The Motor Car Industry Otago Daily Times Issue 20866 5 November 1929 P. 3
81. (1984) Assembly plant closes Christchurch Press 20 August 1984 P. 2
82. Hawkes, Graham On the Road — The Car In New Zealand GP Books Wellington 1990 P. 75
83. (1925) Motor Buses For Wellington The Dominion Volume 18 Issue 218 15 June 1925 P. 10

84. (1926) Commercial - Auckland Star Volume LVII Issue 132 5 June 1926 P.11
85. Coachwork International Palmerston North https://wikijii-com.translate.goog/wiki/Coachwork_International
86. (1946) Advertisements Christchurch Press Volume LXXXII Issue 24995 2 October 1946 P. 10
87. (1948) Splendid New Bus Te Awamutu Courier Volume 77 Issue 6983 29 October 1948 P. 7
88. (1949) Company Floated To Take Over City's Passenger Transport Wanganui Chronicle 11 November 1949 P. 6
89. (1951) Company News Christchurch Press Volume LXXXVII Issue 26436 1 June 1951 P. 9
90. (1960) N.Z. Motor Bodies Christchurch Press Volume XCIX Issue 29221 3 June 1960 P. 15
91. (1963) N.Z. Motor Bodies Profit Rises Christchurch Press Volume CII Issue 30150 6 June 1963 P. 17
92. (1967) N.Z. Motor Bodies Christchurch Press Volume CVII Issue 31397 16 June 1967 P. 17
93. (1970) N.Z. Motor Bodies Confident Christchurch Press Volume CX Issue 32307 27 May 1970 P. 21
94. (1974) Further Problems for N.Z. Motor Bodies Christchurch Press Volume CXIV Issue 33666 16 October 1974 P. 27
95. (1974) Commercials N.Z. Motor Bodies loss $195,408 Christchurch Press Volume CXIV Issue 33719 17 December 1974 P. 26
96. (1975) Two bids for Mtr Bodies Christchurch Press Issue 33841 13 May 1975 P. 26
97. (1975) N.Z. Motor Bodies opts for Moller merger Christchurch Press Issue 33844 16 May 1975 P. 12
98. (1975) N.Z. Motor Bodies acts on Govt assurance Christchurch Press Volume CXV Issue 33977 18 October 1975 P. 18
99. Coachwork International Palmerston North https://wikijii-com.translate.goog/wiki/Coachwork_International
100. (1979) N.Z.M.B. reactivates assembly plant Christchurch Press 8 November 1979 P. 19
101. The New Zealand Gazette No. 199 1 November 1984 P. 4730
102. Coachwork International Palmerston North https://wikijii-com.translate.goog/wiki/Coachwork_International
103. Webster, Mark Assembly — A History of New Zealand Car Production 1921-1998 New Holland Publishers 2021 Pp. 12 & 13
104. Automotive Industry in New Zealand Wikipedia https://en.wikipedia.org/wiki/Automotive_industry_in_New_Zealand
105. (1930) The Motor World Otago Daily Times, Issue 21215, 22 December 1930, P. 4
106. (1929) Name and Reputation Evening Post Volume CVII Issue 118 23 May 1929 P. 15
107. Automotive Industry in New Zealand Wikipedia https://en.wikipedia.org/wiki/Automotive_industry_in_New_Zealand
108. Hawkes, Graham On the Road — The Car In New Zealand GP Books Wellington 1990 P. 84

109. (1932) Rover Company Christchurch Press Volume LXVIII Issue 20480 25 February 1932 P. 10
110. Webster, Mark Assembly — A History of New Zealand Car Production 1921-1998 New Holland Publishers 2021 P. 30
111. (1933) Australian Wine Industry Christchurch Press Volume LXIX Issue 20750 10 January 1933 P. 8
112. (1933) Properties For Sale - Evening Post Volume CXVI Issue 34 9 August 1933 P. 3
113. (1933) Commerce, Mining & Finance Evening Star Issue 21584 2 December 1933 P. 11
114. (1936) Otago Daily Times Issue 22989 18 September 1936 P. 10
115. (1936) Country News Otago Daily Times Issue 22997 28 September 1936 P. 12
116. Hunt, Graeme The Rich List — Wealth and Enterprise in New Zealand 1820-2000 Reed Books Auckland 2000 P. 144
117. Webster, Mark Assembly — A History of New Zealand Car Production 1921-1998 New Holland Publishers 2021 P. 23
118. Todd Corporation History https://toddcorporation.com/history
119. Todd Corporation Wikipedia https://en.wikipedia.org/wiki/Todd_Corporation
120. Webster, Mark Assembly — A History of New Zealand Car Production 1921-1998 New Holland Publishers 2021 P. 31
121. (1979) Todd moves ahead Christchurch Press 8 November 1979 P. 19
122. Todd Corporation History https://toddcorporation.com/history
123. Todd Corporation Wikipedia https://en.wikipedia.org/wiki/Todd_Corporation
124. (1935) Assembling Of Motors Otago Daily Times Issue 22552 22 April 1935 P. 10
125. (1935) Assembly Factory Christchurch Star Volume LXVI Issue 20589 13 April 1935 P. 15
126. (1935) A New Christchurch Industry Christchurch Press Volume LXXI Issue 21626 9 November 1935 P. 1 (Supplement)
127. (1963) Assembly of U.S. Cars Christchurch Press Volume CII Issue 30165 24 June 1963 P. 6
128. (1955) Assembly Of Cars Christchurch Press Volume XCI Issue 27597 2 March 1955 P. 14
129. (1957) Car Assembly Factory Christchurch Press Volume XCV Issue 28271 8 May 1957 P.16
130. (1958) Christchurch Press Volume XCVII Issue 28486 16 January 1958 P. 8
131. ibid.
132. (1962) Car Assembly Plant Christchurch Press Volume CI Issue 29783 28 March 1962 P. 10
133. (1964) Car Plant Cutting Staff, Production Christchurch Press Volume CIII Issue 30385 9 March 1964 P. 17
134. (1964) Car Production In Hutt Still At Peak Level Christchurch Press Volume CIII Issue 30386 10 March 1964 P. 16
135. (1964) Standard-Triumph Buys Cotton Mill Christchurch Press Volume CIII Issue 30494 16 July 1964 P. 1
136. (1964) Cotton, Cars, And Protection Christchurch Press Volume CIII Issue 30497 20 July 1964 P. 10

137. (1965) Car Plant Closes Today Christchurch Press Volume CIV Issue 30836 23 August 1965 P. 1
138. Walker, Ian Around the World: New Zealand — AROnline, Best of British Cars 1 May 2016 http://www.aronline.co.uk/blogs/around-the-world/around-the-world-new-zealand
139. (1970) $2.5M Export Christchurch Press Volume CX Issue 32400 12 September 1970 P. 21
140. Walker, Ian Around the World: New Zealand — AROnline, Best of British Cars 1 May 2016 http://www.aronline.co.uk/blogs/around-the-world/around-the-world-new-zealand
141. (1969) Austin Long Established On N.Z. Market Christchurch Press Volume CIX Issue 32096 18 September 1969 P. 11
142. Webster, Mark Assembly — A History of New Zealand Car Production 1921-1998 New Holland Publishers 2021 P. 30
143. (1969) Austin Long Established On N.Z. Market Christchurch Press Volume CIX Issue 32096 18 September 1969 P. 11
144. ibid.
145. (1939) Finance And Commerce Christchurch Press Volume LXXV Issue 22727 3 June 1939 P. 12
146. (1939) Motor Assembly Factory - Christchurch Press Volume LXXV Issue 22659 14 March 1939 P. 10
147. New Zealand Companies Office
148. (1945) Company Registrations Evening Post Volume CXL Issue 39 15 August 1945 P. 8
149. Walker, Ian Around the World: New Zealand — AROnline, Best of British Cars 1 May 2016 http://www.aronline.co.uk/blogs/around-the-world/around-the-world-new-zealand
150. (1969) Car Distributors To Merge Christchurch Press Volume CIX Issue 32104 27 September 1969 P. 22
151. New Zealand Companies Office
152. Roberts, Neil (Senior Curator) The History of the New Gallery Site — Supplement to the Robert McDougall Art Gallery Bulletin October-November 1996 Pp. 10 to 12
153. (1920) Round the Garages — Phenomenal Growth of Business Christchurch Sun Volume VII Issue 2101 8 November 1920 P. 21 (Supplement)
154. (1937) New Garage Premises Christchurch Press Volume LXXIII Issue 22243 6 November 1937 P. 22
155. Roberts, Neil (Senior Curator) The History of the New Gallery Site — Supplement to the Robert McDougall Art Gallery Bulletin October-November 1996 Pp. 10 to 12
156. (1962) £250,000 Trust Fund For Southland Aged Christchurch Press Volume CI Issue 29937 26 September 1962 P. 17
157. Percy Vickery – P H Vickery Charitable Trust - downloaded 21 December 2022 from: https://www.phvickery.co.nz/#Percy-Vickery
158. (1906) General News The Southern Cross Volume 14 Issue 21 21 July 1906 P. 8
159. (1911) The Latest In Motors Southland Times Issue 16795 26 July 1911 P. 6
160. (1911) Untitled Mataura Ensign 12 October 1911 P. 4
161. (1911) New Motor Bicycle Mataura Ensign 2 November 1911 P. 10
162. (1911) Southland A & P Society Southland Times Issue 16913 13 December 1911 P. 9
163. (1916) The Jubilee Show Southland Times Issue 17897 13 December 1916 P. 7

164. (1919) Untitled Southland Times Issue 18128 1 July 1919 P. 4
165. (1923) English Austin Coy Southland Times Issue 19087 3 November 1923 P. 6
166. (1931) Motordom Southland Times Issue 21395 16 May 1931 P. 13
167. (1935) Obituary Christchurch Press Volume LXXI Issue 21472 14 May 1935 P. 12
168. (1902) The Metropolitan Show Lyttelton Times Volume CVIII Issue 12973 14 November 1902 P. 2
169. (1904) Local And General Christchurch Star Issue 8083 8 August 1904 P. 2
170. (1935) N.Z. Type Hanson Evening Star Issue 22028 14 May 1935 P. 9
171. (1908) Messrs Boon And Company's Exhibit Christchurch Press Volume LXIV Issue 13134 5 June 1908 P. 8
172. (1930) Coachsmith Has Seen Great Changes Caused By Motors Christchurch Star Issue 19013 7 March 1930 P. 11
173. (1930) Trolley-Bus Bodies Christchurch Press Volume LXVI Issue 20106 9 December 1930 P. 15
174. (1900) Cossens and Black (Limited) Otago Daily Times Issue 11626 9 January 1900 P. 2 (Supplement)
175. (1876) Advertisements Otago Daily Times Issue 4333 8 January 1876 P. 1
176. (1879) Otago Daily Times Issue 5518 25 October 1879 P. 2
177. (1882) Mornington Cable Tramway Otago Daily Times Issue 6398 15 August 1882 P. 4
178. (1900) Cossens and Black (Limited) Otago Daily Times Issue 11626 9 January 1900 P. 2 (Supplement)
179. New Zealand Companies Office
180. (1900) Cossens and Black (Limited) Otago Daily Times Issue 11626 9 January 1900 P. 2 (Supplement)
181. (1916) Alexandra Herald & Central Otago Gazette Issue 1051 18 October 1916 P. 4
182. (1917) Otago Metropolitan Show Evening Star Issue 16593 28 November 1917 P. 6
183. (1919) Alexandra Herald & Central Otago Gazette Issue 1178 23 April 1919 P. 4
184. (1921) Cossens & Black Ltd. Otago Daily Times Issue 18164 8 February 1921 P. 8
185. (1924) Cycling & Motor Notes Otago Witness Issue 3690 2 December 1924 P. 62
186. (1926) Special Telegraphic Cromwell Argus 22 November 1926 P. 4
187. (1936) World Economic Conditions --Evening Star, Issue 22240, 18 January 1936, P. 12
188. (1936) New Ford Factory Evening Post Issue 47 25 February 1936 P. 4
189. (1936) Trade Agreement Evening Star Issue 22398 23 July 1936 P. 15
190. Trade Agreement (New Zealand and Canada) Ratification Act 1932 Pp. 81 & 82
191. Customs Acts Amendment Act 1934 No. 14 P. 125
192. ibid. P. 79
193. The New Zealand Gazette No. 86 21 November 1935 P. 3336
194. (1936) Canadian Cars Waipawa Mail Volume LXIII Issue 1 3 January 1936 P. 3
195. (1937) Ford Motors Timaru Herald Volume CXLIII Issue 20700 13 April 1937 P. 9
196. ibid.
197. Hawkes, Graham On the Road — The Car In New Zealand GP Books Wellington 1990 P. 50
198. Ford New Zealand Wikipedia https://en.wikipedia.org/wiki/Ford_New_Zealand
199. Mazda History https://www.mazda.com/en/about/history/1920-1979/

200. (1972) Shipping News Christchurch Press Volume CXII Issue 32805 4 January 1972 P. 15
201. New Zealand Companies Office
202. (1972) N.Z. assembly of Japanese cars Christchurch Press Volume CXII Issue 32882 4 April 1972 P. 14
203. (1974) Criminals at the wheel Christchurch Press Volume CXIV Issue 33614 16 August 1974 P. 4
204. (1979) Motor Holdings confident Christchurch Press 10 August 1979 P. 6
205. (1980) Mazda buys factory Christchurch Press 29 February 1980 P. 14
206. (1984) Mazda, Motor Hlds re-organise Christchurch Press 2 October 1984 P. 22
207. (1985) Motor Holdings sell Mazda Christchurch Press 7 November 1985 P. 28
208. (1986) Mazda to close assembly plant Christchurch Press 27 September 1986 P. 9
209. Motor Verso.com https://www.motorverso.com/does-ford-own-mazda/
210. Mazda Wiki Fandom.com https://mazda.fandom.com/wiki/Partnerships
211. Motor Verso.com https://www.motorverso.com/does-ford-own-mazda/
212. (1986) Mazda, Ford pool assembly resources Christchurch Press 9 October 1986 P. 29
213. New Zealand Companies Office
214. (1987) Ford and Mazda in big N.Z. deal Christchurch Press 11 June 1987 P. 25
215. Ford New Zealand Wikipedia https://en.wikipedia.org/wiki/Ford_New_Zealand
216. (1971) Obituary Mr J. N. Turner Christchurch Press Volume CXI Issue 32741 19 October 1971 P.24
217. Niall, Todd The empty halls of New Zealand's car assembly industry Stuff 6 October 2018
218. Cars and the motor industry Trekka The Encyclopedia of New Zealand Te Ara https://teara.govt.nz/en/photograph/22838/trekka
219. (1971) First exports of vehicles Christchurch Press (N Z Press Association) Volume CXI Issue 32683 12 August 1971 P.14
220. (1966) Motor Hold. Takeover Christchurch Press Volume CV Issue 31010 16 March 1966 P.17
221. (1970) Subaru for N.Z. Christchurch Press Issue 32333 26 June 1970 P.16
222. (1981) Motor Holdings Mazda contract renewed Christchurch Press 23 May 1981 P. 20
223. (1982) Assembly plant to lay off 65 Christchurch Press 28 August 1982 P. 7
224. Volkswagen - downloaded from https://webarchive.org/https://www.volkswagen.co.nz/discover - web page dated 28 July 2017
225. Niall, Todd The empty halls of New Zealand's car assembly industry Stuff 6 October 2018
226. (1945) Advertisements Auckland Star Volume LXXVI Issue 303 22 December 1945 P. 1
227. New Zealand Gazette No. 24 8 May 1947 P. 560
228. (1949) Company Floated To Take Over City's Passenger Transport Wanganui Chronicle 11 November 1949 P.6
229. (1950) Advertisements Wanganui Chronicle 14 September 1950 P. 18 (Supplement)
230. New Zealand Gazette No. 30 13 May 1954 P. 838
231. New Zealand Gazette No. 22 24 March 1955 P. 446
232. New Zealand Gazette No. 15 28 February 1957 P. 328
233. (2017) Grey Lynn site ripe for development The New Zealand Herald 18 February 2017
234. (1957) Beaded Wheels Volume III No. 9 March 1957 P. 20

235. Webster, Mark Assembly — A History of New Zealand Car Production 1921-1998 New Holland Publishers 2021 P. 100
236. New Zealand Gazette No. 51 19 June 1975 P. 1387
237. New Zealand Companies Office
238. Walker, Ian Around the World: New Zealand — AROnline, Best of British Cars 1 May 2016 http://www.aronline.co.uk/blogs/around-the-world/around-the-world-new-zealand
239. (1970) Motor Firm's Agents Meet Christchurch Press Volume CX Issue 32334 27 June 1970 P. 14
240. (1970) Commercial Merger Puts NZMC In Strong Position Christchurch Press Volume CIX Issue 32269 11 April 1970 P. 16
241. (1972) Commercial N.Z.M.C. acquires assets of B.L.N.Z. Christchurch Press Volume CXII Issue 32909 6 May 1972 P. 18
242. (1972) Assembly works changes hands Christchurch Press Volume CXII Issue 32905 2 May 1972 P. 17
243. (1971) Motor industry merger Christchurch Press Volume CXI Issue 32787 11 December 1971 P. 2
244. (1975) N.Z.M.C. leads market with 22.2 per cent Christchurch Press Volume CXV Issue 33915 7 August 1975 P. 16
245. Walker, Ian Around the World: New Zealand — AROnline, Best of British Cars 1 May 2016 http://www.aronline.co.uk/blogs/around-the-world/around-the-world-new-zealand
246. (1968) Motor Firms Merge Christchurch Press Volume CVIII Issue 31581 19 January 1968 P. 9
247. (1919) The New Zealand Herald Volume LVI Issue 17329 28 November 1919 P. 11
248. (1921) Advertisements Feilding Star Volume XVII Issue 4381 30 August 1921 P. 1
249. (1968) Motor Firms Merge Christchurch Press Volume CVIII Issue 31581 19 January 1968 P. 9
250. New Zealand Gazette No. 16 20 March 1969 P. 538
251. (1969) Leyland In N.Z. Christchurch Press Volume CIX Issue 32013 13 June 1969 P. 9
252. CoventryLive Triumph: The rise and fall of an iconic Coventry brand 28 October 2018 downloaded 28 December 2022 from: https://www.coventrytelegraph.net/news/coventry-news/triumph-rise-fall-iconic-coventry-15330637
253. CoventryLive The Standard Motor Company: The rise and fall of a Coventry car giant 10 February 2019 downloaded 28 December 2022 from: https://www.coventrytelegraph.net/news/coventry-news/standard-motor-company-history-coventry-15803806
254. (1931) Personal Items The Dominion Volume 24 Issue 238 4 July 1931 P.6
255. (1931) NZ Finances Christchurch Press, Volume LXVII, Issue 20356, 1 October 1931, P. 10
256. (1931) Advertisements Christchurch Press Volume LXVII Issue 20387 6 November 1931 P. 24 (1932) Advertisements Auckland Star Volume LXIII Issue 163 12 July 1932 P. 15
257. (1932) A Dinner Party Evening Post Volume CXIV Issue 32 6 August 1932 P. 17
258. (1953) Personal Items Christchurch Press Volume LXXXIX Issue 27116 12 August 1953 P. 8

259. (1960) Personal Items Christchurch Press Volume XCIX Issue 29151 11 March 1960 P. 10
260. The New Zealand Gazette No. 15 11 March 1954 P. 388
261. The New Zealand Gazette No. 76 10 December 1959 P. 1898
262. (1957) Advertisements Christchurch Press Volume XCVI Issue 28403 9 October 1957 P. 19
263. The New Zealand Gazette No. 25 13 April 1960 P. 506
264. Walker, Ian Around the World: New Zealand — AROnline, Best of British Cars 1 May 2016 http://www.aronline.co.uk/blogs/around-the-world/around-the-world-new-zealand
265. The New Zealand Gazette No. 8 11 February 1960 P. 167
266. (1961) Changes In Car Firm Christchurch Press Volume C Issue 29602 26 August 1961 P. 17
267. (1967) More Japanese Cars Christchurch Press Volume CVI Issue 31293 13 February 1967 P. 10
268. ibid.
269. (1978) From farm carts to Lotus Sevens Christchurch Press 16 February 1978 P. 11
270. (1977) Wgtn Toyota company buys Steels assembly Christchurch Press 18 February 1977 P. 2
271. (1965) Advertisements Christchurch Press Volume CIV Issue 30656 23 January 1965 P. 22
272. (1978) From farm carts to Lotus Sevens Christchurch Press 16 February 1978 P. 11
273. (1970) Extended car plant opened at Hornby Christchurch Press Volume CX Issue 32442 31 October 1970 P. 3
274. New Zealand Companies Office
275. (1978) From farm carts to Lotus Sevens Christchurch Press 16 February 1978 P. 11
276. (1977) Wgtn Toyota company buys Steels assembly Christchurch Press 18 February 1977 P. 2
277. Steelbro Container Handling Solutions Our History https://steelbro.com/about/history
278. Harlow, Patrick NZ Cars a Cottage Industry/Lotus History downloaded on 8 March 2023 from: https://www.lotusclubqueensland.com/a-history-of-the-lotus-seven
279. Steelbro Container Handling Solutions Our History https://steelbro.com/about/history
280. Nissan History downloaded 1 March 2023 from https://www.nissan.co.nz/about-nissan/about-us.html
281. (1966) Biggest In Japan Christchurch Press Volume CVI Issue 31220 18 November 1966 P. 13
282. New Zealand Companies Office
283. (1965) Datsun Christchurch Press Volume CIV Issue 30786 25 June 1965 P. 25
284. Webster, Mark Assembly — A History of New Zealand Car Production 1921-1998 New Holland Publishers 2021 P. 100
285. Automotive Industry in New Zealand. Wikipedia https://en.wikipedia.org/wiki/Automotive_ industry_in_New_Zealand
286. (1973) New Nissan Plant Christchurch Press Volume CXIII Issue 33378 9 November 1973 P. 14
287. (1974) Central Leader 27 March 1974 Pp. 7-10
288. (1977) Muldoon eye on car sales Christchurch Press 22 October 1977 P. 1
289. (1979) $6M investment opens Christchurch Press 5 November 1979 P. 14

290. (1921) Advertisements New Zealand Herald Volume LVIII Issue 17909 11 October 1921 P. 2
291. (1921) Advertisements New Zealand Herald Volume LVIII Issue 17917 20 October 1921 P. 2
292. (1922) The New Durant Auckland Star Volume LIII Issue 156 4 July 1922 P. 8
293. Durant (automobile) Wikipedia https://en.wikipedia.org/wiki/Durant_(automobile)
294. (1922) Advertisements Auckland Star Volume LIII Issue 178 29 July 1922 P. 22
295. (1923) Campbell Motors Limited New Zealand Herald Volume LX Issue 18455 19 July 1923 P. 6
296. (1926) Advertisements New Zealand Herald Volume LXIII Issue 19251 13 February 1926 P. 11 (supplement)
297. NZ Companies Office
298. (1926) Two New Companies Auckland Star Volume LVII Issue 164 13 July 1926 P. 10
299. (1926) Advertisements The Dominion Volume 20 Issue 65 10 December 1926 P. 8
300. (1927) Advertisements The Dominion Volume 20 Issue 88 8 January 1927 P. 6
301. (1927) Farm & Commercial The Dominion Volume 20 Issue 299 16 September 1927 P. 12
302. (1933) Announcement to Northern Motorists Northern Advocate 18 August 1933 P. 6
303. (1938) Local And General Thames Star Volume LXVI Issue 20389 18 August 1938 P. 2
304. Automotive Industry in New Zealand. Wikipedia https://en.wikipedia.org/wiki/Automotive_industry_in_New_Zealand
305. (1975) Challenge in control of motor group Christchurch Press Volume CXV Issue 33882 30 June 1975 P. 16
306. New Zealand Companies Office
307. ibid.
308. ibid.
309. (1952) William Cable Holdings Christchurch Press Volume LXXXVIII Issue 26792 25 July 1952 P. 12
310. New Zealand Companies Office
311. (1966) Advertisements Christchurch Press Volume CV Issue 30980 9 February 1966 P. 20
312. (1966) Car Assembly Plans Christchurch Press Volume CVI Issue 31119 23 July 1966 P. 1
313. (1967) First Car Assembled Christchurch Press Volume CVI Issue 31285 3 February 1967 P. 1
314. New Zealand Companies Office
315. (1977) C.P.D. most successful in spite of pessimistic forecasts Christchurch Press 8 August 1977 P. 28
316. (1979) Toyota companies in N.Z. share name Christchurch Press 11 October 1979 P. 29
317. New Zealand Companies Office
318. (1977) New firm to have VW franchise Christchurch Press 27 May 1977 P. 16
319. New Zealand Companies Office
320. (1977) New firm to have VW franchise Christchurch Press 27 May 1977 P. 16
321. (1984) Colemans ride into the Rising Sunshine Christchurch Press 8 February 1984 P. 25
322. New Zealand Companies Office
323. (1984) Suzuki sets up firm for N.Z. growth Christchurch Press 4 February 1984 P. 19
324. (1988) Suzuki to shut Wanganui plant Christchurch Press 30 November 1988 P. 5

325. Greenslade, Peter Behind The Wheel New Zealand Industry Plan wins battle Christchurch Press 9 December 1988 P. 38

Chapter Five

1. Pawson, Eric Cars and the motor industry - Demise of the car-assembly and component industries Te Ara - the Encyclopedia of New Zealand
http://www.TeAra.govt.nz/en/cars-and-the-motor-industry/page-4
2. The New Zealand Official Year Book 1920 Main Groups of Imports/Miscellaneous/Automobiles, Motor-cars, and motor cycles, and materials for 1919 — Value £2,244,741
https://www3.stats.govt.nz/New_Zealand_Official_Yearbooks/1920/NZOYB_1920.html
3. The New Zealand Official Year Book 1959 Principal Imports/Motor Vehicle Parts 1957 — Value £2,591,000
https://www3.stats.govt.nz/New_Zealand_Official_Yearbooks/1959/NZOYB_1959.html
4. The New Zealand Official Year Book 1999 Published September 1999 Chapter 21.2 Major manufacturing industry groups/Motor vehicles
https://www3.stats.govt.nz/New_Zealand_Official_Yearbooks/1999/NZOYB_1999.html
5. Webster, Mark Assembly — A History of New Zealand Car Production 1921-1998 New Holland Publishers 2021 Pp. 152 & 178
6. Glass on Web The end of a long era for Pilkington
https://www.glassonweb.com/news/end-long-era-pilkington
7. Isaacs, Nigel The changing shape of window glass Build Magazine June/July 2007 Pp. 118 & 119
8. (1949) Safety Glass For Cars Bay of Plenty Times Volume LXXVII Issue 14971 9 May 1949 P. 2
9. New Zealand Companies Office
10. (2003) Pilkington automotive to close with 130 redundancies The New Zealand Herald 20 May 2003
11. (1960) New McKendrick Company Christchurch Press Volume XCIX Issue 29230 14 June 1960 P. 19
12. Isaacs, Nigel The changing shape of window glass Build Magazine June/July 2007 Pp. 118 & 119
13. (1962) New Glassworks In Difficulties Christchurch Press Volume CI Issue 29940 29 September 1962 P. 10
14. (1963) Advertisements Column 4 Press, Volume CII, Issue 30040, 26 January 1963, Page 28
15. (1963) Whangarei Glassworks Christchurch Press Volume CII Issue 30041 28 January 1963 P. 8
16. (1963) Glass Company's Assets Sold Christchurch Press Volume CII Issue 30142 28 May 1963 P. 12

17. Isaacs, Nigel The changing shape of window glass Build Magazine June/July 2007 Pp. 118 & 119
18. (1971) Advertisements Christchurch Press Volume CXI Issue 32704 6 September 1971 P. 12
19. (1977) Glass firm attacks car model increase Christchurch Press 6 September 1977 P. 7
20. (1981) Laminated glass popular Christchurch Press 5 November 1981 P. 19
21. (1982) Glass factory Christchurch Press 6 May 1982 P. 23
22. (1984) Laminated glass Christchurch Press 2 February 1984 P. 23
23. (1984) Laminated windscreens to be law in new cars Christchurch Press 18 July 1984 P. 24
24. (2003) Pilkington automotive to close with 130 redundancies The New Zealand Herald 20 May 2003
25. ibid.
26. (1939) Death of Lucas Pioneer Bay of Plenty Times Volume LXVII Issue 12766 13 June 1939 P. 6
27. (1922) The Industrial North Evening Post Volume CIV Issue 13 15 July 1922 P. 18
28. (1934) Motoring Christchurch Press Volume LXX Issue 21227 27 July 1934 P. 6
29. (1926) Advertisements The Dominion Volume 19 Issue 218 10 June 1926 P. 5
30. (1927) Motordom Southland Times Issue 20243 30 July 1927 P. 16
31. (1930) The Motor World Otago Daily Times Issue 20935 27 January 1930 P. 5
32. (1933) The Motor World Otago Daily Times Issue 22121 27 November 1933 P. 11
33. (1936) Sydney Exchange The New Zealand Herald Volume LXXIII Issue 22337 7 February 1936 P. 5
34. (1936) Advertisements Auckland Star Volume LXVII Issue 117 19 May 1936 P. 16
35. (1973) Advertisements Christchurch Press Volume CXIII Issue 33330 14 September 1973 P. 13
36. New Zealand Companies Office
37. (1989) Battery deal Christchurch Press 15 March 1989 P. 39
38. New Zealand Companies Office
39. Chloride Electrical Storage Co Limited Science Museum Group Collection https://collection.sciencemuseumgroup.org.uk/people/ap25107/chloride-electrical-storage-company-limited
40. (1911) Tramways For Aramoho Wanganui Chronicle Volume L Issue 12812 23 September 1911 P. 8
41. (1917) Untitled Evening Star Issue 16584 17 November 1917 P. 6
42. (1924) Advertisements Otago Witness Issue 3691 9 December 1924 P. 62
43. (1926) Advertisements Otago Witness Issue 3784 21 September 1926 P. 71
44. (1927) Continuous Service Waikato Times Volume 102 Issue 17115 31 May 1927 P. 8
45. (1928) General News Christchurch Press Volume LXIV Issue 19362 14 July 1928 P. 14
46. (1930) Successful Business Ellesmere Guardian Volume LI Issue 80 7 October 1930 P. 6
47. (1932) Making Known The Goods Poverty Bay Herald Volume LIX Issue 17837 21 July 1932 P. 12
48. (1939) New Local Private Companies Evening Post Volume CXXVII Issue 52 3 March 1939 P. 12

49. (1940) Advertisements Waikato Times Volume 126 Issue 21069 23 March 1940 P. 20 (Supplement)
50. (1940) Situations Vacant Evening Post Volume CXXX Issue 45 21 August 1940 P. 1
51. The New Zealand Gazette No. 52 26 August 1954 P. 1376
52. The New Zealand Gazette No. 37 27 April 1973 P. 843
53. The New Zealand Gazette No. 76 23 November 1967 P. 2146
54. The New Zealand Gazette No. 5 1 February 1968 P. 148
55. (1971) Scientist returns after 40 years Christchurch Press Volume CXI Issue 32570 1 April 1971 P. 15
56. (1970) Advertisements Christchurch Press Volume CX Issue 32346 11 July 1970 P. 20
57. (1972) New Battery Christchurch Press Volume CXII Issue 33058 27 October 1972 P. 11
58. (1973) News In Brief Christchurch Press Volume CXIII Issue 33193 5 April 1973 P. 16
59. (1976) Batteries to Greece Christchurch Press 28 December 1976 P. 16
60. (1977) Successful exporting Christchurch Press 28 September 1977 P. 17
61. (1979) Commercial Export successes continue Christchurch Press 21 August 1979 P. 18
62. (1982) Further dismissals from downturn Christchurch Press 13 December 1982 P. 11
63. (1985) Dunlop Olympic to acquire Chloride Group Christchurch Press 18 September 1985 P. 35
64. Bell, Greg Dunlop Australia Limited Australian National University Archives 22 November 2012 https://archivescollection.anu.edu.au/index.php/dunlop-australia-limited
65. (1988) Transfer of name Christchurch Press 25 February 1988 P. 25
66. (1937) New Companies Auckland Registrations The New Zealand Herald Volume LXXIV Issue 22720 5 May 1937 P. 9
67. (1938) Battery Making Auckland Star Volume LXIX Issue 186 9 August 1938 P. 18
68. (1938) Advertisements The Dominion Volume 31 Issue 277 19 August 1938 P. 41 (Supplement)
69. (1939) Free Battery Service Auckland Star Volume LXX Issue 101 2 May 1939 P. 16
70. New Zealand Companies Office
71. (1940) Amalgamated Batteries Ltd Evening Post Volume CXXX Issue 140 10 December 1940 P. 10 & Advertisements Christchurch Press Volume LXXVI Issue 23044 12 June 1940 P. 13
72. (1960) Storage Batteries Christchurch Press Volume XCIX Issue 29195 4 May 1960 P. 23
73. ibid.
74. (1961) Amalgamated Batteries Christchurch Press Volume C Issue 29486 12 April 1961 P. 19
75. (1933) Advertisements Evening Post Volume CXVI Issue 47 24 August 1933 P. 3
76. New Zealand Companies Office
77. (1934) New Companies Evening Post Volume CXVII Issue 141 16 June 1934 P. 12
78. (1935) Advertisements Evening Post Volume CXX Issue 54 31 August 1935 P. 3
79. (1939) Advertisements The Dominion Volume 32 Issue 233 30 June 1939 P. 3
80. (1962) Amalgamated Batteries Christchurch Press Volume CI Issue 29996 4 December 1962 P. 19
81. (1970) Commercial Successful year for Amalg. Batt. Christchurch Press Volume CX Issue 32454 14 November 1970 P. 20

82. (1971) Good progress by A. Batt Christchurch Press Volume CXI Issue 32608 17 May 1971 P. 18
83. (1979) C.P.D. bid succeeds Christchurch Press 28 March 1979 P. 24
84. (1985) Firms that left the boards Christchurch Press 16 October 1985 P. 41
85. (1988) Workers laid off without warning Christchurch Press 13 February 1988 P. 1
86. (1988) CPD urges Govt action Christchurch Press 26 July 1988 P. 25
87. Willard Storage Battery Company Encylopedia of Cleveland History Case Western Reserve University https://case.edu/ech/articles/w/willard-storage-battery-co
88. (1917) Advertisements Nelson Evening Mail Volume 1 Issue 175 29 December 1917 P. 3
89. (1918) Advertisements Mataura Ensign 19 June 1918 P. 6
90. (1920) Local and General Gisborne Times Volume LII Issue 5503 12 June 1920 P. 4
91. (1920) The Willard Service Station Auckland Star Volume LI Issue 301 17 December 1920 P. 9
92. (1923) Local and General Ashburton Guardian Volume XLIII Issue 9768 8 January 1923 P. 4
93. (1923) Advertisements The New Zealand Herald Volume LX Issue 18529 13 October 1923 P. 11 (supplement)
94. (1928) News And Notes Waikato Times Volume 104 Issue 17511 19 September 1928 P. 4
95. (1929) News & Notes Waikato Times Volume 105 Issue 17729 5 June 1929 P. 11
96. (1939) E.C.C. Waikato Times Volume 124 Issue 20817 30 May 1939 P. 12
97. (1903) Interprovincial News Bush Advocate Volume XIV Issue 272 17 February 1903 P. 3
98. (1890) Electric Traction For Tramways New Zealand Times Volume LI Issue 9005 3 June 1890 P. 1
99. (1893) Untitled Waikato Times Volume XL Issue 3260 20 May 1893 P. 2
100. (1920) Public Works Department Ellesmere Guardian Volume XXIV Issue 4142 24 January 1920 P. 2
101. (1911) Advertisements The New Zealand Herald Volume XLVIII Issue 14817 21 October 1911 P. 4
102. (1921) Electric Power Auckland Star Volume LII Issue 299 16 December 1921 P. 8
103. (1923) Installing Electric Lifts The New Zealand Herald Volume LX Issue 18540 26 October 1923 P. 9
104. (1984) No regulations on escalators Christchurch Press 25 July 1984 P. 14
105. New Zealand Gazette 11 May 2006
106. New Zealand Companies Office
107. (1988) From 1918 to 1988 — Young Brothers have learned the lessons of 70 years in business Christchurch Press 17 June 1988 P. 22
108. (1988) Young Bros celebrate seventy years Christchurch Press 17 June 1988 P. 21
109. (1988) Advertisements Christchurch Press 17 June 1988 P. 21
110. New Zealand Companies Office
111. (1999) A hundred light years Waikato Times 25 June 1999
112. General Electric Britannica Money https://www.britannica.com/money/General-Electric
113. (1936) Trade And Finance Evening Post Volume CXXI Issue 140 15 June 1936 P. 12
114. New Zealand Companies Office
115. AMS Osram History https://ams-osram.com/about-us/history

116. (1909) Advertisements The Dominion Volume 2 Issue 552 6 July 1909 P. 2
117. (1909) Advertisements The Dominion Volume 3 Issue 657 6 November 1909 P. 15
118. New Zealand Gazette No. 83 17 November 1938 P. 2415
119. Who And What Is ACDELCO 21 November 2011
    http://www.overthehillcarpeople.com/whoandwhatisacdelco.htm
120. (1916) Motors And Motoring North Otago Times Volume CIII Issue 13602 24 June 1916 P. 3
121. (1926) Common Faults/Motor Trade Items The New Zealand Herald Volume LXIII Issue 19292 3 April 1926 P. 12 (Supplement)
122. (1926) Notes Christchurch Press Volume LXII Issue 18673 23 April 1926 P. 4
123. (1936) Motordom/Chrysler Chooses Champion Greymouth Evening Star 22 May 1936 P. 4
124. (1930) Motoring & Motorists Evening Star Issue 20649 24 November 1930 P. 15
125. (1965) Spark Plug Factory Christchurch Press Volume CIV Issue 30724 13 April 1965 P. 1
126. New Zealand Companies Office
127. (1988) Partnership Ends Christchurch Press 1 June 1988 P. 46
128. (1988) F. and P. Increases profit to $17.5M Christchurch Press 8 November 1988 P. 27
129. Champion (spark plug) Wikipedia https://en.wikipedia.org/wiki/Champion_(spark_plug)
130. Who And What Is ACDELCO 21 November 2011
    http://www.overthehillcarpeople.com/whoandwhatisacdelco.htm
131. AC Delco History https://acdelco.com.au/gm-b2cau/hundred-years
132. AC Delco History https://acdelco.com.au/gm-b2cau/about
133. Webster, Mark (2021). <u>Assembly - A History of New Zealand Car Production 1921-1998</u>. Sydney/Auckland, New Holland Publishers. P. 118
134. New Zealand Companies Office
135. New Zealand Gazette No. 23 17 April 1969 P. 763
136. Advertisements Christchurch Press Volume CIX Issue 32028 1 July 1969 P. 20
137. (1970) Advertisements Christchurch Press Volume CX Issue 32400 12 September 1970 P. 17
138. (1970) Advertisements Christchurch Press Volume CX Issue 32400 12 September 1970 Pp. 16 & 17
139. (1970) Space! The New Building Christchurch Press Volume CX Issue 32400 12 September 1970 P. 16
140. New Zealand Gazette No. 40 14 April 1976 P. 836
141. New Zealand Rolls-Royce & Bentley Club Inc Issue 17-2 2017 Pp. 26 & 27
142. Experience Blue Gum Consulting Limited
    https://www.bluegumconsultingltd.co.nz/index.phpoption=com_content&view=article&id=3&Itemid=112
143. New Zealand Companies Office
144. Standard Telephones and Cables Wikipedia
    https://en.wikipedia.org/wiki/Standard_Telephones_and_Cables
145. (1927) Advertisements Evening Post Volume CXIII Issue 34 10 February 1927 P. 2
146. (1927) Advertisements Evening Post Volume CXIII Issue 112 14 May 1927 P. 15
147. (1930) Traffic Control Christchurch Press Volume LXVI Issue 19945 4 June 1930 P. 13

148. New Zealand Companies Office
149. (1973) Commercial news in brief Christchurch Press Volume CXIII Issue 33389 22 November 1973 P. 18
150. Webster, Mark (2021). <u>Assembly - A History of New Zealand Car Production 1921-1998</u>. Sydney/Auckland, New Holland Publishers. P. 179
151. (1982) Reduction in staff numbers Christchurch Press 13 November 1982 P. 25
152. New Zealand Companies Office
153. Webster, Mark (2021). <u>Assembly - A History of New Zealand Car Production 1921-1998</u>. Sydney/Auckland, New Holland Publishers. P. 179
154. (1989) Expanding business fills niche Christchurch Press 17 November 1989 P. 16
155. Ben Hall v Pan Pacific Auto Electronics Limited Employment Relations Authority Auckland Determination 21 August 2009
156. Pan Pacific website at: https://www.panpacific.net.nz/Public/Contact
157. New Zealand Companies Office
158. (1936) New Registrations Christchurch Press Volume LXXII Issue 21974 24 December 1936 P. 13
159. (1937) Advertisements Christchurch Press Volume LXXIII Issue 22189 4 September 1937 P. 12
160. (1949) Advertisements Ashburton Guardian Volume 69 Issue 79 13 January 1949 P. 3
161. (1951) Advertisements Christchurch Press Volume LXXXVII Issue 26474 16 July 1951 P. 9
162. (1955) Company News Christchurch Press Volume XCI Issue 27580 10 February 1955 P. 15
163. (1963) New Companies Christchurch Press Volume CII Issue 30209 14 August 1963 P. 17
164. (1965) New Building For Don Agencies Christchurch Press Volume CIV Issue 30824 9 August 1965 P. 8
165. (1976) Offer unconditional Christchurch Press 8 June 1976 P. 18
166. (1977) Extra funds aid A & B profit and sales Christchurch Press 19 April 1977 P. 18
167. (1979) Advertisements Christchurch Press 5 May 1979 P. 19
168. (1983) Scheme to benefit A and B members Christchurch Press 10 June 1983 P. 17
169. (1985) 16 made redundant by rationalisation Christchurch Press 5 November 1985 P. 1
170. New Zealand Companies Office
171. (1973) Milestone for car-seat firm Christchurch Press Volume CXIII Issue 33147 10 February 1973 P. 17
172. (1976) Assistance for firm Christchurch Press 31 August 1976 P. 22
173. (1982) 120 made redundant Christchurch Press 29 October 1982 P. 23
174. (1982) Another 200 redundancies in depressed car industry Christchurch Press 13 November 1982 P. 1
175. (1983) Car workers rehired Christchurch Press 3 November 1983 P. 27
176. Webster, Mark (2021). <u>Assembly - A History of New Zealand Car Production 1921-1998</u>. Sydney/Auckland, New Holland Publishers. P. 152
177. (1985) Briefs Christchurch Press 27 July 1985 P. 21
178. New Zealand Companies Office
179. The New Zealand Gazette No. 84 31 October 1957 P. 2098

180. (1960) National Bank of N.Z. Christchurch Press Volume XCIX Issue 29206 17 May 1960 P. 19
181. The New Zealand Gazette No. 4 29 January 1970 P. 124
182. (1970) Parts Maker Established Christchurch Press Volume CIX Issue 32265 7 April 1970 P. 18
183. (1980) Advertisements Christchurch Press 22 October 1980 P. 3
184. (1982) 120 made redundant Christchurch Press 29 October 1982 P. 23
185. (1985) Fire destroys factory Christchurch Press 29 April 1985 P. 4
186. (1986) Fabco control talks 'advanced' Christchurch Press 16 May 1986 P. 10
187. (1986) Wenrich not yet clear Christchurch Press 22 August 1986 P. 10
188. (1987) Wenrich back to profitability Christchurch Press 17 November 1987 P. 30
189. (1988) Vehicle workers redundant Christchurch Press 7 March 1988 P. 2
190. New Zealand Companies Office
191. (1958) Gracefield Fire Losses May Exceed £1,000,000 Christchurch Press Volume XCVII Issue 28513 17 February 1958 P. 8
192. (1959) Advertisements Christchurch Press Volume XCVIII Issue 28804 27 January 1959 P. 15
193. (1973) Advertisements Christchurch Press Volume CXIII Issue 33138 31 January 1973 P. 12
194. (1978) Advertisements Christchurch Press 5 October 1978 P. 23
195. (1980) Advertisements Christchurch Press 28 May 1980 P. 18
196. (1982) Unique plan to prevent lay-offs Christchurch Press 10 December 1982 P. 3
197. (1985) Advertisements Christchurch Press 1 August 1985 P. 25
198. New Zealand Gazette No. 75 20 September 1951 P. 1411
199. New Zealand Gazette No. 12 18 February 1954 P. 263
200. (1962) Amalgamated Batteries Christchurch Press Volume CI Issue 29996 4 December 1962 P. 19
201. (1966) M. Holdings Moves Christchurch Press Volume CV Issue 30971 29 January 1966 P. 18
202. New Zealand Gazette No. 43 6 July 1967 P. 1183
203. (1967) Restraints Affected Motor Holdings Christchurch Press Volume CVII Issue 31446 12 August 1967 P. 18
204. (1973) Assembly of cars Christchurch Press Volume CXIII Issue 33315 28 August 1973 P. 2
205. (1977) Plant small but efficient Christchurch Press 26 August 1977 P. 8
206. (1979) Motor Holdings to reopen plant Christchurch Press 19 September 1979 P. 28
207. Webster, Mark (2021). <u>Assembly - A History of New Zealand Car Production 1921-1998</u>. Sydney/Auckland, New Holland Publishers. P. 188
208. (1921) Commercial Evening Star Issue 17621 29 March 1921 P. 4
209. (1920) Australian News Hawera & Normanby Star Volume LXXX Issue LXXX 31 January 1920 P. 9
210. (1935) Various Registrations Evening Post Volume CXIX Issue 140 15 June 1935 P. 12
211. (1960) Obituary Mr H D Guthrie Christchurch Press Volume XCIX Issue 29256 14 July 1960 P. 19

212. (1935) Public Notice Auckland Star Volume LXVI Issue 132 6 June 1935 P. 6
213. (1937) Modern Plant Evening Post Volume CXXIV Issue 34 9 August 1937 P. 10
214. (1939) Mr Savage's Itinerary Evening Post Volume CXXVII Issue 47 25 February 1939 P. 11
215. (1940) British Australian Lead Evening Post Volume CXXIX Issue 44 21 February 1940 P. 12
216. New Zealand Gazette No. 2 20 January 1955 P. 48
217. (1960) B.A.L.M. Paints 25th Anniversary Celebration Christchurch Press Volume XCIX Issue 29381 7 December 1960 P. 12
218. (1957) BALM Paints Laboratories Christchurch Press Volume XCV Issue 28290 30 May 1957 P. 11
219. (1959) Developments In Paint Christchurch Press Volume XCVIII Issue 29068 3 December 1959 P. 23
220. (1960) B.A.L.M. Paints 25th Anniversary Celebration Christchurch Press Volume XCIX Issue 29381 7 December 1960 P. 12
221. (1962) Company News BALM Paints Plans Christchurch Press Volume CI Issue 29782 27 March 1962 P. 17
222. (1965) Fibremakers Expected To Help Profits Christchurch Press Volume CIV Issue 30920 29 November 1965 P. 22
223. Dulux in Australia and New Zealand Wikipedia https://en.wikipedia.org/wiki/Dulux
224. New Zealand Gazette No. 72 30 September 1971 P. 2042
225. Dulux in Australia and New Zealand Wikipedia https://en.wikipedia.org/wiki/Dulux
226. Orica 150 History https://www.orica.com/About-Us/Orica-150/history
227. Dulux in Australia and New Zealand Wikipedia https://en.wikipedia.org/wiki/Dulux
228. ibid.
229. (1931) Advertisements Auckland Star Volume LXII Issue 290 8 December 1931 P. 18
230. (1932) Advertisements Christchurch Star Volume XLIV Issue 359 27 February 1932 P. 6
231. Duco Wikipedia https://en.wikipedia.org/wiki/Duco
232. New Zealand Companies Office
233. (1935) New Bus: The New Zealand Herald Volume LXXII Issue 22298 21 December 1935 P. 14 (Supplement)
234. (1973) Advertisements Christchurch Press Volume CXIII Issue 33138 31 January 1973 P. 12
235. New Zealand Companies Office
236. Dulux Group – Acquisition by Nippon Paint Holdings Co. Ltd https://www.duluxgroup.com.au/investor-centre/nippon-acquisition
237. (1916) The New Zealand Herald Volume LIII Issue 16210 22 April 1916 P. 2
238. (1916) The Jubilee Show Southland Times Issue 17897 13 December 1916 P. 7
239. (1917 The New Zealand Herald Volume LIV Issue 16609 4 August 1917 P.2
240. ibid.
241. ibid.
242. (1919) Commercial Items The Dominion Volume 12 Issue 198 16 May 1919 P. 10
243. (1919) The New Zealand Herald Volume LVI Issue 17244 21 August 1919 P.2

244. (1919) The Best In Motoring Comfort And Style Lyttelton Times Volume CXVII Issue 18253 14 November 1919 P. 12
245. (1920) The New Zealand Herald Volume LVII Issue 17511 1 July 1920 P.2
246. (1933) Advertisements Evening Post Volume CXVI Issue 145 16 December 1933 P. 27
247. (1933) Advertisements Evening Post Volume CXVI Issue 145 16 December 1933 P. 27
248. (1986) Sir Philip Proctor Christchurch Press 28 June 1986 P. 22
249. New Zealand Companies Office
250. (1946) Motor Tyres Otago Daily Times Issue 26212 24 July 1946 P. 8
251. (1947) Dunlop (N.Z.) Rubber Ltd. Otago Daily Times Issue 26419 25 March 1947 P. 7
252. (1950) Net Loss Shown By Dunlop (NZ) Ltd. Otago Daily Times Issue 27347 24 March 1950 P. 9
253. (1953) Company News Christchurch Press Volume LXXXIX Issue 27008 7 April 1953 P. 13
254. (1958) Company News Dunlop (N.Z.) Christchurch Press Volume XCVII Issue 28575 2 May 1958 P. 13
255. (1964) Dunlop Profit, Output Higher Christchurch Press Volume CIII Issue 30426 28 April 1964 P. 17
256. (1965) Dunlop Buys Retreader Christchurch Press Volume CIV Issue 30766 2 June 1965 P. 20
257. (1972) Commercial Dunlop served busy market Christchurch Press Volume CXII Issue 32881 3 April 1972 P. 13
258. (1978) Dunlop adds steel to tyre range Christchurch Press 24 February 1978 P. 13
259. (1982) Dunlop profit falls 9 p.c. Christchurch Press 27 February 1982 P. 18
260. (1983) Tyre jobs lost in big Dunlop take-over Christchurch Press 26 March 1983 P. 1
261. Freeth, Martin Govt. prepares for more from import licensing Christchurch Press 6 October 1984 P. 23
262. (1985) Workers think Dunlop may close Chch plant Christchurch Press 20 May 1985 P. 1
263. (1985) Briefs Christchurch Press 13 July 1985 P. 24
264. (1986) Goodyear, Pac. Dunlop to merge activities Christchurch Press 9 December 1986 P. 27
265. (1987) Dunlop approval Christchurch Press 30 March 1987 P. 15
266. (1989) Scope for tyre price cuts - firm Christchurch Press 16 June 1989 P. 37
267. Dick, Allan MTA Centenary Publication — RnR Publishing Limited Martinborough, New Zealand April 2017 P.20
268. New Zealand Companies Office
269. (1947) Firestone To Have Australian Plant Bay of Plenty Times Volume LXXVI Issue14542 10 December 1947 P. 4
270. (1955) Advertisements Christchurch Press Volume XCI Issue 27579 9 February 1955 P. 16
271. New Zealand Companies Office
272. (1975) Firestone last year beset by many problems Christchurch Press Volume CXV Issue 33753 28 January 1975 P. 18
273. (1978) Firestone treads carefully Christchurch Press 24 February 1978 P. 1

274. (1983) Challenge for Firestone Christchurch Press 29 January 1983 P. 18
275. Parliamentary Debates Volume 467 14 November 1985 P. 8119
276. (1987) Firestone waits on tariff issue Christchurch Press 20 February 1987 P. 11
277. Webster, Mark (2021). <u>Assembly - A History of New Zealand Car Production 1921-1998</u>. Sydney/Auckland, New Holland Publishers. P. 177
278. (1989) Firestone profit falls Christchurch Press 9 June 1989 P. 14
279. (1980) Who Owns New Zealand? Christchurch Press 2 July 1980 P. 21
280. New Zealand Companies Office
281. Firestone Factory Te Ara Encyclopedia of New Zealand https://teara.govt.nz/en/photograph/22848/firestone-factory
282. Bridgestone History https://www.bridgestone.com/corporate/history/story/1981-1990.html
283. New Zealand Companies Office
284. (1981) Inquiry welcomed Christchurch Press 29 April 1981 P. 22
285. Parliamentary Debates Volume 443 29 April 1982 P. 647
286. (1982) Tyre support 'deserved' Christchurch Press 22 February 1982 P. 11
287. (1969) Company's 50 Years Christchurch Press Volume CIX Issue 32082 2 September 1969 P. 13
288. (1921) Advertisements The New Zealand Herald Volume LVIII Issue 17748 6 April 1921 P. 2
289. (1921) Advertisements The New Zealand Herald Volume LVIII Issue 17817 25 June 1921 P. 3
290. (1969) Company's 50 Years Christchurch Press Volume CIX Issue 32082 2 September 1969 P. 13
291. (1969) Motor Spec. To Change Name Christchurch Press Volume CIX Issue 32088 9 September 1969 P. 17
292. (1971) Expansion by Motor Specialties Christchurch Press Volume CXI Issue 32705 7 September 1971 P. 21
293. (1971) A and B, Motor Specs in joint venture Christchurch Press Volume CXI Issue 32779 2 December 1971 P. 19
294. (1971) Diversification by Motor Specs Christchurch Press Volume CXI Issue 32789 14 December 1971 P. 25
295. (1976) Motor Specs. Ahead Christchurch Press 7 October 1976 P. 23
296. (1978) Conservation award Christchurch Press 17 March 1978 P. 5
297. (1981) Shake-up for MSI Christchurch Press 26 September 1981 P. 20
298. (1982) MSI Corporation restructures Christchurch Press 5 April 1982 P. 24
299. (1982) Repco moves quickly to raise MSI stake Christchurch Press 12 June 1982 P. 21
300. (1981) ACI and Repco to restructure Christchurch Press 9 December 1981 P. 29
301. (1983) A and B-Repco merger deal Christchurch Press 3 May 1983 P. 1
302. (1879) Advertisements Lyttelton Times Volume LI Issue 5635 18 March 1879 P. 1
303. New Zealand Companies Office
304. (1936) Eighty Years Surveyed Christchurch Press Volume LXXII Issue 21796 30 May 1936 P. 21

305. (1959) Roading Equipment Made In Christchurch Christchurch Press Volume XCVIII Issue 28971 12 August 1959 P. 24
306. (1960) Andrews and Beaven Christchurch Press Volume XCIX Issue 29376 1 December 1960 P. 21
307. (1961) Company News Andrews and Beaven Christchurch Press Volume C Issue 29662 4 November 1961 P. 16
308. (1965) John Chambers Board Changes Christchurch Press Volume CIV Issue 30871 2 October 1965 P. 22
309. (1968) Advertisements Christchurch Press Volume CVIII Issue 31784 14 September 1968 P. 25
310. (1969) Oil Fever Grips Sharemarket Christchurch Press Volume CIX Issue 32147 17 November 1969 P. 24
311. (1973) Andrews and Beaven at record sales levels Christchurch Press Volume CXIII Issue 33358 17 October 1973 P. 18
312. (1983) Chch firm retrenches, 250 lay-offs nationally Christchurch Press 15 September 1983 P. 1
313. (1969) G.A.C. Progressive, NZ-Wide Company Christchurch Press Volume CIX Issue 32140 8 November 1969 P. 19
314. (1914) Advertisements Column 4 New Zealand Herald Volume LI Issue 15504 10 January 1914 P. 14
315. (1915) Advertisements The New Zealand Herald Volume LII Issue 15941 11 June 1915 P. 2
316. (1918) Advertisements The New Zealand Herald Volume LV Issue 16977 10 October 1918 P. 10
317. (1919) Advertisements Auckland Star Volume L Issue 247 17 October 1919 P. 2
318. (1920) Advertisements The New Zealand Herald Volume LVII Issue 17439 8 April 1920 P. 7
319. New Zealand Companies Office
320. (1923) Modern Motoring by Sparkwell Auckland Star Volume LIV Issue 199 21 August 1923 P. 11
321. (1924) Olympia Motor Show The New Zealand Herald Volume LXI Issue 18642 25 February 1924 P. 4
322. New Zealand Companies Office
323. New Zealand Gazette No. 47 4 August 1960 P. 1064
324. Tidd Ross Todd Limited at: https://www.trt.co.nz/about-us/
325. New Zealand Companies Office
326. (1926) Company Affairs Auckland Star Volume LVII Issue 142 17 June 1926 P. 4
327. (1938) Advertisements The New Zealand Herald Volume LXXV Issue 23043 21 May 1938 P. 1
328. (1940) Advertisements The New Zealand Herald Volume LXXVII Issue 23740 21 August 1940 P. 1
329. (1943) Advertisements The New Zealand Herald Volume 80 Issue 24684 9 September 1943 P. 1

330. (1944) Advertisements The Manawatu Standard Volume LXIV Issue 41 17 January 1944 P. 1
331. (1958) Motor Traders Record Profit Christchurch Press Volume XCVII Issue 28717 15 October 1958 P. 19
332. (1958) Advertisements Christchurch Press Volume XCVII Issue 28660 9 August 1958 P. 17
333. (1959) New City Warehouse Sign Of Confidence In Trade Christchurch Press Volume XCVIII Issue 28804 27 January 1959 P. 15
334. (1962) Motor Traders NZ Christchurch Press Volume CI Issue 29992 29 November 1962 P. 22
335. (1965) M. Traders Year Christchurch Press Volume CIV Issue 30911 18 November 1965 P. 21
336. (1971) Expansion pays off for Motor Traders Christchurch Press Volume CXI Issue 32759 9 November 1971 P. 28
337. (1981) MTL board accepts Smiths bid Christchurch Press 14 August 1981 P. 19
338. New Zealand Gazette No. 108 17 September 1981 P. 2609
339. (1982) A and B moves check profit Christchurch Press 30 October 1982 P. 18
340. Commission of Inquiry into the Distribution of Motor Vehicle Parts Wellington 30 November 1977

Chapter Six

1. Such, William B. (Revised Edition 1969). <u>Poverty and Progress in New Zealand - A Re-Assessment</u>. Wellington. A H & A W Reed. P. 97
2. ibid. Pp. 98-99
3. ibid. P. 105
4. ibid. Pp. 141-142
5. ibid. P. 147
6. ibid. P. 341
7. (1907) The Future of Tariff Reform The Thames Star Volume XLIV Issue 10195 18 January 1907 P. 2
8. (1907) Editorial Notes Rangitikei Advocate & Manawatu Argus (Second Edition) Volume XXXI Issue 8712 11 January 1907 P. 2
9. (1907) Auckland Chamber of Commerce Auckland Star Volume XXXVIII Issue 149 24 June 1907 P. 3
10. The New Zealand Gazette Extraordinary 26 September 1907
11. The Tariff Act 1907 25 September 1907
12. ibid.
13. Tariff Revision Evening Star Issue 12754 30 August 1907 P. 2
14. (1907) The Close of the Session Auckland Star Volume XXXVIII Issue 281 25 November 1907 P. 4
15. Witt, Daniel A The New Zealand Motor Car Industry After The Plan - New Zealand Institute of Economic Research Incorporated October 1985 P. 16

16. Rose, William Dennis Development Options in the New Zealand Motor Car Assembly Industry — Research Paper No. 16 of the NZ Institute of Economic Research (Inc.) Wellington 1971 P. 66
17. ibid. P. 14
18. Customs Amendment Act 1921 No. 19 22 December 1921
19. Rose, William Dennis Development Options in the New Zealand Motor Car Assembly Industry — Research Paper No. 16 of the NZ Institute of Economic Research (Inc.) Wellington 1971 P. 15
20. Webster, Mark (2021). <u>Assembly - A History of New Zealand Car Production 1921-1998</u>. Sydney/Auckland, New Holland Publishers. P. 29
21. Customs Amendment Act 1926
22. Rose, William Dennis Development Options in the New Zealand Motor Car Assembly Industry — Research Paper No. 16 of the NZ Institute of Economic Research (Inc.) Wellington 1971 P. 15
23. Customs Amendment Act 1926
24. Webster, Mark (2021). <u>Assembly - A History of New Zealand Car Production 1921-1998</u>. Sydney/Auckland, New Holland Publishers. P. 29
25. (1927) The Tariff Christchurch Press Volume LXIII Issue 19106 15 September 1927 P. 9
26. (1930) Advertisements The Dominion Volume 23 Issue 173 17 April 1930 P. 5
27. (1930) Advertisements The Dominion Volume 23 Issue 255 24 July 1930 P. 8
28. Webster, Mark (2021). <u>Assembly - A History of New Zealand Car Production 1921-1998</u>. Sydney/Auckland, New Holland Publishers. Pp. 28-29
29. (1926) Transport Hawke's Bay Tribune Volume XVI Issue 279 12 November 1926 P. 6
30. Such, William B. (Revised Edition 1969). <u>Poverty and Progress in New Zealand - A Re-Assessment</u>. Wellington. A H & A W Reed. P. 210
31. ibid. P. 213
32. Webster, Mark (2021). <u>Assembly - A History of New Zealand Car Production 1921-1998</u>. Sydney/Auckland, New Holland Publishers. P. 30
33. The Customs Tariff Commission Report 1934 P. 1
34. Statement by the Right Hon. J G Coates, Minister of Customs, when introducing the Customs Resolutions to Parliament 10 July 1934
35. The Customs Tariff Commission Report 1934 Pp. 4-5
36. Statement by the Right Hon. J G Coates, Minister of Customs, when introducing the Customs Resolutions to Parliament 10 July 1934 Pp. 3-5 & 15
37. Maddren, Philip James The Impact of Economic Policies on the Motor Vehicle Assembly Industry of New Zealand: An Effective Protection Analysis — A Thesis Lincoln University 1995 P. 14
38. Customs Acts Amendment Act 1934
39. ibid.
40. New Zealand Gazette No. 78 18 October 1934 P. 3357
41. Rose, William Dennis Development Options in the New Zealand Motor Car Assembly Industry — Research Paper No. 16 of the NZ Institute of Economic Research (Inc.) Wellington 1971 P. 16
42. (1930) Turned Us Down The Dominion Volume 23 Issue 280 22 August 1930 P. 10

43. New Zealand Gazette No. 86 21 November 1935 P. 3336
44. Rose, William Dennis Development Options in the New Zealand Motor Car Assembly Industry — Research Paper No. 16 of the NZ Institute of Economic Research (Inc.) Wellington 1971 P. 17
45. Maddren, Philip James The Impact of Economic Policies on the Motor Vehicle Assembly Industry of New Zealand: An Effective Protection Analysis — A Thesis Lincoln University 1995 Pp. 15 & 22
46. ibid. Pp. 109-110
47. Such, William B. (Revised Edition 1969). <u>Poverty and Progress in New Zealand - A Re-Assessment</u>. Wellington. A H & A W Reed. P. 241
48. (1938) N.Z. Overseas Loan — Apprehends N.Z. Currency Inflation Grey River Argus 14 November 1938 P. 7
49. Such, William B. (Revised Edition 1969). <u>Poverty and Progress in New Zealand - A Re-Assessment</u>. Wellington. A H & A W Reed. P. 227
50. (1938) New Procedure The New Zealand Herald Volume LXXV Issue 23215 8 December 1938 P. 17
51. (1938) Controlled Imports Christchurch Press Volume LXXIV Issue 22579 8 December 1938 P. 10
52. (1939) New Motor-Cars The New Zealand Herald Volume LXXVI Issue 23237 5 January 1939 P. 10
53. (1940) Finance And Commerce — Idle Factory Plants Christchurch Press Volume LXXVI Issue 23081 25 July 1940 P. 4
54. (1940) The Motor Trade Evening Post Volume CXXX Issue 124 21 November 1940 P. 12
55. (1941) Not Recorded — Motor Vehicle Imports Evening Post Volume CXXXI Issue 145 21 June 1941 P. 5
56. (1945) Imports Of New Vehicles Christchurch Press Volume LXXXI Issue 24761 29 December 1945 P. 6
57. (1946) Motor Vehicle Imports Otago Daily Times Issue 26064 30 January 1946 P. 4
58. (1946) Motor Vehicle Imports Christchurch Press Volume LXXXII Issue 24974 7 September 1946 P. 2
59. ibid.
60. (1947) Motor Vehicles — Issue of Import Licences Ashburton Guardian Volume 67 Issue 246 30 July 1947 P. 3
61. (1949) Motor Trade Urges Need for Increased Importation of Cars - Otago Daily Times Issue 27175 2 September 1949 P. 6
62. (1949) New Zealand Requires More Than 100,00 Cars - Bay of Plenty Beacon, Volume 14 Issue 44 28 September 1949 P. 4
63. (1949) Motor Trade Urges Need for Increased Importation of Cars - Otago Daily Times Issue 27175 2 September 1949 P. 6
64. (1949) Motor Vehicle Imports To Be Increased Grey River Argus 9 May 1949 P. 5
65. Rose, William Dennis Development Options in the New Zealand Motor Car Assembly Industry — Research Paper No. 16 of the NZ Institute of Economic Research (Inc.) Wellington 1971 Pp. 17-18
66. Import Licensing In New Zealand Reserve Bank Bulletin March 1981 Pp. 75-76

67. (1970) Convictions Under No-remittance Cases Christchurch Press Volume CIX Issue 32215 6 February 1970 P. 14
68. No-Remittance Licence - Salient, An Organ of Student Opinion at Victoria College, Wellington Volume 17 No. 18 3 September 1953
69. (1972) No-remittance final dates Christchurch Press Volume CXII Issue 32835 8 February 1972 P. 12
70. (1971) No gloom in this Budget Christchurch Press Volume CXI Issue 32630 11 June 1971 P. 8
71. Rose, William Dennis Development Options in the New Zealand Motor Car Assembly Industry — Research Paper No. 16 of the NZ Institute of Economic Research (Inc.) Wellington 1971 P. 20
72. (1950) High Prices for Cars Local And General Te Awamutu Courier Volume 80 Issue 7209 7 June 1950 P. 6
73. (1952) Imports Of Vehicles — Quotas for 1952 Christchurch Press Volume LXXXVIII Issue 26757 14 June 1952 P. 6
74. ibid.
75. (1953) Built-Up Cars — Licensing Decision Deplored Christchurch Press Volume LXXXIX Issue 27032 6 May 1953 P. 11
76. (1954) Motor Vehicle Imports Christchurch Press Volume XC Issue 27428 14 August 1954 P. 8
77. (1955) Assembly Of Cars Christchurch Press Volume XCI Issue 27597 2 March 1955 P.14
78. (1955) Motor-Vehicle Imports Christchurch Press Volume XCI Issue 27660 17 May 1955 P. 11
79. (1955) Cuts In Vehicle Imports Christchurch Press Volume XCII Issue 27789 14 October 1955 P. 6
80. (1958) Light Truck Imports Christchurch Press Volume XCVII Issue 28534 13 March 1958 P. 14
81. (1957) Motor Vehicle Imports: Allocation For 1958 Christchurch Press Volume XCVI Issue 28357 16 August 1957 P. 14
82. ibid.
83. Rose, William Dennis Development Options in the New Zealand Motor Car Assembly Industry — Research Paper No. 16 of the NZ Institute of Economic Research (Inc.) Wellington 1971 P. 21
84. Balance of Payments — Arnold Nordmeyer and his black budget 1958 Te Ara, The Encyclopedia of NZ
85. Customs Acts Amendment Act 1958 - Second Schedule
86. (1958) Christchurch Press Volume XCVII Issue 28486 16 January 1958 P. 8
87. Turnovsky, Stephen J The New Zealand Automobile Market, 1948-63: An Economic Case-Study of Disequilibrium — published The Economic Record June 1966 Volume 42 (1-4) Pp. 256-273
88. Sutch, William B — the quest for security in New Zealand 1840 to 1966 — Wellington, Oxford University Press, 1966 Pp. 418-419

89. Maddren, Philip James The Impact of Economic Policies on the Motor Vehicle Assembly Industry of New Zealand: An Effective Protection Analysis — A Thesis Lincoln University 1995 Pp. 15 & 22
90. (1960) Imports Of Cars Up Slightly Next Year Christchurch Press Volume XCIX Issue 29330 8 October 1960 P. 12
91. Rose, William Dennis Development Options in the New Zealand Motor Car Assembly Industry — Research Paper No. 16 of the NZ Institute of Economic Research (Inc.) Wellington 1971 Pp. 21-23
92. ibid. Pp. 25-27
93. (1970) Car Imports Christchurch Press Volume CIX Issue 32226 19 February 1970 P. 10
94. Rose, William Dennis Development Options in the New Zealand Motor Car Assembly Industry — Research Paper No. 16 of the NZ Institute of Economic Research (Inc.) Wellington 1971 Pp. 8-9, 11, 187
95. (1972) Fewer car models, 'but buyers gain' Christchurch Press Volume CXII Issue 33104 20 December 1972 P. 1
96. Greenslade, Peter Big no-frills Holden smooth traveller Christchurch Press 21 April 1989 P. 29
97. (1974) Shares of market Christchurch Press Volume CXIV Issue 33472 1 March 1974 P. 14
98. (1977) Muldoon eye on car sales Christchurch Press 22 October 1977 P.1
99. (1975) Car duty questioned Christchurch Press Volume CXV Issue 33929 23 August 1975 P. 2
100. Tariff and Development Board Act 1961
101. Industries Development Commission Amendment Act 1975
102. (1975) Chairman for new body Christchurch Press Volume CXV Issue 33904 25 July 1975 P. 13
103. (1975) Economic Strategy Tariff review and industry study Christchurch Press Issue 33837 8 May 1975 P. 5
104. (1981) Tyre factories supported Christchurch Press 9 November 1981 P. 6
105. (1981) Tyre factories safe Christchurch Press 10 December 1981 P. 10
106. (1982) Jobs hit in car industry plan Christchurch Press 11 September 1982 P. 1
107. (1982) Repco head chides IDC Christchurch Press 6 November 1982 P. 19
108. (1982) New cars unlikely to be cheaper — dealers Christchurch Press 9 October 1982 P. 11
109. (1982) Car industry lay-offs Christchurch Press 21 October 1982 P. 6
110. (1982) Car industry lay-offs Christchurch Press 21 October 1982 P. 6
111. (1922) The Motor World Otago Daily Times Issue 18715 20 November 1922 P. 2
112. (1955) Hire-Purchase Regulations Christchurch Press Volume XCII Issue 27719 25 July 1955 P. 10
113. (1958) Hire-Purchase Changes Christchurch Press Volume XCVII Issue 28623 27 June 1958 P. 12
114. (1964) General News Christchurch Press Volume CIII Issue 30407 4 April 1964 P. 12
115. (1968) Lower Deposits On Used Cars Christchurch Press Volume CVIII Issue 31681 17 May 1968 P. 1

116. (1972) Car prices up, down Christchurch Press Volume CXII Issue 33010 1 September 1972 P. 2
117. (1974) Motor-cycle 'discrimination' Christchurch Press Volume CXIV Issue 33640 16 September 1974 P. 12
118. (1976) Slump in car sales Christchurch Press 24 September 1976 P. 1
119. (1977) All woe and little go in car trade Christchurch Press 18 August 1977 P. 1
120. (1978) Economic package announced by P.M. Christchurch Press 3 February 1978 P. 3
121. (1978) New-car sales up 25p.c. Christchurch Press 30 March 1978 P. 5
122. (1978) More buying cars on h.p. Christchurch Press 20 February 1978 P. 5
123. (1981) H.P. on cars to stay Christchurch Press 6 August 1981 P. 4
124. (1982) Regulations attacked by finance houses Christchurch Press 17 February 1982 P. 10
125. (1983) Editorial — No stimulus for car sales Christchurch Press 1 March 1983 P. 20
126. (1983) Dropping of car credit controls welcomed Christchurch Press 9 September 1983 P. 1
127. (1984) Sharp rise in h.p. Christchurch Press 19 June 1984 P. 20
128. (1984) Tasman car talks Christchurch Press 20 September 1984 P. 13
129. (1984) Australians like N.Z. motor industry plan by Chris Peters Christchurch Press 14 December 1984 P. 28
130. (1984) Car dealers welcome new Govt plan Christchurch Press 13 December 1984 P. 6
131. Witt, Daniel A The New Zealand Motor Car Industry After The Plan - New Zealand Institute of Economic Research Incorporated October 1985 P. 36
132. ibid. P. 10
133. ibid. P.12
134. Import Licensing Reserve Bank Bulletin March 1981 Pp. 76 & 78
135. (1985) Car tenderers bid high Christchurch Press 27 February 1985 P. 33
136. (1987) N.Z. car prices Christchurch Press 22 October 1987 P. 14
137. (1987) Motor vehicle tariffs Christchurch Press 18 December 1987 P. 10
138. England, Jane Thousands of dollars off car prices Christchurch Press Volume 6 May 1988 P. 8
139. (1966) Buying More Cars From Japan Urged Christchurch Press Volume CVI Issue 31196 21 October 1966 P. 3
140. (1973) Shiploads Of Cars Christchurch Press Volume CXIII Issue 33373 3 November 1973 P. 20
141. (1973) $3m car shipment Christchurch Press Volume CXIII Issue 33403 8 December 1973 P. 20
142. Witt, Daniel A The New Zealand Motor Car Industry After The Plan - New Zealand Institute of Economic Research Incorporated October 1985 P. 81
143. Dowling, Craig N.Z. car fleet rejuvenated Christchurch Press 30 November 1989 P. 31
144. Webster, Mark (2021). <u>Assembly - A History of New Zealand Car Production 1921-1998</u>. Sydney/Auckland, New Holland Publishers. P. 188
145. Rose, William Dennis Development Options in the New Zealand Motor Car Assembly Industry — Research Paper No. 16 of the NZ Institute of Economic Research (Inc.) Wellington 1971 Pp. 7 & 50

Chapter Seven

1. (1898) Advertisements Auckland Star Volume XXIX Issue 292 10 December 1898 P. 2
2. Hawkes, Graham (1990) On the Road - The Car In New Zealand. Wellington, GP Books. P. 10
3. (1907) Town & Country Timaru Herald Volume XIC Issue 13396 20 September 1907 P. 4
4. (1907) Town & Country Timaru Herald Volume XIC Issue 13457 2 December 1907 P. 4
5. (1907) Untitled Taranaki Herald Volume LIV Issue 13510 11 September 1907 P. 4
6. (1907) Advertising Memoranda Manawatu Times Volume LXIV Issue 106 8 May 1907 P. 5
7. (1972) Pioneer driver dead Christchurch Press Volume CXII Issue 32894 18 April 1972 P. 6
8. (1910) Business Notices Taranaki Daily News Volume LIII Issue 210 14 December 1910 P. 8
9. The New Zealand Gazette No. 4 15 January 1920 P. 191
10. (1909) Advertisements The New Zealand Herald Volume XLVI Issue 14109 10 July 1909 P. 4
11. (1913) Takapuna Sensation Otago Daily Times Issue 15754 3 May 1913 P. 10
12. (1913) Telegrams Feilding Star Volume VIII Issue 2076 17 May 1913 P. 2
13. (1933) Matakana Rodney and Otamatea Times, Waitemata and Kaipara Gazette 9 August 1933 P. 4
14. (1936) Presentation The New Zealand Herald Volume LXXIII Issue 22608 22 December 1936 P. 12
15. (1944) Meteorological The New Zealand Herald Volume 81 Issue 25086 27 December 1944 P. 4
16. (1945) Advertisements Otago Daily Times Issue 26022 10 December 1945 P. 8
17. (1897) Local And General Evening Post Volume LIV Issue 141 11 December 1897 P. 4
18. (1901) West Coast Times, Issue 11972 26 July 1901 P. 2
19. (1913) Social And Personal New Zealand Times Volume XXXVII Issue 8366 28 February 1913 P. 5
20. (1908) Local And General The Dominion Volume 1 Issue 161 1 April 1908 P. 6
21. (1917) Nelson Evening Mail -Volume LI Issue 175 30 July 1917 P. 1
22. (1923) Local and General Hawke's Bay Tribune Volume XIII Issue 119 7 May 1923 P. 6
23. (1934) Evening Post Volume CXVII Issue 35 10 February 1934 P. 26
24. (1970) Commercial Merger Puts NZMC In Strong Position Christchurch Press Volume CIX Issue 32269 11 April 1970 P. 16
25. (1908) Advertisements Christchurch Press Volume LXIV Issue 13029 3 February 1908 P. 2
26. (1908) Advertisements Christchurch Press Volume LXIV Issue 13219 12 September 1908 P. 5
27. (1920) Round the Garages — Phenomenal Growth of Business Christchurch Sun Volume VII Issue 2101 8 November 1920 P. 21 (Supplement)
28. (1915) Advertisements Lyttelton Times Volume CXVI Issue 17037 11 December 1915 P. 1

29. (1925) Whose Assets? Christchurch Press Volume LXI Issue 18485 12 September 1925 P. 7
30. ibid.
31. (1925) Court Of Appeal New Zealand Times Volume LII Issue 12274 21 October 1925 P.6
32. (1971) The Company Christchurch Press Volume CXI Issue 32716 20 September 1971 P. 22
33. (1929) Pioneer And Pauper The New Zealand Herald Volume LXVI Issue 20342 24 August 1929 P. 12 (Supplement)
34. (1971) The Company Christchurch Press Volume CXI Issue 32716 20 September 1971 P. 22
35. (1962) Garage Has Served District For Many Years Christchurch Press Volume CI Issue 29965 29 October 1962 P. 11
36. (1971) The Company Christchurch Press Volume CXI Issue 32716 20 September 1971 P. 22
37. ibid.
38. (1973) Landmarks Christchurch Press Volume CXIII Issue 33299 9 August 1973 P. 13
39. New Zealand Gazette No. 61 21 October 1965 P. 1827
40. (1967) More Japanese Cars Christchurch Press Volume CVI Issue 31293 13 February 1967 P. 10
41. New Zealand Gazette No. 29 21 May 1970 P. 908
42. (1971) The Company Christchurch Press Volume CXI Issue 32716 20 September 1971 P. 22
43. Hunt, Graeme The Rich List — Wealth and Enterprise in New Zealand 1820-2000 Reed Books Auckland 2000 Pp. 148-149
44. (1917) Military Service Christchurch Sun Volume IV Issue 1048 21 June 1917 P. 10
45. (1917) Military Service Christchurch Sun Volume IV Issue 934 7 February 1917 P. 2
46. (1917) Military Service Christchurch Sun Volume IV Issue 1017 16 May 1917 P. 10
47. (1917) Military Service Christchurch Sun Volume IV Issue 1048 21 June 1917 P. 10
48. (1917) Advertisements NZ Truth Issue 636 25 August 1917 P. 2
49. (1930) Tench Brothers Have Dispute Christchurch Star Issue 19019 14 March 1930 P. 9
50. (1928) Scents Libel And Challenges Counsel NZ Truth Issue 1157 2 February 1928 P. 8
51. (1929) Advertisements Christchurch Star Issue 18942 12 December 1929 P. 20
52. (1930) Advertisements Christchurch Press Volume LXVI Issue 19836 25 January 1930 P. 8
53. (1966) Known In Motor Trade Christchurch Press Volume CVI Issue 31069 26 May 1966 P. 20
54. (1953) Advertisements Christchurch Press Volume LXXXIX Issue 27137 5 September 1953 P. 15
55. (1970) Singer Cars To Continue In N.Z. Christchurch Press Volume CX Issue 32208 29 January 1970 P. 10
56. (1971) Motor Firm To Move Christchurch Press Volume CXI Issue 32737 14 October 1971 P. 12
57. (1979) Chch dealers are big, experienced Christchurch Press 5 November 1979 P. 14

58. (1975) Business built on reliability Christchurch Press Volume CXV Issue 33767 13 February 1975 P. 11
59. (1972) Franchise for Chch only Christchurch Press Volume CXII Issue 32888 11 April 1972 P. 14
60. (1983) Tench Bros changes Christchurch Press 17 November 1983 P. 26
61. New Zealand Companies Office
62. (1922) Sensation In Motoring Circles The New Zealand Herald Volume LIX Issue 18196 15 September 1922 P. 9
63. (1926) Advertisements Waikato Times Volume 101 Issue 16875 14 August 1926 P. 21 (Supplement)
64. (1928) Advertisements Waikato Times Volume 104 Issue 17560 15 November 1928 P. 1
65. (1928) New Model Buick Car The New Zealand Herald Volume LXV Issue 20076 13 October 1928 P. 11
66. (1929) Buick Reputation The New Zealand Herald Volume LXVI Issue 20180 14 February 1929 P. 23 (Supplement)
67. The New Zealand Gazette No. 13 20 February 1930 P. 473
68. (1930) Advertisements Auckland Star Volume LXI Issue 49 27 February 1930 P. 16
69. (1930) Advertisements The New Zealand Herald Volume LXVII Issue 20540 15 April 1930 P. 21
70. (1931) Auckland Star Volume LXII Issue 37 13 February 1931 P. 12
71. (1931) Advertisements The New Zealand Herald Volume LXVIII Issue 20814 5 March 1931 P. 2
72. (1938) Stocks And Shares The New Zealand Herald Volume LXXV Issue 23169 15 October 1938 P. 9
73. (1939) Franklin Times Volume XXVIII Issue 99 1 September 1939 P. 6
74. (1940) The New Gazette No. 116 14 November 1940 P. 3421
75. The New Gazette No. 96 29 October 1942 P. 2544
76. The New Gazette No. 34 13 May 1943 P. 530
77. The New Gazette No. 68 19 August 1943 P. 1002
78. (1928) Company Affairs Auckland Star Volume LIX Issue 274 19 November 1928 P. 4
79. (1928) Announcement Waikato Times Volume 104 Issue 17562 17 November 1928 P. 9
80. Ebbett Group at: https://ebbett.nz/timeline/
81. (1937) Company Affairs Auckland Star Volume LXVIII Issue 205 30 August 1937 P. 4
82. Ebbett Group at: https://ebbett.nz/timeline/
83. (1938) Showrooms Opened Waikato Times Volume 123 Issue 20564 30 July 1938 P. 8
84. Ebbett Group at: https://ebbett.nz/timeline/
85. (1973) Commercial news in brief Christchurch Press Volume CXIII Issue 33389 22 November 1973 P. 18
86. (1976) Ebbett sales down Christchurch Press 16 November 1976 P. 24
87. Ebbett Group at: https://ebbett.nz/timeline/
88. Ebbett Group at: https://ebbett.nz/ebbett-dealerships/
89. (1924) Magistrate's Court Hawera Star Volume XLVIII 19 September 1924 P. 5
90. (1926) Advertisements Taranaki Daily News 20 March 1926 P. 1
91. (1929) Advertisements Taranaki Daily News 26 October 1929 P. 3
92. (1930) Advertisements The Dominion Volume 23 Issue 109 1 February 1930 P. 6

93. New Zealand Companies Office
94. (1932) Advertisements Taranaki Daily News 17 October 1932 P. 1
95. New Zealand Companies Office
96. New Zealand Gazette No. 64 30 October 1947 P. 1738
97. (1969) New N.Z. Company Christchurch Press Volume CIX Issue 32151 21 November 1969 P. 11
98. (1975) Advertisements Christchurch Press Volume CXV Issue 33781 1 March 1975 P. 27
99. (1982) Dunedin merger Christchurch Press 8 September 1982 P. 28
100. (1977) Advertisements Christchurch Press 6 January 1977 P. 12
101. (1984) Receivership for two financiers Christchurch Press 10 December 1984 P. 32
102. New Zealand Companies Office
103. Hunt, Graeme The Rich List — Wealth and Enterprise in New Zealand 1820-2000 Reed Books Auckland 2000 P. 221
104. (1923) Advertisements Waipa Post Volume XXIV Issue 1391 12 May 1923 P. 1
105. (1920) Advertisements Waipa Post Volume XVIII Issue 994 16 September 1920 P. 4
106. (1921) Advertisements Waipa Post Volume XIX Issue 1109 25 June 1921 P. 8
107. (1922) Advertisements Waipa Post Volume XXI Issue 1263 4 July 1922 P. 3
108. (1923) Advertisements Waipa Post Volume XXIV Issue 1929 9 August 1923 P. 2
109. (1923) Advertisements Waipa Post Volume XXIV Issue 1421 1 November 1923 P. 2
110. (1925) Advertisements Waipa Post Volume XXIV Issue 1600 27 January 1925 P. 8
111. (1927) Advertisements Waipa Post Volume 35 Issue 2062 24 September 1927 P. 1
112. (1935) New Export Season The New Zealand Herald Volume LXXII Issue 22221 23 September 1935 P. 5
113. (1928) Company Affairs Auckland Star Volume LIX Issue 131 5 June 1928 P. 4
114. (1928) Advertisements Auckland Star Volume LIX Issue 153 30 June 1928 P. 13
115. (1929) Advertisements The New Zealand Herald Volume LXVI Issue 20164 26 January 1929 P. 7
116. Loren, Anna Sixty years on the clock Stuff 2 December 2015 https://www.stuff.co.nz/auckland/local-news/manukau-courier/74443318/sixty-years-on-the-clock
117. New Zealand Companies Office
118. South Auckland Ford https://www.southaucklandford.co.nz
119. (1915) Advertisements The New Zealand Herald Volume LII Issue 16071 10 November 1915 P. 2
120. (1918) Appeals Dealt With Auckland Star Volume XLIX Issue 137 10 June 1918 P. 6
121. (1919) Auckland Motor Company Auckland Star Volume L Issue 302 20 December 1919 P. 8 (Supplement)
122. (1923) Albert Street Land Sale Auckland Star Volume LIV Issue 128 31 May 1923 P. 5
123. (1923) Old Landmark Going The New Zealand Herald Volume LX Issue 18413 31 May 1923 P. 6
124. (1923) Latest Motor Garage The New Zealand Herald Volume LX Issue 18587 20 December 1923 P. 15
125. (1923) Auckland Motor Company Gisborne Times Volume LIX Issue 9649 24 October 1923 P. 7
126. (1930) Advertisements Auckland Star Volume LXI Issue 201 26 August 1930 P. 3

127. (1932) Advertisements Auckland Star Volume LXIII Issue 152 29 June 1932 P. 20
128. (1941) More Candidates Auckland Star Volume LXXII Issue 99 29 April 1941 P. 8
129. (1944) Advertisements Auckland Star Volume LXXV Issue 136 10 June 1944 P. 9
130. (1946) Personal Northern Advocate 10 October 1946 P. 4
131. (1948) Advertisements Northern Advocate 12 October 1948 P. 4
132. (1932) Advertisements The New Zealand Herald Volume LXIX Issue 21289 16 September 1932 P. 2
133. (1933) Advertisements The New Zealand Herald Volume LXX Issue 21599 18 September 1933 P. 15
134. (1937) Advertisements The New Zealand Herald Volume LXXIV Issue 22776 9 July 1937 P. 16
135. (1933) Company Affairs Auckland Star Volume LXIV Issue 226 25 September 1933 P. 4
136. (1937) Advertisements Auckland Star Volume LXVIII Issue 153 30 June 1937 P. 25
137. New Zealand Gazette No. 76 21 September 1972 P. 2005
138. New Zealand Gazette No. 146 10 December 1981 P. 3751
139. New Zealand Companies Office
140. New Zealand Gazette No. 76 21 September 1972 P. 2005
141. (1974) Allied G.R.P. Accounts Christchurch Press Volume CXIV Issue 33575 2 July 1974 P. 16
142. (1974) Tasman seeking more expansion Christchurch Press Volume CXIV Issue 33484 15 March 1974 P. 14
143. (1974) Allied Group doing well Christchurch Press Volume CXIV Issue 33623 27 August 1974 P. 14
144. The New Zealand Gazette No. 72 4 September 1975 P. 2004
145. (1977) All. Fin. sees high rates Christchurch Press 16 September 1977 P. 10
146. (1978) Allied Group to reconstruct Christchurch Press 14 September 1978 P. 14
147. New Zealand Companies Office
148. (1979) Collingwood now out of property lending Christchurch Press 18 July 1979 P. 23
149. New Zealand Companies Office
150. (1925) Advertisements Waikato Times Volume 99 Issue 16678 19 December 1925 P. 12
151. (1926) Advertisements Waikato Times Volume 101 Issue 16946 6 November 1926 P. 2
152. (1928) Austin All-British Car Waikato Times Volume 103 Issue 17415 30 May 1928 P. 2
153. (1927) Advertisements The New Zealand Herald Volume LXIV Issue 19730 1 September 1927 P. 2
154. New Zealand Gazette No. 55 16 May 1957 P. 850
155. Tappenden & Sons, Tauranga - Tauranga Heritage Collection https://view.taurangaheritagecollection.co.nz/objects/29626/slide-tappenden-sons-tauranga
156. New Zealand Gazette No. 15 9 March 1978 P. 500
157. New Zealand Gazette No. 68 6 September 1934 P. 2838
158. (1934) Advertisements Auckland Star Volume LXV Issue 167 17 July 1934 P. 2
159. (1934) Advertisements The New Zealand Herald Volume LXXI Issue 21943 29 October 1934 P. 2
160. (1935) Winter Exhibition The New Zealand Herald Volume LXXII Issue 22164 18 July 1935 P. 19

161. (1937) Company Affairs Auckland Star Volume LXVIII Issue 205 30 August 1937 P. 4
162. (1939) Companies Registered Auckland Star Volume LXX Issue 78 3 April 1939 P. 6
163. (1958) Apprentice Pranks In Early Foundry Christchurch Press Volume XCVII Issue 28575 2 May 1958 P. 12
164. New Zealand Gazette No. 38 16 September 1954 P. 1477
165. Davie Motors Business List: https://www.businesslist.nz/company/496549/davie-motors
166. (1957) Private Share Placement Christchurch Press Volume XCVI Issue 28385 18 September 1957 P. 17
167. (1960) Sydney Share Market Christchurch Press Volume XCIX Issue 29292 25 August 1960 P. 17
168. (1961) Company News Takeover of P. F. Mann Christchurch Press Volume C Issue 29430 4 February 1961 P. 15
169. The New Zealand Gazette No. 19 16 March 1961 P. 436
170. (1961) Engineers' Merchants Form New Subsidiary Christchurch Press Volume C Issue 29474 28 March 1961 P. 19
171. (1964) Tappenden Motors Christchurch Press Volume CIII Issue 30496 18 July 1964 P. 18
172. (1965) Tappenden Take-Over Christchurch Press Volume CIV Issue 30813 27 July 1965 P. 19
173. (1965) Purchase By Tappenden Christchurch Press Volume CIV Issue 30878 11 October 1965 P. 15
174. New Zealand Gazette No. 15 17 March 1966 P. 392
175. (1967) Tappenden More Confident Now Christchurch Press Volume CVII Issue 31554 16 December 1967 P. 18
176. Hunt, Graeme The Rich List — Wealth and Enterprise in New Zealand 1820-2000 Reed Books Auckland 2000 Pp. 251-252
177. (1981) Giltrap expands Christchurch Press 2 May 1981 P. 21
178. (1928) Company Affairs Auckland Star Volume LIX Issue 71 24 March 1928 P. 4
179. (1928) Advertisements The New Zealand Herald Volume LXV Issue 19912 3 April 1928 P. 16
180. (1929) Trainload Of Cars Auckland Star Volume LX Issue 286 3 December 1929 P. 20
181. (1930) Trade-Notes Auckland Star Volume LXI Issue 219 16 September 1930 P. 16
182. (1943) Safebreakers Again Auckland Star Volume LXXIV Issue 252 23 October 1943 P. 6
183. (1944) Garage Thieves Auckland Star Volume LXXV Issue 105 5 May 1944 P. 6
184. (1974) Allied Grp purchase Christchurch Press Volume CXIV Issue 33605 6 August 1974 P. 16
185. (1933) New Zealand Herald Volume LXX Issue 21665 4 December 1933
186. (1933) Advertisements Evening Post Volume CXVI Issue 116 13 November 1933 P. 1
187. (1933) Advertisements Evening Post Volume CXVI Issue 127 25 November 1933 P. 3
188. (1980) Rationalisation move Christchurch Press 16 January 1980 P. 10
189. (1984) The week: rally continues Christchurch Press 14 July 1984 P. 27
190. (1986) GST Manthel Boost Christchurch Press 15 August 1986 P. 8
191. New Zealand Companies Office

192. The Wings Over New Zealand Aviation Forum https://rnzaf.proboards.com/thread/28844/kilkenny-owned-kitset-westport-1930s
193. (1947) Advertisements Gisborne Herald Volume LXXIV Issue 22235 22 January 1947 P. 1
194. (1948) Fair Method Gisborne Herald Volume LXXV Issue 22578 5 March 1948 P. 4
195. (1948) Personal Gisborne Herald Volume LXXV Issue 22740 11 September 1948 P. 6
196. (1949) Advertisements Gisborne Herald Volume LXXVI Issue 23120 6 December 1949 P. 1
197. (1957) Advertisements Christchurch Press Volume XCVI Issue 28364 24 August 1957 P. 17
198. (1959) Advertisements Christchurch Press, Volume XCVIII Issue 29002 17 September 1959 P. 27
199. (1962) Advertisements Christchurch Press Volume CI Issue 29832 26 May 1962 P. 22
200. (1965) Advertisements Christchurch Press Volume CIV Issue 30722 10 April 1965 P. 27
201. New Zealand Gazette No. 17 1 April 1965 P. 462
202. (1971) Advertisements Christchurch Press Volume CXI Issue 32569 31 March 1971 P. 29
203. (1971) Advertisements Christchurch Press Volume CXI Issue 32574 6 April 1971 P. 24
204. Aviation Safety Network Occurrence #62555 16 June 1970 https://aviation-safety.net/wikibase/62555
205. New Zealand Gazette No. 61 6 July 1978 P. 1960
206. New Zealand Gazette No. 103 28 August 1980 P. 2591
207. New Zealand Gazette No. 21 13 March 1975 P. 524
208. New Zealand Gazette No. 67 13 May 1992 P. 1351
209. (1920) Advertisements The New Zealand Herald Volume LVII Issue 17439 8 April 1920 P. 7
210. (1925) Advertisements The New Zealand Herald Volume LXII Issue 18943 14 February 1925 P. 10 (Supplement)
211. New Zealand Companies Office
212. (1925) New Companies Auckland Star Volume LVI Issue 37 13 February 1925 P. 7
213. (1927) Hints For Motorists The New Zealand Herald Volume LXIV Issue 19578 5 March 1927 P. 12 (Supplement)
214. (1928) 1929 Model Motor Spirit Auckland Sun Volume II Issue 534 11 December 1928 P. 9
215. (1926) Three New Companies Auckland Star Volume LVII Issue 99 28 April 1926 P. 9
216. (1928) Used Cars Ltd The New Zealand Herald Volume LXV Issue 20062 27 September 1928 P. 10 (Supplement)
217. (1941) Cars Wanted Putaruru Press Volume XVI Issue 922 20 March 1941 P. 2
218. (1943) Motor Cars, Trucks Wanted Auckland Star Volume LXXIV Issue 22 27 January 1943 P. 5
219. (1958) Obituary Mr E J Schofield Christchurch Press Volume XCVII Issue 28588 17 May 1958 P. 15
220. (1968) Dividends Christchurch Press Volume CVIII Issue 31847 27 November 1968 P. 21
221. Sir Colin Giltrap Business Hall Of Fame 2013 - https://www.businesshalloffame.co.nz/past-laureates/ww2te33en2khc6s-4eh7b-8ew9s-48lzh-d9e4c-gst8m-czd8r?rq=giltrap
222. Giltrap Group History https://www.giltrap.com/about-us/our-history

223. ibid.
224. Hunt, Graeme The Rich List — Wealth and Enterprise in New Zealand 1820-2000 Reed Books Auckland 2000 P. 266
225. Ateco Group NZ https://ateco.co.nz/media
226. New Zealand Companies Office
227. (2012) Queen's Birthday Honours 2012: Neville Crichton — The New Zealand Herald 4 June 2012
228. Morgan, Scott Neville Crichton Weds - autotalk 15 May 2017 - https://autotalk.co.nz/news/neville-crichton-weds

Chapter Eight
1. Petroleum Refining Processes Wikipedia - Downloaded 15 December 2022 from: https://en.wikipedia.org/wiki/Petroleum_refining_processes
2. (1863) Extracts From The Scientific American republished by the Daily Southern Cross Volume XIX Issue 1819 18 May 1863 P. 4
3. (1862) Kerosine The Wellington Independent Volume XVII Issue 1772 27 September 1862 P. 2
4. (1863) Advertisements Otago Daily Times Issue 607 27 November 1863 P. 6
5. (1876) Shipping New Zealand Times Volume XXXI Issue 4895 29 November 1876 P. 2
6. Management of the Petroleum Resource, Report 2011 Pp. 3-4 downloaded from www.waitangitribunal.govt.nz
7. (1968) Murchison Oil Still Unknown Prospect Christchurch Press Volume CVIII Issue 31680 16 May 1968 P. 18
8. Management of the Petroleum Resource, Report 2011 P. 2 downloaded from www.waitangitribunal.govt.nz
9. Petroleum Act 1937 No. 27 11 December 1937
10. Management of the Petroleum Resource, Report 2011 P. 2 downloaded from www.waitangitribunal.govt.nz
11. Management of the Petroleum Resource, Report 2011 Pp. 3-4 downloaded from www.waitangitribunal.govt.nz
12. (1866) Monthly Summary The New Zealand Herald Volume III Issue 740 29 March 1866 P. 5
13. (1866) A Visit To The Sugar-Loaves The Taranaki Herald Volume XIV Issue 713 31 March 1866 P. 3
14. (1866) Taranaki/Petroleum Nelson Evening Mail Volume I Issue 31 10 April 1866 P. 2
15. (1866) Editorial Otago Daily Times Issue 1352 28 April 1866 P. 4
16. (1866) The Petroleum Leases The Taranaki Herald Volume XIV Issue 716 21 April 1866 P. 3
17. Nodding Neddy The Industrious Heart - A History of New Plymouth http://history.new-plymouth.com/5
18. (1866) The Taranaki Petroleum Marlborough Press Volume VII Issue 108 18 April 1866 P. 2
19. (1867) Our Petroleum Borings Taranaki Herald Volume XV Issue 770 4 May 1867 P. 3

20. (1866) Advertisements Taranaki Herald Volume XIV Issue 717 28 April 1866 P. 2
21. (1867) Editorial The Taranaki Herald Volume XV Issue 757 2 February 1867 P. 2
22. (1906) Taranaki Petroleum The New Zealand Herald Volume XLIII Issue 13339 20 November 1906 P. 6
23. (1906) Taranaki Petroleum Company Wairarapa Daily Times Volume XXX Issue 8485 25 June 1906 P. 3
24. (1924) The Quest For Oil The New Zealand Herald Volume LXI Issue 18753 5 July 1924 P. 12
25. (1905) Moturoa Petroleum Company Taranaki Daily News Volume XLVII Issue 7881 25 July 1905 P. 2
26. (1906) Taranaki Petroleum Company Taranaki Daily News Volume XLVII Issue 8122 29 May 1906 P. 2
27. (1906) Death Of A Petroleum Expert The New Zealand Herald Volume XLIII Issue 13345 27 November 1906 P. 6
28. (1907) Petroleum Evening Post Volume LXXIV Issue 98 22 October 1907 P. 2
29. (1907) Mining News Evening Star Issue 12797 13 November 1907 P. 8
30. (1908) Petroleum Taranaki Herald Volume LIV Issue 13709 27 July 1908 P. 2
31. (1909) Untitled Opunake Times Volume XXX Issue 1582 12 October 1909 P. 2
32. (1909) Petroleum Taranaki Daily News Volume LII Issue 215 16 October 1909 P. 5
33. (1909) Taranaki Oil For The Railways Evening Post Volume LXXVIII Issue 93 16 October 1909 P. 9
34. (1910) Taranaki Petroleum Company Evening Post Volume LXXIX Issue 20 25 January 1910 P. 3
35. (1909) Petroleum Taranaki Daily News Volume LII Issue 36 8 March 1909 P. 4
36. (1910) Petroleum Taranaki Herald Volume LV Issue 14118 26 January 1910 P. 7
37. (1910) The Oil Industry Poverty Bay Herald Volume XXXVII Issue 12664 4 February 1910 P. 2
38. (1911) Taranaki's Oil Lyttelton Times Volume CXXII Issue 15608 5 May 1911 P. 6
39. (1911) Taranaki's Oil Taranaki Daily News Volume LIII Issue 296 9 May 1911 P. 4
40. (1911) Petroleum The Taranaki Herald Volume LIX Issue 143494 17 May 1911 P. 2
41. (1911) Taranaki Oil-Fields Ashburton Guardian Volume XXXII Issue 8371 18 May 1911 P. 1
42. (1911) Taranaki Petroleum Company The Taranaki Herald Volume LIX Issue 143497 20 May 1911 P. 2
43. (1911) Taranaki Oilfields The New Zealand Herald Volume XLVIII Issue 14692 29 May 1911 P. 8
44. (1911) Men Of The Day The Taranaki Herald Volume LIX Issue 143629 24 October 1911 P. 2
45. (1911) English Capital And Taranaki Oil Taranaki Daily News Volume LIII Issue 307 22 May 1911 P. 4
46. (1912) Petroleum Taranaki Herald Volume LX Issue 143788 11 May 1912 P. 2
47. New Zealand Gazette No. 8 24 January 1918 P. 265
48. (1911) Petroleum Taranaki Herald Volume LIX Issue 143671 15 December 1911 P. 4
49. ibid.

50. (1912) The Taranaki Oil Wells Coy West Coast Times 9 January 1912 P. 4
51. (1912) An Important Enterprise New Zealand Times Volume XXXVI Issue 8082 10 April 1912 P. 7
52. (1912) Commercial Otago Daily Times Issue 15433 20 April 1912 P. 8
53. (1912) Petroleum Taranaki Herald Volume LX Issue 143890 10 September 1912 P. 3
54. (1912) Taranaki Oil Wells Christchurch Press Volume XLVIII Issue 14375 7 June 1912 P. 8
55. (1912) Telegrams Evening Post Volume LXXXIV Issue 3 3 July 1912 P. 3
56. (1913) Petroleum Taranaki Daily News Volume LVI Issue 2 3 June 1913 P. 4
57. (2013) From oil rags to riches Stuff/Taranaki Daily News 12 October 2013 https://www.stuff.co.nz/taranaki-daily-news/news/9275625/From-oil-rags-to-riches
58. (1924) The Quest For Oil The New Zealand Herald Volume LXI Issue 18753 5 July 1924 P. 12
59. (1913) Local And General News The New Zealand Herald Volume L Issue 15372 6 August 1913 P. 8
60. (1913) Taranaki Oil Wells The New Zealand Herald Volume L Issue 15468 27 November 1913 P. 5
61. (1914) Appropriation Bill Lyttelton Times Volume CXV Issue 16700 5 November 1914 P. 6
62. (1914) House of Representatives Evening Post Volume LXXXVIII Issue 110 5 November 1914 P. 3
63. (1915) Lack Of Capital Evening Post Volume LXXXIX Issue 12 15 January 1915 P. 8
64. (1915) Taranaki Oil Wells Lord Ranfurly's Hopeful Review Evening Post Volume LXXXIX Issue 30 5 February 1915 P. 2
65. (1919) Untitled Southland Times Issue 18000 31 January 1919 P. 4
66. (1919) Local And General News Hawera & Normanby Star Volume LXXIV Issue LXXIV 1 March 1919 P. 4
67. (1919) New Zealand Industries Taranaki Daily News 15 April 1919 P. 6
68. (1919) Commercial The Christchurch Press Volume LV Issue 16643 2 October 1919 P. 9
69. New Zealand Gazette No. 94 18 November 1920 P. 3132
70. (1924) Local And General Wairarapa Daily Times Volume 50 Issue 15069 3 January 1924 P. 4
71. New Zealand Gazette No. 65 24 September 1925 P. 2675
72. (1927) What Is Being Done Evening Post Volume CIV Issue 105 31 October 1927 P. 11
73. (1924) Taranaki Oil Wells Poverty Bay Herald Volume L Issue 16482 15 July 1924 P. 3
74. (1924) Search For Oil Taranaki Daily News 9 July 1924 P. 4
75. (1924) Personal Taranaki Daily News 3 September 1924 P. 4
76. (1924) Search For Oil Otago Witness Issue 3692 16 December 1924 P. 8
77. (1925) Petroleum Prospecting Auckland Star Volume LVI Issue 162 11 July 1925 P. 9
78. (1925) Oil Development Patea Mail Volume XLVIII 6 July 1925 P. 2
79. (1925) Prospecting For Oil Gisborne Times Volume LXIII Issue 10081 21 August 1925 P. 3
80. (1926) Boring For Oil Auckland Star Volume LVII Issue 81 7 April 1926 P. 10
81. (1927) What Is Being Done Evening Post Volume CIV Issue 105 31 October 1927 P. 11
82. (1929) Wellington News Hokitika Guardian 7 January 1929 P. 2

83. (1929) Morere Oil Wells Feilding Star Volume 7 Issue 2296 27 August 1929 P. 4
84. (1930) Taranaki Oil Wells Ltd Evening Post Volume CIX Issue 66 19 March 1930 P. 14
85. (1930) Finance & Markets Auckland Sun Volume IV Issue 1039 1 August 1930 P. 11
86. (1931) Difficulty Experienced Waipukurau Press Volume XXVI Issue 244 31 October 1931 P. 5
87. (1924) The Quest For Oil The New Zealand Herald Volume LXI Issue 18753 5 July 1924 P. 12
88. (1866) Local and General News Taranaki Herald Volume XIV Issue 717 28 April 1866 P. 3
89. Nodding Neddy The Industrious Heart A History of New Plymouth http://history.new-plymouth.com/5
90. (1866) Untitled Grey River Argus Issue 90 9 August 1866 P. 2
91. Nodding Neddy The Industrious Heart A History of New Plymouth http://history.new-plymouth.com/5
92. From oil rags to riches Stuff/Taranaki Daily News 12 October 2013 https://www.stuff.co.nz/taranaki-daily-news/news/9275625/From-oil-rags-to-riches
93. (1906) Advertisements Taranaki Daily News Volume XLVII Issue 8142 26 June 1906 P. 3
94. (1906) Petroleum Taranaki Herald Volume LIV Issue 13214 12 July 1906 P. 7
95. (1906) New Zealand Petroleum The New Zealand Herald Volume XLIII Issue 13287 20 September 1906 P. 6
96. (1906) Petroleum Taranaki Herald Volume LIV Issue 13503 4 September 1906 P. 2
97. (1906) Table Talk Auckland Star Volume XXXVII Issue 269 17 November 1906 P. 1
98. (1908) Local And General Hawera & Normanby Star Volume LVI Issue LVI 15 September 1908 P. 4
99. (1909) The Oil Industry Taranaki Daily News Volume LII Issue 173 25 August 1909 P. 3
100. (1910) Taranaki Oilfields Christchurch Press Volume LXVI Issue 13790 20 July 1910 P. 12
101. (1917) Untitled Taranaki Herald Volume LXV Issue 145878 11 July 1917 P. 2
102. (1918) Advertisements Taranaki Herald Volume LXVI Issue 16145 31 May 1918 P. 7
103. (1907) Petroleum Taranaki Herald Volume LIV Issue 13433 27 March 1907 P. 7
104. (1908) Petroleum Taranaki Herald Volume LIV Issue 13653 7 May 1908 P. 4
105. (1909) Petroleum Taranaki Herald Volume LV Issue 13928 11 June 1909 P. 3
106. (1909) Taranaki Oil and Freehold Co. Evening Post Volume LXXVIII Issue LXVIII 20 November 1909 P. 5
107. (1910) Oil And Freehold Company Taranaki Herald Volume LVIII Issue 14389 21 December 1910 P. 7
108. (1911) Petroleum Taranaki Herald Volume LIX Issue 143678 23 December 1911 P. 4
109. (1923) Answers To Correspondents Taranaki Daily News 7 May 1923 P. 4
110. (1916) Taranaki Oil And Freehold Co Ltd Taranaki Daily News 25 August 1916 P. 8
111. (1906) Bonithon Petroleum and Freehold Company Wanganui Herald Volume XXXX Issue 11982 27 September 1906 P. 7
112. (1906) Taranaki Petroleum New Zealand Mail Issue 1804 3 October 1906 P. 64
113. (1907) Late Telegrams Auckland Star Volume XXXVIII Issue 69 21 March 1907 P. 5
114. (1908) Personal Taranaki Herald Volume LIV Issue 13786 19 October 1908 P. 4
115. (1909) Southern News Auckland Star Volume XL Issue 10 12 January 1909 P. 2
116. (1909) Petroleum Grey River Argus 5 March 1909 P. 4

117. (1909) Petroleum Taranaki Herald Volume LV Issue 13928 11 June 1909 P. 3
118. (1912) Petroleum Prospects NZ Truth Issue 365 22 June 1912 P. 7
119. (1912) Advertisements Evening Post Volume LXXXIII Issue 70 22 March 1912 P. 3
120. (1924) Quest For Oil Taranaki Daily News 4 July 1924 P. 5
121. (1913) The Taranaki Oilfield Taranaki Herald Volume LXI Issue 144157 29 July 1913 P. 4
122. (1915) Taranaki Oilfields Christchurch Press Volume LI Issue 15261 24 April 1915 P. 10
123. (1915) The Bonithon Freehold Petroleum Company Extended Ltd NZ Truth Issue 526 17 July 1915 P. 4
124. (1920) Supreme Court Taranaki Daily News 22 September 1920 P. 8
125. (1913) A Bankruptcy Bother NZ Truth Issue 431 27 September 1913 P. 5
126. (1905) Advertisements Auckland Star Volume XXXVI Issue 104 2 May 1905 P. 6
127. (1913) A Bankruptcy Bother NZ Truth Issue 431 27 September 1913 P. 5
128. (1907) Petroleum Taranaki Herald Volume LIV Issue 13583 14 December 1907 P. 2
129. (1908) Petroleum Taranaki Herald Volume LIV Issue 13653 7 May 1908 P. 4
130. (1908) Petroleum Taranaki Herald Volume LIV Issue 13664 30 May 1908 P. 4
131. (1908) Petroleum Taranaki Herald Volume LIV Issue 13789 22 October 1908 P. 7
132. (1909) e hadley company Taranaki Herald Volume LV Issue 13904 6 March 1909 P. 2
133. (1909) Petroleum Prospects Taranaki Herald Issue 13945 1 July 1909 P. 2
134. (1909) Advertisements The New Zealand Herald Volume XLVI Issue 14178 29 September 1909 P. 1
135. (1909) American Shipping Taranaki Herald Volume LV Issue 14027 5 October 1909 P. 2
136. (1910) Petroleum Prospects Evening Post Volume LXXX Issue 33 8 August 1910 P. 8
137. (1911) Untitled Taranaki Herald Volume LIX Issue 143456 17 March 1911 P. 2
138. (1911) Advertisements The New Zealand Herald Volume XLVIII Issue 14644 1 April 1911 P. 4
139. (1913) Advertisements Auckland Star Volume XLIV Issue 4 4 January 1913 P. 6
140. (1913) Petroleum Taranaki Herald Volume LXI Issue 144076 22 April 1913 P. 3
141. (1913) Taranaki Oilfields Taranaki Herald Volume LXI Issue 144135 3 July 1913 P. 2
142. (1913) A Bankruptcy Bother NZ Truth Issue 431 27 September 1913 P. 5
143. (1913) Standard Oil Company of New Zealand Ltd NZ Truth Issue 431 27 September 1913 P. 2
144. (1915) Taranaki Oilfields Christchurch Press Volume LI Issue 15261 24 April 1915 P. 10
145. (1923) Untitled Hawera & Normanby Star Volume XLII Issue XLII 10 January 1923 P. 8
146. (1924) Disposal Of Oil Shares The New Zealand Herald Volume LXI Issue 18680 9 April 1924 P. 12
147. (1924) Oil Share Ventures The New Zealand Herald Volume LXI Issue 18696 30 April 1924 P. 11
148. (1924) Commercial Christchurch Press Volume LX Issue 18064 5 May 1924 P. 10
149. (1912) Untitled Poverty Bay Herald Volume XXXIX Issue 12715 18 March 1912 P. 4
150. (1916) The Search For Oil Christchurch Sun Volume III Issue 697 5 May 1916 P. 10
151. (1920) Advertisements Lyttelton Times Volume CXVIII Issue 18313 24 January 1920 P. 16
152. (1913) Local And General Evening Post Volume LXXXV Issue 144 19 June 1913 P. 6
153. (1913) The Oil Fields Lyttelton Times Volume CXIV Issue 16331 29 August 1913 P. 5
154. (1922) Advertisements Taranaki Daily News 27 October 1922 P. 1

155. (1912) The Oil Industry Patea Mail Volume XXXV 6 September 1912 P. 2
156. (1913) Local And General Stratford Evening Post Volume XXXVI Issue 8 14 May 1913 P. 4
157. (1916) An Oil Case Lyttelton Times Volume CXVII Issue 17160 5 May 1916 P. 5
158. New Zealand Gazette No. 1 7 January 1918 P. IV
159. (1918) Advertisements Christchurch Press Volume LIV Issue 16406 28 December 1918 P. 14
160. New Zealand Gazette No. 33 27 April 1922 P. 1226
161. (1914) Taranaki Oil Industry Otago Witness Issue 3121 14 January 1914 P. 33
162. (1922) Oil Deposits New Zealand Times Volume XLIX Issue 11109 16 January 1922 P. 8
163. [(1919) New Zealand Industries Taranaki Daily News 15 April 1919 P. 6
164. (1929) Oil At New Plymouth The New Zealand Herald Volume LXVI Issue 20173 6 February 1929 P. 12
165. (1921) Advertisements Taranaki Daily News 4 May 1921 P. 1
166. (1929) Oil At New Plymouth The New Zealand Herald Volume LXVI Issue 20173 6 February 1929 P. 12
167. (1931) Blenheim Oil Company Taranaki Daily News 5 August 1931 P. 6
168. (1931) Commerce And Finance Otago Daily Times Issue 21422 25 August 1931 P. 11
169. (1931) Companies Registered Christchurch Press Volume LXVII Issue 20383 2 November 1931 P. 10
170. (1931) Advertisements Taranaki Daily News 30 November 1931 P. 3
171. (1933) Finance And Commerce Christchurch Press Volume LXIX Issue 20864 25 May 1933 P. 11
172. (1926) Hawke's Bay Tribune Volume XVI Issue 242 29 September 1926 P. 4
173. (1931) Petroleum Quest The New Zealand Herald Volume LXVIII Issue 20982 19 September 1931 P. 9
174. (1930) Advertisements Evening Post Volume CIX Issue 103 3 May 1930 P. 4
175. (1931) Finance And Commerce Taranaki Daily News 17 June 1931 P. 12
176. (1931) Petroleum Quest The New Zealand Herald Volume LXVIII Issue 20982 19 September 1931 P. 9
177. (1931) Suspended Drilling Evening Post Volume CXII Issue 30 4 August 1931 P. 8
178. (1931) Oil Boring At Omata Taranaki Daily News 24 October 1931 P. 6
179. (1932) Shareholders' Action Taranaki Daily News 11 January 1932 P. 9
180. (1932) Exploring Omata Field Taranaki Daily News 5 February 1932 P. 9
181. (1930) Another Oil Company Evening Post Volume CIX Issue 15 18 January 1930 P. 12
182. (1930) Moturoa Oilfields Auckland Star Volume LXI Issue 77 1 April 1930 P. 4
183. (1930) Mining Otago Witness Issue 3985 29 July 1930 P. 32
184. (1933) Moturoa Oilfields The New Zealand Herald Volume LXX Issue 21494 18 May 1933 P. 5
185. (1934) Commerce And Finance Otago Daily Times Issue 22250 1 May 1934 P. 6
186. (1937) Commerce And Finance Otago Daily Times Issue 23344 9 November 1937 P. 15
187. (1946) Moturoa Oilfields Greymouth Evening Star 13 April 1946 P. 6
188. (1947) New Plymouth Oil Wells Sold Wanganui Chronicle 30 January 1947 P. 4
189. (1947) Drilling For Oil Otago Daily Times Issue 26378 5 February 1947 P. 6

190. (1947) Commercial Christchurch Press Volume LXXXIII Issue 25317 17 October 1947 P. 10
191. (1931) Companies Registered Christchurch Press Volume LXVII Issue 20383 2 November 1931 P. 10
192. (1948) Drilling For Oil Bay of Plenty Times Volume LXXVII Issue 14828 16 November 1948 P. 6
193. (1949) Oil Production Otago Daily Times Issue 27022 5 March 1949 P. 6
194. (1949) More Oil in New Plymouth Bay of Plenty Times Volume LXXVII Issue 14951 12 April 1949 P. 3
195. (1949) Petrol Hard To Sell Ashburton Guardian Volume 70 Issue 9 21 October 1949 P. 5
196. (1950) Petrol To Burn Bay Of Plenty Beacon Volume 14 Issue 85 13 January 1950 P. 4
197. New Zealand Gazette No. 11 16 February 1950 P. 188
198. (1953) Oil Prospecting In Taranaki Christchurch Press Volume LXXXIX Issue 26933 8 January 1953 P. 9
199. (1954) Natural Gas From Oil Well Christchurch Press Volume XC Issue 27426 12 August 1954 P. 10
200. (1956) Search For Oil In NZ Christchurch Press Volume XCIII Issue 27978 26 May 1956 P. 13
201. (1957) Oil Production Increases Christchurch Press Volume XCVI Issue 28378 10 September 1957 P. 19
202. (1958) General News Christchurch Press Volume XCVII Issue 28683 5 September 1958 P. 10
203. New Zealand Gazette No. 105 21 July 1983 P. 2354
204. New Zealand Gazette No. 56 21 August 1952 P. 1390
205. (1959) Condensate To Be Refined Christchurch Press Volume XCVIII Issue 29013 30 September 1959 P. 9
206. (1960) General News Christchurch Press Volume XCIX Issue 29142 1 March 1960 P. 14
207. (1962) Taranaki Sites Christchurch Press Volume CI Issue 29723 17 January 1962 P. 12
208. New Zealand Gazette No. 3 18 January 1962 P. 50
209. (1971) NZ oil-prospecting activity in 1970 Christchurch Press Volume CXI Issue 32670 28 July 1971 P. 10
210. The Distribution Of Motor Spirits and Ancillary Products - Report of the Commission of Inquiry Wellington 30 April 1976 P. 20
211. (1972) Production at Moturoa oilfield to cease Christchurch Press Volume CXII Issue 32977 25 July 1972 P. 3
212. Waipatiki oil well, southern Hawkes Bay Manawatu Heritage Palmerston North City Library at: https://manawatuheritage.pncc.govt.nz/item/3e39784c-7be3-452a-ad4c-8edc7edd22f7
213. New Zealand Gazette No. 139 14 December 1916 P. 3851
214. (1931) Search For Oil Gisborne Times Volume LXXII Issue 11492 17 April 1931 P. 2
215. ibid.
216. (1880) New Petroleum Company Auckland Star Volume XI Issue 3117 17 April 1880 P. 2
217. (1880) Australian Summary New Zealand Times Volume XXXV Issue 5968 19 May 1880 P. 3

218. (1880) The Poverty Bay Herald And East Coast News Letter The Poverty Bay Herald Volume VII Issue 1168 10 November 1880 P. 2
219. (1880) Gaining Ground Ashburton Guardian Volume 2 Issue 206 2 December 1880 P. 2
220. (1881) New Zealand Telegrams The New Zealand Herald Volume XVIII Issue 6067 28 April 1881 P. 5
221. (1931) Search For Oil Gisborne Times Volume LXXII Issue 11492 17 April 1931 P. 2
222. (1940) Looking Back Ashburton Guardian Volume 60 Issue 199 31 May 1940 P. 4
223. (1890) The Poverty Bay Herald Volume XVII Issue 5834 2 August 1890 P. 2
224. (1931) Search For Oil Gisborne Times Volume LXXII Issue 11492 17 April 1931 P. 2
225. (1880) The Rotokautuku Oil Block Auckland Star Volume XI Issue 3247 16 December 1880 P. 2
226. (1881) Auckland Poverty Bay Herald Volume VIII Issue 1219 13 January 1881 P. 2
227. (1931) Search For Oil Gisborne Times Volume LXXII Issue 11492 17 April 1931 P. 2
228. (1891) Advertisements Christchurch Press Volume XLVIII Issue 7836 13 April 1891 P. 1
229. (1883) Town and Country New Zealand Mail Issue 620 21 December 1883 P. 17
230. (1884) News Of The Day Christchurch Press Volume XL Issue 5764 10 March 1884 P. 2
231. (1899) Advertisements Evening Post Volume LVII Issue 17 21 January 1899 P. 6
232. (1928) Oil In New Zealand Auckland Sun Volume II Issue 388 23 June 1928 P. 12
233. ibid.
234. (1938) Oil Development Company Formed Northern Advocate 18 May 1938 P. 3
235. (1938) Drilling For Oil Will Start Soon Northern Advocate 23 April 1938 P. 7
236. (1946) Commercial Details Of Wide Search For Oil Greymouth Evening Star 18 December 1946 P. 4
237. (1944) No Oil Found Evening Post Volume CXXXVIII Issue 139 9 December 1944 P. 8
238. The New Zealand Gazette No. 63 2 August 1951 P. 1115
239. (1900) The Kotuku Oil Springs Grey River Argus Volume LVII Issue 10520 1 October 1900 P. 2
240. (1901) Advertisements Greymouth Evening Star Volume XXXI 16 October 1901 P. 3
241. (1902) The Kotuku Oil Field Grey River Argus Volume LVII Issue 10520 20 October 1902 P. 3
242. (1903) Untitled Grey River Argus 19 October 1903 P. 2
243. (1906) News Of The Day Christchurch Press Volume LXII Issue 12573 16 August 1906 P. 6
244. Story: Oil and gas The Encyclopedia of New Zealand at: https://teara.govt.nz/en/map/8917/kotuku-oilfield
245. (1932) Local And General Grey River Argus 14 November 1932 P. 4
246. (1933) Kotuku Oil-Fields Greymouth Evening Star 6 April 1933 P. 5
247. (1934) Advertisements Evening Post Volume CXVII Issue 138 13 June 1934 P. 18
248. (1934) Kotuku Notes Greymouth Evening Star 28 June 1934 P. 3
249. New Zealand Gazette No. 72 27 September 1934 P. 3023
250. (1934) Finance And Commerce Christchurch Press Volume LXX Issue 21228 28 July 1934 P. 10
251. (1936) Untitled Hokitika Guardian 28 July 1936 P. 4
252. (1938) Crude Oil Auckland Star Volume LXIX Issue 124 28 May 1938 P. 12

253. Hill, Brian R Exciting career of an obscure mining entrepreneur: David Ziman (1862-1920) Journal of Australasian Mining History Volume 7 September 2009 P. 155
254. ibid. Pp. 161 & 167
255. (1975) The lost oil of Kotuku Christchurch Press Volume CXV Issue 33761 6 February 1975 P. 16
256. New Zealand Gazette No. 64 12 September 1946 P. 1258
257. (1924) The Search For Oil The New Zealand Herald Volume LXI Issue 18899 23 December 1924 P. 12
258. (1927) What Is Being Done Evening Post Volume CIV Issue 105 31 October 1927 P. 11
259. (1925) Murchison Oil Company The New Zealand Herald Volume LXII Issue 19035 4 June 1925 P. 7
260. (1925) Advertisements The New Zealand Herald Volume LXII Issue 19034 3 June 1925 P. 5
261. (1925) Nelson News Evening Post Issue 119 16 November 1925 P. 9
262. (1925) Murchison Oil Company The New Zealand Herald Volume LXII Issue 19195 8 December 1925 P. 7
263. (1926) Local And General Greymouth Evening Star 15 April 1926 P. 4
264. (1926) Murchison Oil Company The New Zealand Herald Volume LXIII Issue 19414 24 August 1926 P. 7
265. (1927) What Is Being Done Evening Post Volume CIV Issue 105 31 October 1927 P. 11
266. (1927) Late Commercial Poverty Bay Herald Volume LIII Issue 16486 2 November 1927 P. 11
267. (1928) Local And General Nelson Evening Mail Volume LXI 10 August 1928 P. 4
268. (1928) Local And General Nelson Evening Mail Volume LXI 31 August 1928 P. 4
269. (1928) Mines Statement Hokitika Guardian 19 October 1928 P. 7
270. (1930) Murchison Oil Company Directors' Report Nelson Evening Mail Volume LXIV 21 November 1930 P. 2
271. (1931) A Successful Year Christchurch Press Volume LXVII Issue 20401 23 November 1931 P. 10
272. (1932) Company Affairs Auckland Star Volume LXIII Issue 274 18 November 1932 P. 4
273. (1939) Commerce, Mining, Finance Evening Star Issue 23449 14 December 1939 P. 4
274. (1929) Murchison Oil Greymouth Evening Star 15 March 1929 P. 2
275. (1929) Murchison Oil Find Nelson Evening Mail Volume LXIII 11 April 1929 P. 5
276. (1968) Murchison Oil Still Unknown Prospect Christchurch Press Volume CVIII Issue 31680 16 May 1968 P. 18
277. (1960) U.S. Company To Search For Oil In North Island Christchurch Press Volume XCIX Issue 29320 27 September 1960 P. 12
278. (1962) Texans Planning Big Oil Search Christchurch Press Volume CI Issue 29723 17 January 1962 P. 12
279. (1962) Advertisements Christchurch Press Volume CI Issue 29746 13 February 1962 P. 16
280. (1964) No Sign Of Oil Or Gas In Hamilton Bores Christchurch Press Volume CIII Issue 30481 1 July 1964 P. 12
281. (1965) N.Z. Petrol Set-Back Christchurch Press Volume CIV Issue 30664 2 February 1965 P. 19

282. (1967) N.Z. Petroleum Cash Issue Christchurch Press Volume CVII Issue 31491 4 October 1967 P. 18
283. (1968) N.Z. Petroleum Has 25% Interest Christchurch Press Volume CVIII Issue 31684 21 May 1968 P. 19
284. (1968) N.Z. Petrol. Agreement On Murchison Well Christchurch Press Volume CVIII Issue 31688 25 May 1968 P. 18
285. (1969) Hard Rock Struck Canterbury Oil Search Ends Christchurch Press Volume CIX Issue 32111 6 October 1969 P. 1
286. (1971) Commercial news in brief Christchurch Press Volume CXI Issue 32745 23 October 1971 P. 20
287. (1980) Oil well may be drilled off Westland Christchurch Press 5 January 1980 P. 2
288. (1980) Greymouth oil area 'very promising' Christchurch Press 13 August 1980 P. 18
289. New Zealand Companies Office
290. (1985) NZ Pet. loss jumps Christchurch Press 12 January 1985 P. 18
291. (1989) NZP in Indonesia Christchurch Press 7 June 1989 P. 31
292. (1989) NZ Pet. oil search bill $24M Christchurch Press 7 October 1989 P. 32
293. ibid.
294. (1969) Australian Firm In Oil Search Christchurch Press Volume CIX Issue 32067 15 August 1969 P. 1
295. (1970) $4.2m Placement for Bounty's N.Z. Search Christchurch Press Volume CIX Issue 32237 4 March 1970 P. 17
296. (1970) Murchison oil rig being dismantled Christchurch Press Volume CX Issue 32442 31 October 1970 P. 2
297. (1971) Bounty still uncertain Christchurch Press Volume CXI Issue 32627 8 June 1971 P. 12
298. (1971) Bounty Report Christchurch Press Volume CXI Issue 32675 3 August 1971 P. 17
299. (1974) Commercial briefs Christchurch Press Volume CXIV Issue 33723 21 December 1974 P. 21
300. (1973) Commercial Prospecting group under attack Christchurch Press Volume CXIII Issue 38186 28 March 1973 P. 30
301. (1974) Bartons In Gaol Christchurch Press Volume CXIV Issue 33518 26 April 1974 P. 11 & Bartons papers revoked Christchurch Press Volume CXIV Issue 33698 22 November 1974 P. 13
302. (1977) Bartons return to face music Christchurch Press 6 January 1977 P. 4
303. (1985) Petrocorp seeks Murchison oil Christchurch Press 21 September 1985 P. 21
304. (1985) Briefs Christchurch Press 14 December 1985 P. 22
305. Petroleum Corporation of New Zealand Ltd The Fletcher Trust Archives at: https://collection.fletcherarchives.co.nz/persons/304/petroleum-corporation-of-new-zealand-ltd
306. (1979) Hunt for oil gets boost by Petrocorp Christchurch Press 28 July 1979 P. 2
307. (2013) From oil rags to riches Stuff/Taranaki Daily News 12 October 2013 https://www.stuff.co.nz/taranaki-daily-news/news/9275625/From-oil-rags-to-riches
308. New Zealand Companies Office
309. (1960) U.S. Company To Search For Oil In North Island Christchurch Press Volume XCIX Issue 29320 27 September 1960 P. 12

310. Todd Energy at https://toddenergy.co.nz/kapuni/
311. New Zealand Gazette No. 105 21 July 1983 P. 2354
312. Todd Energy at: https://toddenergy.co.nz/our-business/
313. The Distribution Of Motor Spirits and Ancillary Products - Report of the Commission of Inquiry Wellington 30 April 1976 P. 29
314. Oil & gas field profile: Maui Conventional Gas Field, New Zealand Offshore Technology 15 November 2023 at: https://www.offshore-technology.com/marketdata/oil-gas-field-profile-maui-conventional-gas-field-new-zealand/?cf-view
315. Martin, Robin Drilling campaign almost doubles Maui gas field's production - OMV 6 March 2022 Radio New Zealand https://www.rnz.co.nz/news/business/462813/drilling-campaign-almost-doubles-maui-gas-field-s-production-omv
316. (2024) Bill to resume oil and gas exploration set for later this year The New Zealand Herald 9 June 2024
317. (1911) Taranaki Oil Lyttelton Times Volume CXXII Issue 15614 12 May 1911 P. 4
318. (2013) From oil rags to riches Stuff/Taranaki Daily News 12 October 2013 https://www.stuff.co.nz/taranaki-daily-news/news/9275625/From-oil-rags-to-riches
319. (1919) Untitled Southland Times Issue 18000 31 January 1919 P. 4
320. The Distribution Of Motor Spirits and Ancillary Products - Report of the Commission of Inquiry Wellington 30 April 1976 P. 20
321. (1962) Oil Refinery To Begin Early In 1964 Christchurch Press Volume CI Issue 29941 1 October 1962 P. 16
322. The Distribution Of Motor Spirits and Ancillary Products - Report of the Commission of Inquiry Wellington 30 April 1976 P. 20
323. ibid. Pp. 15-16
324. (1983) Pace increasing in work at Marsden Point Christchurch Press 28 April 1983 P. 24
325. (1985) Bitumen to be imported Christchurch Press 14 June 1985 P. 4
326. (1989) Refinery safe for now Christchurch Press 3 May 1989 P. 26
327. New Zealand Companies Office
328. Pullar-Strecker, Tom Reviving Marsden Point oil refinery would likely cost billions, say owner The Post 28 November 2023

Chapter Nine

1. (1995) South China Morning Post 12 December 1995 https://www.scmp.com/article/142527/ingenuity-fuels-history-kerosene
2. The Distribution Of Motor Spirits and Ancillary Products - Report of the Commission of Inquiry Wellington 30 April 1976 P. 18
3. (1897) Harbour Board Auckland Star Volume XXVIII Issue 214 15 September 1897 P. 2
4. (1898) The Agricultural and Pastoral Association's Show The Colonist Volume XLII Issue 9343 1 December 1898 P. 2
5. (1900) Advertisements Mataura Ensign Issue 681 4 January 1900 P. 4
6. (1911) Land And Buildings/Big New Oil Stores The New Zealand Herald Volume XLVIII Issue 14699 2 May 1911 P. 7
7. (1911) Building Progress Auckland Star Volume XLII Issue 74 28 March 1911 P. 7

8. (1995) South China Morning Post 12 December 1995 https://www.scmp.com/article/142527/ingenuity-fuels-history-kerosene
9. The Distribution Of Motor Spirits and Ancillary Products - Report of the Commission of Inquiry Wellington 30 April 1976 P. 18
10. (1962) Vacuum Now Mobil Oil Christchurch Press Volume CI Issue 29788 3 April 1962 P. 17
11. The Distribution Of Motor Spirits and Ancillary Products - Report of the Commission of Inquiry Wellington 30 April 1976 P. 18
12. Shell Historical Archive The University of Melbourne Accession No. 2008.0045 2008
13. Shell In New Zealand — Chemistry in New Zealand June 1986 P. 72
14. (1905) Commercial Otago Daily Times Issue 13343 24 July 1905 P. 4
15. (1909) Shipping Otago Daily Times Issue 14617 1 September 1909 P. 4
16. (1911) Commercial And Financial Evening Post Volume LXXXI Issue 14 18 January 1911 P. 4
17. (1911) Commercial And Financial Evening Post Volume LXXXI Issue 80 5 April 1911 P. 10
18. (1911) Advertisements Evening Post Volume LXXXI Issue 103 3 May 1911 P. 4
19. (1911) Southern News/New Oil Company Auckland Star Volume XLII Issue 117 18 May 1911 P. 2
20. (1911) Commercial Otago Daily Times Issue 15147 19 May 1911 P. 4
21. New Zealand Gazette No. 29 8 March 1928 P. 663
22. New Zealand Gazette No. 91 18 December 1913 P. 3788
23. (1913) County Council Bay of Plenty Times Volume XLI Issue 6032 5 November 1913 P. 3
24. (1922) Local And General Greymouth Evening Star 8 April 1922 P. 4
25. (1922) Untitled Western Star 24 April 1922 P. 3
26. New Zealand Gazette No. 29 8 March 1928 P. 663
27. New Zealand Companies Office
28. (1983) Shell profit $39.5M Christchurch Press 30 August 1983 P. 28
29. (1888) Commercial Evening Star Issue 7708 4 September 1888 P. 3
30. (1888) New Season's Sugar Otago Daily Times Issue 8308 8 October 1888 P. 1
31. (1890) Advertisements Otago Daily Times Issue 8851 8 July 1890 P. 3
32. (1891) Football Evening Post Volume XLII Issue 45 21 August 1891 P. 3
33. (1891) Advertisements Otago Daily Times Issue 9288 2 December 1891 P. 3
34. (1898) Advertisements Auckland Star Volume XXIX Issue 64 17 March 1898 P. 4
35. (1900) Advertisements Marlborough Express Volume XXXIV Issue 204 31 August 1900 P. 3
36. (1902) Advertisements Evening Post Volume LXIII Issue 72 25 March 1902 P. 8
37. New Zealand Companies Office
38. (1912) Advertisements Evening Post Volume LXXXIII Issue 92 18 April 1912 P. 7
39. (1949) Two Well-known Companies Enter Official Stock List Otago Daily Times Issue 27010 19 February 1949 P. 3
40. (1915) Commercial & Financial Evening Post Volume LXXXIX Issue 22 27 January 1915 P. 4

41. (1915) Advertisements King Country Chronicle Volume IX Issue 766 1 May 1915 P. 4
42. (1915) Advertisements Poverty Bay Herald Volume XLII Issue 13740 20 July 1915 P. 2
43. (1915) Big Tree Benzine Bay of Plenty Times Volume XLIII Issue 6138 19 July 1915 P. 2
44. (1915) Passing It On Evening Post Volume XC Issue 54 1 September 1915 P. 8
45. (1915) Advertisements Dominion Volume 8 Issue 2521 23 July 1915 P. 1
46. (1929) Big Tree - Big Figures NZ Truth Issue 1227 6 June 1929 P. 6
47. Shell In New Zealand — Chemistry in New Zealand June 1986 P. 72
48. (1960) Big Tree Petrol Pump Christchurch Press Volume XCIX Issue 29244 30 June 1960 P. 10
49. The Distribution Of Motor Spirits and Ancillary Products - Report of the Commission of Inquiry Wellington 30 April 1976 P. 436
50. (1910) Commercial Evening Star Issue 14421 18 July 1910 P. 6
51. The Distribution Of Motor Spirits and Ancillary Products - Report of the Commission of Inquiry Wellington 30 April 1976 P. 18
52. (1920) Advertisements The Dominion Volume 13 Issue 193 11 May 1920 P. 9
53. New Zealand Companies Office
54. ibid.
55. (1905) Untitled Poverty Bay Herald Volume XXXII Issue 10488 14 October 1905 P. 2
56. (1920) Departures Poverty Bay Herald Volume XLVII Issue 15223 22 May 1920 P. 2
57. (1921) Advertisements The New Zealand Herald Volume LVIII Issue 17753 12 April 1921 P. 8
58. (1921) The Turf Dominion Volume 14 Issue 207 27 May 1921 P. 7
59. (1920) Local And General Waipawa Mail Volume XXXVII Issue 8369 13 August 1920 P. 2
60. (1920) Commercial Otago Witness Issue 3470 14 September 1920 P. 24
61. (1920) Commercial Otago Daily Times Issue 18079 29 October 1920 P. 4
62. New Zealand Gazette No. 68 13 September 1923 P. 2445
63. New Zealand Gazette No. 28 29 April 1937 P. 1082
64. Former Empire Oil Refinery Site U.S. Department of the Interior at: https://www.cerc.usgs.gov/orda_docs/CaseDetails?ID=1018
65. (1909) Advertisements Rangitikei Advocate and Manawatu Argus Volume XXXIV Issue 9480 24 June 1909 P. 8
66. (1910) Advertisements Marlborough Express Volume XLIV Issue 207 7 September 1910 P. 5
67. (1911) Advertisements New Zealand Times Volume XXXIII Issue 7417 20 April 1911 P. 3
68. (1921) Advertisements The Dominion Volume 14 Issue 123 17 February 1921 P. 7
69. (1922) Borough Council Poverty Bay Herald Volume XLVIII Issue 15813 3 May 1922 P. 9
70. (1923) The Power Board Ashburton Guardian Volume XLIV Issue 9851 25 June 1923 P. 8
71. (1931) Foreign Shipping The Dominion Volume 25 Issue 2 28 September 1931 P. 11
72. New Zealand Gazette No. 56 11 September 1958 P. 1219
73. New Zealand Gazette No. 14 5 March 1959 P. 300
74. (1908) Price Of Kerosene The New Zealand Herald Volume XLV Issue 13836 24 August 1908 P. 6

75. (1913) Oil Steamer Ablaze The New Zealand Herald Volume L Issue 15394 1 September 1913 P. 7
76. (1909) Shipping/Oil Despatches From New York The New Zealand Herald Volume XLVI Issue 14063 18 May 1909 P. 4
77. (1912) Starving Motor Cars The New Zealand Herald Volume XLIX Issue 14984 4 May 1912 P. 8
78. (1912) The Petrol Market The New Zealand Herald Volume XLIX Issue 15013 7 June 1912 P. 8
79. (1918) Joyriding Tabooed Christchurch Sun Volume V Issue 1298 11 April 1918 P. 4
80. (1918) The Petrol Shortage Sun (Christchurch) Volume V Issue 1300 13 April 1918 P. 8
81. (1920) Petrol Supplies Southland Times Issue 18772 8 January 1920 P. 5
82. (1920) Control of Petrol Supplies Poverty Bay Herald Volume XLVII Issue 15160 6 March 1920 P. 7
83. (1920) Petrol Supplies Evening Post Volume C Issue 83 5 October 1920 P. 7
84. (1908) The Tin Plate Industry Lyttelton Times Volume CXIX Issue 14856 1 December 1908 P. 7
85. (1932) Petrol Cases And Tins - Nelson Evening Mail Volume LXVI 10 August 1932 P.10
86. (1932) Big Contract Let - Christchurch Press Volume LXVIII Issue 20636 27 August 1932 P. 16
87. (1922) Advertisements Christchurch Press Volume LVIII Issue 17588 18 October 1922 P. 14
88. New Zealand Companies Office
89. (1932) Big Contract Let Christchurch Press Volume LXVIII Issue 20636 27 August 1932 P. 16
90. New Zealand Companies Office
91. (1924) Cycling & Motor Notes Otago Witness Issue 3687 11 November 1924 P. 62
92. (1902) Topics Of The Day New Zealand Times Volume LXXII Issue 4586 14 February 1902 P. 4
93. (1911) Shipping Evening Star Issue 14669 12 September 1911 P. 6
94. (1917) On The Seas Christchurch Press Volume LIII Issue 15794 9 January 1917 P. 7
95. (1926) An Oil Tanker Evening Post Volume CXI Issue 15 19 January 1926 P. 6
96. Auckland Waterfront Development Agency v Mobil Oil New Zealand 13 May 2013 [9]
97. McLean, J G Vigilance at Freeman's Bay Auckland Sun Volume II Issue 329 14 April 1928 P. 17
98. Auckland Waterfront Development Agency v Mobil Oil New Zealand 13 May 2013 [19] to [21]
99. ibid. [1] & [25]
100. Wiri Oil Services Limited at https://www.wosl.co.nz/
101. Energy Supply and Use The Encyclopedia of New Zealand https://teara.govt.nz/en/energy-supply-and-use/page-4
102. Explosive and Dangerous Goods Amendment Act 1920
103. ibid.
104. Gasoline Pump Wikipedia https://en.wikipedia.org/wiki/Gasoline_pump
105. Old Petrol Pumps The Encylopedia of New Zealand at: https://teara.govt.nz/en/photograph/22865/old-petrol-pumps

106. Energy Supply and Use The Encyclopedia of New Zealand https://teara.govt.nz/en/energy-supply-and-use/page-4
107. The Distribution Of Motor Spirits and Ancillary Products - Report of the Commission of Inquiry Wellington 30 April 1976 Pp. 24-26
108. New Zealand Parliamentary Debates, Volume 301 28 October to 27 November 1953 P. 2495
109. The Distribution Of Motor Spirits and Ancillary Products - Report of the Commission of Inquiry Wellington 30 April 1976 Pp. 26-27
110. Gilmore Oil Company Wikipedia https://en.wikipedia.org/wiki/Gilmore_Oil_Company
111. History of Gilmore Gasoline https://www.flickr.com/photos/vaultgarage/4666266911
112. (1924) Advertisements Waipa Post Volume XXIV Issue 1559 9 October 1924 P. 1
113. (1926) Advertisements Taranaki Daily News 6 December 1926 P. 12
114. New Zealand Gazette No. 34 30 April 1931 P. 1410
115. New Zealand Gazette No. 92 13 December 1934 P. 4193
116. New Zealand Gazette No. 34 30 April 1931 P. 1410
117. (1931) Finance And Commerce The Dominion Volume 24 Issue 178 24 April 1931 P. 10
118. (1933) Company Affairs Auckland Star Volume LXIV Issue 45 23 February 1933 P. 4
119. (1933) Electric Welding Christchurch Star Volume XLIV Issue 727 3 April 1933 P. 4
120. (1934) Petrol Price Gutting Evening Star Issue 21865 31 October 1934 P. 14
121. Parliamentary Debates 18 September to 10 November 1934 P. 870
122. History of Gilmore Gasoline https://www.flickr.com/photos/vaultgarage/4666266911
123. (1920) New Incorporations The New York Times 14 December 1920 P. 34
124. Official Gazette of the United States Patent Office Volume 302 September 1922
125. Meteor Oklahoma Motor Spirit Crate https://hibid.com/lot/172317054/meteor-oklahoma-motor-spirit-wooden-crate?ref=lot-list
126. (1921) Advertisements Northern Advocate 29 November 1921 P. 7
127. (1924) Meteor Motor Spirit - Hasell v Texas Foreign Trading Corporation and another Sydney Morning Herald 23 February 1924 P. 14
128. (1877) Shipping The New Zealand Herald Volume XIV Issue 4767 26 February 1877 P. 2
129. (1880) Advertisements The New Zealand Herald Volume XVII Issue 5912 28 October 1880 P. 3
130. (1881) Shipping The New Zealand Herald Volume XVIII Issue 6143 26 July 1881 P. 4
131. New Zealand Gazette No. 46 26 August 1965 P. 1399
132. (1924) The Search After Oil Wanganui Chronicle Volume LXXXI Issue 19124 27 September 1924 P. 9
133. (1927) Oil Merger Auckland Star Volume LVIII Issue 268 12 November 1927 P. 9
134. (1927) Petrol And Oil Supplies Poverty Bay Herald Volume LIII Issue 16523 15 December 1927 P. 5
135. (1928) Branch Of Well-Known Oil Business Sold Auckland Sun Volume II Issue 363 25 May 1928 P. 1
136. (1926) California's Oil Fires Manawatu Times Volume XLIX Issue 3317 12 April 1926 P. 7
137. (1928) Great Benzine Fire The New Zealand Herald Volume LXV Issue 19911 2 April 1928 P. 10
138. (1928) Atlantic Union Oil Evening Post Volume CV Issue 128 1 June 1928 P. 12
139. (1933) Advertisements Northern Advocate 8 November 1933 P. 3

140. (1949) Famous Oil Company Comes To Otago And Southland Otago Daily Times Issue 27175 2 September 1949 P. 8
141. (1959) Advertisements Christchurch Press Volume XCVIII Issue 29089 29 December 1959 P. 12
142. (1960) Company News Christchurch Press Volume XCIX Issue 29395 23 December 1960 P. 14
143. (1980) Oil firms to merge Christchurch Press 23 February 1980 P. 6
144. New Zealand Companies Office
145. (1912) Advertisements Auckland Star Volume XLIII Issue 139 11 June 1912 P. 6
146. New Zealand Companies Office
147. (1920) Advertisements Northern Advocate 26 June 1920 P. 5
148. (1923) Advertisements The New Zealand Herald Volume LX Issue 18529 13 October 1923 P. 11 (Supplement)
149. (1928) Great Benzine Fire The New Zealand Herald Volume LXV Issue 19911 2 April 1928 P. 10
150. (1928) Advertisements Auckland Star Volume LIX Issue 79 3 April 1928 P. 24
151. (1928) Branch Of Well-Known Oil Business Sold Auckland Sun Volume II Issue 363 25 May 1928 P. 1
152. (1946) Farewell Gathering Gisborne Herald Volume LXXIII Issue 22034 30 May 1946 P. 6
153. (1928) Advertisements Manawatu Standard Volume XLVIII Issue 144 18 May 1928 P. 10
154. (1916) New Companies Evening Post Volume XCII Issue 35 10 August 1916 P. 3
155. (1916) Local And General The Dominion Volume 10 Issue 2932 18 November 1916 P. 8
156. The New Zealand Gazette No. 20 21 March 1929 p. 781
157. (1929) Advertisements Wairarapa Age 24 June 1929 P. 1
158. (1930) Advertisements Evening Post Volume CIX Issue 13 16 January 1930 P. 24
159. (1929) Reduction Of Capital Evening Post Volume CVII Issue 15 19 January 1929 P. 12
160. (1929) Advertisements Evening Post Volume CVII Issue 104 7 May 1929 P. 3
161. (1929) Advertisements Evening Post Volume CVIII Issue 4 4 July 1929 P. 3
162. (1930) Advertisements Evening Post Volume CX Issue 130 29 November 1930 P. 27
163. (1930) Advertisements Evening Post Volume CX Issue 142 13 December 1930 P. 8
164. (1930) Advertisements Christchurch Star Issue 19138 2 August 1930 P. 7
165. (1931) Tararua Power Board Pahiatua Herald Volume XXXIX Issue 11653 17 January 1931 P. 3
166. (1931) Advertisements The Dominion Volume 24 Issue 302 17 September 1931 P. 7
167. (1926) Railway Reserve New Zealand Times Volume LIII Issue 12510 28 July 1926 P. 7
168. (1931) Built In New Zealand The Dominion Volume 25 Issue 72 18 December 1931 P. 6
169. (1932) New Companies Evening Post Volume CXIII Issue 6 8 January 1932 P. 10
170. (1932) Big Petrol Cargo The Dominion Volume 25 Issue 99 21 January 1932 P. 10
171. (1932) New Zealand Enterprise Evening Post Volume CXIII Issue 17 21 January 1932 P. 9
172. (1932) Petrol Supplies The Dominion Volume 25 Issue 100 22 January 1932 P. 10
173. (1932) Local Oil Companies Evening Post Volume CXIII Issue 121 24 May 1932 P. 10
174. New Zealand Gazette No. 45 15 June 1933 P. 1637

175. Hunt, Graeme The Rich List — Wealth and Enterprise in New Zealand 1820-2000 Reed Books Auckland 2000 P. 146
176. McCrystal, John 100 Years of Motoring in New Zealand Hodder Moa Beckett 2003 P. 127
177. Webster, Mark (2021) <u>Assembly - A History of New Zealand Car Production 1921-1998</u>. Sydney/Auckland, New Holland Publishers. P. 31
178. Hawkes, Graham (1990) <u>On the Road - The Car In New Zealand</u>. Wellington, GP Books. P. 39
179. The Distribution Of Motor Spirits and Ancillary Products - Report of the Commission of Inquiry Wellington 30 April 1976 P. 19
180. Hunt, Graeme The Rich List — Wealth and Enterprise in New Zealand 1820-2000 Reed Books Auckland 2000 P. 147
181. The Distribution Of Motor Spirits and Ancillary Products - Report of the Commission of Inquiry Wellington 30 April 1976 P. 19
182. ibid. P. 23
183. Dick, Allan MTA Centenary Publication RnR Publishing Limited Martinborough New Zealand April 2017 P. 20
184. (1989) BP (NZ) lifts profit ratio Christchurch Press 18 May 1989 P. 25
185. (2017) How family values fuelled homegrown Gull empire The West Australian 7 December 2017
186. Gull - About Us at https://gull.nz/about-us/
187. Caltex Acquires Gull New Zealand ASX Caltex Australia Release 26 June 2017
188. Smith, Daniel Gull New Zealand sold to Aussie equity firm Stuff 14 March 2022
189. Gull - About Us at https://gull.nz/about-us/
190. Hunter, J S Commissioner of Transport, Transport Department Annual Report for Year Ending 31 March 1930 1 October 1930 P. 81
191. Semple, Robert, Minister of Public Works, Public Works Statement for Year Ending 31 March 1936 20 June 1936 P. 122
192. The Distribution Of Motor Spirits and Ancillary Products - Report of the Commission of Inquiry Wellington 30 April 1976 P. 14
193. ibid. P. 394
194. ibid. P. 20-21
195. Petrol Prices — Parliamentary Debates Volume 237 5 December 1933 P. 675
196. ibid. Pp. 675-676
197. ibid. Pp. 676-677
198. ibid. P. 677
199. ibid. P. 678
200. ibid. Pp. 681-682
201. Motor-spirits (Regulation of Prices) Act 1933 No. 36 22 December 1933
202. Hawkes, Graham (1990) <u>On the Road - The Car In New Zealand</u>. Wellington, GP Books. P. 39
203. New Zealand Gazette No. 49 23 July 1936 P. 1393
204. The Distribution Of Motor Spirits and Ancillary Products - Report of the Commission of Inquiry Wellington 30 April 1976 Pp. 21-22
205. (1950) Petrol Rationing Ends In Dominion Today Gisborne Herald Volume LXXVII Issue 23268 1 June 1950 P. 8

206. (1950) Petrol Rationing Otago Daily Times Issue 27404 1 June 1950 P. 6
207. (1937) Science to the Aid of the Motorist The Dominion Volume 30 Issue 200 20 May 1937 P. 13
208. (1940) Untitled The Dominion Volume 33 Issue 270 9 August 1940 P. 11
209. (1940) Advertisements Evening Post Volume CXXX Issue 39 14 August 1940 P. 2
210. (1941) Advertisements Evening Post Volume CXXXI Issue 120 23 May 1941 P. 2
211. The Industry Licensing (Used Oil Refining) Revocation Notice 1942/32 The New Zealand Gazette No. 19 19 February 1942 P. 85
212. NZ Companies Office
213. (1934) New Companies Auckland Registrations The New Zealand Herald Volume LXXI Issue 21712 30 January 1934 P. 5
214. (1934) Company Affairs Auckland Star Volume LXV Issue 277 22 November 1934 P. 4
215. (1938) Patents Nelson Evening Mail Volume LXXII 6 December 1938 P. 5
216. Material Refining of Used Oils Intellectual Property Office New Zealand Patent Application 1938
217. (1943) Advertisements Auckland Star Volume LXXIV Issue 58 10 March 1943 P. 1
218. (1971) Diversification by Motor Specs Christchurch Press Volume CXI Issue 32789 14 December 1971 P. 25
219. (1973) Motor Specs sales ahead in first three months Christchurch Press Volume CXIII Issue 33343 29 September 1973 P. 13
220. (1975) Difficult year expected by Motor Specs Christchurch Press Volume CXV Issue 33968 8 October 1975 P. 28
221. (1976) Additives vexing reclaimers Christchurch Press Volume CXVI Issue 34139 28 April 1976 P. 18
222. (1976) Motor Specs. ahead Christchurch Press 7 October 1976 P. 23
223. (1977) Oil recycling encouraged Christchurch Press 18 May 1977 P. 20
224. (1978) BP buys M.S.I. firm Christchurch Press 25 February 1978 P. 19
225. (1989) BP (NZ) lifts profit ratio Christchurch Press 18 May 1989 P. 25
226. BP Advertising Complaint 91/57 Advertising Standards Complaints Board Wellington 28 January 1992
227. (1940) New Companies Evening Post Volume CXXIX Issue 112 13 May 1940 P. 12
228. (1982) Obituary Mr Arthur Hilton Christchurch Press 1 March 1982 P. 6
229. (1955) Advertisements Christchurch Press Volume XCI Issue 27648 3 May 1955 P. 7
230. (1974) Five Killed In Explosion In Hutt Valley Chemical Plant Christchurch Press Volume CXIV Issue 33650 27 September 1974 P. 1

Chapter Ten

1. (1865) Editorial The New Zealand Herald Volume II Issue 373 23 January 1865 P. 4
2. (1865) City Board - Monday The New Zealand Herald Volume II Issue 368 17 January 1865 P. 5
3. (1870) Police Court - Monday Auckland Star Volume I Issue 217 19 September 1870 P. 2
4. (1865) The Daily Southern Cross Volume XXI Issue 2439 15 May 1865 P. 4
5. Mexsom, Keith Waka Paddle to Gas Pedal January 2020 P. 105

6. (1877) Main Roads The Bay of Plenty Times Volume VI Edition 528 6 October 1877 P. 2
7. (1904) Opawa Road Christchurch Star Issue 7934 12 February 1904 P. 1
8. Roads and Bridges Construction Act 1882 No. 42 15 September 1882
9. Mair, Sydney A R - Country Roads Evening Post Volume LXXXVII Issue 142 17 June 1914 P. 14
10. (1923) Ashburton Streets Ashburton Guardian Volume XLIV Issue 9928 27 September 1923 P. 5
11. (1928) Highway Finance The New Zealand Herald Volume LXV Issue 20076 13 October 1928 P. 10 (Supplement)
12. (1858) Nelson Improvement Amendment Act Colonist Issue 38 2 March 1858 P. 3
13. (1887) Untitled The New Zealand Herald Volume XXIV Issue 7839 7 January 1887 P. 4
14. (1904) Local And General News The New Zealand Herald Volume XLI Issue 12663 17 September 1904 P. 4
15. (1910) The Work Of The Session Auckland Star Volume XLL Issue 299 17 December 1910 P. 9
16. (1910) Political Notes The New Zealand Herald Volume XLVII Issue 14422 15 July 1910 P. 6
17. (1940) News Of The Day Northern Advocate 29 April 1940 P. 4
18. (1906) Opportunity To Save £20 A Week The Wanganui Herald Volume XXXX Issue 11979 24 September 1906 P. 4
19. (1913) Country News The New Zealand Herald Volume L Issue 15305 19 May 1913 P. 4
20. (1914) Town Board Rodney and Otamatea Times, Waitemata And Kaipara Gazette 30 September 1914 P. 5
21. (1917) Matamata County Council Te Aroha News Volume XXXV Issue 5548 5 October 1917 P. 2
22. (1922) Piako County Council Waikato Times Volume 95 Issue 14951 23 May 1922 P. 7
23. (1926) Drury Notes Franklin Times Volume XVI Issue 33 19 March 1926 P. 8
24. (1926) The Concrete Age Auckland Star Volume LVII Issue 299 17 December 1926 P. 10
25. (1927) New Quarry Opened The New Zealand Herald Volume LXIV Issue 19822 17 December 1927 P. 11
26. (1928) Advertisements Auckland Sun Volume I Issue 248 10 January 1928 P. 3
27. (1928) Quarrying Damage Auckland Sun Volume II Issue 332 18 April 1928 P. 13
28. (1860) Advertisements New Zealander Volume XVI Issue 1480 23 June 1860 P. 2
29. (1863) Advertisements New Zealander Volume XIX Issue 1936 3 August 1863 P. 3
30. (1873) Untitled The New Zealand Herald Volume X Issue 3693 11 September 1873 P. 2
31. (1874) Untitled The New Zealand Herald Volume XI Issue 4031 13 October 1874 P. 2
32. (1912) Metal For City Roads The New Zealand Herald Volume XLIX Issue 14979 29 April 1912 P. 8
33. (1912) Metal For The Roads The New Zealand Herald Volume XLIX Issue 15110 28 September 1912 P. 8
34. (1915) The City Mayoralty The New Zealand Herald Volume LII Issue 15896 20 April 1915 P. 9
35. (1913) City Council Auckland Star Volume XLIV Issue 109 8 May 1913 P. 9

36. (1919) Mount Eden Quarry The New Zealand Herald Volume LVI Issue 17290 14 October 1919 P. 9
37. (1920) Local And General News The New Zealand Herald Volume LVII Issue 17626 12 November 1920 P. 6
38. (1921) The City Council The New Zealand Herald Volume LVIII Issue 17798 3 June 1921 P. 7
39. (1926) Great North Road Auckland Star Volume LVII Issue 228 25 September 1926 P. 11
40. (1929) Take No Risks Auckland Star Volume LX Issue 130 4 June 1929 P. 10
41. (1937) City Enterprises The New Zealand Herald Volume LXXIV Issue 22875 2 November 1937 P. 11
42. (1945) Advertisements The New Zealand Herald Volume 82 Issue 25368 24 November 1945 P. 1
43. Pickmere, Arnold Condemned jail outlasts the critics The New Zealand Herald 30 June 2000
44. Loader, Andy For the love of rock Quarry Mining Magazine 8 November 2017 https://quarryingandminingmag.co.nz/auckland-quarries
45. (1875) Untitled The New Zealand Herald Volume XII Issue 4111 16 January 1875 P. 2
46. (1877) Waste Lands Board The New Zealand Herald Volume XIV Issue 4943 19 September 1877 P. 3
47. (1892) A Visit To Mount Eden Gaol The New Zealand Herald Volume XXIX Issue 8993 26 September 1892 P. 6
48. (1884) Untitled Auckland Star Volume XXIII Issue 4284 15 February 1884 P. 2
49. (1884) Untitled The New Zealand Herald Volume XXI Issue 7042 12 June 1884 P. 4
50. (1921) Sale Of Road Metal Auckland Star Volume LII Issue 279 23 November 1921 P. 4
51. (1922) Prison Labour Auckland Star Volume LIII Issue 87 12 April 1922 P. 9
52. (1923) Mount Eden's Output Auckland Star Volume LIV Issue 191 11 August 1923 P. 13
53. (1923) Local And General News The New Zealand Herald Volume LX Issue 18525 9 October 1923 P. 6
54. (1923) Shortage Of Trucks The New Zealand Herald Volume LX Issue 18587 20 December 1923 P. 10
55. (1927) Trades and the Workers Auckland Sun Volume 1 Issue 84 30 June 1927 P. 7
56. (1932) Auckland Quarries Auckland Star Volume LXIII Issue 87 13 April 1932 P. 5
57. (1932) Price-Fixing Plan Auckland Star Volume LXIII Issue 210 5 September 1932 P. 9
58. (1935) Unfair Competition The New Zealand Herald Volume LXXII Issue 22232 5 October 1935 P. 15
59. (1936) Prices Of Metal The New Zealand Herald Volume LXXIII Issue 22510 29 August 1936 P. 14
60. Pickmere, Arnold Condemned jail outlasts the critics The New Zealand Herald 30 June 2000
61. J J Craig Limited The Fletcher Trust Archives https://collection.fletcherarchives.co.nz/persons/1724/jj-craig-ltd
62. (1885) City Council The New Zealand Herald Volume XXII Issue 7394 31 July 1885 P. 6
63. (1886) Untitled Auckland Star Volume XXVII Issue 12 15 January 1886 P. 3
64. (1900) J J CRAIG The New Zealand Herald Volume XXXVII Issue 11487 26 September 1900 P. 3 (Supplement)

65. J J Craig Limited The Fletcher Trust Archives
    https://collection.fletcherarchives.co.nz/persons/1724/jj-craig-ltd
66. New Zealand Companies Office
67. Craig's Building 100 Queen Street Auckland Heritage New Zealand
    https://www.heritage.org.nz/list-details/4484/Craig
68. (1916) Captain Of Industry Dead Auckland Star, Volume XLVII, Issue 165, 12 July 1916, Page 4
69. J J Craig Limited The Fletcher Trust Archives
    https://collection.fletcherarchives.co.nz/persons/1724/jj-craig-ltd
70. (1921) A Trade Name New Zealand Herald Volume LVIII Issue 17843 26 July 1921 P. 7
71. J J Craig Limited The Fletcher Trust Archives
    https://collection.fletcherarchives.co.nz/persons/1724/jj-craig-ltd
72. (1968) Winstone's Prospects Christchurch Press Volume CVIII Issue 31819 25 October 1968 P. 14
73. New Zealand Companies Office
74. Our Humble Origins The Story of William Winstone - Winstone Aggregates
    https://winstoneaggregates.co.nz/about-us/about-winstone/our-profile
75. (1863) Advertisements The New Zealand Herald Volume I Issue 9 3 December 1863 P. 2
76. (1866) City Board Daily Southern Cross Volume XXII Issue 2706 20 March 1866 P. 5
77. Mount Eden Area Maungawhau Heritage Walks Auckland Council Mount Eden Quarry P.26 www.mounteden.co.nz
78. Our Humble Origins The Story of William Winstone - Winstone Aggregates
    https://winstoneaggregates.co.nz/about-us/about-winstone/our-profile
79. (1872) Advertisements Auckland Star Volume III Issue 855 14 October 1872 P. 3
80. Our Humble Origins The Story of William Winstone - Winstone Aggregates
    https://winstoneaggregates.co.nz/about-us/about-winstone/our-profile
81. (1872) Police Court Auckland Star Volume III Issue 666 29 February 1872 P. 2
82. (1872) Police Court Auckland Star, Volume III Issue 690 28 March 1872 P. 2
83. (1875) Police Court Auckland Star Volume VI Issue 1628 6 May 1875 P. 2
84. (1881) Waikato Times and Thames Valley Gazette Volume XVI Issue 1373 21 April 1881 P. 2
85. (1884) City Council Auckland Star Volume XXVI Issue 4530 5 December 1884 P. 4
86. (1890) Auckland Today Poverty Bay Herald Volume XVII Issue 5715 11 March 1890 P. 2
87. (1890) Consolidation Of The Trades And Labour Councils Evening Post Volume XXXIX Issue 63 17 March 1890 P. 2
88. (1904) Auckland Star Volume XXXV Issue 157 2 July 1904 P. 4
89. (1912) The Coal Trade Hawera & Normanby Star Volume LXVIII Issue LXVIII 28 June 1912 P. 3
90. Our Humble Origins The Story of William Winstone - Winstone Aggregates
    https://winstoneaggregates.co.nz/about-us/about-winstone/our-profile
91. (1924) A Pioneer's Reward Auckland Star Volume 55 Issue 61 12 March 1924 P. 8
92. (1924) Obituary Auckland Star, Volume LV, Issue 147, 23 June 1924, Page 7
93. (1932) Veteran Business Man Auckland Star Volume LXIII Issue 102 2 May 1932 P. 5
94. (1925) Gift Of A Mountain The New Zealand Herald Volume LXII Issue 18999 22 April 1925 P. 8

95. Loader, Andy For the love of rock Quarry Mining Magazine 8 November 2017 https://quarryingandminingmag.co.nz/auckland-quarries
96. Our Humble Origins The Story of William Winstone - Winstone Aggregates https://winstoneaggregates.co.nz/about-us/about-winstone/our-profile
97. New Zealand Companies Office
98. Loader, Andy For the love of rock Quarry Mining Magazine 8 November 2017 https://quarryingandminingmag.co.nz/auckland-quarries
99. Roman cement https://en.wikipedia.org/wiki/Roman_cement
100. Portland cement https://en.wikipedia.org/wiki/Portland_cement
101. (1925) A Century Of Cement Cromwell Argus Volume LVI Issue 2935 17 August 1925 P. 7
102. (1841) Advertisements New Zealand Gazette and Wellington Spectator Volume 17 Issue 53 17 April 1841 P. 2
103. (1843) Advertisements New Zealand Gazette and Wellington Spectator Volume IV Issue 281 16 September 1843 P. 1
104. (1930) Obituary Auckland Star Volume LXI Issue 282 28 November 1930 P. 9
105. (1879) Sheep The New Zealand Herald Volume XVI Issue 5612 11 November 1879 P. 6
106. (1881) Untitled The New Zealand Herald Volume XVIII Issue 6194 21 September 1881 P. 4
107. (1881) City Council Auckland Star Volume XII Issue 3497 21 October 1881 P. 2
108. (1883) Auckland Hydraulic Lime Wanganui Chronicle Volume XXV Issue 9895 7 April 1883 P. 2
109. (1936) Fifty Years Of Progress Northern Advocate 24 June 1936 P. 2
110. (1890) Country News The New Zealand Herald Volume XXVII Issue 8261 21 May 1890 P. 6
111. (1888) Advertisements New Zealand Times Volume L Issue 8373 28 April 1888 P. 5
112. (1893) Current News Wairoa Bell Volume V Issue 196 5 May 1893 P. 2
113. (1897) Untitled South Canterbury Times Issue 8838 22 May 1897 P. 3
114. (1898) Auckland Exhibition The New Zealand Herald Volume XXXV Issue 10937 16 December 1898 P. 3
115. (1936) Fifty Years Of Progress Northern Advocate 24 June 1936 P. 2
116. (1930) Obituary Auckland Star Volume LXI Issue 282 28 November 1930 P. 9
117. (1904) Local And General News The New Zealand Herald Volume XLI Issue 12669 24 September 1904 P. 4
118. (1905) New Plymouth Exhibition New Zealand Mail Issue 1714 4 January 1905 P. 40 (Supplement)
119. (1907) Manufacture Of Cement Lyttelton Times Volume XCVI Issue 14385 30 May 1907 P. 9
120. (1908) Wilsons Portland Cement Company The New Zealand Herald Volume XLV Issue 13760 27 May 1908 P. 5
121. (1910) Commercial Auckland Star Volume XLI Issue 123 26 May 1910 P. 7
122. (1910) Northern Auckland Lime and Cement by Our Special Commissioner The New Zealand Herald Volume XLVII Issue 14471 10 September 1910 P. 5
123. (1911) Cement In New Zealand Auckland Star Volume XLII Issue 30 4 February 1911 P. 10

124. (1911) North NZ Coal And Cement Company's Mine Northern Advocate 24 October 1911 P. 3
125. (1912) Dominion Cement Company Hawera & Normanby Star, Volume XVIII, Issue XVIII, 11 December 1912, Page 8
126. (1912) New Cement Works Waipukurau Press, Volume 4, Issue 486, 12 December 1912, Page 3
127. (1912) Advertisements Dominion Volume 6 Issue 1599 16 November 1912 P. 3
128. (1921) The Cement Industry Auckland Star Volume LII Issue 293 9 December 1921 P. 10
129. Limestone Island Cement Engineering New Zealand https://www.engineeringnz.org/programmes/heritage/heritage-records/limestone-island-cement/
130. (1896) The New Zealand Portland Cement Company Evening Star Issue 10055 11 July 1896 P. 2
131. (1897) New Zealand Portland Cement Company The New Zealand Herald Volume XXXIV Issue 10604 19 November 1897 P. 3
132. (1898) Town Edition Daily Telegraph (Napier) Issue 9265 10 September 1898 P. 3
133. (1902) General Telegrams Evening Post Volume LXIV Issue 66 15 September 1902 P. 5
134. (1904) Commercial The New Zealand Herald Volume XLI Issue 12487 3 February 1904 P. 3 (Supplement)
135. (1905) Local And General News The New Zealand Herald Volume XLII Issue 13038 1 December 1905 P. 4
136. (1906) Whangarei Items The New Zealand Herald Volume XLIII Issue 13251 9 August 1906 P. 7
137. (1908) Untitled Auckland Star Volume XXXIX Issue 21 24 January 1908 P. 4
138. (1912) Portland Cement Company Evening Post Volume LXXXIII Issue 23 27 January 1912 P. 11
139. (1915) Disastrous Fire The Dominion Volume 8 Issue 2359 15 January 1915 P. 6
140. (1915) Local And General Nelson Evening Mail Volume XLVIII Issue XLVIII 21 July 1915 P. 4
141. (1918) New Zealand Cement Company Northern Advocate 8 February 1918 P. 1
142. (1918) Important Amalgamation Evening Star Issue 16685 18 March 1918 P. 8
143. (1918) Control Of Cement Industry Northern Advocate 13 July 1918 P. 2
144. (1924) Cement Works Closing The New Zealand Herald Volume LXI Issue 18860 7 November 1924 P. 8
145. (1925) Concrete Roads The New Zealand Herald Volume LXII Issue 19149 15 October 1925 P. 9
146. (1930) Commercial Nelson Evening Mail Volume LXIV 14 May 1930 P. 2
147. (1932) Cement Works Closing The New Zealand Herald Volume LXIX Issue 21363 12 December 1932 P. 10
148. (1941) Wilsons Cement Waikato Times Volume 128 Issue 21438 4 June 1941 P. 4
149. (1948) Company News Christchurch Press Volume LXXXIV Issue 25535 1 July 1948 P. 8
150. (1965) Cement For Tongariro Christchurch Press Volume CIV Issue 30838 25 August 1965 P. 1
151. Golden Bay Cement Company Amalgamation New Zealand Companies Office 15 August 2000

152. (1926) Valuable Industry Northern Advocate 22 September 1926 P. 4
153. (1926) Company Affairs Auckland Star Volume LVII Issue 243 13 October 1926 P. 4
154. (1926) New Zealand Cement New Zealand Times Volume LIII Issue 12593 2 November 1926 P. 4
155. (1926) The Concrete Age Auckland Star Volume LVII Issue 299 17 December 1926 P. 10
156. (1926) Growth Of The Cement Industry Southland Times Issue 19993 6 October 1926 P. 2
157. (1927) Limestone Deposits Auckland Star Volume LVIII Issue 145 22 June 1927 P. 11
158. (1927) Golden Bay Cement Company Evening Post Volume CIV Issue 148 20 December 1927 P. 11
159. (1928) Chamber Of Commerce Northern Advocate 10 May 1928 P. 3
160. (1931) Colliery Closes Down Auckland Star Volume LXII Issue 284 1 December 1931 P. 3
161. (1907) Advertisements Nelson Evening Mail Volume XLII Issue XLII 27 February 1907 P. 3
162. (1907) Advertisements Colonist Volume XLIX Issue 11939 20 May 1907 P. 2
163. (1907) The Golden Bay Cement Works Limited Colonist Volume XLIX Issue 11966 20 June 1907 P. 1 (Supplement)
164. (1909) Golden Bay Cement Works Limited Evening Post Volume LXXVII Issue 98 27 April 1909 P. 7
165. (1911) Local And General Nelson Evening Mail Volume XLVI Issue XLVI 8 September 1911 P. 4
166. (1912) Local And General News Marlborough Express Volume XLVI Issue 54 29 February 1912 P. 4
167. (1913) The Cement Age The Dominion Volume 6 Issue 1776 14 June 1913 P. 28
168. (1920) News Of The Day New Zealand Times Volume XLVI Issue 10521 24 February 1920 P. 4
169. (1920) Local And General Nelson Evening Mail Volume LIV Issue LIV 16 July 1920 P. 4
170. New Zealand Gazette No. 100 16 December 1920 P. 3304
171. (1921) Cement Works Closed The New Zealand Herald Volume LVIII Issue 17776 9 May 1921 P. 4
172. (1921) Untitled Poverty Bay Herald Volume XLVII Issue 15545 14 June 1921 P. 2
173. (1921) Grave Charges New Zealand Times Volume XLVIII Issue 11019 30 September 1921 P. 5
174. (1921) Monopoly And Exploitation Christchurch Star Issue 16544 30 September 1921 P. 6
175. Cement Industry Commission of Inquiry into the Production, Distribution, Importation, And Price Of Cement - Reported 17 November 1921 Pp. 1-3, 8, & 10
176. (1922) Cement Works Evening Post Volume CIV Issue 22 26 July 1922 P. 2
177. (1923) Work Resumed Evening Post Volume CVI Issue 64 13 September 1923 P. 10
178. (1928) Chamber Of Commerce Northern Advocate 10 May 1928 P. 3
179. (1932) Commercial Evening Star Issue 21281 9 December 1932 P. 7
180. (1932) Company Affairs Auckland Star Volume LXIII Issue 304 23 December 1932 P. 4
181. (1945) Commercial Evening Star Issue 25665 13 December 1945 P. 8
182. (1947) Company News Greymouth Evening Star 4 December 1947 P. 10

183. (1950) Company News Christchurch Press Volume LXXXVI Issue 26062 15 March 1950 P. 9
184. (1954) Company News Christchurch Press Volume XC Issue 27528 9 December 1954 P. 17
185. New Zealand Gazette No. 23 21 March 1957 P. 522
186. Golden Bay Cement Company Limited The Fletcher Trust Archives https://collection.fletcherarchives.co.nz/persons/77/golden-bay-cement-company-ltd
187. New Zealand Gazette No. 105 4 September 1980 P. 2639
188. Golden Bay Cement Company Limited The Fletcher Trust Archives https://collection.fletcherarchives.co.nz/persons/77/golden-bay-cement-company-ltd
189. New Zealand Companies Office
190. Golden Bay Cement Company Amalgamation New Zealand Companies Office 15 August 2000
191. (1877) Advertisements Clutha Leader Volume IV Issue 166 14 September 1877 P. 2
192. (1877) Waste Lands Board Southland Times Issue 2937 23 November 1877 P. 2
193. (1878) Advertisements Bruce Herald Volume XI Issue 1017 11 June 1878 P. 3
194. (1887) Timaru Harbour Board South Canterbury Times Issue 4575 21 December 1887 P. 3
195. (1888) Oamaru Harbour Board Oamaru Mail Volume X Issue 4046 28 February 1888 P. 3
196. (1888) By the Way Mataura Ensign Volume II Issue 773 18 May 1888 P. 6
197. (1888) Advertisements Evening Star Issue 7625 30 May 1888 P. 3
198. (1888) Untitled Western Star Issue 1271 25 July 1888 P. 3
199. (1888) Advertisements Otago Daily Times Issue 8244 25 July 1888 P. 3
200. Tariff Commission Report 31 May 1895 Pp. 80-81
201. ibid. P. 211
202. ibid. P. vi
203. ibid. P. xii
204. (1901) Milburn Lime And Cement Works Otago Witness Issue 2484 23 October 1901 P. 72
205. (1903) Local And General News Tuapeka Times Volume XXXVI Issue 5038 18 February 1903 P. 2
206. (1903) Bruce County Council Bruce Herald Volume XXXX Issue 45 10 June 1903 P. 5
207. (1904) Commercial Otago Daily Times Issue 12883 29 January 1904 P. 4
208. (1911) Untitled Evening Star Issue 14508 7 March 1911 P. 4
209. (1903) The Electric System Otago Daily Times Issue 12846 15 December 1903 P. 3
210. (1905) Local & General Otago Witness Issue 2695 8 November 1905 P. 29
211. (1903) Important Discovery at Burnside Timaru Herald Volume LXXIX Issue 12123 18 July 1903 P. 3 (Supplement)
212. (1905) Advertisements Southland Times Issue 19702 13 November 1905 P. 3
213. (1905) Advertisements Evening Star Volume 12653 Issue 12653 6 November 1905 P. 5
214. (1907) Untitled Evening Star Issue 12632 10 April 1907 P. 4
215. (1909) Our Local Industries Otago Daily Times Issue 14434 29 January 1909 P. 3
216. (1909) Advertisements Otago Daily Times Issue 14461 2 March 1909 P. 6
217. (1910) Burnside Cement Company Evening Star Issue 14425 22 July 1910 P. 4
218. ibid.

219. (1910) Burnside Cement Co. Evening Star Issue 14436 4 August 1910 P. 7
220. (1929) Progress In Industry Otago Daily Times Issue 20663 11 March 1929 P. 5
221. (1947) Milburn Lime Company Otago Daily Times Issue 26575 25 September 1947 P. 9
222. (1950) Milburn Lime Expansion Otago Daily Times Issue 27490 9 September 1950 P. 3
223. (1963) Company News Milburn Cement Christchurch Press Volume CII Issue 30270 24 October 1963 P. 25
224. The New Zealand Gazette No. 51 13 September 1956 P. 1252
225. Cement — a new driver Buller District Council Westport Harbour https://www.westportharbour.co.nz/about/history/
226. The New Zealand Gazette No. 11 5 March 1964 P. 339
227. Cement — a new driver Buller District Council Westport Harbour https://www.westportharbour.co.nz/about/history/
228. (1979) The west port Christchurch Press 14 June 1979 P. 21
229. (1964) NZ Cement Profit Christchurch Press Volume CIII Issue 30558 29 September 1964 P. 21
230. (1964) NZ Cement Plans Christchurch Press Volume CIII Issue 30524 20 August 1964 P. 24
231. (1968) NZ Cement Expects Higher Sales Christchurch Press Volume CVIII Issue 31822 29 October 1968 P. 17
232. (1969) Joint Offer For Wilsons Cement Christchurch Press Volume CIX Issue 32163 5 December 1969 P. 18
233. (1971) A and K Cement in NZ Cement Christchurch Press Volume CXI Issue 32658 14 July 1971 P. 24
234. (1971) NZ Cement in merger Christchurch Press Volume CXI Issue 32791 16 December 1971 P. 9
235. (1975) Cement firm seeks SI price rise Christchurch Press Volume CXV Issue 33866 11 June 1975 P. 2
236. (1984) Cement competitors holding talks on co-operation Christchurch Press 8 March 1984 P. 28
237. (1987) Cement monopoly seen as unlikely Christchurch Press 28 November 1987 P. 32
238. New Zealand Companies Office
239. Built In Dunedin Milburn Lime and Cement Co. Head office https://builtindunedin.com/2015/03/27/milburn-lime-cement-co-head-office/
240. (1988) Milburn split into three Christchurch Press 19 July 1988 P. 21
241. (1988) Milburn buys Ready Mix Christchurch Press 14 December 1988 P. 47
242. Chapple, Irene Parent firm cements out Milburn label The New Zealand Herald 11 September 2002
243. Scanlon, Lee End of an era: Cement works in Westport closes after 58 years The New Zealand Herald 29 June 2016
244. Cement — a new driver Buller District Council Westport Harbour https://www.westportharbour.co.nz/about/history/
245. (1926) Origin and Uses of Asphalte Dunstan Times Issue 3309 22 February 1926 P. 7
246. Demon - Cycling & Motor Notes Otago Witness Issue 3542 31 January 1922 P. 42
247. (1899) Auckland City Council The New Zealand Herald Volume XXXVI Issue 11199 20 October 1899 P. 3

248. Mexsom, Keith Waka Paddle to Gas Pedal January 2020 Pp. 443-444
249. Woolston, A - Equal to the Task - The City of Auckland Traffic Department 1894-1994 Auckland City Council & New Zealand Police Auckland 1996 P. 27
250. (1903) News Of The Day Christchurch Press Volume LX Issue 11695 23 September 1903 P. 6
251. Barr, John The City of Auckland New Zealand 1840-1920 Whitcombe & Tombs Limited Auckland 1922 Pp. 199-200
252. (1916) Local And General News The New Zealand Herald Volume LIII Issue 16414 16 December 1916 P. 8
253. (1917) Gisborne Borough Council Gisborne Times Volume XLVIII Issue 4509 28 March 1917 P. 7
254. (1923) Modern Roads For Auckland - Auckland Star Volume LIV Issue 29 3 February 1923 P. 5
255. (1917) Concrete Paving Auckland Star Volume XLVIII Issue 23 26 January 1917 P. 7
256. (1920) Taihape Borough Council Main Street Improvements Taihape Daily Times Volume XII Issue 3655 17 December 1920 P. 4
257. (1922) Waitoa Roads Te Aroha News Volume XXXIX Issue 6250 14 December 1922 P. 2
258. (1923) Advertisements The New Zealand Herald Volume LX Issue 18553 10 November 1923 P. 10 (supplement)
259. (1921) Advertisements The New Zealand Herald Volume LVIII Issue 17965 15 December 1921 P. 12
260. (1925) Advertisements Auckland Star Volume LVI Issue 264 7 November 1925 P. 11
261. (1859) Daily Southern Cross Volume XVI Issue 1252 16 September 1859 P. 3 (Supplement)
262. Marshall Tufflex New Zealand/Ellis & Co https://www.marshall-tufflex.com/international/australasia/new-zealand/
263. New Zealand Companies Office
264. Marshall Tufflex New Zealand/Ellis & Co https://www.marshall-tufflex.com/international/australasia/new-zealand/
265. (1910) Chamber of Commerce The New Zealand Herald Volume XLVII Issue 14525 12 November 1910 P. 5
266. (1917) Waitotara County Council Whanganui Chronicle Volume LX Issue 18963 17 April 1917 P. 2
267. ibid.
268. New Zealand Gazette No. 162 1 November 1917 P. 4064
269. (1917) Advertisements The New Zealand Herald Volume LIV Issue 16528 2 May 1917 P. 4
270. New Zealand Companies Office
271. (1925) Winter Show Manawatu Standard Volume XLV Issue 167 18 June 1925 P. 5
272. (1931) Marton Wanganui Chronicle Volume 74 Issue 164 14 July 1931 P. 11
273. (1920) Advertisements The New Zealand Herald Volume LVII Issue 17491 8 June 1920 P. 10
274. (1920) Hydro-Electric Scheme Evening Star Issue 17516 23 November 1920 P. 6
275. (1922) Paving Manukau Road The New Zealand Herald Volume LIX Issue 18031 4 March 1922 P. 8

276. (1923) Supplying Engineers Auckland Star Volume LIV Issue 300 17 December 1923 P. 9
277. (1924) Advertisements Auckland Star Volume LV Issue 6 8 January 1924 P. 8
278. (1924) Advertisements Waikato Times Volume 98 Issue 16078 30 August 1924 P. 19 (Supplement)
279. (1964) Kidd Garrett Buys Friar Assets Christchurch Press Volume CIII Issue 30362 11 February 1964 P. 21
280. (1966) Kidd Garrett Take-over Christchurch Press Volume CVI Issue 31177 29 September 1966 P. 16
281. New Zealand Companies Office
282. (1975) Niven acquires Kidd Garrett from Brierley Christchurch Press Volume CXV Issue 33759 4 February 1975 P. 20
283. Vacuum Oil Company Wikipedia https://en.wikipedia.org/wiki/Vacuum_Oil_Company
284. (1910) Commercial Summary Otago Daily Times Issue 14960 10 October 1910 P. 1 (Supplement)
285. (1911) Commercial Lyttelton Times Volume CXXII Issue 15574 25 March 1911 P. 10
286. (1921) Hawera Borough Council Hawera & Normanby Star Volume XLI Issue XLI 12 February 1921 P. 7
287. (1923) Untitled Auckland Star Volume LIV Issue 195 16 August 1923 P. 4
288. John Chambers (businessman) Wikipedia https://en.wikipedia.org/wiki/John_Chambers_(businessman)
289. (1903) Obituary The New Zealand Herald Volume XL Issue 12388 29 September 1903 P. 5
290. (1904) Untitled Auckland Star Volume XXXV Issue 84 8 April 1904 P. 4
291. (1918) Obituary The New Zealand Herald Volume LV Issue 16792 7 March 1918 P. 6
292. (1959) With Firm For 44 Years Christchurch Press Volume XCVIII Issue 28929 24 June 1959 P. 7
293. John Chambers and Son Ltd store interior Tairawhiti Museum https://collection.tairawhitimuseum.org.nz/objects/44878/john-chambers-son-ltd
294. (1965) John Chambers Board Changes Christchurch Press Volume CIV Issue 30871 2 October 1965 P. 22
295. (1879) Advertisements Lyttelton Times Volume LI Issue 5635 18 March 1879 P. 1
296. (1923) Borough Roads Northern Advocate 14 August 1923 P. 8
297. (1914) Maintenance Of Roads Wanganui Chronicle Issue 20025 7 March 1914 P. 6
298. (1914) Best Road For Local Conditions Evening Post Volume LXXXVII Issue 142 17 June 1914 P. 13
299. (1950) Obituary Christchurch Press Volume LXXXVI Issue 26030 6 February 1950 P. 5
300. (1913) Engineer's Report Eltham County Council Hawera & Normanby Star Volume LXV Issue LXV 15 December 1913 P. 6
301. (1914) News Of The Day Christchurch Press Volume L Issue 14886 28 January 1914 P. 8
302. (1914) Eltham County Council Hawera & Normanby Star Volume XLVI Issue XLVI 16 February 1914 P. 5
303. (1914) Tar Manufacture Hawera & Normanby Star Volume XLVI Issue XLVI 6 April 1914 P. 3
304. (1914) Wanganui Restar Company Wanganui Chronicle Issue 20061 22 April 1914 P. 5
305. (1914) Local And General Wanganui Chronicle Issue 20208 29 October 1914 P. 4

306. (1917) Taranaki Tarred Roads Rangitikei Advocate and Manawatu Argus Volume XLI Issue 11292 10 July 1917 P. 4
307. (1917) Restar Ltd The New Zealand Herald Volume LIV Issue 16635 4 September 1917 P. 6
308. (1917) Advance Wanganui - Wanganui Chronicle Volume LX Issue 17116 18 October 1917 P. 6
309. (1918) Advertisements Auckland Star Volume XLIX Issue 59 9 March 1918 P. 7
310. (1918) Restar — The Standard Road Binder Observer Volume XXXVIII Issue 29 23 March 1918 P. 18
311. (1918) Manufacture Of Restar Wanganui Herald Volume LII Issue 15538 15 June 1918 P. 9
312. (1918) Restar Ltd Evening Post Volume XCV Issue 144 18 June 1918 P. 10
313. New Zealand Gazette No. 5 23 January 1920 P. 248
314. New Zealand Gazette No. 67 7 September 1922 P. 2406
315. (1922) A New Industry For Gisborne Poverty Bay Herald Volume XLVIII Issue 15889 31 July 1922 P. 2
316. (1923) Restar Ltd Northland Age Volume 23 Issue 11 2 July 1923 P. 5
317. (1924) Restar For Reliable Roads Hawera Star Volume XLVIII 1 July 1924 P. 4
318. (1929) Wealth From Waste Auckland Sun Volume III Issue 804 26 October 1929 P. 32
319. (1930) Our Industries Auckland Sun Volume III Issue 898 15 February 1930 P. 6
320. (1932) Local And General Hawera Star Volume LII 23 December 1932 P. 4
321. (1933) New Road Seal The Dominion Volume 27 Issue 61 5 December 1933 P. 6
322. (1934) New Companies The New Zealand Herald Volume LXXI Issue 21840 30 June 1934 P. 7
323. (1934) Untitled Evening Post Volume CXVIII Issue 3 4 July 1934 P. 8
324. (1934) Advertisements The New Zealand Herald Volume LXXI Issue 21846 7 July 1934 P. 21
325. New Zealand Gazette No. 80 1 November 1934 P. 3459
326. (1934) Business In Brief Wanganui Chronicle Volume 77 Issue 294 12 December 1934 P. 6
327. (1937) Obituary Auckland Star Volume LXVIII Issue 230 28 September 1937 P. 3
328. (1947) Benzole Catches Alight Christchurch Press Volume LXXXIII Issue 25274 28 August 1947 P. 6
329. (1953) Fire Destroys Factory Christchurch Press Volume LXXXIX Issue 26979 3 March 1953 P. 3
330. New Zealand Gazette No. 89 12 September 1974 P. 1943
331. (1935) Company Registrations Christchurch Press Volume LXXI Issue 21644 30 November 1935 P. 16
332. New Zealand Gazette No. 7 31 January 1974 P. 205
333. (1913) A New Factory The New Zealand Herald Volume L Issue 15311 26 May 1913 P. 4
334. (1913) Rubber-Like Roads Auckland Star Volume XLIV Issue 158 4 July 1913 P. 6
335. (1913) Explosion And Fire The New Zealand Herald Volume L Issue 15362 25 July 1913 P. 7
336. (1913) Untitled Auckland Star Volume XLIV Issue 202 25 August 1913 P. 4
337. (1913) Advertisements Observer Volume XXXIV Issue 5 11 October 1913 P. 22

338. (1915) Local And General Northern Advocate 10 February 1915 P. 4
339. (1916) Borough Council Taranaki Herald Volume LXIV Issue 144889 18 January 1916 P. 4
340. (1916) Borough Council Taranaki Daily News 18 January 1916 P. 8
341. (1916) Local And General Gisborne Times Volume XLVII Issue 4234 9 May 1916 P. 4
342. New Zealand Gazette No. 29 15 February 1917 P. 634
343. (1917) Matiere King Country Chronicle Volume XI Issue 947 10 February 1917 P. 5
344. (1918) Matiere Taranaki Herald Volume LXVI Issue 16124 7 May 1918 P. 5
345. New Zealand Gazette No. 115 18 September 1919 P. 2975
346. Barrett's Road to Innovation: Tarvia Barrett Industries https://barrettemployees.com/2019/06/10/barretts-road-to-innovation-tarvia/
347. (1908) News Of The Day Christchurch Press Volume LXIV Issue 13203 25 August 1908 P. 6
348. (1911) Local And General Hawera & Normanby Star Volume LXII Issue LXII 13 November 1911 P. 4
349. (1913) Tarviated Roads Hawera & Normanby Star Volume LXV Issue LXV 13 March 1913 P. 5
350. (1914) Local And General Pukekohe & Waiuku Times Volume 3 Issue 253 4 December 1914 P. 2
351. (1916) Waimate West County Council Hawera & Normanby Star Volume LXXI Issue LXXI 21 July 1916 P. 5
352. (1916) Reconstruction Of Main Street Ohinemuri Gazette Volume XXVII Issue 3681 9 October 1916 P. 2
353. New Zealand Gazette No. 68 22 July 1920 P. 2246
354. (1914) Untitled Auckland Star Volume XLV Issue 61 12 March 1914 P. 4
355. (1914) Wanganui Borough Council Wanganui Herald Volume XLIX Issue 14309 3 June 1914 P. 8
356. (1914) Fortnightly Meeting Ashburton Guardian Volume XXXIII Issue 8859 9 June 1914 P. 5
357. (1914) The Bituco Preparation The Taranaki Herald Volume LXII Issue 144426 14 July 1914 P. 6
358. (1916) Pukekohe Borough Council Pukekohe & Waiuku Times Volume 5 Issue 186 27 June 1916 P. 4
359. (1916) Reconstruction Of Main Street Ohinemuri Gazette Volume XXVII Issue 3681 9 October 1916 P. 2
360. (1918) Concrete or Bituco? The Waipa Post Volume XII Issue 737 26 April 1918 P. 2
361. (1920) Te Awamutu Borough The Waipa Post Volume II Issue 952 8 June 1920 P. 5
362. (1921) Tamahere Road Board Waikato Times Volume 94 Issue 14720 10 August 1921 P. 7
363. (1921) A Road Trouble Waipa Post Volume XX Issue 1137 3 September 1921 P. 5
364. New Zealand Gazette No. 9 3 February 1921 P. 389
365. (1929) Company Affairs Auckland Star Volume LX Issue 274 19 November 1929 P. 4
366. (1934) Advertisements The New Zealand Herald Volume LXXI Issue 21900 8 September 1934 P. 19
367. (1941) Advertisements Waikato Times Volume 128 Issue 21430 26 May 1941 P. 16 (Supplement)

368. (1966) Tauranga Airport Christchurch Press Volume CV Issue 31019 26 March 1966 P. 19
369. (1979) Bitumen war threatens Canterbury companies by Martin Freeth Christchurch Press 2 November 1979 P. 1
370. (1980) Advertisements Christchurch Press 14 June 1980 P. 53
371. (1949) New Companies In Gisborne And Opotiki Gisborne Herald Volume LXXVI Issue 22996 13 July 1949 P. 9
372. (1982) Advertisements Christchurch Press 31 July 1982 P. 52
373. (1985) Advertisements Christchurch Press 1 June 1985 P. 51
374. (1989) BP (NZ) lifts profit ratio Christchurch Press 18 May 1989 P. 25
375. New Zealand Companies Office
376. (1937) New Private Company The New Zealand Herald Volume LXXIV Issue 22848 1 October 1937 P. 5
377. (1939) Sealing Road to Auckland Hauraki Plains Gazette Volume 48 Issue 2856 30 October 1939 P. 4
378. (1941) To Be Sealed Hauraki Plains Gazette Volume 50 Issue 3059 7 April 1941 P. 5
379. (1942) Capital Increased Auckland Star Volume LXXIII Issue 138 13 June 1942 P. 3
380. (1946) Highway Project Waikato Independent Volume XLIII Issue 6025 9 December 1946 P. 5
381. (1959) New Roading Process Christchurch Press Volume XCVIII Issue 29012 29 September 1959 P. 22
382. (1963) Motorway Contract Christchurch Press Volume CII Issue 30266 19 October 1963 P. 19
383. (1975) Winstone expansion plan trimmed Christchurch Press Volume CXV Issue 33899 19 July 1975 P. 18
384. (1975) No recovery this year Christchurch Press Volume CXV Issue 33915 7 August 1975 P. 16
385. (1977) Bitumix name change Christchurch Press 29 March 1977 P. 18
386. (1979) More rationalisation by Winstone Christchurch Press 30 October 1979 P. 22
387. New Zealand Companies Office
388. The New Zealand Gazette No. 52 24 August 1967 P. 1438
389. The New Zealand Gazette No. 82 18 December 1969 P. 2663
390. The New Zealand Gazette No. 80 10 December 1970 P. 2438
391. The New Zealand Gazette No. 1 13 January 1972 P. 36
392. The New Zealand Gazette No. 57 3 July 1975 P. 1497
393. The New Zealand Gazette No. 107 20 October 1977 P. 2746
394. New Zealand Companies Office
395. (1979) BP subsidiary forcing out roading contractors? Christchurch Press 25 October 1979 P. 1
396. (1984) Ashby sold Christchurch Press 13 October 1984 P. 24
397. Stevenson History https://stevenson.co.nz/history/
398. (1923) Borough Councils New Zealand Herald Volume LX Issue 18377 18 April 1923 P. 7
399. (1924) Northcote Drainage Auckland Star Volume 55 Issue 13 16 January 1924 P. 10
400. (1924) One Tree Hill District New Zealand Herald Volume LXI Issue 18793 21 August 1924 P. 7
401. (1925) Holed Through Auckland Star Volume LVI Issue 257 30 October 1925 P. 3

402. (1926) Auckland Drainage New Zealand Herald Volume LXIII Issue 19338 27 May 1926 P. 14
403. New Zealand Companies Office
404. (1931) New Auckland Company New Zealand Herald Volume LXVIII Issue 20990 29 September 1931 P. 5
405. (1935) Main Road Pahiatua Herald Volume XLII Issue 12921 8 April 1935 P. 3
406. (1938) Road Construction New Zealand Herald Volume LXXV Issue 23030 6 May 1938 P. 12
407. Stevenson History https://stevenson.co.nz/history/
408. (1966) Obituary Christchurch Press Volume CV Issue 30976 4 February 1966 P. 10
409. (1955) Obituary Christchurch Press Volume XCI Issue 27555 12 January 1955 P. 10
410. (1955) Advertisements Christchurch Press Volume XCII Issue 27713 18 July 1955 P. 9
411. (1955) Advertisements Christchurch Press Volume XCII Issue 27717 22 July 1955 P. 15
412. (1960) Farrier-Waimak Christchurch Press Volume XCIX Issue 29154 15 March 1960 P. 23
413. (1960) Council News In Brief Christchurch Press Volume XCIX Issue 29185 21 April 1960 P. 14
414. (1964) Council News In Brief Christchurch Press Volume CIII Issue 30423 23 April 1964 P. 18
415. (1964) Block-making Christchurch Press Volume CIII Issue 30605 23 November 1964 P. 17
416. (1965) Canterbury Branch Now The Biggest In New Zealand Christchurch Press Volume CIV Issue 30832 18 August 1965 P. 9 (Supplement)
417. (1972) Commercial Farrier-Waimak has record profit Christchurch Press Volume CXII Issue 33042 9 October 1972 P. 16
418. (1979) Farrier Waimak attacks BP Christchurch Press 9 November 1979 P. 14
419. (1980) Farrier Waimak loss $140,919 for half Christchurch Press 19 March 1980 P. 18
420. ibid.
421. (1980) Farrier Waimak's prospects better Christchurch Press 17 October 1980 P. 21
422. (1982) Prices soar for road sealing Christchurch Press 27 October 1982 P. 26
423. (1983) Farrier sells road group to Pavroc Christchurch Press 9 November 1983 P. 46
424. (1984) Farrier-W changes approved Christchurch Press 13 April 1984 P. 13
425. Fulton Hogan History https://www.fultonhogan.com/our-story/our-journey/
426. (1936) Registration Of Companies Evening Star Issue 22247 27 January 1936 P. 7
427. (1936) Westport Notes Grey River Argus 29 February 1936 P. 7
428. (1936) Westport Notes Grey River Argus 2 March 1936 P. 7
429. (1938) Hokitika Sports Hokitika Guardian 24 December 1938 P. 2
430. (1939) Public Works Department Otago Daily Times Issue 23995 19 December 1939 P. 5
431. (1941) Commerce And Finance Otago Daily Times Issue 24737 14 October 1941 P. 2
432. (1945) Commercial Christchurch Press Volume LXXXI Issue 24709 29 October 1945 P. 6
433. Fulton Hogan History https://www.fultonhogan.com/our-story/our-journey/
434. (1970) Advertisements Christchurch Press Volume CX Issue 32406 19 September 1970 P. 27
435. (1952) Company News Christchurch Press Volume LXXXVIII Issue 26745 31 May 1952 P. 9

436. (1967) Queenstown Sealing To Start Christchurch Press Volume CVII Issue 31554 16 December 1967 P. 1
437. Fulton Hogan History https://www.fultonhogan.com/our-story/our-journey/
438. (1976) Advertisements Christchurch Press 18 September 1976 P. 44
439. (1981) Advertisements Christchurch Press 29 April 1981 P. 31
440. (1981) All clear for Fulton bid? Christchurch Press 27 May 1981 P. 29
441. Fulton Hogan History https://www.fultonhogan.com/our-story/our-journey/
442. (1987) Advertisements Christchurch Press 18 April 1987 P. 57
443. (1987) Owens to sell Burnett Christchurch Press 26 September 1987 P. 32
444. (1989) Advertisements Christchurch Press 26 January 1989 P. 34
445. (1989) A lot of paving Christchurch Press 6 December 1989 P. 28
446. Fulton Hogan History https://www.fultonhogan.com/our-story/our-journey/
447. ibid.
448. New Zealand Companies Office
449. New Zealand Gazette No. 18 27 February 1975 P. 401
450. New Zealand Gazette No. 13 2 March 1978 P. 430
451. (1978) Firth sales helped by acquisitions Christchurch Press 5 July 1978 P. 18
452. New Zealand Gazette No. 200 23 November 1988 P. 5020
453. The Reliable Group The Fletcher Trust Archives https://collection.fletcherarchives.co.nz/objects/1496/directors-meetings-and-minutes
454. New Zealand Gazette No. 84 17 May 1989 P. 1911
455. (1930) Auckland Companies The New Zealand Herald Volume LXVII Issue 20685 3 October 1930 P. 9
456. (1930) In Liquidation The New Zealand Herald Volume LXVII Issue 20697 17 October 1930 P. 22
457. (1943) Company Registrations Auckland Star Volume LXXIV Issue 56 8 March 1943 P. 5
458. LynnMall Shopping Centre Auckland Libraries Heritage Collections JTD-11A-04016-1
459. New Zealand Gazette No. 4 22 January 1981 P. 117
460. (1982) Castle Hill work soon Christchurch Press 12 August 1982 P. 12
461. (1982) Advertisements Christchurch Press 29 September 1982 P. 33
462. (1938) New Private Companies The New Zealand Herald Volume LXXV Issue 23131 1 September 1938 P. 9
463. (1939) Advertisements Waikato Times Volume 124 Issue 20708 19 January 1939 P. 2
464. (1946) To Be Re-Sealed Hauraki Plains Gazette Volume 55 Issue 32666 21 January 1946 P. 5
465. (1976) Firth into bitumen Christchurch Press 30 September 1976 P. 21
466. (1977) Firth acquisition helped profit rise Christchurch Press 2 June 1977 P. 10
467. (1979) Bitumen war threatens Canterbury companies Christchurch Press 2 November 1979 P. 1
468. arrowhead The magazine of the Fletcher Group Winter 1979 Pp. 1-3
469. (1981) Buyer is Fletcher Christchurch Press 15 May 1981 P. 16
470. arrowhead The magazine of the Fletcher Group Winter 1979 Pp. 1-3
471. (2024) A pothole repair is on Rollins nationwide: transport Minister Simeon Brown unveils for a billion-dollar fund to smooth journeys for motorists The New Zealand Herald 6 June 2024

472. Coughlan, Thomas Transport Minister Simeon Brown unveils fleet of pothole monitoring vans The New Zealand Herald 19 September 2024
473. (1865) The Daily Southern Cross Volume XXI Issue 2439 15 May 1865 P. 4

Chapter Eleven

1. Keillor, Garrison The Writer's Almanac 29 June 2013
2. Donnell, Hayden Streetscapes New Zealand Geographic Issue 174 Mar-Apr 2022 Pp. 56-71
3. Orsman, Bernard Auckland's train chaos highlights national infrastructure worries — The Front Page The New Zealand Herald 15 February 2024
4. (2024) Government officially cancels $15 billion Auckland Light Rail as part of 100-day plan The New Zealand Herald 14 January 2024
5. Dillane, Tom Auckland Light Rail disestablishment to likely cost millions over six months — Cabinet paper release The New Zealand Herald 2 February 2024
6. Wilson, Simon Government plans for Auckland harbour crossings: Transport Minister Simeon Brown on more car lanes, nothing for bikes The New Zealand Herald 9 February 2024
7. Walker, Peter Deputy political editor - Sunak 'backs drivers' with curbs on 20mph limits and bus lanes The Guardian 30 September 2023 at https://www.theguardian.com/politics/2023/sep/29/rishi-sunak-plan-for-motorists-would-limit-travel-choices-campaigners-say
8. Walker, Peter Deputy political editor - Ministers prioritised driving in England partly due to conspiracy theories The Guardian 10 January 2024 at: https://www.theguardian.com/uk-news/2024/jan/10/shift-from-15-minute-cities-in-england-partly-due-to-conspiracy-theories
9. Walton, Felix Westfield Newmarket mall parking chaos prompts calls for Auckland Transport to address road congestion Radio New Zealand 20 November 2023
10. UK M-way's 'bike speed' International Express 27 March 2024 P. 10
11. Bernhard, Adrienne Are cars getting too big for the road? British Broadcasting Corporation 8 February 2024 https://www.bbc.com/future/article/20240207-are-cars-getting-too-big-for-the-road
12. Inquiry into congestion pricing in Auckland — Report of the Transport and Infrastructure Committee August 2021 New Zealand House of Representatives Pp. 2-3
13. Maher, Rachel Auckland Mayor Wayne Brown floats $5 per trip highway congestion charge The New Zealand Herald 14 November 2023 https://www.nzherald.co.nz/nz/auckland-mayor-wayne-brown-floats-5-per-trip-highway-congestion-charge/m7xfjeik65gjnn7d677yi5btre/
14. Government signals replacing Auckland's regional fuel tax with congestion charges will help pay for new highways The New Zealand Herald 30 June 2024
15. Schwenk, Katya; Brewster, Freddy; Santoro, Helen; & Stockton, Lucy Dean - Big Auto And The Death Of Traffic Congestion Reform The Lever 5 June 2024

16. Toussaint, Kristin A million cars have disappeared: What NYC is like after one month of congestion pricing Fast Company Impact
https://www.fastcompany.com/91272434/a-million-cars-have-disappeared-what-nyc-is-like-after-one-month-of-congestion-pricing
17. Trapeznik, Alexander (History Programme, University of Otago) & Gee, Austin 'The Madding Wheels Of Brazen Chariots Rag'd; Dire Was The Noise: Motoring And The Environment In New Zealand Before The Second World War' International Review of Environmental History Volume 6 Issue 1 2020 P. 32
18. ibid. Pp. 33-37
19. Health and air pollution in New Zealand 2016 HAPINZ 3.0: Findings and implications Ministry for the Environment 6 July 2022
https://environment.govt.nz/publications/health-and-air-pollution-in-new-zealand-2016-findings-and-implications/
20. Frame, Kirsty Air pollution from cars killing thousands of NZers yearly: Radio New Zealand 6 July 2022 https://www.rnz.co.nz/news/national/470457/air-pollution-from-cars-killing-thousands-of-nzers-yearly
21. Health and air pollution in New Zealand HAPINZ 3.0 Findings and implications Volume 1 P. 6
22. Turrentine, Jeff What Are the Causes of Climate Change? Natural Resources Defense Council (NRDC) https://www.nrdc.org/stories/what-are-causes-climate-change#agriculture
23. Brogan, Caroline Prioritise tackling toxic emissions from tyres, urge imperial experts Imperial College London - Engineering News 23 February 2023
https://www.imperial.ac.uk/news/243333/prioritise-tackling-toxic-emissions-from-tires/
24. Wiseman, Ed Tyre particles: the invisible poison clouding Britain's roads The Telegraph 25 July 2023 www.telegraph.uk
25. Howse, Imogen Dirty air link to higher risk of Alzheimer's International Express 6 March 2024 P. 40
26. Crimp, Lauren Transport system killing thousands prematurely each year, academic says Radio New Zealand 5 September 2024
27. Dick, Allan (2017) <u>Motor Trade Association of New Zealand Centenary</u> Martinborough, RnR Publishing Pp. 157-158
28. The Clean Car Discount Scheme Inland Revenue Department 16 February 2024
https://www.ird.govt.nz/topics/clean-car-discount-scheme
29. Ministry of Transport Clean Vehicles Act Passed March 2022
https://www.transport.govt.nz/area-of-interest/environment-and-climate-change/clean-cars/
30. Ministry of Transport Changes to the Clean Car Discount agreed for 1 July 2023 May 2023
https://www.transport.govt.nz/area-of-interest/environment-and-climate-change/clean-cars/
31. Smith, Cameron Revving up a record: June smashes all-time car sales as buyers try to beat clean car policy changes The New Zealand Herald 4 July 2023
https://www.nzherald.co.nz/business/biggest-ever-month-for-new-vehicle-sales-as-buyers-try-to-beat-clean-car-policy-changes/

32. Lester, Justin New Zealand's low-emission vehicle revolution is here The Spinoff 6 November 2023 https://thespinoff.co.nz/society/06-11-2023/new-zealands-low-emission-vehicle-revolution-is-here
33. Keall, Chris Tesla South opens in Auckland today as EV sales boom - new facility is the size of three rugby fields The New Zealand Herald 29 July 2023 https://www.nzherald.co.nz/business/tesla-south-opens-in-auckland-today-as-ev-sales-boom-new-facility-is-the-size-of-three-rugby-fields/
34. Keall, Chris $1000/year to drive your EV: Road user charges for electric vehicles from April 1, Transport Minister Simeon Brown confirms The New Zealand Herald 16 January 2024 https://www.nzherald.co.nz/business/1000year-to-drive-your-ev-road-user-charges-for-electric-vehicles-from-april-1-transport-minister-simeon-brown-confirms/
35. Repeal of the Clean Car Discount scheme Ministry of Transport December 2023 https://www.transport.govt.nz/area-of-interest/environment-and-climate-change/clean-cars/
36. Keall, Chris EV sales plunge, petrol and diesel vehicles surge The New Zealand Herald 5 February 2024 https://www.nzherald.co.nz/business/ev-sales-plunge-petrol-and-diesel-vehicles-surge/
37. June new vehicle sales the worst in a decade, possible relief on the way from Transport Minister Simeon Brown The New Zealand Herald 3 July 2024
38. Hassan, Sharif Beyond Local: As some Ontario plants hit the brakes, are Canada's EV ambitions under threat? The Canadian Press 17 September 2024
39. ibid.
40. da Silva, Joao Toyota delays US electric car plans as sales slow BBC 3 October 2024 https://www.bbc.com/news/articles/clylzgmp3zpo
41. Palmer, Russell Labour, Greens warn transport fee increases will impact lower-income families Radio New Zealand 4 March 2024 https://www.rnz.co.nz/news/political/510840/labour-greens-warn-transport-fee-increases-will-impact-lower-income-families
42. Government to spend nearly $33 billion on transport over the next 3 years Radio New Zealand https://www.rnz.co.nz/news/political/526837/government-to-spend-nearly-33-billion-on-transport-over-the-next-3-years
43. Campbell, Georgina Concern Government's National Land Transport Programme will lead to more congestion — The Front Page The New Zealand Herald 6 September 2024
44. Ross, Ben Finally revealed: report shows rail destroys roading for Auckland freight The Spinoff 27 July 2017 https://thespinoff.co.nz/auckland/27-07-2017/finally-revealed-report-shows-rail-destroys-roading-for-auckland-freight
45. MacManus, Joel An 'announcement of an announcement' of two new boats The Bulletin 12 December 2024
46. Coughlan, Thomas Transport giant Mainfreight wants rail on new interisland ferries The New Zealand Herald 25 September 2024

Index

15-minute cities, 369
300 club, 162

A B Donald Ltd, 274–5
Abercrombie, F. N., 150
AC Delco, 103, 105
AC Spark Plugs, 105–6
Adachi, Kaz, 87
Adams, R. M., 183
Adams Limited, 182–3
Adams-Schneider, Lance, 82, 127, 166
advertising
    competitive, 17–18
    and motorised romance, 36
    in newspapers, 18–20
Advertising Standards Complaints Board, 290–1
Aerial motor spirits, 274, 278–80
A. Harvey and Sons Ltd, 267
air pollution, 371–5
Aitken, Peter, 176
Aldridge, A G, 226
Alexander, Dudley, 211
Alexander, T, 246
Alfa Romeo, 188, 199
Allied Asphalt Limited, 363
Allied Group, 191, 195
Alpha oil well, 203–6
Alzheimer's disease, 374
Amalgamated Batteries, 95–9, 114
America
    railways of, 5–6
    road lobby in, 6
AMI (Associated Motor Industries), 67, 77
Ampol, 261, 283
Amuri Motors, 54–5, 62–3, 73, 80
ancillary industries, 88, 111
Anderson, Robert, 11
Anderson, Robert Grant, 186
Andrew, John Watson, 19, 183, 189
Andrews, R S, 347
Andrews, William, 128–9
Andrews and Beaven Ltd, 109–10, 126–31, 133–4, 341
Anglo-American Tire Company, 339
Anglo-Persian Oil Company, 26, 214, 253, 282, 291
    see also BP
Anglo Petroleum Oil Company, 26

Archibald & Shorter, 198–9
Arthur Atkin Vehicle Co, 34
Arthur Burke Limited, 182–3
Ashby Bros Ltd, 357
Asian financial crisis of 1997, 74
Asiatic Petroleum Company Limited, 257
AS Paterson and Co, 259–61
Aspdin, Joseph, 310
asphalt, 210–11, 319, 335–41
Associated Emulsions Limited, 363
Associated Motor Importers of New Zealand, 158
Associated Motorists' Petrol Company, 281–2, 284–5
    see also Europa
Astley, Graham, 112
Aston Martin, 198–9
Ateco Group, 199–200
Atkinson, Harry, 139
Atlantic Refining Co, 275–6
Atlantic Union Oil Company, 254, 269, 275–8, 339
Auckland, 57
    asphalt on roads, 335–7
    first motor cars, 14
    freight rail in, 8–9, 379
    light rail project, 368
    limited circle of, 6–7
    quarries in, 297–8, 304, 309–10
    roads in, 4, 35, 40–1, 292
    suburban rail in, 7–8, 369
    transport infrastructure of, 367–8, 379
    vehicle assembly plants in, 55, 57–60, 65
Auckland Airport, 254, 270
Auckland and Drury Railway, 2, 5
Auckland Automobile Association, 14–15, 190
Auckland Builders, General and Other Labourers' Union, 304–5
Auckland City Council, 16, 190, 293, 311
    and Mt Eden quarry, 299–301
    and road construction, 353
    Technical Advisory Committee, 41–4
Auckland Fibre Manufacturing Company Limited, 311
Auckland Harbour Board, 256, 269, 299, 312–13, 348
Auckland Harbour Bridge, 41–2, 380
Auckland Industrial Association, 302–3

Index **461**

Auckland Motor Company
   first, 189–91
   second, 191, 195
Auckland Quarry Owners' Association, 298
Auckland Town Planning Association, 298
Auckland Transport, 8–9, 370–1, 379
Auckland Waterfront Development Agency, 270
Audi, 86, 198–9
Austin cars, 65–9, 77–8, 81, 125
   dealers for, 184, 188
   local assembly of, 53, 163, 169
Austin Motors (Otago), 67–8
Australia
   free trade agreement with, 65, 166, 172–3
   vehicle imports from, 159
Australian and Kandos Cement Holdings Ltd, 333
Australian Consolidated Industries, 89, 128
Australian Oil Corporation, 245, 247
auto-electrical wiring, 88, 106–8
automatic number plate recognition (ANPR), 370
Automobile Association (AA), 15, 25, 39, 171–2, 190
Automotive Industries Limited, 192–3

Bagley, C, 348
Baigent, H R, 297
balance of payments, 154, 156, 159, 162–3, 287
Ballantyne, J O, 361
Balloch, W, 220
Barber, W H P, 221, 224
Barncastle, H J, 115
Barnet Glass, 96, 120
Barrett, Samuel E, 350
Barrowclough, H E, 92
Barry, John, 227
Bartlam, R, 111
Barton, Alexander and Thomas, 249–50
basalt, 297–9, 301, 309
Basham, Frederick, 342–4
Bassett, John, 242
Bates, Sise and Co, 204
Batt, E A, 281
batteries
   dry cell, 338
   tariffs on, 149
Battery Equipment Manufacturers, 97
Bayly, William Mason, 49–50

Bearing Service Company Ltd, 126
Beaven, Arthur Ward, 128–9
Beaven, E T, 129
Beaven, M W, 129
Beaven, W B, 134
Beck, J H, 273
Bedford, Leslie Frederick, 84
Bedford, Victor Cecil, 84
Bedford Trucks, 57, 186, 192
Begbie, Wilfred E, 42
Begg, Alexander Campbell, 134
Bell, Greg, 96
Bellam, Herbert, 354
Bennett, W S, 23–4
Bentley, 77–8, 198–9
benzine, 17, 24, 201
   demand and supply of, 263, 265–6
   extraction plants, 212
Bernhard, Adrienne, 370
Bett, John, 49–51
bicycles
   importing, 69, 154, 179–80
   manufacturing, 79
Big Tree, 259–61, 285–7
Bing Harris, 112
Bituco Road-binder Company, 351–3
bitumen, 211, 253–4, 319–20, 335–8, 340–1, 347, 354–7, 359, 362
Bitumen Sprayers Limited, 355
bituminous paving, 319, 337, 354
Bitumix Limited, 355–7
Bitural, 347
Black, Alexander John, 70–1
Black, John, 66
Black Budget, 159
Blackwater Valley, 243–5
Blackwell, Walter F, 182
Blackwell Motors Group, 181–3
Bland, Cecil, 41
Blenheim Oil Company, 227–8, 231
Blenheim Oil Well Reclamation Company, 228
Blogg, B D, 183
Blomkamp, Peter, 363, 365
Blue Circle Industries Limited, 325–6
BMW, 55, 175, 198
Board Fabricators Ltd, 112
Board of Trade, 120, 157–8, 166, 324
   and cement, 318, 322–4
   and petroleum supply, 265
Bockaert, Emil, 179

body duty, 142
body shells, 148–9
Bondlite, 90–1
Bonithon Freehold and Petroleum Company, 221–2, 224
Boon, Joseph Kitson, 51, 69
Boon and Company, 62, 66, 69–70
Booth, W E, 218
Bounty Oil, 248–50
Bovill, J O, 249
Bowater, Stuart Waring, 183
Bowron, G, 115, 225
Bowser, Sylvanus, 271
bowsers *see* petrol pumps
Boyce, L B, 42
BP (New Zealand) Ltd, 253–5, 270–2, 282–4
   and road contractors, 354–7, 360–1
   used oil refining, 290–1
   see also Shell BP and Todd Oil Services Limited
Braid, Don, 380
Brailsford, Joseph, 211
brake and clutch parts, 108–10
Brett's Option & New Zealand Oilfields, 237
brickworks, 212, 306
Bridgestone Tire Company, 122, 124
Brierley Investments, 309, 339–40
Briscoe cars, 20, 36, 68, 125
British Australian Lead Manufacturers (BALM), 115–17
   see also Dulux paints
British Electric Construction Company, 129
British Empire Oilfields Limited, 210–11
British Imperial Oil Company, 209, 256–9, 264, 281, 338–9
   see also Shell
British International Oil Company, 278–83
British Leyland, 63, 65, 67, 71, 81, 137
   and NZMC, 77–9
British Pavements, 357, 361
British Preferential Tariff, 71–2, 140, 142, 145–7, 149
British Standard Motor Company, 80
British Standard Portland Cement Company, 320–1, 325–6
Broadbent, W. J., 177
Broadhead, C F, 347
Brooks, Henry, 201
Broue, A E, 215–16

Brown, Athol William Hamilton, 36, 80, 157
Brown, Charles, 205
Brown, D A H, 170
Brown, Henry John, 210–11
Brown, Lloyd, 174
Brown, Simeon, 366, 377–8
Brown, Wayne, 366
Browne, G W, 221
Browne, P C, 348
Brownlee Manufacturing, 267–8
Brugger, Frank, 110–11
Brugger Industries, 110–13
B.S.A. motorcycle, 69
Buckleton brothers, 279–82
Buick cars, 24, 49–50, 56, 181–2, 185–6, 188–9, 194
Bull, Leslie Allen, 347
Bureau of Industry, 98, 287–9
Burgermeister Hackman, 263
Burnett, J L, 40
Burnett Construction Services, 362
Burnside Hydraulic Lime and Cement Company, 330–1
bus bodies, 58–9
buses, in Wanganui, 57
Butcher and Company, 75
Button, C E, 13
Buxton, T, 314
BWH Group, 188

Cable Price Downer Limited, 85–6, 99, 175
Cadillacs, 18, 20, 48, 67–8, 83
Caltex, 254, 261–2, 272, 283
Calvert, Frederick Crace, 201
Campbell, C W, 123
Campbell, George, 20, 192
Campbell, Georgina, 378
Campbell, Wallace B., 72
Campbell, W R, 71
Campbell Motors, 20, 76, 81, 83–6, 149
Campion and Bolton, 114
Canada
   trade agreement with, 71–2
   vehicle imports from, 34–6, 148–9
Canterbury Automobile Association, 25, 281
Canterbury Branch Bitumix Ltd, 357
Cape Foulwind, 332–5
carbon dioxide, 373–6
car dealers, 47, 53
   Campbell Motors, 84
   numbers of, 165

Index **463**

used, 37, 160
Carey, Bruce Reynolds Guyon, 106
Carlton-Carruthers Limited, 80
Carruthers, Robert, 98
Carter, Christopher, 208–9, 212, 214
Carter and Co, 203–6
Carthy Motors Limited, 184–5
casinghead spirit, 202–3
Cavaghan, T B, 71
Caygill, David, 122, 173, 175
CBUs (completely built up cars), 141–3, 147, 164, 174
CCDC (Consistent Condition Data Collection), 366
C C Wakefield & Co Limited, 80
cement, 6, 44, 301, 308–35
  import duties on, 327–9
  raw material for, 314
Cement Industry Commission of Inquiry 1921, 323–4
cement silos, 332–3
Challenge Corporation, 84–6
Chambers, John Moginie, 340–1
Champion, Albert, 104–5
Champion Motors Limited, 54–5, 73
Champion Spark Plug Company, 104–5
Channel Infrastructure NZ, 255
Charles Palmer and Company Ltd, 193
Chasseloup-Laubat, Comte Gaston de, 11, 375
Chemicals Manufacturing Company Limited, 290–1
Chevrolet
  assembly in New Zealand, 48, 56–7
  dealers for, 22–3, 182–4, 186, 188, 194–5, 197
  popularity of, 60
Chevron New Zealand Limited, 261, 270
Chilman, Richard, 205
Chloride Electrical Storage Company, 93–7, 99
Choy, W T, 127
Christchurch
  assembly plants in, 52, 58, 62, 65–6, 80, 109, 178, 267
  roads in, 293
Christchurch City Council, 30, 70
Christchurch Metropolitan Show, 51, 70
Christchurch Oil Company Limited, 225–7
Christiansen, W A, 157
Chrysler, 61, 90, 104, 184, 191

Citroën, 52, 188, 199
City Rail Link, 8–9, 369–71, 378
CKDs (Completely Knocked Down cars), 13, 59–60, 143
  import licences for, 63, 82, 151, 153–6, 161–2
  market share, 174
  requirement to import, 66
  Suzuki, 87
  tariffs on, 53, 62, 72, 145–9, 157–8, 167
Clapp, Frederick G, 215–16
Clarke, C E, 244
Clarke, G T, 153–4
Clarke, William, 235–6
Clean Car Discount, 375–7
Clemow, R K, 355
Coachwork International Limited, 59–60, 191
coal, 201, 314
Coal Oil (NZ) Limited, 229
coal tar, 201, 346, 348
Coates, Gordon, 142, 145–7
Coates, Ken, 32
Cobbe, J G, 304, 331
Coleman, Percy, 86
Coleman Group, 86
Collins, B W, 232
Collom, Charles C, 42
Colonial Motor Company, 55–6, 71, 148, 183, 189, 196, 266
Colyer, Rupert Alexander Maxwell, 242
Combined Buyers Limited, 23–4, 79, 278–9
Commerce Commission, 55, 122, 326, 334
commercial immorality, 322
Commercial Trusts Act 1910, 323–4
commercial vehicles
  assembly, 56–7, 62, 65, 72, 74, 83
  imports, 34, 133, 152–3, 158–9
  sales of, 36
  warranties, 18
Commission of Inquiry into the Distribution of Motor Spirits and Ancillary Products, 254, 284
Commission of Inquiry into the Distribution of Motor Vehicle Parts, 134–8
Companies Act, 128, 277
component manufacturers, 88–106
  Industries Development Commission on, 167
  see also Commission of Inquiry into the Distribution of Motor Vehicle Parts

Compton, R G, 98–9
concrete
  bridges, 321
  buildings made of, 311–12, 331
  pipes, 329–30, 357–8
  for road construction, 298, 300–1, 315, 319–20, 335–7, 339, 344, 353
congestion pricing, 370–1
Congreve, Keith Robert, 134
Connolly, John Alexander, 134
Consolidated Motor Industries Limited, 82, 84–6
Consolidated Oilfields of Taranaki, 225–7
Cooper, Arthur Sidney, 48
Cooper, David Willis, 191
Cooper and Pryce, 48–9, 66, 143
Corkill, F P, 220–1, 252
Cossens, Thomas, 70
Cossens and Black Limited, 54, 62, 70–1
Coughlan, Thomas, 380
Cousins and Aitken, 118
Coutts, P E, 158
Craig, George, 145
Craig, Joseph James, 305–6
Crichton, Neville Alexander, 183, 199–200
Crimp, Lauren, 375
Crow, Ed, 345, 347
Crozier, David, 36, 65–8, 180
Crozier, D. Clive, 66
crude oil, 201–2
Cugnot, Nicolas, 10
Cunningham, David John Edward, 108
Cunningham, Heather Gay, 108
Cunningham, John Lindsay, 108
Customs Acts Amendment Act 1934, 72, 147
Customs Acts Amendment Act 1958, 159
Customs Amendment Act 1921, 142
Customs Amendment Act 1927, 143
Customs determinations, 148–9
customs duties, 69, 72, 139, 166
  on knocked-down cars, 62
  and replacement parts, 137
Customs Tariff Commission 1934, 145–7
Cutler, A R, 63–5, 159
cycle lanes, 368, 371

Daihatsu, 85, 87, 174, 188, 195
Daimler, Gottlieb, 10
Daimler cars, 19, 49, 76, 78, 183, 198
Datsun, 59, 76

Daveys Concrete Limited, 362
David Crozier Limited, 36, 54, 66–9, 77
Davidson, Robert, 11
Davie, Ron, 192
Davie Motors Holden, 192
Davis, Ernest, 301
Deal, R L, 123
Deans, Charles, 55
DELCO (Dayton Engineering Laboratories Company), 105
De Leuw Cather report, 7, 379
Denniston, F. R., 14, 47
Denton, Ethel Catherine, 132
Denton, Harold, 131–2, 197
Deterding, Henry, 257
Dexter, Rueben, 67–8
D F Butler Limited, 85
Dick, Allan, 11, 21, 122, 375
Dickson, A. J., 41–2
Dillane, Tom, 368
Distillation Act 1908, 345
distribution chain, 134, 137
Dobson, Frederick John, 230–2
Dodge cars, 20, 54, 62, 69–71, 83, 180–1, 190
Dominion Battery Company Limited, 25
Dominion Motors, 18, 22, 48, 180, 184, 266
  assembly plants, 60, 67, 77–8
Dominion Oil Refining, 126, 283, 288–90
Dominion Portland Cement Company, 314–15, 317–18
Don Agencies, 108–10
Donald, Alexander Bell, 275
Donald, A W, 215–16, 225
Donnell, Hayden, 367
Dowling, Craig, 177
Drake, Edwin, 201
driveshafts, 127, 149
Drury quarry, 297, 309–10, 358, 363
Dulux paints, 88, 115, 117
Dunedin
  asphalt on roads in, 336
  Moller Holdings and BWH in, 188
  tramway system, 70, 330
Dunlop, John Boyd, 96
Dunlop New Zealand, 119–22
Dunlop Olympic Limited, 96–7, 122
Dunne, D P, 94
Durant, William, 6, 105
Durant cars, 84, 125

East Coast of the North Island, oil exploration, 234–9
Eastern Busway, 371, 378
Ebbett Motors Limited, 185–7
economies of scale, 67, 90, 163, 178
Edwards Motors, 31
Egmont Oil Wells, 232–4, 251
E Hadley Company
    first, 222–3
    second, 224
Eisenhower, Dwight, 367
Electric Construction Company, 100–2
electric vehicles, 11–12, 370, 374–8
electronics manufacturers, 91–106
Elliot, George, 313, 318
Ellis and Co Ltd, 336–8
Eltham County Council, 342–4
Emoleum NZ Limited, 283, 354–5
Empire Oil Company, 262–3
Engineers' Superiority Complex, 42
Engineers' Union, 99, 110, 172
Engine Rebuilders, 127
England, Ken, 184
E Reynolds & Co Limited, 80
Essex motor vehicles, 48, 60, 188, 190
Esso, 277
Europa Oil New Zealand Ltd, 62, 253–4, 272, 282–7
European Motor Distributors, 86, 198–9
Evans, Bill, 121–2
Evans, C W, 359–60
Evans, Ivor, 140
Evans, Lionel, 109–10, 128
Ewing, G C, 235
E W Pidgeon and Company Ltd, 133
E W Tappenden and Sons Limited, 192
exhaust systems, 85, 88, 113–15, 133, 149
Exide Batteries, 88, 93–5
Explosive and Dangerous Goods Amendment Act 1920, 270–1

Fabco Industries, 112–13
Fair, George Charles, 206–7
Fairbairn, George, 38
Fairfield Asphalt Company Limited, 362
Fairweather, G. W., 158, 182
Farmer, Trevor, 194
Farrell, Frederick George, 189–90
Farrier, Henry Edward, 358–9
Farrier-Waimak Limited, 358–61
Fawcett, R B, 18

Fernyhough, John, 194
Fiat, 76, 188, 194, 362
Finance Houses Association, 171
Firestone tyres, 88, 118, 120–4
Firth, Cyril W, 41
Firth, J C, 312
Firth Industries Limited, 363–5
Fisher & Paykel, 104–5
Fitzgerald, J E, 42
Fleming, William, 235
Fletcher, Hugh, 309
Fletcher Challenge, 251, 309, 320, 326
Fletcher Concrete and Infrastructure, 320, 326
Fletcher Group, 364–5
Forbes, George, 60, 144–5, 148, 304
Ford, Henry, 12, 47
Ford Falcon, 91, 155
Ford Model T, 15, 55–6, 91, 127, 148, 182, 350, 357
Ford Motor Company, 18, 64, 71–3
    Canadian factory, 56, 148
    closure of assembly plants, 178
    and Colonial Motors, 55–6
    dealers, 61, 183, 188–9
    Denniston and, 47
    electric vehicles, 377
    import tenders, 175
    market share, 165, 174
    and Mazda, 74–5
    and replacement parts, 136
fossil fuels, 252, 373–6
Fowlds, William, 52
Fowler, R A, 90–1
Fox, W, 225
Frame, Kirsty, 373
Francis, J T F, 112–13
Franklin County Council, 358
Fraser, Colin, 216
Fraser, P E, 42
Fraser, Peter, 273–4
Fraser, Richard, 173
Fraser, William, 4
Free, S L P, 226
Freeman, A, 226
Freemans Bay, 256, 269–70, 276, 348
Freemans Bay Tank Farm *see* Wynyard Tank Farm
Freer, Warren, 163–4, 166, 173
Friar, Richards and Upton Ltd, 339
Friend, H L, 348–9

fuel emissions, 374
fuel tax, 370–1
Fulton, Jules H, 361–2
Fulton Hogan, 358, 361–4

Gadsen, Stanley W, 267
Gair, George, 91
Gardiner, William Ivan, 42
Gardner, Joe, 76–7
Garrett, W, 339
Gee, Austin, 15, 371
General Accessory Company, 129–31, 224
General Electric, 103–4
General Motors (GM), 35, 55–7, 78
   assembly line, 141
   automotive parts brands owned by, 102, 105
   closure of assembly plants, 178
   dealers for, 182, 185–6, 194–5, 197
   and import licences, 64
   import tenders, 175
   market share, 165, 174
   and replacement parts, 136
general parts distributors, 125–34
Genter, Julie Anne, 378
George Fraser and Sons Ltd, 192–3
George Guild and Sons, 193
George Palmer Motors Limited, 86
Gibbes Watson, G G, 71
Gibbons, Sidney, 205
Gibbs, Alan, 194
Gibbs, T A, 126–7
Gibson, R. R., 182
Gibson's Motors, 182
Gilmore Oil Company/Gilmore Lion, 272–4, 282, 284
Giltrap, Colin John, 86, 194, 198–9
Giltrap Group, 198–9
Gisborne Oil Company, 237
Gisborne Oil Proprietary Company, 216–17, 234
Glacier Bearings NZ Ltd, 126
Glanville, John Reed, 51
glass makers, 88–91
Glen Innes, 83
Glico Petroleum Ltd, 26
Goddard, Stephen B, 6, 42
Golden Bay, 318, 320–2, 324–5, 333
Golden Bay Cement Works, 319–26, 333
Goldie, Harry Tinsley, 242
Goodrich tyres, 119

Goodson, Jake, 248
Goodyear Tire and Rubber Company, 120, 122
Goosman, William Stanley, 39, 41, 356
Gough, John, 96
Gould, Garth Hamilton, 54
Gould, George Arthur Churchill, 54
Goulter, R F, 227
Gow, James Burman, 145
Gracefield, Chemicals Manufacturing Company at, 291
Grafton Bridge, 308, 314
Grant, R D, 361
Grant, Vivian, 143
Gray, Charles Eustace, 60
Great Depression, 144–5
Greater New York Automobile Dealers Association, 371
Great South Road, 53, 319, 358
Green, Rodney, 334
greenhouse gas emissions, 373, 375
Greenslade, Peter, 87, 164
Grey, Charles D, 223
Gribble, C R, 42
Griffiths, A T, 42
Griffiths, E, 227
Griffiths, J L, 76
Guardian Cement Company, 332
Guillard Blue Stone Quarry Company Limited, 298
Gull Petroleum, 283
Gunson, James Henry, 274
Guthrie, D H, 17
Guthrie, Hugh Douglas, 115
Guthrie Bowron, 115

Hackathorn Oil New Zealand, 245–9
Hacket, R M, 97
H A D Jannse Ltd, 112
Hadley, Percy, 222–5
Halcrow Thomas report, 7, 43, 379
Hall, J, 42
Hall Service Station Ltd, 192–3
Halstead, E H, 158–9
Hamal Industries, 106–7
Hamer, M B, 216
Hamilton, Austin, 347
Hamilton Borough Council, 303
Hamlet, Joseph, 183
Hanna, Andrew, 225
Hanna, Bertie James, 179

Hanna, James, 189
Hannay, W M, 321
Harbourside Oil, 250
Harrington, John Lane, 211
Hart, S P, 217
Hassan, Sharif, 377
Hatrick & Co, 17, 53, 187, 266
Hauraki Plains County Council, 364
Havard, Charles W, 310
Hawera Borough Council, 340, 350–1
Hawera County Council, 342, 351
Hawkes, Graham, 35, 37, 39
Hazlett, J A, 277
H Denton and Co, 131
Hella New Zealand, 103, 108
H E Melhop Ltd, 77
Henderson, John Henry, 191
Herman, Percy Arthur, 225
H. H. Moller, Ltd, 81
Hickson, John Arnold Einem, 93
Highway Boards, 293, 299, 312
Highway Industries, 126
Hilton, Arthur, 291
Hino, 81, 84
hire purchase, 59, 167–72, 187, 194
Hire Purchase and Credit Sales Stabilisation Regulations 1955, 169
Hitachi, 108, 362
Hoare, P. M., 182
Hochul, Kathy, 371
Hodson, H. H. V., 149
Hogan, Robert, 361–2
Holcim, 334–5
Holden cars, 57, 75, 106
   dealers for, 182, 192, 195
      no-remittance business in, 164–5
      windscreens of, 90–1
Holderbank Financiere Glaris, 333–4
Holland, Sidney, 41, 287
Holloway, John Ferguson, 343–5, 347
Honda, 78, 107, 178, 183
Honda Empisal Distributors, 183
Hope Gibbons, A, 55–6, 71, 93, 266
Hopkins, B P, 114
Hornby, motor assembly plants in, 63, 82
Horner, Andrew L, 211, 214
Horrells Motors Limited, 182
horse-drawn vehicles, 34, 45
horseless carriages, 10–11, 50–1, 168, 306, 375
   see also motor vehicles, first

Hougham, K R, 80
H O Wiles, 276–8
Howland, A G, 45
H T Salter & Co, 189
Hudson motor cars, 48, 60, 183, 188–9
Huels, Anke, 374
Hughes, Andrew, 68
Hunt, Graeme, 282
Hunua quarry, 298, 309–10
Hutchison, George W, 190
H W Smith Ltd, 133–4

ICE (internal combustion engines), 10–13, 93, 266, 374–5, 377
ICI (Imperial Chemical Industries), 116–17
Imperial College London, 373–4
import controls, 132, 139–40
imported vehicles, 16, 34–8
   annual value of, 88, 162
   shortage of, 159–60, 162–3
import licensing, 63–5, 75, 139, 149–50, 178
   for batteries, 99
   end of, 175
   new and used cars, 150–8, 161–2
   no-remittance, 155–6, 160–1, 164–5
   and replacement parts, 137
   for tyres, 120, 123, 125
Import Licensing Committee, 155
import tender scheme, 174–5
Ince, Wesley, 238
India Tyre Distributors Ltd, 126
India Tyres, 119
individualism, 6
industrial base, 160–1
Industrial Efficiency Act 1936, 272, 287–8
Industrial Engineers Ltd, 290
Industries Development Commission, 109, 121, 123–5, 166–8, 171–2, 174
Inglewood Oil Boring and Prospecting Company, 218–19
Inglis, Danny, 108
Inglis, Thomas, 210
Inglis Bros, 266
Ingram, J H, 86
interior trim and fittings, 110–13
Interislander Ferries, 379–80
International Energy Company Ltd of Texas, 247, 249
International Harvester, 81, 182
International Petroleum and Minerals Development Corporation, 224–5

Interstate Highway System, 367
Ironclad Products Company, 365
Isherwood, Henry, 354

Jackson, G. H., 71
Jaguar, 67, 78–9, 106, 188, 199
Japanese cars, 82, 130, 166, 176–7
   domestic assembly of, 81
   market share, 78
   used imports, 37–8, 60
Jas. J. Niven, 339–40
Jay, R. J., 144
J Bett and Bayly Limited, 49–51
Jeantaud electric car, 11, 375
Jewett cars, 125, 278
J Gadsden and Co Limited, 61, 267
Jinyo Maru, 73
J J Craig Limited, 222, 298, 305–6, 320
John Andrew Ford, 183
John Chambers and Son, 101, 129, 337, 340–1
John Hardie, 258
Johns, J B, 182
Johnston, James, 125
Johnston, William, 204
John Wilson and Company, 311–12
Jones, Charles James, 181
Jones, Frederick William Osborn, 42
Jones, Shane, 252
Jordan, W J, 304
Joseph Lucas Limited, 91–2
Jowett Motors, 75
JRA (NZ) Limited, 92–3
J S Hawkes & Co, 181

Kaikoura Express Motor Service, 30
Kamon Petroleum Exploration, 246
Kanagawa Maru, 177
Kapuni oil field, 202, 233–4, 251–2
Keall, Chris, 376–7
Kensley & Co Pty Limited, 80
Kenson Industries Limited, 111
kerosene, 139, 201–2
   discovery of, 256
   suppliers of, 256–8, 260
kerosene tins, 267
Kersey, John Cheverton, 189
Kettering, Charles, 12
Kidd, Douglas Swanston, 339
Kid Garrett Limited, 339–40
King, Thomas, 205

King, W. W., 192–3
Kitson, Joseph, 70
KiwiRail, 8–9, 379–80
Knight, A. E, 347
Knight, C Prendergast, 321
Knight, Cyril Roy, 41
Kohimarama, 295, 357
Kotuku district, overview, 241
Kotuku Oil and Goldfields Company, 240–2
Kotuku Oil Fields Syndicate, 234, 241
Kotuku Oil Springs Association, 239–40
Kotuku Oil Syndicate, 240–1

Labour Government
   first, 66, 149, 166
   second, 282
   third, 368
Lamborghini, 198–9
Land Rover, 77–8, 106, 199
land speculation, 2, 5, 8, 379
Land Transport (Clean Vehicles) Amendment Act 2022, 375–7
Larmour, Charles Corden, 55
Laugesen, Louis Emil, 30–4
Laugesen, Louis Keith, 30, 32
Lawrence & Hanson, 103–4
Lee, E P, 324
Leggett, Nick, 368
L E Laugesen & Co, 30
Lenoir, Etienne, 10
Leslie Friend, H, 348
L F Wallis and Co, 21–4, 26, 30
Licensed Motor Dealers' Association, 169
light trucks, 152, 158, 169–70
lime, 139, 305–6, 317–18, 326–7, 334
   hydraulic, 310–16, 328
limestone, 310, 316, 320–1, 327, 335
Limestone Island, 314–18
L M Silver and Co, 92
Lockwood, Terry, 283
log rolling, 2–3
Lotus cars, 82
Louisson, M G, 225
Lower Hutt, paint factory at, 116
LTNs (low traffic neighbourhoods), 368–9
lubricating oils, 24, 26, 274
   recycling, 127, 288–90
   repackaging, 266–7
   storing, 256
Lucas, Joseph, 91
Lucas Industries Limited, 92–3, 136–7

McArthur, Charles, 321–2
McCorkindale., W H, 97
McCormick, Charles Hewson, 42
MacDonald, Finlay, 5
McDonald, James, 326–7
McDonald's Lime, 334
Macindoe, C G, 225
McIver, G. F., 173
McKay, George, 227
McKendrick, G A R, 89
McKendrick Glass Manufacturing Company, 89
McKibbin, V J, 54
Macky, William G, 42
McLean, Hamish Robert, 106
McLean, J G, 269
McLean, William, 13, 46, 221
McLean Motor-Car Act 1898, 13, 46
McLennan, E D, 298
McLeod, E G, 42
MacManus, Joel, 379
McMillan, R., 182, 186
McNab, Robert, 314
McNeil, F, 235
Magnus, Godfrey William, 7, 80, 180, 266
Magnus Motors Limited, 7, 67, 77, 80, 180
Mangus Sanderson and Co Limited, 180, 266
Mahurangi, 311–15
Main Highways Board, 4, 295, 358, 364
Main Roads Account, 293
Mangere, 83
Mangles River, 242–3
Manthel, Maurice Noel, 195
Manthel Motors, 195
Manukau City *see* Wiri, Ford operations at
Manukau Road, 53, 339
Maoriland Oil Fields, 240–1
Marriott, P W, 277
Marsden Point oil refinery, 233–4, 253–5, 270, 354
Martin, John, 204
Masfen, Peter Hanbury, 191
Mason, H G R, 304
Massey, William (Prime Minister), 141, 213, 265
Massey, William (Soltar worker), 348
Massey-Harris Company, 180
mass production, 12, 47, 91, 116, 141
Master Builders' Federation, 158

Masters, Robert, 322–3
Master Transportation Plan for Metropolitan Auckland, 41–4, 367–9
Matamata County Council, 297
Matiri Valley, 250
Maui offshore gas field, 251–2
Maxwell Bros Limited, 362
Mazda
  and Amuri motors, 54–5
  closure of assembly plants, 178
  dealers for, 188, 194
  import tenders, 175
Mazda Motors of New Zealand Limited, 59, 73–6, 164, 174, 176
Melrose, E J, 277
Mephan's Motor Garage, 118
Mercedes-Benz, 188, 198, 362
Meteor Motor Spirit, 274–5
Metropolitan Gas Company, Melbourne, 346–7
mexphalte, 335, 337–9
M'Hardy Forman, W., 56
Michael, W K, 132–3
Michelin tyres, 69, 118, 189
Michie, F W L, 97
Midland Motorways Services, 30–3
Milburn Lime and Cement Company, 314, 323–4, 326–34
Millar, J B, 124
Miller, Horace G, 123
Mills, C M, 94
Mills, R J, 301
Minerva Petroleum Company, 235
Ministry for the Environment, 373
Ministry of Works, 1, 39, 41, 356, 362
Mitchell, Keith, 283
Mitsubishi, 62, 90–1, 106–8, 176, 178
Mobil Oil Corporation, 253–5, 257, 274, 277, 340
  bitumen business, 283, 355
  and Emoleum, 354
  service stations, 272
  and Wiri oil storage, 270
  and Wynyard Tank Farm, 270
Mogridge, Bryan William, 191
Moir, M, 42
Moline, Arthur H P, 216–17
Moller, Henry H, 187–8
Moller Holdings Limited, 59, 78, 175, 187–8
Moore, R F, 348
Moorhouse Mazda, 54–5

Mordue, Greig, 377
Moreno, Carlos, 369
Morere Hot Springs, 217
Moriarty, Michael James, 134
Morikawa, James, 75
Morningside Deviation, 7, 43–4
Morningside quarry, 302
Mornington Cable Tramway, 70
Morris, Black and Matheson Limited, 193
Morris cars, 60, 67, 77–8, 81, 125, 169
  dealers for, 184, 188
Morrison, J, 226
Mortenson, Nils, 241
Morton, C C, 226
Moseley Tyres, 118
Motor Assemblies (South Island), 62–5, 78, 159
motor-body builders, 17, 54, 82
  Boon and Company, 69
  Midland Motorways and, 31
  New Zealand Motor Bodies, 57
  Stevens and Sons, 51
  and tariffs, 141, 143–6
  transition from horse-drawn transport, 45
  Wilton Motor Bodies, 76
motor clubs, regional, 15–16
Motor Components Limited, 114–15
motor-cycles, 35
  tariff on, 146–7
motor exhausts, 34, 372
motor freight, 16–17
Motor Garage Proprietors' Association, 20, 265–6
Motor Holdings Limited, 73–6, 82–3, 86, 114–15, 174–5, 178
motoring lobby, 14–16
motorised romance, 36, 44
Motor-spirits (Regulation of Prices) Act 1933, 286
motor spirits, imports of, 283–4
Motor Spirits Distribution Act 1953, 272
Motor Spirits Licensing Authority (MSLA), 272
Motor-spirits Prices (North Canterbury) Regulations 1936, 287
Motor Trade Association (MTA), 11, 20–1, 153, 157–8, 168, 196, 272, 375
Motor Traders (NZ) Ltd, 127, 132–4, 266
motor vehicle assemblers
  closure of, 88, 107–8, 177–8
  early, 45–71
  end of protection for, 175
  and hire purchase, 169–72
  and Industries Development Commission, 167
  later, 71–87
  size of industry, 157–8, 162–4
  and tariffs, 141–3, 145–7, 154
Motor Vehicle Dealers Institute, 62, 168, 170, 172–3
motor vehicle importers, 53, 179, 188
  see also imported vehicles
Motor Vehicle Industry Plan, 173
motor vehicles
  first, 13–15, 69, 179
  and road building, 294
  size of, 370
  transition to, 34, 45
  see also commercial vehicles; electric vehicles; imported vehicles; new cars; used cars
motorways, 4–5
  speed on, 369
Motorways Limited, 29, 32–3
Moturoa oilfields, 203, 206–7, 212, 217, 227, 229–34, 252
  refinery at, 212–14
Moturoa Oilfields Limited, 229–31, 238
Moturoa Petroleum Company, 206–7
Mount Albert Borough Council, 357
Mount Eden Borough Council, 300–1
Mount Eden Prison, 301–4, 307
Mount Eden quarry, 296, 298–305, 307–8
Mountfort and Baker, 260
Mount Roskill quarry, 309
Mount Wellington, Motor Bodies plant at, 59, 74, 76, 83, 116
Mount Wellington quarry, 309
Mowbray, John, 13
MSI (Motor Specialties Industries), 109, 125–8, 130, 289–90
Mt Roskill, 83
Mt Smart quarries, 309
mufflers, 12, 84, 114, 126
Muldoon, Robert, 83, 110, 165–6, 170, 172, 368
Murchison Oil Company, 242–5
Murchison oil fields, 239, 242, 244–50
Murex, 268
Murphy, Bernard Edward, 145
Murray, A. S., 35
Myers, A M, 299

Napier Harbour Board, 316, 328
Nash, J A, 273–4
Nash, Walter, 26, 29, 150–4, 159, 282–3
National Party
  in 1954 election, 41
  coalition government of 2023, 370, 376, 379–80
  Fifth Government, 9, 379
  First Government, 39, 155
  Third Government, 368
National Roads Act 1953, 40
National Roads Board, 40, 356, 360, 365
National Service Stations Limited, 25
natural gas, 202–3, 232–3, 245, 251–2
Neal, W F, 185–6
Neal Motors, 185–6
Nelson, assembly plant at, 63–5, 77–8, 178
Nelson Improvement Amendment Act 1858, 295
Neuchatel Asphalt Company, 335–6
Nevada Oil Company Limited, 274
Neville-White, Barry George, 191
new cars
  hire purchase of, 169–72
  imports of, 53, 154, 156, 163, 175
  laminated windscreens in, 91
  prices of, 176
  registration of, 165
  sales of, 150, 170–1
  shortage of, 160, 163
Newmarket
  assembly plant at, 60, 77–8, 178
  roads in, 351–2
  traffic congestion in, 369
New Plymouth Borough Council, 349, 352
New Plymouth Gas Company, 232–3
new prosperity, 36–7
Newspaper Proprietors Association, 285
Newton, Howard Henry, 260
Newton, Isaac, 10
Newton King Limited, 54, 80
New York, congestion pricing in, 371
New Zealand Automobile Association, 38
New Zealand Canister Co, 267
New Zealand Cement Company, 314, 332–3
New Zealand Cement Holdings Limited, 332–4
New Zealand Coach and Motor-body Builders' Association, 143
New Zealand Federated Carters' Union, 308
New Zealand Flex Grip Limited, 26–30
New Zealand Forest Products, 59, 82–3, 112
New Zealand Guarantee Corporation Ltd, 168
New Zealand Institute of Economic Research, 141, 163, 174, 178
New Zealand Motor Bodies, 57–9, 74, 77–8, 83, 188
New Zealand Motor Corporation (NZMC), 53, 69, 77–8, 169, 180, 184
  British origins of, 78–81
  import tenders, 175
  market share, 165, 174
  prices, 176
  redundancies, 111
  and replacement parts, 137
New Zealand Motor Vehicle Importers' Association, 152–3
New Zealand Motor Vehicle Industry Plan, 113, 172–6
New Zealand Oil Refineries, 228, 230–3
New Zealand Petroleum and Iron Syndicate, 218
New Zealand Petroleum Company
  first, 237
  second, 237–9
New Zealand Petroleum Exploration Company, 246–8
New Zealand Portland Cement Company, 315–19
New Zealand Refinery Company, 234, 253–5
New Zealand Retail Motor Trade Association *see* Motor Trade Association (MTA)
New Zealand Tool and Gauge Co, 112
New Zealand Transport Agency, 8, 378–9
New Zealand Tube Mills Limited, 113–14
New Zealand Tyre and Rubber Company, 119
New Zealand Tyre Retreaders' Association, 27–9
New Zealand Wallbords Ltd, 306
New Zealand Window Glass Limited, 89–90
Nippon Paint Holdings Co Ltd, 117
Nisbet, Carrick, 93
Nissan
  electrical wiring, 107
  franchises for, 184, 198
  importing cars, 176–7

  import tenders, 175
  local assembly of, 59, 81–3, 168, 178
  market share, 165, 174
  windscreens, 91
Nissan Motor Distributors, 59, 77, 82–3, 177
Nissan New Zealand, 82–3, 184
NLTP (National Land Transport Programme), 378–9
Nobby Tread Tyres, 119
Noonan, Rosslyn J, 1–2
Nordmeyer, Arnold, 159
no-remittance licences, 155–6, 160–1, 164–5
Northern Automobiles Limited, 20, 54, 80
North Island Main Trunk line, 8, 316, 379
Northland Roadbuilders Limited, 363
Northland Roads Board, 297
North New Zealand Coal and Cement Company, 314
Norton, William, 84
Norwood, C. B., 22, 60, 266
Norwood, Walter, 77–8
NRDC (Natural Resources Defense Council), 373
Nunns, Peter, 43–4

Oakden, Frank, 327–8
Oakland cars, 68, 125, 185–6, 194
Oamaru Harbour Board, 327
Offshore Mining Company, 251
oil
  imports of, 25
  supply of, 12
  see also petroleum products
oil discovery and refining, overseas, 201–2
oil exploration, 62
  in New Zealand, 202–3
  North Island, 203–39
  offshore, 252
  South Island, 239–50
oil filters, 105, 109, 126–7, 176
oil industry, 208, 212–13, 215, 225, 252, 271–2, 275, 282, 287
oil producers, 6, 12, 375
oil refineries, in New Zealand, 211–13, 252–5
oil refining, used, 288–91
oil tanks, 261, 269, 273, 280–1
Oil Trust Limited, 210–11
oil war, 209
Okey, Henry James Hobbs, 208

Oklahoma Trading Corporation, 274–5
Oldfield Tires, 339
Oldsmobile cars, 13–14, 19, 60, 185–6, 194
Omata oil well, 229
OMV New Zealand Limited, 252
One Tree Hill Road Board, 339, 357
Orange, John, 283
Orica, 117
Orsman, Bernard, 368
Osram, 103–4
Otago Motor Association, 15
Otahuhu, assembly plant at, 73–6, 168, 178
Ottawa Agreement, 145–6
Owens, Bob, 113
Owens Group, 111–13, 362

Pacific Dunlop, 97, 122
Pahiatua County Council, 358
Paige Detroit Motor Car Company, 24, 125
Paine, Warren, 194
paint, manufacturers of, 115–17
Pallo, Karl, 271
Palmer, C H T, 193
Palmer, Russell, 378
Panmure, assembly plant at, 60, 77–8, 111, 178
Pan Pacific Auto Electronics, 108
Para Rubber, 119
Parker, James, 310
Parker, Thomas, 11
Parkin, Frank, 167
Pascoe, George Augustus, 145
Patea County Council, 344
Patents Commission, 29
Pavroc Holdings, 361–3
Pawson, Eric, 88
Paykel Brothers Ltd, 126
Peckham, Henry, 292
Pelichet Bay, 327, 331, 334
People's Petroleum Company, 204, 218
Perdriau Rubber, 96, 120
Peter Findlay Motors, 193
Petone
  AMI plant at, 67, 77–8
  General Motors plant at, 56–7, 106, 111, 178
  New Zealand Motor Bodies plant at, 57–9, 178
  Rover Company factory at, 60
  Todd plant at, 61
Petrocorp, 247–8, 250–1

Index **473**

petrol
  price of, 25
  tax on, 30
Petroleum Act 1937, 202–3
petroleum industry, 201, 276, 282
petroleum products
  bulk storage and distribution, 268–72
  consumption of, 254
  demand and supply of, 263–6
  later suppliers, 272
  licensing sellers, 287
  rationing, 287–8
  spending on, 165–6
petrol prices, 268, 279
  regulating, 284–7
petrol pumps, 232, 260–1, 270–1
petrol restrictions, 52, 151, 232
petrol taxes, 5, 30
petrol tins and cases, 266–8
P F Mann Limited, 193
P. H. Vickery Limited, 54, 62, 65–7, 69, 77, 118, 180
Piako County Council, 297
Pilkington Automotive, 88, 90–1
Pilkington Brothers, 88–91
planned obsolescence, 35–6
Plimmer, Clifford, 82
Point Howard, 281
police speed traps, 15
Ponsonby Road, 292, 311, 365–6
Pontiac cars, 56, 77–8, 186, 190, 194
Porirua, Todd Park plant at, 62, 83, 106, 178
Porsche, 86, 198
Portland cement, 310–13, 316, 320, 327–8, 330
Port Taranaki, 203, 218
Pothole Prevention Fund, 365–6
Poverty Bay Petroleum and Kerosene Company, 234
Premier Motors, 194–5
Price, J B, 233
price controls, 136–7, 167–8, 171
Price Tribunal, 27, 120, 333
Prince Motors, 81–2
prison labour, 302–5
Proctor, Philip, 119–21
Prophet, J D, 245
Pryce, William, 48–9
public works, and railways, 1–3
Public Works Act 1928, 5
Public Works Amendment Act 1947, 5

Public Works Department, 1, 33, 293, 338, 355, 361
Public Works Fund, 293
Pukekohe Borough Council, 352–3
puncture seals, 21–2
Putt, Charles Ernest Henry, 42

Quackenbush, Mark, 283
Quarry Owners' Association, 304

Radiola Corporation, 88
Rae, Frederick William, 283
rail electrification, 7, 43–4
rail freight, 8–9, 379
rail network, construction of, 1–3, 5
Railway Commission, 2–3
railways
  competition with motor cars, 17
  customs protection for, 144
  deregulation of, 82
  oil and coal powered, 208
Railways Department, 41–2, 61, 195, 208
Rainster, 112
Ramblers, 76, 84, 183
Ranfurly, Lord, 211, 213
Rangitoto Beacon, 312–13
Raudon Plastics Ltd, 112
Rayner, F J, 14
Read, A F, 195
Ready Mix Concrete, 334
Redmayne, W W, 226
Reed, Vernon, 314
Reform Party, 144–5
Regent Oil Refining Company, 290
Reid, G C W, 97
Reidrubber, 120, 122
Reliable Roads Limited, 363–5
Renault, 84–5, 125, 183
Repco Corporation, 109–11, 126–8, 130, 134, 167
Restar, 342–9, 351
Reynolds & Co Limited, 80
Rhodes, F N, 314
Richardson, H W, 361
Richardson, W, 51
Rich List, 53, 56, 188, 199–200
Ridge Tyre Remoulding Company, 121
road boards, 211, 319
Road Carpets Ltd, 361
road congestion, 35, 369–71, 378–9
road construction, 3–5, 72

474 Index

in Auckland, 40, 43–4
costs of, 294–5
early, 3–4, 295–310
road contractors, 351–65
Road Developments Ltd, 354, 356–7, 360–1
Road Gang, 6–9, 12, 42–4, 366–9, 375–81
Roading Investigation Committee, 39–41
road maintenance, 295, 307, 378
road metal, 16, 296–8, 300–5, 336, 344
roads
discrimination in favour of, 44
quality of, 35
Roads and Bridges Construction Act 1882, 293–4
road-user charges, 144
Robertson, Herbert James Duncan, 242
Robinson, Dove-Myer, 368
Robinson, H. H., 79–80
Robt McLean Limited, 106
Roe, T S, 42
Rolls-Royce cars, 60, 77–8, 180, 198
Roman cement, 310
RoNS (Roads of National Significance), 370, 378
Rootes Group, 61–2, 196
Rose, William Dennis, 141, 154, 162–3, 178
Ross, Ben, 9, 379
Ross, Robert James, 347
Rossiter, J, 235
Rouse & Hurrell, 55
Rover cars, 60–1, 65, 67, 78–9, 198
Roverland, 199
Rowe, William, 298
Roy, J B, 207
Royal Dutch Company, 257
see also Shell
Ruatoria, 217
Rubber Workers' Union, 166
Rundon, K, 357
Rutherford, Duncan, 54
Rutherfurd, Ernest Schaw, 315

sales tax, 59
on motor vehicles, 152, 159, 167, 175
and replacement parts, 136–8
Salmon, J E, 94
Salter, Hudson Taylor, 188–9
Samuel, Marcus, 257
Samuel, Oliver, 218
Sanford, E P, 116
Savage, Michael Joseph, 116

Schofield, Ernest James, 131, 197
Schofield and Co Limited, 131, 197–8
Schofield and Denton, 20, 131
Scott, Charles B, 48
Scott, George H, 65–6
Scott, G. H., 148
Seabrook, John, 52
Seabrook, Philip, 52–3
Seabrook, Fowlds & Company, 52–3, 67, 77, 79, 180
Seaview, Ford plant at, 56, 72–3, 96, 149, 178
Seddon, R J, 4
Semple, Robert, 4, 72
service stations, 6, 32–3, 97, 100, 137
British International Oil Company, 279
as bulk suppliers, 270–1
one-brand, 271–2
Shackell, E H, 216
The Shape of Things to Come, 7
Sharland, J C, 205
Shaw, Caroline, 374–5
Shaw, Peter, 75
Shell BP and Todd Oil Services Limited, 233–4, 247–8, 251–2
Shell Oil New Zealand Ltd, 238, 253–4, 258–9, 268–9, 272, 285
and Fulton Hogan, 362
and Waikato Bitumen, 354, 364
Shell Transport and Trading Company Limited, 257, 268
shingle, 293, 308–9, 355, 359, 361
Shipley, A. E., 47
Shirtcliffe, G, 259–60
Shore, H W, 97
Sim, William Alexander, 323–4
Simca motor vehicles, 75–6
Singer cars, 184
Skeates, Percy, 179
Skeates and Bockaert, 179
Skeates and White, 19, 179–80, 194
Skitrop, C, 349, 352
Skitrop, T E, 337
Skoda, 75–6, 198
Sloan, Alfred P Jnr., 35
Smith, A. G, 341
Smith, Cameron, 376
Smith, Edward Metcalf, 203
Smith, F G, 144
Smith, H S, 348
Smith, H W, 133

Society of Motor Manufacturers and
    Traders, 157
Socony (Standard Oil Company of New
    York), 256, 274, 340
Socony Asphalt, 337, 340
soil-cement stabilisation, 355
Solarc Storage Battery Co, 98
Soltar, 341–3, 348–51
solus trading, 271–2
South Auckland Motors, 188–9
South Eastern Utilities Limited, 54–5
Southern Cross Petroleum Company, 236–
    7, 239
South Island Motors Limited, 52–4, 68
Southland, oil exploration in, 233, 246, 248–
    9
Southland Cement Company Ltd, 333
Southland Motor Association, 15
South Pacific Petroleum Company, 235–7
South Pacific Tyres, 122
South Pacific Vehicle Assemblers, 86
South Road Services, 61
Southward, L, 113
Southward, Roy, 114
Southward Engineering, 88, 113–14
spark plugs, 104–5, 136, 149
Spencer, Christopher Albert, 75
Spencer, John A, 242, 244–5
Spencer, John Berridge, 75
Spencer, Michael Peter, 75
Spencer, Peter Albert, 75
Spencer Allen, James, 196
Spencer Allen Motors, 196–7
Spencer Moulton, 118
Stallworthy, A J, 304
Standard Motor Company, 54, 56, 79–80
Standard Oil Company, 209, 256–8, 260,
    263
    see also Socony
Standard Oil Company of New Zealand,
    223–5
Standard Telephones and Cables, 107–8
Standard-Triumph, 54, 63, 65, 77–8, 80–1
Star Oil Company, 262
    see also Caltex
State Advances Corporation, 26, 29
steel-belted radial tyres, 121
Steel Brothers, 81–2, 85
Steel's Motor Assemblies Limited, 82, 85–6
Steinbeck, John, 367
Stent, N E, 111

Stevens, Frederick Sedgewick, 289
Stevens, William John, 51, 69
Stevens and Sons, 51–2, 54, 57
Stevenson Construction Materials, 358
Stewart, Charles, 321
Stewart, G. D., 58–9
Stewart, W, 182
Stoks, Wieke, 113
Stone, Colin, 168
stone quarries, 295–9, 302
Stone Quarries Act 1910, 295–6
Stratford, Felix, 51
Studebaker cars, 49, 54, 63, 76, 183
Subaru, 73, 76, 91, 106, 115, 174, 195
Sugar Loaf Islands, 203–5
Sumatra, 258, 260, 264
Sunak, Rishi, 368
Superior Oil Company of New Zealand
    Limited, 241, 246
supermarkets, 37
Sutch, William, 1, 7, 44, 139, 149, 160
Suzuki, 86–7, 91, 106, 174, 178, 188
Swarbrick, Chloe, 252
Sylvia Park, assembly plant at, 74–5, 77, 178

Taihape Borough Council, 337
Takapuna, 85, 127, 194
Talbot cars, 91, 106, 183, 189
Tappenden Motors Limited, 192–4
tar, dehydrated, 341–2
Tarakohe, 320–1, 325
Taranaki, oil exploration in, 203–34, 249
    see also Waitara
Taranaki (New Zealand) Oil Wells
    Company, 210–15, 227, 238, 253
Taranaki Oil and Freehold Company, 219–
    21, 252
Taranaki Oil Development Company Ltd,
    215, 225
Taranaki Oil Wells/Fields Limited, 215–18,
    225, 234
Taranaki Petroleum Company
    first, 205–6, 218
    second, 206–11, 252
Tarata district, 215–17
Tariff Act 1907, 140–2
Tariff and Development Board, 166
Tariff Commission 1895, 327–9
tariffs, 139–40
    agreements with Britain, 72, 140
    and components industries, 88, 111

for knocked-down imports, 53, 72
on motor vehicles, 141–4, 146, 172–3, 175–6
and tyres, 123–4
and vehicle assembly, 38, 62, 65, 71
tarmac, 346, 352
tar preparations, 341–51
Tarvia, 294, 342, 349–51
Tasman district, oil exploration in, 242–50
Tasman Rental Cars, 31–2
Tauranga Borough Council, 351
Taylor's Lime, 334
Te Awamutu Borough Council, 353
Teed, D, 351–2
Tench Brothers Limited, 171, 183–5
Terry, W H, 304
Tesla, 376
Tew, Albert Ithiel, 189
Tewsley, H C, 348
Texas Company/Texaco, 261–2, 341
Thames, Campbell Motors plant at, 81, 83–4, 86, 178
Third Main *see* W2W
Thompson, H H, 42
Thomson, Herbert, 225
Thornton, O G, 41
Thornycroft Dump Truck, 16, 53
Three Kings Quarry, 309
Tibbits, E G W, 341
Timaru Harbour Board, 327
tin plate, 266
Todd, Bob, 99, 110
Todd Motors, 61–2, 64
assembly plants, 83
import tenders, 175
market share, 78, 165, 174
and windscreen glass, 91
see also Europa
Tokheim, John J, 271
Tokomaru Bay, 216–17
Tole, D A, 305
Tomlinson, Charles Edward, 125
Totangi oil drilling, 237–8
Totara Lime Works Limited, 361
Toyota
closure of assembly plants, 178
electrical wiring in, 106–7
electric vehicles, 377
franchise for, 82, 85, 198
local assembly of, 81
market share, 78, 165, 174

prices, 176
windscreens of, 91
Toyota Corolla, 84, 91
Toyota Corona, 81–2, 85–6
Toyota Crown, 114, 117
Toyota New Zealand, 86
traffic lights, 107, 369
trams
assembly of, 62, 70
in Auckland, 35, 39, 44, 340, 367
in Christchurch, 30, 48
in Dunedin, 330
electric, 11, 101
Trapeznik, Alexander, 15, 371–2
Treasury, 39, 116, 173
Trekka, 75
Trentham, 57, 112, 178, 321
Trevithick, Richard, 10
Triton Oil and Gas Corp, 247–8, 254
Triumph, 64–5, 67, 78–81, 106, 183, 198
trolley-buses, 58, 70, 188
TRT (Tidd Ross Todd), 131–2
T R Taylor Limited, 80
Tubular Steel, 88
Tudhope, D H, 234
Turnbull, Henry Laidlaw, 84
Turner, Joseph Noel, 75–6
Turner, Peter, 174
Turnovsky, Stephen J, 159
Turrell, L E A, 42
Turrentine, Jeff, 373
two-car families, 20, 37
Tyco Electronics, 106–7
tyre particle pollution, 373–4
tyres, 117
demand for, 264
early importers and retailers, 118–19
imports of, 123, 148
industry study, 125
later importers and retailers, 119–22
manufacturing, 88, 122–4
retreading, 32–4, 121
Tyreways, 30, 34

union asphalt, 336–8, 340
Union Oil Company, 275–6, 278, 336
Unit Concrete Limited, 362
United Concrete, 358
United Oil Company, 226
Universal Motor Company, 183
Unwin, F, 362

Index **477**

Upper Hutt, 111–12, 120, 122, 128
Upper Mahurangi Road Board, 312
urban sprawl, 34, 370
Urquhart's Bay, 320
used cars, 20
   and hire purchase, 169–71
   imports of, 37–8, 75, 124, 151, 177
   market value of, 163
   and warranties, 18

Vacuum Oil Company, 25, 238, 256–7, 260, 262–7, 269, 273–4, 277, 286, 340
   see also Mobil
Vallentine, Edwin James, 242
Vandyke, James, 275
VANZ (Vehicle Assemblers New Zealand), 74–5, 178
Vaughan, William W, 53
Vauxhall cars, 52, 57, 60, 76, 183, 185–6, 192
Vega Batteries, 97
vehicle and parts dealers, 17
vehicle emissions, 372
Vickerman, Neville, 41
Vickery, Percy Harry, 69
Vickery, T W, 69
Victoria bridge, Trentham, 321
Victory Rubber Industries Limited, 26
Vining, Phillip, 48
Vining, William Graeme, 47–8
Vogel, Julius, 1–3, 218
Volkswagen, 75–6, 86, 114, 194, 198
Volvo, 55, 188, 199

W2W (Wiri to Westfield), 8–9, 379
Waihi Borough Council, 295
Waiho Beach, 248
Waikato Bitumen Company, 354, 363–5
Waikato Motors, 187
Waimak Shingle and Sands, 359
Waimea County Council, 16–17
Wainuiomata, 110–11, 113
Waiorongomai, 297
Waipa Borough Council, 352
Waipa County Council, 355
Waipatiki oil well, 234
Waipatiki Oil-Wells Ltd, 241
Waitangi Hill, 217, 237
Waitangi Tribunal, 202
Waitara, assembly plant at, 76, 83, 114–15, 178

Waitotara County Council, 338
Walker, A Greville, 42
Walker, Peter, 368
Wallis, Anthony Bruce, 25
Wallis, John Gregory, 25–6
Wallis, Leonard F, 21–30
Walton, Felix, 369
Walton Park, 327
Wanganui, assembly plant in, 86–7, 178
Wanganui City Council, 57, 76, 296
Wanganui County Council, 344
Ward, Joseph, 144, 168, 208, 320
Waring, George, 310
Warkworth, 312, 315, 318
Warner, F A, 26
warranties, 18, 177
Warren, F M, 225
Warren, F. W., 226
war tariff, 141–2
Warwick Weston, 205
W A Ryan and Company, 12–13
Watts, J T, 156
W Cable and Co, 280–1
Webster, Josiah Daniel, 84
Webster, Mark, 34, 88, 108
Webster, M W, 321
Welch, Tim, 379
Wellington, road access into, 7
Wellington and Marlborough Cement, Lime, and Coal Company, 330
Wellington Automobile Club, 7, 281
Wellington City Council, 79, 101
Wellington Coach and Motor Body Builders' Association, 144
Wenrich Investments, 111–13
West Coast of the South Island
   oil exploration, 239–41, 246–8
   petrol supply, 258
Westport, 229, 332–5, 361
W G Vining Limited, 47
Whangarei Borough Council, 341
Whangarei Harbour, 314–16, 320–1
White, George M, 179
White, John (director), 328
White, John (mechanic), 189
Whyte, D O, 325
Wiles, Harold Oliver, 277
Willard Batteries, 99–103
Williams, Rex, 334
William Scollay and Company Limited, 73
Williamson Jeffrey Ltd, 112

Willie, Christine Rose, 155
Willie, Jack, 155
Wilson, George, 321
Wilson, John, 311–13
Wilson, Nathaniel, 315
Wilson, Stuart H, 288
Wilson, W J, 315
Wilson, Rothery Limited, 298, 363–4
Wilsons (New Zealand) Portland Cement Company, 318–20, 323–4, 326, 332
Wilsons Portland Cement Company, 312–15, 317–18
Wilton Motor Body Company, 76–7
windscreen glass, 90–1
Wines, D P, 116
Winstone, E G, 306
Winstone, George, 307–9, 314, 319
Winstone, William, 307–9
Winstone Civil Construction Limited, 356
Winstone Ltd, 298, 306–9, 326, 356
Winstone's Store fire, 276, 278
Winton, 246, 327
Wiri
  Ford operations at, 72–5, 178
  Nissan plant at, 83, 165, 168
wiring looms, 107, 149
Wiri Oil Storage, 270
Witt, Daniel A, 141, 174
Wix Corporation of Canada, 126–7
Wolseley cars, 49–50, 77–8, 180
Wood, Jane Ingram, 132
Woods, Megan, 255
World War II
  and Amalgamated Batteries, 98
  and petrol, 282, 287–8
  and Steel Bros, 81
  and trade restrictions, 151
  and Willard Batteries, 100
Worley, Ralph P, 42
Wright, E J, 232
Wright, H, 348
Wrightcars Ltd, 55, 85
Wrightson NMA Ltd, 360
Wright Stephenson, 20, 85, 119, 276, 360
  see also Challenge Corporation
WSP/Parsons Brinckerhoff, 8, 379
W Stevenson and Sons, 309, 357–8, 363
W T Trethewey & Sons Ltd, 365
Wynyard Tank Farm, 256, 269–70

Young, David, 5–6
Young Brothers, 102–3
Yuasa Battery Company, 93

Z Energy, 255, 259, 261, 270
Ziman, David, 241

www.ingramcontent.com/pod-product-compliance
Lightning Source LLC
Chambersburg PA
CBHW082336300426
44109CB00045B/2361